Second Edition

Microprocessors and Programmed Logic

Kenneth L. Short

State University of New York
Stony Brook, New York

PRENTICE-HALL, INC., Englewood Cliffs, New Jersey 07632

Library of Congress Cataloging-in-Publication Data

Short, Kenneth L.
  Microprocessors and programmed logic.

  Includes bibliographies and index.
  1. Microprocessors. I. Title.
QA76.5.S496 1987   004.165   86-25385
ISBN 0-13-580606-2

Editorial/production supervision and
  interior design: Mary Jo Stanley
Cover design: 20-20 Services, Inc.
Manufacturing buyer: Rhett Conklin

Printed in the United States of America

10 9 8 7 6 5

ISBN 0-13-580606-2 025

Prentice-Hall International (UK) Limited, *London*
Prentice-Hall of Australia Pty. Limited, *Sydney*
Prentice-Hall Canada Inc., *Toronto*
Prentice-Hall Hispanoamericana, S.A., *Mexico*
Prentice-Hall of India Private Limited, *New Delhi*
Prentice-Hall of Japan, Inc., *Tokyo*
Prentice-Hall of Southeast Asia Pte. Ltd., *Singapore*
Editora Prentice-Hall do Brasil, Ltda., *Rio de Janeiro*

To my parents
Robert F. and Floretta H. Short
and in memory of my brother
Robert M. Short

Contents

Contents

Preface

The single most significant development in digital system design in recent years has been the microprocessor, a central processing unit integrated on a single chip of silicon. The processing power and economics of the microprocessor have had a tremendous impact on the way digital systems are designed and on their scope of application.

This book is about the microprocessor. It is also about its related integrated circuits and the hardware and software design of microprocessor based systems. Its purpose is first to provide the reader with a thorough understanding of the basic hardware and software concepts necessary for the design of microprocessor based systems and, further, to provide the reader with an in-depth knowledge of specific devices and the attendant practical considerations and design techniques necessary to design effectively systems using them.

An important feature of this book is its utilization of a single microprocessor, the 8085A, as the example to illustrate fundamental concepts. Use of a single microprocessor as the instructional example allows an increased depth of coverage of the operation, features, and limitations of an actual device. In addition, it allows use of a single consistent set of signals and signal names for interfacing the many logical devices that constitute a microprocessor system. Use of a single set of signal names simplifies the reader's task in understanding hardware interfacing concepts and the functional operation of various LSI devices.

The 8085A is a general purpose 8-bit microprocessor. This microprocessor was chosen because of its widespread use in industrial applications and its widespread support. This support manifests itself in the form of documentation, application notes, and software and hardware developments aids for the 8085A. In addition, there exists a large family of peripheral LSI devices that are designed to be compatible with the 8085A. Because of its wide applicability, the reader will find that the knowledge gained about the 8085A and its support devices is immediately applicable to many actual designs in industry.

A further advantage of studying a single microprocessor in depth is that the reader not only learns of the features of the device but also learns that with these features come attendant limitations that must be dealt with in any practical application. It should be noted that a reader following a device-specific instructional approach will find that once a specific microprocessor and its application in digital design has been mastered, it is relatively easy to understand the operation and application of other microprocessors from a study of the manufacturers' user's manuals and application notes. This has been the experience of university and industry students who have followed this approach in the author's microprocessor courses over the past several years.

The design of microprocessor systems requires a knowledge of both hardware and software. It is assumed that the reader has a basic knowledge of digital hardware at the gate and flip-flop levels. This material can be found in introductory books on digital system design. The software concepts in this book are illustrated using assembly language for the 8085A. However, prior knowledge of assembly language programming is not necessary. Some general knowledge of computer programming in a high level language is desirable.

The goal has been to introduce the necessary hardware and software concepts in an elementary, systematic, and integrated fashion and to build upon these concepts logically. While the study of no single text can provide mastery in a subject area, it is believed that this book will provide the reader with a solid foundation for the development of proficiency in the design of microprocessor systems.

This second edition is an extensive revision of the first, reflecting important changes in technology that have occurred. However, the overall thrust and structure of the book remain true to the first edition. Two areas in which major technological changes have occurred are programmable logic devices and semiconductor memory. A chapter has been added that is devoted entirely to programmable logic devices and their use in microprocessor based systems. A second chapter on memory has been added that contains new material on dynamic random access memory and nonvolatile memory. Material on read only memory and mass storage systems has also been moved to this chapter. This leaves the introductory chapter on memory to concentrate on basic memory concepts, erasable programmable read only memory, and static random access memory.

Most of the chapters from the original text have undergone substantial revision in order to cover more recent integrated circuit peripheral and support devices, to provide additional application examples, and to place greater emphasis on design.

While advances in microprocessor architecture and technology have led to extremely powerful 16- and 32-bit microprocessors, the complexity of these micro-processors and their nature and software support tools makes them inappropriate for in-depth instructional purposes at the introductory level. Thus, this second edition retains the 8085A as its primary instructional example.

Acknowledgments

Several people have contributed in various ways to the development of the second edition of this text. I would like to express my appreciation to Tim Bozik, Harry Dunham, Bernard Goodwin, Natarajan Gurumoorthy, Emil Sarpa, Kenneth Schachter, and Mary Jo Stanley.

I would especially like to thank Scott Tierno for his suggestions and critical reading of the manuscript.

Kenneth L. Short

1

Introduction

A technological advance which is affecting the practice of logic design is the existence of the LSI microprocessor; a data flow and control on one to several LSI chips. In this case the logic designer's building blocks are data flows, control stores, and read / write memory chips. He arranges the chips and programs the control store.

Glen G. Langdon, Jr.*

*Logic Design: A Review of Theory and Practice (New York: Academic Press, 1974).

1

1.1 THE UBIQUITOUS MICROPROCESSOR

The unabridged second edition of Webster's New Twentieth Century Dictionary defines *microprocessor* (μP) as "the controlling unit of a microcomputer, laid out on a tiny silicon chip and containing the logical elements for handling data, performing calculations, carrying out stored instructions, etc." Ubiquitous is defined as "present, or seeming to be present, everywhere at the same time; existing everywhere; omnipresent." To refer to the microprocessor as ubiquitous is not an exaggeration, particularly to anyone associated with electronic system design.

An ever-increasing number of nontechnical activities also involve individuals with microprocessor systems. While many nontechnical people may associate the microprocessor with only personal computers, chances are they use appliances containing microprocessors and live or work in environments controlled by microprocessor systems. Table 1.1-1 is a partial list of products and systems, for the home, which exist in microprocessor-controlled versions. Only two items on this list are generally thought of as computers, the personal computer and the desktop calculator. In the other items the microprocessor acts primarily as a controller and its existence may be unknown to the user. The microprocessor is said to be *embedded* in such a system. Embedded systems typically implement a fixed or dedicated function. In contrast, the function of a general purpose computer, such as a personal computer, varies, depending on the program the user selects for execution.

Many of the items in Table 1.1-1 existed before the advent of the microprocessor. Microprocessor based versions of these products provide enhanced performance and additional features. Other items in Table 1.1-1 are not technically or economically feasible if not microprocessor based. Microprocessor based products for the home range from the very practical to the frivolous. For example,

TABLE 1.1-1   PRODUCTS AND SYSTEMS FOR THE HOME THAT EXIST IN MICROPROCESSOR-CONTROLLED VERSIONS

Personal computer	Burglar alarm system
Desktop calculator	Microwave oven
Telephone	Dishwasher
Telephone answering machine	Refrigerator
Television	Food processor
Audio amplifier	Blender
Audiocassette deck	Kitchen scale
Turntable	Clock radio
Video camera	Bathroom scale
Videocassette deck	Blood pressure monitor
Video recorder	Clothes washer
Compact disc player	Clothes dryer
Camera	Tape measure
Sewing machine	Lawn sprinkler system
Typewriter	Exercise bike
Thermostat	

health-related products range from a blood pressure and pulse rate monitor, with digital display, to a talking electronic scale that digitally displays weight; stores weights, target weights, and previous weight histories for five people; and has 150 "motivational" messages.

The number of microprocessors in the home is overshadowed by the number in an office environment. And this number is again vastly overshadowed by the number of microprocessors in industrial applications. No area of electronic system design has escaped the impact of the microprocessor. Thus, electronic system designers must have an understanding of the structure, operation, and design of microprocessor systems.

1.2 MICROPROCESSOR SYSTEMS

1.2.1 Conventional Computer Systems

A block diagram representation of a general purpose computer system is shown in Fig. 1.2-1. The computer system consists of a number of subsystems interconnected by paths that transfer data between the subsystems. The *central processing unit, CPU*, controls the operation of the computer system by executing a sequence of instructions. These instructions, stored in the computer's memory, constitute the *program* that the computer executes. This structure is also referred to as a *stored program computer*. The instructions are stored as binary information, patterns of logical 1s and 0s.

The CPU contains a *control section*, which is the clocked sequential machine that controls all the data transfers that take place in the system, including the transfer of instructions from memory to the CPU for execution. The control section decodes an instruction, then carries out the operations specified by the instruction. The operations may transfer data or transform a data value. Transformations of data take place in a CPU subsystem called the *arithmetic and logic unit, ALU*. The ALU executes fundamental arithmetic operations such as addition, subtraction,

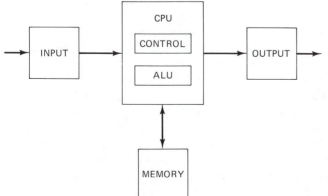

Figure 1.2-1 Simplified block diagram of a stored program digital computer.

multiplication, and division. Logic operations executed by the ALU include complement, AND, OR, and EX-OR.

A particular sequence of instructions causes the computer to implement a specific function. In general, all functions are implemented by the basic operations of inputting data, processing the data, and outputting the results of the processing. ***Programming*** the computer is the process of determining the particular sequence of operations to implement a desired function. ***Coding*** the program is the process of creating a sequence of instructions to implement the required operations. If properly programmed, the computer system can implement any function as long as the time constraints associated with the function's execution are not too stringent.

The input block is the subsystem through which data is transferred from the external world to the CPU. Input data may originate from several sources, including a human operator, another computer, or some other type of electronic system. Data that is input to the CPU may be immediately processed or transferred to the memory to await later processing. Processed data may be immediately output or placed in memory to be output at a later time. The output block represents the devices used to transfer results to the external world. Output devices include displays, printers, and systems for transferring information to other computers or electronic systems.

1.2.2 The Microprocessor

Advances in integrated circuit technology lead to the ability to integrate larger and larger numbers of logic gates on a single integrated circuit chip. ***Small scale integration, SSI***, allowed up to 12 gates to be integrated on a single chip. This resulted in ICs that provide the basic logic functions AND, OR, INVERT, and so on and the basic storage elements D and J-K flip-flops. Computers and other digital systems implemented with SSI required the use of traditional switching theoretic techniques to design cost-effective systems [1]. ***Medium scale integration, MSI***, allowed from 13 to 99 gates or gate equivalents to be integrated on a single IC chip. Since the number of pins associated with an IC package is limited, it was necessary to interconnect these logic gates, on the IC, to implement simple functions such as counters, decoders, registers, comparators, and adders. The decisions, by IC manufacturers, as to what MSI functions to implement, are based on the kinds of functions that frequently appear in systems designed with SSI.

When the capability to integrate 100 or more logic gates on a single chip, ***large scale integration, LSI***, was achieved, the choice of functions to implement became difficult. Because of the significant expense to develop an LSI circuit, the function that the circuit implements has to be one that will find widespread application, and thus a large market. The number of complex fixed functions that meet this requirement is rather limited. A solution to this problem is to integrate a function that is not fixed but is definable by the user of the LSI device. The most general such function is the general purpose computer, a universal logic device. The system designer programs the computer so that it implements the specific function required. The first company to achieve this was the Intel Corporation. In 1971 Intel intro-

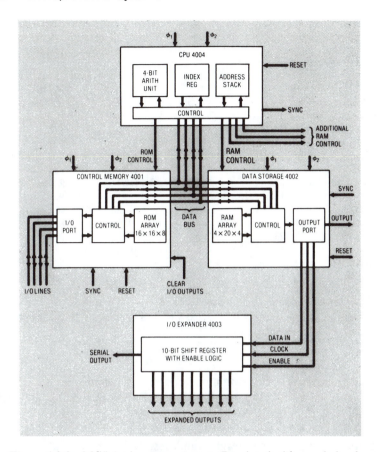

Figure 1.2-2 MCS-4 microcomputer set. (Reprinted with permission from *A History of Microprocessor Development at Intel*, by Robert N. Noyce and Marian E. Hoff, Jr., IEEE MICRO, February 1981. © 1981 IEEE.)

duced a group of four LSI devices that made up a simple but complete computer, the MCS-4 microcomputer set [2, 3, 4].

The MCS-4 microcomputer set consisted of four ICs, each packaged in a 16-pin Dual In-line Package, DIP (see Fig. 1.2-2). The 4004-CPU was the central processing unit IC. This IC, containing the ALU and control on a single chip, became known as a ***microprocessor***. The 4004 had 45 instructions and processed 4-bit data quantities. It interfaced with the other ICs in the set via a 4-bit data bus and five control lines. ***Read only memory, ROM***, which maintained stored data, even when power was removed from the system, was provided by the 4001-ROM. The program was stored in this type of memory and was available for execution as soon as power was applied to the system. Each 4001 contained 256 8-bit words of read only memory. The 4001 also contained a 4-bit input/output (I/O) port that allowed the MCS-4 microcomputer set to communicate with circuits and devices that were not a part of the microcomputer set. The term ***port*** is applied to the circuitry that provides the opening or gateway for the transfer of data between the microcomputer

TABLE 1.2-1   MICROPROCESSOR HARDWARE EVOLUTION: SOME RELATED DEVICES

	4004	8008	8085A	8086	80386
Date	71	71	77	78	85
Class	4 bit	8 bit	8 bit	16 bit	32 bit
Technology	PMOS	PMOS	NMOS	HMOS	CHMOS
Word size data/instr.	4/8	8/8	8/8	16/16	32/32
Address capacity	4 K	16 K	64 K	1 M	4 G
Clock kHz/phases	740/2	800/2	6250/2	8000/2	16,000/2
Add time	10.8 μS	20 μS	1.3 μS	0.375 μS	0.125 μS
Internal regs. ALU/GP	1/16	1/6	1/6	1/8	1/8
Stack size words/bits	3 × 12	7 × 14	RWM	RWM	RWM
Voltages	15 or −10, 5*	−9, 5	+5	+5	+5
Package size	16 pin	18 pin	40 pin	40 pin	132 pin
Instructions	45	48	74†	133	135
Transistors ~	2300	2000	6200	29,000	275,000
Chip size	117 × 159 mil	125 × 170 mil	164 × 222 mil	225 × 230 mil	390 × 390 mil
Manufacturer (original)	Intel	Intel	Intel	Intel	Intel

* The 4004 can be used with a +15 V supply or a −10 V, +5 V supply.

†The number of basic instructions for the 8085A is often given as 80. The number 74 is consistent with the instruction set listing in Appendix C.

and the external world. A minimal operational microcomputer could be constructed with one 4004-CPU and one 4001-ROM. For more complex applications, one CPU could control up to 16 ROMs, providing 4096 8-bit words of read only memory.

Read write memory, RWM, for temporary storage of data after input, intermediate computational results, and results before output, was provided by the 4002-RAM. In addition to providing 20 4-bit words of read write memory, each 4002 also provided four output lines. Sixteen 4002s could be controlled by one 4004, providing 1280 4-bit words of read write memory. Additional I/O was provided by the 4003-SR shift register IC, which was a 10-bit serial-in/parallel-out, serial output shift register.

Comparison of Figs. 1.2-1 and 1.2-2 indicates that the MCS-4 microcomputer set provided the functional equivalent of a computer. The actual distribution of the functions among blocks in the MCS-4 microcomputer set differs from that of Fig. 1.2-1, since I/O, although functionally different from memory, is physically located with memory in the 4001-ROM and 4002-RAM. In addition, the MCS-4 clearly differed from existing computers in terms of its limited amount of memory and I/O and its limited speed of operation.

The power of microprocessors has increased tremendously with advancements in integrated circuit technology and microprocessor systems architecture. *Very large scale integration, VLSI*, allows extremely complex systems, consisting of as many as a million transistors on a single chip, to be realized. These advances are reflected in the listing in Table 1.2-1 of characteristics for a few of the microprocessors introduced by Intel. Though representative of the progress in microprocessor technology, this table lists only a few microprocessors out of the hundreds available from various semiconductor manufacturers. While more powerful microprocessors allow more complex and demanding functions to be implemented, they do not obviate the need for less powerful microprocessors for cost-effective solutions in simpler applications.

Another advance in semiconductor technology was also crucial to the rapid acceptance of microprocessors by digital system designers. The 4001-ROM was a metal mask programmable ROM. A specification of the ROM contents had to be provided by the system designer to the IC manufacturer, because the contents of the ROM were fixed during a step in its manufacturing process. If the designer made an error in the specification or wished to change the program, all the ROMs previously manufactured would be unusable. This adversely impacted the time required to develop or modify a system and increased the cost of design errors. Not long before the introduction of the MCS-4, Intel introduced a new type of ROM, the 1702. This ROM's contents were written by the designer using a special instrument, a device programmer. This ROM also had the unique feature that, once written, it could be erased and rewritten. It is erased by removing the IC from the circuit in which it operates and shining ultraviolet light through a quartz lid on the top of the package and onto the IC itself! Such an erasable ROM is called an *Erasable programmable read only memory, EPROM*. The advantage to the system designer is that the program can be placed in EPROM and the system tested; if errors are found in the program, the EPROM can be erased and reprogrammed. EPROMs could be used for ROM in an MCS-4 system, allowing rapid system development and modification.

1.2.3 Bussed Structure of a Microprocessor System

A simplified block diagram of a microprocessor system is given in Fig. 1.2-3. For simplicity, each block represents a subsystem or hardware module that implements a single primary function such as ROM or input. The important difference between this representation for a microprocessor system and that of a computer in Fig. 1.2-1 is that the subsystems are interconnected by a single common bus, the system bus. A *bus* is simply a group of connections that have a common function. This method of interconnection has a significant impact on the structure and operation of the system.

Each subsystem consists of from one to a large number of ICs. Two conceptual views of each subsystem further aid in understanding the structure and

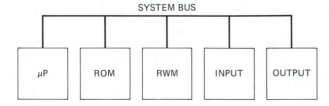

Figure 1.2-3 Simplified block diagram of a microprocessor system.

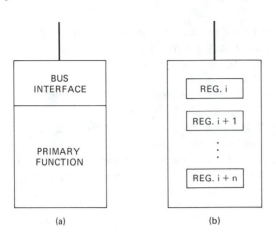

Figure 1.2-4 Conceptual views of microprocessor subsystems: (a) interface and primary function; (b) collection of addressable registers.

operation of the system. All subsystems consist of logic required to implement the primary function of the subsystem and logic required to interface the primary function to the system bus (see Fig. 1.2-4a). Each subsystem can also be viewed as a collection of registers (see Fig. 1.2-4b). Some registers, *operational registers*, are fundamental to the sequential operation of the microprocessor or to the transformation of data. Other registers, *storage registers*, store the binary representation of the program and the data it processes. The single attribute of all of these registers that is important, at this point, is that each one is uniquely identifiable. This is accomplished by assigning each register a unique identifying number, an *address*.

As mentioned previously, the microprocessor system implements its overall function by inputting data, processing the data, and outputting the results. This is accomplished by the microprocessor executing instructions from the program stored in its memory. For many embedded systems the program is stored entirely in ROM. Thus, the system operation can be viewed as *transferring* data, including data that represents instructions, between various registers in the system and *transforming* data in operational registers.

In order to accomplish this, the system bus is divided into an address bus, data bus, and control bus. The *address bus* is used by the microprocessor to specify a memory or I/O register that will be involved in a data transfer. The data is transferred on the *data bus*. The signals that control and synchronize the operation of the subsystems are provided by the *control bus*. The greater the number of address bits provided by the microprocessor the larger the number of registers that can exist in the system. The greater the number of data bits provided by the microprocessor the more data that can be transferred or transformed at one time. As can be seen from Table 1.2-1, the number of microprocessor address bits and data bits has increased with advances in technology, leading to more powerful microprocessors.

A microcomputer system consists of not only the microprocessor but memory and I/O, as seen in Fig. 1.2-3. *Single-chip microcomputers* integrate the microprocessor, memory, and I/O on a single chip. Such devices find widespread use in control applications.

1.3 PROGRAMMABLE SYSTEMS AND DEVICES

The concept of programmability is important in microprocessor systems and appears at many levels. Programmability allows a microprocessor system or other IC device to be tailored to implement a specific function. The application program executed by a microprocessor drives the system hardware in order to implement the desired system function. For a given microprocessor system, different application programs allow different system functions to be implemented, within a range limited by the available system hardware.

At another level, programmable LSI devices in the system, other than the microprocessor, are programmed to specify their mode of operation. For example, programmable LSI devices that provide input and output ports are software programmed to specify the direction, in or out, of each port in the device. This software programming is accomplished by the application program transferring command data to the LSI device to initialize or configure the device. At a lower level, *programmable logic devices, PLDs*, are hardware programmed to implement functions that would otherwise be implemented by hardwired SSI gates, flip-flops, and MSI functions. Hardware programming is done before the device is placed in the circuit in which it operates.

A brief overview of these different types of programmability is given in the following sections. These topics are considered in detail in subsequent chapters.

1.3.1 Application Programs

A microprocessor program consists of a sequence of binary words stored in memory. The number of words in a program is contingent upon the particular application, the system structure, and the ability of the designer to program the system efficiently. A program can be written directly in *machine language*—the form in which it is stored in memory—that is, as patterns of 1s and 0s. While this method of programming may be adequate for very small programs, it becomes very time consuming and error prone as the program size and complexity increase.

Program writing and interpretation are simplified by an *assembly language* that uses mnemonics such as ADD, SUB, or JMP instead of machine language instructions. However, since the microprocessor can only execute the bit patterns of machine language instructions, the assembly language program must ultimately be converted to machine code. This conversion can be carried out by hand, but this procedure, also, is error prone, time consuming, and generally impractical. Special programs are available for each type of microprocessor that convert their assembly language programs to the equivalent machine code. These programs are called *assemblers* and are run either on a microcomputer, a minicomputer, or mainframe computer.

A number of microprocessors have available programs called *compilers*, which allow the system designer to write programs in a *high level language* such as FORTRAN, BASIC, PASCAL, C, or PL/M (similar to PL1). The compiler, using the high level language program as data, then generates machine language code for the microprocessor. Typically, compilers generate machine code that is less efficient

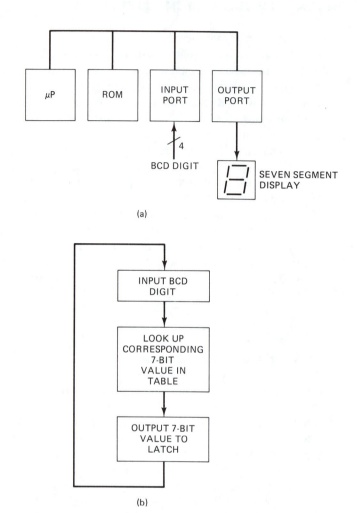

(a)

(b)

```
0000    210F00      START:    LXI H, TABLE    ;SET POINTER TO BEGINNING OF TABLE
0003    DB00                  IN 0            ;INPUT BCD DIGIT
0005    5F                    MOV E, A        ;USE BCD.DIGIT AS OFFSET INTO TABLE
0006    1600                  MVI D, 00H
0008    19                    DAD D           ;ADD OFFSET TO BEGINNING ADDRESS OF TABLE
0009    7E                    MOV A, M        ;TRANSFER 7-SEGMENT CODE FROM TABLE TO A
000A    D300                  OUT 0           ;OUTPUT 7-SEGMENT CODE
000C    C30000                JMP START       ;JUMP BACK TO START OF PROGRAM
000F    7E306D79    TABLE:    DB 7EH, 30H, 6DH, 79H, 33H, 5BH, 1FH, 70H, 7FH, 73H
0013    335B1F70
0017    7F73                  END
```

(c)

Figure 1.3-1 Microprocessor implementation of seven segment display: (a) system block diagram; (b) program flowchart; (c) assembly language program listing.

than code generated from an assembly language program by an assembler, efficiency here being measured in terms of the number of machine language instructions required to perform a particular task. Less efficient programs require more memory and longer execution times.

Without an actual comparison of the machine code resulting from each approach, it is impossible to determine the relative efficiency of programs written in assembly language as opposed to a high level language. High level language programs have been known to generate code anywhere from 10 to 200 percent less efficient than assembly level language programs. In applications where program size or speed of execution is critical, assembly language programming has the advantage of a one-to-one correspondence between each assembly language instruction and each machine language instruction, whereas a single high level language instruction, when compiled, may produce several machine language instructions. Thus, assembly language allows the programmer a greater degree of control over microprocessor operations.

When a microprocessor system is used in a dedicated application, the *control* or *application program* is fixed and stored in ROM. Because changes in the control program are only necessary when the functions implemented by the system are to be altered, the control program in ROM is referred to as *firmware* rather than software. Computations and logical operations performed by the microprocessor under program control produce intermediate results that are stored in registers internal to the microprocessor or in RWM external to the microprocessor. The arithmetic and logical capabilities of a microprocessor allow alternative portions of the control program to be executed based on the results of previous computations or on data from external devices that have been input through I/O circuitry.

The common BCD-to-seven segment decoding function can be easily implemented by a microprocessor system. A microprocessor implements this combinational function in a sequential manner by inputting the BCD digit and using it as an index to a table of values stored in memory. This table specifies those segments of the seven segment display that should be ON and those that should be OFF for each BCD digit. The microprocessor outputs the appropriate value from the table to a latch—the outputs of which drive the various segments in the display. The structure of the microprocessor system, the system operation *flowchart*, the assembly language program, and the machine language code for implementing a seven segment display are shown in Fig. 1.3-1. This method of implementing a BCD-to-seven segment decoder is obviously not economically justifiable on its own. However, if this were only one of a large number of functions that the microprocessor system implemented, such as keyboard scanning, arithmetic operations, or receipt printing, then the resulting system, for example, a point-of-sale terminal, could be easily justified economically.

1.3.2 Programmable Peripheral ICs and Device Controllers

The hardware in microprocessor systems for different applications is distinguished by the number and type of I/O devices required. These devices range from simple electromechanical switches to disk drives that store tens of millions of bits of information. An appropriate interface is required to connect each I/O device to the microprocessor system bus and to synchronize data transfers. In addition, logic is often required to control the basic operation of the I/O device. This logic may be part of the device or may need to be provided by the microprocessor system. LSI circuits are available to provide various peripheral interfaces and device controllers. In order to have wide applicability, these devices are software programmable so that an LSI circuit that handles a class of I/O devices can be configured to handle a specific device in that class. Programmable LSI devices must be initialized by a sequence of software commands before they are used for their intended function.

For example, many microprocessor systems must interface with I/O devices designed for serial data transfer, such as CRT terminals. A USART is an LSI circuit that provides a programmable serial communications interface between a microprocessor and serial I/O device. Data is transferred between the USART and microprocessor as parallel data via the system data bus. Data transfer between the USART and a serial I/O device is in serial form. However, before data transfer between the microprocessor and serial I/O device can take place, the USART must be initialized. The desired data format and synchronization method for the data transfer are specified during initialization by command data written by the microprocessor to the USART.

1.3.3 Programmable Logic Devices

Even with the extensive variety of LSI programmable peripheral and control ICs, the need to implement unavailable hardware functions, from minor logic operations to complex special functions, still exists. These functions can be implemented with SSI and MSI logic using conventional digital system design techniques. However, this results in the need for a large number of IC devices, which increases the manufacturing cost of the system and reduces its reliability. Parts count, the number of ICs, can be reduced by using *programmable logic devices, PLDs*, which provide arrays of gates and flip-flops that are interconnected internally by hardware programming the PLD. Determination of the required internal interconnection of the logic devices in the PLD can be accomplished using conventional digital system design techniques. However, *computer aided design, CAD*, systems translate design specifications, in the form of Boolean equations, truth tables, state diagrams, and so on, into information required to program the PLD on a device programmer.

1.4 AREAS OF APPLICATION

The major areas of microprocessor application are in

1. The replacement of random logic
2. The replacement of custom LSI
3. The replacement of minicomputers
4. New applications not economically feasible with previous technology

TABLE 1.4-1 MICROPROCESSOR APPLICATIONS

Analytical scientific instruments	Computer aided instruction
Smart terminals	On-line control of laboratory instrumentation
Stacker crane controls	Desktop computers
Conveyor controls	Check processors
Word processors	Payroll systems
Point-of-sale systems	Inventory control
Standalone electronic cash registers	Automatic typesetting
Electronic games	Compact business machines
Vending and dispensing machines	Medical instrumentation
Market scales	Automobile diagnostics
Traffic light controls	Data communication processing
Home heating and lighting controls	Optical character recognition
Security and fire alarm systems	I/O terminals for computers
Home appliances	

Table 1.4-1 lists a few specific areas of application where microprocessors have been utilized. Within these areas, the majority of microprocessor applications have been in the replacement of random logic and new applications. *Random logic* systems are implemented with gates and flip-flops interconnected in a manner such that the resulting structure is not regular or repetitive. Randomness here obviously refers to system structure as typified by a logic diagram and not to the methods used to determine the logical interconnections!

For those systems where microprocessors are suitable for the replacement of random logic, certain advantages exist in their utilization: substantial hardware design effort is replaced by programming effort, with an increase in system capability and versatility. Development time is reduced through a programmed approach, and the ability to make changes in the control program greatly enhances the ease with which a design can be modified. For extremely small random logic systems, microprocessors are not an appropriate replacement. A microprocessor system always requires a certain minimum amount of hardware (microprocessor, memory, and I/O circuitry), and thus there is a minimum cost associated with its use independent of the simplicity of the function implemented. With random logic, for all practical purposes, no such base cost exists; i.e., a random logic circuit can consist of as little as a single, small scale integrated circuit. On the other hand, for relatively small digital systems, an implementation structured around ROMs or PLDs can be the most cost effective. Figure 1.4-1 shows how various approaches to system implementation compare in terms of versatility and complexity.[1]

How large should a random logic system be before considering its replacement with a microprocessor? Designers have postulated various rules of thumb in terms of the number of IC packages in the random logic system. Thresholds of 30 to 40 SSI or MSI packages were originally proposed. Such guides are, however, very rough estimates and probably inappropriate. As the costs of microprocessors and associated memory circuits decrease, this threshold decreases. And the availability of single-chip microcomputers produce a significant lowering of the aforementioned thresholds.

[1]An FPLA, field programmable logic array, is one of many types of PLDs.

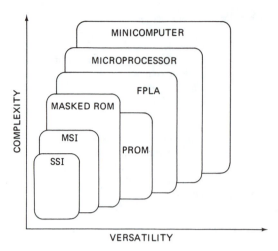

COMPLEXITY

VERSATILITY

Figure 1.4-1 Applicability of various approaches to logic design as a function of system complexity and versatility. (Copyright © 1976 by the Institute of Electrical and Electronics Engineers, Inc. Reprinted by permission, from IEEE SPRECTRUM, Vol. 13, no. 1, January 1976, pp. 50–56.)

Very high speed random logic systems are another category where microprocessors may be an inappropriate replacement. Although progress in LSI technology has provided microprocessors with faster instruction execution times, the sequential operation of a microprocessor system is a fundamental speed limitation. Assuming that the same technology is used, for instance, T^2L, a random logic system can be designed that will operate faster than a microprocessor based system. A random logic system can be designed to operate in parallel, whereas a microcomputer must execute its program sequentially. Given the same clock rate, a random logic system can do more in a single clock period. For example, a microprocessor can change at most a number of bits equal to its word length. A random logic circuit, on the other hand, can change all its memory elements during a single clock pulse.

Custom LSI can be replaced by a microprocessor programmed to implement the same functions. This not only alleviates the relatively long development time associated with custom LSI but also, if a second sourced microprocessor is employed, minimizes the problem of availability.

Microprocessors often are used to replace minicomputers that are under-utilized. However, as more powerful microcomputer systems are developed, those using 16- and 32-bit microprocessors, their performance capabilities approach and often exceed those of the less powerful minicomputers. Soon microcomputers will replace less powerful minicomputers—even in applications where the minicomputer is fully utilized.

The differentiation, however, between minicomputers and microcomputers has become less clear as more powerful microprocessors have been developed. The former criteria for delineation—word length, speed, architecture, instruction set, and cost—can no longer be rigidly applied. For instance, there are microprocessors that are designed to execute the instruction sets of minicomputers and microprocessors with architectural advances and features that supersede those of some

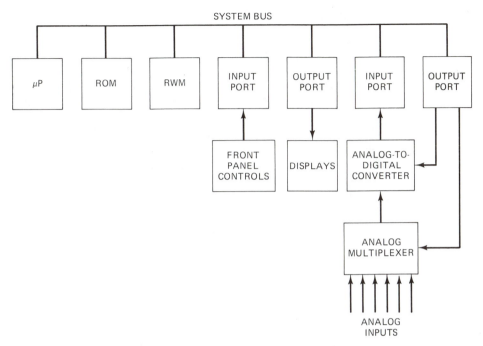

Figure 1.4-2   Generalized microprocessor based instrument.

minicomputers. Microprocessors fabricated with Schottky T^2L, I^2L, and even ECL have fast execution times. Several minicomputers have been designed that contain either catalog or custom microprocessors yet are called minicomputers. The only suitable distinctions between minicomputers and microcomputers are the degree of LSI utilization, the distribution of logic on these circuits, and the resulting smaller cost and size.

Many new products and products with significantly extended capabilities are available because of the small size, low power consumption, and low cost of microprocessors (see Table 1.4-1). Products with extended capabilities are typified by intelligent instrumentation: instrumentation that carries out a significant amount of arithmetic and/or logical processing. Microprocessor based intelligent instrumentation is available that displays computed functions of various measured signals, formats data for the instrument's input/output interface, conducts self-diagnosis, linearizes inputs from nonlinear transducers, and controls the overall system operation. A generalized intelligent instrument is shown in the block diagram of Fig. 1.4-2. New products employing microprocessors include a significant number of applications where digital processing is used for tasks previously handled by nonelectronic means. And applications previously implemented with analog electronic circuits are susceptible to digital implementation as the cost of microprocessors, RWM, ROM, and integrated analog-to-digital and digital-to-analog converters rapidly decreases.

1.5 DESIGN OF MICROPROCESSOR SYSTEMS

The effective design of a microprocessor system requires expertise in three areas: hardware design, software design, and system synthesis (see Fig. 1.5-1). The purpose of this text is to present the fundamental concepts required to develop expertise in these areas. If the designer is also responsible for generating the system specification, a detailed knowledge of the specific application is also required.

It is the nature of microprocessor systems that knowledge in any one of the required areas cannot be pursued in isolation of the others. Thus, each of the following chapters involves varying amounts of hardware design, software design, and system synthesis. Early chapters deal primarily with one area, while later chapters essentially are balanced among two or all three.

Before attempting the hardware design of a microprocessor system, the designer must be familiar with the hardware available for use as system compo-

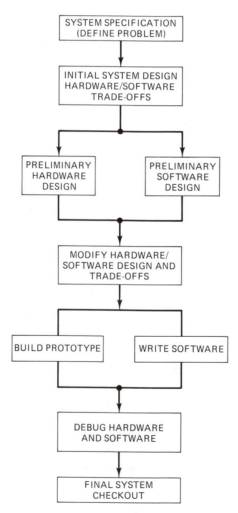

Figure 1.5-1 Steps in designing a microprocessor based system.

nents. Hardware components used range from gates and flip-flops to programmable LSI devices to completely packaged subsystems such as floppy disks. Familiarity with these components includes a knowledge and understanding of their function, logical organization, operation, performance characteristics, limitations, and costs.

Depending on the level at which the design is begun, the designer may be determining the interconnection of individual ICs or the interconnection of pre-manufactured subsystems. In any event, to be really effective, the designer's knowledge of hardware must extend down to the level of individual ICs.

It is assumed that the reader has a basic knowledge of digital system design using gates and flip-flops. The view of a microprocessor system as a collection of addressable registers is central in this text. Therefore, registers are considered in detail before microprocessors. In Chapter 2 the organization and operation of integrated circuit memory devices, including flip-flops, registers, and random access memories are discussed, as is the use of random access memory devices to form a memory system.

In Chapter 3 microprocessor organization and operation are presented using Intel's 8085A microprocessor as an instructional example. The 8085A is a general purpose 8-bit microprocessor that is an enhancement of the popular 8080A. Once a thorough understanding of the operation and application of this microprocessor is developed, it is relatively easy to understand other microprocessors from a study of the manufacturer's data sheets and application notes. Interconnection of a microprocessor to memory and simple I/O structures is also covered in this chapter.

To accomplish software design at the assembly language level, the designer must first have a knowledge of the microprocessor's instruction set and the function of each instruction. The designer must also know how to combine instructions to form a program that carries out a desired function using a particular hardware configuration. Once the program is written, procedures for translating it into machine language for loading into memory and techniques for testing and correcting any errors in the program must be understood.

The instruction set of the 8085A is introduced in Chapter 4. In particular, the instructions that implement data transfer, logical operations, and branching are presented in detail. These instructions are used in simple sequences and programs. The process of translating an assembly language program to machine code and subsequently testing that program is presented in Chapter 5.

A special memory structure common to microprocessors is the *stack*. The operation of the stack and the instructions that control it are introduced in Chapter 6. Among its other uses, the stack provides the hardware mechanism to support subroutines. Subroutines and their associated instructions are covered, which leads to a discussion of the use of subroutines in modular program development and some initial considerations of software design.

Carrying out arithmetic functions in a microprocessor system is considered in detail in Chapter 7. Software approaches, which implement arithmetic computations in the microprocessor itself using its arithmetic instructions, are considered. Binary, two's complement, decimal, and floating point arithmetic are covered. Hardware implementation of arithmetic functions external to the microprocessor is also presented.

The next two chapters deal with various methods of implementing data transfers between a microprocessor and its memory and between a microprocessor and the system's input and output devices. In Chapter 8, the hardware and software to implement I/O transfers that are initiated and completely controlled by the application program are discussed. Both serial and parallel I/O are covered, as is the use of special programmable peripheral LSI devices for implementing I/O interfaces. The important concept of hardware/software trade-off in microprocessor systems as it relates to I/O is illustrated here. In the remainder of the text, hardware/software trade-offs are considered as they relate to different aspects of system design.

In Chapter 9 interrupt and DMA techniques for carrying out I/O are considered. These techniques require additional hardware but have the advantage of providing higher I/O data rates and allowing the microprocessor to carry out other functions concurrently with the I/O transfers.

Because of the diversity of applications for microprocessor systems, they are commonly interfaced to peripheral devices ranging from integrated circuits to complex electromechanical subsystems. These devices are essentially analog or digital in nature. Common digital peripherals for data entry and display and methods for interfacing them to a microprocessor are discussed in Chapter 10. Interfacing analog devices to microprocessors is extensively covered in Chapter 11.

Minimizing the parts count in a microprocessor system is a desirable objective. Chapter 12 discusses the use and hardware programming of LSI programmable logic devices to replace standard SSI and MSI functions in a system. Devices for implementing primary memory systems, in addition to those of Chapter 2, and secondary memory systems are presented in Chapter 13.

The previous chapters having presented the basic concepts of hardware and software design and the integration of hardware and software to implement the synthesis of common subsystems, Chapter 14 ties these concepts together and presents techniques for designing complete systems.

REFERENCES

1. W. I. Fletcher, *An Engineering Approach to Digital Design* (Englewood Cliffs, N.J.: Prentice-Hall, 1980).

2. F. Faggin and M. E. Hoff, Jr., "Standard Parts and Custom Design Merge in Four-Chip Processor Kit," *Electronics*, 45 (April 1972), 112–16.

3. *MCS-4 Microcomputer Set*, *Users Manual* (Santa Clara, Calif.: Intel Corporation, 1974).

4. R. N. Noyce and M. E. Hoff, Jr., "A History of Microprocessor Development at Intel," *IEEE Micro*, 1 (February 1981), 8–21.

2

Random Access Semiconductor Memories

But the microcomputer itself is not the complete source of new ideas and perspectives. Other developments in LSI technology — the LSI ROM, PROM and RAM — form integral parts of the success of microcomputer applications. Without low-cost, low-power and physically small memories, the microcomputer CPU would have a greatly reduced impact. Progress in memory technology is inextricably intertwined into every microcomputer application.

Douglas A. Cassell*

*"Only Small, Clever Programs Need Apply," *Digital Design*, Vol. 5, No. 3, (March 1975), pp. 24 – 26, 30, 32.

Memory is a major consideration in all microprocessor system designs. Program code and constants are typically stored in ROM and data is stored in RWM[1]. In this chapter, the logical operation and timing requirements of random access semiconductor memory devices are presented. The discussion starts with D-type flip-flops and progresses through multibit registers to *static random access memory, SRAM*—the easiest form of RWM to use in microprocessor systems. Next, *erasable programmable read only memory, EPROM*, is presented. An EPROM is a form of ROM, the use of which is particular advantageous during the development of a microprocesssor system. The concept of a data bus and its function in transferring data between registers in a microprocessor system is then developed. These are important preliminary considerations before viewing, in later chapters, the operation of a microprocessor system as consisting, to a large extent, of the transfer of data between various registers that make up the system. This view is utilized throughout this text. Finally, the logic design of memory systems is introduced.

2.1 BASIC MEMORY CONCEPTS

2.1.1 Flip-Flops / 1-Bit Registers

The smallest unit of information a digital system can store is a binary digit, a *bit*, which has a logic value of 0 or 1. A bit of data is stored in an electronic device called a *flip-flop* or a *1-bit register* [1]. A flip-flop is a type of general *memory cell* and, as such, has two stable *states* in which it can remain indefinitely—as long as its operating power is not interrupted—and inputs that allow its state to be changed by external signals. A very simple type of flip-flop is the *D-type flip-flop*, illustrated in Fig. 2.1-1. It has a single data input, D, and two outputs, Q and $\overline{Q}$. Output Q represents the state of the flip-flop, and $\overline{Q}$ represents the complement of the flip-flop's state. The logic value at a flip-flop's D input when a clock signal, CLK, occurs is stored in the flip-flop. If the stored value is equal to 1, (Q = 1), the flip-flop is *set*. If the stored value is equal to 0, (Q = 0), the flip-flop is *clear*.

The logical operation of a D-type flip-flop is expressed by the characteristic equation, $Q_{n+1} = D_n$. This equation indicates that the output of a D-type flip-flop after the occurrence of a clock pulse, Q_{n+1}, is equal to the logic value of the D input before the occurrence of the clock pulse, D_n. But D-type flip-flops differ with regard to the precise time at which the clock pulse causes the input data to be accepted, the output to change in accordance with the input, and the output to be held or latched. This difference is a function of the flip-flop's triggering mechanism, which may be edge or level sensitive.

Two clock pulses, or strobes, are shown in Fig. 2.1-2. The clock pulse in Fig. 2.1-2a is a *positive clock pulse*. This signal is logic 0 in its quiescent state, makes a transition to logic 1, remains at logic 1 momentarily, and then returns to logic 0. The *leading edge* of the pulse is a 0 to 1 or *positive transition*, and the *trailing edge* is

---

[1]Memory inside microprocessors and I/O devices—registers and flags—is discussed in Chapters 3, 8, and 9. Some peripheral devices are mass memories, and these are covered in Chapter 13.

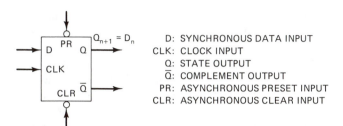

D: SYNCHRONOUS DATA INPUT
CLK: CLOCK INPUT
Q: STATE OUTPUT
$\overline{Q}$:   COMPLEMENT OUTPUT
PR: ASYNCHRONOUS PRESET INPUT
CLR: ASYNCHRONOUS CLEAR INPUT

Figure 2.1-1   D-type flip flop.

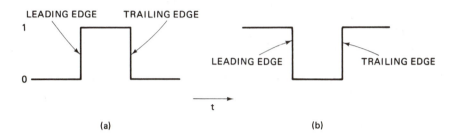

Figure 2.1-2   Single clock pulse: (a) positive clock pulse; (b) negative clock pulse.

a 1 to 0 or **negative transition**. The clock pulse in Fig. 2.1-2b is a **negative clock pulse**; its quiescent value is logic 1, and it makes a momentary negative transition to logic 0 followed by a positive transition back to logic 1. A positive transition is also referred to as a **rising edge**, and a negative transition is also referred to as the **falling edge**.

An **edge triggered** D-type flip-flop latches the logic value at the D input during the clock pulse's transition from one logic value to the other. The sensitivity of the flip-flop to the transition (edge) of the clock is indicated on the flip-flop's logic symbol by a **dynamic indicator**, a triangle, $>$, at the clock input. Positive edge triggered flip-flops latch on the positive transition of the clock (see Fig. 2.1-3a).

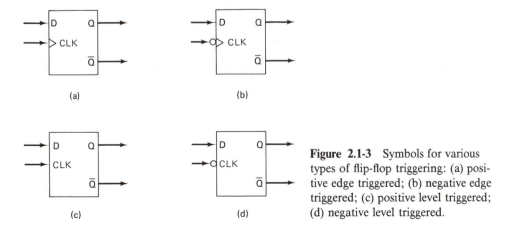

Figure 2.1-3   Symbols for various types of flip-flop triggering: (a) positive edge triggered; (b) negative edge triggered; (c) positive level triggered; (d) negative level triggered.

Negative edge triggered flip-flops latch on the negative transition of the clock. To indicate negative edge sensitivity, an inversion circle is used together with the dynamic indicator at the clock input, as shown in Fig. 2.1-3b.

If the clock pulse of Fig. 2.1-2a is applied to a positive edge triggered D flip-flop, the data is latched at the leading edge of the pulse. If the clock pulse of Fig. 2.1-2b is applied to a positive edge triggered flip-flop, the data is latched at the trailing edge of the pulse. Note that with an edge triggered flip-flop, the input is accepted, and the output changes and is latched during a single clock transition.

A *level triggered* flip-flop, usually referred to simply as a *latch*, has a clock input that is sensitive to the level of the clock signal. The output of a positive level triggered D flip-flop follows the D input when the clock is logic 1. When the clock makes a transition from 1 to 0, the data present at the D input is latched. The output of a negative level triggered D flip-flop follows the input when the clock is logic 0 and latches the input on a 0 to 1 clock transition. Figures 2.1-3c and d show how positive and negative level triggering is indicated at the flip-flop's clock input. Thus, for a level triggered flip-flop, the output follows the input when the clock is at the trigger level. During this condition the flip-flop is referred to as being *transparent*. The input data is latched on the transition from the trigger level to the quiescent level.

The D flip-flop symbol (Fig. 2.1-1) shows two additional inputs common to most IC flip-flops: *preset* and *clear*. The inversion circles on the flip-flop symbol indicate that both these inputs are active low. Preset and clear are asynchronous inputs; they affect the state of the flip-flop independent of the clock's level or transition. Thus, preset and clear override the clocked, or synchronous, input D. A logic 0 at the preset input sets the flip-flop; a logic 0 at the clear input clears it. For proper operation, the preset and clear inputs are not strobed simultaneously.

Figure 2.1-4 is a timing diagram of the clock and data input signals to a positive edge triggered D flip-flop. The waveform representing the data emphasizes when the data may change value, and not its specific value. Thus, the two horizontal lines above and below "data stable" are not to be interpreted as implying that DATA is simultaneously logic 0 and logic 1, an impossible condition, but that DATA can have either value. The crossing of the two lines indicates precisely when a change in state can take place.

In order for a flip-flop to operate correctly, certain timing constraints on the input data and clock signals must be adhered to. The minimum acceptable clock pulse width for proper operation is t_w. The input data must be stable for a minimum time period, t_{su}, before the positive transition of the clock and must remain stable

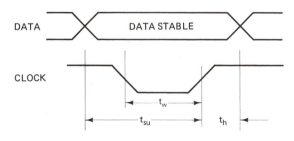

Figure 2.1-4 Timing diagram for a positive edge triggered flip-flop, showing clocking requirements.

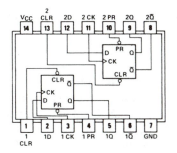

INPUTS				OUTPUTS	
PRESET	CLEAR	CLOCK	D	Q	$\overline{Q}$
L	H	X	X	H	L
H	L	X	X	L	H
L	L	X	X	H*	H*
H	H	↑	H	H	L
H	H	↑	L	L	H
H	H	L	X	Q_0	$\overline{Q}_0$

*The output levels in this configuration are not guaranteed to meet the minimum levels for V_{OH} if the lows at Preset and Clear are near V_{IL} maximum. Furthermore, this configuration is nonstable; that is, it will not persist when either Preset or Clear returns to its inactive (high) level.

(a)   (b)

Figure 2.1-5   74ALS74 dual D-type positive edge triggered flip-flop: (a) pinout; (b) function table. (Courtesy of Texas Instruments Incorporated.)

for a minimum time period, t_h, after this transition. The time period, t_{su}, is called the **setup time**, and the time period, t_h, the **hold time** for the flip-flop.

A 74ALS74 IC that contains two D-type positive edge triggered flip-flops is shown in Fig. 2.1-5 [2]. The minimum clock pulse, t_w, for this device is 14.5 nS. The setup time, t_{su}, is 15 nS, and the hold time, t_h, is 0 nS. A hold time of 0 nS means that the data can change simultaneously with the clock's transition, and if the setup time requirement is met, the data will be properly latched. A variety of other types of IC flip-flops, in addition to the D-type, are available. However, the D-type flip-flop is extensively used in microprocessor systems.

2.1.2 *m*-Bit Registers

To store several bits of data simultaneously, the clock inputs of several D flip-flops are connected in parallel to form an ***m*-bit register** (see Fig. 2.1-6). MSI circuits containing 4-, 6-, or 8-bit registers are readily available. Such registers store m bits

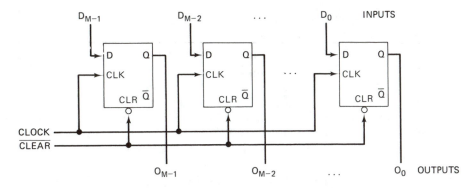

Figure 2.1-6   *m*-bit register consisting of m D-type flip-flops.

of data (D_0 to D_{m-1}) under control of the clock and provide m data outputs (O_0 to O_{m-1}).

The act of storing data in a register is a **write** operation. Determining the value of the contents of a register is a **read** operation.

The m bits of data stored in a register make up a word. A **word** is simply a number of contiguous bits operated upon or considered by the hardware as a group. The number of bits in the word, m, is the **word length**. Frequently, the word length in a digital system is 8 bits. Eight bits of information considered as a unit are referred to as a **byte**. This practice has led to the use of the term **nibble** to refer to smaller, 4-bit units of information.

The m inputs to the register are provided by an m-bit input data bus, and the m outputs by an m-bit output data bus. A **bus** is a number of signal lines, grouped together because of similarity of function, which connect two or more systems or subsystems.

Eight-bit registers are often called **octal registers** and find widespread use in microprocessor systems as input ports and output ports. Both edge and level triggered octal registers are available with either normal or complement outputs. In addition, many of these devices have three-state output buffers.

Three-state buffers are buffers with three output states. Two of the output states are the common logic states 0 and 1. When the buffer is enabled by a control input, its output is either logic 0 or 1. The output impedance is low when the buffer is enabled, allowing the output to source or sink current to the circuits it drives. The third state, which exists when the buffer is disabled, does not provide a conventional logic level output but, rather, causes the output to be a very high impedance. This high impedance state prevents the output from driving or loading any circuit connected to it. Thus, when disabled, three-state outputs are electrically disconnected from any logic circuits to which they are physically connected and are said to be **floating**. The electrical characteristics of three-state outputs are discussed in Appendix A.

Figure 2.1-7 provides the logic diagrams and function tables for the 74ALS573 and 74ALS574 octal flip-flops. The 74ALS574 is an octal D-type positive edge triggered register with three-state outputs. The logic diagram shows eight, negative edge triggered flip-flops with a common clock input. The clock input is driven by an internal inverting buffer. The buffer presents a single standard ALS input load to the CLK pin. The complement output of each flip-flop is inverted by an inverting three-state buffer before it reaches an output pin. To limit the number of pins required on the IC, only the normal form of the stored data is available at the outputs. When the output control input, $\overline{OC}$, is logic 0, the 74ALS574's three-state output buffers are enabled, and each output is either logic 0 or logic 1. When $\overline{OC}$ is logic 1, the outputs are in their high impedance state.

Also shown in Fig. 2.1-7 is the 74ALS573, an octal D-type transparent latch with three-state outputs. The 74ALS573 is functionally similar to 74ALS574 except that it is positive level triggered. One entry in the function tables for the 74ALS574 and 74ALS573 may be somewhat misleading. In row 4, $\overline{OC}$ is logic 1, CLK and D are don't cares, Xs, and the outputs are in the high impedance state, Z. However, it should be noted that the registers can still be written when $\overline{OC}$ is logic 1.

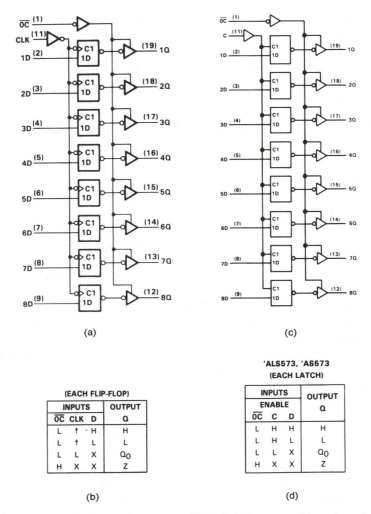

(a)   (c)

'ALS573, 'AS573
(EACH LATCH)

(EACH FLIP-FLOP)		
INPUTS		OUTPUT
$\overline{OC}$ CLK D		Q
L ↑ H		H
L ↑ L		L
L L X		Q_0
H X X		Z

INPUTS		OUTPUT
ENABLE		Q
$\overline{OC}$ C D		
L H H		H
L H L		L
L L X		Q_0
H X X		Z

(b)   (d)

Figure 2.1-7 Octal registers. 74ALS574 octal D-type positive edge triggered flip-flop: (a) logic diagram; (b) function table. 74ALS573 octal
D-type transparent latch: (c) logic diagram; (d) function table. (Courtesy
of Texas Instruments Inc.)

Many other IC registers are available with and without three-state outputs. If
a register with three-state outputs is used where its outputs need never be in the high
impedance state, $\overline{OC}$ is simply grounded.

Like single flip-flops, multibit registers have the same type of timing requirements. The minimum clock pulse, t_w, for the 74ALS574 is 14 nS; the setup time, t_{su},
is 15 nS; and the hold time, t_h, is 0 nS. For the 74ALS573 t_w is 10 nS, t_{su} is 10 nS,
and t_h is 7 nS. Since the 74ALS573 is positive level triggered, the setup time
specifies how long the data must be stable before the negative edge of the clock.

2.1.3 Data Transfer Between Registers

The transfer of data between registers requires a *source register*, from which data is read, and a *destination register*, to which data is written. These two registers must be connected by a data bus. Since there are a large number of possible source and destination registers in a microprocessor system, it is impossible to connect each possible pair of source and destination registers with its own dedicated data bus. Therefore, microprocessor systems use a single shared data bus. Of concern now are the concepts fundamental to the transfer of data between a source and destination register, not how the data may have come to be in the source register in the first place. Consider the transfer of data from any one source register, from among a group of possible source registers, to any one destination register, from among a group of destination registers (see Fig. 2.1-8a). All the source registers are at one end of a data bus and all the destination registers are at the other end. In this structure data is transferred in only one direction on the data bus. Therefore, the data bus is *unidirectional*.

Any single data transfer involves only one source register and one destination register. Three-state output buffers allow the source registers, W, X, Y, and Z to all be physically connected to the shared data bus. However, only one source register can place data on the data bus at a time. Thus, only one source register may have its three-state buffer enabled at a time. The three-state buffers of all other source registers must be disabled. If two registers have their outputs enabled at the same time, bus contention results. *Bus contention* occurs when two or more three-state buffers, with their outputs connected, are enabled simultaneously. If one buffer tries to drive the common connection to logic 1 and the other buffer tries to drive it to logic 0, excessive current in the buffers is the result. At the least, this condition produces invalid data on the bus. It may also produce power supply spikes, which can cause a loss of the data in the registers. The excessive buffer current may affect the life of the device or destroy it immediately.

To distinguish between source registers, each is assigned a unique binary code, an address. The addresses for the source registers are shown in Fig. 2.1-8a. Address decoding logic is required that takes an address as input and generates an output to enable the addressed register's three-state buffer. An additional requirement is that the addressed register only drive the data bus for a period of time defined by a read strobe, $\overline{RD}$. The proper design of decoding logic to prevent bus contention is an extremely important consideration!

In Fig. 2.1-8a, 1-out-of-4 decoders implement the necessary address decoding. Figure 2.1-9 shows the function table for a 1-out-of-4 decoder. The decoder has an enable input, $\overline{G}$, and select inputs, B and A, and four outputs, Y0, Y1, Y2, and Y3. When the enable input is logic 1, all decoder outputs are forced to logic 1 independent of the select inputs. Note that this decoder does not have three-state outputs, and the function of its enable input is different from that of the registers previously discussed. When the decoder is enabled, only one of its outputs is logic 0; all other outputs are logic 1. Which output is logic 0 is determined by the select inputs B and A. For example, if B = 1 and A = 0, then output Y2 is 0. A 74ALS139 provides two independent 1-out-of-4 decoders in a single IC.

3826

16 combinaisons

IC

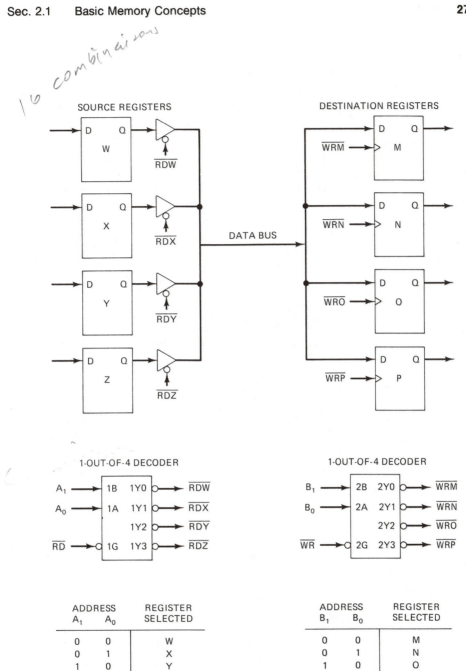

Figure 2.1-8a   Use of three-state buffers to share data bus lines.

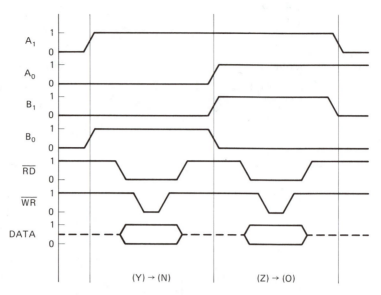

Figure 2.1-8b Timing diagram for two successive data transfers using the logic of Fig. 2.1-8a.

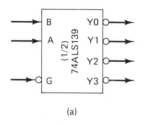

(a)

INPUTS		OUTPUTS			
ENABLE	SELECT				
$\bar{G}$	B A	Y0	Y1	Y2	Y3
H	X X	H	H	H	H
L	L L	L	H	H	H
L	L H	H	L	H	H
L	H L	H	H	L	H
L	H H	H	H	H	L

FUNCTION TABLE

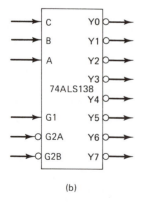

(b)

FUNCTION TABLE

ENABLE INPUTS		SELECT INPUTS			OUTPUTS							
G1	$\bar{G}2$*	C	B	A	Y0	Y1	Y2	Y3	Y4	Y5	Y6	Y7
X	H	X	X	X	H	H	H	H	H	H	H	H
L	X	X	X	X	H	H	H	H	H	H	H	H
H	L	L	L	L	L	H	H	H	H	H	H	H
H	L	L	L	H	H	L	H	H	H	H	H	H
H	L	L	H	L	H	H	L	H	H	H	H	H
H	L	L	H	H	H	H	H	L	H	H	H	H
H	L	H	L	L	H	H	H	H	L	H	H	H
H	L	H	L	H	H	H	H	H	H	L	H	H
H	L	H	H	L	H	H	H	H	H	H	L	H
H	L	H	H	H	H	H	H	H	H	H	H	L

*$\bar{G}2 = \bar{G}2A + \bar{G}2B$

Figure 2.1-9 Logic symbols and function tables for decoders: (a) one-half of a 74ALS139 dual 1-out-of-4 decoder; (b) 74ALS138 1-out-of-8 decoder. (Tables courtesy of Texas Instruments Incorporated.)

Returning to Fig. 2.1-8a, address inputs, A_0 and A_1, of the source decoder, select which register's three-state output buffer will be enabled. As long as $\overline{RD}$ is logic 1, all output buffers are disabled and the output bus is in its high impedance state. When $\overline{RD}$ is logic 0, the output buffer selected by A_0 and A_1 is enabled. Address inputs, B_0 and B_1, of the destination decoder, select the register to be written. The control strobe, $\overline{WR}$, enables the decoder's output, causing the addressed register to be written.

The timing diagram in Fig. 2.1-8b shows the required relative timing relationship between the read and write strobes. Two data transfers take place in this figure, one from register Y to register N, followed by a transfer from register Z to register 0. To meet setup and hold time requirements for the destination register, the read strobe must cause data to be on the data bus for a sufficient time before and after the write strobe. Bus contention is further avoided by separating the data transfer operations by time intervals during which the bus is in its high impedance state. The data bus being in its high impedance state is represented by dashed lines midway between the logic 0 and logic 1 states.

In Fig. 2.1-10 each register has a three-state output buffer. In addition, a connection brings the common output of each group of registers back to a common input. In this structure there are eight possible source registers and eight possible destination registers. Again, only one register may be selected as the source and one as the destination for a single data transfer. Address decoding logic is implemented by two 1-out-of-8 decoders (see Fig. 2.1-9). The data bus can transfer data in either direction, therefore it is *bidirectional*.

2.1.4 Memories

Several equal length registers can be incorporated in a single IC and share a common set of inputs, a common set of outputs, and a single clock line (see Fig. 2.1-11). Such a circuit is simply referred to as a *memory*. It is necessary, of course, to distinguish among the various registers.

Each register occupies a distinct *location*, which has a unique numerical *address*. Thus, memory can be thought of as a collection of *addressable registers*. Logic is necessary in the IC to decode address inputs to ensure that only a single register outputs its contents when data is being read from the memory, and only a single register has data stored in it when data is being written into the memory. This address decoding logic is considered in Section 2.2.2.

A conceptual representation of a memory is shown in Fig. 2.1-12a. In this representation, the addresses of locations are represented by the integers from 0 to $2^n - 1$, and the content of each location is the binary word stored at that address. Memories frequently have word lengths that are multiples of 4 bits. This had led to the convenient practice of specifying memory contents and addresses as hexadecimal quantities. (See Appendix B for a discussion of hexadecimal numbers.) Figure 2.1-12b shows this convention applied to the addresses and memory contents of Fig. 2.1-12a. The letter H is used as a suffix to indicate that the number is expressed in hexadecimal notation.

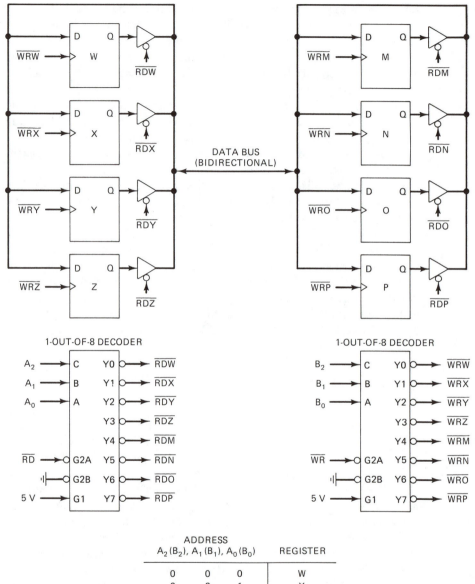

Figure 2.1-10 Registers interconnected by a bidirectional data bus.

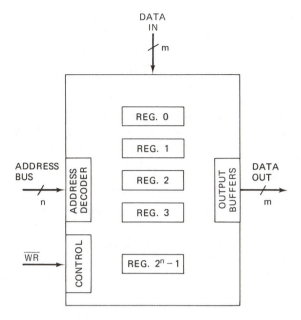

Figure 2.1-11 Register representation of a memory.

MEMORY LOCATION	n-BIT ADDRESS	MEMORY CONTENTS	HEX ADDRESS	HEX CONTENTS
0	000	0 1 1 0	0H	6H
1	001	0 0 1 0	1H	2H
2	010	1 1 0 0	2H	CH
3	011	0 0 0 1	3H	1H
4	100	1 1 1 0	4H	EH
5	101	1 1 1 0	5H	EH
6	110	0 0 0 0	6H	0H
7	111	0 1 1 0	7H	6H

←— m BITS —→

(a)   (b)

Figure 2.1-12 Conceptual representation of $2^n \times m$-bit memory: (a) binary notation; (b) hexadecimal notation.

The *capacity* of a memory is specified in terms of the maximum number of bits or the maximum number of words the memory can store. Assuming that the memory has an n-bit address and each word is of length m, the memory has a capacity of $2^n \times m$ bits, organized as 2^n words each of m bits. Such an organization is referred to as $2^n \times m$ memory. For example, if $n = m = 8$, the memory is called a "two hundred fifty six by eight memory," and is written "256 × 8." The letter K, when used as a suffix in specifying the capacity of a large memory, is equal to 1024 (2^{10}). Therefore, 1 K words represents 1024 words; 2 K words represents 2048 words; and so on. The n address bits are the address inputs to the memory. With n address bits, one of 2^n unique locations (L) can be specified: $L = 2^n$. Thus, the number of locations in a memory is always a power of two. Given L, the number of address bits required to distinguish between L locations is $n = \log_2 L$.

All memories provide a method for reading the contents of a memory location in response to the application of an address and appropriate control signals. The representation of the memory in Fig. 2.1-11 shows a control input, $\overline{OE}$, which, when logic 0, causes a copy of the contents of the location specified by the address inputs to appear at the memory's output. There is a time lag between the application of an address and the appearance at the output of the contents of the addressed location; this time lag is known as the memory's *access time* and is dependent both on the technology and on the structure used to implement the memory. For the memory structure of Fig. 2.1-11, the access time for each read operation is essentially independent of the sequence in which addresses are applied. Such a memory is called a *random access memory, RAM*; thus, with a RAM, the contents of any one location can be accessed in essentially the same time as can the contents of any other location chosen at random.

Writing data into a memory also involves a time delay—following the application of an address, input data, and a write control signal—before the new data is reliably written into the memory. This time period is known as the memory's *write time*. For the memories shown in Fig. 2.1-11, the $\overline{WE}$ control input is momentarily brought to logic 0 for a write operation. This logic 0 strobe is the clock signal that writes the input data. The actual latching of data occurs on the trailing edge of the negative strobe at the $\overline{WE}$ input.

2.2 STATIC READ WRITE MEMORY, SRAM

The easiest type of RWM to use in a microprocessor system is static random access memory, SRAM. The basic memory cell in a static memory is similar to that in a flip-flop. Like a flip-flop, an SRAM is *volatile*: it will retain its data only while its operating power is maintained.

2.2.1 External Organization

The external organization of a memory device refers to the logical organization of the memory as seen at the device's pins. This is the organization of primary concern to the system designer. Static RWMs are typically organized with word lengths of 1, 4, or 8 bits. Memories with 8-bit word lengths are called *byte-wide* memories. Table 2.2-1 lists a number of static memories and their external organization. In simple applications a single SRAM, with word length equal to the data bus width, may provide all the RWM required. For example, an application involving a microprocessor with an 8-bit data bus and requiring no more than 2 K bytes of RWM could be satisfied with a single 2 K × 8 device. In other applications a number of memory devices must be interconnected to provide the required number of words and/or bits per word.

Pins of a RWM accept the address, data, and control signals required to operate the device. Power and ground connections are also required. The devices in Table 2.2.1 require a single +5 V power supply for operation. The n address inputs are designated A_0 to A_{n-1} as shown in Fig. 2.2-1. The binary value at these inputs selects the word that will be written or read.

TABLE 2.2-1 SOME REPRESENTATIVE STATIC READ WRITE MEMORIES

Device	Organization (total words × bits/word)	No. pins	Control lines	I/O type
2115A	1 K × 1	16	$\overline{CS}$, $\overline{WE}$	separate
2147H	4 K × 1	18	$\overline{CS}$, $\overline{WE}$	separate
51C67	16 K × 1	20	$\overline{CS}$, $\overline{WE}$	separate
2114A	1 K × 4	18	$\overline{CS}$, $\overline{WE}$	common
6168	4 K × 4	20	$\overline{CS}$, $\overline{WE}$	common
6116	2 K × 8	24	$\overline{CS}$, $\overline{WE}$, $\overline{OE}$	common
6264	8 K × 8	28	$\overline{CS}$, $\overline{WE}$, $\overline{OE}$	common

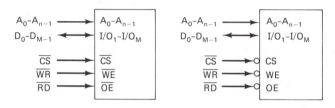

Figure 2.2-1 Equivalent representations of an SRAM with common I/O. One representation uses inversion circles on the control inputs to indicate that they are active low.

To minimize the number of data pins required, common I/O is often used. With **common I / O**, the memory outputs are internally connected, through three-state buffers, back to their corresponding inputs. The m data input/output pins are designated I/O_1 to I/O_m. Such memories are directly compatible with the bidirectional data buses used in microprocessor systems. A memory with **separate I / O**, a separate set of input and output pins, must have its outputs connected back to the corresponding inputs by external three-state buffers when used in a system with a bidirectional data bus.

Control inputs cause write or read operations to take place. Two control schemes are commonly used: the first uses three control lines, $\overline{CS}$, $\overline{WE}$, and $\overline{OE}$; the second uses only $\overline{CS}$ and $\overline{WE}$. Since many applications require more than one memory device, the chip select, $\overline{CS}$, input is provided to select a device for the operation that will take place. This input is active low. If a device is not selected, it cannot be written or read.

To write a device that uses the first scheme, the output enable input, $\overline{OE}$, which controls the memory's three-state output buffers, is held at logic 1, the address of the location to be written is provided at the address inputs, the chip select input is made logic 0, data is provided at the data inputs, and a write strobe, $\overline{WR}$, is provided at the write enable, $\overline{WE}$, input. The write input of the memory is analogous to the CLK input of a flip-flop. For the memory to be properly written, its timing requirements must be met. These requirements are considered in detail in Section 2.2.3.

To read a location, the $\overline{WE}$ input is held at logic 1, the address is applied, the device is selected, and the memory's output buffers are enabled by a $\overline{RD}$ strobe at the $\overline{\text{OE}}$ input. This input is analogous to the output control, $\overline{\text{OC}}$, input of the octal registers. Note that the $\overline{\text{WE}}$ and $\overline{\text{OE}}$ inputs must never be active at the same time.

With the second scheme there is no $\overline{\text{OE}}$ input. Whenever the device is selected, $\overline{\text{CS}}$ low, it will be written or read, depending on the state of the $\overline{\text{WE}}$ input. If $\overline{\text{WE}}$ is low, and the device is selected, it is written. Writing of the device usually occurs on the rising edge of either $\overline{\text{WE}}$ or $\overline{\text{CS}}$, whichever occurs first. If $\overline{\text{WE}}$ is high and the device is selected, it is read. The primary advantage of this scheme is to reduce, by one, the number of pins on the device required for control. The advantage of the first scheme is the simplified interconnection of several devices.

2.2.2 Internal Organization

An understanding of the internal organization of semiconductor memory devices leads to a clearer understanding of their operation and timing requirements. SRAMs are designed so that a single device meets all the functional requirements of a memory system. To do so, a device contains

1. An array of memory cells each of which can store a single bit
2. Logic to address any location in the memory
3. Circuitry to allow reading the contents of any memory location
4. Circuitry to allow any memory location to be written

For easy interconnection of a memory device with other memory devices or logic circuits, memory devices contain input drivers, output buffers, and circuitry for address expansion.

SRAMs are internally organized to obtain a memory with high speed, a large bit capacity, and low peripheral circuit and memory array costs [3]. Conceptually, the simplest organization is a **word organized** array with **linear selection**. The memory array in such an organization has a column length equal to the number of

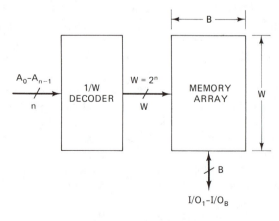

W: NUMBER OF LOGICAL WORDS
B: NUMBER OF BITS PER LOGICAL WORD

Figure 2.2-2 Internal organization of an SRAM using linear selection. Control logic is not shown.

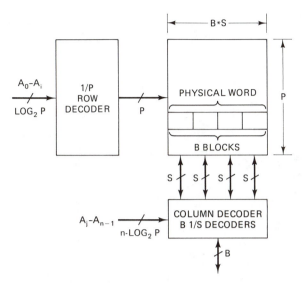

P: NUMBER OF PHYSICAL WORDS
B*S: NUMBER OF BITS IN A PHYSICAL WORD
B: NUMBER OF BITS PER LOGICAL WORD
S: SEGMENTATION

W = P*S

Figure 2.2-3   Two level decoding.

words, W, and a row length equal to the number of bits per word, B (see Fig. 2.2-2). Word selection requires a 1-out-of-W decoder; i.e., a decoder with a mutually exclusive output for each word in the memory. The address inputs to the decoder select one, and only one, of the decoder's outputs—thus selecting one word in the memory array. Clearly, although conceptually simple, the linear selection method requires a large decoder for a large number of words, which is very costly in chip area. For memories with a small number of words, this organization is acceptable and has the advantage of a short access time.

Address decoder size is substantially reduced by organizing the memory array and the word selection logic to allow *coincident selection* or *two-level decoding*. In a memory array utilizing two-level decoding, one level corresponds to a physical word and one to a logical word. A *physical word* consists of the number of bits in a row of the memory array. A *logical word* consists of the number of bits of a physical word that are sensed and gated to the output at one time. Two-level decoding requires two decoders: a row decoder that selects a physical word and a column decoder, actually several multiplexers, that then selects one logical word from the selected physical word. A physical word is divided into S segments (logical words); the row decoder is a 1-out-of-P decoder, where P is equal to W/S; and the column decoder consists of B, 1-out-of-S multiplexers (see Fig. 2.2-3).

The block diagram of an HM6116 SRAM with 2048, 8-bit words (2 K × 8) organized with two-level decoding is shown in Fig. 2.2-4a [4]. The memory array is 128 × 128 bits; thus, it contains 128 physical words. A physical word is selected by decoding the seven address bits A_1 through A_7. Thus, the row decoder is a

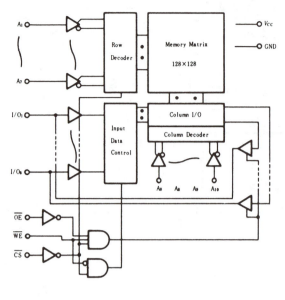

(a)

$\overline{CS}$	$\overline{OE}$	$\overline{WE}$	Mode	I/O Pin
H	×	×	not selected	High Z
L	L	H	Read	D_{out}
L	H	L	Write	D_{in}

(b)

Figure 2.2-4 HM6116, 2 K × 8 SRAM: (a) block diagram; (b) function table. (Courtesy of Hitachi America, Ltd., Semiconductor and I.C. Division.)

1-out-of-128 decoder. Segmentation is accomplished by dividing the physical word into eight blocks of 16 bits. The first block contains the most significant bits of each of the 16 logical words; the next block contains the next most significant bits of each of the 16 logical words, etc., until the eighth block, which contains the least significant bits of each of the 16 logical words. Thus, each physical word is segmented into 16 logical words, and therefore S equals 16. Column decoding, then, requires eight 1-out-of-16 multiplexers to provide an 8-bit output logical word. In this example, address bits A_0, A_8, A_9, and A_{10} control the column decoders.

The HM6116 is an example of a memory device with common I/O and which uses three control lines. The logic associated with the control inputs is shown in Fig. 2.2-4a and the resulting function table is shown in Fig. 2.2-4b.

When the number of segments in a physical word is equal to the number of bits in a physical word, the result is a ***bit organized*** memory; i.e., each logical word is a single bit in length. The bit organized memory has a single output, a square memory array, and row and column decoders of equal complexity. The row and column decoders each decode $n/2$ address bits, resulting in a simplification of the decoders required. A 4 K × 1 bit organized memory, for example, consists of a 64 × 64 memory array, a 1-out-of-64 row decoder, and a 1-out-of-64 column

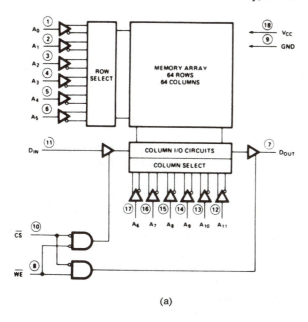

(a)

C̄S̄	W̄Ē	MODE	OUTPUT	POWER
H	X	NOT SELECTED	HIGH Z	STANDBY
L	L	WRITE	HIGH Z	ACTIVE
L	H	READ	D$_{OUT}$	ACTIVE

(b)

Figure 2.2-5   2147H, 4 K × 1 SRAM: (a) block diagram; (b) function table. (Courtesy of Intel Corp.)

decoder. The 2147H SRAM in Fig. 2.2-5a has this organization [5]. The 2147H has separate I/O and uses two control lines. The logic associated with the control inputs is shown in Fig. 2.2-5a and the resulting function table in Fig. 2.2-5b.

2.2.3 Timing Requirements

To ensure proper operation, there are timing constraints on the sequencing of address, data, and control signals to an SRAM device. These constraints are specified on the manufacturer's data sheet in the form of AC characteristics and timing diagrams.

The simplest operation to analyze is a read. The following steps occur in a read:

1. An address is applied to the address inputs.
2. The SRAM is selected by application of the proper logic level at its chip select input.
3. The contents of the selected memory location appear at the data outputs after a period of time equal to the access time.

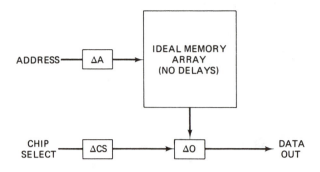

Figure 2.2-6 Lumped delay memory model for a read operation.

A simplified model of an SRAM is shown in Fig. 2.2-6. In terms of timing constraints the memory array in this model is ideal, having no signal propagation delays associated with it. The device delays that exist in any real device are shown as lumped delays associated with the device's inputs and outputs [6]. Two input delays are shown in Fig. 2.2-6: ΔA associated with the address inputs and ΔCS associated with the chip select input. The delay ΔA includes all propagation delays associated with address input buffers, row and column decoders, and the memory array. The delay ΔCS includes all the propagation delays associated with the chip select logic. Delays associated with the output buffers are represented by ΔO. For simplicity, the SRAM has separate I/O and its output buffers are held in their enabled state, $\overline{OE} = 0$.

Assume that the device is selected by the proper logic level at its chip select input. The time elapsed from the subsequent application of an address at the address inputs to the appearance at the memory's output of a stable copy of the addressed data is the address access time, t_A.[2] This time is simply the address to output delay, $\Delta A + \Delta O$.

If a stable address exists at the address inputs and the chip select inputs are changed to select the device, the delay between the application of proper chip select signal and stable output data is $\Delta CS + \Delta O$, the chip select to output delay, t_{CO}, or chip select access time. These two parameters, t_A and t_{CO}, are shown in the timing diagram in Fig. 2.2-7. The diagram shows the application of the address and chip select signals at the latest times for their effects on the output to occur simultaneously. The reference point is the occurrence of valid output data. As shown in the diagram, t_{CO} is usually significantly smaller than t_A. This is due to the fact that the chip select logic is connected directly to the output buffers. This timing diagram uses the 10 and 90 percent points of signal transitions for reference; some timing diagrams use the 50 percent point.

The various access times of a memory indicate its speed. In a microprocessor system, the microprocessor supplies the address and chip select signals to a memory and then must wait a period of time equal to the access time before it can use the output from the memory. Slow memories limit a microprocessor's speed.

---

[2]Although parameter names and symbols vary from manufacturer to manufacturer and among different devices from the same manufacturer, the parameters themselves are common.

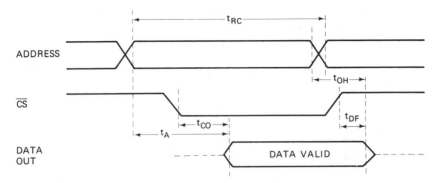

Figure 2.2-7   Timing diagram of a read operation.

Three other parameters are shown in the timing diagram; two of these are the output hold time, t_{OH}, and the chip deselect to output float time, t_{DF}. These parameters are referenced to the time when the valid output data changes to invalid data or to a floating condition. Output hold time, t_{OH}, indicates how long the previous output data is valid after the address is changed. The chip deselect to output float time indicates how long the output data remains valid when the device is no longer selected. The third parameter, read cycle time, t_{RC}, specifies the maximum rate at which different memory locations can be successively read.

The basic sequence of operations for writing an SRAM are as follows:

1. An address is applied to the address inputs of the SRAM.

2. The SRAM is enabled by application of the proper logic level at the chip select input.

3. Data to be written into the memory is applied at the data inputs.

4. The $\overline{WE}$ line is pulsed low.

5. The address and chip select signals can then be changed to select another memory location for reading or writing.

The model for a write operation shown in Fig. 2.2-8 includes two more delays than the read model of Fig. 2.2-6: the input delay, ΔI, and the write enable delay, ΔW.

A *write pulse* must occur at the $\overline{WE}$ input for a minimum length of time, t_{WP}, to guarantee writing into the slowest memory devices. The write pulse begins and ends the write operation and is a convenient reference for specifying other parameters associated with the write operation. It begins when the $\overline{WE}$ line undergoes a 1 to 0 transition. However, in most memories, the levels on the data lines are not important until the $\overline{WE}$ line makes a 0 to 1 transition because most memories accept input data at this transition. This is similar to the situation that exists with a positive edge triggered flip-flop.

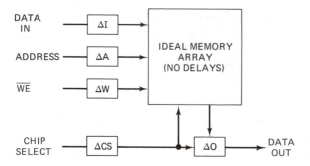

Figure 2.2-8 Lumped delay memory model for a write operation.

When the 0 to 1 transition of the $\overline{\text{WE}}$ line occurs, the data present at the memory array represents the data to be stored. The $\overline{\text{WE}}$ line affects the memory array, ΔW, seconds after the signal is changed at the package pin. Changes in input data values at the package pins reach the memory array, ΔI, seconds later. Thus, data must be stable at the package pins at least $\Delta I - \Delta W$ seconds earlier. This corresponds to a period of time, $\Delta I - \Delta W$, before the 0 to 1 transition of the external $\overline{\text{WE}}$ line. This time, $\Delta I - \Delta W$, is referred to as the data setup time, t_{DW}. Data at the data inputs must be stable for a time equal to or greater than t_{DW} to guarantee proper storage. Figure 2.2-9 shows t_{DW} referenced to the 0 to 1 transition of the $\overline{\text{WE}}$ line. Note that the timing diagrams represent signals at the package pins.

It is also necessary to hold the input data stable for a period of time after the 0 to 1 transition of the $\overline{\text{WE}}$ line; this time period is the data hold time, t_{DH}.

Whenever address inputs are changed, a finite amount of time elapses before the outputs of the address decoders have settled to their final value. During these transients, other memory locations are inadvertently addressed. If the write strobe is applied before these transients end, the data to be written into the memory may be written into several memory locations in addition to that intended. To preclude this,

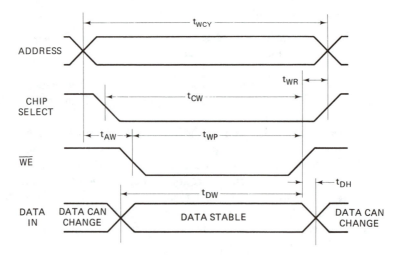

Figure 2.2-9   Write timing diagram for a R/W memory.

A.C. CHARACTERISTICS T_A = 0°C to 70°C, V_{CC} = 5V ± 10%, unless otherwise noted.

READ CYCLE [1]

SYMBOL	PARAMETER	2114AL-1		2114AL-2		2114AL-3		2114A-4/L-4		2114A-5		UNIT
		Min.	Max.	Min.	Max.	Min.	Máx.	Min.	Max.	Min.	Max.	
t_{RC}	Read Cycle Time	100		120		150		200		250		ns
t_A	Access Time		100		120		150		200		250	ns
t_{CO}	Chip Selection to Output Valid		70		70		70		70		85	ns
t_{CX} [3]	Chip Selection to Output Active	10		10		10		10		10		ns
t_{OTD} [3]	Output 3-state from Deselection		30		35		40		50		60	ns
t_{OHA}	Output Hold from Address Change	15		15		15		15		15		ns

WRITE CYCLE [2]

SYMBOL	PARAMETER	2114AL-1		2114AL-2		2114AL-3		2114A-4/L-4		2114A-5		UNIT
		Min.	Max.	Min.	Max.	Min.	Max.	Min.	Max.	Min.	Max.	
t_{WC}	Write Cycle Time	100		120		150		200		250		ns
t_W	Write Time	75		75		90		120		135		ns
t_{WR}	Write Release Time	0		0		0		0		0		ns
t_{OTW} [3]	Output 3-state from Write		30		35		40		50		60	ns
t_{DW}	Data to Write Time Overlap	70		70		90		120		135		ns
t_{DH}	Data Hold from Write Time	0		0		0		0		0		ns

NOTES:
1. A Read occurs during the overlap of a low $\overline{CS}$ and a high $\overline{WE}$.
2. A Write occurs during the overlap of a low $\overline{CS}$ and a low $\overline{WE}$. t_W is measured from the latter of $\overline{CS}$ or $\overline{WE}$ going low to the earlier of $\overline{CS}$ or $\overline{WE}$ going high.
3. Measured at ± 500 mV with 1 TTL Gate and C_L = 5.00 pF

WAVEFORMS
READ CYCLE ③

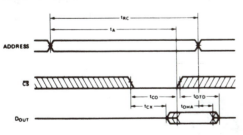

NOTES:
3. $\overline{WE}$ is high for a Read Cycle
4. If the $\overline{CS}$ low transition occurs simultaneously with the $\overline{WE}$ low transition, the output buffers remain in a high impedance state
5. $\overline{WE}$ must be high during all address transitions

WRITE CYCLE

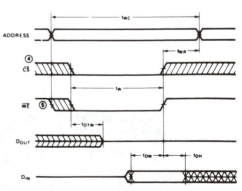

Figure 2.2-10 A.C. characteristics and waveforms for a 2114A SRAM. (Courtesy of Intel Corp.)

the address lines must be stable for a period of time preceding and following the occurrence of the write pulse. The write delay, t_{AW}, indicates how long the address must be stable before the 1 to 0 transition of the write pulse, and the write recovery time, t_{WR}, indicates how long the address must be held stable after the 0 to 1 transition of $\overline{WE}$.

Similar to the address inputs, the chip select must be stable for a period of time referred to as the chip enable to write time, t_{CW}, before the 0 to 1 transition of the $\overline{WE}$ line. A final parameter, t_{WCY}, the write cycle time, specifies the minimum time between write operations. On most static semiconductor memory devices, the read and write cycle times are equal.

Timing parameters for memory devices are specified as A.C. characteristics on the device's data sheet. A specific device is usually available in several different speed versions. The various versions of a device are identified by dash numbers that follow the device type number. The A.C. characteristics and waveforms for a 2114A, 1 K $\times$ 4, SRAM are given in Fig. 2.2-10 [5] on page 41. The A.C. characteristics are specified in two tables; one gives the read cycle parameters and the other gives the write cycle parameters. The parameters are illustrated on the read cycle and write cycle waveforms. The 2114A uses two control lines. Although the notation varies for some parameters, the parameters shown are essentially those of Figs. 2.2-7 and 2.2-9.

The data sheet indicates that the fastest version of the 2114A is the 2114A-1, which has a read and write cycle time of 100 nS. The slowest version is the 2114A-5, which has a read and write cycle time of 250 nS.

2.3 ERASABLE PROGRAMMABLE READ ONLY MEMORY, EPROM

Ultraviolet erasable and electrically reprogrammable read only memory, EPROM, is widely used for storing programs and constants in microprocessor systems. EPROMs are *nonvolatile*; therefore they can store the application program in a dedicated microprocessor system and the program will always be ready for execution. EPROMs must be erased before they can be written—programmed. Both erasure and pro-

Figure 2.3-1   EPROM with quartz window. (Courtesy of Intel Corp.)

gramming are done with the EPROM removed from the microprocessor system. Erasure is accomplished by shining ultraviolet light through the quartz window of the EPROM package and onto the IC chip (see Fig. 2.3-1). Programming is done with an instrument designed for that purpose, an EPROM programmer. Use of EPROMs is particularly advantageous during the development cycle of a microprocessor system. The program, in binary form, can be programmed into the EPROM, the EPROM placed into the circuit, and the system tested. If it is necessary to modify the program, the EPROM is removed, erased, and reprogrammed. This iterative process can be repeated as often as necessary.

When used, in-circuit, the EPROM is only read. It is this mode of operation that is of concern when designing a system that uses an EPROM.

2.3.1 Organization and In-Circuit Operation

Figure 2.3-2a is a diagram of the in-circuit configuration of an EPROM. The external organization is similar to that of an SRAM. However, since the EPROM is a read only memory it has no $\overline{WE}$ input. In the read mode, the program pin, $\overline{PGM}$ is held at logic 1 and the program input voltage, V_{PP}, is held at 5.0 V. Two control lines are used to operate the EPROM; the two control lines are $\overline{CE}$ and $\overline{OE}$. The chip enable input, $\overline{CE}$, is similar in function to the $\overline{CS}$ input of an SRAM. In addition, when the chip is not enabled, $\overline{CE} = 1$, the EPROM is in a low power mode. The output enable input, $\overline{OE}$, controls the three-state output buffers of the EPROM. The first three lines of the mode selection chart in Fig. 2.3-3 relate to the in-circuit operation of the 27128A, 16 K $\times$ 8, EPROM.

EPROMs are usually byte-wide devices. Many devices are available that follow a universal 28-pin memory site standard adopted by the Joint Electronic Devices Engineering Council, JEDEC. This standard defines the pin functions for

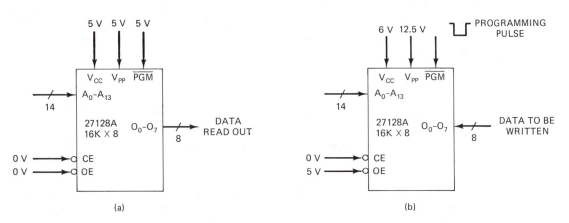

Figure 2.3-2 27128A EPROM external connections: (a) configuration for in-circuit read operation; (b) configuration for programming on an EPROM programmer.

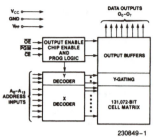

Figure 1. Block Diagram

27256	2764A	2732A	2716
Vpp	Vpp		
A12	A12		
A7	A7	A7	A7
A6	A6	A6	A6
A5	A5	A5	A5
A4	A4	A4	A4
A3	A3	A3	A3
A2	A2	A2	A2
A1	A1	A1	A1
A0	A0	A0	A0
O0	O0	O0	O0
O1	O1	O1	O1
O2	O2	O2	O2
Gnd	Gnd	Gnd	Gnd

27128A

Pin configuration (28-pin):
1 Vpp, 2 A12, 3 A7, 4 A6, 5 A5, 6 A4, 7 A3, 8 A2, 9 A1, 10 A0, 11 O0, 12 O1, 13 O2, 14 GND
28 Vcc, 27 PGM, 26 A13, 25 A8, 24 A9, 23 A11, 22 OE, 21 A10, 20 CE, 19 O7, 18 O6, 17 O5, 16 O4, 15 O3

2716	2732A	2764A	27256
		Vcc	Vcc
		PGM	A14
Vcc	Vcc	N.C.	A13
A8	A8	A8	A8
A9	A9	A9	A9
Vpp	A11	A11	A11
OE	OE/Vpp	OE	OE
CE	CE	CE	CE
O7	O7	O7	O7
O6	O6	O6	O6
O5	O5	O5	O5
O4	O4	O4	O4
O3	O3	O3	O3

230849-2

NOTE: Intel "Universal Site"-Compatible EPROM Pin Configurations are Shown in the Blocks Adjacent to the 27128A Pins

Figure 2. Pin Configurations

Mode Selection

Mode \ Pins	CE (20)	OE (22)	PGM (27)	A9 (24)	Vpp (1)	Vcc (28)	Outputs (11-13, 15-19)
Read	VIL	VIL	VIH	X	Vcc	Vcc	DOUT
Output Disable	VIL	VIH	VIH	X	Vcc	Vcc	High Z
Standby	VIH	X	X	X	Vcc	Vcc	High Z
Verify	VIL	VIL	VIH	X	Vpp	Vcc	DOUT
Program Inhibit	VIH	X	X	X	Vpp	Vcc	High Z
Int₀ligent Identifier	VIL	VIL	VIH	VH	Vcc	Vcc	Code
Int₀ligent Programming	VIL	VIH	VIL	X	Vpp	Vcc	DIN

1. X can be VIH or VIL
2. VH = 12.0V = 0.5V

Pin Names

A_0-A_{13}	ADDRESSES
CE	CHIP ENABLE
OE	OUTPUT ENABLE
O_0-O_7	OUTPUTS
PGM	PROGRAM

Figure 2.3-3 27128A EPROM. (Courtesy of Intel Corp.)

28-pin memory devices. Figure 2.3-3 shows pinouts for the Intel family of EPROMs, which are compatible with the JEDEC standard. Some of these EPROMs are 24-pin devices that conform to the standard when positioned at the "bottom" of the 28-pin universal socket. A socket with connections conforming to the JEDEC standard allows any capacity memory device that conforms to the standard to be placed in the socket. Jumpers must be configured to accommodate the few pins that have different functions for different devices. There are a variety of other types of memory devices that conform to this standard, including the HM6116 SRAM discussed in Section 2.2.

The internal organization of an EPROM is similar to that of an SRAM with programming logic replacing the write logic of the SRAM. Figure 2.3-3 shows the block diagram of the 27128A 16 K × 8 EPROM [5].

2.3.2 The EPROM Memory Cell; Structure, Programming, and Erasure

A memory cell in an EPROM consists of a single floating gate transistor. This transistor resembles an ordinary MOS transistor except for the addition of a floating gate [7, 8] (see Fig. 2.3-4). The floating gate is in the insulator between the substrate and the select gate. Unlike the select gate, the floating gate has no connections to it.

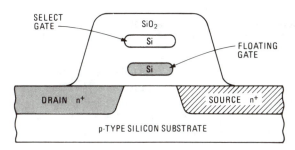

Figure 2.3-4 Floating gate memory cell of an EPROM. (Reprinted from ELECTRONICS, August 16, 1979. Copyright © 1979, McGraw-Hill Inc. All rights reserved.)

The cell is programmed by charging the floating gate via injection of electrons from the drain's pinch-off region. To charge the floating gate, the select gate voltage and the drain voltage are raised to a high positive level, while the source and substrate are held at ground potential. Appropriate drain and gate voltages cause the transistor to operate in saturation. Some of the electrons accelerated in the transistor's pinch-off region acquire enough energy to enter the conduction band of the silicon dioxide and get attracted to the positive potential of the floating gate. The charge on the floating storage gate changes the threshold voltage of the select gate.

The programming procedure for the 27128A is similar to that of other EPROMs. The 27128A is in the programming mode when V_{pp} is 12.5 V, V_{cc} is 6.0 V, and $\overline{CE}$ and $\overline{PGM}$ are both logic 0. The address and data to be programmed are TTL levels. The data to be programmed is applied to the data output pins. When the address and data are stable, a 50 mS active low TTL program pulse is applied to the $\overline{PGM}$ input. Each location must be programmed in a similar manner. Locations may be programmed individually, sequentially, or at random.

The select gate voltage, during reading, results in a drain current that reflects the cell's state. If the gate is charged, the transistor does not conduct, corresponding to the storage of a logic 0. If the floating gate is not charged, is erased, or is unprogrammed, the transistor conducts corresponding to the storage of logic 1. The timing sequence for reading an EPROM is similar to that for reading an SRAM.

The cell is erased by internal photoemission from the floating gate to the select gate and substrate. Erasure is accomplished by exposing the cell to ultraviolet light. The electrons on the floating gate receive enough energy from the ultraviolet light to surmount the energy barrier between the floating gate and the insulator surrounding it. The excited electrons are swept away to the select gate or substrate by the local field. During erasure, the select gate, source, drain, and substrate are all near ground potential. Since the entire silicon chip is exposed to ultraviolet light during erasure, all cells in the memory array are erased simultaneously. It is impossible to erase a single cell or single logical word.

Erasure of an EPROM begins to occur upon exposure to light with wavelengths shorter than 4000 angstroms. Commercial EPROM erasers use mercury arc lamps or mercury vapor lamps. These devices emit strong radiation with a wavelength of 2537 angstroms. A typical eraser will completely erase an EPROM in 15 to 20 minutes. Sunlight, fluorescent light, and incandescent light are all capable of erasing an EPROM if the length of exposure is sufficiently long. After programming, the quartz window of an EPROM is covered with an opaque label to prevent inadvertent erasure.

Many EPROMs are available as *production EPROMs*. A production EPROM uses the same silicon chip as its regular EPROM counterpart. However, production EPROMs use plastic windowless packages. The result is a lower cost "EPROM" that can only be programmed once! Such devices are used in systems that are produced in large quantity and where the code in the production EPROM has been thoroughly tested.

2.3.3 EPROM Programmers and Intelligent Programming

EPROMs are programmed out of circuit by special instruments designed for this purpose. These instruments are called EPROM programmers, PROM programmers, or, generically, device programmers. A dedicated EPROM programmer will only program EPROMs, although it may be capable of programming an entire family of such devices. Universal device programmers are capable of programming a wide range of programmable devices, including EPROMs, PROMs, and PLDs. Universal devices are usually of one of two types, standalone or personal computer driven.

A standalone programmer is capable of programming a device without the aid of a personal computer. These instruments are themselves microprocessor based systems (see Fig. 2.3-5a). The data to be programmed into the EPROM is entered into the programmer from either a front panel keypad, a master EPROM placed in the programming socket, or a serial interface to a computer. The device to be programmed is then placed in the programming socket and programmed. Before programming the EPROM, the programmer verifies that it is erased by reading each location and checking for the erased condition. In order to program other devices such as PROMs and PLDs, hardware personality modules are used. The personality module adapts the programmer to the unique programming voltages, currents, and pin configuration for a particular device.

A personal computer driven system attaches to a personal computer and relies on the execution of software on the personal computer to control its operation (see Fig. 2.3-5b). The programmer is able to control the voltages at each pin of the programming socket as directed by the personal computer. This type of programmer is able to program a wide selection of devices without the need for personality modules.

Early EPROM programming techniques used a nominal 50 mS pulse to program each byte. The 50 mS pulse duration was chosen to ensure that each cell was adequately programmed, even though very few cells in an EPROM actually require more than 8 mS for programming. Thus, programming time was proportional to the number of bytes in the EPROM. For EPROMS with a large number of words, programming time could approach 30 minutes.

Both of the programmers previously described operate under the control of a microprocessor and thus are capable of programming EPROMs using intelligent

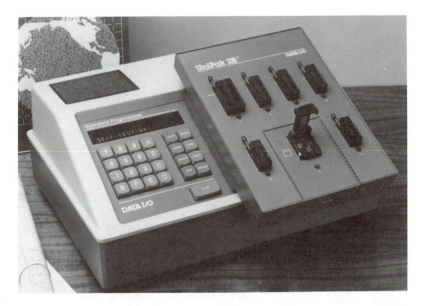

Figure 2.3-5a   (a) A standalone EPROM programmer (Courtesy of Data I/O Corp.).

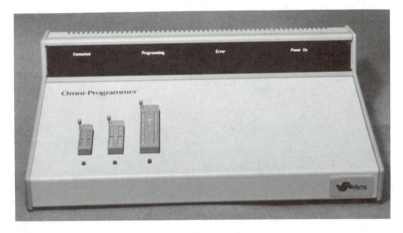

Figure 2.3-5b   (b) Computer driven device programmer (Courtesy of Varix Corp.).

programming algorithms. An intelligent programming algorithm programs an EPROM in the shortest possible time. An intelligent programming algorithm programs a location using short, e.g., 1 mS, programming pulses. After each programming pulse the programmer reads the location it is attempting to program; if the value read differs from the value being programmed, it will apply another programming pulse. Once the value read is the same as that being programmed, it

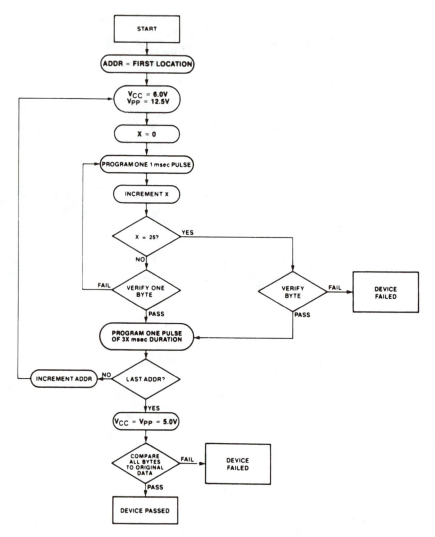

Figure 2.3-6 Flowchart of intelligent programming algorithm. (Courtesy of Intel Corp.)

generates a longer programming pulse to over program the location. Overprogramming ensures that enough charge is placed on the cells in a location to guarantee that the location is reliably programmed.

Figure 2.3-6 is the intelligent programming algorithm for the 27128A. Each location is programmed in sequence starting with the first. After each 1 mS programming pulse the location is read back. If it is not the same as the byte written, this process is repeated up to a maximum of 25 times. After the byte read back is the same, or the maximum number of pulses has been applied, a single pulse of three times the total duration of the previous pulses is applied to overprogram the location. After overprogramming, if the byte read back is incorrect, the device fails. After all locations have been programmed, a final verification of all bytes is made.

2.4 MEMORY SYSTEM DESIGN

The memory requirements of a typical microprocessor system frequently cannot be met with a single memory device. Several memory devices must then be interconnected to form a memory system. In a memory system, capacity is expanded by increasing the number of words and/or by increasing the word length above that attainable from a single memory device. Word length is increased by placing the outputs of two or more memory devices in parallel. For example, m, 16 K $\times$ 1-bit memories can be arranged in parallel to make a 16 K $\times$ m-bit memory system.

The number of words in a memory system is increased by multiplexing outputs from two or more memory devices. Memory devices have features that facilitate this. For example, chip select or chip enable inputs are provided on individual memory devices for this purpose.

A memory system with an increased number of words requires a provision for address expansion: expanding the number of memory address bits to which the memory system responds. The number of address bits that a microprocessor provides dictates its *memory address space* or the range of memory locations it can directly address. A memory system can be designed to fill the entire memory address space of the microprocessor with which it is used, although most applications do not require that much memory.

Depending on the size of the memory system, external address decoding logic, in addition to the memory's chip select inputs, may also be required for address expansion. This external logic decodes the additional address bits required to select a memory device. MSI decoders, which decode two, three, or four inputs are often used for this purpose.

The additional address lines required for memory expansion are connected to the decoder's inputs, and the decoder's outputs provide the signals for the chip select inputs of the memory devices. Decoders, themselves, may also have one or more enable inputs for the purpose of interconnecting decoders to create a larger decoder.

When memory devices are combined to form a memory system, with an expanded number of words, the corresponding data outputs of the memory devices must be multiplexed to form a single set of data outputs for the entire memory system. The output buffers on each memory device are three-state to allow the multiplexing of output data from several memory devices. Address decoding logic decodes the higher order address bits and enables the three-state outputs of only one memory device.

Memory systems are designed to provide the required amount of ROM and RWM needed for a particular application. The design steps may be described as follows:

1. Estimate the amount of ROM and RWM required for the application.
2. Determine the address boundaries for each type of memory. Draw an initial memory map.
3. Select the memory devices to be used.
4. Determine the arrangement of memory devices necessary to provide the required word length and number of words. Draw the detailed memory map.
5. Design the address decoding logic.
6. Determine the buffering required, if any.
7. Determine the required speed of the memory devices.

This section is concerned with steps 4 and 5. The results of steps 1, 2, and 3, which are application dependent, will be assumed as the starting point in this section. Steps 6 and 7 are discussed in Chapter 3.

Microprocessors communicate with external memory via buses: address, data, and control buses. The address bus is unidirectional, providing information to devices external to the microprocessor only. The data bus, on the other hand, is bidirectional, transmitting information from the microprocessor to memory and from memory to the microprocessor. The direction of transfer on the microprocessor's data bus (to or from) is indicated by control signals from the microprocessor. These signals are detailed in Chapter 3. Each of the signals on a control bus is unidirectional. Some of these are outputs from the microprocessor; others are inputs to the microprocessor.

The examples that follow assume that the memory system is interfaced to an 8085A microprocessor with a system bus consisting of a 16-bit address bus, A_0–A_{15}, an 8-bit bidirectional data bus, D_0–D_7, and three control lines. With 16 address bits the microprocessor can address a maximum of 64 K bytes of memory. Thus, the microprocessor is said to have a 64 K byte memory address space. Only a portion of the 64 K byte address space may actually need to contain memory for a particular application. The three control lines from the microprocessor are $\overline{WR}$, $\overline{RD}$, and $IO/\overline{M}$. $\overline{WR}$ and $\overline{RD}$ are strobes that occur when the microprocessor is either writing or reading, respectively, the location corresponding to the address on the address bus. The occurrence of these strobes is mutually exclusive, the microprocessor will never generate both strobes simultaneously. $IO/\overline{M}$ is a control signal from the microprocessor, which when logic 0, indicates that the address is that of a memory location as opposed to an I/O location.

The simplest memory systems are those in which no word length expansion is required and the memory devices have a separate output enable input. Consider an application that requires 8 K bytes of ROM and 2 K bytes of RWM. The ROM must start at location 0000H, and be immediately followed by the RWM. The memory map for the system is shown in Fig. 2.4-1a. It pictorially shows the appropriate memory address boundaries. These storage requirements for this system can be met using only two devices: A 2764A 8 K × 8 EPROM, to provide the

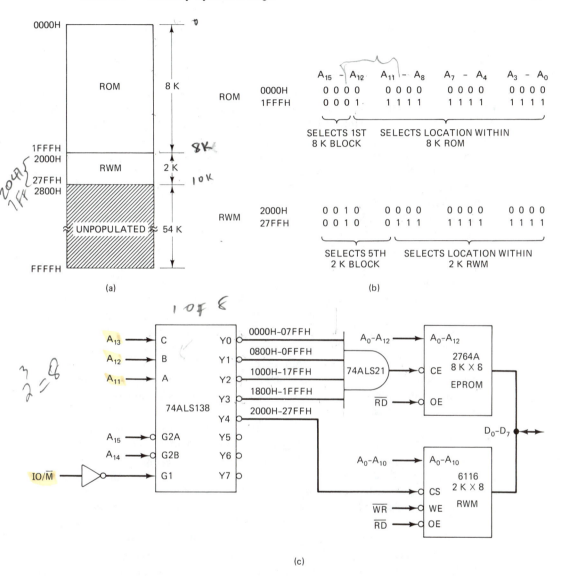

Figure 2.4-1 Exhaustively decoded memory system containing 8 K of ROM and 2 K of RWM: (a) memory map; (b) address bit map; (c) logic diagram.

ROM, and an HM6116 2 K $\times$ 8 SRAM, to provide the RWM. Since these are both byte-wide devices, no word length expansion is required.

Address decoding logic is required to generate the chip enable signal for the EPROM and the chip select signal for the SRAM. The address decoding logic has as its inputs the higher order address bits and the control line IO/$\overline{\text{M}}$. Only one memory device must be enabled, or selected, at a time to preclude bus contention. The EPROM chip must be enabled only when an address in the range from 0000H to 1FFFH is generated and IO/$\overline{\text{M}}$ is logic 0. The SRAM chip must be selected only when the address is in the range 2000H through 27FFH and IO/$\overline{\text{M}}$ is logic 0. The address bit map of Fig. 2.4-1b illustrates which address bits are decoded by the memory devices and which are decoded by the address decoding logic.

Figure 2.4-1c shows an implementation of the required logic. The address decoding logic is simply a multiple-input multiple-output combinational circuit. It could be implemented using SSI or MSI logic. The implementation of Fig. 2.4-1c has been designed to take advantage of the existence of the 74ALS138 1-out-of-8 decoder or its equivalent, the 8205 decoder. The active high enable, G1, of the 74ALS138 is driven by the complement of IO/$\overline{\text{M}}$. Therefore, the decoder is not enabled; none of its outputs is logic 0, unless IO/$\overline{\text{M}}$ is logic 0. The active low enables, $\overline{\text{G2A}}$ and $\overline{\text{G2B}}$, are driven by address inputs A_{15} and A_{14}. This ensures that the decoder is only enabled when both A_{15} and A_{14} are logic 0. The select inputs of the decoder, C, B, and A, are driven by A_{13}, A_{12}, and A_{11}. As a result, each output of the decoder selects a 2 K block in the 64 K address space of the microprocessor. An alternative method to determine the block size is to consider the lower order address bits not connected to the decoder. In this example they are A_0–A_{10}. These 11 address lines correspond to a 2 K block of locations not decoded by the 74ALS138. The first four 2 K blocks of the address space are occupied by the 2764A. The four-input AND will drive the chip enable low when any one of the first four 2 K blocks is selected. The output of the decoder corresponding to the fifth 2 K block, 2000H–27FFH, drives the chip select of the HM6116. The memory device control inputs $\overline{\text{WE}}$ and $\overline{\text{OE}}$ are driven by $\overline{\text{WR}}$ and $\overline{\text{RD}}$, respectively. When a $\overline{\text{RD}}$ strobe occurs only the selected memory device will have its output buffers enabled and drive the data bus.

Address decoding can be exhaustive or partial. With **exhaustive decoding** all address bits are decoded to select a particular location in a memory device. The address bits that go directly to the memory device are decoded by the device's internal decoders. The remaining address bits are decoded by external address decoding logic. Exhaustive decoding leads to a one-to-one mapping of addresses to memory device locations. Thus, each location in a memory device has a single address associated with it. The term **fully decoded** is also used to describe exhaustive decoding. The address decoding logic in Fig. 2.4-1b is exhaustive.

With **partial decoding** all the address bits are not decoded. Not including all of the address bits in the decoding can result in simplified decoding logic. Partial decoding leads to a many-to-one mapping of addresses to memory locations.

Figure 2.4-2 uses partial decoding to implement the same memory system as Fig. 2.4-1. The first output, Y0, of the 74ALS138 is logic 0′ for any address in the first 8 K block of the 64 K address space. The second output, Y1, of the 74ALS138 is logic 0 for any address in the second 8 K block of the address space. Thus, the decoder divides the 64 K address space into eight 8 K blocks. The first 8 K block corresponds to addresses 0000H–1FFFH and the second 8 K block corresponds to addresses 2000H–3FFFH.

In Fig. 2.4-2 the first 8 K memory locations are fully decoded. The internal decoders of the 2764A decode address bits A_0 through A_{12} and the 74ALS138 decodes address bits A_{13} through A_{15}. The 8 K memory locations in the second

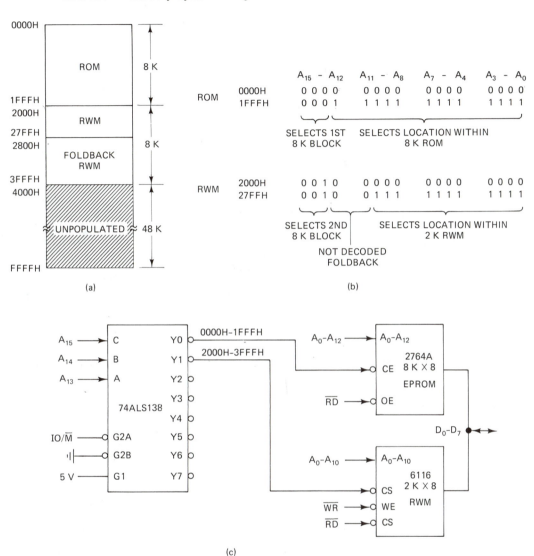

Figure 2.4-2 Partially decoded memory system containing 8 K of ROM and 2 K of RWM: (a) memory map; (b) address bit map; (c) logic diagram.

block are partially decoded. The internal decoders of the HM6116 decode address bits A_0 through A_{10} and the 74ALS138 decodes address bits A_{13} through A_{15}. However, address bits A_{11} and A_{12} are not decoded. The result of not decoding A_{11} and A_{12} is that each byte of memory in the HM6116 responds to four addresses. For example, the first location in the HM6116 responds to addresses 2000H, 2800H, 3000H, and 3800H. These addresses differ only in the values of bits A_{11} and A_{12}. The multiple mapping of the basic locations is called **foldback**.

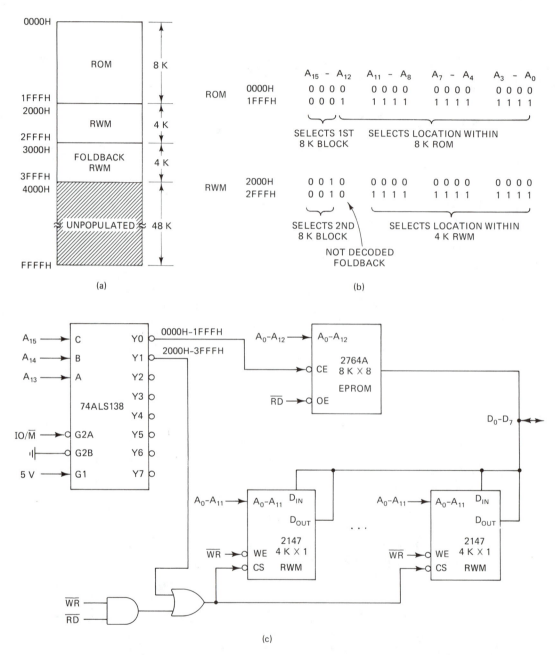

Figure 2.4-3 Partially decoded memory system with 8 K of ROM and 4 K of RWM: (a) memory map; (b) address bit map; (c) logic diagram.

The 2 K byte SRAM occupies only one quarter of the 8 K block in which it resides. The remaining 6 K of memory address space in the 8 K block is foldback. However, a location in the HM6116 will respond to each address in this 8 K block. As the memory requirement was defined this loss of available memory space poses no problem and leads to simple address decoding logic. If additional memory were to be added and this address decoding scheme maintained, then the additional memory would have to start at an address of 4000H or above.

The HM6116 is an example of a RWM that uses three control lines. The 2147H, 4 K × 1, SRAM is an example of a RWM that uses two control lines. In addition, the 2147H also illustrates the use of a "× 1" memory device with separate I/O. Figure 2.4-3 shows a memory system with 8 K bytes of ROM followed by 4 K bytes of RWM. The RWM consists of eight 2147Hs connected in parallel to provide the required 8-bit word length. Each 2147H has a single data input, D_{IN}, and a single data output, D_{OUT}. D_{OUT} is internally driven by a three-state buffer that is enabled when $\overline{WE}$ is logic 1 and $\overline{CS}$ is logic 0. To interface the 2147H to the bidirectional data bus, D_{OUT} is simply connected to D_{IN}, providing a single bidirectional data line. $\overline{WR}$ from the microprocessor drives the 2147H's $\overline{WE}$ input. Since it is required that the memory drive the data bus only during the time that the $\overline{RD}$ strobe is active, the 2147H $\overline{CS}$ input cannot be driven directly from an output of the 74ALS138. The combination of the AND gate and OR gate ensures that the 2147H is selected only during the occurrence of a $\overline{RD}$ or $\overline{WR}$ strobe and a memory address assigned to the 2147H.

As shown by the previous examples, memory systems of the required number of words and word length can be constructed from smaller capacity memory devices. The desired number of words of memory are obtained by using several memory devices and designing the address decoding logic to select the appropriate device for a given address range. The address decoding logic must ensure that only one device is selected at any time in order to preclude bus contention. Timing considerations for memory design are covered in detail in Chapter 3. However, the combined delays of the memory devices and the address decoding logic lead to a slower memory system. Thus it is desirable to design the address decoding logic so that propagation delay of signals through this logic is minimized. Word length expansion is easily achieved by connecting several memory devices in parallel so that they share address and chip select signals. Each device then provides one or more of the data bits in the resulting word.

2.5 MEMORY CLASSES

The SRAM and EPROM memories discussed in the previous sections represent only two of the many types of semiconductor memories available. Other types of semiconductor memories are covered in Chapter 13. This section discusses the classification of the various memory types.

Memories, in general, are classified on the basis of several attributes. Figure 2.5-1 provides an organizational structure for the classification of semiconductor

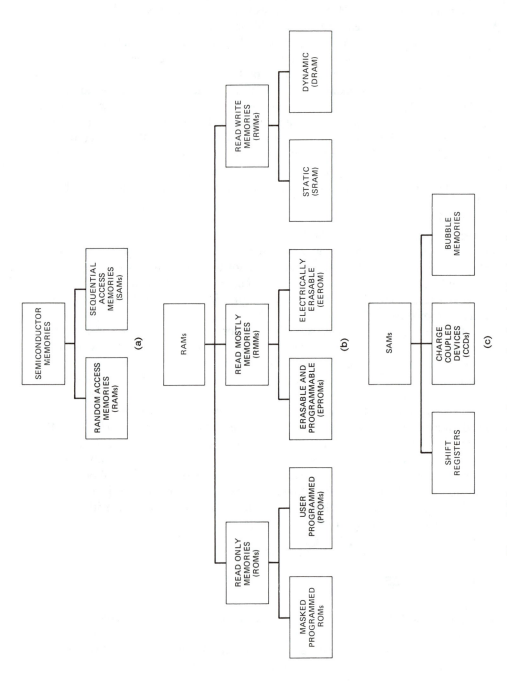

Figure 2.5-1 Organizational structure for the classification of semiconductor memories: (a) subdivision of semiconductor memories into RAMs and SAMs; (b) subdivision of RAMs; (c) subdivision of SAMs.

memories. Access time divides memories into two classes: random access memory, introduced in Section 2.1.4, and sequential access memory. If the access time varies significantly depending upon the order in which addresses are applied, the memory is a *sequential access memory*. Memories composed of shift registers are an example of sequential access semiconductor memories. In this chapter, only random access semiconductor memories were discussed. Sequential access memories are discussed in Chapter 13.

Based on their write times and on the ease with which they can be written, random access memories are further classified as read only memories, read mostly memories, or read write memories. Memories whose contents are specified only once, during manufacture, are read only memories, ROMs. After being written (mask programmed) during manufacture, a ROM's write time is considered infinite, since it cannot be written again. The memory cell used in a ROM is significantly different and simpler than the flip-flop used as a memory cell in an SRAM, since the state of the memory cell is fixed. The application program in most dedicated microprocessor systems is stored in ROM.

A variation of the ROM is the *programmable read only memory, PROM*. Like the ROM, a PROM can be written only once. However, when a PROM is obtained from the manufacturer, all of its bits are fixed at either 1s or 0s, depending on the device. Opposite bit values are programmed into it using the PROM programmer. Bit values, once programmed, cannot be subsequently altered. The production EPROM, of Section 2.3.3, is a type of PROM.

Memories that can be written into more than once and that have short write times, typically on the order of hundreds of nanoseconds or less, are called *read write memories, RWMs*. In dedicated microprocessor based systems, RWMs are used primarily for storing data and intermediate results of computations. RWMs are either static or dynamic in operation. *Static memories* have memory cells that are similar to a common flip-flop. *Dynamic memories* have memory cells that must be *refreshed*, read and rewritten periodically, or the memory cells' contents are lost.

The term "RAM" is often used to signify read write memory to the exclusion of read only memory. However, read only memories are also random access. This exclusive labeling of read write memory as RAM, though not strictly correct, has found widespread usage. RAM is used here in its strict interpretation, i.e., a random access memory, and includes both ROMs and RWMs.

A class of memories exists that lies between ROMs and RWMs in terms of the ase and the speed of writing. Memories in this class are sometimes referred to as *read mostly memories, RMMs*, and include *erasable programmable read only memories, EPROMs*, and *electrically erasable read only memories, EEROMs*. These memories can be written into more than once. They are distinguishable from RWMs by requiring significantly longer write times, some by requiring that all locations be erased simultaneously. The desirability of RMMs stems from the fact that they are, like ROMs, nonvolatile, but are also, in effect, writeable ROMs. The term ROM is used in this text to refer to any of the various types of ROMs and RMMs when the distinction is not important.

The ideal general purpose memory is a low cost, high speed, nonvolatile RWM. The fact that this ideal is still to be met is clearly illustrated by the numerous types of memory just discussed. Each of those memory types is noted for certain advantages in terms of economics and performance in particular applications.

REFERENCES

1. W. I. Fletcher, *An Engineering Approach to Digital Design* (Englewood Cliffs, N.J.: Prentice-Hall, 1980).

2. *The TTL Data Book*, Vol. 3 (Dallas, Tex.: Texas Instruments, Inc., 1984).

3. R. E. Matick, "Memory and Storage," in *Introduction to Computer Architecture*, ed. H. S. Stone (Chicago: Science Research Associates, Inc., 1975), chap. 5.

4. *IC Memories Data Book* (San Jose, Calif.: Hitachi America, Ltd).

5. *Memory Components Handbook* (Santa Clara, Calif.: Intel Corporation, 1985).

6. P. Alfke and I. Larsen, eds., *The T^2L Applications Handbook* (Mountain View, Calif.: Fairchild Semiconductor, 1973).

7. D. Frohman-Bentchkowsky, "A Fully Decoded 2048-Bit Electrically Programmable FAMOS Read-Only Memory," *IEEE Journal of Solid State Circuits*, SC-6, (October 1971), 301–06.

8. M. H. Woods, "An E-PROM's Integrity Starts with Its Cell Structure," *Electronics*, August 14, 1980.

PROBLEMS

2-1. Draw a block diagram showing the common bus structure of a microprocessor based system and the subsystems that the bus connects. Each of the subsystems consists of registers. For each subsystem indicate the nature of the registers that make up the system, i.e., read only, write only, read write, storage, operational, and so on.

2-2. For the clock and data waveforms below draw the output waveform, Q, for a D-type flip-flop for each of the following types of triggering:
(a) positive edge triggered
(b) negative edge triggered
(c) positive level triggered
Assume $Q = 0$ initially.

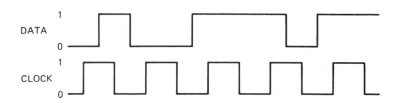

2-3. Draw a logic diagram showing the connection of four 74ALS574 positive edge triggered octal D-type flip-flops, so that the resulting circuit has separate I/O. The input bus is driven by SPST switches and the output bus drives indicator lights. Design logic that will allow any of the registers to be written by a write strobe. $\overline{WR}$, and will allow any register to drive the indicator lights during a read strobe, $\overline{RD}$. Writing and reading of the registers can occur simultaneously. The register written and the register read need not be the same. Use a 74ALS139 dual 1-out-of-4 decoder and any other necessary SSI gates to implement any required logic.

2-4. Give the number of address bits required to address any word in a memory that contains the following number of words:

  (a) 1024
  (b) 4096
  (c) 512
  (d) 8192
  (e) 64,536

2-5. List the hexadecimal equivalents of the following memory addresses specified in decimal:

  (a) 123
  (b) 750
  (c) 2048
  (d) 6743

2-6. Draw a timing diagram showing the relative timing relationships of the data and clock for a positive edge triggered D-type flip-flop. The clock signal is a negative pulse. Label the diagram to show hold time, minimum write pulse width, and setup time. Show the data in the high impedance state except when data must be valid. Draw a second timing diagram for the write operation of a RWM. This diagram should show address, data, and active low write strobe. Label the diagram to show hold time, minimum write pulse width, setup time, and write cycle time.

2-7. A 256 × 4 memory can be organized using linear selection or two-level decoding.

  (a) Draw a block diagram of the logical organization of the memory if linear selection is used.
  (b) If two-level decoding is used and the memory array consists of 32 physical words, draw a block diagram of the logical organization of the memory; specify all appropriate parameters and the method of segmentation.

2-8. Draw a block diagram of the internal structure of a 1024 × 1 SRAM that uses a square memory array and two-level decoding. List the size and number of all required decoders and the address inputs associated with each.

2-9. An SRAM has an external organization of 64 K × 1. Draw a diagram showing the internal organization of the memory. Specifically show the size of the row select, column select, and memory array. Assume that the lower address bits are associated with the row select circuitry. How many bits make up a physical word? How many bits make up a logical word?

2-10. An SRAM has an external organization of 1 K × 4. Draw a diagram of the internal organization of the memory. Show the size of the row select, column select, and memory array. Associate the low order address bits with the row select circuitry. Specify the number of logical words and physical words. Specify the number of bits in a logical word and the number of bits in a physical word. What is the segmentation value? How may multiplexers exist in the circuit, and what is their size?

2-11. An SRAM has an external organization of 4 K × 4. Draw a diagram showing the internal organization of the memory. Specifically show the size of the row select, column select, and memory array. Assume that the lower address bits are associated with the row select circuitry. How many bits make up a physical word? How many bits make up a logical word?

2-12. An SRAM has an external organization of 8 K × 8. Internally the SRAM uses two-level decoding and an optimal memory array geometry. Draw a block diagram showing the functional blocks that make up the SRAM's internal structure and the external connections to these blocks. The memory has common I/O, an active low chip select, $\overline{CS}$, an active low write enable, $\overline{WE}$, and an active low output enable, $\overline{OE}$. Be sure to include in your diagram input buffers, output buffers, and control logic. Also provide the following information about the SRAM: number of logical words, number of physical words, number of bits in a logical word, number of bits in a physical word, and segmentation.

2-13. Draw the block diagram of the internal structure of a 2 K × 8 EPROM that uses two-level decoding. Use the optimal memory array size. Indicate the size of all decoders and the address inputs associated with each. How many physical and logical words exist in this memory organization? What is the segmentation value?

2-14. A 256 × 4 SRAM has separate data input and output lines. The memory has three-state outputs controlled by the chip select. Whenever the memory is selected, the three-state outputs are enabled. Draw a logic diagram to show how this memory can be interfaced to a 4-bit bidirectional data bus using external three-state buffers. Assume the buffers are enabled with an active low control signal.

2-15. The 2114A SRAM is externally organized as a 1024 × 4 memory with common I/O. It has only two control inputs, $\overline{CS}$ and $\overline{WE}$. To read the device, $\overline{CS} = 0$ and $\overline{WE} = 1$. To write the device, $\overline{CS} = 0$ and $\overline{WE} = 0$. Design a 2 K × 8 memory system using the 2114A. This memory system should respond only to addresses 0400H to 0BFFH, and its inputs from the microprocessor are address lines A_0–A_{15}, bidirectional data lines D_0–D_7, and control lines $\overline{WR}$, $\overline{RD}$ and IO/$\overline{M}$. Draw a logic diagram of the memory system and label all connections. For address decoding use a 74ALS138 or similar type of decoder. Implement all other logic with standard gates.

2-16. Design a memory system that provides 4 K of EPROM immediately followed by 2 K of RWM. The EPROM starts at address 0000H. Include a memory map of the system as part of the design. This memory system must interface to an 8085A microprocessor system bus. This bus consists of a 16-bit address bus, A_0–A_{15}, an 8-bit bidirectional data bus, D_0–D_7, and control lines $\overline{RD}$, $\overline{WR}$, and IO/$\overline{M}$. The memory devices to be used include 2732A EPROM's that are 4 K × 8 and have as control inputs an active low chip enable, $\overline{CE}$, and an active low output enable, $\overline{OE}$. The RWM is to be implemented with 2114A SRAMs, which are described in Problem 2-15.

2-17. Design a memory system that contains 4 K × 8 of EPROM followed by 4 K × 8 of RWM. The EPROM starts at address 0000H and is implemented using 2 K × 8 EPROM devices. Include the system's memory map as part of the design. The 2 K × 8 EPROMs have two control inputs, chip enable, $\overline{CE}$, and output enable, $\overline{OE}$. The RWM is implemented using 1 K × 4 SRAMs. These devices have common I/O and control inputs $\overline{CE}$, $\overline{OE}$, and $\overline{WE}$. Decoding must be exhaustive and accomplished using only a 74ALS138 decoder and SSI gates. Use as few gates as possible. Draw the logic diagram of the memory and its interface to the required signals from the 8085A system bus.

2-18. Design a memory that has 16 K × 8 of ROM and 8 K × 8 of RWM. The memory interfaces with an 8085A microprocessor system bus. The ROM is to be constructed using 8 K × 8 EPROMs. These devices have an active low chip enable and an active low output enable. The RWM is to be constructed from 4 K × 4 SRAMs that have two control lines. Each of the SRAM control lines is active low. The SRAM has common I/O. Use a 74ALS138 1-out-of-8 decoder plus as little additional logic as possible to implement address decoding. Address decoding is to be exhaustive. Draw the memory map and logic diagram of the circuit.

2-19. A memory system is to be designed that contains 16 K × 8 of EPROM followed by 16 K × 8 of RWM. The 16 K × 8 of EPROM starts at address 0000H and is implemented using a 27128A EPROM, which is 16 K × 8. The 27128A has two control inputs, chip enable, $\overline{CE}$, and output enable, $\overline{OE}$. The RWM is implemented with 4 K × 4 RWMs. These devices have common I/O and control inputs $\overline{CE}$, $\overline{OE}$, and $\overline{WE}$. Decoding is to be exhaustive and accomplished using only a 74ALS138 decoder and a four-input AND gate. Draw the logic diagram of the memory system and its interface to the required signals from an 8085A system bus.

2-20. A microprocessor based system consists of a number of printed circuit boards that plug into a motherboard. The motherboard carries the system bus, which consists of an address bus (A_0–A_{15}), a bidirectional data bus (D_0–D_7), and a control bus. The control bus consists of $\overline{RD}$, $\overline{WR}$, IO/$\overline{M}$, and other control signals. Each of the memory cards for the system provides 8 K words of memory. The 8 K block of addresses to which a single memory card will respond is determined by a set of switches on the card. Design the on card logic that generates an active low card select signal, $\overline{CARDSEL}$, when the address on the bus is a memory address within the 8 K block assigned to the card by its switch positions.

(a) Draw a block diagram, consisting of a single block, of the required logic showing all inputs and outputs. Indicate the signals that are active low by inversion circles.

(b) Implement the required logic using only two-input EX-OR gates, with open collector outputs. On your logic diagram show the switch positions to select the fifth 8 K block.

3

Microprocessor Architecture and Operation

With circuits, which once would have filled many equipment cabinets, now reduced to a handful of ICs, the formerly awesome computer (in the form of a microprocessor) is today being looked upon simply as a system component, taking its place with power supplies, instruments, transducers, etc. Of course, the similarity exists only in size and possibly cost, not necessarily in complexity or importance.

Gerald Lapidus*

The microprocessor is, of course, the central component in any microprocessor system. It controls the functions performed by the other system devices and provides the system's arithmetic and logic capability. The microprocessor fetches instructions from memory and decodes and executes them. It references memory and I/O devices for data and responds to control signals from external devices.

In this chapter the basic concepts of the structure and operation of microprocessors are presented, and detailed examinations of Intel's 8085A microprocessor illustrate the practical implementation of these concepts. The 8085A is widely second sourced[1] and finds widespread application.

3.1 BASIC MICROPROCESSOR SYSTEM CONCEPTS

The microprocessor system shown in Fig. 1.2-3 is redrawn in Fig. 3.1-1 to emphasize the most fundamental purpose of a microprocessor system: to process digital data that is input from the outside world and to provide as outputs digital data that is a desired function of the input data. Where data in analog form is to be processed or generated by the microprocessor system, suitable analog to digital and digital to analog conversion subsystems are employed to convert analog input data to the required digital form, and vice versa (see Chapter 11).

While this purpose may seem so obvious that it need not be stated, it is for its effective, efficient, and economic accomplishment in different applications that the various microprocessors and various system design techniques for using them have been developed.

To understand microprocessor systems, it is advantageous to view the entire system—microprocessor, ROM, RWM, and I/O ports—as a collection of addressable registers. Those registers that reside within the microprocessor are *internal registers*, and those that exist in the ROM, RWM, and I/O ports are *external registers*.

The collection of registers that constitutes a particular system and the data transfers that are possible among them make up the *system architecture*. The types of registers in the microprocessor and the possible data transfers among them determine the *microprocessor's architecture*.

A microprocessor system implements its functions by *transferring* and *transforming* data in registers of the system. Typically, transformations on data occur in internal registers, many of which are operational registers. *Operational registers* differ from storage registers in that they and their associated circuitry implement arithmetic or logic operations on the data contained in the register, thus transforming the data.

The microprocessor controls and synchronizes the data transfers and transformations according to instructions read into it from the application program in the system's ROM.

---

[1] The original manufacturer of the 8085A is Intel Corporation; second sources include: Advanced Micro Devices, NEC Microcomputers, and Siemens.

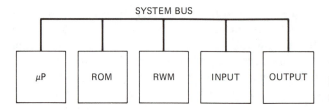

Figure 3.1-1 Microprocessor-based system.

TABLE 3.1-1 A TYPICAL PARTIAL SET OF SYSTEM BUS SIGNALS

Name	Function	Number	Direction*
A_0–A_{15}	Address bus	16	Output
D_0–D_7	Data bus	8	Bidirectional
$\overline{RD}$	Generalized read strobe	1	Output
$\overline{WR}$	Generalized write strobe	1	Output
IO/$\overline{M}$	Status (I/O or memory reference)	1	Output
$\overline{MEMR}$	Memory read strobe	1	Output
$\overline{MEMW}$	Memory write strobe	1	Output
$\overline{I/OR}$	Input device read strobe	1	Output
$\overline{I/OW}$	Output device write strobe	1	Output
Reset	System reset out	1	Output

*The direction is specified with respect to the microprocessor.

The registers in the various subsystems of the microprocessor system are externally interconnected by the *system bus*, which includes the address bus, data bus, and control bus. A typical set of system bus signals is listed in Table 3.1-1. In this case, the system has a 16-bit address bus and an 8-bit data bus. The remaining signals are part of the control bus. The control bus contains additional signals, which are considered in later chapters.

Two equivalent sets of control signals for reading and writing external registers are listed. A particular system uses one or the other or both sets. One set consists of the signals $\overline{RD}$, $\overline{WR}$, and IO/$\overline{M}$. $\overline{RD}$ and $\overline{WR}$ are generalized, active low read and write strobes.

The microprocessor provides an address on the address bus and timing signals on the control bus to synchronize the reading and writing of external devices. A read strobe, $\overline{RD}$, is generated by the microprocessor when it is ready to read data from memory or an input port. A write strobe, $\overline{WR}$, is generated by the microprocessor after the data it has placed on the data bus is stable and can be transferred to memory or an I/O port. The additional status signal, IO/$\overline{M}$, specifies whether an I/O device or memory is being addressed by the microprocessor for reading or writing.

Instead of $\overline{RD}$, $\overline{WR}$, and IO/$\overline{M}$, an equivalent but more specific set of strobes —memory read, $\overline{MEMR}$; memory write, $\overline{MEMW}$; I/O read, $\overline{I/OR}$; and I/O write, $\overline{I/OW}$—can be generated. These strobes are all active low. In some system architectures, this second set of control signals is preferable to the first. This second

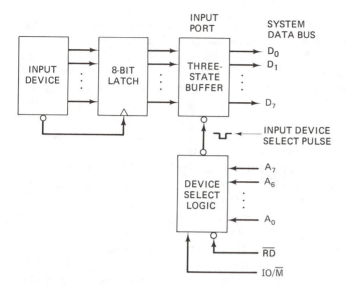

Figure 3.1-2 Simple input port for a microprocessor based system.

set— $\overline{\text{MEMR}}$, $\overline{\text{MEMW}}$, $\overline{\text{I/OR}}$, and $\overline{\text{I/OW}}$—is easily derived from $\overline{\text{RD}}$, $\overline{\text{WR}}$, and IO/$\overline{\text{M}}$ signals. If advantageous, all seven control signals can be used in a single system.

As was shown in Fig. 1.2-4a, each of the subsystems connected to the system bus can be viewed as consisting of a bus interface and primary function. For the SRAM and EPROM, introduced in Chapter 2, the bus interface consists, primarily, of the address decoding logic, which selects the memory devices, and bidirectional buffers for the data bus. The primary function for a memory subsystem is implemented by the memory devices. These memory devices provide the addressable registers considered when viewing the subsystem as a collection of registers. Partitioning a subsystem into a bus interface and primary function, and viewing the subsystem as a collection of registers, will next be considered for input and output subsystems.

External or peripheral devices that generate data for input to a microprocessor system are called *input devices*. Input devices include a large variety of electronic and electromechanical devices. These devices range in complexity from simple switches to other microprocessor systems that preprocess data before transferring it to the main microprocessor. Data generated by an input device is stored temporarily in a register until it can be read by the microprocessor (see Fig. 3.1-2). The loading of the input register with data is done by the input device. Once loaded with data, the input register can later be read by the microprocessor.

In order to place the contents of an input register on the microprocessor system data bus, its outputs are connected to the data bus through a three-state buffer. This buffer is enabled by an *input device select pulse*, obtained by gating the read strobe and the IO/$\overline{\text{M}}$ signal generated by the microprocessor on the control bus with a device address generated by the microprocessor on the address bus. The address is decoded by a decoder that passes the read strobe to the three-state buffer only if that buffer's unique address is present on the address bus. As shown in Fig. 3.1-2 it will be assumed that the port address consists of only 8 bits, A_0–A_7. The use of only 8 of the 16 address bits for port addresses will be described in detail in Chapter 4. The resulting active low device select pulse for address XXH is denoted by $\overline{\text{IDSPXXH}}$. A read strobe is generated by the microprocessor when it executes an instruction inputting data from an input device. The strobe occurs during the instant of time that the microprocessor is ready to input the data on the bus. The input instruction also specifies the address placed on the address bus that selects a single input register from among many in the system.

The three-state buffer alone or the three-state buffer and its associated input register are referred to as an *input port*. A port is simply a "gate" or opening for data to pass from the outside world to the microprocessor system, or vice versa. The 74ALS574 octal D-type flip-flop (see Chapter 2) provides both the 8-bit latch and three-state buffers of an input port in a single package. A single physical input device may contain more than one input port. In such cases, each input port still has a unique address. As discussed in Chapter 2, unique addresses are required to prevent bus conflicts that occur when two or more three-state buffers with common outputs are enabled simultaneously.

Output devices, of which there are a large variety, accept data from the microprocessor system. The data to be output from the system is placed in a register connected to the data bus. This register is called an *output port* and is clocked by an output device select pulse (see Fig. 3.1-3). The *output device select pulse* is obtained by gating the write pulse, $\overline{\text{WR}}$, with $\text{IO}/\overline{\text{M}}$ and the address on the address bus. The address of the output port for which the data is intended is part of the instruction that places data on the bus and creates the write pulse. The convention for representing an active low output device select pulse for output port XXH is $\overline{\text{ODSPXXH}}$. The output port of Fig. 3.1-3 could be provided by a 74ALS574 with its $\overline{\text{OC}}$ input grounded.

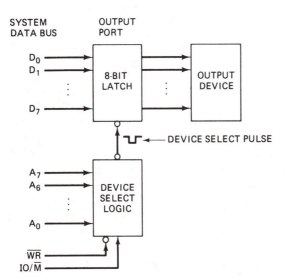

Figure 3.1-3 Simple output port for a microprocessor based system.

Input ports and output ports, as was shown, have a bus interface consisting of address decoding logic. For an input port, the primary function consists of a register and three-state buffer. For an output port, the primary function is simply a register. When viewed as a collection of addressable registers, each port consists of a single register.

3.2 BASIC MICROPROCESSOR ARCHITECTURE AND OPERATION

A simplified representation of a microprocessor's architecture is shown in Fig. 3.2-1. This representation shows two major functional units: the control unit and the arithmetic/logic unit, ALU. In addition to these units, the microprocessor contains a number of registers—instruction register, program counter, stack pointer, general purpose registers, and temporary registers. These components of the microprocessor's architecture are discussed in more detail in the following subsections.

3.2.1 Control Unit

The microprocessor's control unit controls and synchronizes all data transfers and transformations in the microprocessor system and is the key sequential subsystem in the microprocessor itself. All actions attributable to the microprocessor are actions implemented by the control unit.

The control unit uses inputs from a master clock to derive timing and control signals that regulate the transfers and transformations in the system associated with each instruction. The control unit also accepts, as input, control signals generated by other devices in the microprocessor system, which alter the state of the microprocessor (see Fig. 3.2-2).

The basic operation of a microprocessor is regulated by the control unit, is cyclical, and consists of the sequential fetching and execution of instructions. Each

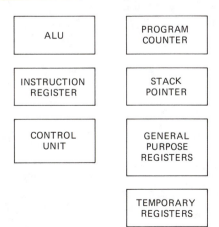

Figure 3.2-1 Simplified representation of a microprocessor's architecture.

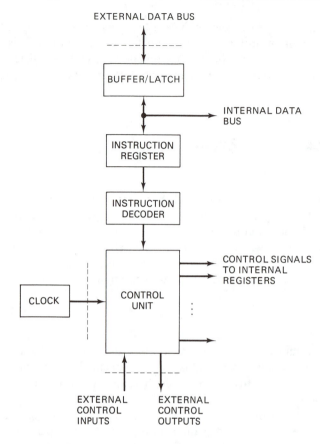

Figure 3.2-2 Microprocessor control unit, instruction register, and instruction decoder.

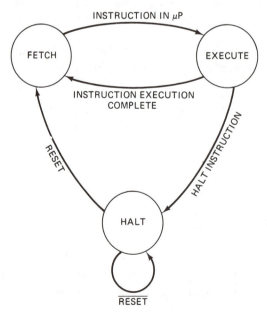

Figure 3.2-3 Alternate fetch and execute cycles of a microprocessor.

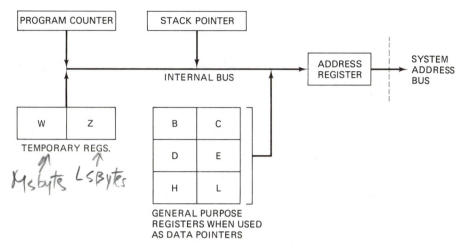

Figure 3.2-4 Various sources of addresses for the address register.

instruction execution cycle has two primary states:[2] the fetch state and the execute state. The fetch state transfers an instruction from memory into the microprocessor, and the execute state executes the instruction. The microprocessor normally cycles between the fetch and execute states unless and until it executes a halt instruction, in which case it enters a halt state and stops (see Fig. 3.2-3).

3.2.2 Internal Registers

To keep track of which instruction is to be executed next, the control unit maintains a special purpose or dedicated register, the *program counter, PC* (see Fig. 3.2-4). The program counter is an operational register that always holds the address of either the next instruction to be executed or the address of the next word of a multiword instruction that has not been completely fetched. In either case, at the completion of the execution of any instruction, the program counter contains the address of the first word of the next instruction to be executed. The operational nature of the program counter allows its contents to be incremented by the control unit.

One of the control inputs to the microprocessor's control unit is the reset input. When the microprocessor is reset, the control unit resets the program counter to zero. This initial value establishes the memory address from which the first instruction is to be obtained.

To actually obtain the first word of the instruction, the address contained in the program counter is placed on the address bus. To do this, the control unit transfers the contents of the program counter to the *address register*. The program counter is then incremented to point to the next memory location. The outputs of the address register are the address pins of the microprocessor. The control unit

---

[2] Each of these states actually consists of a number of substates.

then generates a memory read strobe that transfers the data from the addressed memory location to the microprocessor. The data is transferred into the microprocessor through the data bus buffer/ latch and then into the *instruction register, IR* (Fig. 3.2-2). Registers within the microprocessor are interconnected by an internal data bus.

The first word of an instruction is the operation code for that instruction. The *operation code* indicates to the control unit those operations required to execute the instruction. The output of the IR is decoded and used by the control unit to develop a sequence of operations and register transfers that execute the instruction.

The operation code in the IR addresses a starting location in a control ROM or PLA within the microprocessor where a sequence of very elementary instructions —microinstructions—is located. Each instruction in the fixed instruction set of a microprocessor is implemented by the control unit sequencing through the set of microoperations associated with a particular instruction. For single-chip microprocessors, the microinstructions, and thus the microprocessor's instruction set, are fixed at manufacture.

Microprocessor instructions often require more information than can be provided in a single word of memory. This tends to be the case with 8-bit microprocessors. Therefore, it is common for instructions to consist of two or three words. The first word is always the operation code (OP code). The second and third bytes are data that represent either an address or a data constant. After the OP code is fetched and placed in the instruction register, its decoding indicates whether the instruction consists of additional bytes of data. The bytes of multibyte instructions are contained in successive locations of memory.

To complete the instruction fetch, the additional bytes of the instruction remaining in memory must be copied into the microprocessor. Each memory read or write operation by the microprocessor is called a *memory reference*. If the instruction in question has 2 bytes, a second memory reference is required to input the second byte of the instruction to the microprocessor. The destination of this second byte of data depends on the particular instruction in question. Frequently, it is placed in a temporary register.

Temporary registers are used by the control unit to hold operands or addresses that are part of an instruction, until they are transferred to another register in the microprocessor or used as operands in a computation. For example, two temporary registers shown in Fig. 3.2-4 are labeled W and Z. Each of these is an 8-bit register. When a 3-byte instruction containing a 2-byte address is to be fetched into the microprocessor, the first byte, the operation code, is placed in the IR by the first memory reference. Two additional memory references obtain the two address bytes, which are placed in the temporary registers W and Z. These registers are used together as a register pair. During instruction execution, the address in W and Z is transferred to the address latch to address memory or I/O for a data transfer.

If additional general purpose storage registers are provided in the microprocessor, temporary results from computations can be stored internally, as opposed to storing them in external read write memory. Instructions that transfer data between these general purpose registers require only a few bits to address the internal registers, since the number of internal registers is limited. This results in a shorter instruction execution time because the instruction requires fewer bytes, and fewer memory references are required to fetch it. In addition, the actual transfer of data between the accumulator and a general purpose register does not require a memory reference, since the transfer takes place within the microprocessor.

To allow greater flexibility, instructions can carry out transfers between general purpose registers. The microprocessor in Fig. 3.2-4 has six 8-bit general purpose registers labeled B, C, D, E, H, and L. These registers constitute a register array. Registers in this array are used and operated upon either singly or in pairs.

The address of data to be transferred to or from the microprocessor can be kept in a pair of general purpose registers. Because these registers have a limited operational capability, instructions can increment or decrement their contents, but these instructions do not contain the source or destination address. Another instruction loads the register pair with the source or destination address, and subsequent instructions transfer data to or from the memory location corresponding to that address. The contents of the register pair are then incremented, so the next data transfer involves the next consecutive memory location. When an instruction uses the address in a register pair as the source or destination address in a data transfer, that address is copied into the address latch during the memory reference in which the data transfer occurs. When used in this manner, the register pair is frequently called a *data pointer*.

3.2.3 Arithmetic and Logic Unit

Arithmetic or logic operations on one or two operands constitute the basic data transformations implemented in a microprocessor. The microprocessor contains an *arithmetic and logic unit, ALU*, for this purpose. One of the two ALU registers, the *accumulator*, holds one operand; the other, a temporary register, holds the second (see Fig. 3.2-5). The result of an arithmetic or logic operation is placed in the accumulator at the completion of the operation, replacing one of the original operands.

The ALU is capable of performing the following operations on binary data:

1. Binary addition and subtraction
2. Logical AND, OR, EX-OR
3. Complement
4. Rotate left or right

The ALU also contains a number of flip-flops called *flags*, which store information related to the result of an arithmetic or logic operation. Taken together, these flags constitute a *flag register*. For example, a flag indicates whether a carry occurred out of the most significant bit after an addition operation; another flag indicates that the result left in the accumulator after some arithmetic or logic operation is zero. Most microprocessors contain several flags.

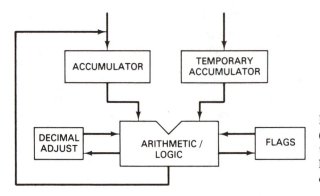

Figure 3.2-5 Arithmetic logic unit (ALU) consisting of the accumulator, temporary accumulator, flags, and logic for the arithmetic and logical operations.

In many applications it is appropriate to represent data in binary coded decimal, BCD, form. The ALU shown contains additional logic to adjust the results of addition operations when the operands are interpreted as BCD data.

3.2.4 The Microprocessor's State

The body of information that completely describes the condition of the micro-processor at any point in the execution of a program is the *status* or *state* of the microprocessor. The state of a microprocessor becomes important when the execu-tion of a program is interrupted and is later resumed. Consider the case of a microprocessor that has two separate programs in memory: task A and task B. At some point during the execution of task A, it is necessary to execute task B. This transfer of control to task B requires that the PC be loaded with the starting address of task B. If, after the execution of task B is complete, task A had to be restarted from the beginning, the results of the processing before the interrupt would be lost. However, if the state of the microprocessor at the time of the interrupt is saved and later restored, processing is switched back to task A with no loss of the results of previous processing.

The information that constitutes the state of the microprocessor includes the contents of the PC, the accumulator, the flag register, and the general purpose registers. Saving and restoring the value of the program counter allow task A to be restarted with the next instruction after the one executed before the interrupt. Because the processing of program task B requires the accumulator, the flag register, and the general purpose registers, their task A contents are saved and later restored.

The interruption of sequential processing is initiated by the execution of a subroutine call instruction or by a signal from an external device. The subroutine call instruction causes a branch from one task to another—the subroutine. The address of the beginning of the subroutine is part of the call instruction. An external device may initiate a hardware interrupt, a branch, to a predetermined memory location when the external device requires servicing. The memory location branched to is the starting location for the interrupting device's service subroutine.

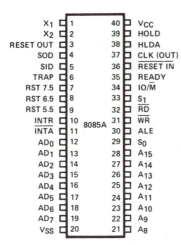

X₁	1		40	Vcc

Figure 3.3-1 8085A microprocessor pin configuration. (Courtesy of Intel Corp.)

A *stack* is a storage structure in which a microprocessor saves its register contents during subroutine calls and interrupts. The stack consists of a group of specifically allocated locations in external read write memory. A *stack pointer* is required to address a register or location in the stack. Depending on the convention used with a given microprocessor, this stack location is either the last location written into or the next location available to be written into. The stack pointer is designed in such a way that items are read from the stack in the reverse order from which they are written into it. This storage structure is referred to as a *last-in, first-out, LIFO*, stack. Access to data stored in the stack is, therefore, sequential, not random.

Writing data into a stack is called a *push* operation, and reading data from a stack is called a *pop* operation. To retrieve a data item pushed onto the stack, all subsequent data items on the stack must be retrieved first.

3.3 THE 8085A MICROPROCESSOR

The 8085A is an 8-bit microprocessor suitable for a wide range of applications. It is a single-chip, NMOS device implemented with approximately 6200 transistors on a 164×222 mil chip contained in a 40-pin dual-in-line package. The package pins and their configuration are shown in Fig. 3.3-1 [1]. The instruction set of the 8085A consists of 74 instructions.

The 8085A operates on a single 5 V power supply connected at V_{CC}; power supply ground is connected to V_{SS}. The frequency of the internal clock generator, which synchronizes the operation of the 8085A, is determined by a crystal or *RC* network connected at pins X_1 and X_2. The internal clock generator oscillates at twice the basic microprocessor frequency. A 50 percent duty cycle, two phase, nonoverlapping clock is derived from the oscillator. A 6.25 MHz crystal provides a 3.125 MHz internal clock frequency. A TTL level clock output, CLK (OUT),

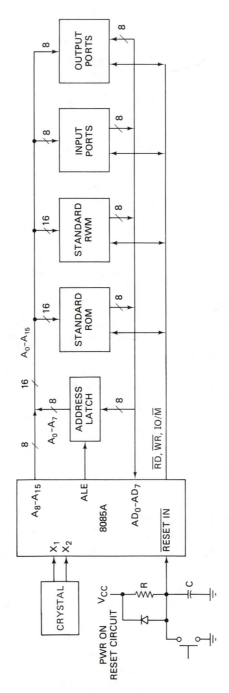

Figure 3.3-2 8085A microprocessor system using standard ROM and R/WM.

derived from one phase of the internal clock, provides a clock signal that can be used for synchronizing external devices. Instead of a crystal or RC network, an external clock can be connected to X_1. The remaining package pins provide the address, data, and control signals.

Intel's later version of the 8085A, the 8085AH, uses an NMOS technology called HMOS. This implementation of the 8085A has improved electrical characteristics, including 20 percent lower power consumption, wider voltage margins, and higher speed versions. CMOS implementations of the 8085A, such as OKI Semiconductor's MSM80C85A, are also available [2]. Architecturally and functionally, these implementations of the 8085A are identical. Where the distinction is not important, the various implementations will simply be referred to generically as the 8085A. Detailed timing calculations in this text use the parameters for the 8085AH.

An 8085A microcomputer system can be constructed with standard ROM and RWM or with specially designed ICs that contain memory and I/O ports. Figure 3.3-2 shows a microcomputer system using standard ROM and RWM. The 8085A is capable of directly addressing up to 64 K memory locations with its 16-bit address. Eight of the 16 bits, A_8–A_{15}, are provided directly on the three-state address pins, A_8–A_{15}. The other eight bits, A_0–A_7, are provided on the bidirectional, three-state address/data pins, AD_0–AD_7. The address/data pins are time multiplexed: at times carrying addresses, at other times carrying data. Address information is provided on the address/data pins by the 8085A at the beginning of each memory reference, and is externally latched and held during the remainder of the memory reference to provide address bits A_0 to A_7. The 8-bit latch in Fig. 3.3-2 latches the address information from the address/data pins when clocked by the address latch enable signal, ALE. The 8085A generates this signal at the appropriate time when providing address information on its address/data pins. At other times during a memory reference, a byte of data is transferred to or from the memory on the address/data pins. The 8085A generates two control pulses to indicate whether it is reading, $\overline{RD}$, or writing, $\overline{WR}$, an external register. Time multiplexing of the address and data reduces the number of pins on the microprocessor package.

I/O ports are basically external registers. They can be interfaced as memory and written to and read from by any instruction that references memory. Alternatively, special instructions can read or write an I/O port. The 8085A directly addresses up to 256 input and 256 output ports, using special I/O instructions with an 8-bit address. This 8-bit address is repeated on pins AD_0–AD_7 and A_8–A_{15} when an I/O device is addressed, and, therefore, the I/O device need only decode one set of these identical address bits. Another control signal, $IO/\overline{M}$, generated by the 8085A indicates whether the microprocessor wants to read or write memory or I/O. When this signal is logic 0, memory is being referenced; when it is logic 1, I/O is being referenced. The signals $\overline{RD}$, $\overline{WR}$, and $IO/\overline{M}$ are used together in the system design to control the reading and writing of external memory and I/O ports. I/O ports and their design and operation are covered extensively in Chapter 8.

Table 3.3-1 summarizes the functions of the 8085A pins discussed in this section. The functions of the other 8085A control signals are discussed later in this chapter and in subsequent chapters when the topics to which they relate are presented.

TABLE 3.3-1 DESCRIPTION OF SOME 8085A PINS (COURTESY OF INTEL CORP.)

Symbol	Type	Name and Function
A_8–A_{15}	O	**Address Bus:** The most significant 8 bits of the memory address or the 8 bits of the I/O address, 3-stated during Hold and Halt modes and during RESET.
AD_{0-7}	I/O	**Multiplexed Address/Data Bus:** Lower 8 bits of the memory address (or I/O address) appear on the bus during the first clock cycle (T state) of a machine cycle. It then becomes the data bus during the second and third clock cycles.
ALE	O	**Address Latch Enable:** It occurs during the first clock state of a machine cycle and enables the address to get latched into the on-chip latch of peripherals. The falling edge of ALE is set to guarantee setup and hold times for the address information. The falling edge of ALE can also be used to strobe the status information. ALE is never 3-stated.
$\overline{RD}$	O	**Read Control:** A low level on $\overline{RD}$ indicates the selected memory or I/O device is to be read and that the Data Bus is available for the data transfer, 3-stated during Hold and Halt modes and during RESET.
$\overline{WR}$	O	**Write Control:** A low level on $\overline{WR}$ indicates the data on the Data Bus is to be written into the selected memory or I/O location. Data is set up at the trailing edge of $\overline{WR}$. 3-stated during Hold and Halt modes and during RESET.
S_0, S_1, and IO/$\overline{M}$	O	**Machine Cycle Status:** IO/$\overline{M}$ S_1 S_0 Status 0 0 1 Memory write 0 1 0 Memory read 1 0 1 I/O write 1 1 0 I/O read 0 1 1 Opcode fetch 1 1 1 Opcode fetch 1 1 1 Interrupt Acknowledge * 0 0 Halt * × × Hold * × × Reset * = 3-state (high impedance) × = unspecified S_1 can be used as an advanced R/$\overline{W}$ status. IO/$\overline{M}$, S_0, and S_1 become valid at the beginning of a machine cycle and remain stable throughout the cycle. The falling edge of ALE may be used to latch the state of these lines.
X_1, X_2	I	**X_1 and X_2:** Are connected to a crystal, LC, or RC network to drive the internal clock generator. X_1 can also be an external clock input from a logic gate. The input frequency is divided by 2 to give the processor's internal operating frequency.
CLK	O	**Clock:** Clock output for use as a system clock. The period of CLK is twice the X_1, X_2 input period.
V_{CC}		**Power:** +5 volt supply.
V_{SS}		**Ground:** Reference.

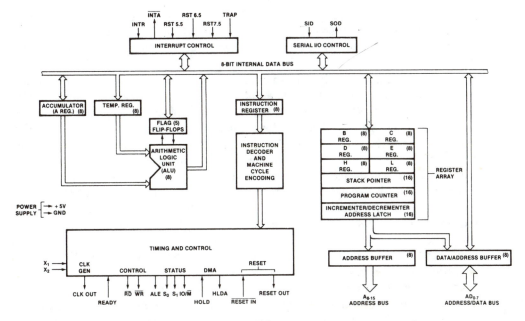

Figure 3.3-3 8085A architecture. (Courtesy of Intel Corp.)

3.3.1 Architecture of the 8085A

A block diagram of the internal architecture of the 8085A is shown in Fig. 3.3-3. The 8085A contains a register array with both dedicated and general purpose registers:

1. A 16-bit program counter (PC)

2. A 16-bit stack pointer (SP)

3. Six 8-bit general purpose registers arranged in pairs: BC, DE, HL

4. A temporary register pair: WZ

The 16-bit program counter addresses instructions in any one of 65,536 possible memory locations. When the $\overline{\text{RESET IN}}$ pin of the 8085A is made logic 0, the program counter is reset to zero; when the $\overline{\text{RESET IN}}$ pin is returned to logic 1, the control unit transfers the contents of the PC to the address latch, providing the address of the first instruction to be executed. Thus, program execution in the 8085A begins with the instruction in memory location zero.

8085A instructions are 1 to 3 bytes in length. The first byte always contains the operation code (OP code). During the instruction fetch, the first byte is transferred from the memory by way of the external data bus through the data bus buffer latch into the instruction register. The PC is automatically incremented so it contains the address of the next instruction if the instruction contains only 1 byte, or the address of the next byte of the present instruction if the instruction consists of 2 or 3 bytes.

In the case of a multibyte instruction, the timing and control section provides additional operations to read in the additional bytes. The timing and control section uses the instruction decoder output and external control signals to generate the state and cycle timing signals and signals for the control of external devices. After all the bytes of an instruction have been fetched into the microprocessor, the instruction is executed. Execution may require transfer of data between the microprocessor and memory or an I/O device. For these transfers, the memory or I/O device address placed in the address latch comes from the instruction which was fetched or from one of the register pairs used as a data pointer: HL, BC, or DE. The timing and sequencing of the 8085A are discussed in detail in the next section.

The six general purpose registers in the register array can be used as single 8-bit registers or as 16-bit register pairs. The temporary register pair, WZ, is not program addressable and is only used by the control unit for the internal execution of instructions. For example, to address an external register for a data transfer, WZ is used to temporarily hold the address from an instruction read into the microprocessor until the address is transferred to the address and address/data latch.

The 16-bit stack pointer, SP, maintains a pointer to the top of the stack allocated in external memory. The stack, as previously indicated, primarily supports interrupt and subroutine programming.

The 8085A's arithmetic logic unit performs arithmetic and logic operations on data. The operands are stored in two registers associated with the ALU: the 8-bit *accumulator* and the 8-bit *temporary register*. The accumulator is loaded from the internal bus and can transfer data to the internal bus. Thus, it serves both as a *destination* and *source* register for data. The temporary register temporarily holds one of the operands during a binary operation. For example, if the contents of register B are to be added to the contents of the accumulator and the result left in the accumulator, the temporary register holds a copy of the contents of register B while the arithmetic operation is taking place.

Associated with the ALU is the 5-bit flag register, F, which indicates conditions associated with the results of arithmetic or logic operations. The flags indicate zero, a carry out of the high order bit, the sign (most significant bit), parity, and auxiliary carry (carry out of the fourth bit).

The 8085A's internal data bus is 8 bits wide and transfers instructions and data among various internal registers or to external devices through the multiplexed address/data bus buffer latch. The bidirectional, three-state *address/data bus buffer latch* isolates the microprocessor's internal data bus from the external system address/data bus. In the output mode, the information on the internal bus is loaded into the 8-bit data latch that drives the address/data bus output buffer. The output buffers are floated during input or nontransfer operations. During the input mode, data from the external data bus is transferred over the internal data bus to an internal register.

A serial I/O register and an interrupt control register are also shown in Fig. 3.3-3. These registers and their functions are discussed in Chapters 8 and 9, respectively.

3.3.2 Timing and Sequencing

During normal operation, the microprocessor sequentially fetches and executes one instruction after another until a *halt* instruction (HLT) is processed. The fetching and execution of a single instruction constitutes an *instruction cycle*, which consists of one or more read or write operations (references) to memory or an I/O device. Each memory or I/O reference requires a *machine cycle*. In other words, every time a byte of data is moved into or out of the microprocessor, a machine cycle is required.

There are seven different types of machine cycles in the 8085A:

1. OPCODE FETCH

2. MEMORY READ

3. MEMORY WRITE

4. I/O READ

5. I/O WRITE

6. INTERRUPT ACKNOWLEDGE

7. BUS IDLE

Three status signals, IO/$\overline{\text{M}}$, S1, and S0, generated at the beginning of each machine cycle, identify each type and remain valid for the duration of the cycle. Figure 3.3-4 shows how the machine cycles are coded with these three bits.

The instruction fetch portion of an instruction cycle requires a machine cycle for each byte of the instruction to be fetched. Since instructions consist of 1 to 3 bytes, the instruction fetch is one to three machine cycles in duration.

The first machine cycle in an instruction cycle is always an OPCODE FETCH, and the 8 bits obtained during an OPCODE FETCH are always interpreted as the

Checking   Command

MACHINE CYCLE			STATUS			CONTROL		
			IO/$\overline{\text{M}}$	S1	S0	$\overline{\text{RD}}$	$\overline{\text{WR}}$	$\overline{\text{INTA}}$
OPCODE FETCH	(OF)		0	1	1	0	1	1
MEMORY READ	(MR)		0	1	0	0	1	1
MEMORY WRITE	(MW)		0	0	1	1	0	1
I/O READ	(IOR)		1	1	0	0	1	1
I/O WRITE	(IOW)		1	0	1	1	0	1
ACKNOWLEDGE OF INTR	(INA)		1	1	1	1	1	0
BUS IDLE	(BI):	DAD	0	1	0	1	1	1
		ACK. OF RST, TRAP	1	1	1	1	1	1
		HALT	TS	0	0	TS	TS	1

Figure 3.3-4   Machine cycle and state information for the 8085A.

OP code of an instruction. Note that to fetch an instruction—i.e., to transfer an entire instruction from memory to the microprocessor—always necessitates an OPCODE FETCH machine cycle. However, one or two MEMORY READ machine cycles are also needed to complete the fetch for 2- and 3-byte instructions, respectively.

The number of machine cycles required to execute the instruction depends on the particular instruction. Some instructions require no additional machine cycles after the instruction fetch is complete; others require additional machine cycles to write or read data to or from memory or I/O devices. The total number of machine cycles required varies from one to five, with no one instruction cycle containing more than five machine cycles. Machine cycles like the MEMORY READ or MEMORY WRITE may occur more than once in a single instruction cycle.

For example, the *store accumulator direct*, STA, instruction transfers the contents of the accumulator to an external register, whose address is specified in the instruction. Since this register can be located anywhere in the 64 K memory space that the 8085A can directly address, 16 bits are required for the address. Thus, the STA instruction contains 3 bytes: a 1-byte OP code and a 2-byte address. The instruction is stored in memory as follows:

OPCODE	byte 1
LO ADDR	byte 2
HI ADDR	byte 3

Three machine cycles are required to fetch this instruction: OPCODE FETCH transfers the OP code from memory to the instruction register. The 2-byte address is then transferred, 1 byte at a time, from memory to the temporary register WZ; this calls for two MEMORY READ machine cycles. When the entire instruction is in the microprocessor, it is executed. Execution entails a data transfer from the microprocessor to memory. The contents of the accumulator are transferred to the external register, whose address was previously transferred to the microprocessor by the preceding two MEMORY READ machine cycles. The address of the memory location to be written is generated as follows: the high order address byte in temporary register W is transferred to the address latch, and the low order address byte in Z is transferred to the address/data latch. This data transfer is effected by a MEMORY WRITE machine cycle. Thus, the 3-byte STA instruction has four machine cycles in its instruction cycle:

Mnemonic	*Instruction byte*	*Machine cycle*
STA	OPCODE	OPCODE FETCH
	LO ADDR	MEMORY READ
	HI ADDR	MEMORY READ
		MEMORY WRITE

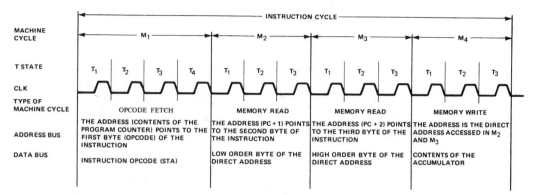

Figure 3.3-5 CPU timing for the store accumulator direct (STA) instruction. (Courtesy of Intel Corp.)

The timing and control section of the microprocessor automatically generates the proper machine cycles required for an instruction cycle from information provided by the OP code. Figure 3.3-5 shows the timing diagram of an STA instruction.

Each machine cycle is divided by the system clock into a number of state transitions, or T states, which correspond to the period between two negative going transitions of that clock. Thus, one complete transition from state T_1 through the state diagram and back to T_1 constitutes a complete machine cycle. A simplified state transition diagram for a machine cycle of the 8085A is given in Fig. 3.3-6. Each machine cycle consists of three to six T states. Each T state, T_1-T_6, is one clock period (state time) in duration. Instruction cycles for various 8085A instructions require from 4 to 18 states.

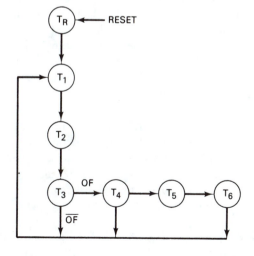

Figure 3.3-6 Simplified state transition diagram for the 8085A.

TABLE 3.3-2 TIMING VALUES FOR 8085AH MICROPROCESSORS

Processor	Crystal MHz (fc)	State Time nS (T)	Add Instruction Execution Time μS
8085AH-1	11.976	167	0.6680
8085AH-2	10.000	200	0.8000
8085AH	6.250	320	1.2800
8085AH	6.144	325.5	1.3020

$$T = \frac{2}{fc}.$$

TABLE 3.3-3 ACTIVITIES ASSOCIATED WITH THE T STATES OF THE 8085A MICROPROCESSOR

T_1: A memory or I/O device address is placed on the address/data bus (AD$_0$–AD$_7$) and address bus (A$_8$–A$_{15}$). An address latch enable, ALE, pulse is generated to facilitate latching the low order address bits on AD$_0$–AD$_7$. Status information is placed on IO/$\overline{M}$, S1, and S0 to define the type of machine cycle. The halt flag is checked.

T_2: Ready and hold inputs are sampled. PC is incremented if machine cycle is part of an instruction fetch. In all machine cycles except BUS IDLE, one of the control strobes— $\overline{RD}$, $\overline{WR}$, or $\overline{INTA}$—makes a 1 to 0 transition.

T_w (optional): This state is entered if the ready line is low. The states of the address, data, and control signals remain the same as at the end of T_2.

T_3: An instruction byte or data byte is transferred to/from the microprocessor. The active control strobe makes a 0 to 1 transition.

T_4: The contents of the instruction register are decoded.

T_5–T_6: These states are used to complete the execution of some instructions.

Table 3.3-2 shows the timing values for several versions of the 8085AH. The third entry in the table is the standard 8085AH, which has a maximum crystal frequency of 6.250 MHz. The first two entries are higher speed selected devices. The highest speed device, the 8085AH-1 can be operated with an 11.976 MHz crystal. Data is also given for an 8085AH operated with a 6.144 MHz crystal. This crystal frequency is often used with the 8085AH because of its advantages in applications involving serial communications. The slowest any version of the 8085AH can be operated is 500 KHz.

The activities associated with each T state are listed in Table 3.3-3. Although the actual states traversed in a single machine cycle depend on the particular instruction and machine cycle within the instruction, the 8085A passes through at least three states in each machine cycle (T_1, T_2, and T_3). All OPCODE FETCH machine cycles consist of either four or six states. All other machine cycles consist of three states. As shown in the state diagram (Fig. 3.3-6), each machine cycle starts in state T_1.

During state T_1, the microprocessor loads the address lines (AD$_0$–AD$_7$ and A$_8$–A$_{15}$) with a memory address or I/O device address. During state T_2 of any machine cycle fetching a multibyte instruction, the program counter is incremented by one. And during T_3 a data transfer from the microprocessor to the external data bus occurs, or vice versa, depending on the type of machine cycle.

OPCODE FETCH: The OP code is transferred from memory to the instruction register of the microprocessor.

MEMORY READ, I/O READ, or INTERRUPT ACKNOWLEDGE: A data byte is transferred from the external data bus to the microprocessor.

MEMORY WRITE, I/O WRITE: A data byte is transferred from the microprocessor to the external data bus.

BUS IDLE:[3] No data is transferred on the external data bus.

At the end of a pass through the state diagram, a machine cycle is complete, and state T_1 is entered to start the next machine cycle. In the simplified diagram of Fig. 3.3-6, this process continues indefinitely, since no provision to stop instruction execution is shown.

For the STA instruction, the number of states required for each machine cycle is as follows:

Instruction	Machine cycle	States
STA	OPCODE FETCH	4
	MEMORY READ	3
	MEMORY READ	3
	MEMORY WRITE	3
		13

STA has a total of 13 states. If the 8085A is operating at a 325.5 nS state time, the STA instruction cycle is executed in 4.23 μS. This time period is the instruction's execution time, although it actually includes both the instruction fetch and the execution times (see Fig. 3.3-5).

The timing diagram of an OPCODE FETCH machine cycle containing six states is shown in Fig. 3.3-7. The timing diagram for a four-state OPCODE FETCH is identical except that states T_5 and T_6 are omitted, and state T_4 is followed by state T_1 of the next machine cycle.

As Fig. 3.3-7 shows, at the beginning of state T_1 the IO/$\overline{\text{M}}$, S1, and S0 status signals indicate the type of machine cycle that has been initiated. For the OPCODE FETCH, IO/$\overline{\text{M}}$ = 0, S1 = 1, and S0 = 1. This status information remains constant for the duration of the machine cycle. The 16-bit address, A_0–A_{15}, of the memory location containing the OP code is obtained from the PC and placed in the address and address/data latches. The high order byte of the address appears on the address bus, A_8–A_{15}, and remains constant until the end of state T_3. During states T_4 through T_6, the data on the address bus is unspecified. The low order byte of the

---

[3] The INTERRUPT ACKNOWLEDGE and BUS IDLE machine cycles are special cases and are detailed in Chapter 9.

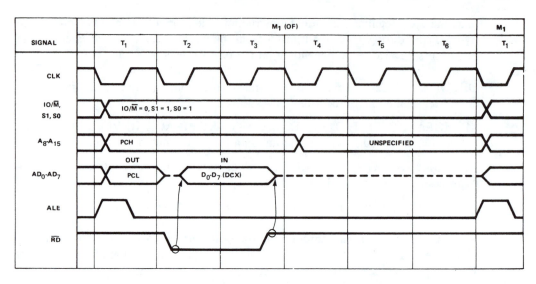

Figure 3.3-7 OPCODE FETCH machine cycle. (Courtesy of Intel Corp.)

address is placed on the address/data bus at the beginning of T_1. This data, however, remains valid only until the beginning of state T_2, at which time the address/data bus is floated. The address latch enable, ALE, clocks an external register that latches the low order address byte on its falling edge.

In Fig. 3.3-8, a 74ALS573 octal D-type transparent latch is used to demultiplex the low address byte, A_0–A_7 from the address/data bus, AD_0–AD_7. Use of a positive level triggered transparent latch has the advantage of making A_0–A_7 available at the latch's output at the beginning of the ALE strobe. With a negative edge triggered latch, A_0–A_7 would not be available until the end of ALE.

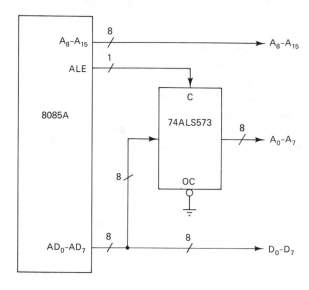

Figure 3.3-8 Use of a 74ALS573 octal D-type transparent latch to demultiplex the address/data bus of an 8085A.

During state T_2, the $\overline{\text{RD}}$ control signal goes low, and the OP code to be fetched is placed on the data bus by the addressed memory location. On the rising edge of the $\overline{\text{RD}}$ control signal in T_3, the OP code obtained from memory is transferred to the microprocessor's instruction register. During T_4 the 8085A decodes the instruction and determines whether to enter state T_5 or to enter state T_1 of the next machine cycle. From the operation code the microprocessor determines what other machine cycles, if any, must be executed to complete the instruction cycle. States T_5 and T_6, when entered, are used for internal microprocessor operations necessitated by the instruction.

MEMORY READ and I/O READ are similar to the OPCODE FETCH machine cycle. However, they use only states T_1 to T_3, and the status signal values appropriate for the particular machine cycle are issued at the beginning of T_1. For MEMORY READ, the source of the address issued during T_1 is not always the program counter but may be one of several other possible register pairs in the microprocessor, depending on the particular instruction of which the machine cycle is a part.

The MEMORY WRITE and I/O WRITE timing diagrams are similar to the corresponding read operations, except that the $\overline{\text{WR}}$ control, instead of $\overline{\text{RD}}$, goes low during T_2.

3.3.3 The HALT State

The state transition diagram of Fig. 3.3-9 includes a provision to stop the microprocessor: the HALT state, T_{HALT}. Assume that an OPCODE FETCH machine cycle is initiated, and the OP code transferred to the instruction register during state T_3 is that of the halt instruction, HLT. During state T_4, the control unit decodes the instruction OP code and sets a halt flip-flop inside the 8085A. Upon exiting state T_4, the microprocessor enters state T_1 of the next machine cycle. As Fig. 3.3-9 indicates, the halt flip-flop is checked in state T_1 of the next machine cycle; if it is set, instead

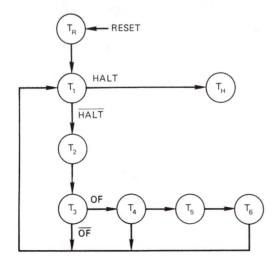

Figure 3.3-9 Simplified 8085A state transition diagram including T_{HALT}.

TABLE 3.3-4 RESET IN AND RESET OUT PIN DESCRIPTIONS (COURTESY OF INTEL CORP.)

Symbol	Type	Name and Function
$\overline{\text{RESET IN}}$	I	**Reset In:** Sets the Program Counter to zero and resets the Interrupt Enable and HLDA flip-flops. The data and address buses and the control lines are 3-stated during RESET and because of the asynchronous nature of RESET, the processor's internal registers and flags may be altered by RESET with unpredictable results. $\overline{\text{RESET IN}}$ is a Schmitt-triggered input, allowing connection to an R-C network for power-on RESET delay (see Figure 3.3-2). Upon power-up, $\overline{\text{RESET IN}}$ must remain low for at least 10 ms after minimum V_{CC} has been reached. For proper reset operation after the power-up duration, $\overline{\text{RESET IN}}$ should be kept low a minimum of three clock periods. The CPU is held in the reset condition as long as $\overline{\text{RESET IN}}$ is applied.
RESET OUT	O	**Reset Out:** Reset Out indicates CPU is being reset. Can be used as a system reset. The signal is synchronized to the processor clock and lasts an integral number of clock periods.

of entering state T_2, the HALT state is entered. Thus, five states are required to reach the HALT state. In the HALT state, the address and address/data buses, along with ALE, $\overline{\text{RD}}$, $\overline{\text{WR}}$, and IO/$\overline{\text{M}}$, are placed in their high impedance states (floated). In this simplified diagram (Fig. 3.3-9), the HALT state can only be exited by resetting the microprocessor, causing the halt flip-flop to be reset and state T_1 to be entered.[4]

3.3.4 Power-ON Reset and Manual Reset

When power is first applied to a microprocessor, the various registers and flip-flops assume random states, and the operation of the microprocessor system is unpredictable. Therefore, the microprocessor must be reset when it is first powered up in order to fetch the first instruction.

The 8085AH is not guaranteed to work until 10 mS after V_{CC} reaches its minimum operating voltage of 4.50 V. The microprocessor is automatically reset at

---

[4] Two other ways of temporarily exiting the HALT state, not shown in this figure, are discussed in Chapter 9.

power on by an *RC* circuit connected to the $\overline{\text{RESET IN}}$ input of the 8085A, as shown in Fig. 3.3-2. When power is first applied to the circuit, the voltage across the capacitor is 0 V. The capacitor charges, at a rate determined by *RC*, to a final voltage of V_{CC}. Values of *R* and *C* are selected to maintain RESET IN at the logic 0 level for the required amount of time. Typical values of *R* and *C* are 75 kΩ and 1 μF respectively. However, these values are a function of the power supply ramp up time and must be determined accordingly.

Once the system is operating, it can be reset manually by the push button switch. Pressing this switch shorts the capacitor and discharges it. For proper resetting, the $\overline{\text{RESET IN}}$ input must remain at logic 0 for three clock pulses. Releasing this switch causes the capacitor to charge, bringing the $\overline{\text{RESET IN}}$ input back to logic 1.

Resetting the 8085A places it in the reset state, T_R, and clears the PC and IR registers and several status flip-flops in the microprocessor, including the halt flip-flop. However, the A, F, B, C, D, E, H, and L registers are not cleared by resetting, although they may be altered.

When $\overline{\text{RESET IN}}$ is logic 0, RESET OUT is logic 1. RESET OUT is used to reset external devices in the microprocessor system. In the reset state, the same pins of the microprocessor that are floated in the halt state are again floated. When $\overline{\text{RESET IN}}$ becomes logic 1, the 8085A enters state T_1 of an OPCODE FETCH machine cycle and fetches the first instruction from memory location 0. The $\overline{\text{RESET IN}}$ and RESET OUT pin functions are summarized in Table 3.3-4

3.4 MEMORY AND I / O SYNCHRONIZATION — THE WAIT STATE

Timing computations must be made to ensure that the memory system and I/O system are compatible with the microprocessor's timing. These computations must include delays introduced by external address decoding logic and buffers. If the timing requirements are not met, several alternatives are available to the designer. One alternative is to select higher speed versions of the memory, I/O, and logic devices where necessary. This approach will not degrade the system's performance but will increase its cost. A second approach is to use a lower frequency crystal, which will increase the value of *T* in all the equations. This approach leads to substantial, and perhaps unacceptable, system performance degradation. Another choice is to design logic to introduce WAIT states when devices that are too slow are read or written.

3.4.1 8085A Read and Write Timing Requirements

When a microprocessor reads external data, the data is clocked into one of the registers in the microprocessor. Thus, like clocking data into any register, certain timing requirements must be met. The microprocessor's registers have setup time,

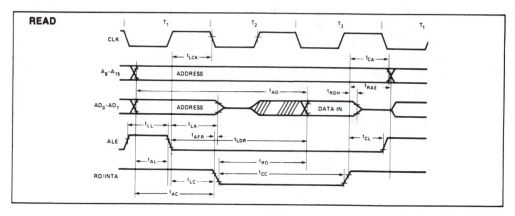

Figure 3.4-1 Timing diagram for an 8085AH read. (Courtesy of Intel Corp.)

hold time, and minimum clock pulse width requirements. However, clocking data into a microprocessor differs from clocking data into a simple register in that the microprocessor provides an address to select the source of the data and generates the clock pulse. This clock pulse is the $\overline{RD}$ strobe. Since the microprocessor dictates the system timing, it is necessary that the memory or I/O device meet the microprocessor's timing requirements. Otherwise, the microprocessor will have to be slowed down to meet the speed limitations of the memory and I/O devices. When a memory or I/O device is referred to in this section, any interface logic; address decoders, buffers, and so on, are considered part of the device.

Figure 3.4-1 is a detailed timing diagram for a read machine cycle for the 8085AH. From this figure it can be seen that the device providing data to the microprocessor must provide valid data at the microprocessor's data pins, AD_0–AD_7, within t_{AD} seconds after the microprocessor provides an address. This parameter, t_{AD}, is the "address valid to valid data in" parameter. The 8085AH data sheet, Appendix F, gives the relationship for t_{AD} as

$$t_{AD} = (5/2 + N)T - 225 \text{ nS}$$

N specifies the number of WAIT states in the machine cycle.

The simplified machine cycle state diagram in Figure 3.3-6 did not indicate the existence of WAIT states; WAIT states are introduced in the next section. Calculations in this section will be made for an 8085AH with a 6.144 MHz crystal (325.5 nS state time) and no WAIT states ($N = 0$). Using the above equation, with $N = 0$ and $T = 325.5$ nS, the device must have an access time of 589 nS or less. An additional timing requirement for the memory or input device is with respect to the beginning of the read strobe. The "$\overline{RD}$ to valid data" timing requirement is specified by t_{RD}:

$$t_{RD} = (3/2 + N)T - 180 \text{ nS}$$

Under the conditions $N = 0$ and $T = 325.5$, $t_{RD} = 308$ nS. The t_{AD} and t_{RD} requirements ensure that the setup time requirement for the 8085AH is met.

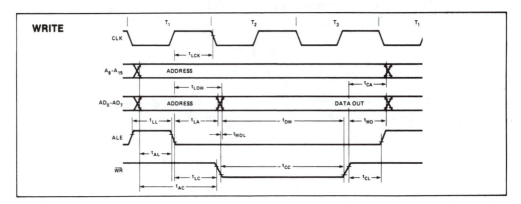

Figure 3.4-2   Timing diagram for an 8085AH write. (Courtesy of Intel Corp.)

The width of the read strobe, "width of control low," is given by t_{CC}:

$$t_{CC} = (3/2 + N)T - 80 \text{ nS}$$

The setup time requirement for the 8085AH is simply $t_{CC} - t_{RD}$, 100 nS, a constant. The hold time, t_{RDH}, is 0 nS.

While t_{RD} specifies the maximum amount of time the external device has to provide valid data at the microprocessor's data pins, another important parameter specifies how quickly the data must be removed. The parameter t_{RAE}, "trailing edge of $\overline{RD}$ to reenabling of address," specifies the time within which the external device must disable its output buffers and cease to drive the microprocessor's data pins. If the external device does not cease to drive the data pins within t_{RAE} nS, then bus contention occurs. This is because the microprocessor will begin driving the data bus with $A_0 - A_7$ for the next machine cycle. The equation for t_{RAE} is

$$t_{RAE} = (1/2)T - 10 \text{ nS}$$

Note that the value of t_{RAE} is not a function of the number of WAIT states.

The write timing diagram for an 8085AH is shown in Fig. 3.4-2. The timing parameters to be considered here are all minimum values. The corresponding memory system and I/O system timing parameters must have smaller values to be compatible.

To preclude writing the wrong memory location or output device, the memory system or output device must decode the address and select the addressed device before the $\overline{WR}$ strobe goes low. If this is not the case, additional memory locations or output devices will be unintentionally written. This time is specified by the parameter t_{AC}, "address valid to leading edge of control":

$$t_{AC} = T - 50 \text{ nS}$$
$$= 275.5 \text{ nS}$$

The time that the address remains valid after the trailing edge of the write strobe is given by t_{CA}, "address valid after control":

$$t_{CA} = (1/2)T - 40 \text{ nS}$$
$$= 122.8 \text{ nS}$$

Other timing parameters of interest here are all specified with respect to the trailing edge of $\overline{\text{WR}}$. The time from the beginning of a valid address to the trailing edge of $\overline{\text{WR}}$ is the sum of t_{AC} and t_{CC}.

$$t_{CC} = (3/2 + N)T - 80 \text{ nS}$$
$$t_{AC} + t_{CC} = (5/2 + N)T - 130 \text{ nS}$$

The setup time available to the memory system or output system is t_{DW}:

$$t_{DW} = (3/2 + N)T - 60 \text{ nS}$$
$$= 428 \text{ nS}$$

And the hold time available to the memory system or output system is t_{WD}:

$$t_{WD} = (1/2)T - 60 \text{ nS}$$
$$= 102 \text{ nS}$$

3.4.2 The WAIT State

To accommodate long access times, the 8085A has a state called the WAIT state, T_{WAIT}, shown in the state diagram of Fig. 3.4-3. When the microprocessor generates an address in state T_1, external control logic monitoring this address can request

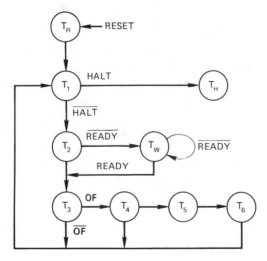

Figure 3.4-3 Simplified 8085A state transition diagram with T_{wait}.

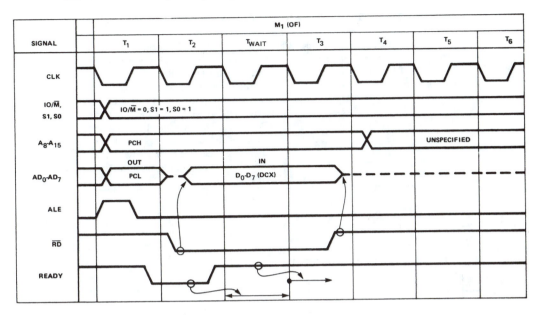

Figure 3.4-4 OPCODE FETCH machine cycle with one WAIT state. (Courtesy of Intel Corp.)

that the microprocessor wait for a period of time equal to an integral number of clock periods. The external control logic does this by making the READY input to the microprocessor logic 0 during state T_2. When this input is logic 0, the microprocessor enters state T_{WAIT} instead of T_3. When the READY line becomes logic 1, the microprocessor's machine cycle continues with a transition to T_3.

The effect of entering a WAIT state is to hold all external signals from the microprocessor in the same state they were in at the end of state T_2. This stretches the duration of the address and the $\overline{RD}$ pulse, so devices with access times greater than 589 nS can be read. If N WAIT states are introduced into the machine cycle, the required access time is $[(\frac{5}{2} + N)T - 225]$ nS. For each clock period that the microprocessor is in the WAIT state, the instruction cycle time is increased by 325.5 nS. The timing diagram of Fig. 3.4-4 shows a single WAIT state transition in a machine cycle. Sampling of the READY line in state T_2 and the transition into the WAIT state allow the microprocessor to synchronize to memories or I/O devices with long access times. Concomitant, of course, is the associated cost of increased instruction cycle time and additional logic to control the READY input to effectively time out the necessary WAIT period. Table 3.4-1 summarizes the READY pin's function.

External logic controlling the READY line can be designed so that none, a fixed number, or a variable number of WAIT states transitions occur during each machine cycle. This logic can also be designed so that these WAIT states occur only for specific addresses and/or for specific types of machine cycles. The circuit in Fig. 3.4-5 will generate a single WAIT state for any machine cycle for which the WAIT

TABLE 3.4-1   8085A READY PIN (COURTESY OF INTEL CORP.)

Symbol	Type	Name and Function
READY	I	**Ready:** If READY is high during a read or write cycle, it indicates that the memory or peripheral is ready to send or receive data. If READY is low, the CPU will wait an integral number of clock cycles for READY to go high before completing the read or write cycle. READY must conform to specified setup and hold times.

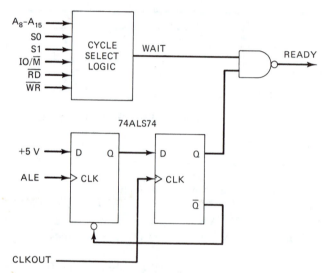

Figure 3.4-5   8085A wait state generator

output of the cycle select circuit is logic 1. If the cycle select circuit is removed and the WAIT signal is fixed at logic 1, the simplified circuit will introduce a WAIT state into all machine cycles. The same effect can be achieved by removing the cycle select circuit and the NAND gate and taking the READY signal from the $\overline{Q}$ output of the rightmost D flip-flop.

To generate a single WAIT state only for specific address ranges and/or types of machine cycles, the cycle select circuit is designed to make WAIT logic 1 when a selected machine cycle is detected. With A_0–A_{15}, S0, S1, and IO/$\overline{M}$ as inputs to the cycle select circuit, any address range and/or type of machine cycle could be detected.

In addition to detecting the desired machine cycles, the cycle select circuit must ensure that the setup and hold times for the READY input are met. The READY input is sampled on the rising edge of CLK during T_2. These times, t_{RYS} and t_{RYH}, are illustrated in Fig. 3.4-6. These values are not dependent on the state time T. For the 8085AH, they are 110 nS and 0 nS, respectively.

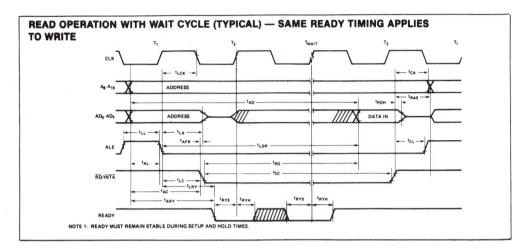

Figure 3.4-6 READY timing requirements for a read operation. (Courtesy of Intel Corp.)

3.4.3 Hardware Single Step

The ability to put the 8085A in its WAIT state is useful when troubleshooting hardware interfaced to the microprocessor. The address, data, and control bits maintain their logic values as long as the microprocessor remains in the WAIT state. If the microprocessor can be caused to enter and then indefinitely reenter the WAIT state, a logic probe can be used to trace signals in the external hardware driven by the address, data, and control buses. Thus, logic design errors or hardware failures can be located without sophisticated test instruments.

The circuit in Fig. 3.4-7 is a *hardware single step circuit*. This circuit allows a user to control the READY line of the 8085A so that program execution is stepped from the WAIT state in one machine cycle to the WAIT state in the next machine cycle. When switch S1 is in the RUN position, the READY output of NAND gate G1 is logic 1 and the microprocessor executes machine cycles without entering the WAIT state. When S1 is in the single step position, the output of G1 depends on the output of the 74ALS74 flip-flop. In T_1 of each machine cycle, the ALE strobe is generated. This strobe is inverted by NAND gate G2 and sets the flip-flop. With the flip-flop set, the READY output of G1 is logic 0. The microprocessor samples its READY input in T_2 and enters the WAIT state. The microprocessor will remain in the WAIT state until pushbutton PB1 is pressed. Pressing PB1 causes the debounce circuit, G3 and G4, to pulse the clock input of the 74ALS74, clearing it. The READY line becomes logic 1; the microprocessor exits the WAIT state and enters T_3. The microprocessor will then continue its state transitions in a normal fashion. When the microprocessor enters state T_1, ALE will again set the flip-flop. The microprocessor will sample its READY input in T_2 and its next transition will be to

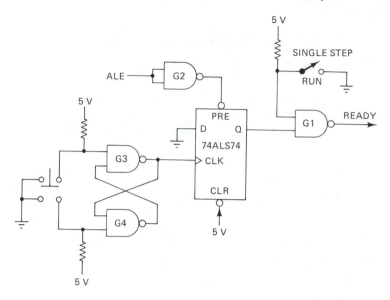

Figure 3.4-7 Hardware single step circuit for the 8085A.

state T_W. It will continue making transitions from T_W back to T_W, staying in the WAIT state until PB1 is pressed again.

The example in Fig. 3.4-8 will be used to illustrate the use of single stepping for hardware troubleshooting and as a further example of instruction execution and machine cycles. Figure 3.4-8 consists of an input device (eight switches), an input port, and address decoding logic. The input port is a 74ALS541 octal buffer. The three-state outputs of the octal buffer are enabled when its enable inputs G1 and G2 are both logic 0. The input device consists of eight single pole switches. Address decoding is implemented using a 74ALS138 1-out-of-8 decoder and a 74ALS30 NAND gate.

A simple *diagnostic program* that can be used to test the input port and its associated address decoding logic is shown below:

LOOP: IN SWITCH

JMP LOOP

This is the assembly language representation of the program. LOOP is the address of the first instruction in the program. The program consists of two instructions. The first instruction, IN PORT, inputs data from the switches. SWITCH is the symbol that represents the port address. The port has an 8-bit address, which is F9H. The second instruction, JMP LOOP, causes the microprocessor to jump back and execute the first instruction again. Thus, the program is an infinite loop that executes the two instructions over and over. Assuming the program begins at

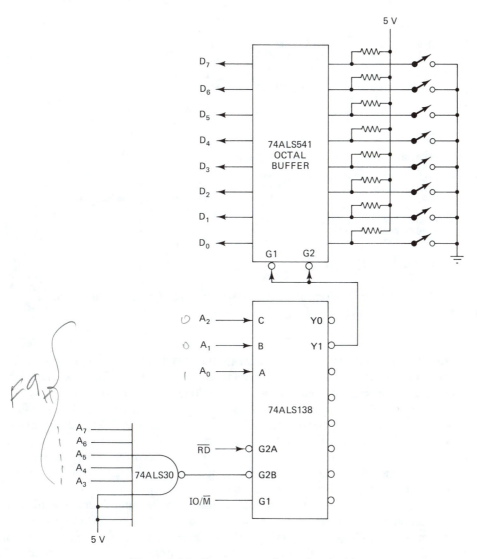

Figure 3.4-8 Input port and associated address decoding logic.

address 0000H, an equivalent representation is

$$\text{IN F9H}$$
$$\text{JMP 0000H}$$

Figure 3.4-9a is a hexadecimal representation of the program code as it appears in memory. The IN instruction is a 2-byte instruction and occupies locations 0000H and 0001H. The first byte, DB, is the opcode for the IN instruction. The second byte, F9H, is the port address. The JMP instruction is a 3-byte

```
ADDRESS    CODE      COMMENT

0000       DB        IN OPCODE
0001       F9        PORT ADDRESS
0002       C3        JMP OPCODE
0003       00        LOW BYTE OF JUMP ADDRESS
0004       00        HIGH BYTE OF JUMP ADDRESS
```

(a)

```
MACHINE CYCLE    ADDRESS BUS    DATA BUS

OPCODE FETCH     0000           DB
MEMORY READ      0001           F9
INPUT            F9F9           XX  ← DATA VALUES READ FROM SWITCH
OPCODE FETCH     0002           C3
MEMORY READ      0003           00
MEMORY READ      0004           00
OPCODE FETCH     0000           DB  ← LOOP REPEATS
```

(b)

Figure 3.4-9   (a) Test program. (b) Machine cycle type and address and data bus contents.

instruction and occupies locations 0002H through 0004H. The first byte, C3, is the opcode for a JMP instruction. The second and third bytes are the low and high bytes of the address from which the next instruction will be fetched.

Execution of the 2-byte IN instruction requires three machine cycles. The first two machine cycles, an OPCODE FETCH and a MEMORY READ, fetch the instruction. The third machine cycle, an I/O READ, inputs the data from the port. Figure 3.4-9b lists the machine cycles in their order of occurrence. This figure also shows the values that would appear on the address bus and data bus during the WAIT state when the program is single stepped.

To troubleshoot the hardware, the program can be single stepped until the third machine cycle. At this point, the address bus should have the value F9F9H. This occurs because during the I/O READ machine cycle the 8085A replicates the port address on both the high and low bytes of the address bus. The occurrence of the port address can be verified by checking the bits of the address bus with a logic probe. During an I/O READ machine cycle, IO/M is logic 1, indicating that the address on the address bus is an I/O address instead of a memory address. During the WAIT state, the RD strobe will be held at logic 0.

With the above conditions present, the enable inputs G1 and G2 of the octal buffer should be logic 0. If this is the case, then the logic value of each switch should appear on its corresponding data bus bit. The switch values can be changed and the corresponding changes should occur on the data bus bits. This test provides reasonable confidence that the address decoding logic, octal buffer, and switches are operating properly. If G1 and G2 are not logic 0 and the inputs to the address decoding logic have the correct values, then either the NAND gate or 1-out-of-8 decoder or their associated connections is the problem. A logic probe can be used to trace through the address decoding logic to determine if a connection or IC is bad.

An alternate approach to verifying proper circuit operation can be taken using the same diagnostic program. In this case the program is not single stepped but is executed in the normal manner. With the program continuously running, signals supplied to and generated by the circuit are again traced using the logic probe. However, with this dynamic approach, pulses or strobes are traced through the circuit rather than static logic levels.

3.5 MEMORY SPEED REQUIREMENTS

In Section 2.4 the logic design of memory systems was presented without consideration of the memory speed required for an application. Since the microprocessor controls the system timing, determination of memory speed requirements can only be made in the context of the microprocessor system in which the memory is used. Figure 3.5-1 shows the memory system of Fig. 2.4-2 interfaced to an 8085AH, and

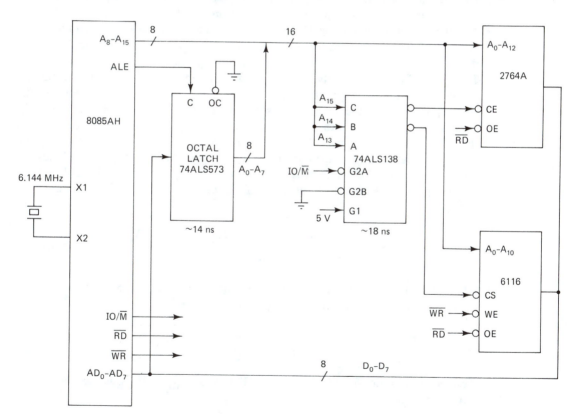

Figure 3.5-1   Memory system interfaced to an 8085AH.

will be used to demonstrate how memory speed requirements can be determined. The memory devices are a 2764A EPROM and a HM6116 SRAM. The objective is to determine the required speeds of these two devices so that no WAIT states are necessary.

The times available for the timing parameters of each memory device must be determined. These times are a function of the timing requirements of the micro-processor and time delays of logic devices that interface the microprocessor to the memory. For each relevant timing parameter of a memory device, a timing equation can be written that relates the memory device's timing parameter to one or more parameters of the microprocessor and time delays of the external logic. For simplicity, the equations are initially written with the time allowed by the micro-processor on the left and the external hardware times on the right. These equations are solved for the memory device's timing parameters. When the times available for each of a memory device's parameters have been found, the slowest memory device that meets these time requirements can be selected.

The times available for the 2764A EPROM will be analyzed first. The timing waveforms and parameter definitions for the 8085AH and 2764A are given in the AC specifications on their data sheets in Appendix F. The 2764A parameter, t_{ACC}, specifies its address to data output delay. From the logic diagram, it can be seen that the address inputs of the 2764A, A_8–A_{12}, are directly driven by the address bits A_8–A_{12} of the microprocessor. However, address inputs A_0–A_7 of the 2764A are driven by address bits A_0–A_7 of the microprocessor, which are delayed by the 74ALS573. Thus, there are two signal paths from the microprocessor to the address inputs of the 2764A. The data outputs of the 2764A are connected directly to the AD_0–AD_7 pins of the microprocessor. The delay allowed from the 8085AH's generation of an address, for a read operation, until valid data must be available at its AD_0–AD_7 pins, is given by the parameter t_{AD}. Thus, the total delay in the external signal path from the 8085AH's address pins back to its data pins must be less than t_{AD} nS. An equation is written for each signal path from the 8085AH's address pins to its data pins and the limiting case determined. The two equations are

$$t_{AD} > t_{ACC} \qquad \text{for address bits } A_8\text{–}A_{12}$$

$$t_{AD} > t_{pdL} + t_{ACC} \quad \text{for address bits } A_0\text{–}A_7$$

where t_{pdL} is the worst case propagation delay of the 74ALS573 latch, 14 nS. Solving each of these equations for t_{ACC} gives

$$t_{ACC} < t_{AD}$$

$$t_{ACC} < t_{AD} - t_{pdL}$$

The second equation is the limiting case. Replacing t_{AD} by its equation and solving with $N = 0$ and $T = 325.5$ nS give

$$t_{ACC} < [(5/2 + N) \times T - 225] - 14$$

$$< 574 \text{ nS}$$

Thus, the access time for the 2764A selected must be less than 574 nS for operation with zero WAIT states.

The parameter t_{CE} for the 2764A specifies the delay from chip enable, $\overline{CE}$, going low until the 2764A provides valid data on the data bus. The signal driving $\overline{CE}$ in the diagram is derived from the A_{13}–A_{15} and $IO/\overline{M}$ outputs of the 8085AH by the 74ALS138. The related 8085AH parameter is again t_{AD}. The equation is

$$t_{AD} > t_{pdD} + t_{CE}$$

where t_{pdD} is the worst case propagation delay of the 74ALS138, 18 nS.

Solving for t_{CE}

$$t_{CE} < t_{AD} - t_{pdD}$$
$$< [(5/2 + N) \times T - 225] - 18$$
$$< 570 \text{ nS}$$

Therefore, t_{CE} for the 2764A selected must be less than 570 nS for zero WAIT state operation.

The 2764A parameter t_{OE} specifies the delay from $\overline{OE}$, going low until its three-state output buffers drive the bus with valid data. Since $\overline{OE}$ is driven directly by $\overline{RD}$ of the 8085AH, and the 8085AH requires valid data within t_{RD} nS after $\overline{RD}$ goes low, the relationship for t_{OE} is simply

$$t_{OE} < t_{RD}$$
$$< (3/2 + N) \times T - 180$$
$$< 308.25 \text{ nS}$$

The delay from either $\overline{CE}$ or $\overline{OE}$ going high until the 2764A's three-state output buffers are disabled is t_{DF}. Since $\overline{OE}$ will go high before $\overline{CE}$ in this system, the related 8085AH parameter is the time from $\overline{RD}$ going high until some device other than the 2764A subsequently drives the data bus. Examination of the 8085AH read timing diagram indicates that the data bus will next be driven by the microprocessor with the address bits A_0–A_7 for the next machine cycle. This time is specified by the parameter t_{RAE}. Thus

$$t_{RAE} > t_{DF}$$

Solving for t_{DF}

$$t_{DF} < t_{RAE}$$
$$< (1/2) \times T - 10$$
$$< 152.75 \text{ nS}$$

If the 2764A selected requires more than 152.75 nS to disable its output buffers, bus contention would result between the 8085AH and the 2764A.

The parameter t_{OH} indicates how long the 2764A will continue to provide valid output data after $\overline{RD}$ goes high. This parameter must be compared to the data

TABLE 3.5-1 SUMMARY OF EQUATIONS AND TIMES AVAILABLE FOR MEMORY PARAMETERS

Memory	Parameter	Equation	Time, nS
2764A	HM6116		$N = 0$, $T = 32.5$ nS
t_{ACC}	t_{AA}	$< t_{AD} - t_{pdL}$	574
t_{CE}	t_{ACS}	$< t_{AD} - t_{pdD}$	570
t_{OE}	t_{OE}	$< t_{RD}$	308.25
t_{DF}	t_{OHZ}	$< t_{RAE}$	152.75
t_{OH}	—	$> t_{RDH}$	0
—	t_{AS}	$< t_{ACL} - t_{pdL}$	231.5
—	t_{WR}	$< t_{CL} + t_{pdL}$	66.75
—	t_{AW}	$< t_{AC} + t_{CC} - t_{pdL}$	669.75
—	t_{CW}	$< t_{AC} + t_{CC} - t_{pdD}$	665.75
—	t_{WP}	$< t_{CC}$	408.25
—	t_{DW}	$< t_{DW}$	428.5
—	t_{DH}	$< t_{WD}$	102.75

hold time for the 8085AH, t_{RDH}.

$$t_{RDH} < t_{OH}$$

Solving for t_{OH}

$$t_{OH} > t_{RDH}$$
$$> 0 \text{ nS}$$

The 0 nS value for t_{RDH} indicates that the 2764A can stop outputting valid data at the instant $\overline{RD}$ makes its zero to one transition. That is, the 8085AH does not require any hold time.

These parameters, their equations, and computed times are summarized in Table 3.5-1. Comparison of these times with those given in the A.C. characteristics of the 2764A data sheet indicate that even the slowest version of the 2764A, the 2764A-45, is fast enough for this application.

Read cycle computations for the HM6116 are similar to those for the 2764A. The correspondences between HM6116 parameters and 2764A parameters are as follows: $t_{AA} = t_{ACC}$, $t_{ACS} = t_{CE}$, $t_{OE} = t_{OE}$, $t_{OHZ} = t_{DF}$. The output hold time for the HM6116 is not explicitly specified on its data sheet.

For write cycle operations the speed requirements can be considered in two groups. The first group of requirements ensures that "unaddressed" memory locations are not inadvertently written. The second group ensures that the selected location is properly written.

To preclude writing "unaddressed" memory locations, two conditions must be met. First, the address inputs to the memory device must be held stable long enough for the memory device's internal address decoders to have selected the addressed location before its $\overline{WE}$ input is driven low. This condition is the memory's address setup time. Second, the memory's address inputs must remain stable for a period of time after the $\overline{WE}$ input signal goes high. This condition is the memory's address hold time. The HM6116's address setup time is specified by its parameter t_{AS}. Two paths exist from the microprocessor to the HM6116 address inputs. The path for the address inputs A_0–A_7 is the critical path. The associated 8085AH parameter is t_{ACL}, "A_0–A_7 valid to leading edge of control." An equation for this parameter is not shown on the 8085AH data sheet. The equation used here is derived from the equation for the parameter t_{AC} and values for t_{AC} and t_{ACL} given for $f_c = 6.25$ MHz.

$$t_{ACL} > t_{AS} + t_{pdL}$$

Solving for t_{AS}

$$t_{AS} < t_{ACL} - t_{pdL}$$
$$< (T - 80) - 14$$
$$< 231.5 \text{ nS}$$

If the address setup time of the HM6116 selected exceeds 231.5 nS, "unaddressed" locations in the memory may be written.

The address hold time for the HM6116 is t_{WR}, its "write recovery time." The critical signal path is again the path for the address bits A_0–A_7. However, in this case the propagation delay of the 74ALS573 is an advantage. The associated 8085AH parameter is t_{CL}, "trailing edge of control to leading edge of ALE." This is the 8085AH parameter of importance, because, after ALE goes high, the address latch will become transparent and the previously latched address will no longer be valid.

$$t_{CL} > t_{WR} - t_{pdL}$$

Solving for t_{WR}

$$t_{WR} < t_{CL} + t_{pdL}$$
$$< [(1/2) \times T - 110] + 14$$
$$< 66.75 \text{ nS}$$

The address hold time or "write recovery time" for the HM6116 selected must be less than 66.75 nS to ensure that no "unaddressed" locations in the memory are written.

The remaining HM6116 parameters are related to ensuring that the addressed memory location is properly written. The time that the address must be valid at the HM6116's address inputs before its $\overline{\text{WE}}$ input goes high is t_{AW}. The related 8085AH time is the sum of its parameters t_{AC} and t_{CC}. Again, the critical path is for the address bits A_0–A_7.

$$t_{AC} + t_{CC} > t_{pdL} + t_{AW}$$

Solving for t_{AW}

$$t_{AW} < t_{AC} + t_{CC} - t_{pdL}$$
$$< (T - 50) + [(3/2 + N) \times T - 80] - 14$$
$$< 669.75 \text{ nS}$$

The minimum time allowed from the HM6116's chip select input going low until its $\overline{\text{WE}}$ input goes high is specified by the parameter t_{CW}. The signal at the HM6116's $\overline{\text{CE}}$ input is derived from the A_{13}–A_{15} and $\text{IO}/\overline{\text{M}}$ outputs of the 8085AH. The resulting equation is

$$t_{\text{AC}} + t_{\text{CC}} > t_{\text{pdD}} + t_{\text{CW}}$$

Solving for t_{CW}

$$
\begin{aligned}
t_{\text{CW}} &< t_{\text{AC}} + t_{\text{CC}} - t_{\text{pdD}} \\
&< (T - 50) + [(3/2 + N) \times T - 80] - 18 \\
&< 665.75 \text{ nS}
\end{aligned}
$$

Since $\overline{\text{WR}}$ directly drives $\overline{\text{WE}}$, and $\overline{\text{CS}}$ is active prior to and after $\overline{\text{WR}}$, the write pulse duration is given by

$$t_{\text{CC}} > t_{\text{WP}}$$

Solving for t_{WP}

$$
\begin{aligned}
t_{\text{WP}} &< t_{\text{CC}} \\
&< (3/2 + N) \times T - 80 \\
&< 408.25 \text{ nS}
\end{aligned}
$$

The setup time computation is straightforward:

$$
\begin{aligned}
T_{\text{DW}}(8085\text{AH}) &> T_{\text{DW}}(\text{HM6116}) \\
T_{\text{DW}}(\text{HM6116}) &< T_{\text{DW}}(8085\text{AH}) \\
&< (3/2 + N) \times T - 60 \\
&< 428.5 \text{ NS}
\end{aligned}
$$

The hold time requirement is

$$t_{\text{WD}} > t_{\text{DH}}$$

Solving for t_{DH}

$$
\begin{aligned}
t_{\text{DH}} &< t_{\text{WD}} \\
&< (1/2) \times T - 60 \\
&< 102.75 \text{ nS}
\end{aligned}
$$

The slowest HM6116 in the data sheet, the HM6116P-4, is compatible with the times allowed by the 8085AH and the external logic.

While the timing margins for both the EPROM and SRAM in this example are substantial, these computations are necessary to ensure that this is the case. Using a faster version of the 8085AH such as the 8085AH-1 at its maximum clock frequency would place significantly greater timing demands on the memory devices. For example, the 2764A-45 would not be compatible with the 8085AH-1 using a 12 MHz crystal. Similar computations must be made to determine the timing compatibility of I/O ports in a system. I/O ports that are part of an MOS or CMOS LSI device are sometimes much slower than typical SRAM memories and may require WAIT states even with relatively slow microprocessors.

3.6 LOGIC LEVELS, LOADING, AND BUFFERING

At the time of the advent of microprocessors, the dominant technology for SSI and MSI devices was standard TTL logic. Since most microprocessors' systems require SSI and MSI logic to complete the system, it was advantageous for microprocessors to be compatible with TTL logic. Thus, even though the early microprocessors were MOS devices, they were designed to be as TTL compatible as possible. In this context, compatibility means that outputs from the microprocessor can directly drive TTL inputs and that outputs from TTL logic can drive the microprocessor's inputs. Early microprocessors achieved this compatibility to varying degrees.

Compatibility with TTL logic requires both voltage level and current drive compatibility. The voltage ranges corresponding to logic 0 and logic 1 for standard TTL are given in Fig. 3.6-1. Two sets of voltage ranges are defined, one for TTL logic outputs (Fig. 3.6-1a), and another for TTL logic inputs (Fig. 3.6-1b). The difference between the minimum output voltage limit for a logic 1, V_{OH}min, and the corresponding minimum input voltage limit, V_{IH}min, provides a small voltage margin for noise immunity. The same is true for the logic 0 case, V_{IL}max $- V_{OL}$max (Fig. 3.6-1c). Input buffers, on a microprocessor chip, buffer the TTL input voltages and shift them to the internal voltage levels required by the microprocessor. Output buffers transform the microprocessor's internal voltage levels to those compatible

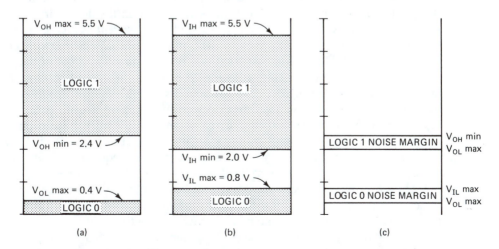

Figure 3.6-1   TTL logic voltage ranges: (a) output voltage levels; (b) input voltage levels; (c) noise margins.

TABLE 3.6-1   TYPICAL WORST CASE VALUES OF PRIMARY INTERFACING PARAMETERS[1]

Parameter	74TTL	74LSTTL	74ALSTTL	HCMOS	HCTMOS	CMOS
V_{IH} min	2.0 V	2.0 V	2.0 V	3.5 V	2.0 V	3.5 V
V_{IL} max	0.8 V	0.8 V	0.8 V	1.0 V	0.8 V	1.5 V
V_{OH} min	2.4 V	2.7 V	2.7 V	4.9 V	3.7 V	4.5 V
V_{OL} max	0.4 V	0.4 V	0.4 V	0.1 V	0.4 V	0.4 V
[2]I_{IH} max	40 μA	20 μA	20 μA	1 μA	1 μA	5 nA
I_{IL} max	−1.6 mA	−400 μA	−100 μA	−1 μA	1 μA	−5 nA
I_{OH} max	−400 μA	−400 μA	−400 μA	−4 mA	−4 mA	−400 μA
I_{OL} max	16 mA	8 mA	4 mA	4 mA	4 mA	400 μA
[3]I_{OZH}	40 μA	20 μA	20 μA	5 μA	5 μA	5 nA
I_{OZL}	−40 μA	−20 μA	−20 μA	−5 μA	−5 μA	−5 nA

[1]All ratings are for device operated at 5.0 V supply, 25°C.
[2]Ratings are for standard outputs; high current output ratings are not listed.
[3]Ratings are for three-state outputs.

with TTL output logic levels. The 8085A microprocessor operates with voltage levels at its pins that are TTL compatible, V_{OH} min = 2.4 V and V_{OL} max = 0.45 V.

The minimum logic 1 and maximum logic 0, worst case voltage levels for standard 74xxx series TTL logic are listed in Table 3.6-1. The corresponding values for other TTL and CMOS families are also given in this table. When TTL devices, or TTL compatible devices, drive CMOS the V_{IH} min voltage level requirement may not be directly met—for example, when a TTL device drives a 74HCMOS device. This incompatibility can be removed by using a pull-up resistor to +5 V on the output of the TTL device [3].

In addition to its input voltage level requirements, the input current requirements of a device must be met by any device that drives it. A logic device's inputs have a current requirement specification for each logic level. When a device's input is logic 1, it may draw a current as high as I_{IH} max from the device driving it (see Fig. 3.6-2a). When an input is logic 0, it may provide a current as high as I_{IL} max to the device that drives it (Fig. 3.6-2b). The minus signs associated with current specifications in Table 3.6-1 indicate that the current's direction is out of the device. The driving device must be able to **source**, or provide, the current required by the inputs it drives at the logic 1 level without its output voltage dropping below V_{OH} min. In the logic 0 case, the driving device must be able to **sink**, or accept, the input current from the device being driven without its output voltage rising above V_{OL} max. The output current drive capability of a device is specified by the parameters I_{OH} max and I_{OL} max. The input current requirements and output current drive capability for several families of logic are given in Table 3.6-1.

In a bused microprocessor system, a device that is driving the bus must meet the current requirements of all the devices connected to it on the bus. This includes current requirements of both inputs and outputs. Input current requirements were discussed above. An output, connected to a common point that is being driven by another device, will be in its high impedance state. Such an output will also draw current when at a logic 1 voltage level and provide current when at a logic 0 voltage

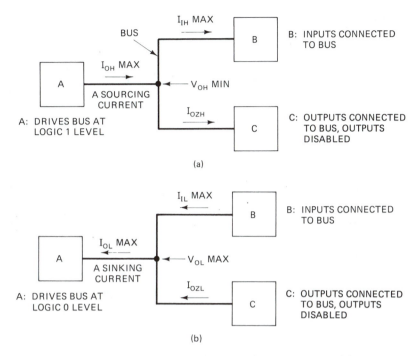

Figure 3.6-2   Input current requirements and output current drive capability: (a) logic 1 case; (b) logic 0 case.

level! These currents are specified as the off-state output current with a high voltage level applied, I_{OZH}, and the off-state output current with a low voltage level applied, I_{OZL}. These worst case values are also given in Table 3.6-1.

If a device that drives the bus cannot meet the total current requirements of the devices to which it is connected, then its output must be buffered. The 8085A has a rather modest output current drive capability. It has an I_{OH}max of -400 μA and an I_{OL}max of 2 mA. The loading on the address, data, and control lines of the 8085A must be calculated to determine if it exceeds the drive capability of the 8085A. Outputs of the 8085A that are excessively loaded must be buffered. Buffers, or devices with buffered outputs, provide higher current drive capability than typical gates in the same family. Buffers typically have three-state outputs.

Figure 3.6-3 shows buffered address, data, and control lines for an 8085A. Since the address lines are unidirectional, their buffering is straightforward. Address buffering for A_8–A_{15} is provided by a 74ALS541 octal buffer. This buffer's output current drive is $I_{OH} = -3$ mA and $I_{OL} = 12$ mA. A 74ALS573 octal transparent latch demultiplexes the address/data bus and provides buffering for A_0–A_7. The octal latch's output drive capability is $I_{OH} = -2.6$ mA and $I_{OL} = 12$ mA. The output drive capability of these buffers significantly exceeds that of the typical 74ALSxxx device in Table 3.6-1. These low and high byte address buffers outputs are always enabled.

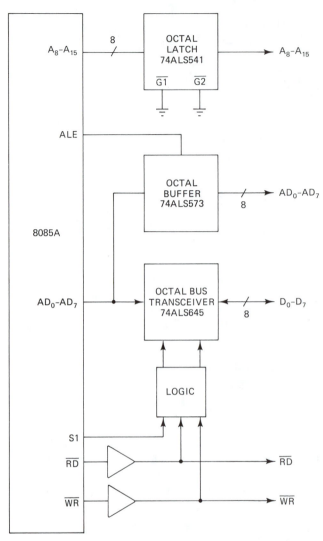

Figure 3.6-3 8085A with buffered address, data, and control bus.

Because the data bus lines are bidirectional, their buffering requires special consideration. Both the direction of transfer through the buffer and the enabling of the buffer must be controlled. Data bus buffers are implemented with octal *bus transceivers*. A 74ALS645 octal bus transceiver consists of eight pairs of back-to-back three-state buffers that share common control logic. The 74ALS645's output drive capability is $I_{OH} = -3$ mA and $I_{OL} = 12$ mA. Figure 3.6-4 shows a representative pair of back-to-back buffers and the common control logic that make up the octal bus transceiver. When the DIR input is logic 1, the bottom buffer is disabled and the top buffer will transfer data from A to B while $\overline{G}$ is logic 0. When DIR is 0 and $\overline{G}$ is 0, data transfer will be from B to A. When $\overline{G}$ is logic 1 both buffers are disabled.

The 8085A does not provide control outputs specifically for controlling a bus transceiver. However, with a minimal amount of logic the existing control and status

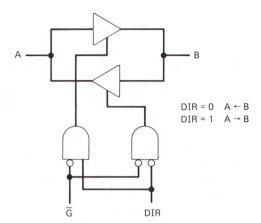

A ———————— B

DIR = 0   A ← B
DIR = 1   A → B

$\overline{G}$ DIR

Figure 3.6-4   One pair of back-to-back buffers from a bus transceiver and the shared buffer control logic.

signals can be used. Three methods of control are shown in Fig. 3.6-5. The first method keeps $\overline{G}$ at logic 0 and controls the direction of the buffer using $\overline{RD}$. Thus, the buffer is enabled and in the output direction until a $\overline{RD}$ strobe occurs. During the $\overline{RD}$ strobe the buffer is in the input direction. Bus contention is possible, when the $\overline{RD}$ strobe makes a 0 to 1 transition at the end of a read operation. The three-state buffers of the device being read must reach their high impedance state before the transceiver turns to the output direction to preclude bus contention. The

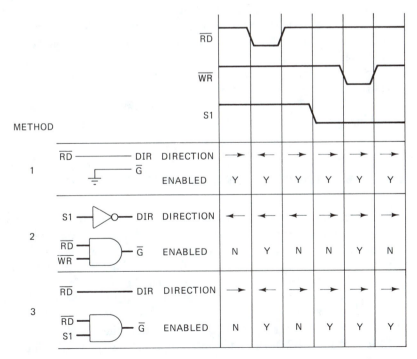

Figure 3.6-5   Three methods for controlling a data bus transceiver for an 8085A system.

"data float time" of all memory and input ports must be checked against this requirement.

The second method only enables the octal transceiver's buffers during the occurrence of a $\overline{RD}$ or $\overline{WR}$ strobe. In this case $\overline{G} = \overline{RD} \cdot \overline{WR}$. The direction of the buffer is controlled by the 8085A status output S1. The status output S1 is 1 for all machine cycles that transfer data to the microprocessor. Since the value of S1 is established at the beginning of each machine cycle, the direction of the buffer is fixed for the entire machine cycle. A potential problem may arise for write operations if the device written has a significant "write hold time" requirement. Since the bus transceiver is disabled on the 0 to 1 transition of the $\overline{WR}$ strobe, and this same signal is being used to clock the device being written, the "data hold time" may be insufficient for some memory or output devices.

The third method controls the direction using $\overline{RD}$, as in the first method. However, for read operations it only enables the buffer for the duration of the read, $\overline{G} = \overline{RD} \cdot S1$. This eliminates the bus contention problem of the first method. For write operations, the transceiver is enabled, S1 = 0, and in the output direction for the entire cycle. This eliminates the possible "write hold problem."

In addition to current loading, capacitive loading must also be considered. The timing specifications of the 8085A are guaranteed as long as the 8085A's 150 pF maximum loading specification is not exceeded. This capacitive load includes device input capacitances, interconnect capacitance, and parasitic capacitance. Capacitive loads as high as 300 pF can be driven by the 8085A. However, this additional load slows down the signal transitions from the 8085A. Correction factors must then be used to adjust the timing. For 150 pF $< C_L <$ 300 pF, 0.13 nS/pF is added. The extra loading capacitance also requires excessive switching currents, which limit the reliability of most MOS devices. The use of buffers significantly reduces the capacitance seen by the 8085A. Capacitive loads below 150 pF result in faster output transitions. A correction factor of 0.1 nS can be subtracted from timing values for 25 pF $< C_L <$ 150 pF.

When buffers are used, their propagation delays must be included when making speed requirement calculations for memory and I/O ports.

3.7 A MINIMUM CONFIGURATION 8085A MICROCOMPUTER

Three special peripheral components designed to be used with the 8085A allow small microprocessor systems to be configured around the 8085A using a minimum number of IC packages. One of these is the 8155, which contains 256 words of R/W memory, two 8-bit and one 6-bit I/O ports, and a 14-bit programmable timer, and is, itself, contained in a 40-pin DIP. The direction of the ports (in or out) is determined by a command word output to the 8155 by the application program.

The other two devices are pin compatible ROMs. One, the 8355, contains 2 K bytes of mask programmed ROM; the other, the 8755, contains 2 K bytes of EPROM. The EPROM device can be used during system development and in low production quantity systems. For high production quantity systems, once the

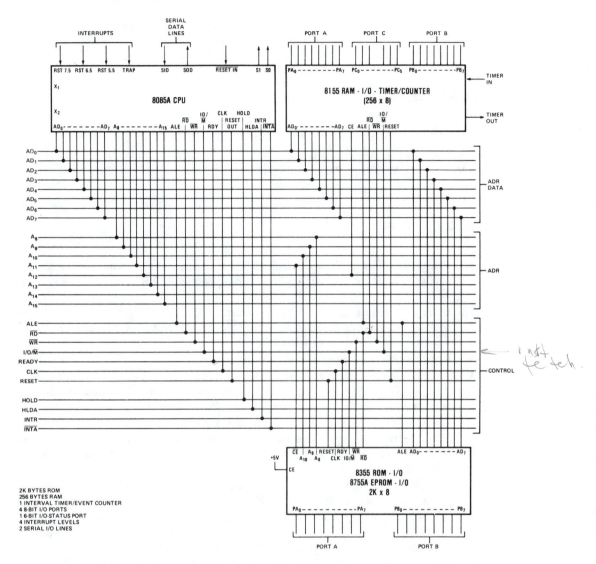

Figure 3.7-1 Three-chip 8085A microcomputer system. (Courtesy of Intel Corp.)

software is debugged, the masked ROM can be used. Each of these devices also contains two 8-bit ports whose directions are programmable. All three of these devices have internal latches that use the ALE strobe to latch the low order byte of the address.

The 3-chip microcomputer system shown in Fig. 3.7-1 attests to the fact that design of the microcomputer portion of a system using this chip set is simple. Merely connect the corresponding signals! More than one 8355/8755 and 8155 can be used in a system by using address lines A_{11} through A_{15} to select the different devices. As the amount of memory required by a system increases, a point is reached beyond which the number of bits of I/O required does not increase proportionally. At this point, it is more cost-effective to use standard ROM and R/W memory.

REFERENCES

1. *The MCS-80/85 Family User's Manual* (Santa Clara, Calif.: Intel Corporation, 1983).
2. *Microcomputer Databook* (Sunnyvale, Calif.: OKI Semiconductor, 1985).
3. *High-speed CMOS Logic Data Book* (Dallas, Tex.: Texas Instruments, Inc., 1984).

PROBLEMS

3-1. Using NAND gates, draw the logic diagram of a circuit that generates the control strobes $\overline{\text{MEMR}}$, $\overline{\text{MEMW}}$, $\overline{\text{I/OR}}$, and $\overline{\text{I/OW}}$ from $\overline{\text{RD}}$, $\overline{\text{WR}}$, and IO/$\overline{\text{M}}$. See Table 3.1-1.

3-2. Using a single quad, 2-line-to-1-line multiplexer (e.g., 74ALS257), draw the connections necessary to generate the control strobes $\overline{\text{MEMR}}$, $\overline{\text{MEMW}}$, $\overline{\text{I/OR}}$, and $\overline{\text{I/OW}}$ from $\overline{\text{RD}}$, $\overline{\text{WR}}$, and IO/$\overline{\text{M}}$. See Table 3.1-1.

3-3. Repeat Problem 3-2 using a 74ALS138 decoder.

3-4. An input device that has its own 8-bit latch is to be interfaced to an 8-bit bidirectional data bus. Draw the logic diagram illustrating how this can be accomplished with an octal three-state buffer (for example, 74ALS541).

3-5. Using a 74ALS138 1-out-of-8 decoder and a minimal amount of additional logic, design a circuit to generate eight active low input device select pulses, $\overline{\text{IDSP}}$(00H) to $\overline{\text{IDSP}}$(07H). These eight pulses should correspond to the input port addresses 00H to 07H.

3-6. Using the same logic as in Problem 3-5, generate and list the eight active low output device select pulses, $\overline{\text{ODSP}}$(00H) to $\overline{\text{ODSP}}$(07H).

3-7. An 8-bit output port is to provide bits to control some external process. The status (logic 0 or 1) of each of these bits must be readable through an input port with the same address FEH. Design this system to interface to an 8085A system bus. Use only the following logic devices: an 8-bit positive edge triggered latch, an 8-bit three-state buffer with active low enable, a 74ALS138 decoder, and an eight-input NAND gate. The address bits to be decoded are A_0–A_7.

3-8. An 8-bit positive edge triggered latch is to be used to construct an output port. This port is to be located in the I/O address space of an 8085A system. Port addresses consist of the bits A_0–A_7. The port's address is to be switch-selectable to respond to any of the possible output port addresses. To provide this capability, use single-pole single-throw switches and two input exclusive OR gates with open collector outputs. No other types of logic gates should be used.

3-9. List the internal registers in an 8085A and their abbreviations and lengths. Describe the primary function of each register.

3-10. List the machine cycles of the 8085A excluding the INTERRUPT ACK. and BUS IDLE machine cycles. For each machine cycle listed specify the value of IO/$\overline{\text{M}}$. Also indicate whether a $\overline{RD}$, $\overline{WR}$, or neither of these control strobes occurs during the machine cycle. For each machine cycle list the source and destination registers as specifically as possible.

3-11. From the written description of each of the following instructions (see Appendix C), list in their order of occurrence the machine cycles that constitute the following instruction cycles:

(a) MOV r_1, r_2

(b) LXI rp, data 16

(c) INR M

(d) LHLD addr

(e) XRA r

3-12. The instruction descriptions in Appendix C list the number of states in each instruction's instruction cycle. Give the instruction cycle time for each of the following instructions if the 8085A is used with a 6.144 MHz crystal.

(a) MOV r, M

(b) LDAX rp

(c) XCHG

(d) ADD r

3-13. The instruction "store H and L direct", SHLD, is a 3-byte instruction. This instruction's mnemonic and its execution can be represented as follows:

$$SHLD\ addr$$
$$((byte\ 3)(byte\ 2)) \leftarrow (L)$$
$$((byte\ 3)(byte\ 2) + 1) \leftarrow (H)$$

The opcode for this instruction is 22H. Assume the instruction appears as follows in memory:

1009H	22H
	06H
	20H

and the 8085A microprocessor's registers are as follows: PC = 1009H and HL = 43C7H. List each machine cycle in the instruction cycle, and for each machine cycle list every register (internal or external) *modified* and its new value (in hex). For simplicity, consider the high order address latch and the external low order address latch as a single 16-bit register, ADRL.

3-14. Draw two timing diagrams that together illustrate the advantage of using a positive level triggered latch to demultiplex the 8085A's address/data bus rather than a negative edge triggered latch. Can the 8085A's address bus be demultiplexed by a positive edge triggered latch?

3-15. Give the clock out frequency and state time, T, of an 8085AH operating with each of the following frequency crystals: 6.25 MHz, 6.144 MHz, 5 MHz, and 4 MHz.

3-16. An 8085AH-2 is operated in a system with a 10 MHz crystal. The system contains a single input port and a single output port. The output port has two control inputs, $\overline{CS}$ and $\overline{WE}$. The register of the output port is positive edge triggered. The data bus and control strobes of the microprocessor are not buffered. What is the setup time, hold time, and clock pulse width available to the output port? The input port has two control inputs, $\overline{CS}$ and $\overline{OE}$. How much time does the input port have to enable its three-state buffers? How much time does it have to disable its three-state buffers? Show all calculations in detail.

3-17. The "address valid to data valid" time parameter, t_{AD}, for a read operation for an 8085AH-2 is given by the expression

$$t_{AD} = (5/2 + N)T - 150 \text{ nS}$$

An 8085AH-2 can be operated with a 10 MHz crystal. If no WAIT states are used, how soon (in nS) after a valid address is generated must the memory output valid data for a read operation? If the memory takes 450 nS to provide valid data after an address is generated, how many WAIT states are required?

3-18. If external logic controls the READY line so that one additional state is introduced for each machine cycle, what is the instruction cycle time for each instruction in Problem 3-12?

3-19. An 8085A is operated with a 6.25 MHz crystal. If three instructions that normally consist of four, seven, and ten states are executed and external logic requests a single WAIT state for each machine cycle, what is the instruction cycle time for each instruction?

3-20. Draw a logic diagram of a circuit that allows the 8085A to be single stepped through either machine cycles or instruction cycles. Indicate the interconnection of this circuit to the 8085A. Include a switch to defeat the circuit and allow the microprocessor to run at full speed.

4

Data Transfer, Logic Operations, and Branching

The use of microprocessors, or MOS / LSI "computers-on-a-chip," requires programming skills. And that may seem to be a disadvantage. Hardware designers once concerned with such matters as latch selection, clock phases and propagation delay must now consider less familiar software-oriented factors like subroutine nesting, indirect addressing and computational algorithms.

Dennis C. Weiss*

*"Software for MOS / LSI Microprocessors," *Electronic Design,* Vol. 22, No. 7, (April 1974), pp. 50 – 57.

Each subsystem in a microprocessor system—the memory, the microprocessor, and the input/output devices—can be thought of in terms of the registers it contains. Random access semiconductor memory is a collection of registers. A microprocessor itself consists of general purpose and dedicated registers. Input and output devices contain registers that hold their data.

The function of a microprocessor system is implemented by a sequence of data transfers between registers in the memory, the microprocessor, and I/O devices and data transformations that occur primarily in registers within the microprocessor. Each register that can be manipulated under program control is addressable in some manner—allowing it to be singled out for use in a data transfer or transformation.

The kinds of individual transfers and transformations possible are specified by the microprocessor's *instruction set*. Each instruction in the set causes one or more data transfers and/or transformations. A sequence of instructions constitutes a program. The control section of a microprocessor decodes the program instructions in turn, and, using timing signals derived from the system clock, controls what register transfers or transformations take place and when.

4.1 INSTRUCTION SET

Each microprocessor is designed to execute a particular instruction set. The 8085A has an instruction set consisting of 74 basic instructions.[1] Many, however, have variations increasing the actual number of distinct operations to 246.

Instructions for the 8085A are 1 to 3 bytes in length. The bit pattern of the first byte is the OP code. This bit pattern is decoded in the instruction register and provides information used by the timing and control section to generate a sequence of elementary operations—microoperations—that implement the instruction. The second and third bytes, the instruction operands, are either addresses or constants.

It is common to divide an instruction set into groups of functionally similar instructions for ease in learning or evaluation. For the 8085A, one such grouping is as follows:

1. Data transfer group: instructions that move data between registers.

2. Logic group: instructions that carry out logic operations, such as AND, OR, or EX-OR, between data in the accumulator and a register, or rotate or complement data in the accumulator.

3. Branch group: instructions that change the execution sequence of a program, such as conditional and unconditional jump instructions and subroutine call and return instructions.

4. Stack and machine control group: instructions for maintaining the stack and internal control flags.

[1] The instruction sets for the 8085A, 8085AH, and 80C85A are identical. The instruction set for the 8080A, the predecessor of the 8085A, consists of all but two of the 8085A instructions.

5. Arithmetic group: instructions that add, subtract, increment, or decrement data in the registers.

The actions that are the result of the execution of each instruction in an instruction set must be precisely specified. A commonly used method is *register transfer expressions*, which concisely represent the transfer of data among registers and the arithmetic and logic operations on data. They do not, however, include those register transfers required to fetch an instruction from memory to the microprocessor prior to its execution. Register transfer expressions are written in a *register transfer language*. There are many of these, and all have relatively similar forms [1]. Symbols used by Intel in its register transfer expressions are defined in Table 4.1-1 [2].

TABLE 4.1-1   SYMBOLS AND ABBREVIATIONS (COURTESY OF INTEL CORP.)

The following symbols and abbreviations are used in the description of the 8085A instructions:

SYMBOLS	MEANING
accumulator	Register A
addr	16-bit address quantity
data	8-bit data quantity
data 16	16-bit data quantity
byte 2	The second byte of the instruction
byte 3	The third byte of the instruction
port	8-bit address of an I/O device
r,r1,r2	One of the registers A,B,C,D,E,H,L
DDD,SSS	The bit pattern designating one of the registers A,B,C,D,E,H,L (DDD = destination, SSS = source):

DDD or SSS	Register Name
111	A
000	B
001	C
010	D
011	E
100	H
101	L

rp   One of the register pairs:
B represents the BC pair with B as the high order register and C as the low order register;
D represents the DE pair with D as the high order register and E as the low order register;
H represents the HL pair with H as the high order register and L as the low order register;
SP represents the 16-bit stack pointer register.

RP   The bit pattern designating one of the register pairs B,D,H,SP:

RP	Register Pair
00	BC
01	DE
10	HL
11	SP

rh   The first (high order) register of a designated register pair.

rl   The second (low order) register of a designated register pair.

PC   16-bit program counter register (PCH and PCL are used to refer to the high order and low order 8 bits, respectively).

SP   16-bit stack pointer register (SPH and SPL are used to refer to the high order and low order 8 bits, respectively).

r_m Bit m of the register r (bits are number 7 through 0 from left to right).

Z,S,P,CY,AC   The condition flags:
Zero,
Sign,
Parity,
Carry,
Auxiliary Carry.

( )   The contents of the memory location or registers enclosed in the parentheses.

←   "Is transferred to"

∧   Logical AND

TABLE 4.1-1 CONTINUED.

∀	Exclusive OR	—	The one's complement, e.g., ($\bar{A}$)
∨	Inclusive OR	n	The restart number 0 through 7
+	Addition	NNN	The binary representation 000
−	Two's complement subtraction		through 111 for restart number 0
*	Multiplication		through 7, respectively.
↔	"Is exchanged with"		

4.2 DATA TRANSFER INSTRUCTIONS

In instruction sets, many instructions are devoted to the transfer of data between two registers of a microprocessor system. One of the registers is always located in the microprocessor itself; the other may be located in one of the following:

1. An I/O device
2. Memory
3. The microprocessor

The various registers which make up an 8085A microprocessor system are shown in Fig. 4.2-1. Registers located in the microprocessor are referred to as

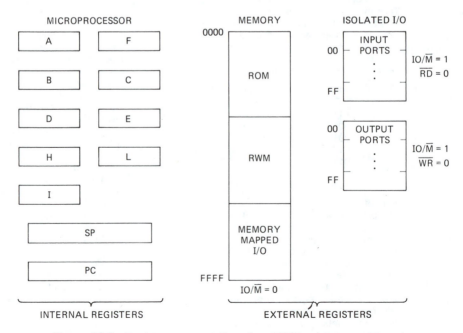

Figure 4.2-1 Register representation of an 8085A microprocessor system.

internal registers, and those in I/O, RWM, or ROM are referred to as external registers. The register from which data is transferred is the **source register**, and the register to which data is transferred is the **destination register**. A transfer involves copying the contents of the source register into the destination register; the contents of the source register are not altered. Each data transfer instruction identifies the source register and the destination register. Identification of one or both of these registers may be implied by the instruction mnemonics or may be explicit. Internal registers, for example, are frequently implied, whereas external registers are usually identified by an explicit address that is part of the instruction.

4.2.1 Data Transfers to and from I/O Devices

Data is transferred from the microprocessor to an output device in an output transfer and from an input device to the microprocessor in an input transfer. Output devices contain one or more registers, each of which is addressable and strobed by the microprocessor to latch the data on the data bus at the appropriate time during an output transfer. Input devices usually contain a register that holds the data to be transferred to the microprocessor and an addressable three-state buffer that is enabled by a strobe from the microprocessor at the appropriate time to place data on the data bus.

I/O structures fall into two categories—*isolated I/O* and *memory mapped I/O*—and each is associated with a specific type of data transfer instruction. An isolated I/O structure uses special input and output instructions, and usually the number of devices addressable by these instructions is limited to a few hundred or less. Memory mapped I/O structures treat I/O registers as memory locations and use memory reference instructions to transfer data to them. All microprocessors are capable of memory mapped I/O. The 8085A, for instance, uses either or both isolated and memory mapped structures in a single system.

Two 8085A instructions are used for isolated I/O: IN for input to the microprocessor and OUT for output from the microprocessor. IN and OUT are the mnemonics for the OP codes. During execution, the *input* instruction places an 8-bit device address on the address bus, where it is repeated as both the low and high order address bytes. An external decoder decodes the device address, the IO/$\overline{\text{M}}$, and the $\overline{\text{RD}}$ strobe in order to generate an input device select pulse to enable the addressed input port's three-state buffer, thus placing the input port's data on the data bus. The register transfer expression for this operation is

$$(A) \leftarrow (port)$$

The parentheses mean "contents of a register," and the left arrow means "is transferred to." Thus, the register transfer expression indicates that the contents of the addressed input port are transferred to the accumulator. In assembly language, the instruction is written as follows, where port is the 8-bit address of the input port:[2]

IN port

IN is a 2-byte instruction; the first byte is the OP code, and the second byte is the 8-bit input device (port) address:

OP CODE
PORT ADDRESS

With eight address bits, any one of 256 possible input devices is addressable with this instruction. If data is input from input port number 12, for example, the IN instruction is written as

IN 12

The destination register, the accumulator, is implied in the IN instruction, whereas the source register is identified by an explicit address that constitutes the second byte of this instruction. If the input device is a switch bank and three-state buffer, the address is used with $IO/\overline{M}$ and $\overline{RD}$ to generate an input device select pulse that enables the three-state buffer (see Fig. 4.2-2).

Data in the accumulator can be output to an I/O device using the 2-byte *output* instruction OUT. Again, the first byte is the OP code, and the second byte is

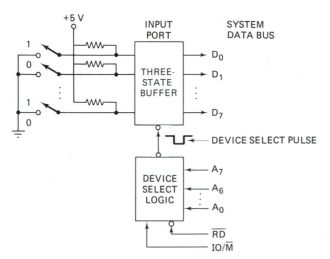

Figure 4.2-2 Simple input switch bank.

[2]Instructions in this text are written in assembly language, and the bit patterns for the OP codes are represented by mnemonics. Addresses and constants are written symbolically or as decimal, octal, or hexadecimal numbers.

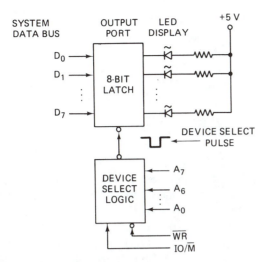

Figure 4.2-3   Output data latch and display.

the 8-bit output port address:

$$\text{OUT port}$$
$$(\text{port}) \leftarrow (A)$$

In the OUT instruction the source register—the accumulator—is implied, and the destination register is explicitly identified by the port address, the second byte of the instruction. The output device decodes the address on the address bus in order to latch the data. For example, if the output device is a data latch and display, the decoded address is used with $IO/\overline{M}$ and $\overline{WR}$ to generate an output device select pulse for strobing the latch (see Fig. 4.2-3).

With only IN, OUT, and HLT, a simple data routing task can be carried out that inputs data from a switch bank and outputs data to two latches, reads data from a second switch bank and outputs data to two other latches, and then halts.

```
IN    1
OUT   1
OUT   2
IN    2
OUT   4
OUT   5
HLT
```

Numbers in the previous IN and OUT instructions are decimal, although numbers used in the assembly language representation of instructions can be decimal, binary, octal, hexadecimal, or symbolic. Binary numbers are written with a B suffix, octal numbers are written with an O or a Q suffix; the hexadecimal numbers are written with an H suffix. Decimal numbers are represented with a D suffix or no suffix at all. This particular notation is compatible with Intel assemblers, which are used in this text for examples. Symbolic names also represent numbers;

for example, the previous program can be written as

```
IN     ONE³
OUT    ONE
OUT    TWO
IN     TWO
OUT    FOUR
OUT    FIVE
HLT
```

Note that there are input and output devices with the same numbers. Both device address decoders respond to the same address; however, the input device's address decoder also requires the $\overline{RD}$ strobe to produce an output strobe, which limits response to the IN instruction. The output device's address decoder requires the $\overline{WR}$ strobe, which limits response to the OUT instruction. Thus, because of distinct strobes for reading and writing, the 8-bit device address can address 256 unique input devices and 256 unique output devices.

The last instruction in the sample program is a *halt*, HLT. When executed, this single-byte control instruction simply stops program execution. If this instruction is not included in the program, the microprocessor fetches the contents of the memory location following OUT FIVE for decoding and execution.

Memory mapped I/O structures use memory reference instructions to transfer data to or from an I/O device. Although the term *memory reference instruction* applies to the group of instructions that transfer data to or from memory, these instructions, in fact, do not distinguish between an addressable register located in memory and one located in an I/O device. Thus, the same instructions that reference memory can be used for I/O if appropriate decoding logic is provided (see Chapter 8). These memory reference instructions use various **addressing modes** to identify the registers involved in the transfer of data. **Direct addressing** is conceptually one of the simplest methods of addressing because the instruction contains the address of the external register involved in the transfer. The 8085A provides a 16-bit memory address, requiring that the address contained in the instruction be 16 bits long. Thus, it must be a 3-byte instruction:

OPCODE
LOW ADDRESS
HIGH ADDRESS

For example, the *load accumulator direct* instruction, LDA, has the following assembly language representation:

LDA addr
(A) ← ((byte 3)(byte 2))

---

[3] The way in which the values associated with these names are assigned is discussed in Chapter 5.

Here the address (addr) is 16 bits long. The effect of the instruction, as indicated by the register transfer expression, is to transfer 8 bits of data from the external register —identified by the 16-bit address contained in bytes 2 and 3 of the instruction—to the accumulator. The register transfer expression is read: "The contents of the register specified by the contents of bytes 2 and 3 of the instruction are transferred to the accumulator." The second byte of the instruction is the low order 8 bits of the address, and the third byte is the high order 8 bits. This ordering of the address bytes is typical of all 8085A instructions that contain 16-bit addresses.

To transfer data from the microprocessor to a memory or output register, the *store accumulator direct* instruction is used.

STA addr

((byte 3)(byte 2)) ← (A)

These two instructions, LDA and STA, when used for I/O, function like IN and OUT instructions. A program equivalent to the previous examples, but using memory mapped I/O, can be written with the LDA and STA instructions:

LDA FIRST
STA FIRST
STA SECND
LDA SECND
STA FORTH
STA FIFTH
HLT

LDA and STA, however, have 16-bit addresses; thus, the number of addressable I/O registers is increased, at the expense of an additional byte required to specify the additional 8 address bits and additional logic to decode these bits.

Transfers to and from external registers using memory mapped I/O are not limited to the accumulator nor do they necessarily involve only a single byte of data. Two instructions that utilize direct addressing involve the H and L register pair and allow the transfer of 2 bytes of data during a single instruction cycle. Two bytes of data in consecutively addressed external registers are transferred to H and L with the *load H and L direct* instruction, LHLD.

LHLD addr

(L) ← ((byte 3)(byte 2))

(H) ← ((byte 3)(byte 2) + 1)

The 16-bit address contained in the instruction specifies the address of the source register for the transfer to register L. The source register for the transfer to H is simply the register with an address one higher than the address contained in the instruction.

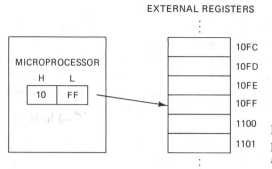

EXTERNAL REGISTERS

Figure 4.2-4 Function of the pointer register in register indirect addressing.

To transfer data from H and L to two external registers with consecutive addresses, the *store H and L direct* instruction, SHLD, is used:

SHLD addr
((byte 3)(byte 2)) ← (L)
((byte 3)(byte 2) + 1) ← (H)

Register indirect addressing is another addressing mode used by the 8085A. Here the address contained in the instruction specifies a register that contains an address instead of the data. This second address is the actual or *effective address* of the external register involved in the transfer. In minicomputers and large computers, both of the registers involved in indirect addressing are usually external registers in RWM. With microprocessors, however, the register that contains the actual address of the operand is usually an internal register; this form of indirect addressing is called *register indirect, pointer*, or *implied addressing*. Since it contains the address of the external register, the internal register points to the external register. The internal register used as a pointer is implied by the instruction. Thus, a particular internal register is the pointer register for a particular instruction that uses register indirect addressing.

The H and L register pair is used as a pointer in many 8085A register indirect instructions (see Fig. 4.2-4). The H register holds the high and the L register holds the low byte of the effective address. The *move from memory* instruction, MOV r, M, transfers a single byte from any external register, M, to any one of the seven internal working registers, r. The specification of M as a register in the instruction actually means the external register pointed to by H and L.

MOV r, M
(r) ← ((H)(L))

The register transfer expression for this instruction indicates that the content of the external register whose address is in H and L is transferred to register r. The corresponding instruction for transfer in the opposite direction is the *move to memory* instruction:

MOV M, r
((H)(L)) ← (r)

Note that in MOV instructions, the destination register is written first, followed by the source register. Before these register indirect instructions are used in a program, a previous instruction must load register pair HL with the appropriate address.

The register pairs BC and DE are also used as pointer registers in two 8085A instructions. The internal register involved in the transfer for these instructions is, however, always the accumulator. These instructions are *load accumulator indirect*

$$LDAX\ rp$$
$$(A) \leftarrow ((rp))$$

and *store accumulator indirect*

$$STAX\ rp$$
$$((rp)) \leftarrow (A)$$

Here rp stands for the register pair. Only rp = B (register pair BC) and rp = D (register pair DE) are allowable values in these instructions.

4.2.2 Additional Data Transfers to and from Memory

The direct and register indirect instructions, which transfer data to and from I/O registers when using memory mapped I/O, also transfer data to and from main memory. The operation of the instruction is the same, the only difference being that the 16-bit address is that of a location in main memory.

Another addressing mode, which transfers data from memory, is *immediate addressing*. With immediate addressing, the data transferred is part of the instruction. After the instruction's OP code is fetched, the program counter contains the effective address of the data. The simplest immediate addressing instruction is the *move immediate*. The second byte of this instruction is the data to be transferred to any general purpose register or to the accumulator.

$$MVI\ r,\ data$$
$$(r) \leftarrow (byte\ 2)$$

This instruction is used for loading a single register with a constant. To load a register pair with a constant, the *load register pair immediate* instruction is used:

$$LXI\ rp,\ data\ 16$$
$$(rl) \leftarrow (byte\ 2)$$
$$(rh) \leftarrow (byte\ 3)$$

The second byte of the instruction is the data to be placed in the low order register, and the third byte is the data for the high order register.

The *move to memory immediate* instruction, a combination of immediate and register indirect addressing, moves data in an instruction to a memory location pointed to by the H and L register pair.

MVI M, data
((H)(L)) ← (byte 2)

4.2.3 Creation of Additional Addressing Modes

Some microprocessors use other addressing modes that are not available via single instructions in the 8085A. However, these addressing modes can be synthesized by combining two or more 8085A instructions. In large computers and minicomputers the term *indirect addressing* traditionally refers to the use of a main memory location to contain the address of data, as opposed to having this address in an internal register—as in the register indirect addressing previously described. Conventional indirect addressing is implemented with two instructions, for example, for an indirect load:

LHLD addr
MOV r, M

The address of the data is contained in the memory location corresponding to the address (addr) in the LHLD instruction. LHLD loads the address of the data into the HL register pair, and the MOV instruction transfers the data from the memory location pointed to by HL to the internal register, r. To store data indirectly, only the MOV instruction is modified:

LHLD addr
MOV M, r

Another mode, *indexed addressing*, is characterized by the effective address being the sum of a base address plus a displacement provided by an index register. The index register is usually incremented or decremented during the execution of a program to access a number of consecutive memory locations.

```
LXI B, BASE    ;load BC with an initial base value
LHLD INDEX     ;load HL from INDEX and INDEX + 1
DAD B          ;add index contained in HL to BC
MOV r, M       ;transfer data
```

The DAD B instruction adds the 16-bit register pairs HL and BC; the result is left in HL. The DAD instruction is described in detail in Chapter 7.

Indirect addressing and indexed addressing can be combined to provide indirect addressing with indexing. For example, to obtain a data value from a table, the indirect address provides the pointer to the beginning of the table, and the index register, an offset into the table.

4.2.4 Transfer of Data within the Microprocessor

Once data has been input to one of a microprocessor's registers, it is often necessary to move it to another register in the microprocessor. The *move register* instruction effects this transfer.

$$\text{MOV r1, r2}$$
$$(r1) \leftarrow (r2)$$

In this instruction, the variables r1 and r2 represent any of the six general purpose registers or the accumulator.

For example, some logic instructions (see Section 4.3) have two operands, each in a different internal register. One of the operands is always in the accumulator, and the other is always in one of the other internal general purpose registers. If the IN instruction inputs both operands from external registers, the first operand input must be transferred from the accumulator to another register before the second operand is input. Here r2 can be A, and r1 can be any of the registers but A. If register B is used for temporary storage of the first operand, the following instruction sequence can be used:

$$\text{IN 1}$$
$$\text{MOV B, A}$$
$$\text{IN 2}$$

If the same register is specified for both r1 and r2, execution of the *move register* instruction does not change the contents of any of the working registers but becomes a null operation. The only use for such an instruction is the generation of delays to allow a certain amount of time to elapse before the next instruction is fetched and executed.

Another data transfer instruction, *exchange H and L with D and E*, allows the contents of these two register pairs to replace each other. This instruction is very useful in alternately pointing to locations in different blocks of memory.

$$\text{XCHG}$$
$$(H) \leftrightarrow (D)$$
$$(L) \leftrightarrow (E)$$

Note that a double arrow in a register transfer expression indicates that the contents of the two registers are exchanged.

4.3 LOGIC OPERATIONS

In all of the logic instructions in the 8085A instruction set, except those operating exclusively on the carry flag, one operand is in the accumulator. In operations requiring two operands, the second operand may be contained in the instruction (as immediate data), in an internal general purpose register, or in an external register.

Information characterizing the result of a logic or arithmetic operation, which is often needed by subsequent instructions for decision purposes, is indicated by the bits in a special register in the microprocessor called the flag register, F. The flag register operates as a 5-bit register: only five of the bits can be set or cleared; the other 3 bits have undefined values. The bits of the F register and their condition codes are

BIT # 7 6 5 4 3 2 1 0

| S | Z | | A C | | P | | C |

bits 5, 3, and 1 have undefined values.

Bits in the microprocessor's registers are labeled from right to left in ascending order. For 8-bit registers, the *most significant bit, msb*, is bit 7; the *least significant bit, lsb*, is bit 0.

S: Sign (bit 7): if the msb of the result is 1, this flag is set; otherwise it is cleared.

Z: Zero (bit 6): If the result is 0, this flag is set; otherwise it is cleared.

AC: Auxiliary Carry (bit 4): If the operation causes a carry out of bit 3 and into bit 4, this flag is set; otherwise it is cleared.

P: Parity (bit 2): If the modulo 2 sum of the bits is 0 (even parity), the flag is set; otherwise it is cleared.

CY: Carry (bit 0): If the operation causes a carry (from addition) or a borrow (from subtraction or comparison) out of the high order bit, this flag is set; otherwise it is cleared.

Certain instructions have no effect on some or any of the flags. For instance, the data transfer instructions affect no flags, whereas the *decrement register* instruction, DCR r, affects four—Z, S, P, and AC. Appendix C describes all 8085A instructions and lists the flags they affect.

Most microprocessor instruction sets, like that of the 8085A, include instructions for carrying out the logic operations NOT, AND, OR, and EX-OR. These operations are equivalent to those commonly used in logic design at the gate level, with one important exception: they are carried out on corresponding bits of two entire bytes of data for binary operations and on all the bits of a single byte for a unary operation.

The instruction that corresponds to the NOT operation is the *complement accumulator*:

$$\text{CMA}$$
$$(A) \leftarrow (\overline{A}) \qquad\qquad\qquad \textit{Flags: None}$$

The 0 bits of the byte in the accumulator become 1, and the 1 bits become 0. Thus, every bit in the accumulator is simultaneously complemented. Another instruction complements a single bit of the flag register, the carry bit. This instruction is the *complement carry* instruction.

$$\text{CMC}$$
$$(CY) \leftarrow (\overline{CY}) \qquad\qquad\qquad \textit{Flags: CY}$$

Another sets the carry, *set carry*:

STC

(CY) ← 1   *Flags:* CY

Execution of the *complement accumulator* instruction, CMA, affects none of the flags, and the *complement carry* instruction, CMC, and *set carry* instruction, STC, affect only the carry flag.

The contents of the accumulator can be ANDed bit by bit with a data byte, using any one of several forms of the AND instruction. The forms differ in terms of the source of the data byte. For instance, with the *AND immediate* instruction, ANI, the second byte of the 2-byte instruction contains the data to be ANDed with the accumulator. The *AND register* version, ANA, ANDs the contents of an internal register with the accumulator, and the *AND memory* ANDs the contents of an external register with the accumulator. The various versions are:

AND immediate	*AND register*	*AND memory*
ANI data	ANA r	ANA M
(A) ← (A) ∧ (byte 2)	(A) ← (A) ∧ (r)	(A) ← (A) ∧ ((H)(L))

Flags: All; CY is cleared and AC is set

The three AND instructions affect all of the flags. The carry flag is always cleared and the auxiliary carry set. The sign, zero, and parity flags are set or cleared, depending on the result left in the accumulator.

The AND function is often used for *masking*. In masking, selected bits of a word are cleared. The bits of the mask byte corresponding to the accumulator bits to be cleared are 0; bits corresponding to those bits to remain unchanged are 1. To clear the most significant 4 bits of a byte in the accumulator, the mask byte, 00001111 = 0FH , is used.

Consider as an example a situation in which ASCII data, representing a decimal digit, is input. The last 4 bits of the ASCII code for decimal digits are the binary equivalent of the decimal digit (see Appendix D). To store only this binary equivalent in a register, the most significant bits of the ASCII code must be cleared. The following program segment accomplishes this, and the mask is the second byte of the ANI instruction, 0FH:

IN ASCII

ANI 0FH

In some applications a logic instruction is used solely to affect flags. For example, since data transfer instructions do not affect the flags, the instruction ANA A can be used after the transfer to affect all the flags of the F register, except the carry. The flags are set or cleared based on the data in the accumulator, without changing the value of that data, and the carry is cleared.

Analogous to the AND are three versions of the OR instruction:

OR immediate	*OR register*	*OR memory*
ORI data	ORA r	ORA M
(A) ← (A) ∨ (byte 2)	(A) ← (A) ∨ (r)	(A) ← (A) ∨ ((H)(L))

Flags: All; CY and AC are cleared

The OR instructions are used to merge the bits of two operands, i.e., to set specific bits of the accumulator. The accumulator is left with 1s in the bit positions corresponding to 1s in either of the operands. For example, the following program segment outputs the ASCII character equivalent of a binary coded decimal digit in register B:

```
MOV A, B
ORI 30H
OUT ASCII
```

To change a single bit of an output port without changing any other bits—a necessity when several bits of an output latch are controlling separate devices—a copy of the last control word output to the port, its *image*, is kept in memory, in location CWORD. To set the bit, bit 4 in this case, the following program segment is used:

```
LXI H, CWORD    ;load address of control word into HL
MOV A, M        ;transfer copy of present control word
                ;to accumulator
ORI 10H         ;set bit 4
MOV M, A        ;update copy of control word
OUT PORT0       ;output new control word to external latch
```

To reset bit 4:

```
LXI H, CWORD    ;load address of control word into HL
MOV A, M        ;transfer copy of present control word
                ;to accumulator
ANI 0EFH        ;reset bit 4
MOV M, A        ;update copy of control word
OUT PORT0       ;output new control word
```

The ORA A instruction is also frequently used to affect the flags following a data transfer to the accumulator without altering the contents of the accumulator.

The EX-OR operation sets the bits of the accumulator corresponding to the bit positions where the two operands differ; the bit positions corresponding to those where the operands are the same are cleared. In other words, the bits of the accumulator that correspond to 1 bits in the data EX-ORed with the accumulator are complemented. The other bits in the accumulator are not altered. The three versions of EX-OR are

EX-OR immediate	*EX-OR register*	*EX-OR memory*
XRI data	XRA r	XRA M
$(A) \leftarrow (A) \veebar (byte\ 2)$	$(A) \leftarrow (A) \veebar (r)$	$(A) \leftarrow (A) \veebar ((H)(L))$

Flags: All; the CY and AC are cleared

When data is EX-ORed with itself, the result is zero. XRA A EX-ORs the accumulator with itself, thus clearing the accumulator and the carry flag.

Frequently, an input port transmits status information to the microprocessor concerning one or more external devices or processes. To ascertain whether any change has occurred in the status of the external process, a copy of the prior status is kept in a memory location and compared with the present status:

```
LXI H, STATUS    ;load HL with address of copy of prior status
MOV B, M         ;transfer copy of prior status to register B
IN PORT1         ;input present status
MOV M, A         ;update status copy
XRA B            ;test for status change
```

At the end of this sequence, the zero flag is set to indicate no change in the status or cleared to indicate a change.

The comparison of 2 bytes to determine which is greater in terms of binary magnitude can be carried out in hardware by using MSI comparator circuits. The software equivalent of the hardware comparator is the compare instruction. This instruction compares 2 bytes, one of which is in the accumulator, by subtracting the second byte from it. This instruction is unusual in that neither of the bytes compared is altered. The compare instruction has three forms:

Compare immediate	*Compare register*	*Compare memory*
CPI data	CMP r	CMP M
$(A) - (byte\ 2)$	$(A) - (r)$	$(A) - ((H)(L))$

Flags: All; Z = 1 if (A) = (r); CY = 1 if (A) < (r)

After execution, the flag register is tested to determine whether the bytes are equal or, if unequal, which is greater. Assuming that the bytes of data being compared are interpreted as unsigned binary numbers, the zero flag is set if they are equal. If the content of the accumulator is greater than the byte with which it is compared, the carry flag is cleared. Since the compare instruction is used exclusively for setting or clearing flags on which branch decisions are made, examples of its application are deferred until branch instructions are introduced later in this chapter.

The remaining logic instructions in the instruction set are those that rotate the contents of the accumulator. The action of the *rotate accumulator left*, RLC, instruction is indicated by the following register transfer expressions and diagram:

RLC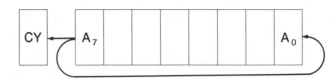

$$(A_{n+1}) \leftarrow (A_n)$$
$$(A_0) \leftarrow (A_7)$$
$$(CY) \leftarrow (A_7)$$

Flags: CY

When the RLC instruction is executed, each bit of the accumulator is shifted left, $(A_{n+1}) \leftarrow (A_n)$, and the most significant bit, A_7, is copied into the least significant bit, A_0, and into the carry, CY.

The corresponding rotate instruction in the opposite direction is the *rotate accumulator right*, RRC, instruction.

RRC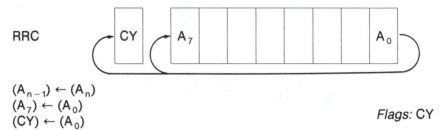

$$(A_{n-1}) \leftarrow (A_n)$$
$$(A_7) \leftarrow (A_0)$$
$$(CY) \leftarrow (A_0)$$

Flags: CY

Two other rotate instructions treat the accumulator and carry together, as if they constitute a 9-bit register. The *rotate accumulator left through carry*, RAL, instruction has the following form:

RAL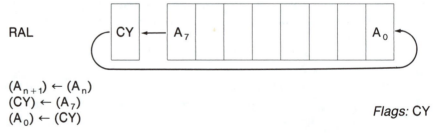

$$(A_{n+1}) \leftarrow (A_n)$$
$$(CY) \leftarrow (A_7)$$
$$(A_0) \leftarrow (CY)$$

Flags: CY

A 9-bit rotation in the opposite direction is implemented with the *rotate accumulator right through carry* instruction.

RAR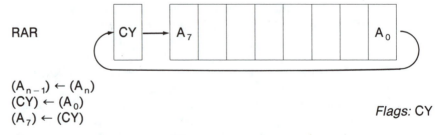

$$(A_{n-1}) \leftarrow (A_n)$$
$$(CY) \leftarrow (A_0)$$
$$(A_7) \leftarrow (CY)$$

Flags: CY

Note the apparent transposition of mnemonics and instruction descriptions for the rotate instructions.

> *RAL*: <u>*R*</u>*otate accumulator* <u>*L*</u>*eft through* <u>*C*</u>*arry*
> *RLC*: <u>*R*</u>*otate* <u>*A*</u>*ccumulator* <u>*L*</u>*eft*

Consider a situation where input port 7 inputs sequentially generated BCD digits, as the least significant 4 bits of a byte. After being input, the BCD digits are packed, two digits to a byte, and stored in memory. The following program segment carries out part of this task: it inputs and packs two digits, leaving the result in the accumulator.

```
IN PORT7      ;input most significant of the two BCD digits
ANI 0FH       ;clear most significant 4 bits of byte input
RLC           ;shift BCD digit four places to the left
RLC
RLC
RLC
MOV B, A      ;store shifted digit in B
IN PORT7      ;input next digit
ANI 0FH       ;clear most significant 4 bits of byte input
ORA B
```

4.4 FLOWCHARTING

Once the functions to be implemented in software have been defined, the designer selects or develops appropriate algorithms for their implementation. An *algorithm* is a computational or logical method of producing a desired result. The development and representation of an algorithm are facilitated by a *flowchart*, a graphic method of representing the order in which operations are carried out and the decisions that determine that order.

The flowchart is the software counterpart of the block diagram used in hardware design. In hardware design, the least detailed block diagram indicates the major hardware subsystems required to implement the overall system function and the information transfer among these subsystems. In software design, the least detailed flowchart indicates the major software subsystems required to implement the overall system function and their order of execution.

Just as the hardware designer must know the function and characteristics of MSI circuits in detail, the software designer must know the functions and characteristics of available instructions in similar detail. For an instruction, its function is represented by its register transfer expressions and a statement of the flags affected by its execution. The characteristics of an instruction are the number of bytes, machine cycles, and states associated with it.

In flowcharts a rectangle represents an operation or process, and a diamond represents a decision (see Fig. 4.4-1). An oval represents the beginning and/or the end of the instruction sequence. Brief statements indicating the operations or decisions associated with each symbol appear inside it. The symbols are interconnected by directed line segments that indicate program flow, just as directed line segments in a hardware block diagram indicate information flow. In an overall

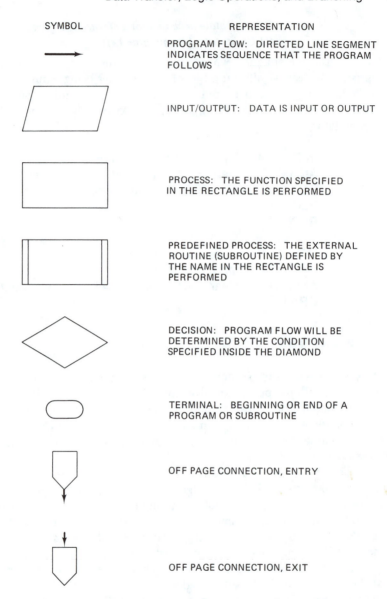

SYMBOL	REPRESENTATION
→	PROGRAM FLOW: DIRECTED LINE SEGMENT INDICATES SEQUENCE THAT THE PROGRAM FOLLOWS
	INPUT/OUTPUT: DATA IS INPUT OR OUTPUT
	PROCESS: THE FUNCTION SPECIFIED IN THE RECTANGLE IS PERFORMED
	PREDEFINED PROCESS: THE EXTERNAL ROUTINE (SUBROUTINE) DEFINED BY THE NAME IN THE RECTANGLE IS PERFORMED
	DECISION: PROGRAM FLOW WILL BE DETERMINED BY THE CONDITION SPECIFIED INSIDE THE DIAMOND
	TERMINAL: BEGINNING OR END OF A PROGRAM OR SUBROUTINE
	OFF PAGE CONNECTION, ENTRY
	OFF PAGE CONNECTION, EXIT

Figure 4.4-1   Flowcharting symbols.

system flowchart, rectangles and diamonds can represent small programs or subroutines. At the most detailed level, each symbol corresponds to a single instruction.

In the process of creating a program, a flowchart is first developed to represent the overall algorithm. Several flowchart examples are given in Section 4.8. This section concentrates on basic program logic structures and their flowchart representation. Flowcharts can be progressively partitioned into more and more detail until each symbol is converted into an instruction or group of instructions.

Knowledge of a set of basic program logic structures that can be combined to implement any algorithm or program facilitates the development of a flowchart. Although these structures and their terminology derive from concepts typically applied to high level language programming, they are useful in studying assembly language program design.

The basis of structured programming is a set of logical structures, each of which has only a single entry and a single exit point. By combining these basic structures, more complex logical structures are formed that also possess a single entry/single exit point. The advantage of this technique is the development of programs that are more reliable and easier to understand, document, and modify.

The syntax of some high level languages directly supports the implementation of the basic logic structures of structured programming. When programming in assembly language, however, it is more difficult to adhere strictly to the structured programming concepts because implementation of the basic logic structures necessitates programs that themselves require more instructions than their unstructured counterparts. However, it is helpful to study these basic structures and how they can be implemented in assembly language. In practice these logic structures and their variations are the foundation of program design.

The basic logic structures are

1. The SEQUENCE structure

2. The IF-THEN/ELSE structure

3. The SELECT structure

4. The DO-WHILE structure

5. The DO-UNTIL structure

The structures are themselves constructed from two elements: the process element and the decision element of Fig. 4.4-1. In a process element, control is transferred into the element, a process is performed, and control is transferred out of the element. In a decision element, control is transferred into the element, a condition is tested, and control is transferred out through one of two possible paths according to the condition.

The simplest basic logic structure consists of one or more process elements in sequence with a single entry and single exit (see Fig. 4.4-2). Each process can be as simple as a single instruction or as complex as an entire algorithm or program.

4.5 BRANCH INSTRUCTIONS

The program segments considered thus far are SEQUENCE structures involving the execution of instructions stored in consecutive memory locations. There are, however, instructions that change program control and fetch the next instruction from a memory location other than the next consecutive one. *Branch instructions* transfer program control by changing the value of the program counter to the address of a

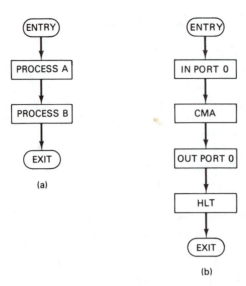

Figure 4.4-2 SEQUENCE structure. (a) Basic structure. (b) Example with four processes each consisting of a single instruction.

nonconsecutive instruction. The next OPCODE FETCH machine cycle uses this new address in the program counter to obtain the next instruction.

Some branch instructions are conditioned on a flag being set or cleared by the execution of a previous instruction. These conditional branch instructions give the microprocessor its capacity for making decisions, i.e., its ability to execute one or another instruction or program segment, depending on previous results.

There are two types of branch instructions: jump instructions and call instructions. Jump instructions are considered in this section, and call instructions are considered in Chapter 6. The execution of an unconditional jump instruction alters the normal sequential program flow by replacing the contents of the program counter with the address contained in the jump instruction. This address is the location of the first byte of the next instruction to be executed, and thus control is transferred to the instruction whose address is specified in bytes 2 and 3 of the jump instruction. The *jump* instruction, JMP, has the form:

JMP addr
(PC) ← (byte 3)(byte 2)   *Flags:* None

In a conditional jump, transfer to the address contained in the jump instruction occurs only if a specified condition is satisfied. If the condition is not satisfied, program execution continues with the instruction following the jump. The conditional jump instruction allows the microprocessor to decide between alternative actions based on the results of previous computations.

Eight conditional jumps are included in the instruction set. The conditions are indicated by the flags of the F register. The *conditional jump* instructions have the general form

J⟨condition⟩addr
If⟨condition⟩ = true, then
(PC) ← (byte 3)(byte 2)   *Flags:* None

Conditions:

$$
\begin{array}{rl}
\text{NZ:} & \text{not zero } (Z = 0) \\
\text{Z:} & \text{zero } (Z = 1) \\
\text{NC:} & \text{no carry } (CY = 0) \\
\text{C:} & \text{carry } (CY = 1) \\
\text{PO:} & \text{parity odd } (P = 0) \\
\text{PE:} & \text{parity even } (P = 1) \\
\text{P:} & \text{plus } (S = 0) \\
\text{M:} & \text{minus } (S = 1)
\end{array}
$$

Conditional branch instructions are often used as decision elements in constructing basic logic structures. However, unlike the sequence element, a decision element cannot by itself be a basic logic structure because of the single entry/single exit requirement. A decision element has two exits.

A sequence element can be combined with one or two process elements to create an IF-THEN/ELSE structure, as shown in Fig. 4.5-1. Based on the condition tested, one of two possible processes occurs. If one of the processes in Fig. 4.5-1 is a null process, a simpler form of the IF-THEN/ELSE, the IF-THEN structure results.

The following program segment, which incorporates an IF-THEN/ELSE structure, inputs a byte of data and determines whether it is less than, greater than, or equal to a previously determined threshold value stored in register B. The result is indicated by lighting one of two light-emitting diodes, LEDs, driven by output port LEDS. If the input is less than the threshold, bit 0 is set. If the input is greater than or equal to the threshold, bit 1 is set.

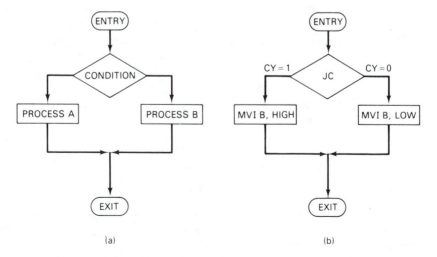

(a)   (b)

Figure 4.5-1 IF-THEN/ELSE structure. (a) Basic structure. (b) Example with the decision based on the carry value.

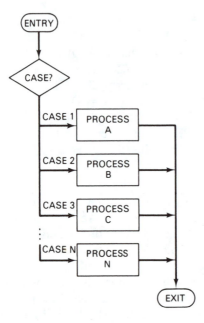

Figure 4.5-2 SELECT structure.

```
TEST:    IN DATA        ;input data byte
         CMP B          ;compare with threshold
         JC LESS
         MVI A, 02H     ;bit pattern for  >  or  =
         JMP DSPLY
LESS:    MVI A, 01H     ;bit pattern for  <
DSPLY:   OUT LEDS       ;turn on LED
```

The selection of one process from among many possible processes is facilitated by nesting several IF-THEN/ELSE structures or simply by placing several IF-THEN/ELSE structures in sequence. Or even more appropriate is the SELECT structure shown in Fig. 4.5-2. This structure tests data for multiple cases and selects the appropriate process for the given case. As the flowchart shows, SELECT has only a single entry and a single exit.

An instruction useful in creating a SELECT structure is the *move H and L to PC*, PCHL, instruction.

$$PCHL$$
$$(PCH) \leftarrow (H)$$
$$(PCL) \leftarrow (L) \hspace{2cm} \textit{Flags:} \text{ None}$$

This is actually a register indirect jump instruction. H and L contain the address to be branched to before the PCHL is executed. With the execution of PCHL, the program counter is set to the value of H and L.

The PCHL instruction can be used to create a *jump table*, which is another type of select structure. The jump table contains starting addresses of alternative processes. Each address has two bytes: the low order address byte is in the first location associated with that entry, and the high order byte is in the second. The determination of which routine to branch to is based on a number that provides an index to the table. To maintain the single exit of a SEQUENCE structure, the last instruction of each routine is an unconditional jump to the same location.

For example, a small keypad on a controller contains eight keys. Each key is associated with a function that the controller carries out when the key is pressed. The input device associated with the keypad contains logic to encode the key pressed to a binary number in the range from 0 to 7. The following program segment implements the required branch:

```
LXI H, TBL      ;load pointer to start of table
IN KEYCDE       ;input encoded binary number
RLC             ;multiply input value by two
MOV C, A        ;create low order byte of offset
MVI B, 0        ;set high order byte of offset to 0
DAD B           ;add offset to H and L
MOV E, M        ;place low order byte of jump address in E
INX H           ;increment pointer to high order jump address
MOV D, M        ;place high order jump address in D
XCHG            ;exchange HL and DE
PCHL            ;jump
```

4.6 PROGRAM LOOPING

A program loop is a sequence of instructions that is executed repeatedly. A jump instruction at the end of the loop transfers program control back to the beginning of the sequence. Conditional jump instructions provide a means for executing a loop a desired number of times and then exiting.

There are two basic loop structures, the DO-WHILE and the DO-UNTIL, both shown in Fig. 4.6-1. In the DO-WHILE structure, the condition that governs loop termination is first tested, and, depending on the results of this test, either the

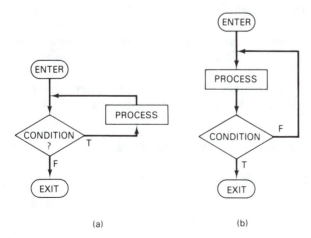

(a)   (b)

Figure 4.6-1 Loop structures: (a) DO-WHILE structure; (b) DO-UNTIL structure.

process is executed or the loop is exited. With this structure, it is possible to enter and exit the loop without ever executing the process. In the DO-UNTIL structure, when the loop is entered, the process is executed and the condition tested. Therefore, the process is always executed at least once when the loop is entered.

There are two methods for controlling the number of times a loop is executed. The first counts the number of passes through the loop. The second tests for some specific event and, when this event occurs, exits the loop. Because counting the number of passes through a loop also requires testing for an event—the occurrence of the required count—the methods may at first appear to be equivalent. However, in the first method, the number of loop executions that will occur is known before the loop is entered; in the second method, it is not.

The first method is simply referred to as **counting**. Counting requires that a register be loaded with some initial value and incremented or decremented for each pass through the loop. A conditional branch instruction determines when the counter register reaches the terminal count and exits the loop.

The following arithmetic instructions increment or decrement a single register. The register can be one of the internal working registers or an external register:

Increment register	*Increment memory*
INR r	INR M
(r) ← (r) + 1	((H)(L)) ← ((H)(L)) + 1

Flags: Z, S, P, and AC

To decrement a register, the following instructions are used:

Decrement register	*Decrement memory*
DCR r	DCR M
(r) ← (r) − 1	((H)(L)) ← ((H)(L)) − 1

Flags: Z, S, P, and AC

The increment and decrement instructions affect all flags except the carry, CY. Note that the flags are set or cleared to indicate the conditions associated with the register or memory location operated upon by the instruction. And for these instructions, the register operated upon is not necessarily the accumulator. It is reasonable to expect that if an 8-bit register containing FFH is incremented, the carry is set—analogous to incrementing an MSI counter and obtaining a carry out; however, this is not the case with the increment instruction. After incrementing the register, its contents are 00H, but the carry flag is unaffected. Thus, when incrementing a register, overflow is determined by testing for the register being zero.

Internal register pairs are incremented or decremented with a single instruction:

Increment register pair	*Decrement register pair*
INX rp	DCX rp
(rh)(rl) ← (rh)(rl) + 1	(rh)(rl) ← (rh)(rl) − 1

Flags: None

These two instructions have no effect on the condition flags. In general, no assumptions concerning the actions or effects of any instructions on the flags can be made; the instruction summary must be referred to for the effect of each instruction.

Either the DO-WHILE or DO-UNTIL structure can be used when counting. The DO-WHILE structure, when used for counting, is frequently called the ***count-then-execute*** method, and the DO-UNTIL is called ***execute-then-count***. The choice determines the value used in presetting the registers to be counted. The two methods are flowcharted in Fig. 4.6-1.

The following DO-UNTIL structure inputs 10 bytes of data from input port DATA and stores them in a buffer area in memory.

```
INDU:   LXI H, BUFF    ;load HL pair with starting address of data buffer
                       ;in memory
        MVI C, 10      ;initialize the count
LOOP:   IN DATA        ;input data
        MOV M, A       ;store data in memory buffer location
                       ;pointed to by HL
        INX H          ;increment pointer to buffer
        DCR C          ;decrement counter
        JNZ LOOP       ;test for last data item
```

The same routine written as a DO-WHILE structure requires an initial value of 11 to input 10 data items:

```
        INDW:   LXI H, BUFF
                MVI C, 11
        LOOP:   DCR C
                JZ FINI
                IN DATA
                MOV M, A
                INX H
                JMP LOOP
        FINI:
```

In other words, to loop N times using a DO-UNTIL structure requires an initial value of N. To loop N times in a DO-WHILE structure requires an initial value of $N + 1$.

If counting is not used, a special character must terminate the loop. In the following example the character used for this purpose is 0DH.

```
        INXX:   LXI H, BUFF
        LOOP:   IN DATA
                MOV M, A
                INX H
                CPI 0DH
                JNZ LOOP
```

The following routine incorporates SEQUENCE structures, an IF-THEN/ELSE, and a DO-UNTIL structure. In this particular program segment, the result is not a properly structured program, as is typically the case in practical assembly language programs.

This routine ascertains whether a 4 K EPROM is completely erased so it can be programmed. As such, this routine can be utilized in a microprocessor based EPROM programmer. The 4 K EPROM is plugged into a socket with starting address EPRM0. When erased, all bits of the EPROM are logic 1. If the EPROM is completely erased, bit 0 of output port DSPLY is set; if not, bit 1 is set. These bits turn LEDs on or off to give a visual display of the result.

```
ERSD?:  XRA A           ;clear accumulator
        OUT DSPLY       ;clear LED display
        LXI H, EPRM0     ;set up pointer to first EPROM location
        LXI B, 1000H     ;set up counter for number of EPROM
                        ;words
NEXT:   MVI A, 0FFH      ;set up constant for comparison
        CMP M           ;compare constant with a word from
                        ;EPROM
        JNZ NO          ;if not equal, test is complete
        INX H           ;increment pointer to next word
        DCX B           ;decrement counter (does not set flag)
        MOV A, C        ;move low byte of counter to A
        ORA B           ;OR with high byte of counter — flags set
        JNZ NEXT        ;if test not complete, loop
        MVI A, 01H       ;test complete; set display to passed
        JMP DONE
NO:     MVI A, 02H       ;set display to indicate not erased
DONE:   OUT DSPLY
```

4.7 SOFTWARE DELAYS

Counting can create time delays. Since the execution times of the instructions used in a counting routine are known, the initial value of the counter register required to obtain a specific time delay can be determined.[4] The following example illustrates how the initial value for the counter register is ascertained.

Consider an output device that consists of a single flip-flop and a device address decoder. The address decoder uses the IO/$\overline{\text{M}}$ and $\overline{\text{WR}}$ signals so that the flip-flop is cleared by an OUT CLR instruction and set by an OUT SET instruction (see Fig. 4.7-1). The output of the flip-flop is programmed to be logic 1 for a desired period of time, thus implementing, in software, the hardware function of a single shot.

---

[4] Instructions in the 8080A instruction set generally require a different number of states for execution than those in the 8085A instruction set.

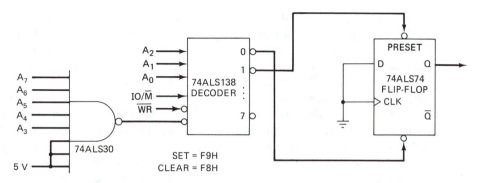

Figure 4.7-1 Setting and resetting an external flip-flop under microprocessor control.

The pulse duration of this software single shot is controlled by the counting loop.

			Number of States
	SSHOT:	MVI B, N	7
		OUT SET	10
N − 1 times	LOOP:	DCR B	4
		JNZ LOOP	7 / 10
	FIN:	OUT CLR	10

The delay loop consists of two instructions, DCR B and JNZ LOOP. The column to the right of the instructions indicates the number of states in the instruction cycle of each instruction. Two values are given for the number of states for the conditional jump instruction. The smaller value applies when the condition is not met, and the larger value applies when it is met. There are $N - 1$ passes through the loop where the condition is met and control is transferred back to the first instruction in the loop. The number of states that elapse while B is not zero is $(N - 1) \times (4 + 10)$. On the last pass through the loop, the condition is not met and the loop is exited. The number of states that elapse on this pass is $4 + 7 + 10$. Since the pulses generated by the output instructions occur at the end of these instructions, the time between the two pulses is

$$t_d = ((N - 1) \times (4 + 10) + (4 + 7 + 10)) \times T \quad \text{for } 0 < N \le 255$$
$$= (N \times 14 + 7) \times T$$
$$= N \times 4.56\ \mu S + 2.28\ \mu S$$

where T = state time of 325.5 nS and

$$t_d = 255 \times 4.56\ \mu S + 2.28\ \mu S \quad \text{for } N = 0$$
$$= 1.165\ mS$$

The shortest delay possible with this routine is 6.84 μS. The longest delay is 1.165 mS. Note that the longest delay actually occurs when N has the value zero because register B is decremented before testing it for zero. When $N = 0$, there are 255 passes through the loop with the jump condition met, and one pass with the condition not met. The resolution of the delay, the smallest change in the delay resulting from a change by 1 in the value of N, is 4.56 μS.

The previous delay used an 8-bit register to hold the loop count. Longer delays can be implemented when a register pair is used to hold the count. For example, the DCX rp, *decrement register pair*, instruction controls a 16-bit counter consisting of a register pair such as BC. However, DCX rp does not affect any of the flags. The following routine uses the register pair BC as the counter and checks it for zero.

```
DELAY:   LXI B, COUNT    ;initialize register pair BC with
                         ;a 16-bit value

         OUT SET
LOOP:    DCX B           ;decrement register pair BC
         MOV A, B        ;check for (B) = (C) = 00H
         ORA C           ;logically OR B and C, set flags
         JNZ LOOP
FIN:     OUT CLR
```

Longer delays can be implemented by counting down a second register pair each time the first register is counted through. Thus, the second register counts multiples of the delay of the first register. In effect, this is a programmed analogy of cascaded presettable hardware counters.

The following routine uses the 16-bit register pair HL to control the inner loop and the 8-bit register B to control the outer loop.

Number of States

		Number of States	
DELAY:	MVI B, NO	7	
OUTER:	LXI H, NI	10	
INNER:	DCX H	6	
	MOV A, L	4	
	ORA H	4	inner loop / outer loop
	JNZ INNER	7 / 10	
	DCR B	4	
	JNZ OUTER	7 / 10	

(annotations: "NO − 1 times", "NI − 1 times", "7", "+", "N0−1")

The loop control variables for the inner and outer loops are NI and NO, respectively. In the routine NI and NO must be assigned constant values. For example, suppose that it is desired that DELAY be capable of generating delays from 10 mS to 2.56 S. NO could then specify the delay in hundreds of a second and the appropriate value of NI would have to be found for this to be the case. This can be done in two steps: the first step is to determine the total number of states required in the inner loop, the second step is to find the value of NI to give this number of states. The equation for the total delay in terms of the total number of states in the inner loop, TSIL, is

$$t_d = (7 + (NO - 1) \times (10 + TSIL + 4 + 10) + (10 + TSIL + 4 + 7)) \times T$$
$$= (4 + NO \times (24 + TSIL)) \times T$$

The resolution of this delay is

$$\Delta t_d = (24 + TSIL) \times T$$

To minimize cumulative error, TSIL can be determined from the above equation. The equation is solved for the value of TSIL that gives a resolution of 10 mS with $T = 325.5$ nS.

$$TSIL = (\Delta t_d - 24 \times T)/T$$
$$= (10{,}000 \ \mu S - 7.812 \ \mu S)/0.3255 \ \mu S$$
$$= 30{,}697.796 \text{ states}$$

An equation can then be written for the total number of states in the inner loop and solved for NI:

$$TSIL = (NI - 1) \times (6 + 4 + 4 + 10) + (6 + 4 + 4 + 7)$$
$$= NI \times 24 - 3$$

or

$$NI = (TSIL + 3)/24$$

for

$$TSIL = 30{,}697.796$$
$$NI = 1279$$

When a very precise delay is required, a loop is written and initialized with a count value that comes as close to the required delay as possible. The delay is then "tuned" by adding instructions outside the loop to bring it to the required time. One instruction that is particularly appropriate for this purpose is the *no operation*, NOP. This instruction carries out no operation and does not affect any of the registers or flags; its only effect is to cause a delay of four clock periods.

NOP   *Flags:* None

Other instructions can be used for this purpose as long as they don't affect register contents that must be preserved.

If WAIT states occur in the execution of the instructions that comprise a delay routine, they must be included in the computation of the initial values of the loop control variables.

4.8 EXAMPLE PROGRAMS

This section contains several complete programs that use the instructions presented in this chapter. In each case a simple microprocessor based system application is described. Each application requires only a few input and/or output ports in addition to the microprocessor and memory. Only the I/O ports and their bit assignments are described in detail. A flowchart gives the overall program logic.

4.8.1 Bar Graph Liquid Level Indicator

A float and transducer generate a voltage that is proportional to the level of liquid in a tank. This voltage is in turn converted to a 4-bit binary value by an analog to digital, A/D, converter. The binary output of the A/D converter is read as bits D_0 to D_3 of input port ADCON (see Fig. 4.8-1a). A bar graph is used to display the

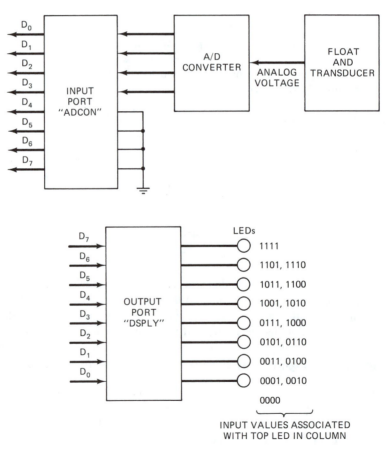

Figure 4.8-1a   Input and output port configuration for liquid level indicator.

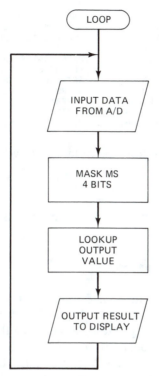

Figure 4.8-1b   Flowchart for liquid level indicator.

liquid level in the tank. The bar graph consists of eight LEDs, which are driven by output port DSPLY. The eight LEDs are positioned to form a column. The desired mapping of A/D outputs to LEDs ON is also shown in Fig. 4.8-1a. The 16 binary values are mapped to 9 possible output conditions. When the output of the A/D converter is 0000 none of the LEDs is ON, indicating an empty tank. As the binary output from the A/D converter increases, the LEDs are turned ON, starting from the bottom. The number of LEDs ON is proportional to the binary output of the A/D converter. For example, when the output from the A/D is 1000, half of the LEDs are ON. The bar graph display immediately changes to indicate changes in the liquid level.

A flowchart of the program is shown in Fig. 4.8-1b and the program appears in Fig. 4.8-1c. The program determines the bit pattern to be output to port DSPLY by a table lookup. The table, TABLE, consists of 16 bytes of data, one for each possible input value. Each byte in the table is the pattern to be output, to control the LEDs, for the corresponding input value from the A/D converter. The binary value input from the A/D converter is the *offset* into the table. The program inputs the offset and adds it to the *base address* of the table to obtain the address of the pattern to be output. The program outputs the pattern to the display port and then jumps to the beginning of the program. The program is an infinite loop. If the object code corresponding to the program and the table were placed in ROM starting at

```
LOOP:    IN ADCON       ;INPUT 4-BIT A/D RESULT
         ANI OFH        ;MASK MS FOUR BITS
         MOV E,A        ;COMPUTE 16-BIT OFFSET IN DE
         MVI D,0
         LXI H,TABLE    ;BASE ADDRESS OF TABLE IN HL
         DAD D          ;ADD OFFSET TO BASE
         MOV A,M        ;GET TABLE ENTRY
         OUT DSPLY      ;OUTPUT TO LEDS
         JMP LOOP       ;REPEAT
TABLE:   DB 00H,01H,01H,03H,03H,07H,07H,0FH
         DB 0FH,1FH,1FH,3FH,3FH,7FH,7FH,0FFH
```

Figure 4.8-1c Program for liquid level indicator.

location 0000H, the program would run continuously after the microprocessor is reset.

4.8.2 Decoder Test System

The I/O port configuration for a system that functionally tests 74ALS138 and 8205, 1-out-of-8 decoders, is shown is Fig. 4.8-2a. The decoder is the device under test, DUT, and is placed in a 16-pin test socket. Since the decoder is a combinational circuit, a complete functional test is achieved by applying all possible input combinations and checking for the correct outputs. The decoder has six inputs and eight outputs. The inputs consist of three enable inputs and three select inputs. The

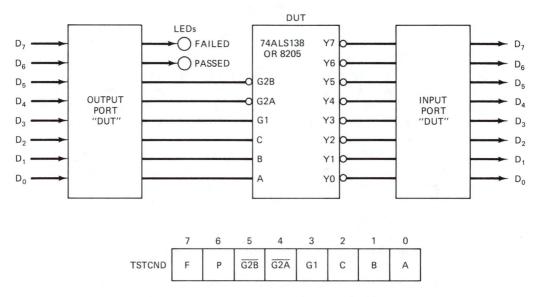

Figure 4.8-2a Input and output port configuration and TSTCND bit assignment for decoder test system.

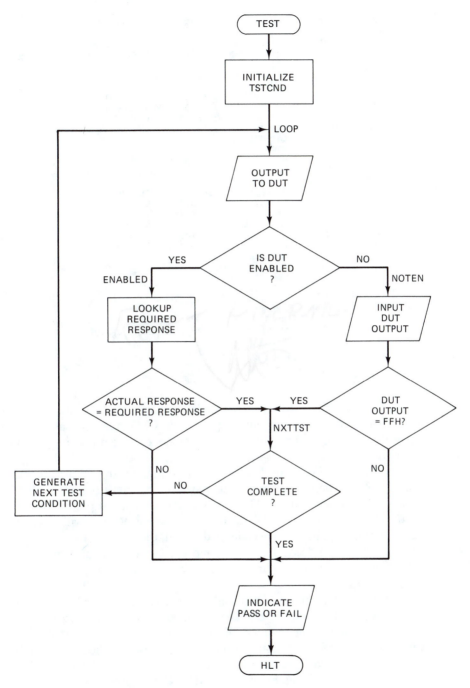

Figure 4.8-2b Flowchart for decoder test system.

```
TEST:     XRA A          ;CLEAR TEST CONDITION
          STA TSTCND     ;SAVE TEST CONDITION
LOOP:     OUT DUT        ;OUTPUT TEST CONDITION TO DUT
          ANI 38H        ;DO TEST CONDITIONS ENABLE DUT?
          CPI 08H
          JZ ENABLD      ;YES,JUMP
NOTEN:    IN DUT         ;NO
          CPI 0FFH       ;IS DUT OUTPUT ALL 1'S
          JNZ FAILED     ;NO, ONE OR MORE OUTPUTS 0
          JMP NXTTST     ;YES, GO TO NEXT TEST
ENABLD:   LDA TSTCND     ;USE SELECT INPUTS AS OFFSET
          ANI 07H
          MOV E,A
          MVI D,0
          LXI H,TABLE    ;COMPUTE TABLE ENTRY ADDRESS
          DAD D
          MOV B,M        ;INPUT REQUIRED RESULT
          IN DUT         ;INPUT ACTUAL RESULT
          CMP B          ;COMPARE
          JNZ FAILED
NXTTST:   LDA TSTCND     ;IS TEST COMPLETE
          INR A
          CPI 40H
          JZ DONE        ;YES
          STA TSTCND     ;NO
          JMP LOOP
FAILED:   MVI A,80H
DONE:     OUT DUT
          HLT
TABLE:    DB 0FEH,0FDH,0FBH,0F7H,0EFH,0DFH,0BFH,07FH
```

Figure 4.8-2c Program for decoder test system.

inputs to the DUT are driven by the six least significant bits of the output port. The most significant bits of the output port drive LEDs that indicate the test result, either PASS or FAIL. This particular assignment of output port bits to inputs of the DUT results in a simple program.

A flowchart for the program is shown in Fig. 4.8-2b and the program appears in Fig. 4.8-2c. The test strategy is to generate, in binary sequence, all 64 possible input combinations to the DUT. A copy of the current test pattern is maintained in the RWM location TSTCND. Each test pattern generated will either enable the decoder or disable it. If the decoder is disabled, then its outputs must all be logic 1. The outputs of the decoder are read, and if they are all logic 1, the test continues with the next test pattern. If any output is logic 0, the test terminates and the FAIL LED is turned ON.

If the test pattern generated enables the decoder, then only one specific output of the decoder should be logic 0. The actual output of the decoder is compared with its required output. The required output is determined by table lookup. The binary value output to the select inputs of the decoder is used as the offset into the table. If the output of the decoder is correct, the test continues. If the decoder output is incorrect, the test terminates and the FAIL LED is turned ON.

After each test pattern is applied and the decoder output tested, a check is made to see if all possible input combinations to the decoder have been tried. If not, the test continues; if so, the test is complete, the PASS LED is turned ON, and the

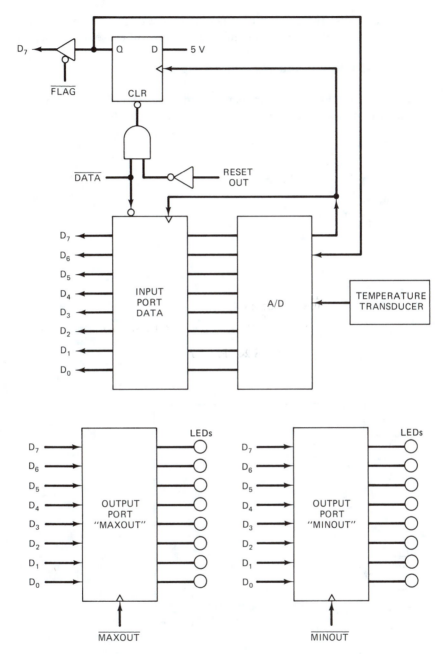

Figure 4.8-3a Input and output port configuration for maximum and minimum display.

program halts. The decoder can then be removed from the test socket and another decoder inserted. Resetting the microprocessor will cause this device to be tested.

4.8.3 Maximum and Minimum Display

The system in Fig. 4.8-3a inputs unsigned binary data from an 8-bit A/D converter and determines whether the data is larger or smaller than all previous values input.

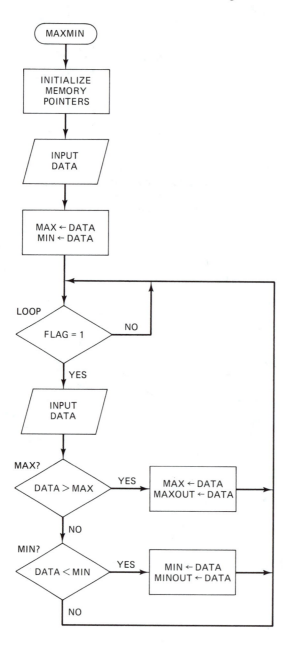

Figure 4.8-3b Flowchart for maximum and minimum display program.

```
START:   LXI H,MAX      ;HL POINTER TO MAX
         LXI D,MIN      ;DE POINTER TO MIN
WAIT1:   IN FLAG        ;CHECK FOR FIRST DATA BYTE
         ORA A          ;SET CPU FLAGS
         JP WAIT1       ;WAIT IF BIT 7 = 0
         IN DATA        ;INPUT DATA
         MOV M,A        ;MAX EQUALS FIRST DATA BYTE
         XCHG           ;SWITCH POINTERS
         MOV M,A        ;MIN EQUALS FIRST DATA BYTE
         OUT MAXOUT     ;OUTPUT INITIAL MAXIMUM
         OUT MINOUT     ;OUTPUT INITIAL MINOUT
NXDATA:  XCHG           ;SWITCH POINTER
WAIT2:   IN FLAG        ;CHECK FOR NEXT DATA BYTE
         ORA A          ;SET CPU FLAGS
         JP WAIT2       ;WAIT IF BIT 7 = 0
         IN DATA        ;INPUT DATA
MAX?:    CMP M          ;NEW DATA > MAX ?
         JC MIN?        ;NO, TEST FOR MIN
         MOV M,A        ;YES, SAVE NEW MAX
         OUT MAXOUT     ;OUTPUT NEW MAXIMUM
         JMP WAIT2      ;GET NEXT DATA BYTE
MIN?:    XCHG           ;SWITCH POINTERS
         CMP M          ;NEW DATA LESS THAN MIN?
         JNC NXDATA     ;NO, GET NEXT DATA BYTE
         MOV M,A        ;YES, SAVE NEW MIN
         OUT MINOUT     ;OUTPUT NEW MINIMUM
         JMP NXDATA     ;GET NEXT DATA BYTE
```

Figure 4.8-3c   Program for maximum and minimum display.

If the data value is larger, it is output to the port MAXOUT; if it is smaller, it is output to the port MINOUT. When the A/D converter generates new data, it writes the data to input port DATA. The strobe from the A/D converter that clocks the data into the port DATA also sets the flip-flop called FLAG. The flip-flop, FLAG, is connected via a 1-bit input port to bit D7 of the data bus. The microprocessor can input from port FLAG and if bit 7 of register A is logic 1 there is new data available in port DATA. When new data is available, the microprocessor will input the data. The strobe that enables the input buffers of port DATA also clears the flip-flop. The A/D converter checks that the flip-flop is logic 0 before writing new data to the port DATA. Thus, there is no chance that the microprocessor will input invalid data due to the A/D converter writing the port simultaneously with the microprocessor attempting to read the previous value of data written. Resetting the microprocessor clears the flip-flop.

The flowchart is given in Fig. 4.8-3b and the program in Fig. 4.8-3c. After the microprocessor is reset, it initializes the registers HL and DE to point to memory locations MAX and MIN, respectively. These memory locations in RWM store the maximum and minimum values input. The microprocessor waits in a loop testing FLAG until it is set. The first byte of data input becomes the initial values of MAX and MIN.

The microprocessor then compares each subsequent data byte input with the present value of MAX. If the value input is greater than MAX, it is written to MAX, becoming the new maximum, and also output to port MAXOUT. If the value input is less than MAX, it is then checked to see if it is less than MIN. If it is less than MIN, it is written to MIN and also to port MINOUT. Note that the comparison of the input data, in register A, is always made with the data in the memory location pointed to by HL. Therefore, the contents of HL and DE are swapped when necessary to point to either MAX or MIN.

The program continues to display the maximum and minimum data values generated from the time it was reset. This system could be used in a number of applications, depending on the transducer used. For example, if the transducer measured temperature, the system could display the maximum and minimum temperatures over some time period.

REFERENCES

1. M. R. BARBACCI, "A Comparison of Register Transfer Languages for Describing Computers and Digital Systems," *IEEE Transactions on Computers*, (February 1975), 137–50.

2. *Intel 8080/8085 Assembly Language Programming Manual* (Santa Clara, Calif.: Intel Corporation, 1979).

PROBLEMS

4-1. Based on the instructions presented in this chapter, rank the general purpose registers A, B, C, D, E, H, and L and all register pairs in terms of computational power or usefulness. In other words, list the registers in terms of usefulness and capability from most powerful to least powerful.

4-2. List the data transfer instructions that transfer 1 byte of data in a single instruction cycle and list those that transfer 2.

4-3. Assume that before each of the following instructions is executed, register A contains 4AH, register B contains 8CH, and register F contains 00X0X0X1B. Specify in binary the contents of registers A, B, and F immediately after each instruction is executed. Use Xs to represent the unspecified bits of F.

   (a) MVI B, 24H

   (b) ANA B

   (c) RLC

   (d) INR A

4-4. Determine the values of the flag bits after the execution of the following instructions. Assume that the initial register conditions are the same for each case: (A) = A7H, (B) = 26H, (C) = FDH, (F) = COH.

   (a) ORI 32H

   (b) MOV A, B

   (c) INR C

   (d) CMP B

   (e) RAL

4-5. Write a program that continually inputs data from two ports, PORT1 and PORT2. When the least significant 4 bits of PORT1 are identical to the most significant 4 bits of PORT2, bit 0 of output port MATCH should be 1; otherwise, it should be 0. Write the program using as few instructions as possible. Comment your program to explain its operation.

4-6. Write a program that inputs a byte of data from an input port, PATRN, and counts the number of 1s in the data byte. The program should store this count in a reserved memory location labeled COUNT. Use as few instructions as possible. Comment your program to explain its operation.

4-7. Write a program that inputs a byte of data from each of two ports, DATA1 and DATA2. The program determines the number of 1s in corresponding bit positions in the 2 bytes and outputs that number to the port ONES. The program then halts.

4-8. Four status signals, S_0, S_1, S_2, and S_3, are connected to bits 0, 1, 2, and 3 of input port 05H. C_2, bit 2 of output port 34H, is to be controlled as specified by the following Boolean equation:

$$C_2 = S_2 \bar{S}_1 S_0 + \bar{S}_2 S_1 \bar{S}_0 + S_3 S_2 S_1 S_0$$

Write a program that controls C_2 as specified. Write the program to loop so that C_2 is continually controlled. The other bits of port 34H should not be modified.

4-9. The following algorithm converts an n-bit Gray code number, $g_{n-1}g_{n-2} \cdots g_0$, to an n-bit binary number, $b_{n-1}b_{n-2} \cdots b_0$:

$$b_{n-1} = g_{n-1} \text{ for the most significant bit}$$
$$b_i = g_i \forall b_{i+1} \quad 0 \le i < n - 1$$

Write a program that inputs an 8-bit Gray code number, computes the binary equivalent of this number using the above algorithm, and outputs the binary equivalent. Compare the advantages and disadvantages of this approach with that of a table lookup approach in terms of execution speed and memory requirements.

4-10. The following algorithm converts an n-bit binary number, $b_{n-1}b_{n-2} \cdots b_0$, to an n-bit Gray code number, $g_{n-1}g_{n-2} \cdots g_0$.

$$g_{n-1} = b_{n-1} \text{ for the most significant bit}$$
$$g_i = b_{i+1} \forall b_i \quad 0 \le i < n - 1$$

Write a program that inputs an 8-bit binary number, computes its Gray code equivalent using the above algorithm, and outputs this equivalent.

4-11. Write a program to find the smallest element in a block of data, the length of which is in memory location 2001H, and which itself begins in memory location 2002H. The numbers in the block are 8-bit unsigned binary numbers. Store the smallest element in memory location 2000H.

4-12. Write a program that inputs data from the port DATA. All values input are discarded until the first occurrence of the value 02H. The first occurrence of 02H is written into a buffer that starts in location TXTBUF. The program continues inputting data and storing it in successive locations in the buffer until it inputs and stores the first occurrence of the value 03H. At this point, the program halts.

4-13. Write a program that generates a single logic 1 pulse with a duration of 0.1 to 25.0 S in 0.1 S steps. Have this program input the desired length of the pulse as a binary number from input port 20H. Also, have it generate the pulse as bit 0 of output port 08H.

4-14. Write a program that measures the duration of a pulse generated by an external source, samples the pulse as bit 7 of input port 03H, and outputs to output port 06H a binary number equal to the measured pulse duration in mS. Assume that the maximum pulse duration is < 256 mS.

4-15. For the program ERSD? of Section 4.6, compute and give the length of time it takes to determine if an EPROM is completely erased. Assume a state time of 325.5 nS.

4-16. For the delay routine below, write an expression that gives the total delay time of the routine as a function of N and the state time, T. Determine the value of N required for a 1 mS delay assuming an 8085A processor with a 6.144 MHz crystal.

```
DELAY:   LXI B, N
LOOP:    DCX B
         MOV A, B
         ORA C
         JNZ LOOP
```

4-17. Write an expression for the delay routine of Problem 4-16 that gives the total delay time as a function of the loop control variable, N, the state time, T, and the number of wait states, W.

4-18. A four-input "threshold gate" is to be implemented. This gate has a logic 1 output when the number of its inputs that are logic 1 is greater than or equal to a threshold. The threshold is specified in binary by two inputs $T1$ and $T0$. When the inputs or threshold change, the output should change accordingly. Specify the assignment of signals to input and output ports. Write the required program.

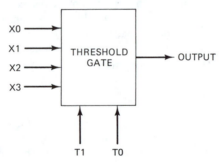

4-19. A 4-bit binary comparator is to be implemented. The comparator provides a continuous comparison of two 4-bit binary words $A_3A_2A_1A_0$ and $B_3B_2B_1B_0$. The binary words are input on switches. Three outputs are to be generated $A > B$, $A = B$, and $A < B$. Only one input port and one output port are to be used. Specify the assignment of signals to the input port and the output port. Write the required program.

4-20. Design a frequency counter that measures input frequencies between 0 and 127 Hz. The input waveform is a periodic TTL signal but is not necessarily a square wave. Use a sample interval of 1 S. The measured frequency should be output in binary to LEDs. The measurement cycles should be continuous with the display updated at the end of each. An LED should be toggled by the program at the beginning of each cycle of the input waveform. This LED provides an indication from the program that it is detecting a nonzero frequency input.

5

Program Assembly and Testing

Software for the microprocessor can be generated using a time-share service, dedicated minicomputer, large computer system, manual methods, or a microcomputer built around a specific microprocessor. Each has advantages and disadvantages.

Eli S. Nauful*

*"Software Support for Microprocessors Poses New Design Choices," Computer Design, Vol. 15, No. 10, (October 1976), pp. 93 – 98.

After an application program is written in assembly language, it must be translated—assembled—into machine code. Machine or binary code consists of 0s and 1s and is, of course, the only language that can be stored in the microprocessor's memory and interpreted by its instruction decoder. With the exception of very short programs that can be assembled by hand, a special program called an *assembler* is necessary for efficient translation.

Once the machine code is obtained, the program is tested to determine whether it functions as logically intended. The test may be conducted by loading the machine code into the microprocessor system and executing it under the control of a *monitor*. Alternatively, another special program, a *simulator*, can be run on a different computer to simulate execution of the machine code by the microprocessor in order to locate logical errors in the program. Another approach requiring special support hardware and software is in-circuit emulation. *In-circuit emulation* allows the application software and its interaction with the prototype hardware to be tested, usually in real time. In either case, an editor program is then used to correct any errors in the application program, which is subsequently reassembled and tested again. Once all apparent errors are corrected, the assembled program is loaded into a hardware prototype of the microprocessor system for final testing.

5.1 PROGRAMMING LANGUAGES

Programs can be written in any one of three languages: machine language, assembly language, or high level language. Machine language alone is directly executable by a microprocessor. Programs written in assembly language or a high level language must be translated to machine language for execution.

The instruction set for the 8085A microprocessor in Appendix C gives the binary code for each instruction. Consider the following program written in machine language:

Binary
00111010
00001100
00000000
01000111
00111010
00001101
00000000
10000000
10000000
00001110
00000000
01110110

Although it is probably not apparent from scanning, this machine language program adds two numbers obtained from memory, stores the result in memory, and then halts. One disadvantage of a machine language program is obvious: it is difficult to read; it is equally difficult and tedious to write.

The machine language program listing can be simplified somewhat by converting the binary code to octal or hexadecimal:

Binary	Octal	Hexadecimal
00111010	072	3A
00001100	014	0C
00000000	000	00
01000111	107	47
00111010	072	3A
00001101	015	0D
00000000	000	00
10000000	200	80
00110010	062	32
00001110	016	0E
00000000	000	00
01110110	166	76

And, although such a shorthand notation alleviates some of the difficulty of writing the codes, it does not improve the understandability of the program's function. Machine code is usually represented in hexadecimal for conciseness. However, it must be converted back to binary to be loaded into memory. Programs of any appreciable length are not written directly in machine language.

Assembly language uses mnemonic representations for operation codes, data, and addresses. These mnemonics are abbreviations of the names or descriptions of the instructions, addresses, or data and are used as an aid in remembering their function. The program given in the previous example is written using 8085A assembly language mnemonics as follows:

Assembly Language	Binary
LDA AUGND	00111010
	00001100
	00000000
MOV B, A	01000111
LDA ADDND	00111010
	00001101
	00000000
ADD B	10000000
STA SUM	00110010
	00001110
	00000000
HLT	01110110

This assembly language program is much more understandable than the corresponding machine language program, which makes the writing and modification of the program easier. The memory reference instructions are represented by the mnemonics introduced in Chapter 4; the addition instruction is represented by ADD; and AUGND, ADDND, and SUM are symbolic names for the memory locations 0CH, 0DH, and 0EH in the hexadecimal version of the program. If an assembler program is available, the translation of the assembly language program to machine code is automatic.

When writing a program in machine language, all addresses used in memory references for data transfers or transfers of control must be specified as absolute addresses. That is, the actual address of the memory location must be specified. The use of symbolic names for addresses in assembly language programs not only makes it easier to write a program but also facilitates the insertion or deletion of instructions. If instructions are inserted or deleted in a machine language program, the absolute addresses in memory reference and branch instructions must be checked to see whether their values require changing because of the shifting of the actual location of instructions in memory caused by this insertion or deletion. When a program is written in assembly language using symbolic addresses, insertion or deletion causes no problems because, as the modified program is assembled, the correct addresses of all memory references and branch instructions are automatically computed and substituted for their symbolic representations.

Programming ease is further enhanced by a high level language,[1] where a single instruction is equivalent to several machine language instructions. For example

High Level Language	*Binary*
I = J + K	00111010
	00001100
	00000000
	01000111
	00111010
	00001101
	00000000
	10000000
	00110010
	00001110
	00000000
	01110110

High level language programs must also be translated to machine code for microprocessor execution.

[1] High level languages are discussed in Chapter 14.

5.2 SOFTWARE DEVELOPMENT

Software development is a process that culminates with the creation and verification of a pattern of 0s and 1s, which, when placed in the appropriate memory locations of a specific microprocessor system and executed, cause the system to implement its intended function. In general, software development consists of five steps:

1. Design: the determination from the functional specification of the overall structure of the program and the data, as well as a determination of the algorithms to implement the necessary functions.

2. Coding: the actual writing of instructions in a specific programming language to implement the algorithms of the previous step.

3. Translation: the creation of the patterns of 0s and 1s (the object code) from the program (source program) created in step 2.

4. Testing: the determination of whether the object code, when executed, actually causes the system to implement its intended function.

5. Debugging: the process of determining the source of any failures found during testing in order to eliminate them. Correction of a failure requires a repetition of these steps, starting with the first or second one.

Although software can be developed by hand, practical development for any but the smallest programs requires computer assistance. Software development costs often constitute the major portion of system development cost, and the use of computer aids reduces development cost and time and improves software and system reliability.

There are two fundamental approaches to computer assisted software development. One uses a large computer or minicomputer with a number of software development support programs. The other uses a microprocessor based software development system and a functionally similar software development support package. The microprocessor based software development system is a microcomputer that contains a microprocessor of the type for which the software is being developed.

Computer assisted software development typically includes the use of several software development programs: monitor, text editor, translator, loader, simulator, and debugger.

The *monitor* is a program that controls, at an elementary level, the overall operation of the computer system: the inputting and outputtting of programs to and from the computer system and the initiation of their execution. It also contains software to control the system peripheral devices: the CRT terminal and printer. In microcomputer development systems, the monitor is contained in ROM and is immediately available when the system is turned on. On computer systems with sophisticated peripherals, an enhanced monitor, referred to as an operating system, is also used. This is true for advanced microcomputer development systems, personal computers, and large computers.

The *text editor* facilitates the creation and modification of a source program file. Editor commands create, modify, or reposition lines of text and add them to or delete them from the program file. This file is usually saved on the computer floppy or hard disk and can be recalled for processing whenever necessary.

The *translator* takes the program file—the source program—and translates its instructions into machine code. Since this code is the object (result) of the translation process, it is referred to as *object code*. The translator produces a listing of the source program and indicates violations of the grammatical rules of the language.

There are several different types of translators: assemblers, cross assemblers, self assemblers, and compilers. Assemblers accept source programs written in a specific assembly language and generate object code for the corresponding microprocessor. Cross assemblers run on one processor but assemble programs written for another processor. An assembler that runs on a microprocessor and creates object code for that same microprocessor is called a self assembler. Cross assemblers are usually written in a high level language and are more powerful than self assemblers because of the additional features that can be supported.

If the source program is written in a high level language, a compiler is used for translation. High level languages are essentially independent of a particular microprocessor; thus, the details of the microprocessor's architecture on which the object code is executed are not important during the writing of the high level language program. The compiler determines the sequence of assembly language instructions necessary for a particular microprocessor to implement the operation indicated by each instruction in the high level language program. The compiler creates, as well, the actual object code that, when executed, carries out the function specified by the high level language program.

A *loader* transfers the object code from some external medium, such as a floppy disk, to the microprocessor memory. Loaders vary, depending on the configuration of the microprocessor system on which the object code is executed. In the case of a software development system, for example, the loader is a program that runs on the microprocessor and loads the object code into R/W memory for execution. Or if the object code is loaded into ROM for execution on the system prototype, the PROM programmer functions as the loader.

A *simulator* is a program that runs on a large computer or minicomputer and emulates a microprocessor's operation. It uses memory locations in the computer on which it runs to simulate the registers and memory of the microprocessor system. The simulator reads each instruction in the object code and simulates its execution, modifying the simulated microprocessor registers and memory as appropriate.

The simulator executes one or more instructions for each instruction in the object code, and therefore its execution speed differs from that of the actual microprocessor. Real-time operation differences notwithstanding, a simulator can effectively carry out substantial testing of the object program without requiring the presence of the microprocessor.

A *debugger* is a program that facilitates testing the execution of the object program on the microprocessor. It stops execution at the occurrence of specified events and thus allows the examination and modification of the contents of registers and memory locations and/or allows the execution of one instruction at a time for analysis.

When a simulator is used, the debugger is part of the simulator. And, in a microcomputer development system, debugging capabilities are often included in the monitor.

There are pros and cons to the use of large computers as opposed to microcomputer development systems for software development. A large computer or minicomputer eliminates the cost of a software development system; however, the cross software—particularly the assembler and simulator—must be available for the particular microprocessor for which the software is being developed. If cross software is available for several different microprocessors, their software developments can be compared for a particular application.

The use of a large computer system becomes costly if many iterations through the software design steps are required. Since simulators are usually appropriate only for initial testing of the software, due to limitations in simulating the real-time nature of external operations such as input/output and interrupts, a final testing of the software on the actual prototype is a necessity.

If access to a large computer is not available, then a dedicated microprocessor based software development system involves the smallest initial investment. Here problems associated with inadequate simulation are eliminated since initial tests are carried out on the actual microprocessor. Many sophisticated microprocessor development systems provide features for translation and testing that are superior to those possible using cross software.

Coding, translation, testing, and debugging are basically the same whether software is developed with cross software on a large computer or minicomputer or with a microcomputer development system. The only major difference occurs in the initial testing and debugging stage: in the first case the object program's execution is only simulated; in the second case the program is executed on the actual microprocessor. Detailed examples of the implementation of the various approaches are given in Section 5.9.

The steps in software development using a cross assembler and simulator on a large computer, with the final program testing on a hardware prototype, are outlined in Fig. 5.2-1. First, the assembly language program file, the *source program*, is developed, generally from an interactive device such as a CRT terminal. Development and any corrections or changes are facilitated by the editor program.

The source program is input to the assembler program, which produces the equivalent machine code along with a listing of the original source program. In the process of assembling the source program, the assembler checks for *syntactic errors*—violations of the rules governing the structure of instructions—and for consistency and completeness of the program. Syntax errors are indicated on the program listing to the left of each incorrect program statement. The editor is then used to make any required corrections in the source program statements; the program is then reassembled. It may take several iterations of assembly followed by use of the editor to locate and correct all the syntax errors in a program.

Logical errors are mistakes in the use of instructions to implement the required algorithm. They are detected by using a simulator program, which executes

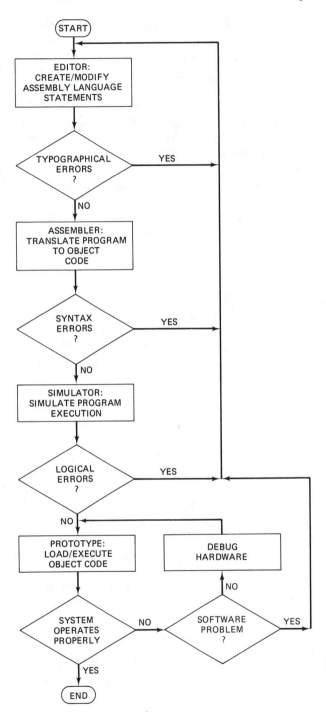

Figure 5.2-1 Steps in software development, using a cross assembler and simulator.

the object code resulting from the assembly. In addition, the simulator provides the user with a number of execution monitoring commands. After logical errors are detected using the simulator, the original source program is corrected using the editor, reassembled, and simulated again.

When all detectable errors are corrected, the object code is loaded into the memory of the microprocessor system hardware prototype, and hardware and software are tested together for proper system operation.

5.3 ASSEMBLER SOURCE PROGRAMS

Three types of statements are common in an assembly language source program:

1. Microprocessor instructions that are to be translated into machine language instructions resulting in object code.

2. Directive statements or pseudo instructions to the assembler program directing the translation of the symbolic microprocessor instructions.

3. Comment statements that are reproduced in the program listing for documentation purposes but have no effect on the translation of the program.

Symbolic microprocessor instructions and pseudo instructions usually are separate lines of the source program. A comment statement can also be a separate line, but may be included as part of a microprocessor instruction or assembler directive.

Whether it is to be assembled on a self assembler or on a cross assembler, the assembly language program must be written to conform to the strict syntax of the assembler in order to be assembled automatically. Most assemblers require that instructions consist of four separate fields, one or more of which may be blank.

1. The label field: containing the name to be assigned to an instruction's location.

2. The operation code field: specifying the operation to be performed.

3. The operand field: providing address and/or data information when required by an operation code.

4. The comment field: describing the way in which the instruction relates to the purpose of the program.

To facilitate use with terminals, most assemblers have a *free-field format* that allows any number of blanks between separate fields on a line of code. The fields are, however, separated by some type of delimiter. The delimiters used with Intel's ASM80 assembler and their placements are the following [1]:[2]

---

[2] The Intel ASM80 assembler assembles source programs for the 8085A and 8080A microprocessors.

Delimiter	Placement
: (colon)	After each label
(space)	Between an operation code and operand
, (comma)	Between operands in an operand field
; (semicolon)	Preceding comments

A label on an instruction is optional but, if used, is one to six characters long. The label begins with a letter of the alphabet or with the special characters @ or ? and is terminated with a colon. Operation codes, assembler directive names, and register names are *reserved words* and cannot be used as labels.

The operation field contains the instruction mnemonic and is delimited by a space. If the operand field for an instruction requires two operands, they are separated by commas. Operand field data specifies a register or register pair, immediate data, or an 8- or 16-bit address. There are many ways of expressing operands: as binary, octal, decimal, or hexadecimal numbers; as symbolic names with assigned values; as labels of instructions or data; as ASCII constants; or as arithmetic and logic expressions. For example, to specify the bit pattern of an ASCII code character, the character is placed in quotes, and the assembler substitutes for it the actual bit pattern. To load the accumulator with the ASCII code for a period (.), the single instruction

MVI A, '.'

suffices. The assembler makes the second byte of the resulting object code 2EH, the ASCII code for period.

Assemblers that allow operands to be specified as expressions containing arithmetic or logic operations evaluate the expression during assembly and replace it with its binary equivalent in the object code representation of the instruction. The specific arithmetic and logic operators allowed in expressions and their method of evaluation are determined by the particular assembler used.

Some of the arithmetic and logic operations allowed in expressions include addition, subtraction, multiplication, division, modulo division, NOT, AND, OR, EX-OR, shift right, and shift left. Note that these are operations carried out by the assembler program during translation and have nothing to do with the arithmetic and logic operations available as instructions in the microprocessor's instruction set.

5.4 MANUAL ASSEMBLY OF PROGRAMS

The procedure for manual assembly is simple and parallels that performed by an assembler program. A knowledge of manual assembly facilitates understanding of the operation of two-pass assemblers and the need for assembler directives. Hand assembly is important in its own right when obtaining object code for small programs or when making quick patches to larger programs that have been previously assembled.

For hand assembly, two blank columns are allocated to the left of the label field: after assembly the address column contains the address of the first byte of each instruction, and the object code column contains the hexadecimal representation of the 1, 2, or 3 bytes of code that comprise the instruction. See Fig. 5.4-1a.

Manual assembly is carried out in two steps, each requiring a complete scan or **pass** through the program. The first pass determines the memory location into which the first byte of each instruction is assembled and creates a table for the values of all symbolic names in the program. A starting address in memory, or **origin**, is assigned to the first byte of the first instruction and is recorded in the address column. This is the initial value for a count that is incremented by the number of bytes in each instruction. This count corresponds to the location in memory for which the first byte of each instruction is to be placed. A counter, referred to as the **location counter, LC**, keeps track of the count.

The count, or location of the first byte of each instruction, is recorded in the address column. The label, for each instruction that has one, is recorded in a **symbol table**, together with the address of the first byte of the instruction. See Fig. 5.4-1b. These labels are symbolic names used as addresses in various program instructions. For example, if the operand in a jump instruction is represented symbolically, then it appears as a label somewhere in the program. Operands other than addresses are also written symbolically, but values must be explicitly assigned to these. For example, COUNT, which is the value to be loaded into the register pair BC is a symbolic value—not an address. These symbolic names and their assigned values are also entered in the symbol table.

At the completion of the first pass through the assembly language program, all the symbolic labels and operands appear in the symbol table along with their assigned values. Thus, at the end of the first pass, the address column and symbol table are complete.

The second pass of the assembly process fills in the object code column. During this pass, each instruction is examined, and the instruction mnemonic is replaced by its machine code written in hexadecimal notation. If the instruction consists of more than a single byte, and the address or constant constituting the additional bytes is written symbolically, the symbol table is consulted to determine the hexadecimal code for the symbolic operand. At the end of the second pass, the assembly process is complete. See Fig. 5.4-1c. The operation code is found in the listing of machine codes for the various mnemonic instructions (see Appendix C). The resulting object code can be loaded into the microprocessor's memory and executed.[3]

To complete the manual assembly process, all instruction mnemonics and symbolic addresses and constants are replaced with their absolute values. Insertion or deletion of instructions requires program reassembly. Some modifications, such as changing the value of a constant, can be made in the object code without involving another assembly.

---

[3]Instruction mnemonics used in this book are those recognized by the Intel ASM80 assembler. Assemblers are available that use different mnemonics for the same instructions but generate identical object code.

ADDRESS	OBJECT CODE	LABEL	OPERATION	OPERAND(S)	COMMENT

(a) SOURCE

ADDRESS	OBJECT CODE	LABEL	OPERATION	OPERAND(S)	COMMENT
		DELAY:	LXI	B, COUNT	; INITIALIZE REGISTER PAIR BC
			OUT	1	; WITH A 16-BIT VALUE
		LOOP:	DCX	B	; DECREMENT REGISTER PAIR BC
			MOV	A, B	
			ORA	C	; SET FLAGS
			JZ	FIN	; COUNT = 0?
			JMP	LOOP	
		FIN:	OUT	0	

Symbol Table

DELAY	0000H
LOOP	0005H
FIN	000EH
COUNT	0100H

(b) PASS 1

ADDRESS	OBJECT CODE	LABEL	OPERATION	OPERAND(S)
0000H		DELAY:	LXI	B, COUNT
0003H			OUT	1
0005H		LOOP:	DCX	B
0006H			MOV	A, B
0007H			ORA	C
0008H			JZ	FIN
000BH			JMP	LOOP
000EH		FIN:	OUT	0

(c) PASS 2

ADDRESS	OBJECT CODE	LABEL	OPERATION	OPERAND(S)
0000H	010001H	DELAY:	LXI	B, COUNT
0003H	D301H		OUT	1
0005H	0BH	LOOP:	DCX	B
0006H	78H		MOV	A, B
0007H	B1H		ORA	C
0008H	CA0E00H		JZ	FIN
000BH	C30500H		JMP	LOOP
000EH	D300H	FIN:	OUT	0

Figure 5.4-1 Steps in assembly of a program: (a) source; (b) first pass; (c) second pass.

5.5 ASSEMBLER DIRECTIVES — PSEUDO INSTRUCTIONS

To assemble a program automatically, the assembler needs information in the form of *assembler directives* or *pseudo instructions* that control the assembly. Pseudo instructions are commands placed in the program by the designer that provide information to the assembler. They are not part of the instruction set of the microprocessor nor are they translated into executable code. Each assembler has its own unique pseudo instructions and corresponding mnemonics.

Although the mnemonics and details vary, most assemblers contain an essentially equivalent set of pseudo instructions, written in assembly language format. For example, the *origin*, ORG, pseudo instruction tells the assembler the location in memory for which the next instruction or data byte should be assembled. When different parts of a program are to be placed in different areas of memory, an ORG pseudo instruction is used before each part of the program to specify the starting location for assembly of that part of the program. The *origin* pseudo instruction has the following form, where expression evaluates to a 16-bit address:

ORG expression

If no origin pseudo instruction appears before the first instruction in the program, assembly will begin, by default, at memory location 0.

When an assembler scans the program to be assembled, it must know where the program ends. It cannot depend on a *halt* instruction for this because some programs don't contain a *halt* as the last instruction, and others don't contain a *halt* at all. An application program used, for example, in process monitoring or control might run continuously and therefore not contain a *halt* instruction. Thus, an *end assembly*, END, directive must be the last instruction to explicitly indicate the end of the program. This directive has the form:

END

The ORG and END assembler directives, in effect, frame the program to be assembled.

ORG 0000H
[Assembly Language Instructions
END

When there is more than one *origin* assembler directive, the assembly of each group of instructions starts at the location specified by the *origin* assembler directive that precedes it. For example

ORG 0000H

This block of instructions is assembled starting at location 0000H [Assembly Language Instructions

ORG 0100H

This block of instructions is assembled starting at location 0100H [Assembly Language Instructions

END

Symbolic names, which appear in assembly language programs as labels, instruction mnemonics, and operands, are translated to binary values by the assembler. As illustrated by the hand assembly of a program in Section 5.4, labels are assigned the current value of the assembler's location counter when encountered in the first pass of the assembly. Instruction mnemonics have predefined values that the assembler obtains from a table that is part of the assembler.

A symbolic operand can be a register name, an address, or a data constant. Register names have predefined values. All addresses correspond to labels in the program, and thus their values are defined. Data constants, on the other hand, are defined by the designer using an *equate* or *set* assembler directive. *Equate* assembler directives usually appear as a group at the beginning of a program and have the form:

name   EQU   expression

"Name" stands for the symbolic name. The assembler evaluates the expression and equates the symbolic name to it by placing the name in its symbol table along with the value of the expression. From that point on, wherever the name appears in the program, it is replaced by the value of the expression in the *equate* pseudo instruction. For example, the value of COUNT in Fig. 5.4-1 can be defined as follows:

COUNT   EQU   0100H

Note that the symbolic name is not followed by a colon and is not a label, even though it appears in the label field. The symbolic name in one equate assembler directive cannot be used in another, nor can it be used as the label of another instruction. That is, the name in an equate assembler directive cannot be redefined. If its value is changed, the equate assembler directive must be changed and the program reassembled.

There are a number of advantages in using symbolic data constants when writing a program. Obviously, just as with symbolic addresses, it makes reading the program easier; the designer chooses symbolic names that are meaningful to the application and thus more easily recognizable than their binary equivalents. The equate assembler directives that define the values of all symbolic data constants are typically grouped together at the beginning of the program. Thus, if it is necessary to change the value of a data constant, it can be done by simply changing the expression in a single equate assembler directive and reassembling the program. If, instead, the actual value of the data constant is used in the operand field, any change necessitates locating and correcting it throughout the entire program. A final advantage of using a symbolic data constant is that its value need not be known before assembly. It can be specified as an expression in the operand field of the equate directive and evaluated by the assembler.

A variation of the *equate* assembler directive is the *set* assembler directive, SET. This directive also assigns a value to the name associated with it; however, the same symbol can be redefined at various points in the program using SET. Thus, more than one SET instruction can have the same name. The SET assembler directive has the form:

name   SET   *expression*

Another pseudo instruction, the *define storage*, reserves or allocates read/write memory locations for storage of temporary data. The first of the locations allocated can be referred to by an optional symbolic label. The *define storage* instruction has the form:

opt. label: DS   *expression*

A number of bytes of memory equal to the value of the expression are reserved. However, no assumption can be made about the initial values of the data in these reserved locations. If a symbolic name is used with the DS pseudo instruction, it has the value of the address of the first reserved memory location. For example, to establish two 1-byte storage registers in R/W memory with the names TEMP1 and TEMP2, the instruction is written:

TEMP1:   DS   1
TEMP2:   DS   1

During the first pass, the assembler assigns the values of its location counter to TEMP1 and TEMP2, respectively, and thus, an address is associated with each label. Instructions in the program can read or write these locations, using memory reference instructions such as STA TEMP1 or LDA TEMP2.

A memory buffer is a collection of consecutive memory locations also used to store data temporarily. When a buffer is established using a DS pseudo instruction, the contents of the memory locations are undefined. For example, the following establishes a buffer consisting of 80 memory locations:

BUFF: DS   80

The address of the first location is BUFF. Such a buffer is usually written and read sequentially using register indirect addressing.

When a table of fixed data values is required, memory must also be allocated. However, unlike the *define storage* assembler directive, each memory location must have a defined data value that is assembled into it. The pseudo instruction for this is the *define byte*, DB, pseudo instruction:

opt. name: DB   list

"List" refers either to one or more arithmetic or logic expressions that evaluate to 8-bit data quantities or to strings of characters enclosed in quotes that the assembler replaces with their equivalent ASCII representations. Assembled bytes of data are stored in successive memory locations until the list is exhausted. The operands of the DS and DB pseudo instructions are defined before the instruction is encountered in the assembly process; forward references cannot be made for these operands.

A pseudo instruction similar to *define byte* is the *define word* instruction:

opt. name: DW   list

The difference between *define byte* and *define word* is that each expression in the *define word* list is evaluated to a 16-bit quantity and stored as 2 bytes. It is stored with the low order byte in the lower of the two memory locations and the high order byte in the next higher one. This is consistent with the convention for storing 16-bit quantities in 8085A systems.

The *conditional assembly* pseudo instruction allows certain assembly language instructions to be assembled, depending on the value of an expression. The instruction has the following form:

IF expression
[Assembly Language Statements
ENDIF

The assembler evaluates the expression: if it is 0, the assembly language statements between IF and ENDIF are ignored; if it is 1, these statements are assembled.

The *conditional assembly* pseudo instruction facilitates configuring a microprocessor system with optional features. Microprocessor hardware is structured in a modular manner so that the hardware for an optional feature is contained on a separate PC card and can simply be plugged into the basic system. To preclude main memory containing code to handle all optional features, whether included or not, a single program is written that handles all options. Software associated with the optional features is also modular; the conditional assembly pseudo instruction is used so certain subroutines are assembled only if required.

For the pseudo instructions presented, except EQU and SET, labels are optional. EQU and SET require names.

5.6 TWO-PASS ASSEMBLERS

Many assemblers are two-pass assemblers. On pass one, a symbol table is generated that defines the value of all symbols, labels, and symbols assigned values by pseudo instructions. Figure 5.6-1 is a simplified flowchart of the first pass of a two-pass assembler.

The assembler contains an *operation code table* that has an entry for each operation code in the instruction set. Each table entry contains an assembly language instruction mnemonic, its machine code equivalent, and a descriptor word. The descriptor word indicates the number of bytes in the instruction and the format of the data in the operand.

The assembler maintains a location counter, LC, in memory, which is initially set to 0. Each line of the program is scanned in turn. If the line has a label, that label is added to the symbol table along with the value of the location counter,

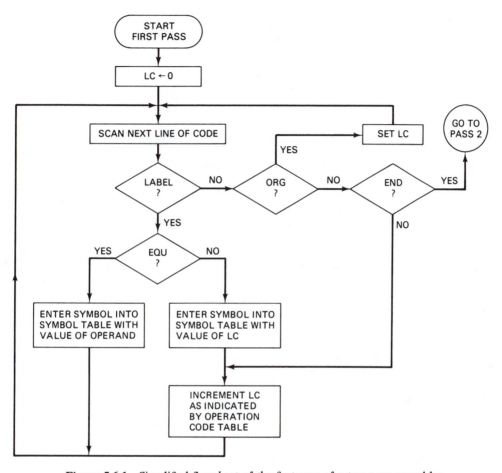

Figure 5.6-1 Simplified flowchart of the first pass of a two-pass assembler.

which defines its value. The operation code is extracted from the operation code table, and the location counter is incremented by the value specified for it in its descriptor word. In this way the location counter keeps track of the memory locations assigned to each instruction. If a program contains an *origin* pseudo instruction, the location counter is set to the value specified by the operand of the *origin* pseudo instruction. If an attempt is made to set the location counter to a value less than its present value, an error occurs. When the last line of the program is scanned, the *end of assembly* pseudo instruction is detected, and the first pass of the assembly is complete.

The second pass of a two-pass assembler scans the program again. Using the operation code table and the symbol table created in the first pass, it replaces all the symbols with their machine code equivalents and thus generates the binary object code. Figure 5.6-2 is a simplified flowchart for the second pass of an assembler. In addition to the object code, the assembler provides a program listing of both the

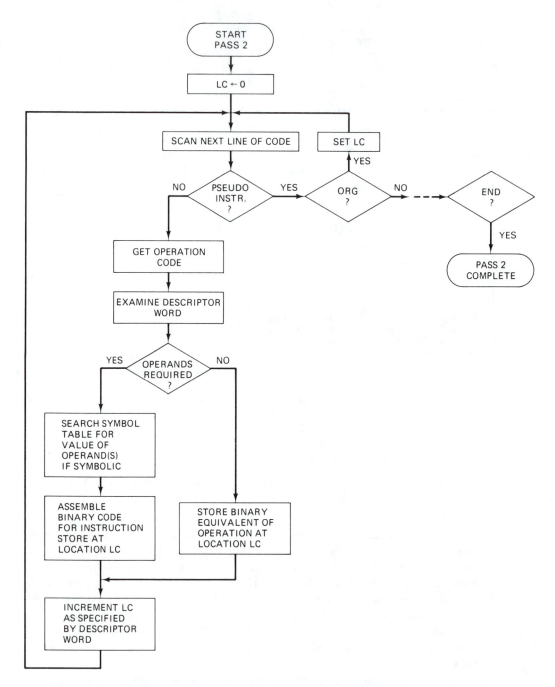

Figure 5.6-2 Simplified flowchart of the second pass of a two-pass assembler.

```
ASM80 :F1:LEVEL.ASM DEBUG MACROFILE MOD85


ISIS-II 8080/8085 MACRO ASSEMBLER, V4.0          MODULE   PAGE   1


 LOC  OBJ         LINE        SOURCE STATEMENT

 0000                1 ADCON    EQU 00H
 0000                2 DSPLY    EQU 00H
                     3
 0000                4          ORG 0000H
 0000 DB00           5 LOOP:    IN ADCON                 ;INPUT 4-BIT A/D RESULT
 0002 E60F           6          ANI 0FH                  ;MASK MS FOUR BITS
 0004 5F             7          MOV E,A                  ;COMPUTE 16-BIT OFFSET IN DE
 0005 1600           8          MVI D,0
 0007 211100         9          LXI H,TABLE              ;BASE ADDRESS OF TABLE IN HL
 000A 19            10          DAD D                    ;ADD OFFSET TO BASE
 000B 7E            11          MOV A,M                  ;GET TABLE ENTRY
 000C D300          12          OUT DSPLY                ;OUTPUT TO LEDS
 000E C30000        13          JMP LOOP                 ;REPEAT
                    14
 0011 00            15 TABLE:   DB 00H,01H,01H,03H,03H,07H,07H,0FH
 0012 01
 0013 01
 0014 03
 0015 03
 0016 07
 0017 07
 0018 0F
 0019 0F            16          DB 0FH,1FH,1FH,3FH,3FH,7FH,7FH,0FFH
 001A 1F
 001B 1F
 001C 3F
 001D 3F
 001E 7F
 001F 7F
 0020 FF
                    17
                    18          END


PUBLIC SYMBOLS


EXTERNAL SYMBOLS


USER SYMBOLS
ADCON  A 0000   DSPLY  A 0000   LOOP  A 0000   TABLE  A 0011


ASSEMBLY COMPLETE,   NO ERRORS


ISIS-II ASSEMBLER SYMBOL CROSS REFERENCE, V2.1          PAGE 1


ADCON     1#    5
DSPLY     2#   12
LOOP      5#   13
TABLE     9    15#
CROSS REFERENCE COMPLETE
```

Figure 5.6-3 List file for bar graph liquid level indicator program.

source and binary object code and a listing of all errors found in the source program.

Intel's ASM80 assembler is used on its development systems to assemble programs for 8085A and 8080A microprocessors [2]. The assembler can produce several files as output. One file, the list file, is a formatted file that can be printed. The list file contains the assembled object code, the source program, a table of symbols and their values, a summary of assembly errors, and a cross-reference table. The list file resulting from the assembly of the liquid level display program of Section 4.8.1 is shown in Fig. 5.6-3. Note that several assembler directives were added to the source program so that it could be assembled. Equate directives appear at the beginning of the program to assign actual port addresses to the symbolic addresses used later in the program. An *origin* directive specifies that the first byte of object code is to be placed in memory location 0000H. Define byte directives are used to set up the 16-byte table of bit patterns to be output to the display. Finally, the end directive is used to indicate the end of the source file. The source program in the listing file is simply an exact copy of the source program that was assembled.

For each assembly language instruction, the two leftmost columns in the listing provide the location and the object code bytes assembled starting in that location. The two leftmost columns serve the same purpose for assembler directives that directly generate object code. Only the define byte directive directly generates object code in this program. Values associated with directives that don't directly generate code are shown in the location column.

The symbol table is divided into categories: public symbols, external symbols, and user symbols. Public symbols and external symbols are associated with programs that consist of a number of modules that are assembled separately and, after assembly, are linked together into a single object file. This concept is appropriate for large programs and will be considered later. The user symbol table lists all of the symbols created by the writer of the program and their values. The letter A preceding a value indicates that the value is absolute, the final value to be used in the object code.

The cross-reference table lists all the user symbols and the lines in the program in which they are defined or referenced. The line number where a symbol is defined is followed by the pound sign (#). The cross-reference table is used as an aid in debugging program logic errors.

Figure 5.6-4 is a printout of the list file for the assembly of the maximum and minimum display program of Section 4.8.3. The necessary assembler directives have been added. Unlike the previous program, this program requires read/write memory for storage of the maximum and minimum values. Values for the *origin* directives assemble the program so that it can be executed on a system with ROM starting at location 0000H and RWM starting at location 2000H. The define storage directives following the second *origin* directive allocate 2 bytes of RWM to hold the values MAX and MIN.

Another file created by the assembler is the object code file. The object code file contains the instructions and data that can be loaded into memory for execution. The assembler is also able to include the symbol table in the object file so that debugging, simulation, or emulation can be done symbolically.

ISIS – II 8080 / 8085 MACRO ASSEMBLER, V4.0   MODULE   PAGE 1

```
LOC OBJ       LINE            SOURCE STATEMENT


0000          1 FLAG          EQU 0     ;PORT ADDRESSES
0001          2 DATA          EQU 1
0000          3 MAXOUT        EQU 0
0001          4 MINOUT        EQU 1
              5
0000          6               ORG 0000H
              7
0000 210020   8 START:        LXI H,MAX       ;HL POINTER TO MAX
0003 110120   9               LXI D,MIN       ;DE POINTER TO MIN
0006 DB00    10 WAIT1:        IN FLAG         ;CHECK FOR FIRST DATA BYTE
0008 B7      11               ORA A           ;SET CPU FLAGS
0009 F20600  12               JP WAIT1        ;WAIT IF BIT 7 = 0
000C DB01    13               IN DATA         ;INPUT DATA
000E 77      14               MOV M,A         ;MAX EQUALS FIRST DATA BYTE
000F EB      15               XCHG            ;SWITCH POINTERS
0010 77      16               MOV M,A         ;MIN EQUALS FIRST DATA BYTE
0011 D300    17               OUT MAXOUT      ;OUTPUT INITIAL MAXIMUM
0013 D301    18               OUT MINOUT      ;OUTPUT INITIAL MINOUT
0015 EB      19 NXDATA:       XCHG            ;SWITCH POINTER
0016 DB00    20 WAIT2:        IN FLAG         ;CHECK FOR NEXT DATA BYTE
0018 B7      21               ORA A           ;SET CPU FLAGS
0019 F21600  22               JP WAIT2        ;WAIT IF BIT 7 = 0
001C DB01    23               IN DATA         ;INPUT DATA
001E BE      24 MAX?:         CMP M           ;NEW DATA > MAX?
001F DA2800  25               JC MIN?         ;NO, TEST FOR MIN
0022 77      26               MOV M,A         ;YES, SAVE NEW MAX
0023 D300    27               OUT MAXOUT      ;OUTPUT NEW MAXIMUM
0025 C31600  28               JMP WAIT2       ;GET NEXT DATA BYTE
0028 EB      29 MIN?:         XCHG            ;SWITCH POINTERS
0029 BE      30               CMP M           ;NEW DATA LESS THAN MIN?
002A D21500  31               JNC NXDATA      ;NO, GET NEXT DATA BYTE
002D 77      32               MOV M,A         ;YES, SAVE NEW MIN
002E D301    33               OUT MINOUT      ;OUTPUT NEW MINIMUM
0030 C31500  34               JMP NXDATA      ;GET NEXT DATA BYTE
             35
2000         36               ORG 2000H
2000         37 MAX:          DS 1            ;RESERVED LOCATION FOR CURRENT MAXIMUM
2001         38 MIN:          DS 1            ;RESERVED LOCATION FOR CURRENT MINIMUM
             39
             40               END
```

PUBLIC SYMBOLS

EXTERNAL SYMBOLS


```
USER SYMBOLS
DATA   A 0001   FLAG   A 0000   MAX    A 2000   MAX?   A 001E   MAXOUT A 0000   MIN
A 2001   MIN?  A 0028
MINOUT A 0001   NXDATA A 0015   START  A 0000   WAIT1 A 0006   WAIT2  A 0016
```

Figure 5.6-4   List file for maximum and minimum display program.

```
ASSEMBLY COMPLETE, NO ERRORS


ISIS - II ASSEMBLER SYMBOL CROSS REFERENCE, V2.1              PAGE 1
DATA        2#     13     21
FLAG        1#     10     18
MAX         8      35#
MAX?        22#
MAXOUT      3#     25
MIN         9      36#
MIN?        23     27#
MINOUT      4#     31
NXDATA      17#    29     32
START       8#
WAIT1       10#    12
WAIT2       18#    20     26


CROSS REFERENCE COMPLETE
```

Figure 5.6-4   Continued.

When object code is transferred from one system to another, such as from a development system to a PROM programmer, it is frequently transferred as ASCII characters. The machine language object code is converted to ASCII for this purpose. The format used by Intel is the Intel HEX-ASCII format. In HEX-ASCII format, each byte of data is divided into two hex digits. Each hex digit is then converted to ASCII. The object code is formatted as a number of data records and an end-of-file record. Every byte in these records is an ASCII character. Figure 5.6-5 shows the format. Each data record begins with a nine-character prefix and ends with a two-character suffix. The prefix starts with a colon. The next two ASCII characters, BC, represent the number of data bytes in the record. Each data record can contain from 1 to 16 data bytes. The next four characters, AAAA, are the

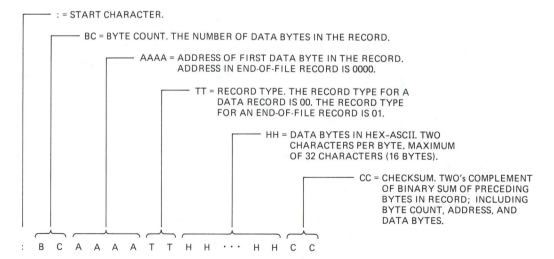

Figure 5.6-5   Intel HEX-ASCII format. Characters represent hexadecimal numbers encoded in ASCII.

```
:10000000DB00E60F5F1600211100197ED300C3004C
:10001000000000101030307070F0F1F1F3F3F7F7FF2
:01002000FFE0
:00000001FF
```

Figure 5.6-6 Intel HEX-ASCII object code file for the program of Fig.
5.6-3.

hexadecimal address of the first data byte in the record. The next two characters,
TT, are the record type and have the value 00. This completes the nine-character
prefix. The next characters, a maximum of 32, are the data bytes in HEX-ASCII.
The record is terminated with a two-character HEX-ASCII checksum, CC. The
checksum is the two's complement of the sum of all the preceding bytes in the
record. This sum includes the byte count, address, record type, and data bytes.

The end-of-file record has a byte count equal to 00H, an address equal to
0000H, and a record type of 01H.

The Intel HEX-ASCII form of the object code file for the program in Fig.
5.6-3 is shown in Fig. 5.6-6. A utility program, OBJHEX, is available on Intel
development systems to create this file from the object file.

5.7 MACROS

The ASM80 assembler introduced in the previous section is a *macro assembler*; it
has the capability to process macro instructions. A *macro instruction* is a single
instruction that the macro assembler replaces with a group of instructions wherever
it appears in an assembly language program. The macro instruction and the
instructions that replace it are defined by the system designer only once in the
program. Macros are useful when a small group of instructions must be repeated
several times in a program, with only minor or no changes in each repetition.

The use of a macro in assembly language programming entails three steps:

1. The macro definition
2. The macro reference
3. The macro expansion

The *macro definition* defines the group of instructions equivalent to the macro
instruction. A *macro reference* is the use of the macro instruction as an instruction
in the program. A *macro expansion* is the replacement of the macro instruction by
the group of instructions defined to be its equivalent.

The first two steps are carried out by the system designer and the third by the
macro assembler.

The macro definition has the following format:

Label	*Code*	*Operand*
name	MACRO	list
	[macro body	
	ENDM	

"Name" stands for the name of the macro that appears in the label field of the macro definition. A list of dummy parameters may be specified, and, if so, these parameters also appear in the macro body. The macro body is the sequence of assembly language instructions that replace the macro reference in the program when assembled. The macro definition produces no object code; it simply indicates to the assembler what instructions are represented by the macro name.

Consider the use of a macro in a program involving a large amount of indirect addressing. An indirect addressing input capability (see Section 4.2.3) is provided by the two instructions:

```
LHLD addr
MOV r, M
```

This sequence can also be written as a macro named LDIND, with a macro definition of

```
LDIND   MACRO REG,ADDR
        LHLD ADDR
        MOV REG,M
        ENDM
```

To have the macro body appear at any given point in the program requires a macro reference. Its format is identical to that of an assembly language instruction:

Label	Code	Operand
optional label	name	parameter list

"Name" is the label by which the macro is referenced.

The following macro instructions load register C indirectly through the address PTR

```
LDIND C, PTR
```

and load register E indirectly through the address ENTRY

```
LDIND E, ENTRY
```

When a program containing macros is input to a macro assembler, the assembler carries out a text substitution, the macro expansion; substituting for each macro reference the macro body specified in the macro definition. And for each dummy parameter in the macro body, the appropriate parameter from the parameter list of the macro reference is substituted. Therefore, when the macro assembler encounters the macro instruction

```
LDIND C, PTR
```

it replaces it with the instructions

```
LHLD PTR
MOV C, M
```

The following macro rotates the contents of the accumulator to the left through the carry, N times. This is done with a loop that is terminated when a register is counted down to zero. The number of rotations, N, and the register to be used as the counter are parameters in the macro definition:

```
RALN    MACRO N, REG
        MVI REG, N
LOOP:   RAL
        DCR REG
        JNZ LOOP
        ENDM
```

If this macro appears in a program, which references it twice, a problem results. When the macro is expanded, the label LOOP will appear twice in the program listing, resulting in a multiply defined symbol error when the program is assembled.

```
ASM80  :F1:MACRO1.ASM DEBUG MACROFILE MOD85



     ISIS-II 8080/8085 MACRO ASSEMBLER, V4.0        MODULE    PAGE   1



     LOC OBJ        LINE            SOURCE STATEMENT
                       1RALN        MACRO N,REG
                       2            LOCAL LOOP
                       3            MVI REG,N
                       4 LOOP:      RAL
                       5            DCR REG
                       6            JNZ LOOP
                       7            ENDM
                       8
     0000 DB00          9           IN 0
                       10           RALN 2,C
     0002 0E02         11 +         MVI C,2
     0004 17           12 +??0001:  RAL
     0005 0D           13 +         DCR C
     0006 C20400       14 +         JNZ ??0001
     0009 D300         15           OUT 0
     000B DB01         16           IN 1
                       17           RALN 3,C
     000D 0E03         18 +         MVI C,3
     000F 17           19 +??0002:  RAL
     0010 0D           20 +         DCR C
     0011 C20F00       21 +         JNZ ??0002
     0014 D301         22           OUT 1
     0016 76           23           HLT
                       24           END



     PUBLIC SYMBOLS



     EXTERNAL SYMBOLS



     USER SYMBOLS
     RALN   +0000
     ASSEMBLY COMPLETE,    NO ERRORS
```

Figure 5.7-1 List file of a program referencing the RALN macro twice.

This problem is avoided by use of the LOCAL directive, which is placed in the macro definition. The LOCAL directive has the form

Label	*Code*	*Operand*
—	LOCAL	label names

The specified label names are defined to have meaning only within the current macro expansion. Each time the macro is referenced and expanded, the assembler assigns each local symbol a unique symbol in the form ??nnnn. The assembler assigns ??0001 to the first symbol, ??0002 to the second, and so on. The most recent symbol name generated always indicates the total number of symbols created for all macro expansions. These symbols are never duplicated by the assembler.

Figure 5.7-1 is the list file for a program that references the RALN macro twice. The RALN macro has been modified to include a LOCAL directive to define LOOP as a local variable. As a result, the program assembles without error.

5.8 SOFTWARE DEVELOPMENT ENVIRONMENTS

The type and power of software development aids available to the designer depend on the hardware host used for software development. These hosts can be categorized as

1. Large computers
2. Dedicated development systems
3. Personal computers
4. Evaluation kits

Used alone, each of these hosts has advantages and disadvantages with respect to cost and performance. In addition, software and hardware are available to link a host from one category to a host from another category, to provide a desired total software development environment. The first three categories are represented in Fig. 5.8-1.

Large computers include mainframes and large minicomputers. When using such systems, the designer is typically one of many users served by the system on a time-shared basis. However, the designer is usually not aware of the time-shared nature of the system's operation. The designer interacts with the computer system through a CRT terminal that is often remote from the computer. In some cases the CRT terminal is connected to the large computer by telephone lines via a modem.

Dedicated development systems are designed and optimized specifically for the development and testing of microprocessor software. They provide the most complete form of support for microprocessor software development. Development systems are provided by microprocessor manufacturers for their specific microprocessors and by instrument manufacturers for microprocessors from a variety of sources. These systems are completely self-contained for standalone operation. They can also be linked to large computers to serve as high performance work stations in a development network.

Figure 5.8-1   Various hardware hosts for microprocessor software development. (Courtesy of Intel Corp.)

Personal computers are increasingly used for microprocessor software development as the available cross software and add-on hardware designed for microprocessor software development increases.

Evaluation kits are typically single board microcomputers with very limited power. They are provided by the microprocessor manufacturers primarily for evaluation of a specific microprocessor. As shown in Fig. 5.8-2, operator interaction with the system is usually via a keypad and seven-segment display. Optionally, a CRT terminal may be used. Software support is limited to a monitor program in ROM. Application program object code is entered into the system in binary form. If an assembler is not available, the object code is obtained by hand assembly. Evaluation kits are appropriate only for very limited software development.

Large computers and personal computers usually have several line and screen editor programs available. The computer manufacturer provides at least a line editor or a screen editor. Depending on the popularity of the computer and its operating system, many more screen editors and word processors may be available from independent software houses. Dedicated development systems usually provided a single screen editor. Since most dedicated development systems use a proprietary operating system, editors and word processors from independent software houses are rarely available. Most evaluation kits don't provide any editing capability.

Cross assemblers, which run on large computers and personal computers, are available for most microprocessors. They are provided by independent software

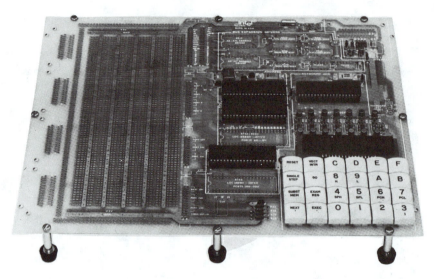

Figure 5.8-2 SDK-85 single-board microcomputer system. (Courtesy of Intel Corp.)

vendors and by microprocessor manufacturers. Dedicated development systems provide assemblers for the microprocessors supported by the system. Most assemblers for a given microprocessor use the same instruction mnemonics and same assembler directives used in the assembler provided by the microprocessor manufacturer. Assemblers similar to the ASM80 assembler for the Intel development system are available for personal computers and large computers. Evaluation kits usually have no assembler capability or at most a primitive line assembler. However, many evaluation kit monitors have routines that will load object code output from an assembler run on a computer or development system.

Relocatable assemblers allow large programs to be assembled in parts or modules. These modules exist as separate files that are functionally coherent pieces of the total program, such as subroutines (which will be introduced in the next chapter). Each module can be written, assembled, and tested individually. The modules are then linked together by a linker program to form the final object code. An advantage of a relocatable assembler is that when a change in a single module is required only that module must be reassembled, not the entire program. The modified module is then linked with the other modules. Linking a group of modules is a much faster operation than reassembling an equivalent program that exists as a single file. ASM80 is a relocatable assembler [3]. Some personal computer versions of the ASM80 assembler provide a relocatable object output file format that is identical to that of the ASM80. This allows modules developed on a personal computer to be linked to modules developed on a dedicated development system.

High level language compilers are provided by microprocessor manufacturers and independent software houses. To use a specific high level language, a compiler must be available that compiles the high level language and produces object code for the specific microprocessor. In addition, the compiler must be able to run under the host's operating system. Compilers are available that produce object code output files with the same format as an assembler for the target microprocessor. This allows object code modules that result from compiling a high level language to be linked with object modules from assembly language programs.

As discussed, there are a number of ways of obtaining object code for an application, ranging from hand assembly for very simple programs to automatic translation of a source file in either assembly or a high level language.

5.9 SOFTWARE TESTING

Obtaining assembler output with no program errors simply means that the assembler has detected no errors in syntax. It is not an indication that the program does what the designer intends it to do. A testing method is required that allows logical errors in the program to be detected. Attempting to test software, for the first time, after it has been placed in EPROM in the microprocessor system prototype is not appropriate. If the system prototype appeared to operate properly, it would be difficult to subject it to a large enough set of test conditions to be sure that it operates properly. For some systems it is impossible to test the system during development using the actual I/O devices the system will ultimately be connected to. In addition, if the prototype system fails, there may be no clue as to the source of failure. This is particularly true for systems that do not have output displays. For large programs it is also desirable to be able to test portions of the program as they are developed.

What is required is the ability to execute the program in a controlled manner and to be able to observe the software and the system's operation in a step-by-step fashion. To be useful, the contents of the system's registers must be observable as the program operation is sequenced.

A minimum capability for testing is represented by the SDK-85 single board computer shown in Fig. 5.8-2. The SDK-85 is controlled by a monitor program that provides commands that allow an application program's object code to be loaded into the SDK-85 and executed in a controlled manner [4]. The SDK-85's system bus is brought out to connectors on its printed circuit board. This allows input and output devices to be interfaced to the SDK-85 to provide a system prototype.

The SDK-85 is operated using its keyboard and display or a CRT terminal. The keyboard commands are listed in Table 5.9-1. The SDK-85 can be thought of as always operating in one of two modes. In the command mode it accepts commands from the keyboard. In the execution mode it executes the application program. When the system is RESET the monitor is automatically executed and the SDK-85 is in the command mode. Using the SUBST MEM command, the designer can load the application program's object code in hexadecimal. After the program is loaded it can be executed using the GO command. To return to the command mode, the user presses the RESET key.

The application program's operation can be observed using the SINGLE STEP command. In the single step mode, each time the NEXT key is pressed, one

TABLE 5.9-1   SDK-85 COMMAND SEQUENCES

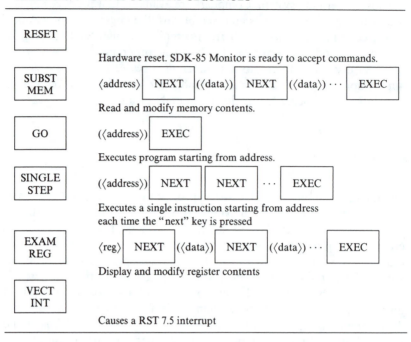

RESET

Hardware reset. SDK-85 Monitor is ready to accept commands.

SUBST MEM   ⟨address⟩ NEXT ⟨⟨data⟩⟩ NEXT ⟨⟨data⟩⟩ ⋯ EXEC

Read and modify memory contents.

GO   ⟨⟨address⟩⟩ EXEC

Executes program starting from address.

SINGLE STEP   ⟨⟨address⟩⟩ NEXT NEXT ⋯ EXEC

Executes a single instruction starting from address
each time the "next" key is pressed

EXAM REG   ⟨reg⟩ NEXT ⟨⟨data⟩⟩ NEXT ⟨⟨data⟩⟩ ⋯ EXEC

Display and modify register contents

VECT INT

Causes a RST 7.5 interrupt

instruction in the application program is executed and control is then returned to
the monitor. The EXEC key terminates the command. The EXAM REG command
can then be used to examine, and if desired modify, any of the microprocessor's
registers. The SUBST MEM command is used to examine, or if desired modify, the
contents of any memory location. These commands allow program execution to be
monitored and the program to be modified in order to detect and correct errors.

It is often desirable to examine register contents at a certain point in a
program or to start single stepping a program from a particular point. To stop a
program's execution at a certain point, without having to single step to that point,
a breakpoint is required. A *breakpoint* can stop the execution of a program at a
specified instruction and turn control over to the monitor. With the SDK-85, a
breakpoint is implemented by replacing the first byte of the instruction, where the
breakpoint is to be placed, with a RST 1 instruction. The program can then be
executed from its beginning using the GO command. When the RESTART instruction is executed, control will be returned to the monitor. All the microprocessor's
registers and user memory contents are preserved by the monitor in the state they
were in at the time of execution of the RST 1 instruction. Registers and memory can
be examined and modified as desired. To continue execution, the RST 1 instruction
is replaced with the OP code of the instruction it originally replaced. Execution is
continued with the GO or SINGLE STEP command. The address that appears on
the display when either of these commands is used is the value of the microprocessor's program counter. This is the location from which these commands will
start execution and must be manually decremented by one to start execution at the
instruction's OP code.

For learning about a microprocessor or testing very simple systems, evaluation kits are adequate. However, for more complex systems this method of testing is tedious and slow.

Simulators are available to test microprocessor programs on large computer systems and personal computers. A simulator is a program, run on the large computer or personal computer, which accepts the object code and symbol table output of a cross assembler as input. Under direction of user-supplied commands, the simulator provides a software simulation of the microprocessor's execution of the object code. The simulator uses memory locations in the computer to simulate the microprocessor's internal registers, memory, and I/O ports. It simulates execution of the object code, modifying the simulated microprocessor's internal registers, memory, and I/O exactly as they would be modified if the microprocessor itself were executing the code. The simulation is, of course, not real time. Simulators are written in high level languages and many instructions in the high level language are executed to simulate the execution of one instruction in the microprocessor's program.

A subset of the commands for an 8085A simulator is given in Table 5.9-2. A simulator provides for greater control over the execution of the application program than does a monitor. For example, the breakpoint command, SET BREAK, in Table 5.9-2 allows a variety of breakpoint types to be set. An EXEC breakpoint causes execution to be stopped if the program makes an attempt to execute the contents of a specified location. An ALTER breakpoint stops program execution if an attempt is made to alter the contents of a specified memory location. Finally, a reference breakpoint causes the program to be stopped if any reference, other than execution, is made to the location. The SET BREAK command also allows an address range to be specified over which a breakpoint will apply.

The display commands allow a memory location or range of memory locations (using DISPLAY MEM) or any of the microprocessor's registers (using DISPLAY

TABLE 5.9-2   SIMULATOR COMMAND SUMMARY SUBSET

LOAD [object file]
DISPLAY SYMBOL [symbol name]
MAP MEMORY [address range] = [memory or I / O type]
MAP IO [port range] = [I / O type]
MAP CLOCK [time designator]
SET REGISTER [register designator] = [value]
DISPLAY REGISTER [register designator]
SET TIME [time designator]
DISPLAY TIME
RESET
SET MEMORY [address range] = [value list]
DISPLAY MEMORY [address range]
SET BREAK [break type] AT [address range]
REMOVE BREAK [break type] FROM [address range]
TRACE [address range]
REMOVE TRACE [address range]
DISPLAY LAST [number]
GO [number]

REG) to be displayed. The trace feature, TRACE, can be turned on to cause the instruction and the contents of all the microprocessor's registers to be listed each time an instruction is executed. The DISPLAY LAST command allows the designer to view the execution of the program after it has run. This feature is particularly helpful in determining the program execution that lead to the occurrence of a particular event. For example, if the value of a reserved memory location is being modified when it should not be, an ALTER breakpoint can be set that will occur only when that memory location is written. The program is then executed, and when the breakpoint occurs the DISPLAY LAST command is used to see which instruction or instruction sequence caused the memory location to be written.

During the simulation of the program, if data is output to a port, the port is identified and the value output is displayed. When input is required from a port, the simulator identifies the port and requests the input value from the designer. Input

```
@SB*8085.SIMULATE
SB = 85 SIMULATOR            REV 1.2         5 / 19 / 81
    MAP MEMORY 0000H to 0020H = ROM
    MAP OK
    LOAD
    LOAD OK
    MAP IO ADCON = INPUT
    MAP OK
    MAP IO DSPLY = OUTPUT
    MAP OK
    TRACE 0000H to 000EH
    TRACE OK
    SET BREAK EXEC AT LOOP
    SET OK
    GO 100
    BREAKPOINT: EXECUTE AT 0000H (ADCON + 0000H)
    GO 100
    DATA REQUESTED ON PORT ADCON
    05H

CY   V   P  AC  X5   Z   S   A    B    C    D    E    H    L    PC     SP
 0   0   0   0    0   0   0   00H  00H  00H  00H  00H  00H  00H  0000H  0000H

 0000H    IN       00H
 0   0   0   0    0   0   0  *05H 00H  00H  00H  00H  00H  00H*0002H  0000H
 0002H    ANI      0FH
 0   0  *1   0    0   0   0   05H  00H  00H  00H  00H  00H  00H*0004H  0000H
 0004H    MOV EA
 0   0   1   0    0   0   0   05H  00H  00H  00H*05H 00H  00H*0005H  0000H
 0005H    MVI D    00H
 0   0   1   0    0   0   0   05H  00H  00H  00H  05H  00H  00H*0007H  0000H
 0007H    LXI H    0011H
 0   0   1   0    0   0   0   05H  00H  00H  00H  05H  00H*11H*000AH  0000H
 000AH    DAD D
 0   0   1   0    0   0   0   05H  00H  00H  00H  05H  00H*16H*000BH  0000H
 000BH    MOV AM
 0   0   1   0    0   0   0  *07H 00H  00H  00H  05H  00H  16H*000CH  0000H

    PORT DSPLY = 7H
 000CH    OUT      00H
 0   0   1   0    0   0   0   07H  00H  00H  00H  05H  00H  16H*000EH  0000H
 000EH    JMP      0000H
 0   0   1   0    0   0   0   07H  00H  00H  00H  05H  00H  16H*0000H  0000H

    BREAKPOINT: EXECUTE AT 0000H (ADCON + 0000H)
    SIMULATION TERMINATED
```

Figure 5.9-1 Simulation of liquid level program of Fig. 5.6-3.

values are provided by the designer to achieve a particular test objective. This aspect of a simulator can be a drawback if the input device is complex and its responses difficult to determine.

A simulation of the liquid level program of Fig. 5.6-3 is shown in Fig. 5.9-1. Before the program's object code can be loaded, the memory into which it will be loaded must be mapped. Mapping indicates to the simulator the existence of the desired memory in the system to be simulated. Initially, all the memory available in the simulator is mapped as protected or nonexistent. The memory locations where the program is to be loaded are mapped as being ROM. Once mapped as ROM, any attempt to write these locations by the program when it executes will cause the automatic occurrence of a breakpoint. The program's object code and symbol table are then loaded. Input and output ports must be mapped also. Mapping an input port causes a request for input data from the designer when an IN instruction for the port is executed. Mapping an output port causes the data which the program outputs to the port to be displayed. Once the symbol table has been loaded, all references to ports or memory locations can be done symbolically. The trace feature is enabled over the entire program address range. An execution breakpoint is set at the beginning of the program.

Program execution is begun by the GO command. An execution breakpoint immediately occurs. The GO command is repeated and a request for data for port ADCON occurs. The data value input in response to this request is 05H. For each instruction's execution there are two lines in the trace. The first line gives the address of the instruction and the instruction. The next line gives the contents of the microprocessor's registers after the instruction's execution. If the contents of a register are modified by the instruction's execution, an asterisk appears in front of the register's contents. When the out instruction is executed, the data output to the port DSPLY is displayed. When the jump instruction is executed, control is transferred to the beginning of the program and execution breakpoint occurs again. At this point the simulation is terminated.

Dedicated microprocessor development systems were the first to provide a complete test environment adequate for real-time testing of a microprocessor system prototype. This is accomplished with an in-circuit emulator. In-circuit emulation allows software, which is being developed, to be executed on the actual system prototype under control of the designer. In-circuit emulators provide an extensive set of debugging commands, including commands similar to those available with simulators.

An *in-circuit emulator* is a development system option that includes hardware and software for emulation of a specific microprocessor. For example, the Intel Series IV development system has in-circuit emulator options available for all the various Intel microprocessors, including the 8085A [5]. With in-circuit emulation the microprocessor in the prototype is removed from its socket and a connector from the in-circuit emulator is plugged into the socket (see Fig. 5.9-2). The object code is loaded into the development system and executed under control of in-circuit emulator commands. However, the execution of the program is not simulated; the program is actually executed on a microprocessor of the same type used in the prototype but that is part of the in-circuit emulator. Input and output devices in the prototype can actually be used for input and output. As development of the

Figure 5.9-2 Series IV development system with ICE 85b in-circuit emulator for 8085A microprocessor. (Courtesy of Intel Corp.)

system progresses, the application program can be placed in ROM in the prototype and executed, in real time, under control of the development system.

One feature of in-circuit emulation that speeds the software and hardware development cycle is its ability to substitute the development system's resources for the prototype's. At the very beginning, software development can begin without a prototype. Read/write memory in the development system is used in place of the ROM and RWM of the prototype. Development system I/O replaces prototype I/O. At this stage the in-circuit emulator is similar to a simulator. As the prototype is constructed, hardware in the prototype replaces the resources in the development system that simulated them. For example, once the prototype's read/write memory has been interfaced to the prototype's system bus, it can be used in place of the read/write memory in the development system that simulated it. This is accomplished with the in-circuit emulator's MAP command, which allows memory or I/O ports in the system being developed to be specified as existing in the development system or in the prototype for the purpose of software execution. This allows the simultaneous integration of software with prototype hardware throughout the system's development cycle. All the debug capabilities of the in-circuit emulator are also available to locate hardware problems in the prototype.

In-circuit emulators are also available for large computers and personal computers. These consist of separate instruments that communicate with the computer via a serial communications link. Object code is downloaded from the computer to the in-circuit emulator. Capabilities on these systems are often more limited than those provided by dedicated microprocessor development system in-circuit emulators.

REFERENCES

1. *Intel 8080/8085 Assembly Language Programming Manual* (Santa Clara, Calif.: Intel Corporation, 1979).
2. *ISIS-II 8080/8085 Macro Assembler Operator's Manual* (Santa Clara, Calif.: Intel Corporation, 1980).
3. *MCS 80/85 Relocatable Object Module Formats* (Santa Clara, Calif.: Intel Corporation, 1981).
4. *SDK-85 System Design Kit User's Manual* (Santa Clara, Calif.: Intel Corporation, 1978).
5. *ICE-85b In-Circuit Emulator Operating Instructions for ISIS-II Users* (Santa Clara, Calif.: Intel Corporation, 1981).

PROBLEMS

5-1. Describe the effect or purpose of each of the following assembler directives. For each corresponding example, list the entries generated in the symbol table and the code generated in the object code. Write all code in hexadecimal.

	Assume value of assembler location counter is
(a) TTY EQU 27Q	LC = 0H
(b) BLOCK: DS 16D	LC = 0200H
(c) CON: DB 11B, 10Q, 8, 'A'	LC = 02FFH
(d) ADDR: DW 1024, 0FA4H	LC = 4000H

5-2. Hand-assemble the following program assuming a starting address of 0000H. List each symbol in a symbol table with its associated value. The port addresses are

```
PORT 0 = 00H
PORT 1 = 01H
Location BUFF is at 1000H
```

Assuming the program is to be moved in memory so that it starts at location 0400H, which instruction's object code, if any, would have to be modified. Indicate the new values for any changes in the object code and symbol table.

```
            MVI C, 0
            LXI H, BUFF
LABEL1:     IN PORT 0
            CMP M
            JZ LABEL2
            INX H
            DCR C
            JNZ LABEL1
LABEL2:     MOV A,L
            OUT PORT 0
            MOV A,H
            OUT PORT 1
            HLT
```

5-3. Write all the required assembler directives to assemble the program in Problem 5.2. The starting location of the program is 0400H. The address for BUFF is 0800H. Briefly describe what the program does and write an appropriate set of comments for the program.

5-4. Assemble the following program by hand and create a symbol table for it.

```
TTY       EQU   10Q
          ORG   1024D
LINE:     LXI   H,BUFF
LOOP:     IN    TTY
          MOV   M,A
          INX   H
          CPI   0DH
          JNZ   LOOP
          HLT
          ORG   600H
BUFF:     DS    01010000B
          END
```

5-5. Assemble the following program by hand. Give the object code and addresses in hexadecimal. List the entries in the symbol table and their values.

```
          ORG 100H
SLEN:     LXI H, STRNG −1    ;set pointer to byte before string
          MVI C, OFFH        ;set byte counter = −1
          MVI A, 0DH         ;load A with CR
SRCH:     INX H              ;scan string
          INR C
          CMP M
          JNZ  SRCH
          MOV A, C           ;store string length
          STA LNGTH
          HLT
          ORG 400H
LNGTH:    DS 1
STRNG:    DS 80
          END
```

5-6. Hand-assemble the following program. List all entries in the symbol table.

```
X         EQU 0
Y         EQU 0
DJNZ      MACRO R,ADDR
          DCR R
          JNZ ADDR
          ENDM
          MVI B,X
L1:       MVI C,Y
L2:       NOP
          DJNZ C,L2
          DJNZ B,L1
          HLT
          END
```

5-7. Hand-assemble the following program. Provide the starting address of each instruction in memory and its object code. List each symbol table entry and its value.

```
PORTA       EQU 80H
PORTB       EQU 81H
            ORG 2000H
START:      XRA A
            LXI H, RSRV1
            MOV M,A
            LXI H, RSRV2
            MOV M,A
            MVI C, 100
LOOP:       IN PORTA
            ORA A
            JP LOOP
            IN PORTB
            RAR
            JC LABEL2
LABEL1:     LXI H, RSRV2
            JMP LABEL3
LABEL2:     LXI H, RSRV1
LABEL3:     INR M
            DCR C
            JNZ LOOP
            HLT
RSRV1:      DS 1
RSRV 2:     DS 1
            END
```

5-8. Briefly describe what the program in Problem 5-7 does. Also write a set of comments for the program to indicate how it accomplishes its task.

5-9. Write a routine that implements a code conversion. The input code must be read from an input port, INCDE, and the equivalent output code is written to an output port, OTCDE. Both the input and output codes are 8 bits in length. The input and output ports are not memory mapped.

Since there is no simple mathematical or logical relationship between the input and output codes, the conversion process is to be accomplished by a table lookup. The table, CDEWD, consists of a listing of each input code followed by its corresponding output code. How would the assembler be instructed to generate the object code for the table?

5-10. Using as few instructions as possible, write a macro, SWAP, that exchanges the most significant and least significant 4 bits of the accumulator. If other registers in the microprocessor are required to implement the macro, specify them as parameters in the macro definition. Show the complete macro definition, an example of a reference to the macro, and the macro's expansion.

5-11. Write a macro definition and a sample expansion for each of the following macros.
   (a) Macro CLC clears the carry flag;
   No other registers or flags are affected.
   (b) Macro ANIP computes the logic AND of the data from an input port and a mask. The address of the input port and the mask pattern are specified in the macro instruction. The result is left in the accumulator; no other registers are altered except the flag register.

(c) Macro DJNZ decrements a register specified in the instruction and jumps to an address, also specified in the instruction, if the register is not zero after being decremented.

5-12. Write a macro, SWAP Q,R, that exchanges (Q $\leftrightarrow$ R), the contents of any two of the six general purpose registers B, C, D, E, H, and L. Macro execution should not alter any of the general purpose registers other than the two being swapped. In addition, write the macro expansion for the following two references:

(a) SWAP B, C

(b) SWAP E, L

5-13. Write a macro, JGE, that transfers program control to a specified address, ADDR, if the contents of the accumulator are greater than or equal to the contents of register R. Interpret register contents as unsigned binary numbers. Write the macro in such a way that if the contents of the accumulator are less than R, the instruction that follows the macro reference is executed. Thus the macro implements a conditional jump. The macro should leave all internal registers unaltered with the possible exception of the flag register and PC. In addition to the macro definition, give an example of a reference to it, and give the macro expansion that causes a jump to location STOP if the contents of the accumulator are greater than or equal to the contents of register L.

5-14. Write a macro, FILL, that fills a block of memory with a constant. The length of the memory block can be up to 64 K long. The starting address, length, and constant are specified by the macro reference.

5-15. Write a macro, PEDGE, that loops until a 0 to 1 transition is detected on a single bit of an input port. The macro is parameterized to allow the port address and the bit to be tested to be specified. The bit to be tested is specified by a mask byte that is all 0s except for the desired bit. Write a macro reference that checks bit 3 of a port with address 27H. Write the sequence of instructions that comprise the expansion of this macro reference. If this macro was referenced more than once in a program, how would the assembler avoid the problem of a multiply defined label?

5-16. Write a macro, RHLR, that rotates the contents of the carry, CY, and registers H and L 1 bit to the right. Thus the macro treats CY, H, and L as a 17-bit register with the CY as the most significant bit, H as the next most significant 8 bits, and L as the least significant 8 bits. The macro should use as few instructions as possible.

5-17. A macro, EQLTY, compares the contents of register A and another register r and computes a result that is stored in A. The result is a 1 in each bit position where the bits of the operands A and r are equal and is 0 otherwise.

$$A_i \leftarrow A_i r_i + \overline{A}_i \overline{r}_i$$

Write the macro definition. Write a reference and expansion of the macro for the case where r = B.

5-18. Write the macro definitions for two macros, CLR and STT, that allow a specified bit in a specified memory location to be cleared or set, respectively. Bits in the memory location of interest other than the specified bit are not to be altered. The macro should take advantage of the existence of eight equates of the following form:

```
B0   EQU   00000001B
B1   EQU   00000010B
        ⋮
B7   EQU   10000000B
```

Show a macro reference and expansion that sets bit 3 of the memory location CTRLI.

6

The Stack and Subroutines

The best place to start is at the top — with the entire software requirement. Working from the top down, just as in many hardware designs, the engineer breaks up the overall requirement into major system blocks and further subdivides these into functional modules — in other words, software subroutines. The next step is to define exactly how these modules interface with one another (in terms of parameter passing) and with system hardware (in the input / output driver routines). Subsequently, the debugging process works back upwards through the design, from the lowest-level elements up through the major blocks to the complete, integrated system.

William F. Dalton*

*"Design Microcomputer Software Like Other Systems — Systematically," Electronics, Vol. 51, No. 2, (January 19, 1978), pp. 97 – 102. Copyright © McGraw-Hill, Inc., 1978.

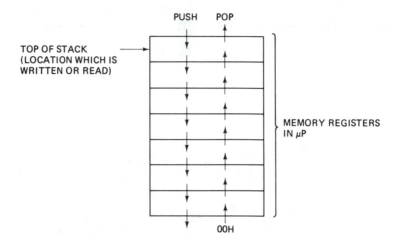

Figure 6.1-1   Representation of a cascade stack storage structure.

6.1 THE STACK AND STACK OPERATIONS

The use of subroutines is a very important technique in designing software for microprocessor systems. And central to their use is a storage structure called a *stack*, which is a collection of registers organized in such a manner that the last data item written is the first item available to be read. In other words, a stack is a last-in/first-out memory buffer, or LIFO buffer. The single register accessible for writing or reading at a particular time is the *top* of the stack. When information is written to the top of the stack, the operation is called a *push*. When information is read from the top of the stack, the operation is called a *pop*.

A conceptual representation of a stack is shown in Fig. 6.1-1. This stack consists of a collection of registers, of which only the top register can be written or read. Pushing data onto, or writing data to, the top register causes the contents of each register in the stack to be shifted to the register below. Initially, the stack is empty; there is no data in any of the registers. The number of registers in the stack is the stack's length. If a stack has a length of N, N words can be pushed onto the stack, with no intervening pop operations, without data loss. The next word pushed onto the stack would cause the first word pushed to be shifted out of the bottom register and lost.

Popping data from, or reading, the top register in the stack causes the data in each register in the stack to be shifted to the register above it. The bottom register is cleared by a pop operation. A number of push operations, on an empty stack, followed by an equal number of pop operations, leaves the stack empty.

To implement the stack directly would require registers and logic, between each pair of registers, to control the direction that data is shifted. This direct method of implementation becomes costly as the required stack length increases. A less costly implementation is to use common RWM and a special memory pointer register. A register in RWM used as part of the stack is considered empty if it has

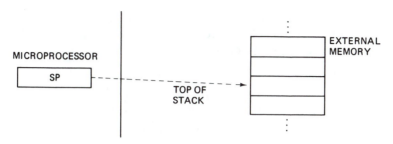

Figure 6.1-2   Stack pointer indicating "top of stack," the last written and not subsequently read memory location.

never been written or has been read after being written. The special pointer register is called the ***stack pointer***. The stack pointer's contents are automatically manipulated to point to an empty RWM register, the new top of the stack, when a write operation takes place. When a read operation takes place, the stack pointer points to the register most recently written but not subsequently read, the current top of the stack. In this implementation the shift that takes place is a shift in terms of which register is considered the top of the stack and not a shift of data among registers.

This method of stack implementation is used by the 8085A. The stack pointer, SP, is a 16-bit register in the 8085A that is properly manipulated by the microprocessor's control section (see Fig. 6.1-2). The RWM used for the stack is external memory provided by the designer. This implementation method allows the stack length to grow as needed, provided it does not exceed the RWM allocated for stack use.

The base of the memory area allocated for the stack is specified by loading the stack pointer with an initial value. This specification is necessary because different applications use different memory configurations. The stack pointer is initialized by the *load register pair immediate* instruction, with the register pair SP specified:

LXI SP, data16

The stack pointer must be initialized before any instructions that use the stack are executed. Therefore, stack initialization is one of the first instructions in a program. Instructions in the 8085A that place data onto the stack, decrement the stack pointer, and, as more data is pushed on the stack, the stack expands into memory locations with lower addresses. Therefore, the stack pointer is commonly initialized to the highest RWM location available.[1]

When a designer wishes to set the stack pointer to a value that has been computed by the program, this value is placed in H and L and then moved to the stack, using the *move HL to SP* instruction:

SPHL

(SP) ← (H)(L)   *Flags:* None

---

[1]Since the 8085A's stack pointer is decremented before data is written to the stack, the stack pointer can actually be initialized to a value one higher than the highest RWM location available.

With push and pop operations, the stack can be used as a temporary data storage area. For example, the contents of internal register pairs (BC, DE, or HL) are saved by the *push* instruction.

$$\text{PUSH rp}$$
$$((SP) - 1) \leftarrow (rh)$$
$$((SP) - 2) \leftarrow (rl)$$
$$(SP) \leftarrow (SP) - 2 \qquad\qquad \textit{Flags: None}$$

Register pair rp = SP cannot be specified in a *push* because it creates an invalid instruction. PUSH transfers the contents of the high order register of the pair, rp, to the memory location whose address is one less than the initial value of the stack pointer, and the contents of the low order register to the memory location whose address is two less than its initial value. The stack pointer is left with a value two less than the stack pointer's initial value. The *push* instruction is another example of register indirect addressing, with SP as the pointer register. All stack instructions in the 8085A involve the transfer of 2 bytes of data. Thus, with this implementation, the top of the stack actually consists of two registers.

Data is transferred from the stack to a microprocessor register pair by the 1-byte *pop* instruction:

$$\text{POP rp}$$
$$(rl) \leftarrow ((SP))$$
$$(rh) \leftarrow ((SP) + 1)$$
$$(SP) \leftarrow (SP) + 2 \qquad\qquad \textit{Flags: None}$$

POP is the reverse of PUSH. However, popping a stack implemented in external RWM does not actually remove data from the stack; it simply copies the data into an internal register pair. But the memory locations from which the data is copied are considered empty, and when a subsequent push operation occurs, these locations are written over. It is clear from the register transfer expressions that the stack pointer in the 8085A points to the last filled (written and not subsequently read) location in the stack.

There are special push and pop instructions that place on or remove from the stack the contents of register A and the flag register, F. These instructions treat A and F as a register pair, with A as the high order register. This pair is referred to as the processor status word, so the *push processor status word* instruction places the contents of registers A and F on the stack:

$$\text{PUSH PSW}$$
$$((SP) - 1) \leftarrow (A)$$
$$((SP) - 2) \leftarrow (F)$$
$$(SP) \leftarrow (SP) - 2 \qquad\qquad \textit{Flags: None}$$

The *pop processor status word* transfers the contents of the top of the stack to registers A and F:

POP PSW
F ← ((SP))
A ← ((SP)) + 1
(SP) ← (SP) + 2   *Flags:* All

Instructions that push data onto the stack or pop data from it automatically
increment or decrement the stack pointer. Thus, once the stack is initialized, the
designer does not have to keep track of the address at which data is stored in the
stack.

External stacks of microprocessors other than the 8085A may grow in the
opposite direction: successive push operations causing data to be written in successively higher memory locations and successive pop operations reading from successively lower ones. Regardless of the direction in which the stack grows, the basic
concepts and uses of all stacks are the same.

As an example of *push* and *pop* instructions and their effects on internal
registers and the stack, a routine that exchanges the contents of register pairs BC
and HL, using the stack for temporary storage, is illustrated in Fig. 6.1-3. Here the
contents of the various registers are shown after the instruction listed beneath them
is executed. The routine assumes that the stack pointer has been initialized (i.e.,
LXI SP 1000H), after which four single-byte instructions are required for the

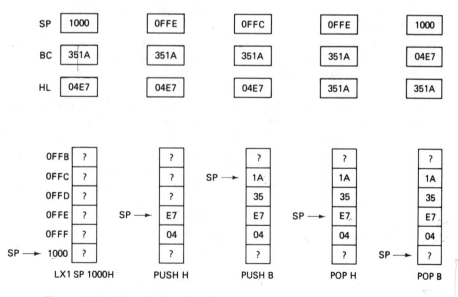

Figure 6.1-3 Use of the stack as temporary storage to implement an
exchange of the contents of register pairs BC and HL.

exchange:

```
PUSH H
PUSH B
POP H
POP B
```

Another instruction, the *exchange top of stack with H and L*, interchanges the data on the top of the stack with the contents of the registers H and L:

XTHL
$(L) \leftrightarrow ((SP))$
$(H) \leftrightarrow ((SP) + 1)$ *Flags:* None

It does not change the value of the stack pointer and, therefore, allows access to the contents of the stack without changing the position of the stack pointer or losing the contents of H and L.

6.2 SUBROUTINES

It is frequently necessary, at several points in a program, to carry out a task that requires the execution of the same group of instructions or, in several different programs, to carry out the same task. Programming such a task, if it is sufficiently short, can be simplified by writing the group of instructions as a macro (see Chapter 5). However, each macro reference is expanded by the assembler into the group of instructions it represents, thus generating a large amount of object code if many references are made. It is more cost effective in terms of memory usage if the needed group of instructions appears only once in the object code but can be executed from several points in a program. Subroutines provide this capability.

A subroutine is written like any other group of assembly language statements, and it is referred to by name—the label associated with its first instruction. The subroutine is referenced by a *subroutine call* instruction in the main program. CALL saves the address of the instruction following it and then transfers control to the first instruction in the subroutine. Essentially a CALL is a push of the program counter followed by a jump. When subroutine execution is complete, the last instruction, a subroutine return, transfers control back to the instruction following the CALL.

The exact manner in which the transfer of control to a subroutine is made in the 8085A is indicated by the register transfer definition of the *CALL* instruction:

CALL addr
$((SP) - 1) \leftarrow (PCH)$
$((SP) - 2) \leftarrow (PCL)$
$(SP) \leftarrow (SP) - 2$
$(PC) \leftarrow (byte\ 3)(byte\ 2)$ *Flags:* None

The address contained in the CALL (bytes 2 and 3) is the label of the first instruction of the subroutine. Recall that during execution of an instruction, the program counter contains the address of the next instruction. Thus, pushing the program counter onto the stack saves the address of the instruction following the CALL, the return address. The stack pointer is decremented by 2 so that it points to the new top of the stack. The actual transfer to the subroutine, a jump, is implemented by replacing the contents of the program counter with the address of the first instruction of the subroutine.

The execution of the CALL instruction is now complete. The next machine cycle is an OPCODE FETCH, which uses the contents of the program counter (the address of the subroutine) as the location from which to fetch the OP code of the next instruction. The transfer of control to the subroutine is now complete.

The last instruction executed in a subroutine is always a *return*, which transfers control back to the instruction following the CALL. One type of return instruction is the unconditional *return*, RET:

$$RET$$
$$(PCL) \leftarrow ((SP))$$
$$(PCH) \leftarrow ((SP) + 1)$$
$$(SP) \leftarrow (SP) + 2$$

Execution of the RET instruction transfers the address of the instruction following the CALL from the stack to the program counter. When the OPCODE FETCH of the next instruction cycle is executed, it fetches the operation code of the instruction following the CALL.

In Fig. 6.2-1a, the transfer of control to two subroutines, SUBA and SUBB, is illustrated. The first subroutine is exited (returned from) before the second sub-

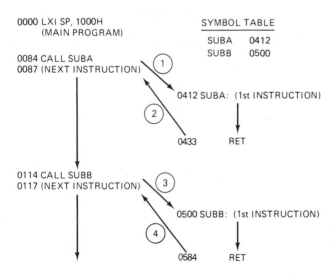

Figure 6.2-1a   Transfer of control in a program segment containing two subroutine calls.

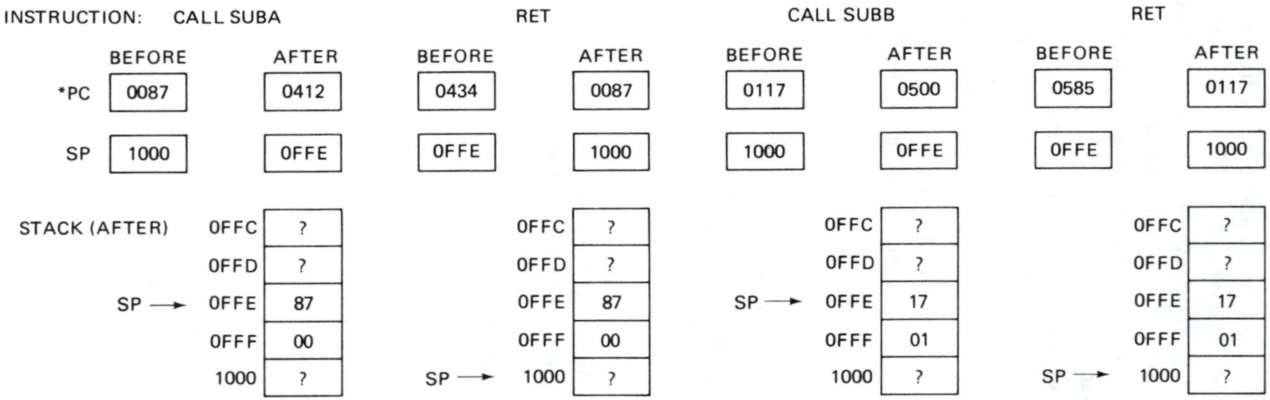

INSTRUCTION: CALL SUBA

	BEFORE	AFTER
*PC	0087	0412
SP	1000	0FFE

STACK (AFTER):

0FFC	?	
0FFD	?	
SP → 0FFE	87	
0FFF	00	
1000	?	

RET

	BEFORE	AFTER
	0434	0087
	0FFE	1000

0FFC	?	
0FFD	?	
0FFE	87	
0FFF	00	
SP → 1000	?	

CALL SUBB

	BEFORE	AFTER
	0117	0500
	1000	0FFE

0FFC	?	
0FFD	?	
SP → 0FFE	17	
0FFF	01	
1000	?	

RET

	BEFORE	AFTER
	0585	0117
	0FFE	1000

0FFC	?	
0FFD	?	
0FFE	17	
0FFF	01	
SP → 1000	?	

*NOTE: PC CONTENTS ARE THOSE BEFORE THE EXECUTION OF THE INSTRUCTION, NOT BEFORE ITS FETCH.

Figure 6.2-1b Program counter, stack pointer, and stack contents before and after execution of call and return instructions of Fig. 6.2-1a.

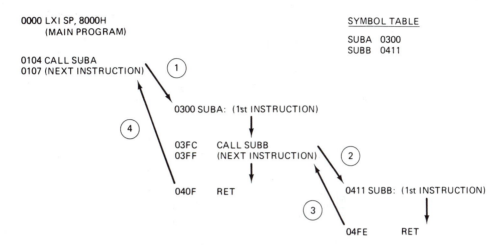

Figure 6.2-2a   Transfer of control with nested subroutines.

routine is called. Figure 6.2-1b shows the contents of the program counter (PC) and the stack pointer (SP) before and after CALL and RET are executed.

When one subroutine calls another subroutine to complete its processing task, the operation is called **nesting**. The second subroutine may in turn call a third subroutine and so on. Each successive CALL without an intervening return creates an additional **level of nesting**. The effect of each *call* instruction is to store the appropriate return address on the stack. The *return* instructions and their effects on the stack ensure that program control eventually returns to the instruction following the original CALL.

The level of subroutine nesting cannot exceed that supported by the available stack memory in the system. Since the stack pointer is usually initialized to the highest available RWM location, and the stack grows toward lower addresses, it is possible that too many PUSH or CALL operations without a sufficient number of intervening POP or RET operations result in the overwriting of nonstack data in lower addresses. Care must be taken in memory allocation and program design to prevent this.

Figure 6.2-2a illustrates the transfer of control in a program containing one level of nesting. The contents of the program counter, stack pointer, and stack are shown before and after the execution of each CALL and RET instruction in Fig. 6.2-2b.

In these examples, it is assumed that only return addresses are placed on the stack and that each subroutine is properly exited via a *return* instruction. In fact, however, after a subroutine is called, it can place other data on the stack: for example, if push instructions are part of the subroutine. If it does place other data on the stack, that data must be popped from the stack leaving the return address on the top of the stack when the RET instruction is executed. If this is not done the microprocessor will use the data on the top of the stack as a return address and

INSTRUCTION: CALL SUBA

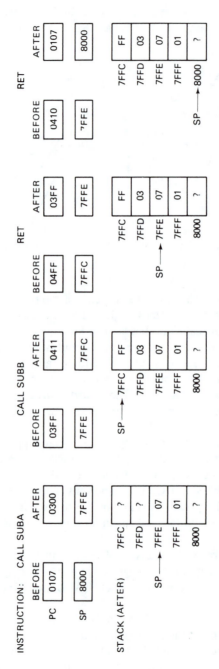

Figure 6.2-2b Program counter, stack pointer, and stack contents for Fig. 6.2-2a.

control will be transferred to a location in memory other than that of the instruction following the CALL, causing a logical error. The program logic must ensure that when a RET instruction is executed, the proper return address is at the top of the stack. This is easily ensured if PUSH and POP instructions are properly paired.

When a subroutine is called, it uses some of the microprocessor's registers to implement its intended function. If data in a microprocessor's registers before a subroutine call is needed by the calling program after execution of the subroutine, the data must be saved. Register contents are saved by either the calling program or by the subroutine itself. If the subroutine is called from several different places in the main program, less program memory is required if the subroutine saves the register contents. To save all of the microprocessor's registers at the beginning and restore them at the end, the following instruction sequence can be used:

```
SUBX:   PUSH H          ; save all internal registers
        PUSH D
        PUSH B
        PUSH PSW
        : (other instructions of subroutine)
        .
        POP PSW         ; restore register values
        POP B
        POP D
        POP H
        RET             ; return (i.e., restore) PC
```

Note the reverse order of the PUSH and POP instructions above.

A special form of call instruction is the *restart* instruction. This is a 1-byte call instruction that can transfer control to one of only eight possible locations. The instruction is defined as follows:

$$RST\ n$$
$$((SP) - 1) \leftarrow (PCH)$$
$$((SP) - 2) \leftarrow (PCL)$$
$$(SP) \leftarrow (SP) - 2$$
$$(PC) \leftarrow 8 \times n$$

The location to which control is transferred is $8 \times n$, where $0 \le n \le 7$. This instruction is used primarily in interrupt applications (see Chapter 9) and to establish breakpoints when debugging software.

6.3 CONDITIONAL CALLS AND RETURNS

Similar to *conditional jump* instructions—in which transfers are predicated on the result of a previous operation—are conditional forms of call and return. In the

8085A these conditions are the same as for conditional jumps:

NZ: not zero
Z: zero
NC: no carry
C: carry
PO: parity odd
PE: parity even
P: plus
M: minus

The *conditional call* instruction has the form

C ⟨condition⟩ addr

If ⟨condition⟩ = true then
((SP) − 1) ← (PCH)
((SP) − 2) ← (PCL)
(SP) ← (SP) − 2
(PC) ← (byte 3)(byte 2)

If the condition associated with the conditional CALL is not met, the instruction following the CALL is executed. If the condition is met, the program counter is saved on the stack, and the address contained in the *call* instruction is transferred to the program counter. The number of machine cycles and states required by a *conditional call* depends on whether or not the condition is satisfied. When the condition is not satisfied, two machine cycles with a total of nine states are required to fetch and execute the instruction. When the condition is satisfied, five machine cycles and 18 states are required.

Conditional return instructions have the form

R ⟨condition⟩

If ⟨condition⟩ = true then
(PCL) ← ((SP))
(PCH) ← ((SP) + 1)
(SP) ← (SP) + 2

These conditions are the same as those for *conditional jumps* and *conditional calls*. When *conditional returns* are used in a subroutine, the last instruction in the subroutine listing is not necessarily a *return* instruction. This presents no problem as long as subroutine execution is terminated at some point by a return or a conditional return instruction. Conditional returns also require a varying number of machine cycles and states, depending on whether the associated condition is or is not satisfied. When the condition is not satisfied, the instruction cycle requires one machine cycle and six states; when the condition is satisfied, three machine cycles and 12 states are required.

6.4 PASSING PARAMETERS

Many subroutines accept data inputs and provide as output results that are a function of the input data. Subroutines with greater applicability, i.e., greater general usefulness, can be written if the subroutine is parameterized. The data, also called the subroutine *parameters* or *arguments*, must be transferred or passed to the subroutine by that portion of the program that calls the subroutine. In addition, results generated by the subroutine must be passed back to the calling program. There are a number of ways of passing data between the calling program and subroutine. The method is often determined by the quantity of data involved. Data can be passed via

1. Internal registers
2. Reserved memory locations
3. Pointers to parameter lists in memory
4. The stack

When the number of data items to be passed is fewer than the number of internal general purpose registers, it is convenient to transfer data via internal registers. In this case, when transferring parameters to a subroutine, instructions that load the data into specific internal registers precede the actual CALL instruction. These instructions and the subroutine CALL itself are together referred to as the *subroutine linkage* or *calling sequence*.

The subroutine obtains its parameters from predetermined registers when called. The results generated by a subroutine are placed in predetermined registers before the return instruction is executed. For example, the 8085A microprocessor's instruction set does not contain a multiply instruction, but a subroutine can be written for this purpose (see Chapter 7). If a subroutine, MULT, computes the 16-bit product of two 8-bit operands, one operand, the multiplicand, is in register B, and the other, the multiplier, is in register C when the subroutine is called. The subroutine leaves the computed product in registers DE before it returns to the main program. Subsequent instructions in the main program can then use the computed result as desired.

Parameters and results are also passed between the main program and a subroutine or between subroutines by reserved memory locations. A *reserved memory* location is one in RWM set aside to hold the value of a specific variable or parameter. These locations are established by the *define storage*, DS, assembler directive. Instructions in the calling sequence and in the subroutine refer to the parameter by its symbolic name, the label on the assembler directive that reserves its storage.

When a subroutine requires a large number of arguments, they can be placed in RWM, and pointers to the data can be provided in internal registers—or in reserved memory locations—before the subroutine is called. For example, a subroutine that computes the mean of N data items requires that HL and DE be loaded with data to be used as pointers to a parameter list in memory. Thus, HL points to a

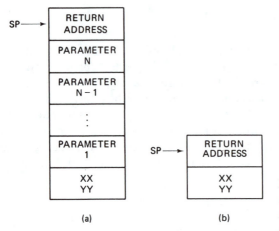

Figure 6.4-1 Stack frame: (a) before subroutine call; (b) after subroutine call.

location containing the value of N and the subsequent N locations contain the data to be averaged. The pointer in DE indicates where the computed mean is to be placed before the subroutine returns.

The stack can be used to pass parameters. The parameters required by a subroutine are placed on the stack by the calling sequence, using push instructions. These parameters, together with the return address, which is automatically pushed onto the stack by the CALL instruction, comprise a *stack frame* (see Fig. 6.4-1a). After a subroutine is called, the stack pointer points to its return address, which is followed by the required parameters. The subroutine obtains the parameters from the stack, leaving the return address on the stack, as shown in Fig. 6.4-1b. The number of parameters passed on the stack when calling a particular subroutine can be fixed, or the last parameter placed on the stack can be a count of the parameters.

A straightforward approach to implement this method of parameter passing is to have the subroutine pop the return address from the stack and save it in an internal register or reserved memory location. The subroutine then pops the parameters from the stack as needed. When all the parameters are removed and processed, the subroutine pushes the return address back onto the stack and executes a return instruction. For example,the following instructions use a reserve memory location to save the return address:

```
POP H         ;pop return address into H and L
SHLD RADDR    ;save return address, remove and use
              ;parameters
    .
    .
    .
LHLD RADDR    ;obtain return address and
PUSH H        ;place it on top of stack
RET
```

If all of the parameters pushed onto the stack are popped off, before executing the PUSH H instruction, the stack looks like the example shown in Fig. 6.4-1b. If, on the other hand, they are not all popped off, the stack is left with one or more unused parameters under the return address, which causes a permanent shift of the base of the stack to a memory location numerically lower than its initial value. This condition, referred to as *stack creep*, is cumulative; if each time the subroutine is called, one or more unused parameters is left on the stack, eventually the stack will move into ROM or into RWM locations not allocated for it. In either case, the program will fail.

The XTHL instruction provides a means of obtaining parameters from the stack one at a time while leaving the return address on the top of the stack:

```
POP H   ;pop return address from stack
XTHL    ;place parameter in H and L and place return
         address back on top of stack
```

After control has been transferred to the subroutine, this sequence pops the return address from the stack and places it in H and L, then exchanges the return address in H and L with the parameter on top of the stack. As a result, the top 2 bytes of the parameter are in H and L, and the return address is on the top of the stack. This instruction sequence can be repeatedly executed until all parameters placed on the stack have been removed.

Results of a subroutine execution can also be returned by the same technique. Before the subroutine returns, it pushes the results onto the stack, leaving the return address on the top. Execution of the return instruction pops the return address from the stack. The calling program then pops all the results from the stack.

A parameter stack exclusively for subroutine parameter passing can be established. This stack is in addition to the primary one established when the stack pointer is first initialized by the program. The pointer value for the parameter stack is kept in reserved memory until the stack is manipulated, at which point it is transferred from reserved memory to the stack pointer. The following subroutine saves the primary stack address in SPTR and loads the stack pointer with the parameter stack address. At the beginning of the main program, the reserved memory location, PARAM, is initialized with the base address for the parameter stack.

```
LXI H, 0       ;save primary stack pointer value
DAD SP
SHLD SPTR
LHLD PARAM     ;load SP with parameter stack pointer value
SPHL
```

The subroutine then pops the parameters from the parameter stack. Before it executes the return instruction or calls another subroutine, it reinstates the primary stack pointer value:

```
LXI H, 0
DAD SP
SHLD PARAM
LHLD SPTR
SPHL
RET
```

Of the various methods discussed for passing parameters, the easiest is the use of reserved memory locations. Each value passed is referred to by its symbolic name in both the calling program and the subroutine. This is also true of a parameter list when the pointer is kept in a reserved memory location. However, there are disadvantages: for some applications, this type of parameter passing necessitates the allocation of a large number of RWM locations. And since a memory reference is required to pass each parameter in a reserved memory location, this method is slower than using internal registers.

Subroutines can be written in such a manner that they can be called again before executing a return from the first call. These *reentrant* subroutines are required when recursive algorithms are implemented or when a subroutine can be called by both the main program and interrupt routines (see Chapter 9).

6.5 SUBROUTINE DOCUMENTATION

Careful documentation ensures that subroutine functions are clear, as are their responses to error conditions. It also obviates the necessity for closely examining the actual instruction listing when using an established subroutine in a new program or when studying the overall structure of a large program containing many subroutines. Subroutine documentation specifies the parameters and the methods by which they are passed to the subroutine, what results are generated and how, and the method by which results are returned to the calling program. Documentation also indicates what registers, if any—other than those used to pass back the results —are modified by the subroutine.

Adequate subroutine documentation also facilitates subroutine testing and debugging, independent of the program which calls it. And, it allows the designer to accumulate a library of useful subroutines which can be used in later work.

Because subroutines can be nested, any particular subroutine may be called by other subroutines and/or make calls to others. Consequently, documentation for a subroutine in a particular application requires a list of subroutines which it calls and a list of subroutines that call it. The list of subroutines that a particular subroutine calls is fixed and indicates that these subroutines must be included in any program using the subroutine that calls them. On the other hand, the list of subroutines that call a particular subroutine changes from application to application. This procedure helps in determining the effects of any changes made to any subroutine on the overall program.

A *subroutine header* concisely documents the subroutine in a program listing, for example:

```
;FUNCTION: name and function
;
;CREATED: date originally written
;REVISED: last revision date
;
;ASSUMES: parameters passed to subroutine
;RETURNS: results passed back
```

```
;REGS. MODIFIED: list of internal registers and reserved
;   memory locations modified by subroutine
;CALLS: list of all subroutines that this subroutine
;   calls to carry out its function
;CALLED BY: list of all subroutines that call
;   this subroutine for a given application
;STACK LEVEL: maximum depth of stack required to
;   support this subroutine
;
;DESCRIPTION: description of subroutines operation
```

The total number of bytes of stack storage required to support the subroutine is indicated by the stack level. The minimum stack level is two—the 2 bytes that hold the return address. The maximum value includes the return address plus the amount of stack used for parameter passing and the amount used by nested subroutines. A worst case approximation of the required stack level is established by adding the maximum value for nested subroutines to the value computed for the subroutine itself. The largest stack level value is then checked against allocated RWM to determine whether the space is sufficient.

6.6 DETAILED SUBROUTINE EXAMPLE

Examples of subroutines appear throughout the remaining chapters. These examples illustrate the parameter passing techniques discussed. However, these subroutines are most often described in the text and therefore not documented in the manner they would be in a standalone program listing. This section provides an example RWM test subroutine with standalone documentation. Since this example also illustrates many of the techniques of this chapter, additional detailed explanation is given. First, the subroutine listing, Fig. 6.6-1, should be read thoroughly to see if the subroutine's operation can be completely understood from the listing alone. Then the detailed explanation that follows should be read.

A general understanding of the purpose of the subroutine and the algorithm that it implements is prerequisite to understanding the programming details. For our purposes a RWM operates properly if each bit can be set and cleared, by a write operation, independently of the value of any other bit. Further, each location in the memory must be uniquely addressable, a write or read operation should affect only the location addressed and no others.

Because failures in semiconductor RWMs may be pattern sensitive, memory test techniques involve a trade-off between the time required to run the test and the thoroughness of the test. The goal here is a test that executes quickly and provides reasonable assurance of proper memory operation. A simple test to check that the bits in a memory can be independently set and cleared is the checkerboard test. The checkerboard test involves writing a checkerboard pattern of 1s and 0s throughout the memory and then reading the pattern back for verification. After the checker-

```
ASM80  :F1:RWMCK.ASM DEBUG MACROFILE MOD85

ISIS-II 8080/8085 MACRO ASSEMBLER, V4.0          MODULE    PAGE    1

LOC  OBJ         LINE        SOURCE STATEMENT

                    1  ;*******************************************************
                    2  ;
                    3  ; FUNCTION: RWMCK-READ WRITE MEMORY TEST
                    4  ;
                    5  ; CREATED: 12/08/85
                    6  ; REVISED:
                    7  ;
                    8  ; ASSUMES: HL-STARTING ADDRESS OF RWM, DE-MEMORY BYTE COUNT
                    9  ; RETURNS: CY=1, TEST FAILED, HL-MEMORY LOCATION THAT FAILED
                   10  ; MODIFIES: ALL UP REGISTERS AND MEMORY TESTED
                   11  ;
                   12  ; CALLS: NONE
                   13  ; CALLED BY:
                   14  ; STACK LEVEL: 6
                   15  ;
                   16  ; DESCRIPTION: IMPLEMENTS A CHECKERBOARD TEST AND AN ADDRESS TEST
                   17  ; FOR RWM. THE NUMBER OF BYTES IN THE BLOCK OF RWM TO BE TESTED
                   18  ; MUST BE EVEN. WRITES ENTIRE MEMORY BLOCK SPECIFIED WITH CHECKER-
                   19  ; BOARD PATTERN. THEN READS BLOCK BACK TO COMPARE. IF THIS TEST
                   20  ; IS PASSED, IT THEN WRITES THE COMPLEMENT CHECKERBOARD PATTERN
                   21  ; AND READS IT BACK. IF THE COMPLEMENT CHECKERBOARD PATTERN TEST
                   22  ; IS PASSED AN ADDRESS TEST IS RUN. THE ADDRESS TEST WRITES THE
                   23  ; LOW ADDRESS BYTE OF EACH MEMORY LOCATION INTO THAT LOCATION.
                   24  ; AFTER ALL LOCATIONS IN THE BLOCK ARE WRITTEN THE BLOCK IS READ
                   25  ; BACK AND COMPARED.
                   26  ;
                   27  ;:::::::::::::::::::::::::::::::::::::::::::::::::::::::::::::::::::
                   28
                   29
                   30  ;INITIALIZATION
0000 7B            31  RWMCK:  MOV A,E  ;CHECK FOR AN EVEN NUMBER OF BYTES TO BE TESTED
0001 1F            32          RAR       ;SET CY IF NUMBER OF BYTES IS ODD
0002 D8            33          RC        ;RETURN IF NUMBER OF BYTES IS ODD
0003 0E00          34          MVI C,00H  ;CLEAR PASS INDICATOR, 0=PASS1, FF=PASS2
0005 3EAA          35          MVI A,10101010B ;LOAD TEST PATTERN FOR EVEN LOCATIONS
                   36
                   37  ;WRITE CHECKERBOARD PATTERN
```

Figure 6.6-1 Assembler listing of RWM test subroutine.

```
0007 E5      38 WRCKBD: PUSH H          ;SAVE STARTING ADDRESS OF RWM
0008 D5      39         PUSH D          ;SAVE BYTE COUNT
0009 77      40 WRCK:   MOV M,A         ;WRITE MEMORY LOCATION
000A 2F      41         CMA             ;CREATE TEST PATTERN FOR NEXT MEMORY LOCATION
000B 47      42         MOV B,A         ;SAVE IT
000C 23      43         INX H           ;INCREMENT POINTER TO NEXT MEMORY LOCATION
000D 1B      44         DCX D           ;DECREMENT BYTE COUNTER
000E 7B      45         MOV A,E         ;SET ZERO FLAG IF BYTE COUNTER=0
000F B2      46         ORA D
0010 78      47         MOV A,B         ;GET PATTERN FOR NEXT MEMORY LOCATION
0011 C20900  48         JNZ WRCK        ;GO BACK AND WRITE NEXT MEMORY LOCATION
             49 ;READ CHECKERBOARD PATTERN
0014 D1      51 RDCKBD: POP D           ;GET BYTE COUNT
0015 E1      52         POP H           ;GET STARTING ADDRESS OF RWM
0016 E5      53         PUSH H          ;SAVE STARTING ADDRESS OF RWM
0017 D5      54         PUSH D          ;SAVE BYTE COUNT

ISIS-II 8080/8085 MACRO ASSEMBLER, V4.0          MODULE     PAGE   2

LOC OBJ         LINE         SOURCE STATEMENT
0018 BE      55 RDCK:   CMP M           ;SET ZERO FLAG IF MEMORY BYTE EQUALS PATTERN
0019 C24E00  56         JNZ FAILCB      ;MEMORY BYTE INCORRECT, MEMORY FAILS
001C 2F      57         CMA             ;CREAT TEST PATTERN FOR NEXT MEMORY LOCATION
001D 47      58         MOV B,A         ;SAVE IT
001E 23      59         INX H           ;INCREMENT POINTER TO NEXT MEMORY LOCATION
001F 1B      60         DCX D           ;DECREMENT BYTE COUNTER
0020 7B      61         MOV A,E         ;SET ZERO FLAG IF BYTE COUNTER=0
0021 B2      62         ORA D
0022 78      63         MOV A,B         ;GET PATTERN FOR NEXT MEMORY LOCATION
0023 C21800  64         JNZ RDCK        ;GO BACK AND COMPARE NEXT MEMORY LOCATION
             65 ;INITIALIZATION AND TRANSFER FOR NEXT PASS OR ADDRESS TEST
0026 D1      67         POP D           ;GET BYTE COUNT
0027 E1      68         POP H           ;GET STARTING ADDRESS OF RWM
0028 E5      69         PUSH H          ;SAVE STARTING ADDRESS OF RWM
0029 D5      70         PUSH D          ;SAVE BYTE COUNT
002A 79      71         MOV A,C         ;SET ZERO FLAG IF LAST PASS WAS PASS0
002B B7      72         ORA A
002C C23600  73         JNZ WRADDR      ;CHECKERBOARD TEST COMPLETE, DO ADDRESS TEST
002F 0EFF    74         MVI C,0FFH      ;CHECKERBOARD TEST NOT COMPLETE, MODIFY PASS COUNTER
0031 3E55    75         MVI A,01010101B ;EVEN BYTE TEST PATTERN-REVERSE TEST
```

Figure 6.6-1 Continued.

211

```
0033 C30900    76         JMP WRCK        ;GO BACK AND WRITE REVERSE PATTERN
               77
               78    ;ADDRESS TEST
0036 75        79    WRADDR: MOV M,L      ;WRITE LOW ADDRESS BYTE TO EACH MEMORY LOCATION
0037 23        80         INX H           ;INCREMENT MEMORY POINTER
0038 1B        81         DCX D           ;DECREMENT BYTE COUNTER
0039 7B        82         MOV A,E         ;SET ZERO FLAG IF BYTE COUNTER=0
003A B2        83         ORA D
003B C23600    84         JNZ WRADDR      ;GO BACK AND WRITE NEXT MEMORY LOCATION
               85
               86    ;COMPARE WRITTEN ADDRESS AND MEMORY LOCATION
003E D1        87         POP D           ;GET BYTE COUNT
003F E1        88         POP H           ;GET RWM STARTING ADDRESS
0040 7D        89    RDADDR: MOV A,L      ;GET LOW ADDRESS BYTE OF MEMORY LOCATION
0041 BE        90         CMP M           ;SET ZERO FLAG IF LOW ADDRESS BYTE=MEMORY CONTENTS
0042 C25000    91         JNZ FAIL        ;ADDRESS TEST FAILED
0045 23        92         INX H           ;INCREMENT MEMORY POINTER
0046 1B        93         DCX D           ;DECREMENT BYTE COUNTER
0047 7B        94         MOV A,E         ;SET ZERO FLAG IF BYTE COUNT=0
0048 B2        95         ORA D
0049 C24000    96         JNZ RDADDR      ;GO BACK AND COMPARE NEXT LOW ADDRESS BYTE WITH MEMORY
               97
               98    ;SET UP RESULTS FOR RETURN, CLEAN UP STACK IF NECESSARY
004C B7        99    PASS:  ORA A         ;CLEAR CY TO INDICATE ALL TESTS PASSED
004D C9        100        RET
004E D1        101   FAILCB: POP D        ;CHECKERBOARD TEST FAILED, CLEAN UP STACK
004F D1        102        POP D
0050 37        103   FAIL:  STC           ;SET CY TO INDICATE MEMORY FAILED TEST
0051 C9        104        RET
               105        END

PUBLIC SYMBOLS
```

Figure 6.6-1 Continued.

board pattern is written, the memory would contain the following pattern of 1s and 0s:

10101010
01010101
10101010
01010101

In the pattern each bit is surrounded by bits that are its complement. If any bit cell adversely affects adjacent cells it should be detected by this test. However, with memories using two level decoding, logically adjacent cells are not physically adjacent. Because of its simplicity and speed this type of test is still useful. Writing the checkerboard once is not sufficient; it simply indicates that any cell can store one of the two logic values that it must be able to store. Thus, it is also necessary to write and read the complement of the previous checkerboard:

01010101
10101010
01010101
10101010

A deficiency of the checkerboard test is that it does not determine if the memory's address decoding logic is working properly. A failure of on-chip or external address decoding logic could cause a single write operation to write more than one location. If the separation between the multiple locations written is a power of 2, the checkerboard test would not detect a problem. The address test attempts to overcome this problem by writing the address of each memory location into that location. For 8-bit memory words and a 16-bit memory address, the low byte of the address is written into memory. Memory locations starting at 4000H would be written with the following values:

4000H   00000000
4001H   00000001
4002H   00000010
4003H   00000011

Only a multiple write of locations that are exactly 256 bytes apart would not be detected when this data is read back.

The example RWM test subroutine implements both a checkerboard and an address test on a specified block of memory. The block of memory must be specified by the calling program. This is accomplished by passing the starting address of the memory block and the block length, in bytes, to the subroutine as parameters via the microprocessor's registers. The starting address is passed in HL and the block length in DE. The block length must be even.

The CY is used to indicate the results of the test to the calling program. If the CY is set when the subroutine returns, the test was failed. The test will be failed if the number of bytes specified for test is odd or if the memory does not operate properly. If the number of bytes specified for test is even and the test is failed, the HL registers will contain the address of the first memory location to fail. If the test is passed the subroutine returns with the CY cleared.

The operation of the subroutine is now explained in detail. An instruction is referred to by its line number, Lnnn, in the listing. L31–L33 check that the block length is even. Since DE contains the block length, the least significant bit of E must be 0. The least significant bit of E is placed in the CY and a return is executed if the CY is set.

The checkerboard test is executed first. This test is accomplished in two passes using the same instructions. The first pass writes the checkerboard pattern and reads it back. The second pass writes the complement checkerboard pattern and reads it back. Register C is used as a flag to keep track of which pass is in progress. L34 clears the pass flag for pass1. The pattern for the even memory bytes is placed in A by L35.

The entire block of memory must be written with the checkerboard pattern before it is read back. To write the block, register HL is used as a memory pointer and DE is used as a byte counter to determine completion. When the data is read back, the starting address of memory and the block length will again be needed. Therefore, the contents of HL and DE are saved on the stack, L38–L39, before the memory is written.

L40–L48 comprise the loop that writes the checkerboard pattern. The pattern in A is written to memory, L40. It is then complemented and saved to be written to the next location, L41–L42. The memory pointer is incremented for the next write operation, L43. Next the byte counter is decremented and the flags effected, L44–L46. The effect of L46 is to set or clear the zero flag. The actual test of the zero flag, the conditional branch, L48, is not encountered until after the test pattern for the next memory location is moved back to A in anticipation that the write loop is not complete, L47. In this case the fact that a data transfer does not effect the flags is used to advantage. During the last iteration of the loop the last memory location in the block will be written and DE will be decremented to 0. The conditional jump, L48, will not be executed and control will pass to the instruction following the jump, L51.

Since the block length is even, the pattern moved to A by L47 on the last loop iteration will be the same as the pattern written into the first location of the block. This is the pattern needed for the first comparison at the start of the readback from the block. The block length and the starting address of the block are on top of the stack. These values are placed in DE and HL by L51–L52. However, they will be needed again for the second pass of the checkerboard test and for the address test. Therefore, they are also placed back on the stack by L53–L54.

The checkerboard read loop consists of L55–L64. This loop is similar to the write loop, except that L55–L56 compare the data read with the pattern in A. If they are not the same the test is failed and control is transferred to L101. If this occurs, the starting address and block length will still be on the stack and must be removed before the subroutine returns. This is accomplished by L101–L102. Note that both these instructions are POP D instructions. Use of a POP H instruction would leave the starting address in HL instead of the address of the memory location that failed. The CY flag is then set, L103, and the subroutine returns, L104.

If the checkerboard read back is successful, the next operation is either the second pass of the checkerboard test or the address test. In either case, the starting address and block length are again needed and again must be saved for later operations, L67–L70. The C register is checked to determine which operation is next, L71–L73. If the C register is not 0, both checkerboard tests are complete and control is transferred to address test, L79. If C = 0, it is loaded with FFH, L74, the reverse checkerboard pattern put in A, L75, and control transferred to L40 to begin the reverse checkerboard test, L76.

L79–L84 comprise the address write loop. Since the low byte of the address is in L during each pass through the loop, the contents of L are simply written to memory, L79. Each time through the loop the memory pointer is incremented, the byte counter decremented, the zero flag effected, and tested, L80–L84.

To read back the addresses, the starting address and block length are required. These are obtained by L87–L88. Since they will not be needed again, they are not saved back on the stack. The subroutine's return address is now on the top of the stack. L89–L96 comprise the address readback loop. If the comparison, L90, fails, control is transferred to L103. At this point the return address is at the top of the stack and it is only necessary to set the CY flag and return, L103–L104.

If the address test is passed, L99 is encountered, the CY is cleared, and the subroutine returns, L99–L100.

The use of the stack to save the starting address and block length requires careful consideration. When any of the return instructions in the program is executed these parameters must no longer be on the stack. And the return address must be on the top of the stack. There are several paths through the subroutine to a return:

1. Byte count is odd, return at L33 executed.
2. Checkerboard test fails, return at L104 executed via L101.
3. Complement checkerboard fails, return at L104 via L101.
4. Address test fails, return at L104 executed via L103.
5. Test passed, return at L100 executed via L99.

The use of the stack through each of these paths has to be examined to ensure that it is manipulated properly.

6.7 MODULAR PROGRAM STRUCTURE

Using subroutines, programs can be structured in a modular fashion: as a main program containing numerous calls to subroutines. A modular program structure reduces the complexity of the software development because

1. The overall program function is implemented by the execution of a number of subfunctions—subroutines—in the proper order.
2. The order in which subroutines are executed is controlled by the order in which they are called by the main program.

3. The programming effort is reduced by writing and debugging smaller programs—subroutines.

4. Previously written subroutines are often used in implementing required subfunctions.

5. Changes in the program are easier to implement.

A typical modular program layout follows:

1. *Program Header*: A comment field provides a summary of the program's function and operation and describes the hardware environment on which the software runs.

2. *Symbolic Constant Definitions*: Symbols representing constants in the program are assigned values using EQU and SET assembler directives.

ROM:

3. *System Hardware Initialization*: Instructions that write appropriate control words into system hardware to initialize or configure that hardware under software control (see Chapter 8).

4. *Macro Definitions*: The definition of all macros.

5. *Branch Tables*: If branch tables are used to structure the program, the jump instructions that comprise the table appear here.

6. *Main Program*: Instructions that control the overall program and also control the calling of subroutines.

7. *Subroutines*: All the subroutines required by the main program are collected together in this area.

8. *Data Tables*: Tables of data constants, lookup tables, are used in conversion, linearization, etc., and storage of ASCII for printable messages. The tables are constructed with the use of the DB and DW assembler directives.

RWM:

9. *Reserved Storage*: Reserved memory locations referred to by symbolic names, which store particular temporary data, are established by using a DS assembler directive with labels.

10. *Scratch Storage*: Memory locations that are used for temporary storage in an unrestricted manner by the main program or subroutines.

11. *Stack*: Section of RWM allocated for the stack.

6.8 SIMULATION OF SUBROUTINES

A modular program structure simplifies program development, testing, and debugging. Subroutines can be written and simulated separately, allowing a program to be tested in stages from the bottom up. In bottom-up testing, *elemental subroutines*—those that don't call other subroutines—are written and tested first.

Input data for test cases must not only test the subroutine's performance with typical parameter values but also with values at the extremes of the range of data for which the subroutine is designed. In some applications, the subroutine will have to take appropriate action for invalid input data values or results that exceed representable ranges of values. These cases must also be tested.

After an appropriate set of test cases is determined, the actual simulation is conducted. The subroutine is loaded into the simulator or into a microcomputer development system. Breakpoints are established at the return instructions and at any desired intermediate points. Appropriate commands set the registers (microprocessor, memory, or stack) that pass parameters to the values corresponding to those of each test case. After the parameter values are initialized, the PC is set to the starting address of the subroutine, and the subroutine is executed. When the breakpoint associated with the subroutine's return instruction is reached, those registers that return the results are displayed and compared with the expected result.

After all elemental subroutines are tested, the next level of subroutines is tested in combination with the subroutines they call. When all nested subroutines are tested, they are combined with the main program, and the entire software system is tested.

BIBLIOGRAPHY

DALTON, W. F., "Design Microcomputer Software Like Other Systems—Systematically," *Electronics*, 51, (January 1978), 97–102.

HETZEL, W., *Program Test Methods*. Englewood Cliffs, N.J.: Prentice-Hall, 1973.

LEVENTHAL, L. A., and W. SAVILLE, *8080/8085 Assembly Language Subroutines*. Berkeley, Calif.: Osborne/McGraw-Hill, 1983.

MAZOR, S., and C. PITCHFORD, "Develop Cooperative μP Subroutines," *Electronic Design* (June 1978), 116–18.

ROSENFELD, P., and S. J. HANNA, "Developing Modular Hardware for the 8080A," *Electronics* (September 1976), 83–87.

YOURDON, E., *Techniques of Program Structure and Design*. Englewood Cliffs, N.J.: Prentice-Hall, 1976.

PROBLEMS

6-1. Write a macro, RDEL, that rotates DE left through the carry. In other words, this macro implements the following register transfers:

$$(CY) \leftarrow (D_7)$$
$$(D_{n+1}) \leftarrow (D_n)$$
$$(D_0) \leftarrow (E_7)$$
$$(E_{n+1}) \leftarrow (E_n)$$
$$(E_0) \leftarrow (CY)$$

Leave only registers DE and F altered by the macro.

6-2. Write a macro definition for the macro XBCDE. This macro swaps the contents of the register pairs BC and DE without altering the values in any of the other general purpose registers.

6-3. Write a subroutine that compares two equal length blocks of memory to see whether they are identical. Write your subroutine such that the starting address of block 1 is in HL and of block 2 in DE, and the block length is in register C when the subroutine is called. If the blocks are identical, have the subroutine return with the carry set. If the blocks differ, have it return with the carry cleared and the address of the first location of block 2 that differs from that of block 1 in HL and the contents of that location in register B.

6-4. Modify the subroutine of Problem 6-3 so that the starting addresses are obtained from reserved memory locations BLOC1 and BLOC2 and the block length from reserved memory location BLEN. If the blocks are identical, have the subroutine set reserved memory location DIFF to FFFFH; otherwise, it should be set to the address of the first location in block 2 that differs.

6-5. Write two macros, SAVE and RSTOR, that use the stack to save and restore the contents of the microprocessor's registers. These macros would be used at the beginning and end of subroutines that save and restore the microprocessor register contents.

6-6. Subroutine, STATE, is part of a monitor program that, among other things, saves, in reserved memory locations, the values of registers A, B, C, D, E, H, L, F, and SP, which exist when the subroutine is called. The PC value pushed on the stack by the calling instruction is also saved in reserved memory. Using as few instructions as possible, write that part of the subroutine that saves the register contents. Provide adequate comments so that your program can be understood. The assembler directives that provide the storage for the register contents are as follows:

```
VDE:   DS 2    ; Storage for E and D registers
VBC:   DS 2    ; Storage for C and B registers
VAF:   DS 2    ; Storage for A and F registers
VHL:   DS 2    ; Storage for L and H registers
VPC:   DS 2    ; Storage for PC
VSP:   DS 2    ; Storage for SP
```

6-7. Write a programmable subroutine, DELAY, that counts down register pair HL to zero and then returns. The initial value of HL is passed to the subroutine via reserved memory locations called INIT. Indicate how the reserved memory locations are established in assembly language. Write the subroutine and give an example of a calling sequence that gives HL an initial value of 0123H. Explain how the total elapsed time of the delay is determined so that a given value for INIT could be obtained for a desired delay.

6-8. Write a macro, LHLX (load H and L indirect through DE), that loads L with the contents of the memory location pointed to by the contents of DE and that loads H with the contents of the succeeding memory location. In other words, write the macro to implement the following register transfer expressions:

$$(L) \leftarrow ((D)(E))$$
$$(H) \leftarrow ((D)(E) + 1)$$

The macro should leave all the microprocessor registers except H and L unaltered, including the flag register.

6-9. Write a macro, SHLX (store H and L indirect through D and E), that stores the contents of HL in the memory location specified by the contents of DE. In other words, write the macro to implement the following register transfer expressions:

$$((D)(E)) \leftarrow (L)$$
$$((D)(E) + 1) \leftarrow (H)$$

The macro should leave all the microprocessor registers unaltered, including the flag register.

6-10. The instruction SPHL transfers the contents of register pair HL to the stack pointer SP. Write a macro, HLSP, that transfers the contents of SP to HL. No other registers in the microprocessor should be altered.

6-11. Write a subroutine that when called will output the contents of the flag register to port 0. The subroutine should return with the CPU registers containing the same values that existed at the execution of the call.

6-12. Write a subroutine, FLBLK, that fills a block of memory with a constant. Parameters are passed to the subroutine via the microprocessor's registers: (A) = constant, (HL) = starting address of memory block, (C) = memory block length in bytes. Data in the microprocessor's registers, which are not used to pass parameters, must be preserved. This includes the contents of the F register. The subroutine must be written to use as few instructions as possible.

6-13. The call instructions provided for the 8085A microprocessor transfer control to an address that is fixed, specified when the program is written. Write a macro definition for a macro, CALLI, that transfers control to an address that is computed when the program is executed. The computed address is placed in HL by the program before the program encounters the macro reference.

6-14. Write a macro, GET, that is used after a subroutine call to extract a 2-byte parameter from beneath the return address on the stack and place it in HL.

6-15. A calling sequence passes two 16-bit parameters to a subroutine using a stack frame. Before being passed, the parameters are in register pairs BC and DE. The parameter in register pair BC is passed first. Assuming the following values at the start of the calling sequence—(SP) = 400H, (PC) = 20AH, (BC) = 1234H, (DE) = C320H—draw a diagram of memory showing all information placed on the stack by the calling sequence along with the associated memory addresses.

6-16. Write a subroutine that implements a data transfer with time out. When the subroutine is called, it waits for bit 7 of input port STATUS to be logic 1. When that is the case, it inputs data from input port DATA, leaves this data in register A, and returns with the carry flag set. If bit 7 of port STATUS does not become 1 in a fixed length of time, the subroutine returns with the carry cleared. The length of time the subroutine waits is determined by a constant that is specified by an equate directive.

6-17. A subroutine is to be written that inputs data from two memory mapped input ports and places the data in a memory buffer. The 8-bit data values from the two ports together make up a 16-bit data value. On port, LPORT, provides the low byte of the 16-bit value; the other port, HPORT, provides the high byte. The address of HPORT is equal to LPORT + 1. The buffer in memory that receives the data is 128 bytes long and starts at location BUFFER. In order to transfer data from the I/O ports to the buffer as fast as possible, the LHLD instruction is to be used to get data from the ports and the PUSH instruction is to be used to write it into the buffer. Assume that the input ports will always have valid data available. When the subroutine is executed, it is to transfer 128 bytes from the ports to the buffer. The buffer is filled from its higher addresses to its lower addresses. The subroutine can modify any of the microprocessor's registers but it cannot modify any memory locations other than those making up the buffer. After the subroutine returns, the SP must have the value it had before the call.

7

Arithmetic Operations

Digital arithmetic refers to the algorithms which implement the arithmetic operations of a digital machine. These algorithms have been developed to take into account many factors, such as binary circuit operation, method of representing a negative number, the finite range of numbers representable in the computer, the limited (and usually fixed) number of digits in a computer word, and location of the digit point (such as the binary point of a binary number).

Yaohan Chu*

Digital Computer Design Fundamentals (New York: McGraw-Hill, 1962).

The operation of many microprocessor systems requires both simple (addition and subtraction) and more complex (multiplication, division, etc.) arithmetic computations. One or more instructions for binary addition are always provided in a microprocessor's instruction set, and instructions for subtraction are usually, but not always, provided. Multiplication and division instructions are not included in the instruction sets of all 8-bit microprocessors but are usually included in those of 16-bit microprocessors. When specific arithmetic functions are not provided as individual instructions in an instruction set, they can be implemented in software or hardware: in software as macros or subroutines; in hardware with arithmetic processing units implemented as MSI and LSI circuits.

Prior to developing macros or subroutines, the designer determines the range of the values to be represented numerically and their required degree of precision. After this, a method for representing these numbers is selected. The length of a macro or subroutine varies significantly with the choice of number representation. If an inadequate representation is selected, calculations are in error. If too powerful a representation is chosen, the additional memory required for the longer subroutine and data representation is wasted.

Methods of numerical representation include unsigned binary numbers, two's complement numbers, BCD numbers, fractional numbers, and floating point numbers.

7.1 UNSIGNED BINARY INTEGER NUMBERS

Unsigned binary integer numbers represent positive integer quantities only, because all bits represent the number's magnitude. Unsigned binary is also the simplest of the number representations. With n-bit binary numbers, interpreted as unsigned integers, representable values range between 0 and $2^n - 1$ (see Fig. 7.1-1). When a single byte represents a number, it is called a *single precision number*. Single precision unsigned binary numbers range in value from 0 to 255 (0 to $2^8 - 1$).

For the general case of an n-bit integer, the number is written in positional notation:

$$X = x_{n-1}x_{n-2} \ldots x_0$$

n	$2^n - 1$
1	1
2	3
3	7
4	15
8	255
12	4095
16	65,535
24	16,777,215
32	4,294,967,295

Figure 7.1-1 Largest value representable by an n-bit binary number.

and has the value

$$V(X) = \sum_{i=0}^{n-1} x_i 2^i$$

Thus, the value of the n-bit integer equals the sum of the products of each bit, x_i, and the weight associated with its position, 2^i. For example, the 8-bit number

$$N_2 = 10110110$$
with bit positions 76543210

is equal to

$$N_{10} = 1(2^7) + 0(2^6) + 1(2^5) + 1(2^4) + 0(2^3) + 1(2^2) + 1(2^1) + 0(2^0)$$
$$= 128 + 0 + 32 + 16 + 0 + 4 + 2 + 0$$
$$= 182_{10}$$

The subscripts 2 and 10 on N indicate that the number is represented in base 2 (binary) and base 10 (decimal). This subscript notation is used only when the base of a number is not clear from the context in which it is used.

7.1.1 Addition

The addition of two 1-bit numbers is defined as follows:

Augend	Addend	Carry	Sum
0 +	0	= 0	0
0 +	1	= 0	1
1 +	0	= 0	1
1 +	1	= 1	0

For an n-bit number, addition starts with the least significant bits of the augend and addend and continues with the addition of successively higher order bits and the carry from the previous lower order bit's addition. As long as the sum of two unsigned integers is less than 256, it can be represented by a single byte. For example

Carries		00100001	
Augend	X	10110001	177
Addend	Y	00100101	$+37$
Sum	$X + Y$	0] 11010110	214

In general, for n-bit unsigned numbers, the sum ranges from 0 to $2^{n+1} - 2$.

$$(2^n - 1) + (2^n - 1) = 2(2^n - 1) = 2^{n+1} - 2$$

```
SBADD:   LXI B,AUGND    ;LOAD BC WITH ADDRESS OF AUGND
         LXI H,ADDND    ;LOAD HL WITH ADDRESS OF ADDND
         LXI D,SUM      ;LOAD DE WITH ADDRESS OF SUM
         LDAX B         ;MOVE AUGND TO A
         ADD M          ;ADD ADDND
         STAX D         ;STORE IN SUM
         RET
          . . .
AUGND:   DS 1H          ;RESERVED MEMORY FOR OPERANDS
ADDND:   DS 1H
SUM:     DS 1H          ;RESERVED MEMORY FOR RESULT
```

Figure 7.1-2   Single byte addition subroutine.

However, for single byte operands specifically, sums range from 0 to 510. The maximum sum results from the following case:

Carries	11111111	
X	11111111	255
Y	11111111	255
$X + Y$	1] 11111110	510

When the sum of two n-bit unsigned binary integers exceeds $2^n - 1$, it produces an **arithmetic overflow**: the sum cannot be represented with n bits, and a carry bit is required. When adding binary numbers with pencil and paper, this carry represents no problem. The sum is simply represented by $n + 1$ bits. However, in a microprocessor with n-bit registers, the sum cannot be stored in a single register.

For example, when single byte addition is carried out in the 8085A, the sum is left in the accumulator, and, if greater than 255, the carry flip-flop is set. In such a case, two memory locations are required to store the sum properly.

Two types of 8085A instructions add single byte binary numbers: one (add), which merely adds the two bytes, and another (add with carry), which not only adds the two bytes but also adds the value of the carry from a previous operation. In both cases, the second operand can be immediate data or data contained in an internal or external register. The instructions for add are[1]

Add immediate	*Add register*	*Add memory*
ADI data	ADD r	ADD M
$(A) \leftarrow (A) + \text{byte } 2$	$(A) \leftarrow (A) + (r)$	$(A) \leftarrow (A) + ((H)(L))$

Flags: Z, S, P, CY, AC

See Fig. 7.1-2 for a subroutine, SBADD, which adds the contents of two memory locations—AUGND and ADDND—and stores the result in the location SUM.

If a system requires greater range or precision, several bytes of data can represent a single number. To add multibyte numbers, the carry that results from

---

[1] The 8085A addition instructions implement straight binary addition, without any regard to the number representation chosen by the programmer.

```
;N ASSUMED PREVIOUSLY DEFINED
MBADD:    MVI D,N        ;INITIALIZE BYTE COUNTER
          LXI B,AUGND    ;LOAD BC WITH ADDRESS OF AUGND
          LXI H,ADDND    ;LOAD HL WITH ADDRESS OF ADDND
          XRA A          ;CLEAR CARRY
LOOP:     LDAX B         ;ADD TWO BYTES
          ADC M
          MOV M,A        ;STORE SUM
          DCR D          ;DECREMENT BYTE COUNTER
          RZ             ;RETURN AFTER LAST BYTES ARE ADDED
          INX B          ;INCREMENT POINTERS
          INX H
          JMP LOOP
          . . .
AUGND:    DS N
ADDND:    DS N
```

Figure 7.1-3   Multibyte addition subroutine.

the lower order byte addition is included in the next higher order byte addition. The add with carry instructions are used for this purpose:

Add immediate with carry

ACI data

$(A) \leftarrow (A) + \text{byte } 2 + (CY)$

Add register with carry

ADC r

$(A) \leftarrow (A) + (r) + (CY)$

Add memory with carry

ADC M

$(A) \leftarrow (A) + ((H)(L)) + (CY)$

Flags: Z, S, P, CY, AC

See Fig. 7.1-3 for a subroutine, MBADD, which adds two *N*-byte numbers. The value of *N* has been previously defined with an EQU instruction. The numbers are stored low order byte first in memory buffers, beginning at AUGND and ADDND. The computed sum is stored in the memory buffer, ADDND, low order byte first, replacing the original addend. The routine is written so that when control is returned to the calling program, the carry flag indicates whether an arithmetic overflow has occurred. Note that the only instruction within the loop that affects the carry flag is the ADC M instruction.

As Fig. 7.1-3 shows, single byte addition instructions and looping implement multibyte additions. However, a very useful double precision (16-bit) addition instruction in the 8085A instruction set also implements multibyte addition:

Add register pair to H and L

DAD rp

$(H)(L) \leftarrow (H)(L) + (rh)(rl)$ *Flags:* CY

The contents of the register pair, rp, are added to the contents of the register pair H and L. The sum is left in H and L. The carry is the only flag affected.

7.1.2 Subtraction

The following rules define the subtraction operation for two, 1-bit numbers:

Minuend	Subtrahend	Borrow	Difference
0	$-$ 0	= 0	0
0	$-$ 1	= 1	1
1	$-$ 0	= 0	1
1	$-$ 1	= 0	0

For an n-bit number, subtraction starts with the least significant bits of the minuend and subtrahend and continues with the subtraction of successively higher order bits, including a borrow from the previous lower order bit. If the subtrahend is greater than the minuend, an ***arithmetic underflow*** condition exists and results in a borrow out of the higher order bit; for example

Borrows		10011000	
Minuend	X	00110101	53
Subtrahend	Y	10011101	-157
Difference	$X - Y$	1] 10011000	-104

There is a single byte subtraction operation analogous to each of the single byte addition operations.[2]

Subtract immediate	Subtract register	Subtract memory
SUI data	SUB r	SUB M
$(A) \leftarrow (A) -$ byte 2	$(A) \leftarrow (A) - (r)$	$(A) \leftarrow (A) - ((H)(L))$

Flags: Z, S, P, CY, AC

However, in unsigned binary representations, although a borrow flag indicates a negative difference, this difference cannot be represented for subsequent storage. Therefore, unsigned binary is inappropriate and cannot be used as a method for handling subtraction requiring a borrow. This holds true in 1-bit, n-bit, single byte, and multibyte subtraction of unsigned binary numbers.

The subroutine for single byte subtraction shown in Fig. 7.1-4 parallels that for single byte addition. The calling program checks the carry flag for arithmetic underflow after the subroutine is executed.

For multibyte subtraction, the 8085A has instructions that subtract the carry flag, which represents a borrow from the previous lower order byte. These instructions are

Subtract immediate with borrow	Subtract register with borrow	Subtract memory with borrow
SBI data	SBB r	SBB M
$(A) \leftarrow (A) -$ byte 2 $- (CY)$	$(A) \leftarrow (A) - (r) - (CY)$	$(A) \leftarrow (A) - ((H)(L)) - (CY)$

Flags: Z, S, P, CY, AC

---

[2] The 8085A subtraction instructions implement straight binary subtraction, without any regard to the number representation chosen by the programmer.

```
SBSUB:    LXI B,MINU      ;LOAD BC WITH ADDRESS OF MINUEND
          LXI H,SUBTR     ;LOAD HL WITH ADDRESS OF SUBTRAHEND
          LXI D,DIFF      ;LOAD DE WITH ADDRESS OF DIFFERENCE
          LDAX B          ;MOVE MINU TO A
          SUB M           ;SUBTRACT SUBTR
          STAX D          ;STORE DIFFERENCE IN DIFF
          RET
          . . .
MINU:     DS 1H           ;RESERVED MEMORY FOR OPERANDS
SUBTR:    DS 1H
DIFF:     DS 1H           ;RESERVED MEMORY FOR RESULT
```

Figure 7.1-4   Subroutine for single byte subtraction.

```
;N ASSUMED PREVIOUSLY DEFINED
MBSUB:    MVI D,N         ;INITIALIZE BYTE COUNTER
          LXI B,MINU      ;LOAD BC WITH ADDRESS OF MINU
          LXI H,SUBTR     ;LOAD HL WITH ADDRESS OF SUBTR
          XRA A           ;CLEAR BORROW (CARRY)
LOOP:     LDAX B          ;SUBTRACT TWO BYTES
          SBB M
          MOV M,A         ;STORE DIFFERENCE
          DCR D           ;DECREMENT BYTE COUNTER
          RZ              ;RETURN AFTER LAST BYTES ARE SUBTRACTED
          INX B           ;INCREMENT MEMORY POINTERS
          INX H
          JMP LOOP
          . . .
MINU:     DS N
SUBTR:    DS N
```

Figure 7.1-5   Multibyte subtraction subroutine.

The SBB instruction implements multibyte subtraction in the subroutine represented in Fig. 7.1-5. The subroutine is similar to the program for multibyte addition and is written so that when control is returned to the calling program, the carry flag is examined for arithmetic underflow.

7.1.3 Logical Shifts

An arithmetic operation not implemented in the 8085A instruction set and therefore must be implemented by a macro or subroutine is the logical shift. Logical shifts multiply and divide unsigned binary integer numbers.

A logical left shift moves each bit of data in a register one position to the left. The bit shifted out of the left end of the register is lost, and a 0 bit is shifted into the right end.

If the data in the register is an unsigned binary integer, if the bit shifted in is a 0, and if the bit shifted out is a 0, the number is multiplied by two. A left shift does not multiply a number by two if the bit shifted out is a 1. For example, shifting the number

$$00011011 = 27$$

three places to the left results in

$$11011000 = 216$$

or

$$27 \times 2^3 = 27 \times 8 = 216$$

An additional shift to the left, however, gives

$$10110000 = 176$$

which is not equal to 27×2^4 because a 1 bit was shifted out and lost.

Each logical shift to the right divides a number by two, assuming the bit shifted in is a 0. Since the resulting number is always an integer, any fractional part is lost. Shifting the number 27 three places to the right results in

$$00000011 = 3$$

which is the integer quotient of

$$\frac{27}{2^3} = \frac{27}{8} = 3.38$$

The subroutine in Fig. 7.1-6 implements a logical right shift of n places. The subroutine is entered with the data to be shifted in the accumulator and the desired number of shifts in B.

The analogous left shift is implemented similarly, with RAR replaced by RAL. A 16-bit logical left shift of the contents of register pair H and L is carried out by the DAD H instruction. DAD H adds the contents of register pair H and L to itself, thus doubling its original value, or, in effect, shifting the contents one place to the left.

In general, multipliers and divisors are rarely powers of two, thus limiting the applicability of logical left and right shifts for multiplying and dividing unsigned binary integers. Other methods, however, are available.

7.1.4 Multiplication

Since some microprocessors do not contain multiplication instructions, multiplication is implemented by subroutines or external hardware. A simple subroutine for unsigned binary numbers carries out multiplication by repeated addition. The

```
          SUBROUTINE ENTERED WITH N IN REGISTER B
     SRN:     ORA  A      ;CLEAR THE CARRY IN ORDER TO SHIFT IN O'S
              RAR         ;SHIFT RIGHT
              DCR  B      ;DECREMENT COUNTER
              JNZ  SRN    ;IF COUNTER IS NOT ZERO, SHIFT AGAIN
              RET
```

Figure 7.1-6 Subroutine for n-bit logical right shift.

multiplier is loaded into an internal register as an initial count, the accumulator is cleared, and the multiplicand is added to the accumulator. The multiplier register is then decremented; if it is not zero, the multiplicand is again added to the accumulator, and the process is repeated. When the multiplier register is finally decremented to zero, the multiplication is complete.

If the multiplier is large, the subroutine for multiplying unsigned binary numbers requires the execution of a large number of instructions, and therefore this method is only appropriate in applications where execution speed is not critical.

The multiplication rules for single bit arithmetic provide the basis for faster algorithms that multiply n-bit numbers:

Multiplicand		Multiplier		Product
0	×	0	=	0
0	×	1	=	0
1	×	0	=	0
1	×	1	=	1

An m-bit unsigned number multiplied by an n-bit unsigned number produces an $m + n$-bit result. Multiplication of binary numbers on paper is carried out by examining each bit of the multiplier in turn: the bit is multiplied by the multiplicand, producing a partial product that is written in a position that reflects the weight of the multiplier bit. After each multiplier bit has been examined, the partial products are summed to provide the final product:

$$
\begin{array}{lrl}
\text{Multiplicand} & X & 1011 \\
\text{Multiplier} & \times Y & 1001 \\
\hline
& & 1011 \\
& & 0000 \\
& & 0000 \quad \text{Partial} \\
& & 1011 \quad \text{products} \\
\hline
\text{Product} \quad Z = Y \times X = & & 1100011
\end{array}
$$

The subroutine shown in Fig. 7.1-7 implements multiplication in a manner similar to manual multiplication. The essential difference is that partial products are not summed simultaneously but are added to an accumulated partial product in registers H and L as they are generated, except when a multiplier bit is 0, in which case addition of the multiplicand to the partial product is not necessary. The subroutine is entered with the multiplicand in register E and the multiplier in register C. The product is returned in registers H and L. The multiplier is shifted right to check the value of each multiplier bit by moving the bit into the carry. During the right shift, a zero is moved into the most significant bit of the multiplier. Before each iteration, the multiplier is checked for a value of zero; if zero, the subroutine is exited. The time required for this multiplication varies, depending on the value of the multiplier.

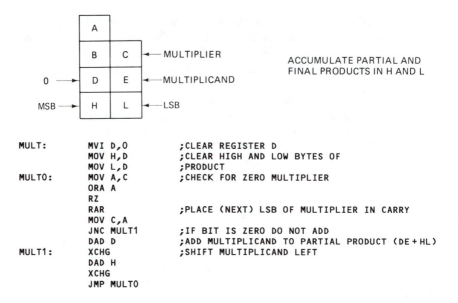

```
MULT:       MVI D,0           ;CLEAR REGISTER D
            MOV H,D           ;CLEAR HIGH AND LOW BYTES OF
            MOV L,D           ;PRODUCT
MULT0:      MOV A,C           ;CHECK FOR ZERO MULTIPLIER
            ORA A
            RZ
            RAR               ;PLACE (NEXT) LSB OF MULTIPLIER IN CARRY
            MOV C,A
            JNC MULT1         ;IF BIT IS ZERO DO NOT ADD
            DAD D             ;ADD MULTIPLICAND TO PARTIAL PRODUCT (DE+HL)
MULT1:      XCHG              ;SHIFT MULTIPLICAND LEFT
            DAD H
            XCHG
            JMP MULT0
```

Figure 7.1-7 Multiplication subroutine for 8-bit positive integers.

7.1.5 Division

As in the case for multiplication, some microprocessors do not contain division instructions. And, in the same manner in which multiplication is implemented in software as repeated addition, division is implemented as repeated subtraction of the divisor from the dividend. The number of times the divisor is subtracted from the dividend without a borrow occurring is the quotient, Q, and the difference after the last successful subtraction is the remainder, R. This method of division is appropriate when execution time is not critical.

Algorithms can, however, be developed that implement division faster than the repeated subtraction method. The division rules for two 1-bit numbers are as follows:

Dividend	Divisor		Remainder	Quotient
0	÷	0	=	Undefined	Undefined
0	÷	1	=	0	0
1	÷	0	=	Undefined	Undefined
1	÷	1	=	0	1

In general, if Y is the dividend and X is the divisor, Q the quotient, and R the remainder, their relationship is expressed as[3]

$$\frac{Y}{X} = Q + \frac{R}{X} \quad \text{and} \quad R < X$$

[3]To preclude Q being extremely large, some restriction must be placed on the value of X. Since this section deals only with unsigned integers, the restriction is $X \geq 1$.

or

$$Y = QX + R$$

For n-bit unsigned binary integers, the equation is written as

$$Y = \left(Q_{n-1}2^{n-1} + Q_{n-2}2^{n-2} + \cdots + Q_0 2^0\right) X + R$$

$$= Q_{n-1}2^{n-1}X + Q_{n-2}2^{n-2}X + \cdots + Q_0 2^0 X + R$$

This equation indicates that division is accomplished by repeatedly subtracting the highest power of the divisor from the dividend and then from the resulting partial remainders. First, Q_{n-1} is determined by subtracting $2^{n-1}X$ from Y. If the difference is positive; i.e., there is no borrow, then $Q_{n-1} = 1$, and the first partial remainder is the difference between Y and $2^{n-1}X$. If a borrow occurs, then $Q_{n-1} = 0$, meaning that $2^{n-1}X$ is larger than Y, and the first partial remainder is equal to Y itself. The next highest power of the divisor is then subtracted from the previous partial remainder to obtain the next bit of the quotient. This process is repeated until all the remaining bits of the quotient are determined. R is the final partial remainder.

Division of binary numbers by hand is simply a shorthand version of this algorithm, as shown in the following example:

```
                    0100      Quotient
   Divisor:    0011|1110      Dividend
               11
               ----
                001           Partial remainder
                000
               -----
                0010          Partial remainder
                0000
               -----
                0010          Remainder
```

It can, however, be written to resemble a machine implementation:

```
                  0100
         0011|0001110
              0000
             ------
              0011
              0011
             ------
              0001
              0000
             ------
              0010
              0000
             ------
              0010
```

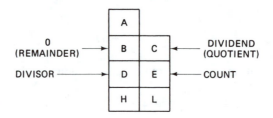

```
DIV:   MVI B,0
       MVI E,8        ;SET UP COUNTER
       MOV A,C        ;SET UP DIVIDEND DIVIDED BY 2⁷ (RELATIVE TO BC)
       RAL
       MOV C,A
       MOV A,B
       RAL
DIV0:  SUB D          ;SUBTRACT DIVISOR FROM PARTIAL REMAINDER
       JNC DIV1
       ADD D          ;IF DIFFERENCE IS NEGATIVE, RESTORE PARTIAL REMAINDER
       STC            ;SET CARRY SO THAT WHEN LATER COMPLEMENTED IT WILL DICTATE
DIV1:  MOV B,A        ;QUOTIENT BIT
       CMC            ;COMPLEMENT CARRY TO INDICATE DIVISOR BIT
       MOV A,C        ;MULTIPLY LOW ORDER DIVIDEND BY TWO
       RAL
       MOV C,A
       DCR E          ;CHECK FOR END OF DIVISION
       RZ
       MOV A,B        ;MULTIPLY HIGH ORDER DIVIDEND BY TWO
       RAL
       JMP DIV0
```

Figure 7.1-8 Division subroutine.

In this form the divisor is first tested against the dividend divided by 2^{n-1}, which is equivalent to testing 2^{n-1} times the divisor against the dividend. If it is equal to or smaller than the dividend divided by 2^{n-1}, the divisor is subtracted from the dividend; if not, zero is subtracted from the dividend. The divisor is shifted right after each test. In the division routine that appears in Fig. 7.1-8, this final step is accomplished by shifting the dividend to the left, relative to the divisor.

The subroutine in Fig. 7.1-8 divides two 8-bit numbers and generates an 8-bit quotient and an 8-bit remainder. Register B is initially zero and at the completion of the subroutine contains the remainder. Register C initially contains the dividend and at the completion of the subroutine contains the quotient. Register D contains the divisor, and register E contains the count.

The subroutine, as written, has no check for a 0 divisor; instead, the calling routine checks the divisor and only calls the subroutine if it is not zero. Alternatively, the division subroutine can be written to make this check itself.

If a routine divides a 16-bit dividend by an 8-bit divisor, a restriction has to be set on their relative sizes, if the quotient and remainder are to be single byte quantities: the value of the most significant byte of the dividend must be less than the divisor. If this condition is not met, the quotient requires more than 8 bits.

Errors occur when operands are outside of the range of allowed values or when results are too large or small to be expressed in the number representation. In systems that involve sufficient operator intervention, error messages can be provided to the operator. In other applications, operands or results that are out of range are replaced with either the largest or smallest value expressable in the representation. However, in many systems it is critical for proper operation that no such error conditions ever be allowed to occur. In these systems, the only possible response to an error condition is to shut down the system. Since the range of inputs in most dedicated systems is known, these errors can be avoided by the proper choice of number representation and the correct development of algorithms.

7.2 TWO'S COMPLEMENT NUMBERS

Two's complement numbers provide a binary representation of both positive and negative values, and can be added and subtracted by the same addition and subtraction instructions used for unsigned binary numbers. In an n-bit two's complement number, the most significant bit is the sign. The sign bit of a positive number is $X_{n-1} = 0$. The remaining $n - 1$ bits represent its magnitude. Thus, n-bit positive numbers range from 0 to $+(2^{n-1} - 1)$. The value of the n-bit positive number $x_{n-1}x_{n-2} \cdots x_0$ is

$$V(X) = + \sum_{i=0}^{n-2} x_i 2^i$$

Two's complement negative numbers have a sign bit, x_{n-1}, equal to 1. In two's complement, n-bit negative numbers range from -1 to -2^{n-1} and have the value

$$V(X) = -2^{n-1} + \sum_{i=0}^{n-2} x_i 2^i$$

For the general case of positive and negative two's complement numbers, the value of the number is given by

$$V(X) = \left(-x_{n-1}2^{n-1}\right) + \sum_{i=0}^{n-2} x_i 2^i$$

As an example, several 8-bit numbers are listed below in two's complement form with their decimal equivalent. As this listing shows, with 8-bits numbers from $-128(-2^{n-1})$ to $+127(+2^{n-1} - 1)$ can be represented. This range of values is not symmetrical since there is one more negative integer than there is positive.

	Sign Bit								Decimal Equivalent
Weight	-2^7 -128	2^6 64	2^5 32	2^4 16	2^3 8	2^2 4	2^1 2	2^0 1	
	0	1	1	1	1	1	1	1	$+127$
	0	1	1	1	1	1	1	0	$+126$
					$\vdots$					
	0	0	0	0	0	0	0	1	$+1$
	0	0	0	0	0	0	0	0	0
	1	1	1	1	1	1	1	1	-1
	1	1	1	1	1	1	1	0	-2
					$\vdots$					
	1	0	0	0	0	0	0	1	-127
	1	0	0	0	0	0	0	0	-128

Given a two's complement number, X, represented with n bits (a sign bit, x_{n-1}, and $n-1$ magnitude bits), its negative equivalent, $-X$, is equal to $2^n - X$. The computation of $2^n - X$, given X, is referred to as "taking the two's complement of X."[4]

The determination of $2^n - X$ is as follows:

$$X = x_{n-1}x_{n-2}x_{n-3} \cdots x_0$$

The two's complement of X is

$$2^n - X$$

$$\underbrace{1\,00 \cdots 0}_{n \ 0s} - \left(x_{n-1}x_{n-2}x_{n-3} \cdots x_0 \right)$$

or

$$\underbrace{11 \cdots 1}_{n \ 1s} + 1 - \left(x_{n-1}x_{n-2}x_{n-3} \cdots x_0 \right)$$

or

$$(1 - x_{n-1})(1 - x_{n-2})(1 - x_{n-3}) \cdots (1 - x_0) + 1$$

However, $1 - x_i$ equals $\bar{x}_i$, the logical complement of x_i.

In simpler terms, the two's complement of X is obtained by complementing each bit of X and adding 1 to the result. Any carry out of the high order bit position resulting from the addition is ignored. The resulting n bits represent the two's complement of X.

---

[4]A careful distinction must be drawn between the two's complement representation of a number, positive or negative, and the action of "taking the two's complement of a number." The latter refers to the computation of the negative of a number that is already encoded in two's complement form, regardless of whether the number was originally negative or positive.

Consider the following encoding of negative numbers originating as 7-bit unsigned magnitudes. The two's complement representation requires 8 bits:

	Sign	*Magnitude*	*Decimal*
	$-$	1001101	-77
Concatenate 0 sign bit		01001101	
Complement		10110010	
Add 1		1	
Two's complement representation		10110011	

	Sign	*Magnitude*	*Decimal*
	$-$	1111111	-127
Concatenate 0 sign bit		01111111	
Complement		10000000	
Add 1		1	
Two's complement representation		10000001	

When the two's complement procedure is applied to a number (positive or negative) initially represented in two's complement form, the negative of that number is obtained:

	Magnitude	*Decimal*
	11100110	-26
Complement	00011001	
Add 1	1	
Two's complement representation	00011010	$+26$

There is one exception to the above rule: For a given n, the two's complement of the most negative number generates a positive number not representable with n bits. For example, $n = 8$.

	10000000	-128
Complement	01111111	
Add 1	1	
	10000000	This is not $+128$, as desired but -128

7.2.1 Addition of Two's Complement Numbers

Two's complement numbers are added without considering the sign bit. The sum is correct if it is within the allowed range; however, errors arise if the result exceeds this range, producing arithmetic overflow. Consider the addition of two 8-bit two's complement numbers. It is possible to add two positive two's complement numbers and obtain an incorrect negative two's complement number or to add two negative two's complement numbers and obtain an incorrect positive two's complement number. When a positive two's complement and a negative two's complement number are added, the result is always correct. Consider the following addition:

$$
\begin{array}{r}
00010101 \\
+01110111 \\
\hline
10001100
\end{array}
\quad = \quad
\begin{array}{r}
21 \\
+119 \\
\hline
140
\end{array}
\quad \text{when interpreted as unsigned integers}
$$

When these two numbers are unsigned positive integers, an accurate sum expressable with 8 bits results from the addition. However, when these same numbers are two's complement, the sum is -116, not $+140$, because of arithmetic overflow.

$$
\begin{array}{r}
00010101 \\
+01110111 \\
\hline
10001100
\end{array}
\quad
\begin{array}{r}
21 \\
+119 \\
\hline
-116
\end{array}
\quad
\begin{array}{l}
\text{when interpreted as a two's} \\
\text{complement number (overflow!)}
\end{array}
$$

Similarly, the addition of two negative two's complement numbers can produce an erroneous positive result:

	Unsigned Positive Integers	*Two's Complement*
11001010	202	-54
$+10100011$	$+163$	$+(-93)$
1] 01101101	$+109$ (8 bit result)	$+\quad 109$
carry		
lost		

Here, however, neither addition is correct. If adding two unsigned positive numbers, the 8-bit result is incorrect unless the carry is included and it is represented with nine bits. And if the bit patterns are interpreted as two's complement numbers, then the result is a positive number and is obviously incorrect.

Thus, it is the responsibility of the designer to include instructions that not only detect overflow conditions but also take whatever steps are necessary to handle these conditions. The subroutine shown in Fig. 7.2-1 adds two 8-bit numbers in two's complement and checks for overflow.

The subroutine is called with the augend in register B and the addend in register C. The sum is left in register A when the subroutine is exited. If arithmetic overflow occurs, register D contains all 1s; if not, it contains all 0s. To ascertain an arithmetic overflow condition, the sign of the result is checked to determine whether it is appropriate, given the signs of the operands. The signs of the operands are determined by adding the addend to the accumulator, which contains only the sign bit of the augend with the remaining augend bits set to 0. The carry and sign bits

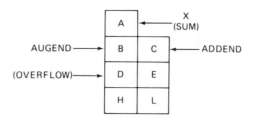

```
TCADD:   MVI D,0
         MOV A,B
         ANI 80H      ;MASK OUT ALL BUT SIGN BIT OF AUGEND
         ADD C        ;ADD ADDEND TO SIGN BIT OF AUGEND
         JC BNEG      ;IF A CARRY OCCURS BOTH ARE NEGATIVE
         JP BPOS      ;BOTH POSITIVE
         MOV A,B      ;HERE IF SIGNS ARE OPPOSITE AND THERE IS NO CHANCE OF OVERFLOW!
         ADD C
         RET
BNEG:    MOV A,B      ;BOTH AUGEND AND ADDEND ARE NEGATIVE
         ADD C
         JP ERROR     ;IF RESULT IS POSITIVE--ARITHMETIC OVERFLOW
         RET
BPOS:    MOV A,B      ;BOTH NUMBERS ARE POSITIVE
         ADD C
         JM ERROR     ;IF RESULT IS NEGATIVE--ARITHMETIC OVERFLOW
         RET
ERROR:   MVI D,0FFH
         RET
```

Figure 7.2-1   Two's complement addition subroutine.

from this addition indicate the operand sign bits as follows:

Sign of Augend	Sign of Addend	Carry	Sign Bit
Negative	Negative	1	0
Negative	Positive	0	1
Positive	Negative	0	1
Positive	Positive	0	0

Multibyte two's complement addition is a direct extension of single byte addition. The most significant bit of the most significant byte is the sign of the number. Once the multibyte numbers are in two's complement form, the same subroutine used for unsigned multibyte addition is used. However, no check for arithmetic overflow is provided by this subroutine.

7.2.2 Subtraction of Two's Complement Numbers

As previously stated, taking the two's complement of a number produces the negative of that number. Thus, taking the two's complement of Y produces $-Y$. This allows two's complement numbers to be subtracted by addition; i.e., the two's complement of the subtrahend is *added* to the minuend. The sum is the correct two's complement representation of the difference—if it is within the range of values expressable by the *n*-bit two's complement number. For example

Minuend	01110100	(+116)
Subtrahend	00011101	−(+29)
		(+87)

Take the two's	00011101	
complement of	11100010	Complement
the subtrahend	1	Add 1
	11100011	
Minuend + two's	01110100	(+116)
complement of	11100011	+(−29)
the subtrahend	1] 01010111	(+87)

As another example, consider the subtraction of a negative number from a positive one:

Minuend	00000111	(+7)
Subtrahend	11000011	−(−61)
		(+68)

Take the two's	11000011	
complement of	00111100	Complement
the subtrahend	1	Add 1
	00111101	
Minuend and two's	00000111	(+7)
complement of the	00111101	+(+61)
subtrahend	0] 01000100	(+68)

Or consider a subtraction that creates a negative difference:

Minuend	00011000	(+24)
Subtrahend	00100000	−(+32)
		(−8)

Take the two's	00100000	
complement of	11011111	Complement
the subtrahend	1	Add 1
	0] 11100000	
Minuend and two's	00011000	(+24)
complement of the	11100000	+(−32)
subtrahend	0] 11111000	(−8)

```
TWOSC:   MVI C,N          ;SET COUNTER FOR NUMBER OF BYTES
         LXI H,SUBTR
         STC              ;SET CARRY FOR ADDITION OF 1 TO LSB
LOOP:    MOV A,M
         CMA              ;COMPLEMENT BYTE
         ACI 00H          ;ADD PREVIOUS CARRY
         MOV M,A          ;STORE TWO'S COMPLEMENT
         DCR C            ;DECREMENT COUNTER
         RZ               ;RETURN IF 0
         INX H
         JMP LOOP
```

Figure 7.2-2 Subroutine to compute the two's complement of an N-byte number.

The 1 in the most significant bit of this result indicates that it is the two's complement representation of a negative number.

In microprocessors that do not have subtraction instructions, subtraction is carried out by the previous technique. Assume that the subtrahend is in register A and the minuend in register B,

```
CMA       ;complement the subtrahend
ADI 01H   ;add one, obtaining the two's complement
ADD B     ;add minuend, leaving the difference in A
```

Multibyte subtraction using two's complement is the same as multibyte addition once the complement of the subtrahend has been obtained. The subroutine in Fig. 7.2-2 obtains the two's complement of an N-byte number stored least significant byte first, starting at location SUBTR.

The 8085A subtraction instructions directly subtract two's complement numbers. The difference from the subtraction of two's complement numbers, using these instructions, will be correct if it is within the allowed range. In fact, the 8085A's subtraction instructions actually compute the difference between the minuend and subtrahend by taking the two's complement of the subtrahend and adding it to the minuend. This sequence of operations is implemented as microoperations by the 8085A's control section when it executes a subtract instruction. Subtraction is implemented in this manner because it eliminates the need for subtraction logic in the ALU of the microprocessor. Thus, logic in the ALU for addition and complement is sufficient to implement subtraction also.

There is, however, one difference between subtraction by two's complement implemented by the previous sequence of 8085A instructions and subtraction implemented directly by an 8085A subtraction instruction. The 8085A subtraction instructions complement the carry that results from the addition microoperation, so that it represents the borrow that occurs in straight binary subtraction. For instance, in the last example of subtraction implemented by two's complement, $(+24) - (+32)$, the carry bit was 0. If, instead, the 8085A SUB instruction is used to subtract $+32$ from $+24$, the 8085A carry bit is set to indicate a borrow.

7.2.3 Arithmetic Shifts

The shifting of a two's complement number left or right to multiply or divide the number by two is referred to as an *arithmetic shift*. In arithmetic shifts, unlike the logical shifts of Section 7.1.3, the sign bit is treated in a special manner. In a left shift, the sign bit is never changed. For a left shift of an 8-bit number, bits shifted out of bit 6 never enter bit 7 (the sign bit). For example, if the two's complement number

$$11100101 = -27$$

is shifted left two positions, the result is

$$10010100 = -108$$

or

$$-27 \times 2^2 = -27 \times 4 = -108$$

An additional left shift of this result gives

$$10101000 = -88$$

which is not equal to -27×2^3. An n-bit left shift of a negative two's complement number results in an arithmetic overflow if the most significant $n + 1$ bits are not equal to 1. For positive two's complement numbers arithmetic overflow occurs when a 1 is shifted out of bit 6.

In an arithmetic right shift, the sign bit is also left unchanged. In addition, the bit shifted into the vacated position is the same as the sign bit. For positive numbers, this is equivalent to the logical shift for unsigned numbers. For negative numbers, some rather interesting results occur. If the two's complement number

$$11100101 = -27$$

is shifted three places to the right, the result is

$$11111100 = -4$$

but

$$\frac{-27}{2^3} = -3.38$$

An additional right shift by two gives

$$11111111 = -1$$

but

$$\frac{-27}{2^5} = -0.84$$

```
ARN:    RLC             ;SAMPLE THE SIGN (MSB) BIT
        RAR             ;RESTORE A
        RAR             ;SHIFT A RIGHT
        DCR B           ;DECREMENT COUNTER
        RZ              ;DONE WHEN ZERO
        JMP ARN
```

Figure 7.2-3 Subroutine for n-bit right arithmetic shift.

Finally, one more right shift gives

$$11111111 = -1$$

Additional shifting to the right always gives a result of -1. It is clear from these examples that shifting a signed two's complement number (positive or negative) one place to the right results in division by two, with the result rounded to the next most negative integer.

The subroutine shown in Fig. 7.2-3 implements an n-bit right arithmetic shift. The subroutine is entered with the number to be shifted in A and the number of positions it is to be shifted in B.

7.2.4 Multiplication and Division of Two's Complement Numbers

Two's complement numbers cannot be multiplied with the algorithm for unsigned binary numbers because if either or both of the operands is negative, the result is incorrect. One method for multiplying two's complement numbers first determines and saves the signs of the operands. Negative operands are made positive, and the operands are multiplied using the add and shift algorithm of Section 7.1.4. If the operand signs are different, the two's complement of the product is taken.

Booth's algorithm is a more direct method of multiplying either unsigned or two's complement numbers [1, 2]. In the previously considered add and shift algorithm for unsigned binary integers, each multiplier bit was examined in turn; when the multiplier bit was 1, the multiplicand was added to the accumulated partial product. For each multiplier bit there was a relative 1-bit shift between the multiplicand and partial product, whether or not an addition was required. In Booth's algorithm, however, more than one shift can be made at a time, depending on the grouping of 0s and 1s in the multiplier.

Booth's algorithm is based on the fact that a string of 0s in the multiplier requires no addition, just shifting, and a string of 1s running from bit 2^p to 2^q (where $q > p$) is treated as $2^{q+1} - 2^p$. Consider the multiplier

$$X = 00011110$$
$$p = 1$$
$$q = 4$$

Then $2^{q+1} - 2^p = 2^5 - 2^1 = 32 - 2 = 30$, is the value of X. With Booth's al-

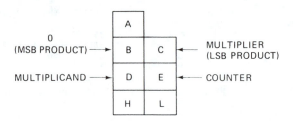

```
SMULT:    MVI B,0       ;CLEAR MSB OF RESULT
          MVI E,8       ;SET COUNTER
          XRA A         ;CLEAR CARRY (SET X(-1)=0)
          MOV A,C       ;PLACE MULTIPLIER IN A
LLA:      JC LLB        ;CHECK X(I-1)
          RRC           ;X(I-1)=0, PLACE X(I) IN CY
          MOV A,B       ;MOVE PARTIAL PRODUCT TO A
          JNC LLC       ;CHECK X(I)
          SUB D         ; X(I)=1 and X(I-1)=0, SUBTRACT MULTIPLICAND
          JMP LLC
LLB:      RRC           ;X(I-1)=1, PLACE X(I) IN CY
          MOV A,B       ;MOVE PARTIAL PRODUCT TO A
          JC LLC        ;CHECK X(I)
          ADD D         ;X(I)=0, and X(I-1)=1, ADD MULTIPLICAND
LLC:      MOV B,A       ;SAVE MSB OF PARTIAL PRODUCT
          RAL           ;SET CY TO MSB
          MOV A,B       ;LOAD MSB OF PARTIAL PRODUCT
          RAR           ;ARITHMETIC RIGHT SHIFT
          MOV B,A       ;SAVE SHIFTED MSB
          MOV A,C       ;LOAD LSB OF PARTIAL PRODUCT
          RAR           ;RIGHT SHIFT LSB, NEW X(I-1) IN CY
          MOV C,A       ;SAVE
          DCR E         ;CHECK FOR COMPLETION
          JNZ LLA
          RET
```

Figure 7.2-4 Subroutine to implement multiplication, using Booth's algorithm.

gorithm, this multiplication requires only two operations in addition to the shifts—one subtraction and one addition—whereas the add and shift method requires four additions plus the shifts. Booth's algorithm thus results in a faster multiplication because fewer operations are needed.

Booth's algorithm is as follows: let x_i be the ith bit of an n-bit multiplier. Bit x_{n-1} is the most significant bit, and x_0 is the least significant bit. A bit, $x_{-1} = 0$, is assumed. The multiplicand is Y. Starting with $i = 0$, x_i and x_{i-1} are compared. Depending on the comparison, one of the following actions occurs:

x_i	x_{i-1}	
0	0	Shift Y (left with respect to partial product)[5]
0	1	Add Y to partial product, then shift Y
1	0	Subtract Y from partial product, then shift Y
1	1	Shift Y

The process is repeated until n comparisons are made, completing the multiplication. The procedure is valid for the two's complement numbers Y and X. It is valid

[5]Note that Y is shifted left relative to the partial product. Thus, in an actual implementation Y may remain fixed, and the partial product is shifted to the right.

for Y because the logic for addition and subtraction of unsigned and two's complement numbers is identical. For X it is valid because if X ends in a string of 1s, the last operation (excluding shifting) is a subtraction of Y at the appropriate weight.

The subroutine shown in Fig. 7.2-4 implements Booth's algorithm for an 8-bit multiplicand and an 8-bit multiplier. The subroutine is entered with the multiplicand in register D and the multiplier in register C; the 16-bit product is returned in register pair BC. Booth's algorithm is also used with multibyte operands.

Several different algorithms are used in the software division of two's complement numbers. The simplest one examines the signs of the dividend and divisor to determine the signs of the quotient and remainder. The magnitudes of the quotient and remainder are determined by making both the dividend and divisor positive and then dividing. This divides the magnitudes of the numbers, and the magnitudes of the quotient and remainder are then converted to the appropriate signed two's complement representation.

Other algorithms directly divide two's complement numbers [3, 4, 5]. Most of these, developed to carry out division more quickly by manipulating the operands as signed quantities, are designed for implementation with hardware. Therefore, if programmed on a microprocessor, the improvement in execution time may be negligible or nonexistent.

7.2.5 Unspecified 8085A Two's Complement Arithmetic Instructions

Two of the ten unspecified instructions (see Appendix G) in the 8085A instruction set are for two's complement arithmetic. These instructions illustrate and extend concepts presented in the previous sections.

One of the additional unspecified flag bits is the two's complement overflow flag, V. This flag indicates the occurrence of arithmetic overflow from the addition of two's complement numbers. This flag is bit 1 of the flag register, F. The overflow flag's value is a function of the carries out of bit 6, cy_6, and bit 7, cy_7, positions as a result of an addition:

$$V = cy_7 \,\forall\, cy_6$$

For a two's complement number this corresponds to the EX-OR of the carry out of the sign bit position and the carry into the sign bit position. The existence of an overflow flag obviates the need for the checking of the signs of the operands and sign of the result to determine if arithmetic overflow occurred, as was done in Fig. 7.2-1. Many microprocessors have an overflow flag.

The RST V instruction in the unspecified instruction group is used to test the V flag and transfer control based on its value. The instruction has the following form:

$$\text{RST V}$$
$$\text{If V} = 1, \text{ then:}$$
$$((SP) - 1) \leftarrow (PCH)$$
$$((SP) - 2) \leftarrow (PCL)$$
$$(SP) \leftarrow (SP) - 2$$
$$(PC) \leftarrow 40H$$

If the V flag is set when the RST V instruction is executed, the address of the instruction following the RST V is saved on the stack, the stack pointer is decremented, and control is transferred to location 40H. If the V flag is not set when RST V is executed, control is transferred directly to the instruction following RST V. In effect, RST V is a conditional call. The RST V instruction is placed after the instructions that add two's complement numbers and will transfer control to a subroutine written to handle the overflow condition.

The instruction ARHL implements an *arithmetic right shift* of register pair HL:

$$
\begin{aligned}
&\text{ARHL} \\
&(H_7) \leftarrow (H_7) \\
&(H_{n-1}) \leftarrow (H_n) \\
&(H_0) \leftarrow (L_7) \\
&(L_{n-1}) \leftarrow (L_n) \\
&(CY) \leftarrow (L_0)
\end{aligned}
$$

The sign bit is maintained and also shifted right with the remaining bits of HL. The least significant bit of L is shifted to the CY.

7.3 BCD NUMBERS

Each of the decimal digits, 0 through 9, can be coded in binary by using four bits. The resulting numerical representation is called *binary coded decimal*, or *BCD*. The BCD code for decimal digits is shown in Table 7.3-1.

Many data input devices represent numbers as decimal digits and encode them in BCD. For example, a thumbwheel switch is basically a 10 position switch labeled in decimal, whose output is the BCD code corresponding to the selected decimal digit (see Chapter 10). Output displays, as well, for numerical data frequently require BCD inputs. A seven segment display, for example, is driven by a BCD-to-seven segment decoder driver IC. Some dot-matrix decimal displays have an internal display decoder that accepts BCD inputs. And in systems that require the frequent input and output of decimal data but not a substantial amount of calculation to produce outputs, it is advantageous to have the microprocessor carry out computa-

TABLE 7.3-1 BCD CODE FOR DECIMAL DIGITS

Decimal Number	BCD Code
0	0000
1	0001
2	0010
3	0011
4	0100
5	0101
6	0110
7	0111
8	1000
9	1001

tions in decimal arithmetic rather than binary. In cases of substantial or complex calculation, on the other hand, it is advantageous to convert the BCD input to binary—such as two's complement—carry out the required computations and then convert the results from binary to BCD for outputting.

7.3.1 Addition of Unsigned BCD Numbers

Special instructions for decimal addition are not available in the 8085A instruction set, and those addition instructions that are available implement only straight binary addition. For BCD, operands are added in binary, and the result is changed to a valid BCD representation. A single data byte can store or pack two BCD digits, but when 2 bytes of data, each representing two decimal digits, are added, the result is generally incorrect if interpreted as two BCD digits. Consider the following addition:

$$
\begin{array}{ccc}
 & 0000 \quad 0111 & 07 \\
 & 0000 \quad 0110 & +06 \\
\hline
AC = 0 \quad 0] & 0000 \quad 1101 & 13
\end{array}
$$

It is incorrect because 1101 is not a valid code for a BCD digit (see Table 7.3.1). As another example, consider the following:

$$
\begin{array}{ccc}
 & 0000 \quad 1001 & 09 \\
 & 0000 \quad 1000 & +08 \\
\hline
AC = 1 \quad 0] & 0001 \quad 0001 & 17
\end{array}
$$

The BCD result is 11 and not 17 as it should be. Note that the auxiliary carry flag is set, indicating a carry out of bit 3 into bit 4 as a result of the addition.

It is clear that when the sum of two BCD numbers, added using binary arithmetic, is greater than 9 or when a carry out of the most significant of the 4 bits occurs, the result is not valid in BCD. This is true for the least and most significant BCD digit in the byte. If the two previous examples are examined closely, it also becomes apparent that whenever the sum is erroneous, it can be corrected by adding 6 (0110).

	0000	0111		07
	+0000	0110		+06
AC = 0 0]	$\overline{0000}$	$\overline{1101}$	sum > 9, add 6	$\overline{13}$
	+0000	0110		
AC = 1 0]	$\overline{0001}$	$\overline{0011}$	Adjusted BCD sum	
	0000	1001		09
	0000	1000		+08
AC = 1 0]	$\overline{0001}$	$\overline{0001}$	AC = 1, sum > 9, add 6	$\overline{17}$
	+0000	0110		
AC = 0 0]	$\overline{0001}$	$\overline{0111}$	Adjusted BCD sum	

The 8085A obviates this problem with an instruction that adjusts the results of an addition when the numbers added are interpreted as BCD. This instruction is the *decimal adjust accumulator*, or DAA. It uses two steps to adjust the contents of the accumulator after an addition in order to represent a two-digit BCD result:

1. If the least significant 4 bits of the accumulator represent a number greater than 9, or if the auxiliary carry (AC) is equal to 1, then 6 is added to the accumulator. Otherwise no addition occurs.

2. After step 1 is completed, if the most significant 4 bits of the accumulator represent a number greater than 9 or if the normal carry (CY) is 1, then 6 is added to the most significant 4 bits of the accumulator. Otherwise no addition occurs. The following example shows the effect of executing a DAA instruction after an addition:

		0110	0111	67
Addition		0011	0100	34
	AC = 0	0] 1001	1011	101
	DAA step 1	0000	0110	
Decimal	AC = 1	0] 1010	0001	
adjust				
accumulator	DAA step 2	0110	0000	
	AC = 1	1] 0000	0001	

The previous multibyte addition routine for unsigned binary numbers is easily modified to handle unsigned BCD numbers by inserting a DAA instruction after the addition instruction.

7.3.2 Ten's Complement and Subtraction of BCD Numbers

Because the DAA instruction only works after an addition operation, BCD subtraction is implemented with complementary arithmetic. Signed decimal numbers are represented in *ten's complement* in a manner analogous to two's complement for signed binary numbers. An n-digit positive ten's complement number, $d_{n-1}d_{n-2} \cdots d_0$, has a sign digit of 0, and $n - 1$ decimal digits represent its magnitude. Each of these digits is encoded in BCD when stored in the microprocessor's memory. The representation of a negative decimal number, $-D$, is determined from the ten's complement representation of the positive number of the same magnitude, $+D$, by the process of taking its ten's complement.

The ten's complement of an n-digit decimal number, D, is defined as

$$10^n - D$$

$$\underbrace{1\,00 \cdots 0}_{n \ 0s} - (d_{n-1}d_{n-2} \cdots d_0)$$

```
TENSC:    MVI A,9AH      ;SET FIRST MINUEND DIGIT PAIR TO 9AH
LOOP:     SUB M          ;SUBTRACT
          ADI 00H        ;DECIMAL ADJUST DIFFERENCE
          DAA
          MOV M,A        ;STORE 10'S COMPLEMENT DIGITS
          DCR C          ;DECREMENT DIGIT PAIR COUNTER
          RZ             ;RETURN IF DONE
          INX H          ;SET POINTER TO NEXT PAIR OF DIGITS
          MVI A,99H      ;SET MINUEND DIGIT PAIR TO 99H
          ACI 0          ;OR 9AH IF PREVIOUS DIGIT PAIRS=0
          JMP LOOP
```

Figure 7.3-1   Subroutine to compute the ten's complement of a multidigit BCD number.

or

$$\underbrace{99\cdots9}_{n\ 9s} + 1 - (d_{n-1}d_{n-2}\cdots d_0)$$

or

$$(9 - d_{n-1})(9 - d_{n-2})\cdots(9 - d_0) + 1$$

$$(9 - d_{n-1})(9 - d_{n-2})\cdots(10 - d_0)$$

The latter equation shows the way in which the ten's complement of a decimal number is computed by subtracting the least significant digit of the number from 10 and each of the remaining digits from 9. For a negative ten's complement number, the sign bit is $9 - d_{n-1}$, or 9.

In subtracting ten's complement numbers, the ten's complement of the subtrahend is added to the minuend. Assuming that the decimal digits are encoded in BCD, the subroutine shown in Fig. 7.3-1 computes the ten's complement of a multidigit decimal number of $2 \times N$ digits stored two digits to the byte, least significant two digits first, starting at location SUBTR. The subroutine is entered with N in register C and the address of the least significant byte of the subtrahend in H and L. The ADI 00H and DAA instructions following SUB M convert the difference to BCD before storing it in memory. This sequence correctly adjusts the accumulator contents after subtraction only because in this particular application each minuend digit is either 9 or A. Thus, no borrow occurs between BCD digits and, therefore, adjustment of the result is based only on whether digit values are greater than 9. The ADI 00H instruction sets the auxiliary carry to 0. The only case requiring correction occurs when the least significant digit of the number to be complemented is 0. Then 0 is subtracted from A, leaving a result of A. The ACI 00H instruction propagates any carry resulting from this case.

The ten's complement subroutine can be used with a BCD addition subroutine to implement subtraction. Alternatively, as illustrated in Fig. 7.3-2, a single subroutine can be written that implements BCD subtraction of two $2 \times N$-digit BCD

```
BCDSB:   STC              ;INITIALIZE CARRY
LOOP:    MVI A,99H        ;OBTAIN 10'S COMPLEMENT OF SUBTRAHEND
         ACI 0
         SUB M
         XCHG             ;SWITCH SUBTRAHEND AND MINUEND POINTERS
         ADD M            ;ADD MINUEND TO SUBTRAHEND COMPLEMENT
         DAA              ;DECIMAL ADJUST DIFFERENCE
         XCHG             ;SWITCH POINTERS AGAIN
         MOV M,A          ;STORE DIFFERENCE
         DCR C            ;DECREMENT DIGIT PAIR COUNTER
         RZ               ;RETURN IF DONE
         INX H            ;INCREMENT POINTERS
         INX D
         JMP LOOP
```

Figure 7.3-2   Subroutine for subtraction of multidigit BCD numbers.

numbers directly. Here the ten's complement of the subtrahend is taken and added to the minuend. The computed difference replaces the subtrahend. The subroutine is entered with N in register C, a pointer to the subtrahend in registers H and L, and a pointer to the minuend in registers D and E.

In this routine the ten's complement is formed by initially setting the carry, placing 99 in the accumulator, and adding 0 with carry to form 9A. The first byte of the subtrahend is then subtracted from 9A, forming its ten's complement, and the minuend is added to the result, providing the difference for that byte. Additional bytes of the subtrahend are subtracted from 99 or 9A to form the ten's complement of each byte. Subtraction from 9A occurs if all previous bytes of the subtrahend are zero, and the DAA instruction propagates the carry into the next loop.

7.3.3 Multiplication and Division of BCD Numbers

Multiplication and division of unsigned BCD numbers are carried out by algorithms that implement repeated addition or subtraction, respectively. The execution times of these routines tend to be long, but more sophisticated algorithms are not only slow but also require inordinate amounts of memory. In all but the simplest cases, therefore, it is more efficient to convert BCD data into binary, carry out complex calculations, and then convert the results back to BCD.

7.3.4 BCD / Binary Conversion

There are many ways to convert BCD digits to binary. The slowest and simplest method is to count the BCD number down to zero using decimal arithmetic and, for each count, to increment in binary another register that is initially zeroed. The register containing the BCD number is counted down by adding -1 in ten's complement to the BCD value and then decimal adjusting the result. When this register is counted to zero, the other register contains the binary equivalent of the decimal number.

Faster methods utilize the fact that a decimal number, $d_{n-1}d_{n-2} \cdots d_0$, can be written as

$$D = \left(\cdots ((d_{n-1}) \times 10 + d_{n-2}) \times 10 + \cdots \right) \times 10 + d_1) \times 10 + d_0$$

```
BCDTB:    LXI  H,0H        ;CLEAR H and L
          MVI  C,4H        ;SET DIGIT COUNTER
LOOP:     LDAX D           ;LOAD POINTER TO DECIMAL NUMBER BUFFER
          ADD  L           ;ADD DECIMAL DIGIT TO H AND L
          MOV  L,A
          MVI  A,0H
          ADC  H
          MOV  H,A
          DCR  C           ;CHECK FOR LAST DIGIT
          RZ
          CALL TEN         ;MULTIPLY H AND L BY TEN
          INX  D           ;POINT TO NEXT DECIMAL DIGIT
          JMP  LOOP
TEN:      PUSH B           ;SAVE COUNTER
          DAD  H           ;HL*2
          PUSH H           ;SAVE
          DAD  H           ;HL*4
          DAD  H           ;HL*8
          POP  B           ;LOAD BC WITH HL*2
          DAD  B           ;HL*10
          POP  B           ;RESTORE COUNTER
          RET
```

Figure 7.3-3   Subroutine for BCD to binary conversion.

An algorithm based on this expression starts with the most significant decimal digit, d_{n-1}, multiplies it by 10, and adds the next most significant decimal digit. This result is then multiplied by 10, and so on, until the least significant digit is added. Subroutine BCDTB, shown in Fig. 7.3-3, converts a four-digit decimal number to a 16-bit binary result. The BCD digits are stored in 4 bytes—one digit per byte—with the most significant byte first (lowest address). The routine is entered with DE containing a pointer to the most significant digit of the BCD number to be converted.

Subroutine BCDTB calls subroutine TEN, which multiplies the contents of register pair HL by 10. The multiplication is carried out by generating $2 \times HL$ and $8 \times HL$—through repeated doubling of HL (DAD H)—and then adding these results to obtain $10 \times HL$.

Frequently, binary data is converted to BCD before being output because many display devices accept data in BCD. Binary numbers are easily converted to BCD through repeated division by binary ten (1010). The remainder after each division is a BCD digit. The remainder from the first division provides the low order BCD digit of the number, and each subsequent division provides the next higher order digit. This technique is particularly appropriate if the microprocessor being used has a divide instruction, although a divide subroutine can also be used.

A binary to decimal conversion method that is useful when a divide instruction is not available is repeated subtraction of powers of ten in binary. The highest power of ten possible in the binary number is repeatedly subtracted from the number until the difference becomes negative. The number of times the subtraction can be accomplished without a negative difference provides the digit associated with the power of ten being subtracted. The next highest power of ten is then subtracted from the positive binary difference resulting from the determination of the previous digit. When the digit associated with 10^1 is obtained, the positive remainder is the

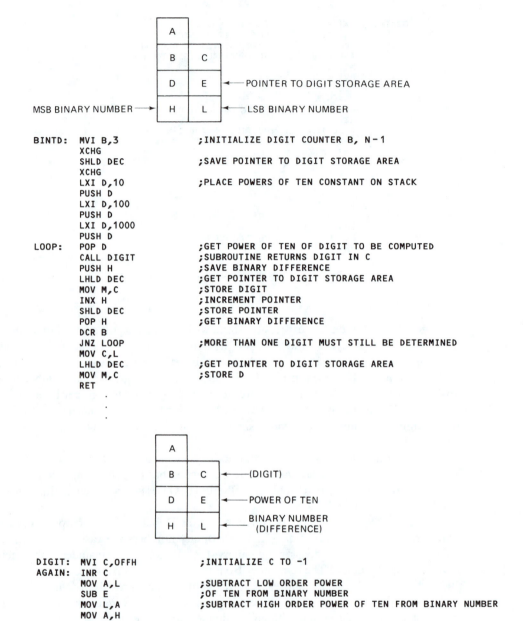

```
                    ┌─────┐
                    │  A  │
                    ├─────┼─────┐
                    │  B  │  C  │
                    ├─────┼─────┤
                    │  D  │  E  │◄────── POINTER TO DIGIT STORAGE AREA
                    ├─────┼─────┤
MSB BINARY NUMBER ─►│  H  │  L  │◄────── LSB BINARY NUMBER
                    └─────┴─────┘
```

```
BINTD:  MVI B,3          ;INITIALIZE DIGIT COUNTER B, N-1
        XCHG
        SHLD DEC         ;SAVE POINTER TO DIGIT STORAGE AREA
        XCHG
        LXI D,10         ;PLACE POWERS OF TEN CONSTANT ON STACK
        PUSH D
        LXI D,100
        PUSH D
        LXI D,1000
        PUSH D
LOOP:   POP D            ;GET POWER OF TEN OF DIGIT TO BE COMPUTED
        CALL DIGIT       ;SUBROUTINE RETURNS DIGIT IN C
        PUSH H           ;SAVE BINARY DIFFERENCE
        LHLD DEC         ;GET POINTER TO DIGIT STORAGE AREA
        MOV M,C          ;STORE DIGIT
        INX H            ;INCREMENT POINTER
        SHLD DEC         ;STORE POINTER
        POP H            ;GET BINARY DIFFERENCE
        DCR B
        JNZ LOOP         ;MORE THAN ONE DIGIT MUST STILL BE DETERMINED
        MOV C,L
        LHLD DEC         ;GET POINTER TO DIGIT STORAGE AREA
        MOV M,C          ;STORE D
        RET
            .
            .
            .
```

```
                    ┌─────┐
                    │  A  │
                    ├─────┼─────┐
                    │  B  │  C  │◄────── (DIGIT)
                    ├─────┼─────┤
                    │  D  │  E  │◄────── POWER OF TEN
                    ├─────┼─────┤
                    │  H  │  L  │◄────── BINARY NUMBER
                    └─────┴─────┘        (DIFFERENCE)
```

```
DIGIT:  MVI C,0FFH       ;INITIALIZE C TO -1
AGAIN:  INR C
        MOV A,L          ;SUBTRACT LOW ORDER POWER
        SUB E            ;OF TEN FROM BINARY NUMBER
        MOV L,A          ;SUBTRACT HIGH ORDER POWER OF TEN FROM BINARY NUMBER
        MOV A,H
        SBB D
        MOV H,A
        JNC AGAIN        ;IF DIFFERENCE IS POSITIVE GO BACK TO SUBTRACT AGAIN
        DAD D            ;IF DIFFERENCE IS NEGATIVE, RESTORE
        RET
DEC:    DS 2
```

Figure 7.3-4 Subroutine for binary to decimal conversion.

units digit. The subroutine shown in Fig. 7.3-4 converts a 16-bit unsigned binary number to a 4-digit decimal number. The subroutine is entered with the 16-bit binary number to be converted in HL and the address of the first digit of the result buffer in DE.

The conversion routines discussed above deal with unsigned numbers. For signed conversions, the sign is determined and saved. The magnitude of the number to be converted is determined, and the conversion is carried out on the unsigned magnitude. After the magnitude conversion is complete, the number is complemented if it is negative.

7.4 FRACTIONAL NUMBERS

To represent unsigned fractions, simply imagine a binary point in front of the most significant bit of the number. This corresponds to shifting the binary point—imagined in an 8-bit integer to follow x_0—eight places to the left, which is equivalent to dividing the number by 2^8, or 256. The value of an unsigned 8-bit number is

$$X = \cdot x_7 x_6 \cdots x_0$$

— Imagined binary point

$$V(X) = x_7 2^{-1} + x_6 2^{-2} + \cdots + x_0 2^{-8}$$

And the range of representable unsigned fractions is

$$.00000000 = \frac{0}{256} = 0$$

to

$$.11111111 = \frac{255}{256} = 0.99609375$$

To represent signed fractions, imagine a binary point after the first bit of the representation; the first bit indicates the sign.

$$X = x_{n-1} \cdot x_{n-2} \cdots x_0$$

— Imagined binary point

For the two's complement representation of signed fractions

$$V(X) = (-x_{n-1}) + \sum_{i=0}^{n-2} x_i 2^{-(n-(i+1))}$$

with $n = 8$, $X = x_7 \cdot x_6 \cdots x_0$. Values of X range from $-1.$ to $+0.99218750$. And, as with the integer two's complement case, the range of values is not symmetrical. There is one additional representable negative "fraction": $-1(+1$ is not representable).

An integer decimal number can be exactly represented by a binary number as long as the range of the binary number is not exceeded. Fractional representation of decimal numbers is only exact in unusual cases where the decimal fraction to be represented has an exact binary representation in n or fewer bits. When there is no exact representation, the binary equivalent is approximate. The approximation is obtained by retaining only the first n bits of the binary equivalent of the decimal fraction and dropping any others. The error that results from **truncating** the binary approximation at n bits is less than 2^{-n}.

Another approach, which provides a more accurate approximation, involves *rounding* the binary approximation to the nearest representable value. With rounding, the error is less than $2^{-(n+1)}$.

Arithmetic operations on fractions, even if the original fractions are exactly representable, include errors because, generally, the result must be truncated or rounded. The designer must ensure, in a particular application, that truncation or roundoff error does not produce unacceptable inaccuracy in the result. These errors are reduced by using more bits to represent the operands.

Arithmetic operations on unsigned and two's complement fractions are carried out in a manner analogous to those operations on integers and two's complement integers.

7.5 FLOATING POINT NUMBERS

In some applications, the required range of numbers is very large. While it is possible to represent such numbers as multibyte integers or multibyte fractions, the memory required for storage is excessive. And when the number of significant bits required is small, the use of a multibyte representation is wasteful of memory. In addition, most very large or very small numbers do not require the precision of a multibyte representation.

On paper, a more efficient representation of very large or very small decimal numbers is **scientific notation**, which minimizes the number of necessary digits. This notation consists of a **mantissa** multiplied by the decimal base that has been raised to a power represented by an exponent, E:

$$N = M \times 10^E$$

For example, the number 65,535 is represented by all of the following:

$$65{,}535 \times 10^0$$

$$6553.5 \times 10^1$$

$$655.35 \times 10^2$$

$$65.535 \times 10^3$$

$$6.5535 \times 10^4$$

$$0.65535 \times 10^5$$

$$0.065535 \times 10^6$$

Of course, an unlimited number of representations is possible by using different exponents.

Scientific notation delineates the precision and the range of a number. Precision is determined by the number of digits in the mantissa, and range is determined primarily by the base and the number of digits in the exponent.

7.5.1 Floating Point Formats

In digital systems, the counterpart of scientific notation is ***floating point notation***. A binary floating point number usually has a base of 2, although others are used in some representations, 10 and 16 being fairly common. In all cases, however, the base is implied, and representation requires only the mantissa (also called ***coefficient*** or ***fraction***) and the exponent (also called ***characteristic*** or ***power***). Similar to scientific notation, the number of bits used in representing the mantissa and exponent determines the precision and range of representable numbers.

The choice of base and format varies widely. It is application-dependent and involves such considerations as precision and range, memory size, computation speed, ease of implementation with a given microprocessor architecture, and ease of interface to other software. For this discussion, a base of 2 is used. The mantissa and exponent are signed quantities and therefore require a signed number representation. The exponent is represented by seven bits of a single byte in excess-64 (XS-64) form. This is equivalent to a 7-bit two's complement representation with 64 added to it. Or it is the same as a 7-bit two's complement representation with the sign bit inverted (see Fig. 7.5-1). Thus, exponents range from -64 to $+63$. Using the excess-64 representation with the msb (most significant bit) of the exponent word makes it easy to distinguish between exponent overflow and underflow.

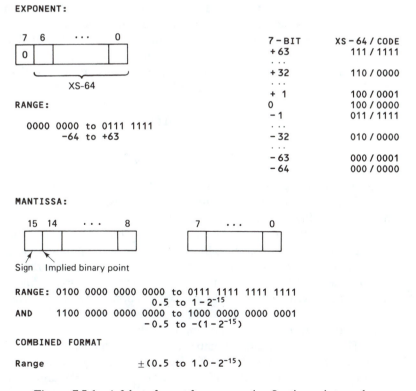

Figure 7.5-1 A 3-byte format for representing floating point numbers.

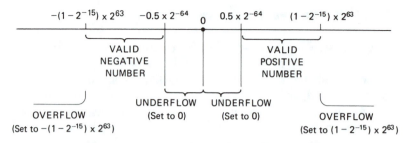

Figure 7.5-2 Range of representable numbers for the floating point format of Fig. 7.5-1.

In this example the mantissa is represented as a 2-byte two's complement fraction. The msb of the 16 bits is the sign bit. An implied binary point is assumed immediately to the right of the sign bit, leaving 15 bits available to represent the magnitude.

To avoid multiple representations of the same number and to maintain as many significant bits as possible in the mantissa, a floating point number is normalized. In a normalized nonzero number, the bit following the binary point must be a 1. A normalized nonzero number has a fractional mantissa such that $0.5 \le |M| \le 1$. Zero is a special case because $0 = 0 \times 2^E$ for all E and therefore cannot be represented in the same manner as nonzero numbers. The convention used for zero is a 0 mantissa and the most negative possible exponent (-64 in the XS-64 representation). Floating point numbers are generally stored in their normalized form, and routines that process them require normalized operands. The normalized range of the mantissa is $\pm(0.5$ to $1.0 - 2^{-15})$.

Combining these representations of the exponent and mantissa, the range of representable numbers in the format of Fig. 7.5-1 is

$$\pm\left(0.5 \times 2^{-64} \text{ to } \left(1 - 2^{-15}\right) \times 2^{63}\right)$$

or

$$\pm\left(2.7105 \times 10^{-19} \text{ to } 0.9223 \times 10^{19}\right)$$

This range of values is illustrated in Fig. 7.5-2.

There are four ranges of numbers that correspond to arithmetic overflow and underflow in Fig. 7.5-2. If a result exceeds the largest positive or negative value representable, the overflow condition means that the result is incorrect. When overflow occurs it may be possible in subsequent computations to use the largest expressible positive value where positive overflow has occurred and the largest possible negative value where negative overflow has occurred. And in cases where the value of a result is too small to be expressed, positive or negative underflow, the result is also incorrect. Underflow may not be a serious problem because in most applications zero is a satisfactory approximation.

There are only a finite number of representable values in the four ranges. If the result of a calculation cannot be expressed exactly in the given representation, it must be truncated or rounded off to the nearest expressable number. Roundoff error

```
OUFLW:    XRA A          ;TEST CARRY STORED IN MSB OF C
          ADD C
          JM UFLW
OFLW:     CALL EOFLW     ;CALL ERROR ROUTINE FOR OVERFLOW
          LXI H,7FFFH    ;SET TO LARGEST POSITIVE VALUE
          MVI B,7FH
STSGN:    MOV A,C        ;CHECK IF VALUE SHOULD BE NEGATIVE
          RAR
          XCHG           ;PLACE MANTISSA IN DE
          CC NGDE1       ;NEGATE
          RET
UFLW:     CALL EUFLW     ;CALL ERROR ROUTINE FOR UNDERFLOW
          LXI D,0H       ;SET MANTISSA TO ZERO
UFLWE:    MVI B,0H       ;SET EXPONENT TO ZERO (2⁻⁶⁴)
          RET
```

Figure 7.5-3   Subroutine for handling overflow and underflow conditions for floating point operations.

in floating point numbers is dependent on the exponent. The error in the mantissa can be limited to half the spacing between fractions: for an m-bit mantissa, excluding sign, the error is less than $2^{-(m+1)}$. The actual error is less than $2^{-(m+1)} \times 2^E$. The error is the smallest when E is the smallest, which is the case with floating point numbers in normalized form. The problem of truncation or roundoff errors in complex floating point calculations can be extreme and must be considered carefully. This problem falls in the domain of numerical analysis.

7.5.2 Floating Point Arithmetic Routines

A typical floating point arithmetic software package contains routines for handling overflow and underflow, negation, addition, subtraction, multiplication, and division. In the floating point routines used here,[6] the following register allocation is used: the first operand at the beginning of a calculation and the result at completion of the calculation are placed in registers B and DE, respectively. The second operand, if any, is placed in registers A and HL. In both cases the exponent is in the first register, the msB (most significant byte) of the mantissa in the second, and the lsB (least significant byte) of the mantissa in the third. Register C stores a count of the negations performed and a copy of the carry bit from the exponent calculation for determining overflow or underflow. Floating point quantities are stored in ascending memory by using 3 bytes of memory: the exponent first, followed by the lsB and msB of the mantissa. This particular register allocation allows optimal use of 8085A instructions in the floating point routines.

Both overflow and underflow conditions are handled by the subroutine OUFLW (see Fig. 7.5-3, which has several entry points. OUFLW checks the msb of register C—a copy of the carry produced during an exponent calculation before OUFLW is called. If this bit is 0, an overflow condition exists and a call is made to a user subroutine, EUFLW, which takes whatever actions are appropriate in the

---

[6]The routines discussed here follow those developed at Oxford [6]. These routines were selected as a basis of illustration because of their conciseness but have been modified somewhat for instructional purposes.

```
NGDE:     INR C      ;INCREMENT NEGATION COUNT
NGDE1:    XRA A      ;SUBTRACT DE FROM 0
          SUB E
          MOV E,A    ;LEAVE RESULT IN DE
          MVI A,0
          SBB D
          MOV D,A
          RET
```

Figure 7.5-4 Subroutine to negate a floating point number.

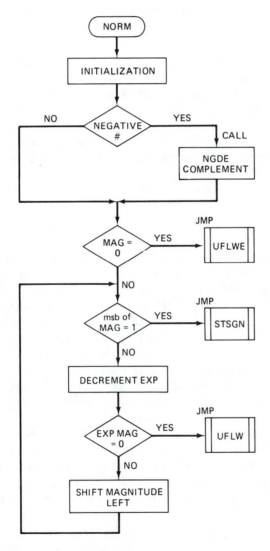

Figure 7.5-5 Flowchart for normalization subroutine.

```
NORM:     XRA A
          MOV C,A          ;CLEAR C FOR NORMALIZATION
          ORA D            ;CHECK FOR NEGATIVE NUMBER
          CM NGDE          ;MAKE POSITIVE
          ORA E            ;CHECK FOR ZERO MAGNITUDE
          JZ UFLWE         ;IF MAGNITUDE IS ZERO, SET EXPONENT TO 0
          XCHG             ;NORMALIZE IN HL
NORM1:    MOV A,H          ;ENTRY FOR POSITIVE NONZERO NUMBERS
          ADD H
          JM STSGN         ;NORMALIZATION COMPLETE; SET SIGN
          DCR B            ;DECREMENT EXPONENT
          JM UFLW          ;UNDERFLOW
          DAD H            ;SHIFT LEFT
          JMP NORM1
```

Figure 7.5-6 Subroutine to normalize a floating point number; assume number is in B and DE—can be positive or negative; C must be initialized, C = 0.

particular application. Upon return from this subroutine, the result registers are loaded with either the largest possible positive or largest possible negative value.

If the msb of C is 1 when the subroutine OUFLW is entered, a call is made to the user subroutine, EUFLW, which takes whatever actions are appropriate to the application in the case of underflow. Upon return from this subroutine, the result registers are all set to zero, giving a value of 0×2^{-64} and making zero less significant than the smallest nonzero number. The entry point UFLWE sets the result exponent to zero if the result of a calculation is zero. No call is made to EUFLW when the entry point UFLWE is used.

The subroutine OUFLW and the subroutine NORM, which normalize a floating point number, require an additional subroutine that negates a floating point number. This subroutine, NGDE, has two entry points: one that increments the negation count in C and another that does not (see Fig. 7.5-4).

A floating point number is normalized by making the number positive and then shifting it left until its magnitude msb is 1. Each time the number is shifted left, the exponent is decremented, thus maintaining the original value of the number. If the original number is negative, the normalized floating point number must be negated. A flowchart for a normalization routine, NORM, is shown in Fig. 7.5-5 and the subroutine listing in Fig. 7.5-6.

To add two floating point numbers, they must be aligned. Alignment refers to equal exponents and is accomplished by shifting the smaller number to the right and incrementing its exponent until the values of the two exponents are equal. If the shift requires more than 16 places, the addition is unnecessary because the larger number, when added to the smaller number, does not change. Therefore, the sum is simply the larger of the two numbers. A flowchart for the floating point addition routine, FADD, is shown in Fig. 7.5-7.

When aligned numbers are added, their signs and the sign of the result and the carry bit are checked for magnitude overflow. If the modulo-2 sum of the carry and three sign bits is 1, there is overflow. The overflowed bit is the same as the sign bits of the operands. The overflowed bit must be shifted into the result, and the exponent of the result must be incremented. After incrementing the exponent, it is also checked for overflow. In all computations, whether or not they involve overflow, the result may need normalizing—in which case the subroutine NORM is called. The floating point addition subroutine is shown in Fig. 7.5-8.

In floating point subtraction, the subtrahend is negated and added to the minuend. Algorithms for floating point multiplication and division can be developed by using the rules of scientific notation.

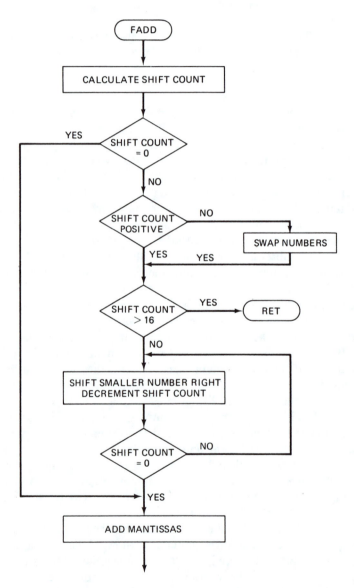

Figure 7.5-7   Flowchart for a floating point addition subroutine.

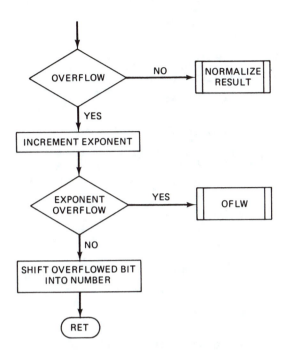

Figure 7.5-7 Continued

Additional routines are required to convert decimal numbers input to the system to floating point numbers in the desired format, and vice versa.

When greater precision or range is required, formats that require more than 3 bytes of data represent each floating point number. In such a case, operands, partial results, and the final result are maintained in memory locations.

7.6 HARDWARE IMPLEMENTATION OF MATHEMATICAL FUNCTIONS

Arithmetic functions implemented with hardware external to the microprocessor are advantageous in certain instances. For example, when the execution time of a software implementation exceeds that allowable in the particular application, a faster microprocessor or a hardware approach obviates the problem. Or, in the case of some complex arithmetic functions, special hardware eliminates the need for assembly language algorithms.

Hardware that implements arithmetic functions is interfaced to the microprocessor through I/O ports and is, in effect, a peripheral device. The microprocessor transfers operands and commands to the external arithmetic hardware and receives status information and computed results from it.

Four types of external hardware are commonly used to implement arithmetic in microprocessor systems:

1. Limited function high speed arithmetic ICs.
2. Calculator ICs.

```
FADD:   MOV C,A     ;SAVE EXPONENT
        MOV A,B
        SUB C
        JZ FADD3    ;NO SHIFT REQUIRED
        JP FADD1    ;OPERANDS IN RIGHT ORDER
        CMA         ;MAKE SHIFT COUNT POSITIVE
        ADI 01H
        XCHG        ;SWAP OPERANDS
        MOV B,C
FADD1:  CPI 16
        RP          ;SHIFT>16 ADDITION UNNECESSARY
        MOV C,A     ;SAVE SHIFT COUNT
FADD2:  MOV A,H     ;LOOP TO SHIFT SMALLER NUMBER RIGHT
        RAL          GET SIGN
        MOV A,H
        RAR
        MOV H,A
        MOV A,L
        RAR         ;LEAVES LSB IN CARRY
        MOV L,A
        DCR C
        JNZ FADD2
FADD3:  MOV C,H     ;SAVE SIGN OF H, L
        DAD D       ;ADD MANTISSAS
        XCHG
        SBB A       ;SAVE CARRY / OVERFLOW A = 0 OR FF
        XRA C
        XRA D
        XRA H
        JP NORM
FADD4:  MOV A,H     ;SUPER NORMAL OR NEGATIVE MAX
        RLC
        MOV C,A
        INR B       ;ADJUST EXPONENT FOR CARRY
        JM OFLW     ;REAL OVERFLOW
        MOV A,D     ;SHIFT OVERFLOW BIT INTO RESULT
        RAR
        MOV D,A
        MOV A,E
        RAR
        MOV E,A
        RET
```

Figure 7.5-8   Subroutine for floating point addition.

3. LSI arithmetic processing units (APUs).

4. High speed bit slice microprocessors.

7.6.1 Limited Function High Speed Arithmetic ICs

Some real-time microprocessor applications require that only certain arithmetic functions—such as multiplication and/or division—be implemented at speeds exceeding those possible with the system's microprocessor. This is often the case even if the microprocessor contains instructions for multiplication and division. There are several ICs that implement one or a very limited number of mathematical operations at these high speeds. One example is an LSI multiplier.

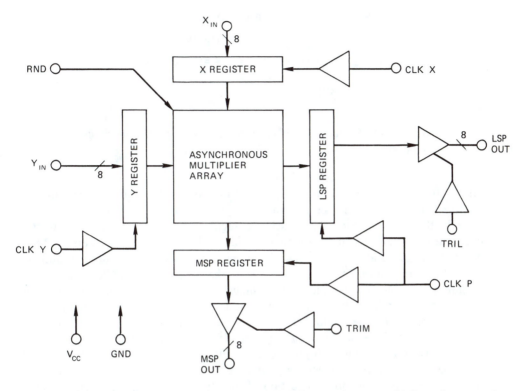

Figure 7.6-1 An LSI 8 × 8-bit parallel two's complement multiplier. (Courtesy of TRW.)

An 8 × 8-bit parallel two's complement multiplier, the TRW MPY-8, is shown in Fig. 7.6-1. This multiplier is contained in a 40-pin package and executes multiplication in 130 nS, providing a 14-bit plus sign result. In operation X_{IN}, Y_{IN}, MSP_{OUT}, and LSP_{OUT} are connected in common to the data bus. If used with an isolated I/O structure, the X and Y registers are output ports, and CLKX and CLKY are controlled by their device select pulses. The registers MSP and LSP are input ports, and TRIM and TRIL—the enable lines for these ports—are controlled by their device select pulses. Assume that the multiplier is in register C and the multiplicand in register D; the subroutine in Fig. 7.6-2 implements the multiplication using the external hardware multiplier. The subroutine leaves the product in B and C. The format of the product duplicates the sign bit as the most significant bit of B and of C. This subroutine requires 84 states or 26.9 μS (8085AH) for execution, including the subroutine call.

The actual hardware multiplication time, 130 nS, is overshadowed by the time required to load and read the registers of the hardware multiplier, which, in effect, becomes the multiplication time. This time can be minimized by reducing the load and read times by using memory mapped, instead of isolated, I/O; using registers H

```
HTCM:       MOV A,C      ;LOAD MULTIPLIER
            OUT X
            MOV A,D      ;LOAD MULTIPLICAND
            OUT Y
            IN LSP       ;STORE LOW BYTE OF PRODUCT
            MOV C,A
            IN MSP       ;STORE HIGH BYTE OF PRODUCT
            MOV B,A
            RET
```

Figure 7.6-2 Subroutine to implement multiplication using the hardware multiplier of Fig. 7.6-1.

and L for transferring the multiplicand, multiplier, and product; and writing a routine that transfers the operands and result as a macro.

In the memory mapped I/O scheme, registers X and Y are allocated to two consecutive memory locations, the first of which is labeled MPY. Registers LSP and MSP are also allocated to these two locations. Thus, a write operation to address MPY loads the multiplier into register X of the hardware multiplier, and a read operation from MPY reads the least significant byte of the product from register LSP of the multiplier. A write operation to address MPY + 1 loads the multiplicand into register Y of the multiplier, and a read from MPY + 1 reads the most significant byte of the product from register MSP of the multiplier.

To use a macro, the multiplicand and multiplier are placed in registers H and L, respectively, before the macro is referenced. The macro leaves the product in H and L. The memory mapped allocation of the hardware multiplier registers allows the loading and reading of the multiplier with only two instructions. The macro is

```
MULT    MACRO
        SHLD MPY
        LHLD MPY
        ENDM
```

Memory mapping transfers the operands directly between an internal register pair and external registers without being routed through the accumulator. And use of a macro, instead of a subroutine, eliminates the time required for the subroutine call and return. The multiplication time is now only 10.2 μS.

7.6.2 Calculator ICs

The first hardware devices used with microprocessors to implement complex arithmetic were LSI calculator ICs, which predated the advent of general purpose microprocessors. A calculator IC is simply a microprocessor with a built-in microprogram for evaluating arithmetic functions and is designed for use in a hand calculator. These ICs are slow because the technology used in their manufacturer is PMOS and because they incorporate features that are advantageous for interfacing to hand calculators but that are undesirable when used with microprocessors.

Most LSI calculator ICs accept data from a key matrix and are equipped with input logic for scanning and debouncing key closures. The debouncing logic introduces delays in the tens of milliseconds range for each digit of data entered.

The output of a typical calculator chip is a multiplexed 7-bit code for each digit of the result and a set of digit strobes that control display multiplexing. Because of this, additional logic is necessary to interface a calculator IC to a microprocessor. Hardware conversion of the seven segment output is facilitated by a MM74C915 seven-segment-to-BCD converter IC. A few calculator chips are designed for BCD input and output. In addition, most calculators have input and output signal levels that are not TTL compatible and, therefore, require level shifting circuitry in order to interface with microprocessors that have TTL compatible inputs and outputs. Even with their low speed and the necessity for additional interface logic, calculator chips are advantageous in applications where speed is not important and where reducing the cost of software development is.

If the interface is designed so that the calculator chip is loaded with the operands by the microprocessor, and, when the computation is complete, the calculator interface interrupts the microprocessor (see Chapter 9), the resulting concurrent processing capability minimizes the effect of the calculator IC's slowness on the system throughput. Several arithmetic subsystems are manufactured as printed circuit (PC) boards that use calculator ICs and provide the hardware and software for interfacing to a particular microprocessor. In most of these systems, the execution speed is only comparable to that achievable via software by the particular microprocessor; however, they do avoid additional software development.

Special calculator-type devices are designed for ease of interfacing to a microprocessor. National's MM57409 Super Number Cruncher, SNC, is a device that is essentially an enhanced calculator chip. It implements arithmetic, trigonometric, logarithmic, and exponential functions. Its data format is floating point decimal with up to a 12-bit mantissa and a 2-digit exponent. Unlike most calculator chips, data is input to and output from the SNC in BCD. Instructions are input as a 6-bit code. Instruction execution times range from 1 to 500 mS, with 5 to 10 mS being typical.

7.6.3 Arithmetic Processing Units (APUs)

LSI devices specifically designed as computational adjuncts to a microprocessor are also manufactured. The block diagram of one such device, the Am9511A arithmetic processing unit (APU) (Intel 8231A), is shown in Fig. 7.6-3. [7, 8] This is an NMOS device contained in a 24-pin DIP. It uses binary data formats and is capable of fixed and floating point calculations. Fixed point numbers are either 16 or 32 bits in two's complement form. Floating point numbers are 32 bits with the most significant byte containing the sign (1 bit) of the mantissa and the exponent (7 bits in two's complement form). The remaining 3 bytes contain the 24-bit mantissa.

Operands and commands are transferred to and results and status transferred from the APU through its 8-bit data bus buffer. The $C/\overline{D}$ input of the APU's bus control logic determines whether the data transferred is a command or status,

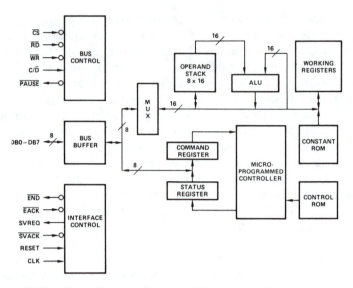

Figure 7.6-3 Block diagram of an Am9511A arithmetic processing unit. (Copyright © 1979 Advanced Micro Devices, Inc. Reproduced with permission of copyright owner.)

$C/\overline{D} = 1$, or an operand or result, $C/\overline{D} = 0$. The $\overline{PAUSE}$ output of the APU synchronizes read and write operations between the microprocessor and APU. A simple interconnection between a microprocessor and APU to support programmed I/O transfers is shown in Fig. 7.6-4.

Reverse Polish Notation is used for the data and command input sequence to the APU. Data is written a byte at a time into the APU's 8×16 operand stack, least significant byte first. APU commands implement addition, subtraction, multiplication, division, trigonometric and inverse trigonometric functions, square roots, logarithms, exponentiation, and floating to fixed and fixed to floating point conversion. Some commands require two operands and use the top two on the stack; those

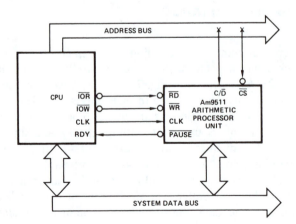

Figure 7.6-4 Programmed I/O interface to the Am9511A APU. (Copyright © 1979 Advanced Micro Devices, Inc. Reproduced with permission of copyright owner.)

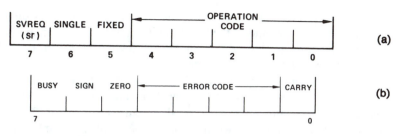

BUSY: Indicates that Am9511 is currently executing a com-
    mand (1 = Busy).

SIGN: Indicates that the value on the top of stack is negative
    (1 = Negative).

ZERO: Indicates that the value on the top of stack is zero (1
    = Value is zero).

ERROR CODE: This field contains an indication of the va-
    lidity of the result of the last operation. The error
    codes are:

0000 – No error

1000 – Divide by zero

0100 – Square root or log of negative number

1100 – Argument of inverse sine, cosine, or e^x too large

XX10 – Underflow

XX01 – Overflow

CARRY: Previous operation resulted in carry or borrow from
    most significant bit. (1 = Carry/Borrow, 0 = No Carry/
    No Borrow)

Figure 7.6-5   Command (a) and status (b) word format for the Am9511A
APU (Copyright © 1979 Advanced Micro Devices, Inc. Reproduced with
permission of copyright owner.)

that require a single operand use only the one on the top of the stack. Operation
results are left on top of the stack. The command format is shown in Fig. 7.6-5a.
Commands are also available that manipulate the contents of the stack, and a read
operation can then retrieve the result from the stack. If an attempt is made to read
the result before the computation has been completed, the $\overline{\text{PAUSE}}$ output forces the
microprocessor to wait until the computation is complete.

Status of the APU is held in its status word register (See Fig. 7.6-5b). A BUSY
bit indicates whether the Am9511A is executing a command. When using programmed I/O, this bit can be polled to determine when a computation is complete.
If the BUSY bit is 1, the other status bits are not defined. If it is 0, the remaining
bits of the status word provide information relating to the data on the top of the
stack. The error code indicates whether an error occurred in the last operation and,
if so, what type.

The APU has handshaking signals used when interrupts or DMA implement
data transfers (see Chapter 9). The $\overline{\text{END}}$ signal indicates completed execution of a
previously entered command and can be used as an interrupt request. $\overline{\text{EACK}}$ clears

the $\overline{END}$ signal. The service request output, SVREQ, indicates the completion of a command execution only if the SVREQ bit, bit 7, of the command is set. For greater throughput, operand transfers can be handled by a DMA controller and CPU coordination handled by interrupts.

When operand transfer is included, execution time for the various operations is dependent on the method of transfer. Versions of the Am9511A are available at 2 MHz, 3 MHz, and 4 MHz. Typical execution times for 32-bit floating point operands are listed as follows, in terms of the number of Am9511A clock cycles:

Operation	Clock Cycles
Multiplication	168
Square root	800
Cosine	4118
Log	4490
Power	9292

REFERENCES

1. A. D. BOOTH, "A Signed Binary Multiplication Algorithm," *Quarterly Journal of Mechanics and Applied Mathematics*, 4, pt. 2 (1951), 236–40.

2. J. R. MICK, *Understanding Booth's Algorithm in 2's Complement Digital Multiplication* (Sunnyvale, Calif.: Advanced Micro Devices, Inc.).

3. H. H. LOOMIS, JR., "Data Representation," in *Introduction to Computer Architecture*, ed. H. Stone (Chicago: Science Research Associates, Inc., 1975), 23–73.

4. Y. CHU, *Digital Computer Design Fundamentals* (New York: McGraw-Hill, 1962).

5. O. L. MACSORLEY, "High-Speed Arithmetic in Binary Computers," *Proceedings of the IRE*, 49 (1961), 67–91.

6. S. N. COPE, *Floating-Point Arithmetic Routines and Macros for an Intel 8080 Microprocessor*, O.U.E.L. Report no. 1123/75 (Springfield, Va.: National Technical Information Service, 1975).

7. *Am9511 Arithmetic Processor* (Data Sheet) (Sunnyvale, Calif.: Advanced Micro Devices, Inc., 1978).

8. R. O. PARKER and J. H. KROEGER, *Algorithm Details for the Am9511 Arithmetic Processing Unit* (Sunnyvale, Calif.: Advanced Micro Devices, Inc., 1978).

PROBLEMS

7-1. Add the following unsigned binary integers. If the result is to be stored as a single byte, indicate those sums that involve arithmetic overflow. Give the decimal equivalents of the unsigned binary sums.

(a) 10110011
   + 01100001

(b) 01011101
   + 01100010

(c) 10010101
   + 01101011

(d) 10010011
   + 10101100

7-2. Subtract the following unsigned binary integers. If the result is to be stored as a single byte, indicate those differences that involve arithmetic underflow.

(a)   01100101
       − 10010011

(b)   11010111
       − 01101100

(c)   00110010
       − 00010110

(d)   00101111
       − 01011101

7-3. Write a macro, LDHI DATA, that loads DE with the sum of the contents of HL and DATA. In other words, write a macro that implements the register transfer expression

$$(D)(E) \leftarrow (H)(L) + DATA$$

Assume that DATA is an 8-bit constant. This macro should leave all the registers except DE and HL unaltered.

7-4. Write a subroutine, DSUB (double subtraction), that subtracts the contents of register pair BC from the contents of register pair HL, leaving the difference in HL. Indicate those flags that are valid for the result after returning from the subroutine. Use available subtraction instructions.

7-5. Using the DAD instruction, write a subroutine that carries out an n-bit logical left shift of a 16-bit quantity in register HL. Include a provision for the calling program to detect whenever an overflow occurs.

7-6. Write a subroutine that multiplies two 8-bit unsigned integers using repeated addition. Give the maximum execution time if the state time is 325.5 nS.

7-7. Write a subroutine that divides a 16-bit unsigned integer by an 8-bit unsigned integer. Give the maximum execution time if the state time is 325.5 nS.

7-8. Write a subroutine, ARHL, that implements a 1-bit arithmetic right shift of the contents of HL.

7-9. Compute the sum of the following two's complement numbers using binary arithmetic. Indicate those cases, if any, that involve arithmetic overflow or underflow. Convert all operands to decimal and add them again to check for accuracy.

(a)   10110011
       + 01101011

(b)   00100100
       + 11110101

(c)   11101110
       + 11110100

(d)   01110010
       + 00101101

7-10. Determine the bit pattern of all the following decimal numbers when represented as 8-bit two's complement numbers. Write the bit patterns in hexadecimal.
(a) − 1
(b) + 126
(c) − 13
(d) − 74

7-11. A register initially contains the bit pattern 34H. Give the contents of the register (in hexadecimal) after each of the following operations takes place.
(a) left logical shift two places
(b) left arithmetic shift two places
(c) right logical shift two places
(d) right arithmetic shift two places
Repeat this problem with an initial register value of E8H.

7-12. List the steps in the operation of the decimal adjust accumulator instruction, DAA. Also list each step of the operation of DAA when executed following the execution of an ADD B instruction with (A) = 87H and (B) = 96H.

7-13. Write a subroutine that subtracts two 16-bit unsigned integers. Enter the subroutine with the minuend in HL and the subtrahend in BC. At its completion have the subroutine leave the difference in HL. What restrictions must be placed on the operands for the result to be valid? Describe what, if any, modification would have to be made in the subroutine to subtract 16-bit two's complement numbers. Also what restrictions must be placed on the two's complement operands for a valid result?

7-14. Repeat Problem 7-10 representing each decimal number as a 16-bit two's complement number.

7-15. Write the bit patterns that represent each of the following decimal numbers as 16-bit ten's complement numbers. Write these bit patterns in hexadecimal.

   (a) + 49
   (b) − 312
   (c) − 1
   (d) − 67

7-16. Without using subtraction instructions write a subroutine, DIFF, that subtracts the content of register pair DE from the content of register pair HL and leaves the difference in HL. Assume that the operands are 16-bit numbers represented in two's complement form.

7-17. Write a subroutine that adds two 4-digit BCD numbers. Assume that the operands are in register pairs BC and DE before the subroutine is called. The subroutine should leave the least significant four digits of the BCD result in register pair DE and the value of the carry in the least significant 4 bits of register C.

7-18. Multiply by hand the following 4-bit two's complement numbers using Booth's algorithm. Multiplicand $Y = 0101$, multiplier $X = 1011$. Write each step of the multiplication. For each step indicate the bit(s) of the multiplier examined and the operation dictated by Booth's algorithm.

7-19. Write a subroutine that uses repeated addition to multiply two 8-bit binary unsigned numbers. The multiplier is in register C, the multiplicand in register E, and the result is returned in register pair HL. Write an equation that gives the maximum execution time of the subroutine as a function of the state time, T.

7-20. Write a subroutine that uses repeated subtraction to divide two numbers. The dividend is in register D and the divisor is in register E. The subroutine should return with the quotient in register H and the remainder in register L. Assume that the divisor is never zero. Write an equation that gives the maximum execution time of the subroutine as a function of the state time, T.

8

Program Controlled I/O

Since the processor usually talks to all its peripherals over only one or two main interconnecting busses, the interface must insure that processor outputs reach only the intended peripheral. In the reverse direction, the interface must provide a means for information from each peripheral to reach the processor without interfering with other units hanging on the system busses. In addition, the interface must reconcile any differences between microprocessor and peripheral timing. The microprocessor runs on its own internal clock. Peripherals may, or may not, have internal clocks of their own.

Howard Falk*

8.1 INTRODUCTION

Any application of a microprocessor system requires the transfer of data between circuitry external to the microprocessor and the microprocessor itself. This transfer of data is in addition to transfers between the microprocessor and memory and is referred to as *input/output*, or *I/O*.

There are many ways that the transfer of information is initiated and controlled; however, these can be placed in one of three primary categories:

1. Program controlled I/O
2. Interrupt-program controlled I/O
3. Hardware controlled I/O[1]

These three methods differ in the degree to which the microprocessor initiates and controls the transfer of data. With program controlled I/O operations, the transfer of data is completely under the control of the microprocessor program; i.e., an I/O operation takes place only when an I/O transfer instruction is encountered in the execution of the program. In many cases it is necessary to determine the "readiness" of the device before the data transfer occurs. This involves testing one or more external flags or status bits associated with the I/O device, which, of course, requires a transfer of status information to the microprocessor—an additional I/O operation.

In contrast, with an interrupt-program controlled approach, an external device indicates directly to the microprocessor its readiness to transfer data by a logic signal at an interrupt input of the microprocessor. Most microprocessor interrupt inputs can be disabled under program control. Interrupts that occur while the interrupt input is disabled are ignored.

When a microprocessor program is interrupted, control is transferred to an interrupt service subroutine. This subroutine performs the data transfer, then returns control to the program at the point it was interrupted, and processing continues. Thus, with an interrupt-program controlled I/O operation, the transfer is requested by external hardware and then implemented by an interrupt service subroutine.

Hardware controlled transfers, commonly referred to as *direct memory access* (*DMA*), are direct transfers between an I/O device and memory: data is not routed from an I/O device to one of the microprocessor's registers and then to memory, or vice versa, but routed directly between the external device and memory. The microprocessor still sets up the transfer in the sense that it sends initialization information—the starting address in memory and the number of words to be transferred—to the DMA device. However, subsequent to this, hardware associated with the DMA device requests and controls the actual data transfer. DMA is used primarily to transfer a number of words or a block of data at high speed. Interfacing

---

[1] This chapter considers program controlled I/O only. Interrupt-program controlled I/O and DMA are presented in Chapter 9.

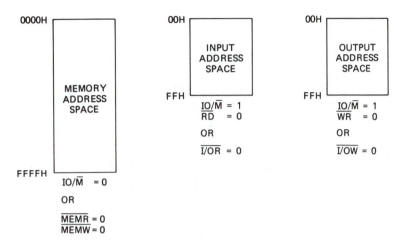

Figure 8.1-1 Control signals and strobes determine to which address space an address refers.

some peripheral devices to a microprocessor includes the use of a combination of these primary data transfer methods.

As discussed in Chapter 3, input ports and output ports are basically external registers. Some microprocessors provide control signals that allow external registers associated with I/O devices to occupy a separate address space—distinct from the address space of the external registers that comprise main memory. When I/O ports are assigned to a separate address space, they are referred to as *isolated* or *standard I/O*. When assigned to the same address space as memory, they are referred to as *memory mapped I/O*.

The $IO/\overline{M}$ control signal of the 8085A determines whether the address generated during a data transfer refers to memory ($IO/\overline{M} = 0$) or to the separate I/O address space ($IO/\overline{M} = 1$). I/O address space is further divided by control strobes into an input address space ($\overline{RD} = 0$) and an output address space ($\overline{WR} = 0$). Figure 8.1-1 shows how the address space of the 8085A is partitioned by these control signals.

8.2 ISOLATED I/O AND DEVICE SELECT DECODING

Only the IN and OUT instructions provide data transfer for isolated I/O. IN and OUT each require three machine cycles for execution. The first is, of course, an OPCODE FETCH. The second is a MEMORY READ, during which the 8-bit port address is transferred from memory to the microprocessor and placed in both the W and Z temporary registers. And the third is either an I/O READ or I/O WRITE machine cycle, during which the actual data transfer from or to the I/O device occurs.

During the I/O READ and I/O WRITE machine cycles, the 8-bit port address, in W and Z, is output from the 8085A on address/data bus lines AD_0–AD_7 and on address lines A_8–A_{15}. See the IN and OUT instruction cycle timing diagrams for the 8085A in Fig. 8.2-1. The read ($\overline{RD}$) and write ($\overline{WR}$) control strobes from the 8085A specify the exact time at which an input port's three-state buffer is enabled to drive the data bus or the exact time at which an output port latches the data placed on the data bus by the microprocessor, respectively. Figure 8.2-1a shows the timing relationship for the 8085A between the availability of the port address and the $\overline{RD}$ during an I/O READ machine cycle, and Fig. 8.2-1b shows the timing relationship between the port address and $\overline{WR}$ control strobes for an I/O WRITE machine cycle.

For input ports, external decoding logic combines $\overline{RD}$, IO/$\overline{M}$, and the port address and generates a unique *input device select pulse* for each input port (see Fig. 3.1-2). This pulse occurs only during the I/O READ machine cycle of an IN instruction that addresses the specific port. The input device select pulse enables the input port's three-state buffer. If, through design or programming error, the three-state buffers of two or more ports or a port and a memory device are simultaneously enabled, both drive the data bus and cause bus contention.

For output operations, external decoding logic combines $\overline{WR}$, IO/$\overline{M}$, and the port address and generates a unique *output device select pulse* for each output port (see Fig. 3.1-3). This pulse occurs only during the I/O WRITE machine cycle of an OUT instruction that addresses the port and clocks the output port's register. Typically, each output device select pulse clocks a single output port; however, it is possible and often useful to have two or more output ports selected simultaneously.

The design of device selection logic varies, depending on how many I/O devices are required in a system and the logic provided by the ICs that comprise the input and output ports. If only a single input port and a single output port are required, address decoding is unnecessary. The IO/$\overline{M}$ control signal is simply combined with $\overline{RD}$ to generate an input read strobe ($\overline{I/OR}$) and with $\overline{WR}$ to generate an output write strobe ($\overline{I/OW}$). These strobes directly control the input buffer and the output latch, respectively. The port address byte of the I/O instruction is, in cases requiring only a single port, a don't care, but cannot be omitted from the instruction or its object code. IN and OUT are 2-byte instructions, and both bytes must appear in the program wherever the instruction is used.

When more than one input or output port is required in a system, which is usually the case, the port address is decoded to generate device select pulses for each input and output port. The simplest form of decoding is the *linear selection method*. This requires the smallest amount of logic but can only be used for eight or fewer input and eight or fewer output ports. Here, one address bit is associated exclusively with each I/O port and is logically combined with IO/$\overline{M}$ and $\overline{RD}$ or $\overline{WR}$ to generate an input or output device select pulse (see Fig. 8.2-2). Note that the device select pulse occurs during the machine cycle at essentially the same time as the $\overline{RD}$ or $\overline{WR}$ strobe, delayed only by the propagation time of the device selection logic. For example, in Fig. 8.2-2, address bit $A_4 = 1$ selects port 16. If the $\overline{RD}$ strobe is inverted and NANDed with A_4 and IO/$\overline{M}$, an active low input device select pulse, $\overline{IDSP10H}$,[2] is generated. $\overline{IDSP10H}$ is connected to the active low enable of a three-state buffer and determines when the buffer drives the bus. If the IC three-state buffer has multiple enable inputs, the internal decoding logic of the three-state buffer itself may be sufficient, requiring no external gates.

---

[2] Note that port address is specified here in hexadecimal.

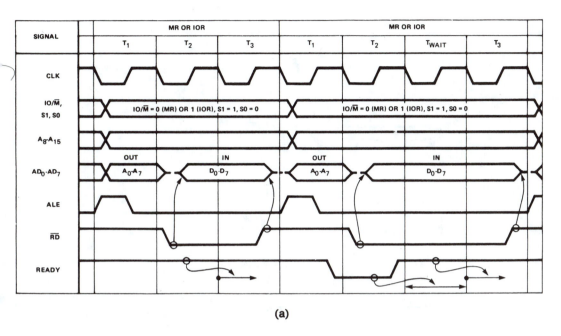

(a)

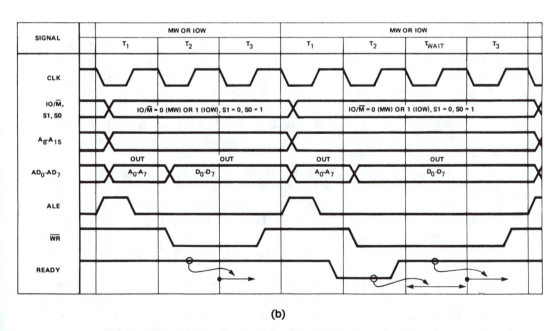

(b)

Figure 8.2-1 Timing diagrams for the 8085A: (a) read timing diagram; (b) write timing diagram. (Courtesy of Intel Corp.)

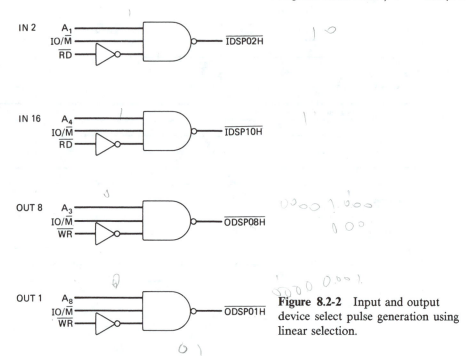

Figure 8.2-2 Input and output device select pulse generation using linear selection.

A disadvantage of linear selection is the possibility that a programming error will damage the hardware. If the port address is not exhaustively decoded, two or more input ports can drive the data bus simultaneously. Suppose, for example, a particular design using linear selection contains an input port 4 and an input port 8, selected by address bits A_2 and A_3, respectively. If a programming error results in the use of an IN 12 instruction instead of, for instance, an IN 8, execution causes input ports 4 and 8 to be selected simultaneously, possibly damaging the three-state buffers. *When linear selection is used, extra care must be taken to ensure that two ports are not selected simultaneously!*

Since there are only eight unique address bits in the port address, only eight input and eight output ports can be selected with the linear select method. However, the elimination of the decoders required to decode combinations of address bits is an important savings in small systems. To select from a larger number of I/O devices requires decoding port addresses. With exhaustive decoding, the maximum number of device select pulses that can be generated is 512: 256 associated with IN instructions, 256 with OUT instructions.

When decoding address bits to generate more than one device select pulse, decoders with enable inputs are particularly useful because they reduce the package count. If an application requires four or fewer input and four or fewer output device select pulses, a 74ALS139 Dual 1-of-4 Decoder can be used. The active low enable of one of the decoders is connected to the $\overline{I/OR}$ strobe, and the select inputs to address bits A_0 and A_1, providing four input device select pulses (see Fig. 8.2-3). All four outputs remain high until the $\overline{I/OR}$ strobe occurs. The active low strobe enables the decoder, and an active low device select pulse occurs at the output

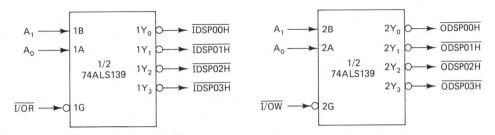

Figure 8.2-3 Four input and four output device select pulses generated with a single 74ALS139 1-of-4 decoder.

selected by A_0 and A_1. The unselected outputs remain high. The active low enable of the other 1-of-4 decoder is connected to the $\overline{I/OW}$ strobe, and the select inputs to address bits A_0 and A_1, thus providing four output device select pulses.

Because only the least significant two address bits are connected to the decoder, the most significant six port address bits in the second byte of the instruction are don't cares. The effect of these don't cares is the generation of the same device select pulses by a number of IN or OUT instructions with different port addresses. For example, the $\overline{IDSP00H}$ device select pulse is generated by executing an IN 0 instruction or any of the following: IN 4, IN 8, IN 12, IN 16, IN 20, etc.

Decoders with both active low and active high enable inputs provide even greater flexibility. The 74ALS138 (8205), for instance, is a 1-out-of-8 binary decoders with two active low and one active high enable inputs (see Fig. 8.2-4). When the required input combination is not applied to the enables, all outputs of the decoder are high, regardless of the select or address input values. When a 74ALS138 generates device select pulses for the 8085A, the $\overline{RD}$ or $\overline{WR}$ strobe is connected to one of the active low enables, the second active low enable is grounded, and the $IO/\overline{M}$ signal is connected to the active high enable. This arrangement requires no

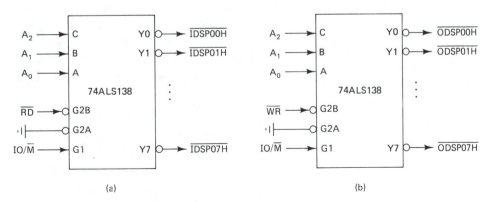

Figure 8.2-4 Generation of (a) input device select strobes and (b) output device select strobes for an 8085A system.

additional logic to generate an $\overline{\text{I/OR}}$ or $\overline{\text{I/OW}}$ because generation is, in effect, accomplished by the internal enable gating of the 74ALS138. If no more than eight input and eight output ports are required, the circuit of Fig. 8.2-4 is adequate. For larger numbers of input and output ports, the active low enable, which is grounded in Fig. 8.2-4, is controlled by combinational logic that decodes additional address bits. For exhaustive decoding, A_3–A_7 would be decoded to generate an active low enable. Decoders with enable inputs can be cascaded to generate larger numbers of device select pulses. As shown in Fig. 8.2-5, nine 74ALS138 provide 64 device select

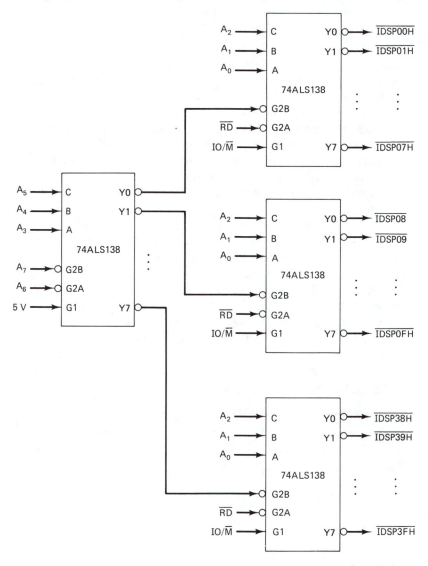

Figure 8.2-5 Using nine 74ALS138 decoders to generate 64 exhaustively decoded input device select pulses.

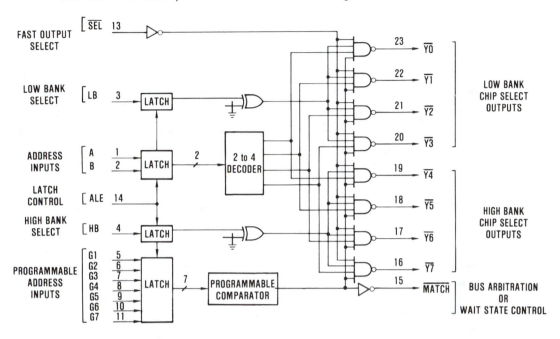

Figure 8.2-6 Block diagram of HPL-82C339 Programmable Chip Select Decoder. (Courtesy of Harris Corp.)

pulses. Generation of device select pulses can also be accomplished using various programmable logic devices (PLDs), as described in Chapter 12.

The need for device select logic is so common in microprocessor systems that a special circuit has been designed for this purpose. The Harris HPL-82C339 Programmable Chip Select Decoder is a superset of the 74ALS138 and 74ALS139 [1]. It is used to generate memory or I/O device select signals. The 82C339 is a CMOS device with TTL compatible inputs and outputs. The block diagram of the 82C339 is shown in Fig. 8.2-6. On the input side are several transparent latches that permit the 82C339 to be used with both multiplexed and nonmultiplexed address/data bus microprocessors. In 8085A systems that don't have a separate latch for address/data bus demultiplexing, the ALE input of the 82C339 is driven by ALE from the 8085A, if address bits A_0–A_7 are to be decoded. If a separate latch is used for address/data bus demultiplexing, ALE is fixed at logic 1.

Figure 8.2-7a shows the 82C339 configured to generate eight device select pulses. In this configuration, the 82C339 obtains the port address by demultiplexing the address/data bus, AD_0–AD_7. The address and IO/$\overline{M}$ are latched on the falling edge of ALE. The outputs of the latch with inputs G1–G7 (see Fig. 8.2-6) are inputs to a hardware programmable comparator. The latches' outputs are compared with values that have been programmed into the 82C339 comparator by blowing fuses within the device. This programming is carried out on a device programmer prior to the 82C339 being placed in the circuit. If there is a match, the $\overline{MATCH}$ output is logic 0. This output can be used as an input to READY generation logic to indicate

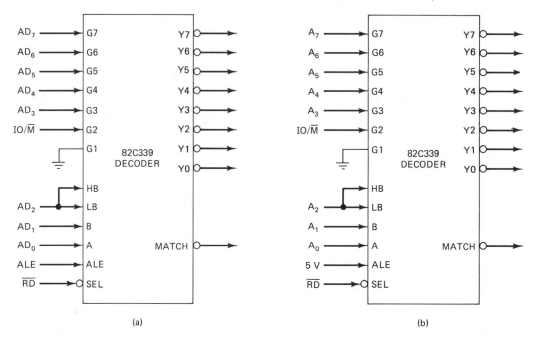

Figure 8.2-7 Generation of eight input device select pulses using an HPL-82C339 Programmable Chip Select Decoder. (a) 8085A system without separate address/data bus demultiplexer latch; (b) 8085A system with separate address/data bus demultiplexer latch.

that one of the eight I/O devices associated with this 82C339 has been addressed, so that WAIT states can be generated if required.

When the $\overline{\text{SEL}}$ input, which is driven by $\overline{\text{RD}}$, is logic 0, the selected output, $\overline{\text{Y0}}$– $\overline{\text{Y7}}$, will be logic 0. The output selected is determined by inputs at A, B, LB, and HB. The latched inputs at A and B are decoded by a 2-to-4 decoder, which selects one output in the low bank, $\overline{\text{Y0}}$– $\overline{\text{Y3}}$, and one output in the high bank, $\overline{\text{Y4}}$– $\overline{\text{Y7}}$. The determination of whether an output in the low bank or the high bank or both is selected is based on the low bank select, LB, and high bank select, HB, inputs and the programming of 1-bit comparator associated with each bank. As shown in Fig. 8.2-6, the inputs at LB and HB are latched on the falling edge of ALE. The EX-OR gate at the output of each latch serves as a 1-bit comparator for the output of that latch. One input of each EX-OR gate is connected to ground via a fuse. If the fuse is left intact, a logic 1 output from the latch will select the associated bank. If the fuse is programmed open (burned), a logic 0 at the output of the latch will cause the associated bank to be selected. To configure the 82C339 as a 1-out-of-8 decoder, as in Fig. 8.2-7, the LB input is programmed to be active low and the HB input is programmed to be active high. To generate output device select pulses, $\overline{\text{SEL}}$ is driven by $\overline{\text{WR}}$.

If the 8085A's address/data bus is demultiplexed by a separate latch or if address bits A_8–A_{15} are decoded, ALE is hardwired to logic 1 and the appropriate address inputs, A_0–A_7 or A_8–A_{15}, are used (see Fig. 8.2-7b).

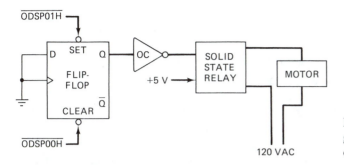

Figure 8.2-8 Use of program generated device select pulses to control an external device.

Device select pulses are also useful as control pulses when controlling external devices where no actual data transfer is intended. The OUT instruction is preferable for generating such pulses because IN causes whatever is on the data bus when the instruction is executed to replace the contents of the accumulator. In Fig. 8.2-8, software generated device select pulses control an external device by setting or clearing a flip-flop. Execution of OUT 1 sets the flip-flop and makes the output of the open collector inverter logic 0, turning ON the solid state relay, which acts like a closed switch. Current flows from the 120 V A.C. source through the solid state relay and motor. Execution of an OUT 0 instruction clears the flip-flop, turning OFF the motor. Note that the data placed on the data bus during the execution of the OUT instruction is not latched and has no effect on the system.

8.3 MEMORY MAPPED I/O

Any instruction that references memory can also transfer data between an I/O device and the microprocessor, as long as the I/O port is assigned to the memory address space rather than to the I/O address space. The register associated with the I/O port is simply treated as a memory location.

Consider an example in which address bit A_{15} designates whether instructions reference memory or an I/O device. If $A_{15} = 0$, a memory register is addressed; if $A_{15} = 1$, then a memory mapped I/O device is addressed. This assignment devotes the first 32 K of memory address space to memory and the second 32 K to memory mapped I/O, and address decoder logic enables either main memory or memory mapped I/O devices. External logic generates device select pulses for memory mapped I/O only when $IO/\overline{M} = 0$, the appropriate address is on the address bus, and a $\overline{RD}$ or $\overline{WR}$ strobe occurs.

Input and output transfers using memory mapped I/O are not limited to the accumulator. For example, some of the 8085A instructions that can be used for input from memory mapped ports are the following:

Instruction	Interpretation for memory mapped I / O
MOV r,M	input from a port to any register
LDA	input from a port to accumulator
LHLD	input from two ports to H and L
ADD M	input from a port with arithmetic operation to accumulator
ANA M	input from a port with logical operation to accumulator

ADD M and ANA M provide input data transfer and computation in a single instruction. Some instructions that output data from memory mapped ports are

Instruction	Interpretation for memory mapped I / O
MOV M, r	output any register to a port
STA	output accumulator to a port
SHLD	output H and L to two ports
MVI M, data	output immediate data to a port

LHLD and SHLD carry out 16-bit I/O transfers with a single instruction, which reduces program execution time considerably. The price paid for this added capability is a reduction in directly addressable main memory and the necessity of decoding a 16-bit rather than an 8-bit port address.

When a microprocessor puts out an address and generates a control strobe for a memory read, it has no way of determining whether the device that responds with data is a memory device or an I/O device, nor does it care. It only requires that the device that responds does so within the allowable access time or uses the READY line to request a sufficient number of WAIT states. The same is true when a microprocessor executes a write to memory. It supplies an address, data, and a write strobe, and continues its operation. External logic determines whether memory, I/O, or anything at all receives the data transferred.

Many commercially available digital and analog I/O devices (see Chapters 10 and 11) are equipped with interfaces that respond like memory locations, so they are directly compatible with microprocessors.

8.4 MSI I / O PORTS

I/O ports can be implemented with SSI, MSI, or LSI circuits. However, to minimize parts count, MSI or LSI circuits are generally used. Certain MSI circuits provide input and output ports in a single package.

An output port must be able to store data output from the microprocessor until the output device associated with the port can accept the data. An output port in its most basic form is a simple register or latch. An 8-bit output port can be implemented with a single 8-bit register such as the 74ALS574 or 74ALS573 shown in Fig. 2.1-7. The 74ALS574 is an octal D-type positive edge triggered flip-flop with three-state outputs. When used as an output port, the output device select pulse is the clock signal for the 74ALS574 (see Fig. 8.4-1a). Data from the microprocessor's data bus will be clocked into the 74ALS574 on the rising (trailing) edge of the output device select pulse. Since the device select pulse is derived from $\overline{WR}$, the time at which the data is latched corresponds to the time of occurrence of the rising edge of $\overline{WR}$ in Fig. 8.2-1b. Data should be latched on the trailing edge of an output device select pulse, because data is not valid, on the data bus, at the leading edge of the pulse. The three-state output buffers of the 74ALS574 must be maintained in their enabled state. This is accomplished by grounding the active low output control input, OC.

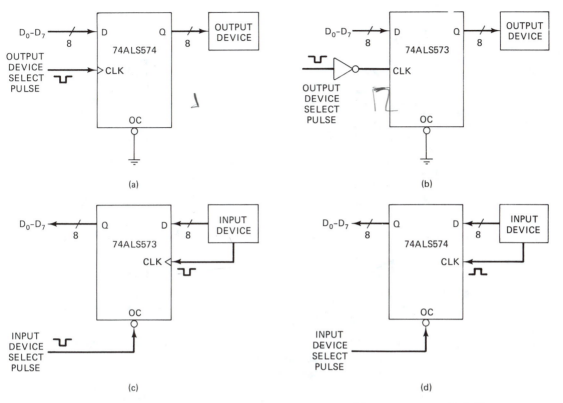

Figure 8.4-1 Octal D-type flip-flops as output and input ports: (a) 74ALS574 as an output port; (b) 74ALS573 as an output port; (c) 74ALS574 as input port; (d) 74ALS573 as input port.

The 74ALS573 is an octal D-type positive level triggered latch. If the device select logic creates an active low device select pulse, the pulse must be inverted so that the 74ALS573 is clocked on the pulse's trailing edge.

A variety of hex and octal registers can be used as output ports. The two devices just discussed have noninverting, or *true*, *outputs*; other devices are available with inverting outputs. Some octal devices are split into two quad registers, each with separate clock and output control inputs. Some registers, like the 74ALS574 and 74ALS573, have *flow through* pin arrangements—all input pins are on one side of the chip, and all output pins are on the other side. Generally, this makes printed circuit board layout easier.

Data from an input device must be stored until input by the microprocessor. The input port must isolate the data from the microprocessor's data bus until the microprocessor is ready to input the data. The simplest input port is a three-state buffer. An input port consisting of only a three-state buffer is appropriate when the input device stores the input data, for example, when the input device is a group of mechanical switches. The input device select pulse provides the signal that enables

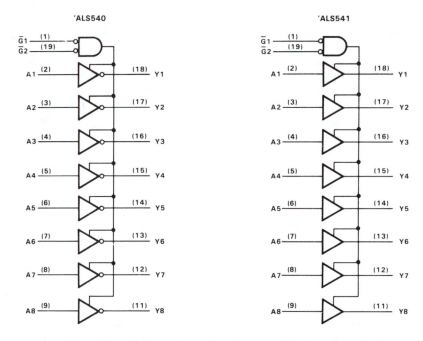

Figure 8.4-2 Inverting and noninverting octal three-state buffers. (Courtesy of Texas Instruments Inc.)

the three-state buffer. Octal buffer/drivers are available in noninverting and inverting forms. For example, the 74ALS541 is a noninverting octal buffer/driver and the 74ALS540 is an inverting octal buffer/driver. As shown in Fig. 8.4-2, the output buffers of the 74ALS541 and 74ALS540 are enabled when both $\overline{G}1$ and $\overline{G}2$ are logic 0.

If the input device does not store the input data, a register with three-state buffers can serve as the input port. If a 74ALS574 or 74ALS573 is used for this purpose, the input device provides data and the clock signal to the register. The input device select pulse controls the enabling of the register's three-state buffers.

8.5 UNCONDITIONAL AND CONDITIONAL PARALLEL TRANSFER OF INFORMATION

Under program control, data transferred on the data bus between a microprocessor and an I/O device is transmitted in parallel, a word at a time. Two types of program controlled transfer are possible: unconditional and conditional.

An unconditional transfer is one in which an instruction transfers data to or from an I/O port without determining whether the port is ready to receive or transmit the data. Unconditional transfers handle command information, status information, or other data. Command information is transferred from the microprocessor to control the operation of an I/O device. Status information is transferred from an I/O device and is used by the microprocessor to monitor the state of the I/O device. Data is transferred in both directions and is distinguished from command or status information by the manner in which it is used by the microprocessor.

An example of an unconditional output data transfer is the transmission of BCD data from a microprocessor to a display. The microprocessor does not ascertain whether the display is ready to receive the data; it simply assumes the display is ready. Illustrative of an unconditional input data transfer is the input of data from a set of manual switches. Here again the microprocessor assumes the switches are set to their desired positions.

In conditional data transfers, execution of the I/O instruction transferring the data is conditioned on the I/O device being ready for the data transfer. Readiness is determined by an unconditional transfer of status information from the I/O device to the microprocessor that precedes the actual data transfer. Status information, in a bit pattern, indicates the present state of the I/O device hardware. Often fewer than 8 bits indicate the status of an I/O device; the software simply ignores the unused bits.

A single bit of status information indicates when a single input port has information available for input or when a single output port is ready to receive information. The software that tests the status flag increases the time associated with the I/O operation; the additional time is the *I/O overhead*.

Consider, for example, an input device that has data available at input port 1 (DATA) for transmission to a microprocessor (see Fig. 8.5-1). To indicate availabil-

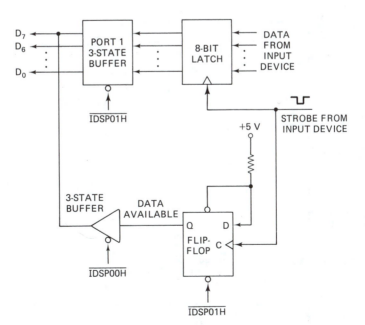

Figure 8.5-1 Handshaking using a data available flag.

```
PIN:  IN STATUS   ;INPUT STATUS BYTE
      ORA A       ;SET FLAGS
      JP PIN      ;CHECK DATA AVAILABLE STATUS BIT (BIT 7), IF DATA IS NOT
                  ;AVAILABLE, WAIT
      IN DATA     ;DATA IS AVAILABLE, INPUT DATA, CLEAR DATA AVAILABLE FLAG
      MOV M,A     ;TRANSFER DATA TO MEMORY BUFFER
      INX H       ;INCREMENT MEMORY POINTER
      DCR B       ;DECREMENT COUNTER
      JNZ PIN     ;BACK TO PIN IF MORE DATA IS TO BE INPUT
      RET
```

Figure 8.5-2 Subroutine to synchronize data transfer using the hardware
of Fig. 8.5-1.

ity, the input device sets a flag, bit 7 of input port 0 (STATUS). The use of flags in
controlling conditional transfers is referred to as *handshaking*. With programmed
I/O, it is the only way of knowing when new data is available for input to the
microprocessor.

To determine availability of data for input, the microprocessor periodically
inputs the status word at input port 0 and tests bit 7; if bit 7 is 1, data is available,

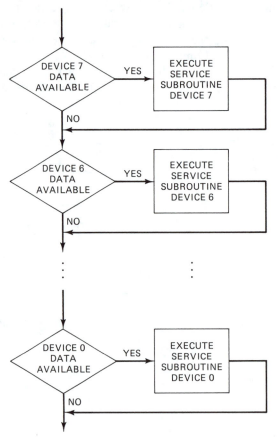

Figure 8.5-3 Polling subroutine
flowchart.

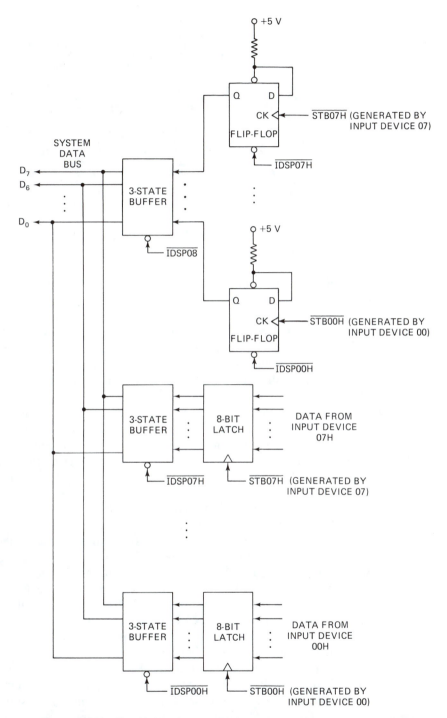

Figure 8.5-4 Combining data available flags of eight input devices into one status byte.

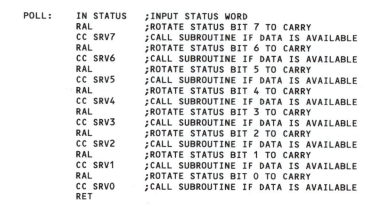

```
POLL:   IN STATUS       ;INPUT STATUS WORD
        RAL             ;ROTATE STATUS BIT 7 TO CARRY
        CC SRV7         ;CALL SUBROUTINE IF DATA IS AVAILABLE
        RAL             ;ROTATE STATUS BIT 6 TO CARRY
        CC SRV6         ;CALL SUBROUTINE IF DATA IS AVAILABLE
        RAL             ;ROTATE STATUS BIT 5 TO CARRY
        CC SRV5         ;CALL SUBROUTINE IF DATA IS AVAILABLE
        RAL             ;ROTATE STATUS BIT 4 TO CARRY
        CC SRV4         ;CALL SUBROUTINE IF DATA IS AVAILABLE
        RAL             ;ROTATE STATUS BIT 3 TO CARRY
        CC SRV3         ;CALL SUBROUTINE IF DATA IS AVAILABLE
        RAL             ;ROTATE STATUS BIT 2 TO CARRY
        CC SRV2         ;CALL SUBROUTINE IF DATA IS AVAILABLE
        RAL             ;ROTATE STATUS BIT 1 TO CARRY
        CC SRV1         ;CALL SUBROUTINE IF DATA IS AVAILABLE
        RAL             ;ROTATE STATUS BIT 0 TO CARRY
        CC SRV0         ;CALL SUBROUTINE IF DATA IS AVAILABLE
        RET
```

Figure 8.5-5 Polling subroutine for the flowchart of Figure 8.5-3.

and an instruction inputs it from port 1. The input device select strobe that enables the data from port 1 also resets the data available flag.

The frequency with which the status flag is checked determines the minimum length of time it takes to transfer the data. An input subroutine executes a tight loop to check the status flag. The subroutine of Fig. 8.5-2 for the system shown in Fig. 8.5-1 assumes that the number of bytes of data to be transferred is B and that HL points to the starting address of the data buffer in memory when the subroutine is called.

Use of a tight loop to check the status bit creates a problem in systems where no method is provided for exiting the loop if the input device malfunctions and cannot set the status flag. A software solution programs the test loop as a *controlled timeout*. This ensures that if the status flag is not set within a given time, the loop is exited, and appropriate actions are taken for a no response condition from the I/O device.

When several input devices are used in a system with programmed I/O, a subroutine checks the ready flag of each device, in turn, to see which has data available for the microprocessor. This process is known as *polling*. Figure 8.5-3 shows the flowchart of a polling subroutine for Fig. 8.5-4, which has eight input devices with their data available flags combined into one status byte.

The polling subroutine in Fig. 8.5-5 checks the status flag of each input device and branches to a service subroutine for the device if its flag is set. It also sets up a priority among the eight input devices by the order in which it tests the service request bits, with input device 7 having the highest priority. The service subroutine for each input device saves the contents of the accumulator, A, then inputs the data byte and stores it in memory or processes it. Before returning from the service subroutine, A is restored. For output operations, a ready flag in the output device indicates when the device can accept the next data byte. This is necessary when an output device requires time to process the data previously transferred to it before it can accept new data.

8.6 PROGRAMMABLE LSI PORTS

Combinations of latches, buffers, and flags constituting I/O ports are available in LSI. Due to the number of pins available on larger 40-pin LSI packages, a single package can contain several ports. And for greater versatility in application, LSI devices are software programmable, i.e., the mode of operation of each port is established under program control.

Programmable LSI ports are implemented in two ways: as part of an LSI circuit that also serves other functions and as a peripheral circuit whose exclusive function is providing I/O ports.

8.6.1 The 8155H; Programmable I / O Ports, RWM, and Counter Timer

An example of the first case is the 8155H, an LSI circuit containing three programmable I/O ports, 256×8 RWM, and a 14-bit binary counter timer [2] (see Fig. 8.6-1). This circuit is directly compatible with the 8085A, as shown in Fig. 3.7-1. The 8155H contains an internal latch to demultiplex the low order address byte, A_0–A_7, from the address/data bus, AD_0–AD_7. The logic value of the $IO/\overline{M}$ input determines whether the address refers to memory or I/O. The address and value of $IO/\overline{M}$ are latched by the 8155H on the falling edge of ALE. The chip enable signal is derived from the high order address byte. For a memory reference, $IO/\overline{M} = 0$, the latched low order address byte selects one of the 256 RWM locations.

The 8155 contains six registers that are addressed as I/O. These are the command/status register; three ports A, B, and C; and the high and low bytes of the timer.

The *command/status register (C/S)* serves two purposes: (1) it programs the function of the I/O ports when the command/status register is written by an I/O

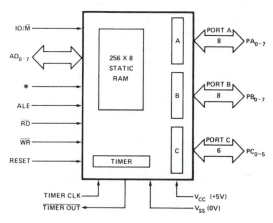

*: 8155/8155-2 = $\overline{CE}$, 8156/8156-2 = CE

Figure 8.6-1 Block diagram of an 8155. (Courtesy of Intel Corp.)

write operation, and (2) it provides information on the status of the ports and timer when the command/status register is ready by an I/O read. Actually, the command/status register is really two registers with the same I/O address, differentiated by the operation—write or read. The function of the various bits of the registers for command and status are specified in Fig. 8.6-2.

Ports A and B (PA and PB) are 8-bit ports and can be programmed for input or output. Bits 0 and 1 of the command word specify the directions of these ports. When an 8155H I/O port is programmed for output, its contents can still be read by an input operation (see Fig. 8.6-3). This eliminates the need to keep an image of the port's contents in memory, as discussed in Chapter 4, when a simple latch is used as an output port to provide independent control signals. Port C, a 6-bit port, can also be input (ALT1) or output (ALT2), or it can supply handshaking signals for ports A and B (ALT3 and ALT4) (see Fig. 8.6-4). Port C's operation is defined by bits 2 and 3 of the command word. In ALT1 and ALT2 input ports do not latch the input data. In ALT3 and ALT4 input data is latched in input ports. Bits 4 through 7 affect the interrupt signals and timer (see Chapter 9). When reset, the three ports, A, B, and C, of the 8155H are in the input mode.

The following addresses are assigned to the command/status register, ports, and timer:

Register	Address
C / S	XXXXX000
PA	XXXXX001
PB	XXXXX010
PC	XXXXX011
TIMER LOW	XXXXX100
TIMER HIGH	XXXXX101

The chip enable signal is derived from the high order address byte. However, the fact that the 8085A repeats the port address on AD_0–AD_7 and A_8–A_{15} during I/O references and the fact that in the 8155H memory and I/O share the same chip enable limits the number of bits in the high address byte that are decoded to select the 8155H. In other words, the 8-bit port address is repeated as the low and high address byte, and the least significant 3 bits provide the I/O register address, leaving only the most significant 5 bits of the high address byte for chip enable decoding.

For example, if address decoding logic enables an 8155H when A_{15}–A_8 = 01000XXX, then the address of the C/S register on this 8155H is 40H. To program the 8155H, the appropriate command word is written into the command status register by an output to port 40H.

Consider the configuration of the 8155H in Fig. 8.6-5: port A is input, port B is output, and alternative 4 is chosen for port C. (Port C provides handshaking signals for ports A and B; see Fig. 8.6-4.) Assume also that the interrupt outputs and timer are not enabled. The required command word to program the ports of the

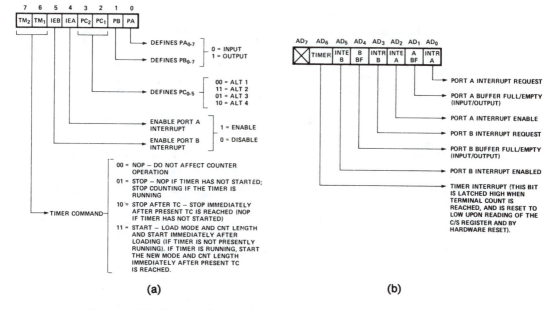

Figure 8.6-2 Command/status register (a) bit assignment and (b) status word format. (Courtesy of Intel Corp.)

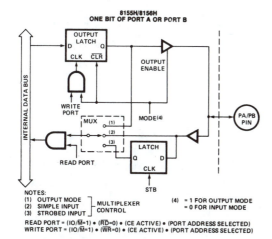

Figure 8.6-3 Logic associated with a single bit of port A or port B of an 8155H. (Courtesy of Intel Corp.)

8155H is then

$$00001010 = 0AH$$

And the following two instructions initialize the 8155H:

```
MVI A, 0AH    ;load A with command word
OUT 40H       ;output to C / S register
```

Pin	ALT 1	ALT 2	ALT 3	ALT 4
PC0	Input Port	Output Port	A INTR (Port A Interrupt)	A INTR (Port A Interrupt)
PC1	Input Port	Output Port	A BF (Port A Buffer Full)	A BF (Port A Buffer Full)
PC2	Input Port	Output Port	A $\overline{STB}$ (Port A Strobe)	A $\overline{STB}$ (Port A Strobe)
PC3	Input Port	Output Port	Output Port	B INTR (Port B Interrupt)
PC4	Input Port	Output Port	Output Port	B BF (Port B Buffer Full)
PC5	Input Port	Output Port	Output Port	B $\overline{STB}$ (Port B Strobe)

Figure 8.6-4   Table of port control assignment. (Courtesy of Intel Corp.)

When a port is in the input mode in ALT4 (for instance, port A) the input device places data on the 8155H inputs PA_0–PA_7, then provides an active low strobe to PC2 (see Figs. 8.6-5 and 8.6-6). This loads the data into input port A and sets the port A buffer full flag (ABF), bit 1 of the status register. The buffer full condition is tested by reading the C/S register with an IN 40H instruction and testing bit 1. If the buffer is full, an IN instruction for port A, IN 41H, transfers the data from port A to the 8085A's accumulator. The read strobe generated by IN 41H

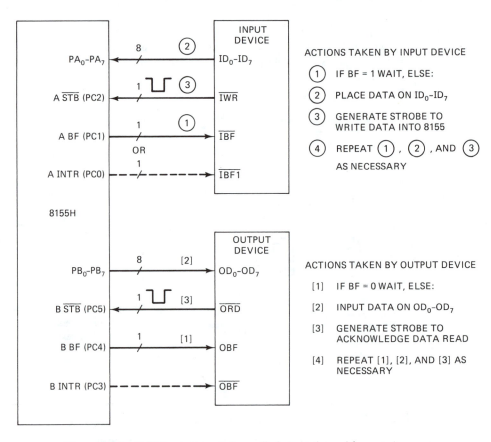

Figure 8.6-5   8155H configured for polled operation with port A as an input port and port B as an output port.

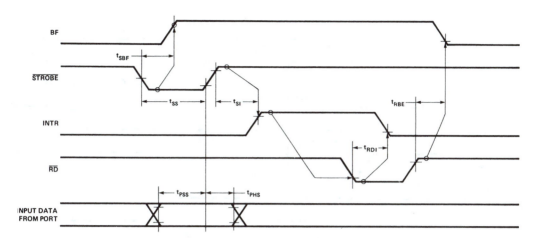

Figure 8.6-6 Timing diagram for strobe input mode of 8155H. (Courtesy of Intel Corp.)

clears the BF signal for port A. Inclusion of handshaking logic in the same IC as the port saves constructing such logic with additional ICs.

When the input device generates a long strobe at pin PC2 of the 8155H, there is a problem if the BF flag of the status register is tested by a program loop. When the strobe from the input device occurs, the BF flag is set. Assume that the strobe remains low for a relatively long period of time. The software being executed by the microprocessor tests the BF flag, finds it set, and executes an IN instruction to input the data from the port. The $\overline{\text{RD}}$ strobe during the input machine cycle of the IN instruction clears the BF flag; however, if the strobe from the input device is still low, the BF flag is set again, and the microprocessor again inputs the same data from the port. Thus, if the software is in a loop to read 10 bytes of data from the input port, it instead reads the same byte of data 10 times!

This problem can be prevented by designing logic to limit the duration of the strobe from the input device. An easier solution, however, is to test the INTR flag instead of BF, since INTR is set only when $\overline{\text{STROBE}}$ returns to logic 1.

Since the BF flag is also available as an output from the 8155H, the input device can test this signal to determine whether the microprocessor has input the previous byte strobed into port A. Thus, the input device can use the BF output to synchronize its operation with that of the microprocessor. To use the INTR output for this purpose, instead of BF, the initialization command to the 8155H must enable the interrupt output (IEA = 1). Note that the internal INTR A flag in the status register is not affected by IEA.

The control signals also provide handshaking for an output port. In the previous example, where port B was an output port, bits PC3–PC5 provide the handshaking control signals. In the output mode, contents of the 8085A's accumulator are transferred to output port B of the 8155H by an OUT instruction that addresses this port. The $\overline{\text{WR}}$ strobe resulting from the OUT instruction makes B BF

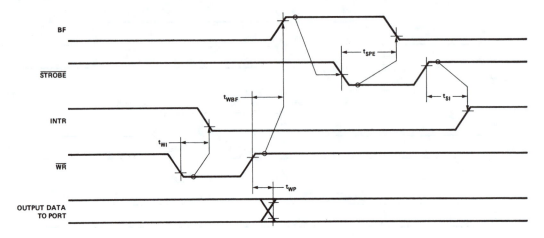

Figure 8.6-7 Timing diagram for strobed output mode of 8155H. (Courtesy of Intel Corp.)

(PC4) logic 1 (see Fig. 8.6-7). The output device monitors B BF to determine when there is valid output data. When the output device is ready to take the data, it strobes PC5, and the strobe signal at PC5 clears B BF. The 8085A reads the status word and tests bit 4 to see whether the output device has accepted the data.

8.6.2 The 8755A; Programmable I/O Ports and EPROM

Another multifunction LSI device containing I/O ports is the 8755A [2]. This device contains two general purpose 8-bit I/O ports and 2 K × 8 of EPROM (see Fig. 8.6-8). Each bit of the two 8-bit ports can be independently programmed for input

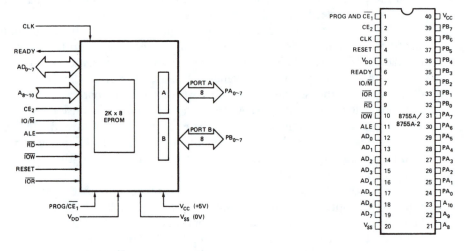

Figure 8.6-8 Block diagram (a) and pin configuration (b) of 8755A EPROM with I/O. (Courtesy of Intel Corp.)

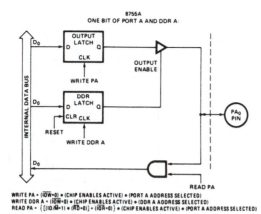

Figure 8.6-9 Logic detail of a single I/O pin on 8755A. (Courtesy of Intel Corp.)

or output. Output data is latched but input data is not. The direction of each bit of each I/O port is controlled by writing two data direction registers, DDR A and DDR B. The ports and the data direction registers are addressed by the values of AD_0–AD_1 latched during I/O operations:

Register	Address
PA	XXXXXX00
PB	XXXXXX01
DDR A	XXXXXX10
DDR B	XXXXXX11

A 1 in a bit of a DDR register establishes the corresponding port bit as an output; a 0 establishes the corresponding port bit as an input. The effect of each bit of a data direction register on the corresponding port bit is shown in Fig. 8.6-9. When a port is read, the logic values of bits in both the input and output mode are returned. The 8755A does not have a status register and does not provide for strobed input or output handshaking.

8.6.3 The 8255A Programmable Peripheral Interface

The 8255A Programmable Peripheral Interface provides programmable I/O ports exclusively [2][3]. It can be used with the 8085A or any of a number of other microprocessors. The 8255A contains a control register and three 8-bit I/O ports: A, B, and C, as shown in Fig. 8.6-10. Port C is actually two separately programmable ports: C-upper (C_4–C_7) and C-lower (C_0–C_3). An 8-bit data bus buffer transfers data between the external data bus and the control register or one of the I/O ports.

The 8255A is selected by a low signal at its chip select input, $\overline{CS}$. When not selected, the data bus buffers that connect the 8255A to the system data bus are floated. The source of the $\overline{CS}$ signal depends on whether isolated or memory mapped I/O is used. For isolated I/O, bits A_2 to A_7 are decoded to provide $\overline{CS}$, and bits A_1 and A_0 are used for selecting the control register or one of the ports. If

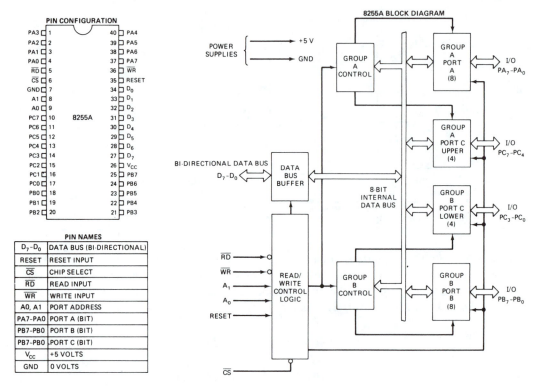

Figure 8.6-10 Block diagram of 8255A Programmable Peripheral Interface. (Courtesy of Intel Corp.)

the six address bits, A_2–A_7, are exhaustively decoded, as many as sixty-four 8255As can be used in a system. With isolated I/O, selection of the 8255A is further conditioned on $IO/\overline{M} = 1$.

Linear selection saves decoders and can select six 8255As, using isolated I/O with device and port selection as shown below.

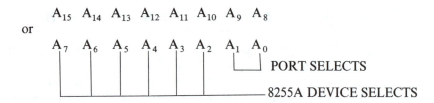

However, in order to condition the selection to isolated I/O, $\overline{I/OR}$ is connected to the $\overline{RD}$ input of the 8255A, and $\overline{I/OW}$ to the $\overline{WR}$ input of the 8255A.

With memory mapped I/O, $\overline{MEMR}$ is connected to the $\overline{RD}$ input of the 8255A and $\overline{MEMW}$ is connected to the $\overline{WR}$ input of the 8255A. And the address bits A_2–A_{15} are decoded to provide the $\overline{CS}$ signal.

TABLE 8.6-1   8255A BASIC OPERATION [3]

A_1	A_0	$\overline{RD}$	$\overline{WR}$	$\overline{CS}$	INPUT OPERATION (READ)
0	0	0	1	0	PORT A ⇒ DATA BUS
0	1	0	1	0	PORT B ⇒ DATA BUS
1	0	0	1	0	PORT C ⇒ DATA BUS
					OUTPUT OPERATION (WRITE)
0	0	1	0	0	DATA BUS ⇒ PORT A
0	1	1	0	0	DATA BUS ⇒ PORT B
1	0	1	0	0	DATA BUS ⇒ PORT C
1	1	1	0	0	DATA BUS ⇒ CONTROL
					DISABLE FUNCTION
X	X	X	X	1	DATA BUS ⇒ 3-STATE
1	1	0	1	0	ILLEGAL CONDITION
X	X	1	1	0	DATA BUS ⇒ 3-STATE

In both the isolated I/O and memory mapped schemes, when the 8255A is selected, inputs A_0 and A_1, in turn, select the control register or one of the ports (A, B, or C) for the data transfer (see Table 8.6-1).

At system power up, a reset signal applied to the 8255A clears the control register and sets all ports to the input mode. The 8255A stays in this condition until the application program writes a word into the control register that defines the 8255A's subsequent mode of operation. The three basic modes of operation are:

1. Mode 0: basic input-output
2. Mode 1: strobed input-output
3. Mode 2: bidirectional bus

The mode definition format of the control word is shown in Fig. 8.6-11.

Mode 0 provides two 8-bit ports (A and B) and two 4-bit ports (C-upper and C-lower). Any port can be input or output; outputs are latched, inputs are not. There are 16 possible input-output configurations in this mode. For example, the control word 8AH sets port A for output, port C-upper for input, port C-lower for output, and port B for input. An 8255A used for isolated I/O and selected when A_2 to $A_7 = 0$, is initialized by the following instructions to the above configuration.

```
MVI A,8AH       ;load A with control word
OUT 03H         ;write control word into control
                ;register of 8255A
```

Mode 1 also provides two 8-bit ports, A and B, but here both inputs and outputs are latched. The two 4-bit ports (C) provide handshaking for ports A and B.

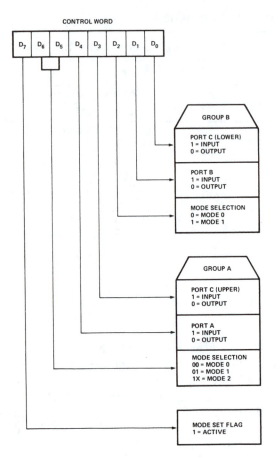

CONTROL WORD

| D$_7$ | D$_6$ | D$_5$ | D$_4$ | D$_3$ | D$_2$ | D$_1$ | D$_0$ |

GROUP B

PORT C (LOWER)
1 = INPUT
0 = OUTPUT

PORT B
1 = INPUT
0 = OUTPUT

MODE SELECTION
0 = MODE 0
1 = MODE 1

GROUP A

PORT C (UPPER)
1 = INPUT
0 = OUTPUT

PORT A
1 = INPUT
0 = OUTPUT

MODE SELECTION
00 = MODE 0
01 = MODE 1
1X = MODE 2

MODE SET FLAG
1 = ACTIVE

Figure 8.6-11 Mode definition format of control word for 8255A. (Courtesy of Intel Corp.)

Figure 8.6-12 shows the configuration of the 8255A for input and output in mode 1 operation along with the necessary control word.

For input in mode 1, port A is an input port, and bits C_3, C_4, and C_5 are used for associated handshaking. Port B is an input port with C_0, C_1, and C_2 used for handshaking. C_6 and C_7 can be used as input or output ports. The input device places 8 bits of data at A_0–A_7 (or B_0–B_7), then generates an active low strobe, $\overline{STB}$, which loads data into the input latch. This makes the input buffer full signal, IBF, logic 1. The microprocessor reads port C and checks the IBF signal to determine whether data is available for input to the microprocessor. In mode 1, port C provides status information. The mode 1 status word format is shown in Fig. 8.6-13. If IBF is logic 1, the microprocessor reads port A (or B), which inputs the data and resets the IBF flag.

For output in mode 1, the microprocessor writes data to port A (or B), and the output buffer full flag, $\overline{OBF}$, goes low to indicate this. The output device monitors $\overline{OBF}$ to determine when output data is available. And it acknowledges acceptance of the data by bringing the acknowledge input, $\overline{ACK}$, low, thus clearing the output buffer full flag.

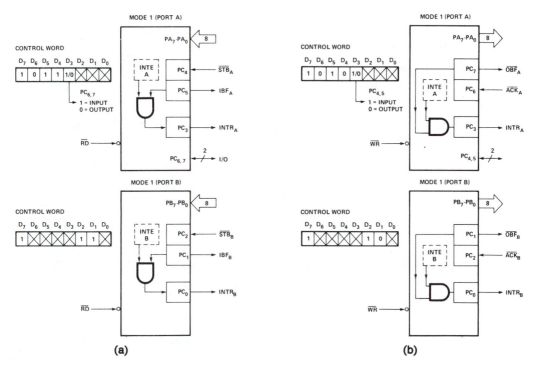

Figure 8.6-12 Mode 1 (a) input and (b) output configuration for an 8255A. (Courtesy of Intel Corp.)

Figure 8.6-13 Mode 1 status word (port C) for 8255A. (Courtesy of Intel Corp.)

Mode 2 provides a single 8-bit bidirectional bus: port A. Five bits of port C are used for status and control of port A, thus providing a handshaking capability similar to that of mode 1. Figure 8.6-14 illustrates the control word and the configuration of the 8255A in mode 2. The format of the status word when the 8255A is in mode 2 is shown in Fig. 8.6-15.

Various combinations of mode operation are possible. For example, while port A and C_5 to C_7 are used for bidirectional data transfer with handshaking in mode 2, port B can be used for input in mode 0.

The 8255A also has a bit set/reset capability for port C. When bit 7 of the control word is 0, the control word is interpreted by the 8255A as a port C bit set/reset command. Any bit of port C can be set or cleared. The bit set/reset format is shown in Fig. 8.6-16. The ability to directly set or reset a single bit is advantageous in applications where individual bits control separate external functions.

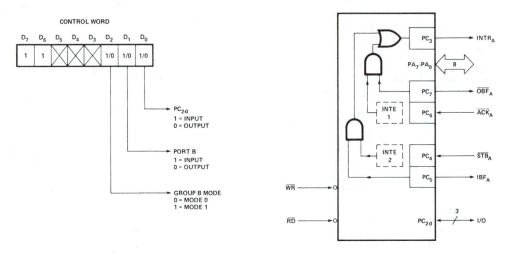

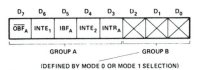

Figure 8.6-14 Mode 2 bidirectional port configuration for an 8255A. (Courtesy of Intel Corp.)

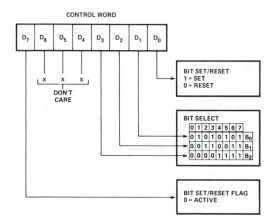

Figure 8.6-15 Mode 2 status word (port C) for 8255A. (Courtesy of Intel Corp.)

Figure 8.6-16 Bit set/reset format of 8255A. (Courtesy of Intel Corp.)

8.7 SERIAL TRANSFER OF INFORMATION

Although the data bus of a microprocessor is designed to transfer data to and from I/O devices in parallel—all bits of a data word being transferred simultaneously—there are cases when it is preferable to transfer data serially (1 bit

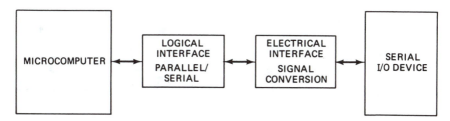

Figure 8.7-1   Interface between microprocessor and I/O device for serial transfer.

at a time). Data transferred serially is often sent in groups of bits that constitute a character or word. Frequently, the characters are coded in ASCII. *Serial transfer* requires only one signal line or communications channel and is appropriate when

1. The I/O device to/from which the data is transferred is inherently serial in operation.
2. The distance between the microprocessor and the I/O device is great.

Many I/O devices such as CRT terminals and magnetic tape cartridges and cassettes are constrained by their design to receive or transmit data a bit at a time and thus operate in a serial fashion.

As the distance between a microprocessor and an I/O device increases, the cost differential between running a cable with a number of conductors equal to the data bus width and running a single cable becomes very significant. Not only is the multiple conductor cable more costly, but multiple line drivers and receivers are necessary. A point is reached beyond which it becomes more economical to use serial data transfer, even though it may require additional hardware and/or software, than to use a multiple conductor cable. In other applications, the distance may be so great that common carrier facilities such as telephone lines are required, and thus the data must be transmitted in serial form. In general, an interface is required between the microprocessor and an I/O device for serial data transfer (see Fig. 8.7-1). The interface provides two functions:

1. The logical formatting of data, including serial-to-parallel/parallel-to-serial conversion.
2. Translation of logic signals to the electrical signals appropriate for transmitting data over the communications channel connecting the microprocessor and I/O device.

Voltage and current levels used for data communication are seldom TTL compatible. Electrical signal translation is implemented by hardware. Logical formatting of data, however, may be implemented by software or hardware or by a combination of the two.

Serial data transfer systems are simplex, half duplex, or full duplex. In a *simplex* system, data is transferred only in one direction. In a *half duplex* system, it

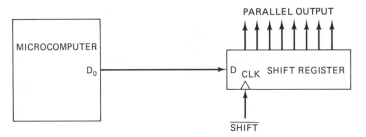

Figure 8.7-2 Serial data transmission to shift register receiver. The output device select pulse clocks the shift register.

is transmitted in either direction, but in only one direction at a time. In a *full duplex* system, data is transferred in both directions simultaneously.

Consider the example of simplex serial data transfer shown in Fig. 8.7-2. A microprocessor transfers data to a shift register in an I/O device. The shift register is within several feet of the microprocessor, and the communications channel is a twisted pair of wires. The formatting of data is done by software. Data input to the shift register is connected to bit D_0 of the data bus, and the clock input of the shift register is driven by logic that generates an output device select pulse $\overline{\text{SHIFT}}$. Assuming that the data byte to be transferred is in A, the following subroutine formats the data and implements the transfer, least significant bit first:

```
SO8:        MVI C,8
LOOP:       OUT SHIFT
            RAR
            DCR C
            JNZ LOOP
            RET
```

This example illustrates an important aspect of serial data transfer: the receiver has to have some means of determining when its data input should be sampled, thus defining the occurrence of a new data bit. In this example a clock signal from the transmitter tells the receiving device when it should sample the data input line, thus synchronizing the data transfer. Use of the device select pulse for synchronization ensures that the data on the interconnecting line is sampled at the proper time. However, transferring a separate clock signal from the transmitter to the receiver for synchronization requires an additional connection between the devices. Techniques for the serial transfer of data that do not require a separate clock line from transmitter to receiver are considered in the following sections.

The *baud rate* is the rate at which data is transferred. It denotes the number of signal changes per second. When the signals being transmitted are binary, the baud rate is equivalent to the number of bits per second. Communications channels are rated by baud rate. If data is transmitted on a channel at a baud rate beyond the channel's capacity, the error rate of the transmission is unacceptably high.

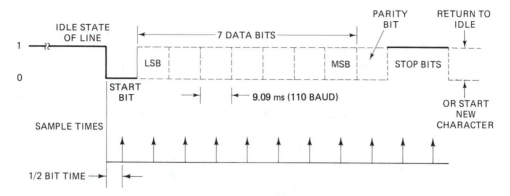

Figure 8.7-3   Seven bit asynchronous data character format, 110 baud.

Serial transfer of data is asynchronous or synchronous. In asynchronous transmission, a character is sent whenever it is available. Thus, the time interval between two characters is variable; however, the time interval between bits in a single character is fixed. When no character is available for transmission, the line is idle. With synchronous character transmission, one character is followed immediately by another. Whenever another data character is not immediately ready for transmission, the transmitter repeatedly sends a special SYNC character until it can transmit the next data character.

8.7.1 Asynchronous Serial Character Transfer

Asynchronous data transfer is used for low speed, low data rate transfers. Such transfers typically occur at 110, 300, 600, 1200, 2400, 4800, 9600 or 19.2 K baud, values commonly used by manufacturers of commercial communications equipment. The transfer of information between a CRT terminal and microprocessor is asynchronous. For instance, a CRT terminal may transmit and receive data at 110 baud or 110 bits per second. At this rate, each bit duration or *bit time* is 9.09 mS. Data is transferred as a group of serial bits constituting a character. The character is coded in ASCII as 7 bits, or *seven level code*, and transmitted in the format shown in Fig. 8.7-3.

Even though the receiver and transmitter in an asynchronous data transfer are not synchronized with respect to the time at which a character is transmitted, once the transmitter starts to send a character, the receiver synchronizes itself with the bit times of the character in order to sample them at the correct time. The baud rate of the transmitter and receiver are set to the same value.

A *start bit* synchronizes the transmitter and receiver. It is the first bit of any character sent and is logic 0. When no character is being sent, the transmitter's output is logic 1, and the data line is *idle* or *marking*. The receiver synchronizes its operation with the transmitter on the 1 to 0 transition of the data line. It waits one-half a bit time, checks the input to make sure it is still logic 0—and therefore a valid start bit—and begins sampling the data line at intervals equal to one bit time. The data line is sampled at the center of each transmitted bit. This eliminates errors that might occur if sampling takes place at the beginning of each bit time, since the leading or trailing edges of transitions on the data line are distorted in transmission. Following the start bit, the seven data bits of the ASCII character are transmitted—least significant bit first—followed by a parity bit, which is set or cleared to provide even or odd parity. For odd (even) parity, the parity bit is set to make the total number of bits (data bits and parity bit) in the ASCII character odd (even). Finally, two stop bits are transmitted.[3] The start bit, logic 0, and two stop bits, both logic 1, *frame* the ASCII character.

On the microprocessor side, the logical formatting of data for serial transfer can be implemented in software, including the 9.09 mS delay and the other features required for transmitting or receiving. Hardware only provides electrical interfacing between the microprocessor and CRT terminal signals.

The disadvantage of software formatting and timing of a serial transfer is that the microprocessor is completely tied up during each character transfer. It takes 100 mS to transfer a single character at 110 baud; in this period of time, assuming an average instruction execution time of 2 μS, 50,000 instructions could be executed.

Parallel-to-serial conversion for transmitting and serial-to-parallel conversion for receiving and formatting with hardware use the microprocessor's time more effectively. The microprocessor transfers data in parallel to external hardware, which provides the necessary formatting and parallel-to-serial conversion. This hardware also receives serial data, removes the parity and framing information, and supplies the data in parallel to the microprocessor.

8.7.2 Synchronous Serial Character Transfer

Synchronous character transmission eliminates the noninformation-carrying start and stop bits associated with asynchronous transfers and allows faster data transmission. It usually occurs at rates of 3800 and 9600 baud. Synchronization between the receiver and transmitter is provided by one or two (bisync) synchronization characters. When transmitting in ASCII, for example, the SYN character is used.

In synchronous transmission, the data received is a continuous stream of bits with no indication of character boundaries. The receiver operates in a hunt mode—making a bit-by-bit comparison of the input stream with the values of the desired sync character(s)—until it detects the sync character(s). Once the desired sync character(s) is detected, the receiver treats each subsequent group of *n* bits as a character. The transmitter continues to send characters to maintain the synchronization, even if the source of data characters does not have data ready for transmission. In this case, the transmitter sends the sync code or the code for a null character, and thus the time interval between two characters is fixed. The clocks in the transmitter and receiver operate at exactly the same frequency and must be very stable to maintain synchronization for a long period of time. Typically, thousands of blocks of characters can be sent without resynchronizing the receiver.

---

[3] Data transmitted at 110 baud typically requires two stop bits and data transmitted at 300 baud and above requires only one stop bit.

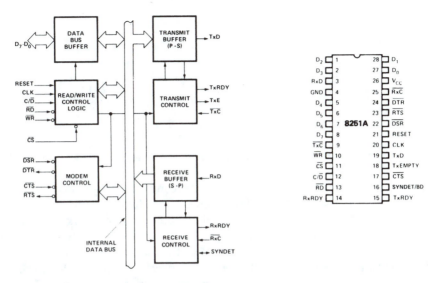

Figure 8.7-4 Block diagram (a) and pin configuration (b) for 8251A USART. (Courtesy of Intel Corp.)

Single-chip LSI devices are available that provide the required logic for a bidirectional synchronous serial interface in a single package. The functional configurations of the device are programmed by writing information into the control registers. Devices, such as the Intel 8251A Programmable Communication Interface, provide both a synchronous and asynchronous interface in a single package.

8.7.3 The 8251A USART; Universal Synchronous / Asynchronous Receiver / Transmitter

The 8251A USART is a programmable communications interface designed to provide serial data communications in microprocessor systems [4], [5]. The 8251A supports synchronous and asynchronous communication. It converts parallel data from the microprocessor to serial format for transmission and converts incoming serial data to parallel for input to the microprocessor. The block diagram and pin configuration of the 8251A is shown in Fig. 8.7-4. The 8251A interfaces with the microprocessor through its bidirectional data bus D_0–D_7 and control signals RESET, CLK, C/$\overline{D}$, $\overline{RD}$, $\overline{WR}$, and $\overline{CS}$. It provides serial data out at TxD and inputs serial data in at RxD. Full duplex operation is supported, allowing data to be transmitted and received simultaneously. It also has signals to support modem control for interface to telephone lines, $\overline{DSR}$, $\overline{DTR}$, $\overline{CTS}$, and $\overline{RTS}$.

The functional definition of the 8251A must be programmed by the microprocessor before the 8251A transmits or receives data. The 8251A contains control registers, a status register, transmit data register, and received data register. The selection of these registers is accomplished using the control signals as shown in Table 8.7-1. The input C/$\overline{D}$ selects the control register or status register when it is

TABLE 8.7-1 8251A REGISTER SELECTION

$\overline{CS}$	$C/\overline{D}$	$\overline{RD}$	$\overline{WR}$	REGISTER
0	1	1	0	CONTROL
0	1	0	1	STATUS
0	0	1	0	TRANSMIT DATA
0	0	0	1	RECEIVED DATA

logic 1, and the transmit data or received data register when it is logic 0. $C/\overline{D}$ is typically driven by A_0.

After a hardware reset, the 8251A must be programmed for asynchronous or synchronous operation. The discussion that follows considers asynchronous operation. Two control words are required, after reset, to configure the 8251A, the mode instruction and the command instruction. The first byte written to the control register after a reset is interpreted by the 8251A as a mode instruction. All subsequent bytes written to the control register are interpreted as command instructions. The format for the mode instruction is shown in Fig. 8.7-5. Bits B_2 and B_1 program the baud rate factor. For synchronous operation these bits are 00. For asynchronous operation these bits specify the factor by which the transmit and receive clocks, $\overline{TxC}$ and $\overline{RxC}$, exceed the baud rate. These clock inputs are provided by an external user supplied clock, the ***baud rate generator***. The other clock input to the 8251A, CLK, is used to generate internal device timing and must simply be greater than 30 times the transmitter or receiver baud rates. For an 8085A system CLK is usually CLK (OUT) of the 8085A.

Bits L_2 and L_1 specify the number of data bits in the character to be sent or received. This number excludes the parity bit if parity has been enabled. Bit PEN enables the parity and bit EP selects even or odd parity. Bits S_2 and S_1 specify the number of stop bits for transmission. Data transmitted at 110 baud typically

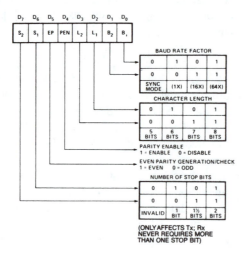

Figure 8.7-5 Mode instruction format, asynchronous mode, 8251A. (Courtesy of Intel Corp.)

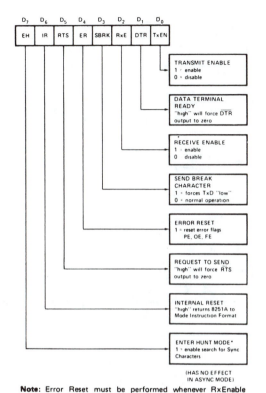

Figure 8.7-6 Command instruction format, 8251A. (Courtesy of Intel Corp.)

requires two stop bits and data transmitted at 300 baud and above requires only one stop bit.

A command instruction must follow the mode instruction and controls the actual operation of the selected format. Functions such as Enable Transmit/ Receive, Error Reset, and modem control are provided by the command instruction (see Fig. 8.7-6). To transmit or receive data the TxEN and RxEN bits in the command instruction must be set.

The 8251A can be operated in a polled or interrupt mode. In the polled mode status, bits in the 8251A are monitored by the microprocessor to determine when a character has been received or when a character can be transmitted. The format of the status register is given in Fig. 8.7-7. If the receiver has been enabled by the command instruction, it will sense a start bit at RxD and assemble the serial data into parallel format. The 8251A strips the start bit, parity bit, and stop bit(s) from the received character before placing it in the received data register. When the parallel data is ready for transfer to the microprocessor, the 8251A will set the RxRDY bit of the status word. If a parity error, framing error, or overrun error is detected the appropriate bit(s) in the status word, PE, FE, or OE, will be set. When the microprocessor detects RxRDY set, it inputs the data from the received data register. Reading the received data register clears RxRDY. If the receiver is not enabled by the command instruction, RxRDY will be held at logic 0.

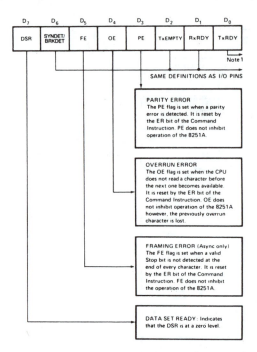

Note 1: TxRDY status bit has different meanings from the
         TxRDY output pin. The former is not conditioned
         by $\overline{CTS}$ and TxEN; the latter is conditioned by both
         $\overline{CTS}$ and TxEN.

         i.e. TxRDY status bit = DB Buffer Empty
             TxRDY pin out - DB Buffer Empty · ($\overline{CTS} = 0$)·
             (TxEN=1)

Figure 8.7-7   Status read format,
8251A. (Courtesy of Intel Corp.)

To transmit data with polled operation, the microprocessor reads the status byte and checks TxRDY. If the TxRDY status bit is set, the transmitter buffer is empty and the microprocessor can write a character to it. The TxRDY status bit indicates the status of the transmit data register regardless of the value of the TxEN bit. TxRDY is automatically cleared when a data character is written to the transmit data register. If the microprocessor is sending an ASCII character, it outputs only the seven data bits that make up the character. This character is output right-justified, with the most significant bit a don't care. The 8251A adds the start bit, parity bit (if required), and the number of stop bits specified, then transmits the character.

Figure 8.7-8 is a block diagram showing the interface of an 8251A to an 8085A. This interface is for polled operation and no modem control. The baud rate generator can be implemented using a programmable baud rate generator chip, such as the Standard Microsystems COM8146T [6], or by counting down CLK (OUT) of the 8085A using a programmable counter timer. Implementation of a baud rate generator using a counter timer is given in Chapter 9. The baud rate desired is selected by switches that are read from an input port. The subroutine in Fig. 8.7-9

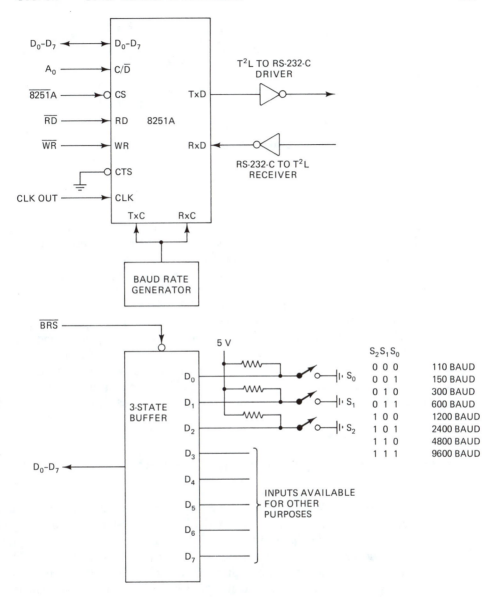

Figure 8.7-8   Interface of 8251A to an 8085A microprocessor.

reads the baud rate selection switches and initializes the 8251A for asynchronous operation at the selected baud rate with a 16 × baud rate clock, even parity, a seven bit data word, and one or two stop bits, depending on the baud rate selected.

Because of the time that elapses between characters for serial data transfer, it is particularly advantageous to use interrupt driven data transfer as opposed to polled operation with the 8251A. RxRDY is available as an output signal from the 8251A. This signal has the same characteristics as the status bit RxRDY. If

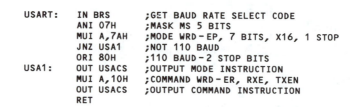

```
USART:    IN BRS        ;GET BAUD RATE SELECT CODE
          ANI 07H       ;MASK MS 5 BITS
          MUI A,7AH     ;MODE WRD-EP, 7 BITS, X16, 1 STOP
          JNZ USA1      ;NOT 110 BAUD
          ORI 80H       ;110 BAUD-2 STOP BITS
USA1:     OUT USACS     ;OUTPUT MODE INSTRUCTION
          MUI A,10H     ;COMMAND WRD-ER, RXE, TXEN
          OUT USACS     ;OUTPUT COMMAND INSTRUCTION
          RET
```

Figure 8.7-9 Subroutine to initialize an 8251A for polled asynchronous operation.

the receiver is enabled and a character has been received, this signal becomes logic 1. RxRDY is connected to one of the microprocessor's interrupt pins. When the microprocessor is interrupted, it transfers control to a subroutine that reads the character from the 8251A and processes it. The microprocessor then continues with its other tasks until the next character is received.

TxRDY is available as an output signal from the 8251A that can be used to interrupt directly the microprocessor when the transmit data register in the 8251A is empty. The TxRDY signal is masked by the TxEN bit of the command instruction and the CTS input of the 8251A. Thus, when the 8251A is ready to transmit a character, it interrupts the microprocessor. In response to the interrupt, the micro-processor outputs the next character to be transmitted and then continues with its other tasks. The details of interrupt driven data transfer are covered in Chapter 9.

8.8 DIRECT MICROPROCESSOR SERIAL I/O PINS

Some microprocessors have one or more pins for serial input and output of data. The 8085A, for instance, has a single serial input data, SID, pin and a single serial output data, SOD, pin [7]. Data is input to the microprocessor at the SID pin by the RIM instruction and output from the SOD pin by the SIM instruction. The RIM instruction reads the data at the SID input into bit 7 of the accumulator. The remaining six bits of the accumulator provide information on the status of the microprocessor's interrupt system (see Chapter 9).

The SIM instruction loads the value of bit 7 of the accumulator into the SOD latch, if bit 6 of the accumulator is logic 1. If bit 6 is logic 0, the SOD latch is unaffected. The other six bits of the accumulator set the interrupt masks of the 8085A (see Chapter 9). When the 8085A is reset, the SOD latch is set to logic 0. Appropriate program control of the SOD pin provides serial data directly to an output device. A subroutine for asynchronous serial data transfer using the SOD pin of the 8085A is given in Fig. 8.8-1. The subroutine is called with the 7-bit ASCII character and the parity bit in register B. The parity bit is bit 7 of register B.

```
SRLD    MVI  C, 10D      ;INITIALIZE BIT COUNTER
        MVI  A, SODO     ;SET BIT 7 OF A TO 0 (SODO = 01XXXXXX)
        SIM              ;OUTPUT START BIT
LOOP:   CALL DELAY       ;DELAY ONE BIT TIME
        MOV  A, B        ;LOAD A WITH DATA AND PARITY
        STC              ;SET CARRY FOR STOP BITS
        RAR              ;PUT BIT TO BE SENT IN CY
        MOV  B, A        ;SAVE REMAINING BITS
        RAR              ;PUT BIT TO BE SENT IN A7
        ANI  80H         ;ZERO ALL BUT 7 OF A
        ORI  SODO        ;OR REMAIN BITS REQUIRED FOR SIM
        SIM              ;OUTPUT BIT 7
        DCR  C           ;DECREMENT BIT COUNTER
        JNZ  LOOP
        RET
```

Figure 8.8-1 Subroutine for asynchronous serial data transmission using the SOD pin of the 8085A.

8.9 SERIAL TRANSFER ELECTRICAL CHARACTERISTICS

As the physical distance between an I/O port and its associated I/O device increases, special consideration must be given to the electrical characteristics of the interconnection in order to minimize the error rate of the data received. As the propagation delay of the interconnection increases relative to the rise and fall time of the signal, interconnection lines cease to respond like simple interconnections and take on the aspects of transmission lines.

Three conditions produce a voltage at the receiving end significantly different from that at the transmitting end, causing received data to be invalid:

1. A noise voltage can be induced into the interconnection via capacitive and inductive coupling, or electrical noise sources, such as motors, in the environment.

2. The transmitting and receiving ends may have different ground connections between which a ground shift voltage exists.

3. The interconnection may act as a transmission line, and reflections of the transmitted voltage may occur on the line.

Typically, standard TTL gates are restricted to driving lines of a maximum 2 feet in length. In electrically noisy environments, the small noise margin of TTL voltage levels can result in seriously degraded performance.

8.9.1 Line Drivers and Receivers

Line driver ICs are available that convert TTL levels into signals for driving transmission lines. Line receiver circuits convert these signals back to TTL levels. There are three kinds of line driver and receiver interconnections: single-ended, balanced differential, and unbalanced differential (see Fig. 8.9-1).

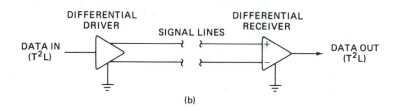

(a)

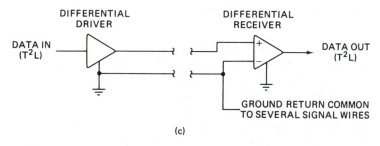

(b)

DIFFERENTIAL   DIFFERENTIAL
DRIVER   RECEIVER

DATA IN   DATA OUT
(T²L)   (T²L)

GROUND RETURN COMMON
TO SEVERAL SIGNAL WIRES

(c)

Figure 8.9-1   Line driver and receiver interconnections: (a) single-ended;
(b) balanced differential; and (c) unbalanced differential.

A single-ended circuit uses one signal line and a common ground return to transmit the signal V_O. Although advantageous in that only one signal wire is required per data channel, the performance of the circuit can be degraded by a noise voltage, V_N, induced by inductive or capacitive coupling from adjacent signal lines or noise generators such as motors. There may be a voltage between the receiver and transmitter grounds due to a finite resistance between the driver and receiver ground points. The return signal current and possibly other system currents cause a voltage drop, V_G, across this resistance. The voltage at the receiver, V_R, equals $V_O \pm V_N \pm V_G$. The receiver cannot distinguish what portion of the signal is V_O and may assign it an incorrect logic value.

A balanced differential system uses a differential driver and a differential receiver. The driver produces the logic value of the data to be transmitted on one output and its complement on the other. The receiver converts the differential signal into a TTL level at its output.

The driver and receiver are connected by a twisted pair of wires that cancel magnetically induced currents. Electrostatically coupled noise equally affects both lines of the twisted pair and thus appears at both inputs of the differential receiver. This noise voltage, common to both inputs, is referred to as a ***common mode signal***.

The ground potential voltage also appears to the receiver as a common mode signal. The voltage at the plus input of the differential receiver is $V_O \pm V_N \pm V_G$, and at the minus input terminal is $\pm V_N \pm V_G$. The differential receiver takes the difference of the signals at its plus and minus inputs, eliminating the noise and ground shift voltage, and leaves V_O, which it converts to a TTL logic level, at the output.

In the unbalanced differential method, the minus input of the differential amplifier is connected to the ground return, eliminating one wire. However, performance is diminished because inductive coupling is increased by the use of the common ground return.

Improperly terminated transmission lines are subject to errors from reflections of the transmitted signals. When data bit duration is long in comparison with the propagation delay of the line, the effects of the reflection die away in a relatively short period of time. However, when the data bit duration is short in comparison with the propagation time, the line must be properly terminated.

The characteristic impedance of a transmission line, R_O—which is a function of its geometry and dimension—typically falls between 50 and 200 ohms. To preclude reflections, a transmission line must be terminated by a resistance equal to its characteristic impedance. Line receivers have a high input impedance and thus require the addition of resistors for proper termination.

8.9.2 Standards

Commercial I/O devices, particularly data communications devices, are frequently designed to meet the requirements of one or more formal interface standards. Such standards specify the electrical characteristics and the protocol for transferring data between devices adhering to the standard (see Table 8.9-1). A commonly used standard is the RS-232-C [8]. The electrical interface is simplex, single-ended, and unterminated. Line length and slew rate limit control reflections. The recommended maximum line length is 50 feet, and the maximum data rate is 20 K baud; logic 1 is -3 to -15 V, and logic 0 is $+3$ to $+15$ V. IC line drivers and receivers are available that meet the electrical requirements of this standard.

More recent standards allow longer line lengths and higher data rates. Standard RS-422-A [9] covers the electrical characteristics of a balanced differential interface. This standard allows line lengths of 1200 meters (4000 feet) and data rates of 10 M baud. Standard RS-423-A [10] pertains to unbalanced differential circuits and allows a line length of 1200 meters (4000 feet) and data rates of 100 K baud. IC drivers and receivers are also available that meet these standards. Standard RS-485 is an upgraded version of standard RS-422-A which allows as many as 32 driver and receiver combinations on a single twisted pair line.

8.9.3 RS-232-C IC Drivers and Receivers

Integrated circuit drivers and receivers are available for each of the standards previously discussed. Devices for the RS-232-C standard are considered here. A commonly used pair of ICs for this purpose are the MC1488 and MC1489A. The MC1488 contains four drivers in a 14-pin package. Each driver converts a TTL

TABLE 8.9-1 POPULAR GENERAL PURPOSE EIA LINE CIRCUIT STANDARDS (COURTESY OF TEXAS INSTRUMENTS, INC.)

PARAMETER		RS-232-C	RS-423-A	RS-422-A	RS-485
Mode of operation		Single-ended	Single-ended	Differential	Differential
Number of drivers and receivers allowed		1 Driver 1 Receiver	1 Driver 10 Receivers	1 Driver 10 Receivers	32 Drivers 32 Receivers
Maximum cable length (ft)		50	4000	4000	4000
Maximum data rate bits per second		20k	100k	10M	10M
Maximum common-mode voltage		±25 V	±6 V	6 V −0.25 V	12 V −7 V
Driver output		±5 V min ±15 V max	±3.6 V min ±6.0 V max	±2 V min	±1.5 V min
Driver load		3 kΩ to 7 kΩ	450 Ω min	100 Ω min	60 Ω min
Driver slew rate		30 V/μs max	Externally controlled	NA	NA
Driver output short circuit current limit		500 mA to V_{CC} or GRD	150 mA to GRD	150 mA to GRD	150 mA to GRD 250 mA to 8 V or 12 V
Driver output resistance (High Z state)	Power on	NA	NA	NA	120 kΩ
	Power off	300 Ω	60 kΩ	60 kΩ	120 kΩ
Receiver input resistance Ω		3 kΩ to 7 kΩ	4 kΩ	4 kΩ	12 kΩ
Receiver sensitivity		±3 V	±200 mV	±200 mV	±200 mV

input signal to an output signal compatible with the RS-232-C standard. The MC1489A contains four receivers that convert RS-232-C level inputs into TTL outputs. While the MC1489A requires only a $+5$ V supply voltage for operation, the MC1488 requires a V_{CC} supply voltage of from $+9$ V to $+15$ V and a V_{EE} supply voltage from -9 V to -15 V. In microprocessor systems that include analog circuits, supply voltages in this range are usually required for the analog circuits and therefore are not an additional requirement. However, in microprocessor systems without analog circuitry, these supply voltages would be required simply to handle the RS-232-C drivers.

For systems that only have a $+5$ V supply, the MAXIM MAX232 provides two RS-232-C transmitters and two RS-232-C receivers in a single IC that requires only a $+5$ V supply [11]. This CMOS IC contains an on chip charge pump that generates $+10$ V and -10 V supplies from its $+5$ V supply input. The drivers convert TTL inputs to ± 10 V outputs.

REFERENCES

1. HPL-82C399 Programmable Chip Select Decoder data sheet (Melbourne, Fla.: Harris Corporation, 1985).

2. *Microsystem Components Handbook*, Vol. I (Santa Clara, Calif.: Intel Corporation, 1985).

3. A. EBRIGHT, *8255A Programmable Peripheral Interface Applications* (Application Note AP-15) (Santa Clara, Calif.: Intel Corporation, 1976).

4. *Microsystem Components Handbook*, Vol. II (Santa Clara, Calif.: Intel Corporation, 1985).

5. L. SMITH, *Using the 8251 Universal Synchronous/Asynchronous Receiver/Transmitter* (Application Note AP-16) (Santa Clara, Calif.: Intel Corporation, 1976).

6. *Standard Microsystems Corporation Data Catalog* (Hauppauge, N.Y.: Standard Microsystems Corporation, 1984).

7. J. WHARTON, *Using the Intel 8085 Serial I/O Lines* (Application Note AP-29) (Santa Clara, Calif.: Intel Corporation, 1977).

8. *Interface Between Data Terminal Equipment and Data Communications Equipment Employing Serial Binary Data Interchange* (Washington, D.C.: Electronic Industries Association, 1969).

9. *Electrical Characteristics of Balanced Voltage Digital Interface Circuits* (Washington, D.C.: Electronic Industries Association, 1978).

10. *Electrical Characteristics of Unbalanced Voltage Digital Interface Circuits* (Washington, D.C.: Electronic Industries Association, 1978).

11. *MAX232 RS-232 Dual Transmitter-Receiver data sheet* (Sunnyvale, Calif.: Maxim Integrated Products, Inc., 1985).

PROBLEMS

8-1. List the eight unique hexadecimal port addresses possible using isolated I/O and linear selection. Assume that the address line associated with each port is logic 1 when the port is selected.

8-2. Repeat Problem 8-1 assuming that the address line associated with each port is logic 0 when the port is selected.

8-3. List all the instructions that will create each of the following device select pulses with the hardware of Fig. 8.2-4. Specify the instructions' addresses in hexadecimal.

   (a) $\overline{\text{IDSP00H}}$

   (b) $\overline{\text{IDSP05H}}$

   (c) $\overline{\text{ODSP03H}}$

   (d) $\overline{\text{ODSP06H}}$

8-4. Using three 74ALS138s, NAND gates, and inverters, draw the logic diagram of a circuit that generates 24 output device select pulses, $\overline{\text{ODSP00H}}$ to $\overline{\text{ODSP17H}}$.

8-5. Using 74ALS138s and common gates, design the logic required to generate 24 input device select pulses, $\overline{\text{IDSP08H}}$ to $\overline{\text{IDSP1FH}}$.

8-6. Design the logic necessary to generate eight device select pulses for input and eight device select pulses for output using memory mapped I/O. Make the port addresses FFF0H to FFF7H. Use 74ALS138s, NAND gates, and inverters.

8-7. List the advantages and disadvantages of isolated and memory mapped I/O.

8-8. An input device generates an active low 100 nS pulse each time it has new data available for the microprocessor. The input device contains a register to hold the data until it generates new data. Draw a logic diagram of an interface of this device to the microprocessor using handshaking. A status input port must provide a data available status bit, DAV, and an overrun status bit, OVRN. The OVRN status bit should be logic 1 if the microprocessor does not input a byte of data from the input device before the input device generates another byte.

8-9. An input device is interfaced to an 8085A microprocessor. The device has one input, RUN, which when high, operates the device. The device then outputs bytes of data asynchronously on its eight data lines. It has one data valid status output, DAV, which indicates valid data each time it makes a 1 to 0 transition. The RUN, DAV, and eight data outputs are the only connections to the device. These inputs and outputs are TTL. Design the hardware and draw the logic diagram for this interface with the following port assignments:

RUN	bit 7	output port 0
DAV	bit 7	input port 0
DATA (8 bits)		input port 1

Write a subroutine that starts the device, inputs 64 bytes of data, stores them in a memory buffer, BUFF, and then turns the device off.

8-10. There are certain types of registers that are common to all programmable devices, including the 8155, 8255, and 8251A. Describe, in general, these registers and their functions. For the 8155, describe the function and/or information provided by these registers in detail.

8-11. Design the interface between seven input devices and an 8085A microprocessor system that transfers data using programmed I/O. The devices are numbered 1 through 7; device number 1 has the highest priority. Use a 74LS148 priority encoder to speed up priority arbitration. The 74LS148 has eight active low inputs and three outputs. Input 7 of this encoder has the highest priority. The output of the priority encoder is the complement of the binary equivalent of the number of its highest priority active input.

   (a) Draw a logic diagram of the interconnection of the data available flip-flops to the priority encoder and a single input port that provides the microprocessor with the status of all the input devices. Also show the logic necessary to clear the data available flip-flops.

   (b) Write a program that checks the status and jumps to the appropriate service routine via a jump table.

8-12. Modify subroutine PIN, shown in Fig. 8.5-2, for conditional data transfer to provide a controlled timeout feature. If the input device does not respond in 100 mS with each byte of data, the subroutine, PIN, should be returned from, with the carry cleared. If all bytes of data are transferred successfully, the subroutine returns with the carry set.

8-13. An 8155 is used with port A as output, port B as input, and with port C used for handshaking for ports A and B. The 8155 is enabled when A_{15} to A_8 = 00110XXX. Write the instruction sequence to program the 8155 for this mode of operation.

8-14. For the 8155 of Problem 8-13, write a subroutine that outputs 40 bytes of data from a memory buffer labeled LINE, to port A using handshaking. The subroutine should check the 8155's status word to determine when the output device has accepted the data.

8-15. Determine the control words necessary to put an 8255 in mode 0 with the following configuration:

   (a) port A, input; ports B and C output

   (b) ports A and C lower, output; ports B and C upper, input

   (c) ports A and C upper, input; ports B and C lower, output

   (d) ports A and B, input; port C, output

8-16. Draw a logic diagram of the interface of an 8251A to an 8085A bus. The 8251A is to be IO mapped and respond to addresses 0FEH and 0FFH. Use only an eight-input NAND for address decoding. The receiver and transmitter are to to be operated in the polled mode. Write the sequence of instructions required to initialize the 8251A to receive and transmit 7-bit ASCII characters at 300 baud with even parity. Assume that the transmit and receive clock inputs to the 8251A are driven by a 19.2 KHz square wave.

8-17. Write a macro, PE, that treats the last significant 7 bits of the accumulator contents as an ASCII character. The initial value of the eighth bit is undefined. The macro makes the eighth bit of the accumulator the value necessary to achieve even parity for the entire contents of the accumulator.

8-18. A microprocessor transmits ASCII data, in serial, at 1200 baud with even parity. What is the maximum number of characters that can be transmitted per second? Write a sequence of 1s and 0s that represents the logic level of the serial line when the two ASCII characters "SB" are transmitted at the highest possible character rate. The sequence is written with time increasing from left to right. What is the time duration of a single bit?

8-19. A printer has a single 8-bit data input register that is negative level triggered. A character to be printed must be loaded into this register. The printer can print characters at a rate of 10 per second. The printer creates a 100 nS negative pulse simultaneously with the completion of the printing of a character. Design the hardware and software required to synchronize an 8085A microprocessor to the printer. The transfer of data is to be program controlled. A subroutine, PRTR, is to be written that operates with the hardware you designed to output a character to the printer. The character to be printed is passed to the subroutine in register A. When the printer is ready to accept a new character the subroutine outputs the character and returns to the calling program. Briefly describe how the subroutine would be modified to handle a situation where it is desired to return to the calling program with an error indication if the printer is not ready in 200 mS.

9

Interrupts and DMA

Interrupts increase processor system efficiency by letting an
I / O device request CPU time only when that device needs
immediate attention. Main-line programs can then perform
routine tasks without continually checking I / O device status.
Among routine duties, interrupts generally accomplish programmed I / O upon device demand; respond to time-critical
events; establish a time base with a timer or clock; or count
external events.

Ronald L. Baldridge*

*"Interrupts Add Power, Complexity to μC-System Design," *EDN*, Vol. 22, No. 14, (August 5,
1977), pp. 67 – 73.

9.1 INTERRUPTS

Polling of I/O service request flags monopolizes a significant amount of a microprocessor's time. This reduces system *throughput*—the total, useful information
processed or communicated during a specified time period. Therefore, it is advantageous, in terms of increasing throughput as well as reducing program complexity, if
an I/O device demands service directly from the microprocessor.

Interrupts provide this capability. Essentially, an *interrupt* is a subroutine call
initiated by external hardware. A simple structure that allows a single device to
interrupt a microprocessor is shown in Fig. 9.1-1.

When an I/O device requires service, it sets its interrupt request flip-flop. This
flip-flop is functionally the same as the service request flip-flop of Chapter 8, except
that instead of its output being connected to an input port, it is connected to an
interrupt pin of the microprocessor. Thus, this flip-flop stores the I/O device's
interrupt request until it is acknowledged by the microprocessor.

Since the interrupt request is asynchronous, it may occur at any point in a
program's execution. When an interrupt occurs, the execution of the current
instruction is completed, the interrupt is acknowledged by the microprocessor, and
control is transferred to a subroutine that services the interrupt (see Fig. 9.1-2).
When the microprocessor responds to the interrupt, the interrupt request flip-flop is
cleared by a signal directly from the microprocessor (Fig. 9.1-1) or by a device select
pulse generated by the service subroutine. To resume program execution at the

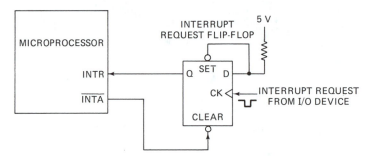

Figure 9.1-1 Generation of microprocessor interrupt for a single I/O
device via an interrupt request flag.

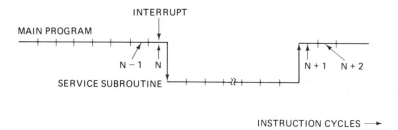

Figure 9.1-2 Transfer of program control in response to an interrupt.

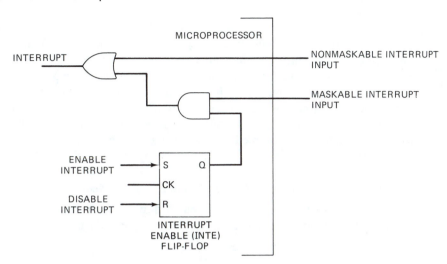

Figure 9.1-3   Representation of maskable and nonmaskable interrupts.

proper point when the I/O service subroutine is finished, the program counter is automatically saved before control is transferred to the service subroutine. The service subroutine saves the contents of any registers it uses on the stack and restores the register's contents before returning. The contents of the program counter, flag register, accumulator, and general purpose registers together represent the state of the microprocessor.

There are two types of interrupt inputs: nonmaskable and maskable (see Fig. 9.1-3). When a logic signal is applied to a nonmaskable interrupt input, the

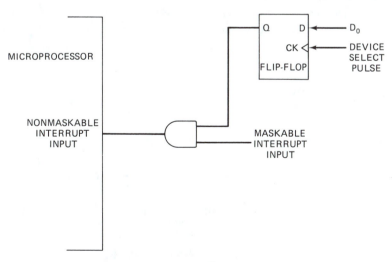

Figure 9.1-4   Creating a maskable interrupt from a nonmaskable interrupt.

microprocessor is immediately interrupted. When a logic signal is applied to a maskable interrupt input, the microprocessor is interrupted only if that particular input is enabled. Maskable interrupts are enabled or disabled under program control. If disabled, an interrupt request is ignored by the microprocessor.

A nonmaskable interrupt input can be masked externally by an interrupt mask signal from an output port. The mask bit from an output port shown in Fig. 9.1-4 gates the interrupt signal. If an output instruction writes a 1 in the mask bit position, the interrupt is enabled; if it writes a 0, it is disabled.

In response to an interrupt, the following operations occur:

1. The processing of the current instruction is completed.

2. An interrupt machine cycle is executed during which the program counter is saved and control is transferred to an appropriate memory location.

3. The state of the microprocessor is saved.

4. If more than one I/O device is associated with the location transferred to, the highest priority device requesting an interrupt is identified.

5. A subroutine is executed which services the interrupting I/O device. This subroutine clears the interrupt service request flip-flop if it was not cleared in step 2.

6. The saved state of the microprocessor is restored.

7. Control is returned to the instruction that follows the interrupted instruction.

Figure 9.1-5 illustrates the above sequence. Each step requires a certain amount of time. The combined times for a given microprocessor and external interrupt logic determine how quickly the microprocessor responds to an I/O device's request for service.

The time that elapses between the occurrence of the interrupt and the beginning of the execution of the interrupt-handling subroutine is the *response time*,

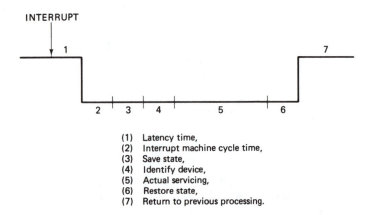

INTERRUPT

(1) Latency time,
(2) Interrupt machine cycle time,
(3) Save state,
(4) Identify device,
(5) Actual servicing,
(6) Restore state,
(7) Return to previous processing.

Figure 9.1-5 Sequence of actions associated with servicing an interrupt.

the sum of the times of steps (1) through (4). The difference between the total time that the microprocessor is interrupted and the actual execution time of the service subroutine is referred to as *overhead*. Interrupt structures with low overhead allow greater throughput.

9.2 8085A INTERRUPT STRUCTURE

The 8085A has five interrupt inputs: TRAP, RST7.5, RST6.5, RST5.5, and INTR (see Table 9.2-1). TRAP is nonmaskable; the others are maskable. When the 8085A is reset, its internal interrupt enable flip-flop, INTE FF, is reset and the RST MASK bits are set. This disables all the maskable interrupts, so the microprocessor only responds to TRAP. For maskable interrupts to be effective, they must be enabled under program control.

Two program steps are required to enable the RST7.5, RST6.5, and RST5.5 interrupts: (1) clearing the interrupt masks and (2) enabling the interrupts.

TABLE 9.2-1   8085A INTERRUPT INPUT AND OUTPUT PINS (COURTESY OF INTEL CORP.)

Symbol	Type	Name and Function
TRAP	I	**Trap**: Trap interrupt is a nonmaskable RESTART interrupt. It is recognized at the same time as INTR or RST5.5-7.5. It is unaffected by any mask or Interrupt Enable. It has the highest priority of any interrupt.
RST 5.5 RST 6.5 RST 7.5	I	**Restart Interrupts**: These three inputs have the same timing as INTR except they cause an internal RESTART to be automatically inserted. The priority of these interrupts is ordered as shown in Table 9.2-2. These interrupts have a higher priority than INTR. In addition, they may be individually masked out using the SIM instruction.
INTR	I	**Interrupt Request**: Is used as a general purpose interrupt. It is sampled only during the next to the last clock cycle of an instruction and during Hold and Halt states. If it is active, the Program Counter (PC) will be inhibited from incrementing and an $\overline{\text{INTA}}$ will be issued. During this cycle a RESTART or CALL instruction can be inserted to jump to the interrupt service routine. The INTR is enabled and disabled by software. It is disabled by Reset and immediately after an interrupt is accepted.
$\overline{\text{INTA}}$	O	**Interrupt Acknowledge**: Is used instead of (and has the same timing as) $\overline{\text{RD}}$ during the Instruction cycle after an INTR is accepted. It can be used to activate an 8259A Interrupt chip or some other interrupt port.

Each interrupt can be masked independently by the *set interrupt mask*, SIM, instruction:

SIM (Set Interrupt Masks) [1]

During the execution of the SIM instruction, the contents of the accumulator will be used in programming the restart interrupt masks. Bits 0–2 will set/reset the mask bit for RST5.5, 6.5, 7.5 of the interrupt mask register, if bit 3 is 1 ("set"). Bit 3 is a "mask set enable" control.

Setting the mask (i.e., mask bit = 1) *disables* the corresponding interrupt.

	Set	Reset
RST5.5 MASK	if bit 0 = 1	if bit 0 = 0
RST6.5 MASK	bit 1 = 1	bit 1 = 0
RST7.5 MASK	bit 2 = 1	bit 2 = 0

The RST7.5 (edge triggered) internal request flip-flop will be reset if bit 4 of the accumulator = 1; regardless of whether or not RST7.5 is masked.

A hardware RESET of the 8085A will set all RST MASKs and reset/disable all interrupts.

SIM can also load the SOD output latch. Accumulator bit 7 is loaded into the SOD latch if bit 6 is set. The latch is unaffected if bit 6 is a zero. $\overline{\text{RESET IN}}$ input sets the SOD latch to zero.

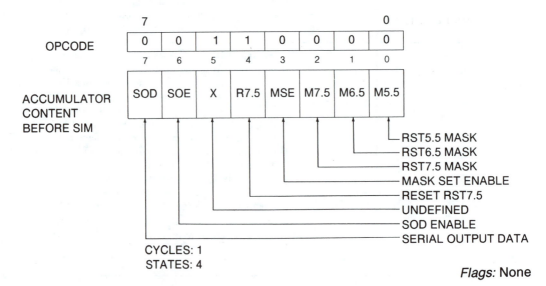

CYCLES: 1
STATES: 4

Flags: None

For example, the following instruction sequence enables RST7.5 and RST5.5 and disables RST6.5:

```
MVI A, 00011010B    ;load A with interrupt mask
SIM                 ;set interrupt mask
```

In step (2), the microprocessor's interrupt enable flip-flop, INTE FF, is set by the *enable interrupt* instruction, after execution of the instruction *following* EI:

$$\text{Enable interrupts}$$
$$\text{EI}$$
$$(\text{INTE FF}) \leftarrow 1$$

The *disable interrupts* instruction disables all maskable interrupts:

$$\text{Disable interrupts}$$
$$\text{DI}$$
$$(\text{INTE FF}) \leftarrow 0$$

Maskable interrupts are disabled immediately after the execution of the DI instruction. They are also automatically disabled when the microprocessor enters an interrupt machine cycle, which prevents it from responding to further interrupts until the EI instruction is executed.

The interrupt input, INTR, is not affected by SIM and requires only execution of the EI instruction to be completely enabled. Thus, in the 8085A the conditions for a valid interrupt are

$$\text{VALID INT} = \text{TRAP} + \text{INTE} \cdot (\text{INTR} + \text{RST7.5} \cdot \overline{\text{M7.5}}$$
$$+ \text{RST6.5} \cdot \overline{\text{M6.5}} + \text{RST5.5} \cdot \overline{\text{M5.5}})$$

where $M(n)$ refers to the mask bit for $RST(n)$ controlled by the SIM instruction.

Most microprocessor interrupt inputs are level sensitive; however, some are edge sensitive, and others are both edge and level sensitive. Interrupt inputs to the 8085A encompass all three types. The TRAP input, for example, is both edge and level sensitive and must make a low to high transition and remain high until acknowledged. After acknowledgment, it is not recognized again until it goes low, then high again and remains high—this avoids false triggering due to noise or logic glitches.

RST7.5 is rising edge sensitive: only a pulse is required to set the interrupt request. This request is remembered until the 8085A responds to the interrupt or until the request is reset by the SIM instruction or a $\overline{\text{RESET IN}}$ signal. In effect, the interrupt request flip-flop for RST7.5 is internal to the microprocessor. RST6.5 and RST5.5 are high level sensitive. The signal at these pins must be maintained until the interrupt is acknowledged. Thus, external interrupt request flip-flops are required for TRAP, RST6.5, and RST5.5. Service request flip-flops must be cleared at system power ON to prevent erroneous interrupts. This can be accomplished using RESET OUT of the 8085A or by system initialization software.

read interrupt mask
RIM

ACCUMULATOR
CONTENT
AFTER RIM:

SID	17.5	16.5	15.5	1E	M7.5	M6.5	M5.5

INTERRUPT MASKS
INTERRUPT ENABLE FLAG
INTERRUPTS PENDING
SERIAL INPUT DATA

Flags: None

The *read interrupt mask*, RIM, instruction loads the status of the interrupt masks, the pending interrupts, and the contents of the serial input data line, SID, into the accumulator. Thus, their respective statuses can be monitored under program control. When interrupts are disabled but pending, the program can selectively enable a particular interrupt to service it.

Using interrupts, the programmed polling of service flags is, effectively, replaced by an automatic hardware polling. As shown in Fig. 9.2-1, the interrupt inputs are checked by the 8085A during the clock of the next to last state of each instruction cycle and during every clock pulse if the microprocessor is in the HALT state. Automatic polling of interrupt requests allows completion of the current instruction cycle before an interrupt. When there is a valid interrupt request, the INTE FF is cleared, and the interrupt acknowledge flip-flop (INTA FF) is set. The next machine cycle is a special one for handling the interrupt. For TRAP, RST7.5, RST6.5, and RST5.5, it is the BUS IDLE, BI, machine cycle. For INTR, it is the INTERRUPT ACKNOWLEDGE, INA.

Latency time, t_{LAT}, is the time between the occurrence of an interrupt request and the beginning of the interrupt machine cycle (see Fig. 9.1-5). As shown in Fig. 9.2-2, the interrupt signal must be valid for a time greater or equal to the interrupt setup time, t_{INS}, before the falling edge of CLK for the last state of the instruction cycle in order for the next machine cycle to be an interrupt machine cycle. For the 8085AH, the minimum value of t_{INS} is 160 nS.

If the interrupt becomes valid precisely t_{INS} seconds before the beginning of the next instruction cycle, then that cycle is an interrupt cycle with a minimum latency time, $t_{LATMIN} = t_{INS}$. If, however, the interrupt signal becomes valid just after this setup time, then it is not responded to until after the next instruction is executed. This provides a worst case latency time of

$$t_{LATMAX} = t_{INS} + t_{MAX\ INSTRUCTION\ CYCLE}$$
$$= 160 \text{ nS} + 18T$$

Maximum, or worst case, latency time is an important factor in determining response time.

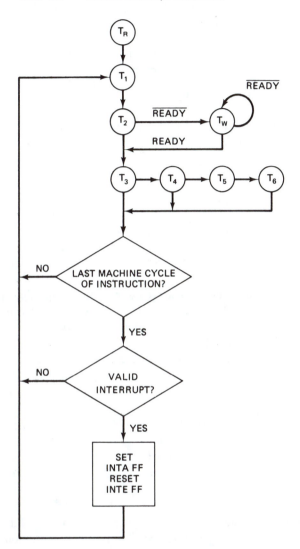

Figure 9.2-1 Simplified machine cycle of 8085A, including interrupt logic.

This relationship assumes there are no WAIT states or HOLD[1] states in the instruction cycle during which an interrupt request occurs. If, in fact, there are WAIT or HOLD states, then the maximum times for these conditions are included when determining t_{LATMAX}. A further assumption is, of course, that the interrupt is enabled when the interrupt request occurs. If this is not the case, the t_{LATMAX} additionally includes the longest period of time that the interrupt(s) is disabled during program execution.

The interrupt machine cycle has a fixed duration of $12T$ during which the value of the PC—the address of the instruction following the interrupted instruction

---

[1] The HOLD state is discussed in Section 9.7.

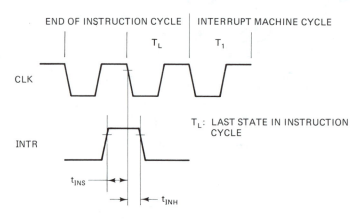

Figure 9.2-2 Setup and hold times, t_{INS} and t_{INH}, for an interrupt signal with respect to the microprocessor's clock.

—is saved on the stack, and control is then transferred to an address associated with the specific interrupt. This implements a hardware initiated subroutine call. The method for transferring control to the address associated with the interrupt differs, depending on which interrupt is involved.

For TRAP, RST7.5, RST6.5, and RST5.5, the mechanism is the same: the microprocessor transfers control to a predetermined address associated with each of these inputs:

Interrupt	Restart address
TRAP	24H
RST5.5	2CH
RST6.5	34H
RST7.5	3CH

The interrupt machine cycle for these is a BUS IDLE, BI, during which the microprocessor internally generates the operation code for a restart instruction with the appropriate restart address. The PC is not incremented during BI and thus contains the address of the instruction following the one being executed when the interrupt occurs. The action of this internally generated instruction is as follows:

$$RST \text{ (internal)}$$
$$((SP) - 1) \leftarrow (PCH)$$
$$((SP) - 2) \leftarrow (PCL)$$
$$(SP) \leftarrow (SP) - 2$$
$$(PC) \leftarrow restart\ address$$

The BI machine cycle is like an OPCODE FETCH, OF, except the $\overline{RD}$ line remains high. The operation code, which is generally read in during OF, is instead generated internally during the BI machine cycle by the microprocessor.

After an RST is executed, the PC contains the address of the starting location for the subroutine that handles the interrupt. This procedure for identifying the interrupting device and directly transferring control to the starting location is called a *vectored interrupt*. Since only a few memory locations separate the different vector addresses, there is usually a jump instruction at the vector address that transfers control to another memory location where the actual service subroutine begins.

In the case of an INTR interrupt, the interrupt machine cycle entered is an INTERRUPT ACKNOWLEDGE, INA. INA is similar to OF except that $IO/\overline{M}$ = 1, instead of a $\overline{RD}$ the microprocessor generates an $\overline{INTA}$ strobe, and the value of the program counter is not incremented during INA. Thus, the PC contains the address of the instruction following the one being executed when the interrupt occurred.

In response to the $\overline{INTA}$ strobe, external logic places an instruction OP code on the data bus. In the case of a mutibyte instruction, additional INA machine cycles are generated by the 8085A to transfer the additional bytes into the microprocessor. Theoretically, the external logic can place any instruction on the data bus in response to the $\overline{INTA}$. However, only CALL and RST, which save the PC contents before transferring control, allow a proper return from a service subroutine. The *restart* instruction, RST *n*, has $0 \leq n \leq 7$.

$$RST\ n$$
$$((SP) - 1) \leftarrow (PCH)$$
$$((SP) - 2) \leftarrow (PCL)$$
$$(SP) \leftarrow (SP) - 2$$
$$(PC) \leftarrow 8*n$$

This instruction is essentially the same as the previously mentioned internal restart, except for the restart address and the fact that it is generated by external hardware. *Restart* has the following bit pattern, frequently referred to as the *restart* or *interrupt vector*:

$$1\ 1\ N\ N\ N\ 1\ 1\ 1$$

where $n = NNN$ is a 3-bit binary number. When this instruction is executed, the program counter is saved on the stack, thus saving the return address. And control is transferred to a location with an address which is eight times *NNN*, thus facilitating a branch to any one of eight fixed addresses—00H, 08H, 10H, 18H, 20H, 28H, 30H, or 38H—depending on the value of *NNN*. These addresses are referred to as *restart locations*, 0, 1, 2, . . . to 7.

External logic controls a three-state buffer with the $\overline{INTA}$ signal in order to place a restart vector onto the data bus. In Fig. 9.2-3 a single I/O device is connected to the microprocessor's interrupt structure. The output of its interrupt request flip-flop is directly connected to the INTR interrupt pin of the microprocessor. When the interrupt request flip-flop of the I/O device is set, the microprocessor completes execution of the current instruction and then initiates an

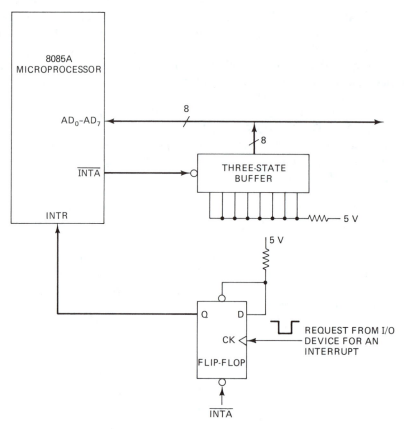

Figure 9.2-3 Vectored interrupt with RST 7 "jammed" on interrupt acknowledge.

interrupt acknowledge machine cycle. During this cycle, the internal INTE FF is cleared, disabling further interrupts from affecting the microprocessor. The $\overline{\text{INTA}}$ signal that is generated enables the three-state buffer whose data inputs are hardwired to the value of the interrupt vector, RST7, in this example. $\overline{\text{INTA}}$ also clears the interrupt request flip-flop. The microprocessor inputs the restart vector, saves the program counter, and branches to memory location 38H. The subroutine that starts at that location services the I/O device.

In the discussion of Fig. 9.2-3, two assumptions were made: (1) only the INTR interrupt input was involved in creating the valid interrupt condition and (2) only one interrupting device is associated with this input. Given these conditions, once an interrupt occurs, control is transferred to the restart location for that interrupt. Execution of a restart during the interrupt machine cycle saves the value of the PC. The remainder of the information that comprises the state of the microprocessor is saved by pushing the program status word (registers A and F) and the other register pairs onto the stack.

TABLE 9.2-2 8085A INTERRUPT CHARACTERISTICS

Interrupt	Priority	Branch Address (1)	Trigger Type	Maskable	Disabled by (3)	Enabled by	Service Request Flip-Flop Location	SR F-F Cleared by
TRAP	1	24H	Rising edge AND high level until sampled	No	Cannot be Disabled	Always Enabled	Internal (edge) AND External	Automatic AND Service subroutine
RST7.5	2	3CH	Rising edge (latched)	Yes	M7.5 = 1 (SIM) OR DI	M7.5 = 0 (SIM) AND EI	Internal	Automatic
RST6.5	3	34H	High level until sampled	Yes	M6.5 = 1 (SIM) OR DI	M6.5 = 0 (SIM) AND EI	External	Service subroutine
RST5.5	4	2CH	High level until sampled	Yes	M5.5 = 1 (SIM) OR DI	M5.5 = 0 (SIM) AND EI	External	Service subroutine
INTR	5	(2)	High level until sampled	Yes	DI	EI	External	Service subroutine

(1) For TRAP and RST 5.5-7.5, the contents of the Program Counter are pushed onto the stack before the branch occurs.

(2) Address depends on the instruction provided to the 8085A by an 8259A or other logic when the interrupt is acknowledged.

(3) All maskable interrupts are disabled by the occurrence of a valid interrupt.

The following four instructions save the entire state of the microprocessor:

PUSH PSW
PUSH B
PUSH D
PUSH H

The time required to execute these instructions constitutes the save state of step (3) of Section 9.1. Any registers not used by the service subroutine do not have to be saved, thus reducing this time period.

This sequence of instructions is executed at the beginning of the I/O service routine. Once the state of the microprocessor has been saved, the interrupt service subroutine is free to use any of the microprocessor's registers. With only one I/O device connected to each interrupt input, identification of the interrupting device is automatic, in that each restart location is associated with only a single device. Thus, step (4) of Section 9.1 requires no additional time. At the end of the I/O service subroutine, the state of the processor that has been stored on the stack is restored by executing the first four of the following sequence of instructions:

POP H
POP D
POP B
POP PSW
EI
RET

Note that the order of the POP sequence is the reverse of the PUSH since the stack is a last-in/first-out type. The *pop processor status word*, POP PSW, instruction restores the accumulator and flag registers from the stack.

The enable interrupt instruction in the previous instruction sequence allows the microprocessor to respond to interrupts again only after the execution of the return instruction. RET replaces the contents of the program counter with the return address, thus completing the last step of the sequence. Table 9.2-2 summarizes the characteristics of the 8085A's interrupts.

9.2.1 Interrupt Driven I/O Examples

Two examples will illustrate the details of interrupt driven I/O. One implements data transfer to a parallel printer using an 8155H as the interface; the other implements asynchronous serial data transfer to a serial printer using an 8251A as the interface. In both examples, data to be output is in a memory buffer and is transferred as parallel data to the interface IC. An interrupt, from the interface, initiates the transfer of each data byte. The software for both examples is nearly identical.

Figure 9.2-4a shows the hardware interface of a parallel printer to an 8085A via an 8155H. The printer has an 8-bit data input. When the printer's data valid input, DAV, makes a 0 to 1 transition the printer latches the input data and

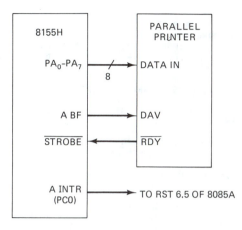

Figure 9.2-4a 8155H to parallel printer interface for interrupt driven I/O.

proceeds to print it. After printing a character the printer generates a negative strobe, $\overline{\text{RDY}}$, to indicate that it is ready to receive the next character.

The program is given in Fig. 9.2-4b. Only those instructions that directly relate to the interrupt driven data transfer are shown. Since the addresses associated with interrupt vectoring range from 0000H to 003CH, the main program starts after this address range at 0040H. The jump instruction at address 0000H transfers control to the main program when the 8085A is reset. Occurrence of an RST6.5 interrupt transfers control to address 0034H. A jump instruction at this address transfers control to the service subroutine.

During execution of the main program, the microprocessor fills the memory buffer, OUTBUF, with ASCII characters that make up one line to be printed. The last two characters in the line are the ASCII carriage return, CR, and ASCII line feed, LF, characters, ODH and OAH, respectively. After the microprocessor has filled the output buffer, it calls the subroutine PRINT to initiate the interrupt driven transfer of the buffer contents. PRINT initializes the buffer pointer to the start of the buffer, clears the output buffer empty flag, OBMT, and enables the interrupt output pin of the 8155H.

Since the PORT A output buffer of the 8155H is initially empty, the microprocessor will be immediately interrupted. The 8155H strobed output timing diagram, Fig. 8.6-7, indicates that the interrupt output pin, INTR A (PCO), remains logic 1 until the microprocessor outputs data to PORT A. Thus, this output serves as the service request and no service request flip-flop is needed. The interrupt service subroutine, BYTOUT, will transfer a byte from the memory buffer to the 8155H, clearing the service request. The buffer pointer is incremented in preparation for the next interrupt. If the byte output is the LF character, the service subroutine will disable the 8155H interrupt pin and set OBMT before returning.

When the printer completes the printing of a character, it generates a ready strobe, $\overline{\text{RDY}}$, to indicate that it is ready to print another character. This signal provides the $\overline{\text{STROBE}}$ input to the 8155H that clears the A BF output and sets INTR A.

```
;EQUATE STATEMENTS
COMND   EQU     20H     ;ADDRESS 8155H COMMAND REGISTER
DATA    EQU     21H     ;ADDRESS PORTA 8155H
EIPIN   EQU     00010101B       ;PORTA STROBED OUTPUT, ENABLE INTERRUPT
DIPIN   EQU     00000101B       ;PORTA STROBED OUTPUT, DISABLE INTERRUPT
;REVECTORING
        ORG 0000H
        JMP START       ;START PROGRAM AFTER INTERRUPT STARTING ADDRESSES
        ORG 0034H
        JMP BYTOUT      ;JUMP TO START OF INTERRUPT SERVICE SUBROUTINE
;SYSTEM INITIALIZATION IN MAIN PROGRAM
        ORG 0040H
START: LXI SP,4000H     ;INITIALIZE STACK POINTER
        MVI A,DIPIN     ;DISABLE INTR A PIN OF 8155
        OUT COMND
        MVI A,00001101B ;ENABLE RST6.5
        SIM
        EI
;SUBROUTINE TO INITIATE PRINTING OF BUFFER
PRINT: LXI H,OUTBUF     ;INITIALIZE POINTER TO START OF BUFFER
        SHLD OBPTR      ;SAVE  POINTER
        XRA A           ;CLEAR BUFFER EMPTY FLAG
        STA OBMT
        MVI A,EIPIN     ;ENABLE 8155H INTRA A OUTPUT PIN
        OUT COMND
        RET
;PRINTER SERVICE SUBROUTINE
BYTOUT: PUSH PSW        ;SAVE REGISTERS TO BE USED
        PUSH H
        LHLD OBPTR      ;GET OUTPUT BUFFER POINTER
        MOV A,M         ;GET BYTE FROM BUFFER
        OUT DATA        ;OUTPUT DATA BYTE TO PORTA
        INX H           ;INCREMENT BUFFER POINTER
        SHLD OBPTR      ;SAVE BUFFER POINTER
        CPI 0AH         ;WAS BYTE OUTPUT A LF?
        JNZ RESTOR      ;NO, ADDITIONAL BYTES IN BUFFER
        MVI A,0FFH      ;YES,BUFFER IS EMPTY
        STA OBMT        ;SET BUFFER EMPTY FLAG
        MVI A,DIPIN     ;DISABLE 8155H INTR A OUTPUT PIN
        OUT COMND
RESTOR: POP H           ;RESTORE REGISTERS
        POP PSW
        EI              ;ENABLE 8085A INTERRUPTS
        RET

;ALLOCATION OF RESERVED MEMORY
        ORG 3C00H
OUTBUF: DS 80   ;OUTPUT BUFFER
OBPTR:  DS 2    ;BUFFER POINTER
OBMT:   DS 1    ;OUTPUT BUFFER EMPTY FLAG
        END
```

Figure 9.2-4b   Program for interrupt driven printer interface using 8155H.

To print a line of characters, the microprocessor calls the subroutine PRINT to initiate the interrupt driven transfers. After this, characters are printed at a rate determined by the printer. Each time the printer is ready to print another character the microprocessor is interrupted. If there are N characters in the buffer, N interrupts occur and the interrupt service subroutine is executed N times. On the Nth execution, the service subroutine disables the interrupts, terminating the transfers.

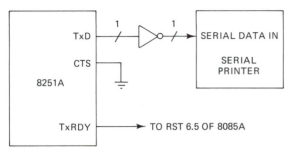

Figure 9.2-5 8251A to serial printer interface for interrupt driven I/O.

The second example uses the 8251A to interface an 8085A to a serial printer (see Fig. 9.2-5). Again the RST6.5 interrupt is used. The microprocessor transfers data in parallel to the 8251A, which converts the data to serial and transmits it to the printer. The serial printer does not indicate to the microprocessor when it is ready. Initialization of the 8251A's baud rate must be compatible with the printing rate of the serial printer. The 8085A is interrupted whenever the transmitter buffer of the 8251A is empty. This condition is indicated by the TxRDY output of the 8251A.

With the exception of the initialization of the interface, the software for the data transfer in this example is essentially the same as in the first example. The addresses of the command and data registers in the interfaces are different as are the command words to disable and enable the interrupt request pins of the interface ICs. The subroutine to initialize an 8251A for polled asynchronous operation given in Fig. 8.7-9 can be modified to handle the interrupt driven case. The only change required is that the transmit enable bit, TxEN, in the command word be set. If this bit is low it would hold the TxRDY output of the 8251A low.

9.3 PRIORITY INTERRUPT STRUCTURES

In reality, interrupts are asynchronous; they do not occur one at a time in an orderly fashion. Microprocessors have certain priorities established for their various interrupt inputs. A *priority interrupt* structure arbitrates among several devices simultaneously requesting service and assures that the device with the highest assigned priority is serviced first.

The five interrupt inputs of the 8085A have an internally established, fixed, multilevel priority structure. From highest to lowest they are TRAP, RST7.5, RST6.5, RST5.5, and INTR. TRAP, since it is not maskable, is usually reserved to handle catastrophic events such as power failures. I/O devices are associated with the other four interrupt inputs in such a way that the highest priority device is connected to RST7.5, the next highest priority device to RST6.5, and so on. Devices that require the fastest response time or that interrupt the microprocessor with the greatest frequency are usually given the highest priority.

Once an interrupt occurs, the internal interrupt enable flip-flop, INTE FF, is automatically cleared, allowing no more interrupts until an EI instruction is

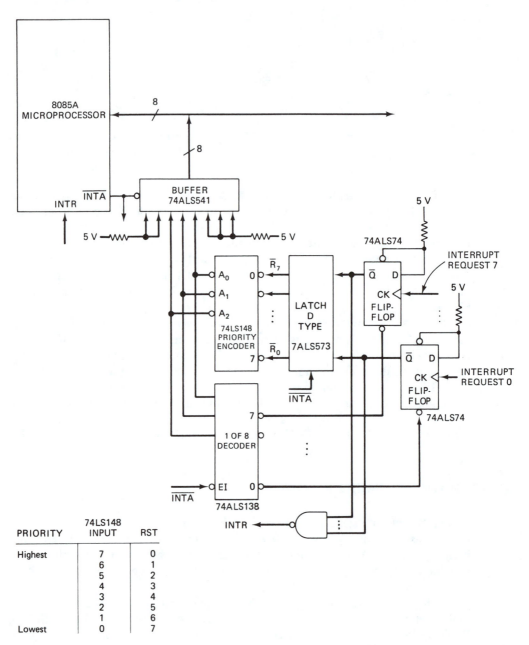

Figure 9.3-1   Priority vectored interrupt.

executed. However, if, for example, an RST7.5 interrupt occurs, and the service subroutine for that interrupt subsequently enables the microprocessor interrupt feature before its completion, the microprocessor can be interrupted by a lower priority interrupt, for instance, an RST5.5.

Several I/O devices can be connected to a single microprocessor interrupt input by ORing their interrupt service request flags. When an interrupt request occurs at such an input, the particular device requesting an interrupt must be identified. For INTR of the 8085A, identification and transfer of control to the starting address of the service subroutine are done in a vectored manner for as many as eight devices. Each of the eight is assigned a different interrupt vector in the RST n instruction. The appropriate RST n instruction OP code is placed on the data bus in response to $\overline{\text{INTA}}$. The I/O device's interrupt request flip-flop outputs are ORed together and connected to the microprocessor's interrupt input (see Fig. 9.3-1). In that figure, the *restart* instruction is generated with the aid of a priority encoder that supplies the three bits, NNN, of the interrupt vector. An 8-line-to-3-line priority encoder allows the highest priority device, with its interrupt request flag set, to generate NNN, and thus be identified immediately.

The truth table for an SN74LS148 priority encoder is shown in Fig. 9.3-2. There are eight active low inputs to the priority encoder. When an input is held low, the 3-bit code representing its complement appears at outputs $\overline{A}_2$, $\overline{A}_1$, and $\overline{A}_0$. When two or more inputs are active, the output is the complement of the input with the highest numerical value.

The D-type positive level triggered latch shown in Fig. 9.3-1 allows the inputs to the priority encoder to follow the $\overline{Q}$ outputs of the interrupt flags until an interrupt acknowledge, $\overline{\text{INTA}}$, occurs. The $\overline{\text{INTA}}$ signal forces the latch outputs to retain the values that existed at the leading edge of $\overline{\text{INTA}}$, and enables the three-state buffer, placing an RST instruction on the data bus. The microprocessor inputs this instruction on the rising edge of $\overline{\text{INTA}}$, and control is transferred to the location associated with the RST n instruction.

The instruction RSTO 0 transfers control to the first memory location, the same location used when an external reset is applied to the system. Thus, RST 0 is usually not used for interrupts.

The priority encoder shown in Fig. 9.3-2 establishes priority among interrupts that occur simultaneously. That is, if one device sets its interrupt request flag, causing an interrupt, and another device also sets its flag before the interrupt acknowledge ($\overline{\text{INTA}}$) occurs, the device serviced is the one connected to the highest numbered input of the priority encoder.

The INA machine cycle automatically disables the INTE FF so that no other interrupts can occur until the one being processed is completed. The interrupt request flip-flop of the device being serviced must be cleared. In Fig. 9.3-1 $\overline{\text{INTA}}$ is gated with a 1-out-of-8 decoder to clear the appropriate flip-flop; however, a programmed pulse generated by each device's service subroutine would have the same effect. The next to last instruction in the service subroutine enables the interrupt, and the last instruction transfers control back to the instruction following the one that was interrupted. The lower priority of the two interrupt requests will

'148, 'LS148

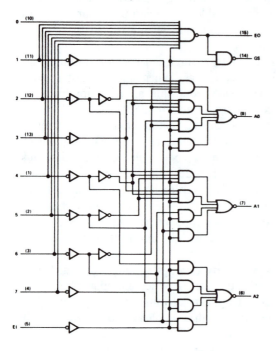

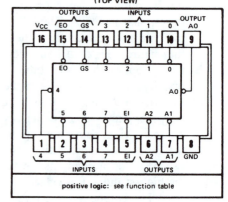

SN54148, SN54LS148 . . . J OR W PACKAGE
SN74148, SN74LS148 . . . J OR N PACKAGE
(TOP VIEW)

positive logic: see function table

'148, 'LS148
FUNCTION TABLE

	INPUTS									OUTPUTS				
EI	0	1	2	3	4	5	6	7		A2	A1	A0	GS	EO
H	X	X	X	X	X	X	X	X		H	H	H	H	H
L	H	H	H	H	H	H	H	H		H	H	H	H	L
L	X	X	X	X	X	X	X	L		L	L	L	L	H
L	X	X	X	X	X	X	L	H		L	L	H	L	H
L	X	X	X	X	X	L	H	H		L	H	L	L	H
L	X	X	X	X	L	H	H	H		L	H	H	L	H
L	X	X	X	L	H	H	H	H		H	L	L	L	H
L	X	X	L	H	H	H	H	H		H	L	H	L	H
L	X	L	H	H	H	H	H	H		H	H	L	L	H
L	L	H	H	H	H	H	H	H		H	H	H	L	H

Figure 9.3-2 An 8-line-to-3-line priority encoder, 74LS148. (Courtesy of Texas Instruments, Inc.)

then cause another INA machine cycle to occur. The low priority interrupt will then be serviced.

When several I/O devices are associated with a single interrupt vector or interrupt input, their interrupt request flip-flops can be ORed together to create a single interrupt. The outputs of each of these interrupt flip-flops are connected to an input port. The service subroutine then inputs the status of the interrupt request flip-flops from this port to determine which of the I/O devices to service. In the case of simultaneous interrupts, priority is implemented in software, as was illustrated in Chapter 8 when polling devices for programmed I/O.

9.3.1 The 8259A Programmable Interrupt Controller

The 8259A Programmable Interrupt Controller provides, in a single IC, priority arbitration and vector generation for up to eight interrupt inputs [2]. The 8259A has several modes of operation and can be used with either 8085A or 8086/8088 microprocessors. Nine 8259As can be cascaded in a master slave configuration to handle 64 interrupt inputs. The discussion here will be limited to a single 8259A in an 8085A system.

The block diagram and pin configuration of the 8259A is shown in Fig. 9.3-3. The 8259A has eight interrupt request inputs, IR0–IR7. The 8259A uses its INT output to interrupt the 8085A via the 8085A's INTR pin. The 8259A receives interrupt acknowledge pulses from the microprocessor at its INTA input. Vector information, used by the 8085A to transfer control to the service subroutine of the interrupting device, is provided by the 8259A on the data bus.

The 8259A is a programmable device that must be initialized by initialization command words sent by the microprocessor. After initialization, the 8259A's mode of operation can be changed by operation command words from the micro-processor. Three 8-bit registers in the 8259A each have bits associated with the eight interrupt request inputs. The interrupt request register, IRR, stores all the interrupt inputs that are requesting service. The in service register, ISR, stores all the interrupt requests that are being serviced. And the interrupt mask register, IMR, stores the bits that mask the interrupt requests. Each of these three registers can be

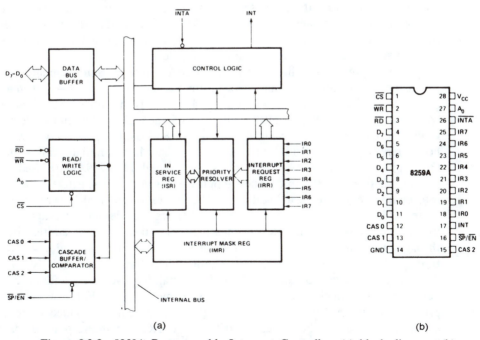

(a)   (b)

Figure 9.3-3   8259A Programmable Interrupt Controller: (a) block diagram; (b) pin configuration. (Courtesy of Intel Corp.)

read as status registers. The command and status registers of the 8259A are written and read as I/O ports. The 8259A interfaces to the 8085A through the system's data bus.

Before considering the details of initializing the 8259A, the sequence of events that occur in response to an interrupt request at one of the IR inputs of an initialized 8259A are considered. One or more of the interrupt request lines, IR0–IR7, is made logic 1 by device(s) requesting service. The corresponding bit(s) in the interrupt request register, IRR, is set. The priority resolver and control logic use information from the ISR and IMR to determine if the microprocessor should be interrupted. If so, INT becomes logic 1. If the 8085A's INTR interrupt is enabled and this is the highest priority interrupt request, the microprocessor completes the execution of the current instruction and then executes an interrupt acknowledge, INA, machine cycle. During the INA the 8085A acknowledges the interrupt with an $\overline{INTA}$ pulse.

In response to the $\overline{INTA}$, the 8259A sets the highest priority ISR bit and resets the corresponding IRR bit. The 8259A also places the CALL instruction OP code on the data bus. When the 8085A receives a CALL instruction OP code during the INA machine cycle, it generates two more INA machine cycles. During the second and third INA machine cycles, a second and a third $\overline{INTA}$ pulse are generated by the 8085A. In response to the second $\overline{INTA}$ pulse, the 8259A places the low address of a preprogrammed subroutine address on the data bus. The high address of the subroutine address is placed on the bus in response to the third INA pulse. If the 8259A is in the AEOI (automatic end of interrupt) mode, the ISR bit is reset at the end of the third $\overline{INTA}$ pulse. Otherwise the ISR bit remains set until an appropriate EOI command is issued by the 8085A at the end of the interrupt service subroutine. The 8085A executes the CALL instruction by saving the PC on the stack and transferring control to the preprogrammed address.

The 8259A is initialized by a sequence of initialization command words, ICWs. The initialization command word format is shown in Fig. 9.3-4. When a byte is sent to the 8259A with $A_0 = 0$ and bit 4 = 1, it is interpreted as initialization command word 1, ICW1. If bit 0 of ICW1 = 0, then all the functions selected by ICW4 are cleared. This puts the 8259A in the 80/85 mode, with no AEOI, and nonbuffered operation. No ICW4 would then be sent in this initialization sequence. Other bits in ICW1 specify whether a single or multiple 8259As are used in the system, whether the interrupt request inputs are edge or level sensitive, and provide information about the vector addresses. The separation interval between the eight vector addresses is selected to be either 4 or 8 bytes. The desired interval is selected by bit 2 of ICW1. If the interval chosen is four, the values of address bits A_5 through A_{15} must be specified. If the interval chosen is eight, address bits A_6 through A_{15} must be specified. Bits A_5 through A_7 are specified in ICW1. Bits A_8 through A_{15} are specified in ICW2. The remaining five or six address bits are determined by which interrupt request is being serviced. For example, if the programmed interval is eight, and IR0 is the request being responded to, the least significant six address bits would be 000000B. If IR1 is being responded to, these bits would be 001000B. For a system with a single 8259A no ICW3 is required.

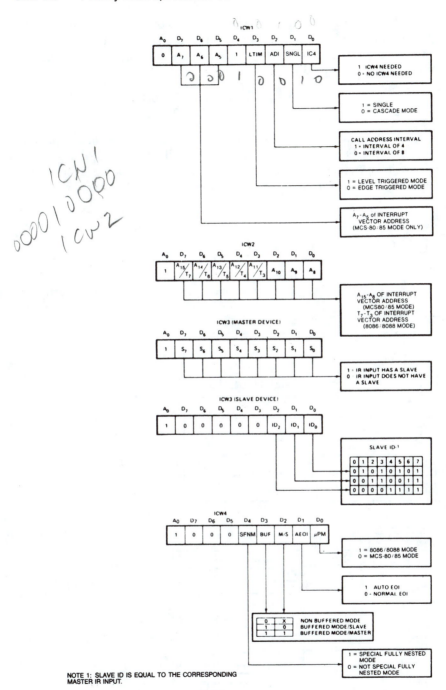

Figure 9.3-4   8259A initialization command word format. (Courtesy of Intel Corp.)

Thus, an 8085A system using a single 8259A could be programmed with only two ICWs: ICW1 and ICW2. For example, if a service subroutine starting address interval of eight is desired with the first address 0400H, the required initialization command words would be

$$\text{ICW1} = 00010010B$$
$$\text{ICW2} = 00000100B$$

With these initialization command words, the interrupt request inputs are programmed for edge triggered mode. In addition, the 8259A's priority structure would be operating in the fully nested mode. In this mode the interrupt requests are ordered in priority from 0 through 7, with 0 having the highest priority.

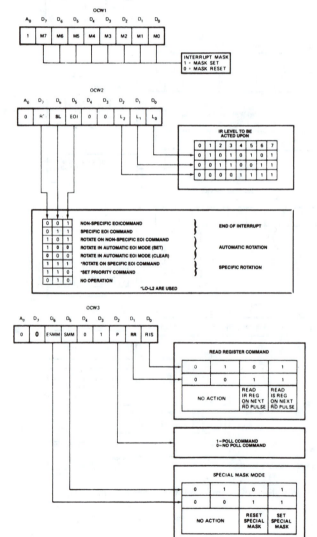

Figure 9.3-5 8259A operation command word format. (Courtesy of Intel Corp.)

After the 8259A has been initialized, it is ready to accept interrupt requests at its input lines. During operation the 8259A can be commanded to operate in different modes using operation command words, OCWs. Figure 9.3-5 shows the operation command word formats. OCW1 sets and clears the mask bits in the interrupt mask register. When no ICW4 is used, the 8259A operates in the non-AEOI mode. In this mode the bit in the ISR corresponding to the interrupt request whose service has been completed must be reset by software. This can be accomplished by the 8085A issuing a nonspecific EOI command using OCW2. In response to receiving a nonspecific EOI command, the 8259A will automatically reset the highest ISR bit of those that are set. In the fully nested mode the highest ISR bit is the last request acknowledged and serviced.

OCW3 is used to read the IRR and ISR registers. The register to be read is selected by sending the 8259A an OCW3 with the appropriate "read register" bit pattern. A read of the 8259A with $A_0 = 0$ will return the contents of the selected register. To read the IMR, no OCW3 is required; a read of the 8259A with $A_0 = 1$ will return the contents of the IMR.

Features of the 8259A, which are not discussed in detail here, allow the system priority structure to be dynamically altered and also allow several 8259As to be cascaded in a master slave configuration to handle as many as 64 interrupt request inputs.

9.4 FIFO BUFFERS

Thus far, two handshaking methods have been discussed that synchronize the data transfer between an I/O device and a microprocessor: polling and interrupting. Each technique transfers a single word of data every time it is invoked, and each involves a certain amount of overhead. In some applications, however, it is more efficient to transfer data between an I/O device and a microprocessor in blocks. A hardware device, the *first-in / first-out, FIFO*, buffer or memory facilitates this.

A FIFO is a memory unit with separate data inputs and outputs but no address inputs. Data is read from the memory in the same order in which it is written into it; i.e., the first word written in is the first word read out. An important feature of the FIFO is that it can be written into and read from at two different data rates, simultaneously and independently.

When placed between an I/O device and a microprocessor, a FIFO accepts data at the I/O device's rate and is read from at the microprocessor's rate. One of two conditions exists: either the I/O device is slower than the microprocessor or it is faster. If the I/O device is slower, e.g., an electromechanical device, it loads data into the FIFO at a slow rate. When the FIFO is filled with a block of data, the FIFO interrupts the microprocessor, and the service subroutine inputs the entire block. This substantially reduces the overhead per data word transferred.

In a situation where the I/O device generates bursts of data at a high data rate, the FIFO accepts the data at the faster rate and the microprocessor reads the data at a slower rate. Of course, the average data rate of the I/O device must be low

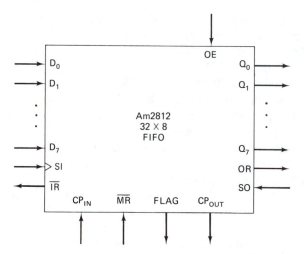

Figure 9.4-1 Logic symbol for a 32 × 8 FIFO Am2812.

enough to be handled by the microprocessor, and the capacity of the FIFO must be great enough to average out the data rate of the burst data appropriately.

The logic symbol for a 32 × 8 FIFO, Am2812, is shown in Fig. 9.4-1 [3]. Initially, the device is reset by pulsing the master reset input, $\overline{MR}$. After resetting, the input ready output, $\overline{IR}$, is low—indicating that the FIFO is ready to receive new data. The output ready, OR, is also low—indicating that valid data is not available at the output. A low to high transition at the shift input, SI, loads data into the first register of the FIFO and sets $\overline{IR}$ high. When SI is brought low again, data in the first register is automatically shifted toward the output register of the FIFO. Once the data word in the first register is shifted to the second register, $\overline{IR}$ goes low and new data can be entered. The amount of time required for the data at the input to be shifted to the output is the *ripple through time* and is proportional to the number of registers in the FIFO.

Internal logic associated with each register in the FIFO determines whether the next register, closer to the output, is empty; if so, it shifts data into it, and the source register's control logic enters its empty state. Thus, data entered into the FIFO is shifted or rippled from the input register to the last empty register. When the FIFO is full, $\overline{IR}$ remains high, and additional data cannot be input until a word is read.

When the output read, OR, signal is high, valid data is available to be read from the FIFO. A pulse on the shift out input, SO, reads the data in the output register and shifts data from the next register into it. This starts a ripple process whereby the remaining data in the FIFO shifts one register closer to the output.

The Am2812 has three-state outputs controlled by an output enable input, OE. If the output is not enabled, data cannot be read out of the FIFO. The FLAG output on the Am2812 also indicates whether it is more or less than half full. FLAG goes high when the 15th ± 1 word is loaded into the FIFO and remains high until there are fewer than 15 ± 1 words in the memory.

Am2812 FIFOs are cascaded by connecting the OR and SO outputs of one FIFO to the SI and $\overline{IR}$ inputs of the next FIFO. When an SI signal loads the last

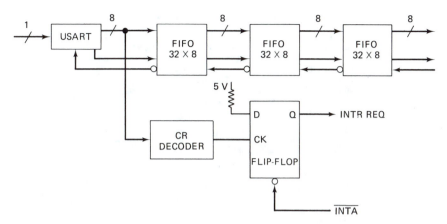

Figure 9.4-2 94 × 8 FIFO constructed from three 32 × 8 FIFOs cascaded and used to buffer serial data received from a UAR/T.

register in an Am2812, the $\overline{\text{IR}}$ output stays high, so no pulse is applied to the preceding FIFO. As a result, its output and the input of the filled FIFO contain the same word until a word is read from the FIFO. Thus, the total number of words that can be stored in n cascaded FIFOs in $31n + 1$, not $32n$. In Fig. 9.4-2, three Am2812s are cascaded, making a 94 × 8 FIFO. This FIFO receives data from a USART connected to a terminal. Characters received from the terminal are stored in the FIFO until a carriage return, CR, indicates the end of a line of data. A combinational decoder detects the CR (0DH) and generates an interrupt request to the microprocessor. The service subroutine then inputs an entire line of data each time it is invoked.

The Am2812 is also capable of accepting serial data at its D_0 input and outputting that data at D_7. In this configuration, the device looks like a 256 × 1 FIFO. Inputs CP_{in} and CP_{out} strobe data into and read data from the FIFO.

9.5 REAL-TIME CLOCKS AND INTERVAL TIMERS

For microprocessor systems, time is generally measured for two reasons: to keep a record of the time of day and to chart the elapsed time between two events. Several approaches, with varying hardware/software trade-offs, can be used in these measurements.

A *real-time clock* keeps track of the passage of time (e.g., the time of day) and can be implemented either in software or in hardware. One software implementation uses three RWM locations to store the decimal digits corresponding to seconds, minutes, and hours. The routine counts pulses from an external, 1-second pulse generator and updates the three memory locations. A pulse train with a 1-second period is obtained by converting a 60 Hz AC power line signal to a TTL level pulse train or by counting down the output of a crystal oscillator. The pulse from the

```
TOD:        PUSH PSW    ;SAVE REGISTERS THAT WILL BE MODIFIED
            PUSH B
            PUSH H
            MVI C,2H    ;SET UP SEC-MIN LOOP COUNTER
            LXI H,SEC   ;SET POINTER TO SECONDS LOCATION
LOOP:       MOV A,M
            INR A       ;INCREMENT SECS (MIN)
            DAA         ;CORRECT RESULT TO BCD REPRESENTATION
            MOV M,A     ;STORE SECS (MIN)
            CPI 60H     ;IF NOT EQUAL TO 60, RETURN
            JNZ FIN
            MVI M,0     ;IF EQUAL TO 60, SET TO 0
            INX H       ;POINT TO NEXT MEMORY LOCATION
            DCR C       ;IF PREVIOUS PASS INCREMENTED SECONDS TO 60, THEN LOOP AND
                        ;INCREMENT MIN
            JNZ LOOP
            MOV A,M     ;IF PREVIOUS PASS INCREMENTED MIN TO 60, THEN HRS MUST BE
                        ;INCREMENTED
            INR A
            DAA
            MOV M,A
            CPI 24H     ;IF HOURS LESS THAN 24, THEN FINISH
            JNZ FIN
            MVI M,OH    ;IF HOURS EQUAL 24, THEN SET TO 0
FIN:        POP H       ;RESTORE PRE-INTERRUPT STATE
            POP B
            POP PSW
            EI
            RET
            .
            .
            .
            ORG XXX     ;RESERVED MEMORY FOR SEC, MIN, AND HRS MUST BE IN RWM
SEC:        DS 1
MIN:        DS 1
HRS:        DS 1
```

Figure 9.5-1   Service subroutine for time of day clock.

generator is counted via an interrupt; i.e., the pulse creates an interrupt, and the interrupt service routine then increments the stored time. An additional routine initially sets the clock. The interrupt service subroutine shown in Fig. 9.5-1 keeps time in response to interrupts from the 1-second oscillator. Other routines that need to know the time read it from the three memory locations, e.g., an indication of the time of day along with data being output to a printer. The clock reading routine disables the interrupt before reading the seconds, minutes, and hours. Typically, the highest priority interrupt is used for the clock. If it is nonmaskable, then the clock routine must provide a mechanism to prevent time read errors caused if another clock interrupt occurs during reading. For example, a simple mechanism requires two successive, identical clock readings.

A real-time clock can also be implemented in hardware. The hardware clock, an input device whose time is read through input ports, uses clock or calendar ICs. Hardware implementation is advantageous during a power failure because the clock or calendar IC can be powered from a battery backup system.

Elapsed time can also be measured with a software real-time clock, if a resolution of 1 second is adequate. The time at the start of the interval is simply saved in a block of memory. At the end of the interval, the start time is subtracted from the finish time, giving the elapsed time. For greater resolution a faster pulse train is used, and another memory location records fractions of a second.

As the required resolution for elapsed time measurements increases, use of an interrupt-driven, software, real-time clock becomes inefficient because the processor is continually servicing interrupts from a fast pulse generator used as a clock. An alternative approach uses external counters to count pulses (either directly or stepped down) from the microprocessor's clock or a pulse generator. A pulse at the start of the interval clears and enables the counter, and a pulse at the end of the interval disables the counter and interrupts the microprocessor. The counter contents are then input by the microprocessor.

9.5.1 The 8155H's Timer

The 8155H discussed in Chapter 8 contains a 14-bit programmable counter/timer in addition to RWM and I/O ports (see Fig. 8.6-1). The timer counts pulses at the TIMER IN input and provides either a square wave or a pulse when the terminal count is reached at the TIMER OUT output. The 8155H timer is primarily a square wave generator, not an event counter. To facilitate the generation of square waves, the counter counts down by two for each pulse at the TIMER IN input. This procedure is repeated twice, for one complete cycle.

This 14-bit counter is part of the 16-bit count length register, CLR, which can be either written or read. The most significant two bits of the CLR determine the counter's mode of operation (see Fig. 9.5-2). The address for the low order byte of the CLR is XXXXX100, and for the high order byte, XXXXX101.

In operation, the 8155H is first loaded with a code that defines the timer mode and the desired count lenth. The possible modes are

M_2	M_1	
0	0	Timer output low during second half of count.
0	1	Square wave output with period equal to the count length and automatic reload of count length at terminal count.
1	0	Single pulse when terminal count is reached.
1	1	Single pulse at terminal count with automatic reload.

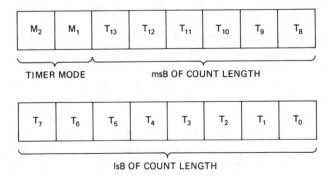

M_2	M_1	T_{13}	T_{12}	T_{11}	T_{10}	T_9	T_8

TIMER MODE   msB OF COUNT LENGTH

T_7	T_6	T_5	T_4	T_3	T_2	T_1	T_0

lsB OF COUNT LENGTH

Figure 9.5-2 Bit designation of the 8155H timer's count length register.

The counter is started or stopped when a control word is written into the command status register of the 8155H (see Fig. 8.6-2). Bits 6 and 7 of the control word program the counter as follows:

C/S_7	C/S_6	
0	0	NOP: Does not affect counter's operation.
0	1	STOP: Stop counting if timer is running; NOP if timer has not been started.
1	0	STOP AFTER TC: Stop immediately after present terminal count is reached; NOP if timer has not started.
1	1	START: Load mode, count length, and start immediately after loading. If timer is already running start new mode and count length immediately after present TC is reached.

When the counter has reached its terminal count—when operating in mode two, $M_2 = 1$, $M_1 = 0$—the single pulse generated at TIMER OUT can interrupt the microprocessor. Otherwise, the end of a count is determined by software polling of bit 6 of the command/status register (see Fig. 8.6-2). This bit is latched high when a terminal count is reached and reset when the C/S register is read or a new count is started.

In a microcomputer system, a programmable timer generates accurate time delays under software control without requiring software loops. Thus, the overhead is minimized, and the microprocessor can carry out other processing tasks during the delay. Once the delay is counted out, the timer interrupts the microprocessor and indicates the end of the delay period. The timer can be programmed so that its output implements several functions, such as a square wave generator or a divide by N counter.

To use the timer as an event counter, for example, to measure the period of a waveform, the pulses from a clock oscillator, the event, that occur during one period of the waveform are counted. The waveform is input to a toggle flip-flop (Fig. 9.5-3), which creates a square wave with a period twice that of the signal to be measured. (It is assumed that the original waveform is not necessarily a square wave; i.e., its duty cycle is not necessarily 50 percent.) Thus, the square wave is logic 1 for a length of time equal to the period of the original waveform. The output of the toggle flip-flop gates the signal from the clock oscillator to the TIMER IN input of the 8155H. To count pulses during one period, the subroutine, HTOL, waits for a high to low transition of the flip-flop output and starts the counter. However, no clock pulses are gated to the counter until the flip-flop's output is logic 1 again. Since the flip-flop's output is logic 1 for one period of the original waveform, pulses are counted during this period (see Fig. 9.5-4).

At the same time the counter is counting pulses, the microprocessor monitors the output of the flip-flop for the next 1 to 0 transition. When this occurs, the microprocessor stops the counter, and clock pulses are accumulated for only one period of the original waveform. The count in the CLR is then input to the

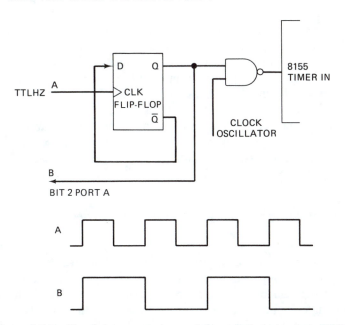

Figure 9.5-3 Circuit for measurement of the period of waveform TTLHZ.

```
PERIOD: XRA A           ;LOAD COUNT LENGTH REGISTER WITH 0, SET MODE=0
        OUT CLRL
        OUT CLRH
        CALL HTOL       ;WAIT FOR 1-TO-0 TRANSITION
        MVI A,START     ;START COUNTER
        OUT CSR
        CALL HTOL       ;WAIT FOR 1-TO-0 TRANSITION
        MVI A,STOP      ;STOP COUNTER
        OUT CSR
        IN TIMEL        ;INPUT LOW BYTE OF COUNT
        MOV C,A         ;LEAVE IN C
        IN TIMEH        ;INPUT HIGH BYTE OF COUNT
        ORA MSKPD       ;SET BITS 14 AND 15 (MODE) TO 1S
        MOV B,A         ;LEAVE IN B
        RET
        ;HTOL-IMPLEMENTS A WAIT VIA LOOPING
        ;UNTIL A 1-TO-0 TRANSITION OCCURS IN THE
        ;BIT OF PORT A INDICATED BY THE MASK TTLHZ
HTOL:   IN PORTA
        ANI TTLHZ
        JZ HTOL         ;IF LOW WAIT IN LOOP
TTLH:   IN PORTA
        ANI TTLHZ
        JNZ TTLH        ;IF HIGH WAIT IN LOOP
        RET
```

Figure 9.5-4 Subroutine to measure the period of a waveform using the hardware of Fig. 9.5-3.

microprocessor, and the most significant two of the 16 bits are set. Registers B and C, therefore, contain the two's complement of twice the number of clock pulses.[2]

This technique allows a very precise measurement of elapsed time. However, it requires polling the flip-flop output while the counter is running, and this adds software overhead to the measurement. An alternative technique, which reduces software overhead, uses the 1 to 0 transition of the flip-flop output to interrupt the microprocessor and a service subroutine to start the counter. At the next 1 to 0 transition, the flip-flop causes a second interrupt and the service subroutine stops the counter. The service subroutine complements and tests one bit of a reserved memory location to determine whether it should start or stop the counter.

9.5.2 The 8254 Programmable Interval Timer

The 8254 Programmable Interval Timer provides three independent 16-bit counters in a single 24-pin package (see Fig. 9.5-5). Each counter can be operated in any one of six programmable modes and count in binary or BCD. Each counter has a clock input, gate input, and counter output. Depending on the mode of operation programmed, the counter output may consist of a change in level after a programmed initial count is counted down to zero or it may consist of a repetitive pulse

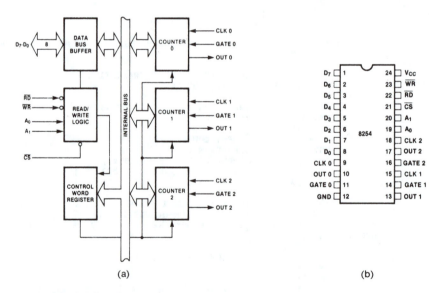

(a)   (b)

Figure 9.5-5 8254 Programmable Interval Timer: (a) block diagram; (b) pin configuration. (Courtesy of Intel Corp.)

---

[2] The timer circuit of the 8155 is designed to be a square wave timer, not an event timer. To achieve this, it counts down by two twice in completing one cycle.

D$_7$	D$_6$	D$_5$	D$_4$	D$_3$	D$_2$	D$_1$	D$_0$
SC1	SC0	RW1	RW0	M2	M1	M0	BCD

SC — Select Counter:

SC1	SC0	
0	0	Select Counter 0
0	1	Select Counter 1
1	0	Select Counter 2
1	1	Read-Back Command (See Read Operations)

RW — Read/Write:

RW1	RW0	
0	0	Counter Latch Command (see Read Operations)
0	1	Read/Write least significant byte only.
1	0	Read/Write most significant byte only.
1	1	Read/Write least significant byte first, then most significant byte.

NOTE: DON'T CARE BITS (X) SHOULD BE 0 TO INSURE COMPATIBILITY WITH FUTURE INTEL PRODUCTS.

M — MODE:

M2	M1	M0	
0	0	0	Mode 0
0	0	1	Mode 1
X	1	0	Mode 2
X	1	1	Mode 3
1	0	0	Mode 4
1	0	1	Mode 5

BCD:

0	Binary Counter 16-bits
1	Binary Coded Decimal (BCD) Counter (4 Decades)

Figure 9.5-6   8254 control word format. (Courtesy of Intel Corp.)

train that is related to the input pulse train by the programmed count. The six modes of operation are

Mode 0:   interrupt on terminal count
Mode 1:   hardware retriggerable one-shot
Mode 2:   rate generator
Mode 3:   square wave mode
Mode 4:   software triggered strobe
Mode 5:   hardware triggered strobe

The mode of operation of each counter must be specified by programming each counter before use. To program a counter a control word must be written to the 8254's command register followed by an initial count, written to the selected counter. The sequence in which the initial count is written must follow the format specified in the control word. The control word format is given in Fig. 9.5-6. The addresses of the control word register and counters are listed in Fig. 9.5-7. For example, to program counter 0 to operate in mode 3, with the initial count to be written as two bytes, and to count in binary, the command word would be 00110110B. The initial count would then be output to counter 0 by two output operations, least significant byte first. Mode 3 produces a square wave. The period of the square wave output for an initial count of N is N times the period of the input clock. Once the initial count is loaded, the 8254 continues to automatically reload it and count it down again when it reaches zero.

$\overline{CS}$	$\overline{RD}$	$\overline{WR}$	A_1	A_0	
0	1	0	0	0	Write into Counter 0
0	1	0	0	1	Write into Counter 1
0	1	0	1	0	Write into Counter 2
0	1	0	1	1	Write Control Word
0	0	1	0	0	Read from Counter 0
0	0	1	0	1	Read from Counter 1
0	0	1	1	0	Read from Counter 2
0	0	1	1	1	No-Operation (3-State)
1	X	X	X	X	No-Operation (3-State)
0	1	1	X	X	No-Operation (3-State)

Figure 9.5-7 8254 register addresses. (Courtesy of Intel Corp.)

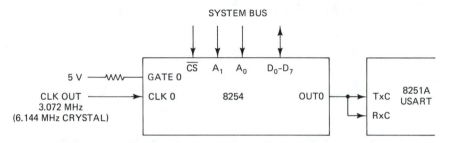

Figure 9.5-8 Counter 0 of an 8254 used as a baud rate generator.

```
CNTROI:     IN  BRS         ;GET BAUD RATE SELECT CODE
            ANI 07H         ;MASK MS 5 BITS
            RLC             ;MULT *2 FOR OFFSET
            MOV E,A         ;PUT OFFSET IN DE
            MVI D,0
            LXI H,BRDTBL    ;GET TABLE BASE ADDRESS
            DAD D
            MOV C,M         ;PUT COUNT IN BC
            INX H
            MOV B,M
            MVI A,36H       ;COMMAND WORD
            OUT CMWD        ;OUTPUT COMMAND WORD
            MOV A,C         ;OUTPUT COUNT LOW BYTE
            OUT CNTR0
            MOV A,B         ;OUTPUT COUNT HIGH BYTE
            OUT CNTR0
            RET

BRDTBL:     DW  1746        ;110 BAUD,        1.760 KHz
            DW  1280        ;150             2.400 KHz
            DW  640         ;300             4.800 KHz
            DW  320         ;600             9.600 KHz
            DW  160         ;1200            19.20 KHz
            DW  80          ;2400            38.40 KHz
            DW  40          ;4800            76.80 KHz
            DW  20          ;9600            153.6 KHz
```

Figure 9.5-9 8254 Counter 0 mode 3 initialization for baud rate generation.

Figure 9.5-8 shows counter 0 of an 8254 used as a baud rate generator. The input to CLK 0 is CLK OUT of an 8085AH operated with a 6.144 MHz crystal. The OUT 0 of the 8254 provides the transmit and receive clock for the 8251A USART. Thus, counter 0 provides the baud rate generator required in Fig. 8.7-8. The other two counters, in the 8254, are available to implement other timing functions required in the system. The program in Fig. 9.5-9 initializes counter 0. To do so, it reads the baud rate selection switches in Fig. 8.7-8 and uses a table to find the required initial count for the selected baud rate. The values in the table assume that the 8251A is programmed for $\times 16$ operation. It can now be seen why the slower crystal frequency of 6.144 MHz is often used with the 8085AH, which can be operated at 6.25 MHz. The 6.144 MHz frequency divides down, by integer values, to produce the $\times 16$ clock rates needed for asynchronous serial communication at standard baud rates.

9.6 CONSIDERATIONS FOR USING INTERRUPTS

Although the use of interrupts is advantageous for allowing concurrent processing while I/O is performed and/or external events are responded to, interrupts must be used with considerable care. For example, suppose a subroutine used by the main program is also used by an interrupt service subroutine, or by two or more interrupts at different priority levels. Assume that the subroutine is being executed as the result of a call by the main program, that an interrupt occurs, and that the interrupt service subroutine calls the same subroutine. This process of calling a subroutine that is only partially through execution is referred to as *reentering* the subroutine. The result of reentering can be the loss of data and subsequent failure of the system.

9.6.1 Shared Subroutines

Three techniques preclude these problems. By the first method, the subroutine is duplicated rather than shared. Duplicated subroutines are totally independent of each other; not only must they have different names and instruction labels, but they cannot share reserved memory. The cost of duplication is the additional memory required.

Not all subroutines that need to be shared can be duplicated. I/O driver subroutines, for instance, cannot be duplicated because the I/O device is a single resource and must be shared. In such cases, the second method, described next, is employed.

By the second method, reentry of shared subroutines is prevented by disabling the interrupts before the subroutine is called and enabling them after the return from the subroutine. This increases the interrupt response time to a value greater than the execution time of the shared subroutine. In a system where critical response times must be met, such a solution may not be acceptable.

By the third method, for situations other than those where a single physical device is being controlled by a subroutine, a reentrant subroutine can be written and shared. *Reentrant subroutines* can be reentered without loss of temporary results. They are written in pure code, with a separate temporary storage or work area for each entry into the subroutine. *Pure code* does not modify itself in any way. All but the simplest subroutines require temporary storage for parameters, data, and intermediate results. This storage, or work area, is unique for each call of a reentrant subroutine. If the only temporary storage needed is provided by general purpose registers in the microprocessor, then this work area is effectively separate from the main program and interrupt service routines for different levels, since the contents of these registers are saved and restored by the interrupt service routine. If the subroutine requires a larger work area, the address of the work area can be provided in one of the register pairs in the microprocessor. Alternatively, the stack can be used to provide temporary work areas.

9.6.2 Disabling Interrupts

Often during the execution of time critical routines, interrupts must be disabled. If software delay routines and interrupts are used, the interrupts must be disabled before any delay is initiated; otherwise, the delay may be of unpredictable duration. Subroutines that act as drivers for certain I/O devices may also need to function uninterrupted.

Situations where interrupts are disabled must be taken into consideration when determining worst case response time. And, as the number of interrupt sources increases, so does the complexity of the design and timing analysis. Software delay routines can be eliminated entirely by implementing timing functions in hardware with programmable timers, such as the 8254.

9.6.3 Priority Assignments

Generally, it is advisable to avoid the use of interrupts in a design unless the need for concurrent processing, fast response time, or other restrictions makes them necessary. If used, it is advantageous in limiting complexity to have all interrupts on a single level, when possible. If a multilevel or priority interrupt structure is essential, the assignment of interrupts is usually made as follows. The unmaskable interrupt, which is the highest level, is used for catastrophic events such as power failures. If a high resolution real-time clock is used, it is associated with the next highest interrupt so that clock ticks will not be lost. The remaining devices or events are associated with priority levels such that devices or events requiring the shortest response times are assigned the highest levels.

Another reason for avoiding interrupts is the difficulty of debugging a system. Since interrupts are asynchronous events and unpredictable in terms of time of occurrence, it is hard to simulate worst case conditions to determine whether the system will respond properly to combinations of interrupts.

9.7 DIRECT MEMORY ACCESS (DMA)

Program controlled data transfers require a significant amount of a microprocessor's time to transmit a rather small amount of data per unit time, i.e., a low data rate. And the microprocessor cannot execute any other processing functions during program controlled I/O operations. Although interrupts increase the attainable data rate, require less software, and allow concurrent processing, applications exist where the required data rate is simply too high to be achieved by using interrupts or where the data rate is such that the time spent in interrupt service routines impacts the concurrent processing to an unacceptable degree.

However, *direct memory access, DMA*, facilitates maximum I/O data rate and maximum concurrency. Unlike programmed I/O and interrupt I/O that route data through the microprocessor, DMA directly transfers data between an I/O device and memory. For DMA transfers, the microprocessor must have a DMA feature. Additional external logic is also necessary. This additional logic, the *DMA controller*, contains its own address register, word count register, and logic for reading or writing data to or from memory. Figure 9.7-1 illustrates the basic components of a DMA controller.

DMA is commonly used for three types of data transfer: burst, cycle stealing, and transparent. *Burst* DMA transfers a block of data at the highest rate possible. The steps in the execution of a data transfer using burst DMA are as follows:

1. The microprocessor loads the DMA controller with a starting address for the memory transfer and the number of words to be transferred.

2. When the input device has the data ready to be transferred to the memory or when the output device is ready for the transfer from the memory, the DMA controller sends a DMA request to the microprocessor.

3. The microprocessor acknowledges the DMA request, floats its address and data buses and appropriate control lines, and suspends any processing that requires use of the address and data bus.

4. The DMA controller provides an address and control strobes to read or write memory. The I/O device provides or accepts the data on the data bus. After a data byte is transferred, the DMA controller increments its address register and decrements its word count register. If the required number of words has not been transferred, the DMA controller repeats this step when the I/O device is ready.

5. When the required number of words has been transferred, the DMA controller terminates the DMA request and interrupts the microprocessor to indicate that the DMA transfer is complete.

The maximum data rate of a burst DMA transfer is limited only by the read or write cycle time of the memory and by the speed of the DMA controller. Below this maximum, the data rate is limited by the rate at which the I/O device can supply or receive data. Burst data transfers are commonly used in transferring data

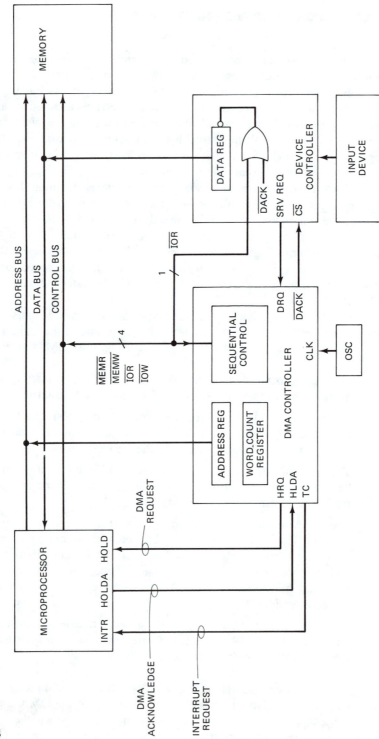

Figure 9.7-1 DMA controller controlling an input device.

TABLE 9.7-1   8085A HOLD AND HOLD ACKNOWLEDGE PINS (COURTESY OF INTEL CORP.)

Symbol	Type	Name and Function
HOLD	I	**Hold**: Indicates that another master is requesting the use of the address and data buses. The cpu, upon receiving the hold request, will relinquish the use of the bus as soon as the completion of the current bus transfer. Internal processing can continue. The processor can regain the bus only after the HOLD is removed. When the HOLD is acknowledged, the Address, Data $\overline{RD}$, $\overline{WR}$, and $IO/\overline{M}$ lines are 3-stated.
HLDA	O	**Hold Acknowledge**: Indicates that the cpu has received the HOLD request and that it will relinquish the bus in the next clock cycle. HLDA goes low after the Hold request is removed. The cpu takes the bus one half clock cycle after HLDA goes low.

to or from a floppy disk mass storage unit or for refreshing a CRT display (see Chapters 10 and 13).

In *cycle stealing* DMA, data is transferred concurrently with other processing being carried out by the microprocessor. The steps in execution are similar to those for burst DMA except that after one word of data is transferred in step 4, if the required number of data words have not been transferred, then steps 2, 3, and 4 are repeated for each data byte, until the requisite number of bytes has been transferred. Thus, the DMA controller steals cycles (state times) from the microprocessor, during which it transfers data. The processing carried out by the microprocessor is slowed accordingly.

For some microprocessors, external logic can be designed so that cycle stealing occurs during internal processing when the system address and data buses are not being used. Such DMA transfers are transparent to the microprocessor in that they do not interfere with or slow down its normal rate of instruction execution. *Transparent* DMA, in addition to the normal logic, requires logic to detect the occurrence of microprocessor states that involve only internal processing.

For the three types of DMA transfer, the only software required is that necessary for initializing the DMA controller's address and word count registers. With the 8085A, a DMA controller requests a DMA operation by bringing the HOLD input of the microprocessor high (see Table 9.7-1). The microprocessor then synchronizes the asynchronous hold request and, at the proper time in the machine cycle, provides a hold acknowledge (HLDA) signal to the DMA controller and floats its address and data buses and the $\overline{RD}$, $\overline{WR}$, and $IO/\overline{M}$ control lines. The microprocessor continues internal processing and then enters a hold state (see Fig. 9.7-2). By floating its address, data, and control buses, the microprocessor effectively

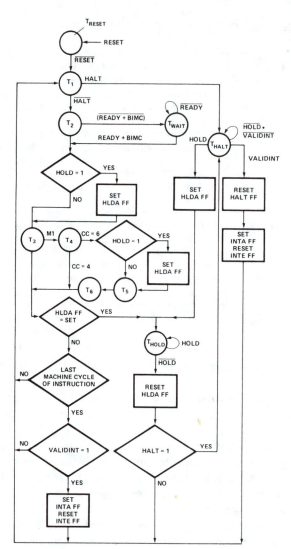

Figure 9.7-2 Complete state transition diagram for 8085A. (Courtesy of Intel Corp.)

disconnects itself from the system. From this point on, it is up to the DMA controller to provide addresses, data, and control signals to the memory and I/O port to implement the data transfer. The DMA controler then enables its three-state buffers, which connect it to the address, data, and control buses. When the DMA processor is through using memory, it floats its address, data, and control buses, and then brings the HOLD input of the microprocessor low. The microprocessor exits the hold state and continues its previous operation from the point at which it was suspended by the hold request. The DMA controller subsequently interrupts the microprocessor, indicating that the DMA transfer is complete.

DMA controllers range from random logic structures to special LSI devices and even to dedicated microprocessors. An LSI DMA controller such as the Intel

8257-5 is programmable and controls the DMA operations of several I/O devices [4].

The only additional hardware this four-channel device requires is an 8212 latch to demultiplex the addresses it generates.[3] The 8257-5 uses a clock input with a minimum clock period of 320 nS. Four clock cycles are required to transfer 1 byte of data. With a 3 MHz clock, a transfer rate of 750,000 bytes per second is achieved.

Figure 9.7-3 shows how the 8257-5 and the 8212 are interfaced to an 8085A to provide DMA capability for up to four I/O devices.[4] Consider the case of a DMA read operation, a transfer from memory to a peripheral. Assume that only a single DMA channel (channel 0) is used in the system. Prior to a DMA transfer, both the DMA controller and the controller of the output device are initialized.

The DMA controller contains two 16-bit registers, a DMA address register and a terminal count register, for each channel, that must be initialized. It also contains an 8-bit mode register and an 8-bit status register that are shared by the four channels. The data required for initialization is written into the DMA controller by the microprocessor. The microprocessor treats the DMA controller as an I/O device and uses its address inputs A_0–A_3 to select the register to be written.

The address and terminal count registers for channel 0 are initialized by loading the DMA address register with the address of the first memory location to be accessed. The least significant 14 bits of the terminal count register are loaded with the number of DMA cycles[5] (words to be transferred) before the terminal count output is activated. The two most significant bits of this register are loaded with a code indicating that channel 0 is to operate in the DMA read mode. To load a 16-bit channel register, the low order byte is written first and then the high order byte.

Each 16-bit register has a single address because the DMA controller contains a first/last, F/L, flip-flop that is cleared when the controller is reset. Whenever a channel register (DMA address or terminal count register) is written, the F/L flip-flop is toggled. This flip-flop provides the additional address bit necessary to select the low or high byte of the 16-bit register. The mode register is loaded with an appropriate bit pattern to enable channel 0.

The microprocessor then initializes the output device's controller, the requirements for initialization varying with the nature of the output device. When the output device is ready to accept the first byte of data, its controller makes the request input of the DMA controller logic 1. The DMA controller then outputs a hold request, HRQ, to the 8085A, which returns a hold acknowledge, HLDA, indicating that it has relinquished control of the system bus. The DMA controller then takes control of the system bus, and addresses memory with the address in its DMA address register. The high address byte is output by the DMA controller onto

---

[3] The 8212 is an 8-bit latch that has triggering options. When used with the 8257-5, as shown in Fig. 9.7-4, it operates as a positive level triggered latch. When used in this manner STB is the clock input. Input DS2 enables the three-state output buffers of the latch.

[4] Throughout the remainder of this section, any reference to a DMA controller means the 8257-5 controller.

[5] For N DMA cycles, the actual value loaded into the terminal count register is $N - 1$.

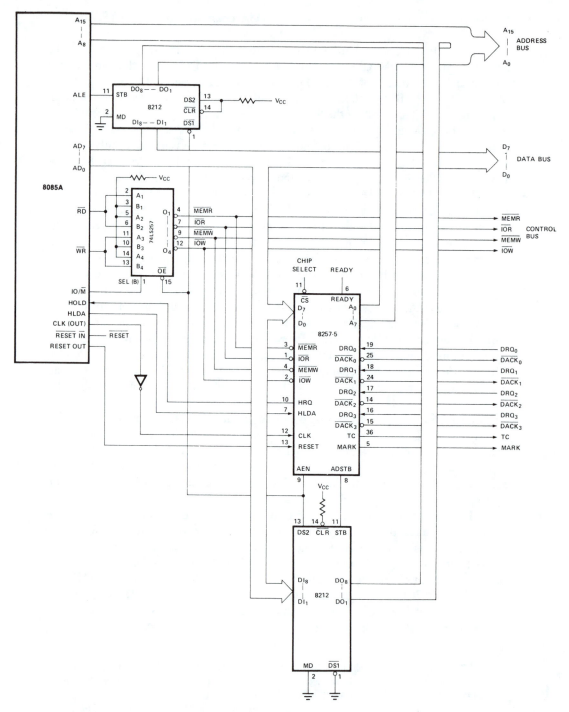

Figure 9.7-3 8257-5 DMA controller interface to an 8085A microprocessor. (Courtesy of Intel Corp.)

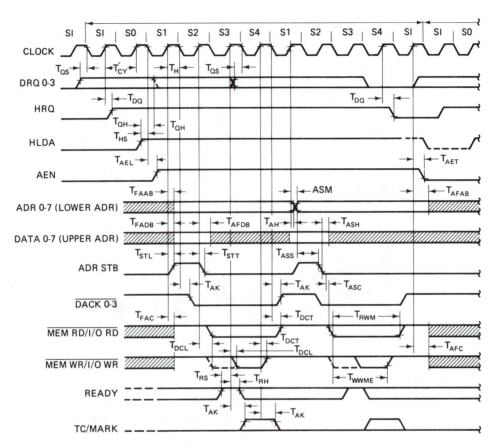

Figure 9.7-4   8257-5 timing diagram for DMA cycles. (Courtesy of Intel Corp.)

the data bus and latched by its associated 8212. Pins A_0–A_7 provide the low address byte. The DMA controller then generates a $\overline{\text{MEMR}}$ strobe, and the memory drives the data bus with the data to be transferred (see Fig. 9.7-4).

Note that address lines A_0–A_3 of the DMA controller are bidirectional. These lines serve as address inputs when the registers of the DMA controller are loaded by the microprocessor. At such a time the DMA controller operates as a slave device. When it operates as a master (controlling the system bus), these address lines are outputs.

The DMA controller also generates a DMA acknowledge signal, $\overline{\text{DACK}_0}$, which selects the output device and, after the data is stable on the data bus, generates an $\overline{\text{I/OW}}$ strobe, which writes data into the output device. Channel 0's DMA address register is incremented and the terminal count register decremented.

For a burst DMA transfer, the controller of the output device keeps the DRQ_0 input logic 1 until the DMA controller indicates that the last byte of data has been transferred, TC = 1. On the other hand, for cycle stealing DMA, the output device's controller returns the DRQ_0 line to logic 0 when it receives $\overline{DACK}_0$, and only a single byte is transferred. The output device's controller subsequently requests a sufficient number of DMA cycles to transfer the remaining bytes.

The terminal count, TC, output of the DMA controller interrupts the microprocessor, indicating that a block of data has been transferred. The interrupt service subroutine takes whatever action is appropriate for the particular application. Note that if the microprocessor is not interrupted at the completion of a block transfer, it has no way of knowing when the transfer is complete.

REFERENCES

1. *MCS-80/85 Family User's Manual* (Santa Clara, Calif.: Intel Corporation, 1983).
2. R. JIGOUR, *Using the 8259A Programmable Interrupt Controller* (Application Note AP-59) (Santa Clara, Calif.: Intel Corporation, 1979).
3. J. SPRINGER, *Application of First-In First-Out Memories* (Application Note) (Sunnyvale, Calif.: Advanced Micro Devices, Inc., 1973).
4. G. ALEXY and G. MILLER, *Direct Memory Access with the 8257 DMA Controller* (Application Note AP-48) (Santa Clara, Calif.: Intel Corporation, 1979).

PROBLEMS

9-1. Describe how each step in the list of operations that occur in response to an interrupt is implemented by an 8085A system.

9-2. Interrupt request flip-flops should be cleared when a microprocessor is first powered up or reset. Why? In what ways can this be accomplished?

9-3. Design the external hardware necessary to make the TRAP interrupt of an 8085A maskable. Write two macros: ENAT to enable the TRAP interrupt and DAT to disable the TRAP interrupt.

9-4. Write a sequence of instructions that enables the RST6.5 and RST7.5 interrupts and disables the RST5.5 interrupt of an 8085A.

9-5. To interrupt an 8085A microprocessor, an I/O device generates a 100 nS positive pulse. Design the logic to interface this device to each of the following interrupts of an 8085A:
(a) RST5.5
(b) RST6.5
(c) RST7.5

9-6. The BI and INA machine cycles are similar to the OF machine cycle in that they load the instruction register with an OP code. However, OF increments the PC, and BI and INA do not. Explain why the PC is handled differently by BI and INA.

9-7. Assume eight I/O devices are to share a single interrupt input, RST5.5. Design the logic to interface the interrupt request flip-flops to an 8085A. Implement priority arbitration with a 74LS148 priority encoder whose outputs are available through an input port. Write a subroutine that uses the priority encoder's output as an index into a jump table for the purpose of transferring control to the individual service subroutines.

9-8. Is it possible to devise a software method to establish a rotating priority among the interrupt inputs RST5.5, RST6.5, and RST7.5 so that lower priority interrupts cannot be completely locked out by the continual occurrence of higher priority interrupts? If it is possible, write a program that establishes this rotating priority. If it is not possible, discuss why.

9-9. Assume that the USART in Fig. 9.4-2 receives ASCII encoded characters at a rate of 10 characters per second. Assume that up to 80 characters can be received before a carriage return occurs and the microprocessor is interrupted. Write an interrupt service subroutine that transfers data from the FIFO buffer to the microprocessor system's RWM. Compare the software overhead required to transfer 80 characters using this structure with that required using a hardware structure without FIFOs, where the USART interrupts the microprocessor to transfer each byte of data.

9-10. Two bytes of reserved memory are used to store a 16-bit count of the number of times an external event occurs. The least significant of the 2 bytes is stored in location CNT, and the most significant is stored in location CNT + 1. An interrupt service subroutine starting in location 38H increments the 16-bit events counter each time it is called. Write this interrupt service subroutine, and draw a complete logic diagram of the external hardware required to interrupt an 8085A and directly vector to the interrupt service subroutine. Use the 8085A interrupt input, INTR.

9-11. Using the real-time clock of Fig. 9.5-1, write a pair of interrupt service subroutines that together compute the elapsed time between two events and store this elapsed time in three reserved memory locations: ELSEC, ELMIN, and ELHRS. The first event generates an RST5.5 interrupt and the second event generates an RST6.5 interrupt.

9-12. Repeat Problem 9-11 with both events generating an RST6.5 interrupt.

9-13. Write a subroutine to set the real-time clock of Fig. 9.5-1. Assume that the time is input through a port, TSET, by inputting two digits for hours, two for minutes, and two for seconds. The format of the input data is shown in the diagram.

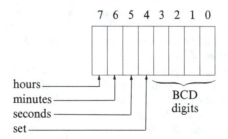

Write the subroutine assuming that only one of the most significant 4 bits is set at a time and only the last two digits input for any particular parameter (hours, minutes, or seconds) are valid. The actual setting of the clock should take place when bit 4 is 1; this would be the last data byte entered.

9-14. In a microprocessor system using CMOS RWM with a battery backup, the contents of the RWM are not lost if the system's power is interrupted. Assume that a system of this type has external circuitry that detects the initial loss of power and interrupts the microprocessor. Write a service subroutine that saves the microprocessor's state before the power supply output drops below the operating level. Also design software and hardware that automatically restore the microprocessor's state when the supply of power is reestablished. Note that upon a power On reset, a determination must be made as to whether it is a normal power ON reset or whether it is a power On reset following a power failure.

9-15. An output device generates a 200 nS negative pulse whenever it can receive another data byte from an 8085A. This device is to be interfaced to the INTR interrupt input of the 8085A. The output device contains an 8-bit positive edge triggered latch to receive the data from the 8085A. The address that control is to be transferred to when this interrupt occurs is 30H. Draw the logic diagram of this interface. Show any address decoding logic in block diagram form only.

9-16. Write an interrupt service subroutine that outputs a byte of data to the output device of problem 9-15. The byte of data is in a 256-byte buffer, BUFF. The offset of the particular byte to be output is in the location OFFSET. The service subroutine must take the byte from the memory buffer location and output it to the output device, OUTDEV. The service subroutine must also increment the offset so that it points to the next byte in the buffer to be output. This next byte to be output is the next sequential location in the buffer, unless the current byte being output is the last byte in the buffer. In this case the next byte to be output is the first byte in the buffer. Because of the slow speed of the output device, other interrupts must be allowed to interrupt the servicing of OUTDEV at any time.

9-17. An input device generates bytes of data for a microprocessor. The data lines from the input device do not have three-state outputs. For each new byte of data the input device generates a 100 nS negative control pulse. The data byte is valid 100 nS before the leading edge of the pulse and remains valid for 100 nS after the trailing edge of the pulse. Draw a diagram of the logic to interface the input device to the microprocessor using the RST5.5 interrupt input. The logic diagram must show all the logic required to implement the interrupt driven data transfer. Any address decoding logic can be shown as a single block. However, all inputs and outputs of the block must be completely specified.

9-18. Write an interrupt service subroutine, for the hardware in problem 9-17 that inputs a single data byte each time an RST5.5 interrupt occurs. This interrupt subroutine should not itself be interrupted. The byte of data input must be placed in a buffer in memory. A 16-bit pointer to the buffer is kept in the reserved memory location BPTR. The number of bytes left to be input before the data in the buffer is processed is an 8-bit number that is kept in the reserved memory location BCNT. If the buffer is full after a byte of data is transferred to the buffer, the service subroutine must call another subroutine, PROCES, to process the data. When called, the subroutine PROCES processes the data in the buffer and initializes BPTR and BCNT. Do not write the subroutine PROCES.

9-19. Assuming that a single channel DMA controller has gained control of the system bus (HLDA received from the 8085A), list the sequence of operations the DMA controller carries out to cause the transfer of 1 byte of data during a DMA read. Draw a timing diagram showing the relationship of the appropriate system bus signals for the transfer.

10

Digital Data Entry
and Display

10.1 MANUAL DATA ENTRY

Methods of digital data entry to a microprocessor are either manual or automatic. Manual entry is the direct input of data by an operator, whereas automatic entry involves input by another machine or process. In both methods, the provision of appropriate input data signals from a digital source requires one or more of the following operations:

1. Conversion: distinguishing between two states of the input and generating an electrical signal with the appropriate logic level for that state.
2. Sensing: detecting a change in an output signal or the occurrence of new data.
3. Debouncing: providing a single transition for each change of state in an electromechanical device that inherently creates multiple output changes during its transition from one state to another.
4. Encoding: converting a multivalued input state to a desired binary code.

10.1.1 Mechanical Switches

Mechanical switches are used for manual data entry in many microprocessor systems. Such systems require a provision for an operator to input data to the system. The amount of data input varies from very little at system initiation only, as in some controllers, to large amounts during the entire operation, as in interactive systems. The selection of devices for manual data entry, therefore, should be based on the type and quantity of data to be entered and the time and frequency at which data entry is required.

A large number of mechanical switches are available, which vary significantly in design. Single-pole/single-throw (SPST) and single-pole/double-throw (SPDT), toggle, and momentary contact (pushbutton) switches are considered here (see Fig. 10.1-1).

When using mechanical switches for data entry, the position of the switch must be converted to an electrical signal compatible with the system's logic circuits.

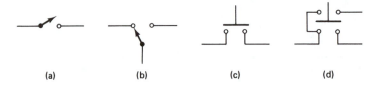

(a)   (b)   (c)   (d)

Figure 10.1-1 Simple mechanical switches: (a) single-pole/single-throw; (b) single-pole/double-throw; (c) single-pole/single-throw momentary contact switch; (d) single-pole/double-throw momentary contact switch.

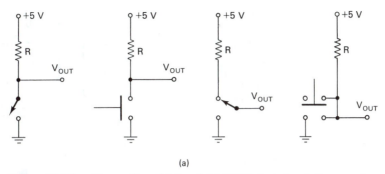

(a)

Figure 10.1-2a   Generation of LS and ALS TTL logic levels from mechanical switch positions.

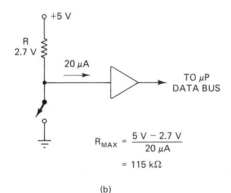

$$R_{MAX} = \frac{5\ V - 2.7\ V}{20\ \mu A}$$

$$= 115\ k\Omega$$

(b)

Figure 10.1-2b   Computation of maximum value of pull up resistor.

Figure 10.1-2 shows how a switch and pull up resistor to +5 V provide a signal compatible with TTL circuits for various switch configurations. When the switch is closed, it provides an output voltage of 0 V. When open, it provides a voltage $V_{OUT} = 5\ V - IR$, where I is the logic 1 current required by the load connected to the switch output. The value of R limits the power dissipated when the switch is closed and provides a voltage above 2.7 V at the required input current of the load when it is open. This load is the input of a three-state buffer if the switch's logic state is to be input on the microprocessor's data bus.

When a mechanical switch opens or closes, the **contacts bounce**, actually opening and closing many times before coming to rest. A typical switch bounces for many milliseconds—5–20 mS is common—resulting in a sequence of logic signal transitions at the switch output instead of a single, smooth transition (see Fig. 10.1-3). If a microprocessor repeatedly inputs the switch output during the bounce period, it appears to the microprocessor that the switch has been operated several times instead of once. To preclude this possibility, the switch must be debounced. Debouncing can be accomplished by using either hardware or software.

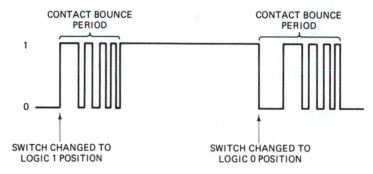

Figure 10.1-3 Multiple signal transitions caused by contact bounce of a mechanical switch.

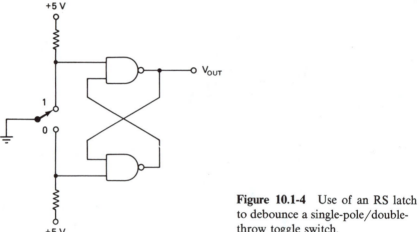

Figure 10.1-4 Use of an RS latch to debounce a single-pole/double-throw toggle switch.

An RS latch, as shown in Fig. 10.1-4, can debounce a single-pole/double-throw switch. The output of the latch changes state only once when the switch position is changed. RS latches are available, four to a package, as quad debouncer ICs (74LS279A).

Both SPST and SPDT switches can be debounced with software. For example, a microprocessor can repeatedly input the output of a switch and, if its value remains the same for a period of time in excess of the switch's bounce period, accept the input value as valid. The same technique provides noise immunity when inputting data from a bounce-free source: the microprocessor repeatedly samples the input line until it remains at the same logic value a fixed number of times in succession before interpreting the value as valid.

Another method of software debouncing is carried out by the subroutine PBCNT, which counts the number of times a pushbutton is pressed. The pushbutton output, wired as in Fig. 10.1-2, is connected to bit 7 of input port 0. The operation of the subroutine is flowcharted in Fig. 10.1-5, and the actual subroutine

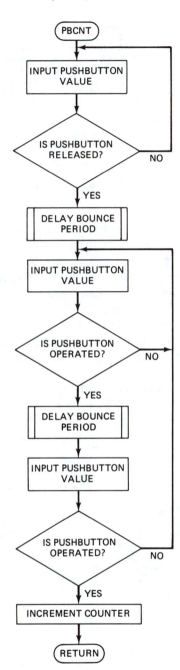

Figure 10.1-5 Flowchart of push-button debounce subroutine.

```
PBCNT:     IN PB          ;INPUT PUSHBUTTON OUTPUT
           ORA A          ;SET FLAGS
           JP PBCNT       ;IF BUTTON NOT RELEASED LOOP
           CALL DELAY     ;BUTTON RELEASED TIMEOUT BOUNCE
PBNP:      IN PB          ;INPUT PUSHBUTTON OUTPUT
           ORA A          ;CHECK FOR PUSHBUTTON PRESSED
           JM PBNP        ;IF PUSHBUTTON NOT PRESSED LOOP
           CALL DELAY     ;PUSHBUTTON PRESSED TIMEOUT BOUNCE
           IN PB          ;INPUT PUSHBUTTON OUTPUT
           ORA A          ;SET FLAGS
           JM PBNP        ;CHECK FOR ERRONEOUS SIGNAL TRANSITION
CLOSURE    INX D          ;PUSHBUTTON CLOSURE VERIFIED, INCREMENT COUNTER
           RET
```

Figure 10.1-6   Subroutine to debounce a mechanical switch.

appears in Fig. 10.1-6. The subroutine first checks that the pushbutton has been released; if not, it waits in a loop until it is released. The subroutine then waits a period of time in excess of the pushbutton's bounce by calling a delay subroutine, after which it waits in a second loop to detect the pressing of the button. When the button press is detected, a second delay is initiated, and the pushbutton's value is input and checked one more time to verify that the button was actually pressed—as opposed to a noise pulse having been detected.

Regardless of whether a switch is debounced by hardware or software, the microprocessor must sense the switch's output with sufficient regularity to detect its operation and release.

When several bits of data are provided to a microprocessor via mechanical switches, the data can be entered in parallel from a bank of single switches. Another

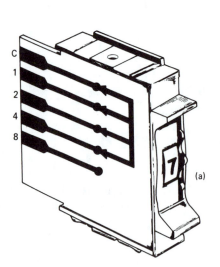

BCD, 1-POLE, 10-POSITION				
D I A L	COMMON C CONNECTED TO TERMINALS INDICATED			
	1	2	4	8
0				
1	●			
2		●		
3	●	●		
4			●	
5	●		●	
6		●	●	
7	●	●	●	
8				●
9	●			●

(a)

(b)

Figure 10.1-7   Thumbwheel switch: (a) pictorial; (b) truth table indicating which terminals are connected to common for each dial position.

method employs a rotary switch that mechanically generates a binary code representing the switch position. One type of rotary switch with this capability is the ***thumbwheel***. As shown in Fig. 10.1-7, a thumbwheel switch indicates the switch setting by a symbol on the wheel. The output of the switch is a parallel set of contact closures that provides a binary code corresponding to the switch position. Thumbwheel switches that provide a number of different binary output codes are readily available; ten-position thumbwheel switches with BCD coded outputs are commonly used for the entry of decimal data. These switches can be stacked (thus using minimal panel space) to accommodate several decades of input. Other commonly available codes include octal, hexadecimal, excess-3, and ten's complement.

10.1.2 Keypads and Keyboards

When manual entry of a large number of data symbols is essential, keyboards containing up to 100 pushbutton switches, or keys, are commonly used. The term "keypad" is applied to keyboards containing a small number of keys. In keypads and keyboards each key is associated with a particular symbol or binary value. When a key is pressed it generates a corresponding binary code. When the number of keys is less than or equal to 16, key closures are efficiently encoded into parallel data by using combinational circuitry. For example, an IC encoder, which encodes eight inputs, has a special output that is active if any one of its inputs is low. This output can be used by circuitry or software that debounces the encoder's output or can be latched and used to generate an interrupt, allowing the microprocessor to read the encoder's output. The 74LS148 priority encoder presented in Chapter 9 encodes eight contact closures into a 3-bit code, as shown in Fig. 10.1-8. The keys in Fig. 10.1-8 have one contact connected in common.

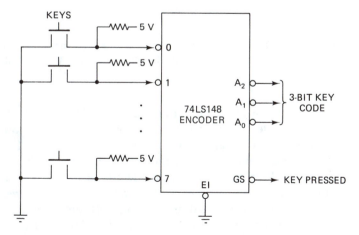

Figure 10.1-8   Use of a 74LS148 priority encoder to encode an eight-key keypad.

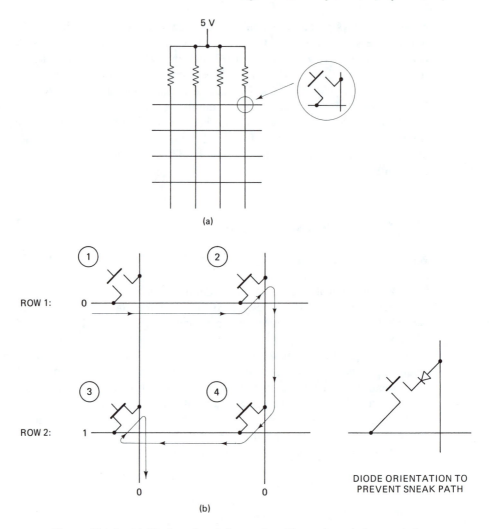

Figure 10.1-9 (a) Keyboard switch matrix; (b) sneak path in a switch matrix: key 1 appears pressed when keys 2, 3, and 4 are actually pressed.

As an alternative to the linear arrangement of keys in Fig. 10.1-8, keys can be arranged at the intersection of wires that form a matrix, as shown in Fig. 10.1-9a. This arrangement is advantageous when a large number of keys are involved because it allows a reduction in the amount of hardware for encoding. To determine that a key has been pressed, and to identify that key, the matrix is *scanned*. Associating a digital code with each key is referred to as *encoding* the keyboard.

The key matrix is scanned, using either software or hardware, by making all the rows of the matrix logic 0 and sensing the logic values of the columns. If one or more columns is logic 0, then one or more keys has been pressed. To encode the key, each horizontal wire is, in turn, made logic 0 with all other horizontal wires logic 1.

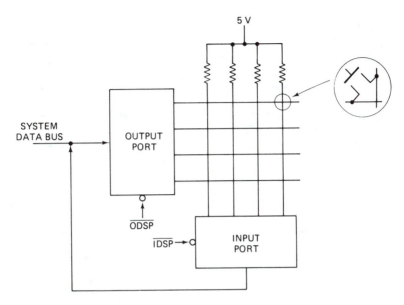

Figure 10.1-10   Hardware structure for software scanning of key matrix.

While a single horizontal wire is logic 0, each of the vertical wires is examined to see whether it is logic 0. When a vertical line is logic 0, the number of that line, together with the number of the logic 0 row, identifies the pressed key.

An example of the hardware used in key closure detection and key scanning with software is shown in Fig. 10.1-10. The rows of the key matrix are controlled by an output port, and its columns are sensed through an input port.

To preclude a key being pressed and released without detection, the software scan subroutine is called repetitively. In addition, the routine that calls the scan algorithm must provide debouncing and must distinguish between a single key being operated several times or simply being pressed and held for a long period of time.

Problems arise when two or more keys are depressed simultaneously. This situation is called *rollover*. In the previous scan algorithm, if rollover occurs, the value of the key returned depends on the order of detection by that subroutine and not on the order in which the keys are depressed.

To prevent the problems inherent in rollover, two methods are used: two-key and N-key rollover—both of which describe the manner in which the keyboard is scanned and key closures are accepted. Two-key rollover handles cases where two keys are pressed simultaneously. In *two-key rollover*, a key closure is accepted, provided all other keys are released. When a key is pressed, that closure is processed, and the keyboard is ignored until it is released. If a second key is pressed before the first is released, it will be recognized only after the first is released.

N-key rollover processes each key closure in the order in which it is detected in the scan, regardless of the status of all other keys. This mode of operation is used when data entry is rapid, and the operator may press a second and possibly a third key before releasing the first.

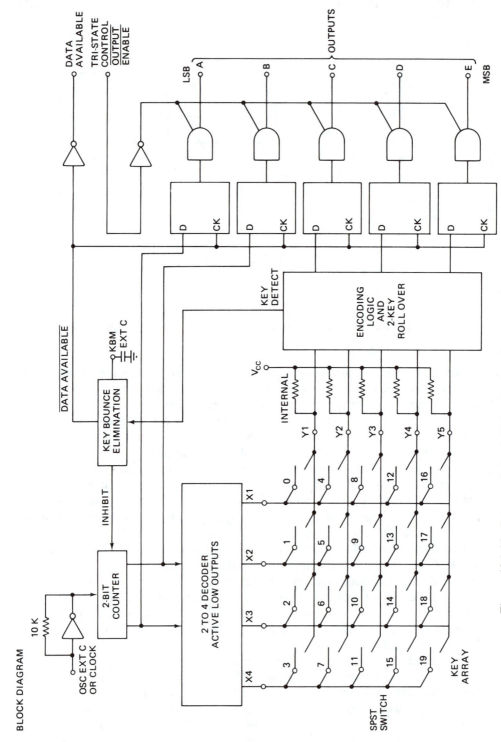

Figure 10.1-11 Integrated circuit 20-key keyboard scanner MM74C923. (Courtesy of National Semiconductor Corp.)

372

TRUTH TABLE

DATA OUT	SWITCH POSITION	0 Y1,X1	1 Y1,X2	2 Y1,X3	3 Y1,X4	4 Y2,X1	5 Y2,X2	6 Y2,X3	7 Y2,X4	8 Y3,X1	9 Y3,X2	10 Y3,X3	11 Y3,X4	12 Y4,X1	13 Y4,X2	14 Y4,X3	15 Y4,X4	16 Y5*,X1	17 Y5*,X2	18 Y5*,X3	19 Y5*,X4
	A	0	1	0	1	0	1	0	1	0	1	0	1	0	1	0	1	0	1	0	1
	B	0	0	1	1	0	0	1	1	0	0	1	1	0	0	1	1	0	0	1	1
	C	0	0	0	0	1	1	1	1	0	0	0	0	1	1	1	1	0	0	0	0
	D	0	0	0	0	0	0	0	0	1	1	1	1	1	1	1	1	0	0	0	0
	E*	0	0	0	0	0	0	0	0	0	0	0	0	0	0	0	0	1	1	1	1

Figure 10.1-11 Continued.

Implementation of N-key rollover requires additional components in the key matrix. As shown in Fig. 10.1-9a, each intersection of conductors in the matrix simply contains a switch between the row and column that electrically connects the two when closed. Consider the situation in Fig. 10.1-9b, where row 1 has been selected in the scan, and switches 2, 3, and 4 are pressed. There is an electrical path, called a *sneak path*, through switches 2-4-3, which makes column 1's output logic 0. Since row 1 is selected and column 1 is 0, it appears that switch 1 has been pressed when, in reality, it has not. A diode connected in series with each switch prevents sneak paths in the matrix.

For hardware scanning of a key matrix, LSI keyboard encoders are available that scan small and large keyswitch arrays and produce an encoded output corresponding to the key pressed. Typical devices handle 16, 20, 64, 78, and 90 key matrices. A single IC keyboard encoder, the MM74C923, is shown in Fig. 10.1-11. This device handles 20 SPST keys. A 2-bit counter and a two-to-four decoder scan the columns of the switch matrix. Scan frequency is set by an external oscillator or by a capacitor for the internal oscillator. Encoding logic senses the rows and detects key closure. Additional circuitry provides contact bounce elimination and two-key rollover. The debounce period can be set by an external capacitor. When a key closure is accepted, three bits from the encoding logic and two bits from the counter are latched into a 5-bit register by a data available signal that provides a high output as long as the accepted key remains pressed. When the key is released, the data available signal goes low even if another key is depressed. The data available signal goes high again after a debounced period to indicate the availability of new data for the second key.

Use of hardware eliminates the requirement that the microprocessor scan the keyboard constantly within a prescribed time interval. The data available signal interrupts the microprocessor, allowing keyboard scanning to take place concurrently with other microprocessor operations.

Larger keyboard scanners, such as MM5740 keyboard encoder, can scan a 90-key array at a rate controlled by an external clock.[1] Internal ring counters select rows and columns of the array for scanning. These counters also address an internal ROM that provides the code corresponding to the key position being scanned. If the key is pressed, the code is placed in a single character register and a data available signal is generated. That signal can interrupt a microprocessor. The keyboard encoder has three-state outputs controlled by an output enable input. That input enables the three-state buffers and places the encoded character on the data bus.

The keyboard encoder debounces key closures and provides a number of other features useful in modern keyboard design. The encoder's inputs and outputs are all TTL compatible. Versions of the MM5740 are available with the internal ROM programmed with the ASCII character set. Alternatively, the devices can be mask programmed with any desired character set.

---

[1]*Application Note AN-80 MOS Keyboard Encoding* (Santa Clara, Calif.: National Semiconductor Corp.).

10.1.3 Digital Potentiometers

A digital potentiometer is an optical incremental shaft encoder designed for applications where a hand-operated panel mounted encoder is required. Like other optical incremental encoders, it translates the rotation of a shaft into interruptions of a light beam that are then output as electrical pulses. Thus, a shaft encoder converts rotary mechanical motion directly to a digital output. Physically, the digital potentiometer looks like a common analog electrical potentiometer (see Fig. 10.1-12). It produces two TTL compatible digital waveforms as output. These waveforms, channel A and channel B, are in quadrature (a phase difference of 90 degrees). For clockwise (CW) shaft rotation of the device in Fig. 10.1-12, B leads A as shown in Fig. 10.1-13b. For counterclockwise (CCW) rotation, A leads B. The digital potentiometer shown produces 16 pulses for one complete revolution of its shaft. Other digital potentiometers are available that provide from 16 to 256 pulses per revolution.

A common use of a digital potentiometer in a microprocessor based system is to allow an operator to increment or decrement a parameter stored in memory. For example, CW rotation of the shaft might cause the parameter to be incremented and CCW rotation cause it to be decremented. Optical incremental shaft encoders are used in other operator and mechanical input devices. For example, a track ball input device uses two optical encoders to provide X and Y position information. Optical encoders are also used in a variety of mechanical motion and position sensing devices.

Internally each channel of the digital potentiometer consists of a light-emitting diode, LED, and two phototransistors or photodiodes. LEDs are discussed in detail

Figure 10.1-12 Digital potentiometer. (Courtesy of U.S. Digital Corp.)

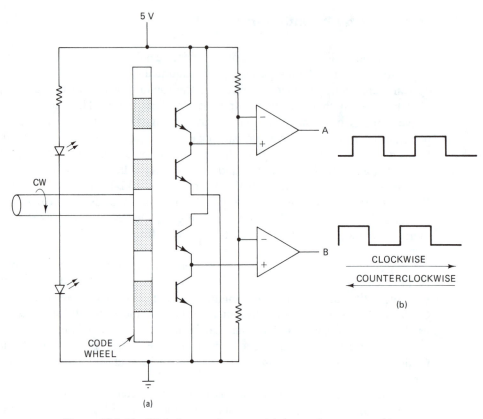

Figure 10.1-13 Digital potentiometer: (a) internal structure; (b) output waveforms.

in Section 10.2.1. These elements are arranged as shown in Fig. 10.1-13a. When light from the LED strikes a phototransistor, it conducts, i.e., is turned ON. When light is blocked from the phototransistor, it turns OFF. The phototransistors are separated from the LEDs by a code wheel that is connected to the shaft of the digital potentiometer. The code wheel is a metal disk with N equally spaced apertures around its circumference. The physical positioning of each LED and phototransistor pair is such that as the disk is rotated one transistor in the pair and then the other is exposed to light from the LED. When one transistor in the pair is fully exposed, the other transistor is fully blocked. The output from a phototransistor pair is input to an analog comparator that compares it with a reference voltage level. The output from the comparator is a signal with TTL logic levels. Each pair of phototransistors creates a square wave, as shown in Fig. 10.1-13b, as the shaft is rotated. The relative positioning of the two transistor pairs creates two square waves with a phase difference of 90 degrees.

An interface of the digital potentiometer to a microprocessor system bus, for polled operation, is shown in Fig. 10.1-14a. With polled operation, the micro-

NEW BA	OLD BA	COMPOSITE	ROTATION
10	00	08H	CW
11	10	0EH	CW
01	11	07H	CW
00	01	01H	CW
01	00	04H	CCW
11	01	0DH	CCW
10	11	0BH	CCW
00	10	02H	CCW

Figure 10.1-14a Determination of rotation direction from new and old values of B and A from digital potentiometer.

```
DPOT      EQU    00H
INITDP:   IN DPOT            ;GET INITIAL POSITION STATUS
          ANI 03H            ;MASK
          STA STATUS         ;SAVE
POLLDP:   LDA STATUS         ;GET OLD POSITION STATUS
          MOV B,A            ;SAVE IN B
          IN DPOT            ;GET NEW POSITION
          ANI 03H            ;MASK
          CMP B              ;IF NEW POSITION IS SAME AS OLD RETURN
          RZ
          STA STATUS         ;UPDATE OLD POSITION STATUS
          RLC                ;CREATE COMPOSITE POSITION STATUS
          RLC
          ORA B
          LXI H, PARAM       ;POINTER TO PARAMETER IN MEMORY
          CPI 08H            ;CHECK COMPOSITE POSITION STATUS AGAINST
          JZ INCR            ;COMPOSITE CODES FOR CW ROTATION
          CPI 0EH
          JZ INCR
          CPI 07H
          JZ INCR
          CPI 01H
          JZ INCR
          DCR M              ;POSITION STATUS IS FOR CCW ROTATION
          RET                ;DECREMENT PARAMETER AND RETURN
INCR:     INR M              ;INCREMENT PARAMETER
          RET
STATUS:   DS 1               ;POSITION STATUS
PARAM:    DS 1               ;PARAMETER
          END
```

Figure 10.1-14b Subroutine to poll digital potentiometer.

processor must continually input A and B to detect a change in the shaft's position. Once a change is detected, a determination must be made as to whether the shaft rotation is CW or CCW.

The program in Fig. 10.1-14b handles the digital potentiometer for polled operation. The routine INITDP initializes a memory location with the positional

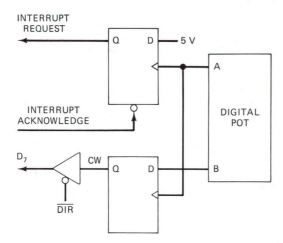

Figure 10.1-15 Interrupt interface of digital potentiometer to microprocessor system bus.

status of the digital potentiometer at power ON. The positional status is simply the values of A and B from the digital potentiometer. The subroutine POLLDP is called to poll the digital potentiometer. This subroutine inputs the values of A and B and compares them with the old values of A and B. If they are the same, the shaft has not been rotated and the subroutine is exited.

If the new values of A and B differ from the previous values, it must be determined whether the rotation of the shaft is CW or CCW. This is done by creating a composite positional status byte that consists of the new values of A and B as bits 3 and 2 and the old values of A and B as bits 1 and 0. This value is compared with the four composite codes that correspond to CW rotation. If the composite positional status corresponds to one of these values, a memory location, PARAM, is incremented; if not, it is decremented.

Figure 10.1-15 is an interrupt interface of the digital potentiometer to the microprocessor system bus. The rising edge of A sets the interrupt request flip-flop. In addition, this edge is used to clock a second flip-flop that stores the value of B. The interrupt service subroutine clears the service request flip-flop and reads the direction flip-flop to determine whether the shaft was being rotated CW or CCW when the interrupt occurred.

In either of the previous interface approaches the amount that the parameter is incremented for, each pulse from A is fixed. For fine tuning a parameter, this is very efficient. However, if the parameter must be changed by a large amount, many turns of the shaft would be required. This problem can be solved by making the amount that the parameter is incremented a function of the angular velocity of the shaft. This can be accomplished by measuring the time between successive A pulses. When the time between the A pulses is short, the velocity is high, and the parameter is changed by a large value. If the time between pulses is long, the velocity is low, and the parameter is changed by a small value. The time between pulses can be measured using software timing loops. Alternatively, this time can be measured using hardware such as the 8254 Programmable Interval Timer.

10.2 DISPLAYS

Information displays for microprocessor systems range from simple annunciators (ON-OFF lights) to alphanumeric displays such as cathode ray tubes (CRTs). A wide range of technologies is used to implement these display devices and, also, to control such devices. The two most common classes of displays use light-emitting diodes (LEDs) and cathode ray tubes.

10.2.1 LED Displays

The most common and simplest display device used with IC logic is the *light-emitting diode, LED*. LEDs are solid state devices, p-n junctions, which emit light energy when stimulated by a low voltage direct current. LEDs can be designed to emit light from ultraviolet, through the visible spectrum, to infrared. The most efficient LED is in the visible spectrum and emits red light; it is the most commonly used for LED displays. Amber and green LEDs are also available.

LEDs are popular display devices for many reasons. Because they can be operated from low voltages, they are compatible with systems that use integrated circuits. They are small, lightweight, and mechanically rugged. As solid state devices, they are highly reliable and have a typical operating life of more than 100,000 hours. LEDs are available as single devices or packaged together in various arrangements and are designed for displaying binary, numeric, and alphanumeric information.

The circuit symbol for an LED is shown in Fig. 10.2-1. The LED emits light when forward biased, and the intensity of the light is a function of the forward current through the LED. The voltage drop of a forward biased LED is essentially fixed, typically 1.6 or 2.4 V. When driven as shown in Fig. 10.2-1, a resistor limits the current to the desired value. For DC operation, the nominal operating current is typically 20 mA for red LEDs and 25 mA for amber and green.

In general, the output of most logic circuits cannot directly drive an LED at rated current because they can't sink 20 to 25 mA. For example, a standard

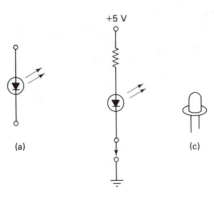

(a)

(b)

(c)

Figure 10.2-1 Light-emitting diode, LED: (a) circuit symbol; (b) drive circuit using a mechanical switch and current limiting resistor; (c) actual diode.

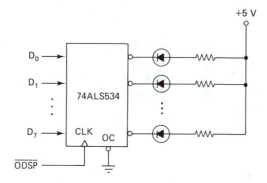

Figure 10.2-2 Using a 74ALS534 Octal D-type flip-flop to directly drive LEDs.

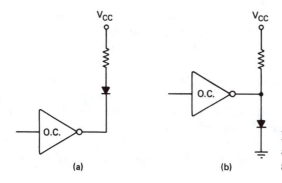

Figure 10.2-3 Driving a LED with an open collector inverter: (a) series switching: (b) shunt switching.

74ALSXXX series device can only sink 8 mA. However, some with output buffers, like the 74ALS534, can sink 24 mAs (see Fig. 10.2-2). Logic circuits with open collector outputs can drive an LED by using series or shunt switching, as shown in Fig. 10.2.3. The series switching configuration dissipates less power when the LED is OFF.

10.2.1.1 Seven Segment Displays

Decimal digits and some letters of the alphabet can be displayed by using seven segments in the font (arrangement) shown in Fig. 10.2-4. Seven segment LED displays use an LED (or sometimes two) for each segment; they are represented in Fig. 10.2-5. Here there are two variations of seven segment displays. In one all of the anodes are connected in common; in the other all of the cathodes are connected

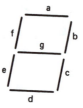

Figure 10.2-4 Seven segment display format.

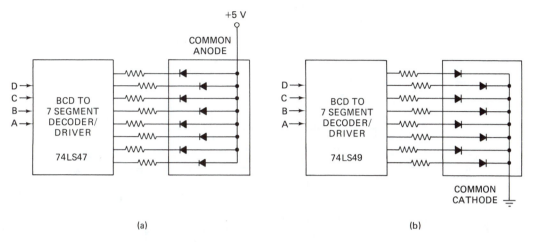

Figure 10.2-5   Driving seven segment LED displays from BCD inputs, using decoder drivers: (a) common anode circuit; (b) common cathode circuit.

in common. These variations require different drive arrangements. Each segment can be driven with 1 bit of an output port, as shown in Fig. 10.2-2, or decoder-driver ICs can be used.

BCD-to-seven segment and hex-to-seven segment decoder drivers are available for driving seven segment displays. Figure 10.2-5 shows the connection of a common anode and common cathode seven segment display to appropriate drivers. In one the anode is connected to the 5 V supply, and a logic 0 decoder-driver output turns a segment ON. In the other, the cathodes are connected to ground. In this case, a logic 1 decoder-driver output turns a segment ON.

10.2.1.2 Multiplexed Displays

To display a small number of digits each segment can be directly driven from an output port or by a decoder driver connected to an output port. In this arrangement, however, since each digit requires its own port and/or decoder driver, the number of ports and drivers increases in direct proportion to the number of display digits.

Multiplexing techniques allow one set of decoding and driving circuitry to be shared among the digits in a display. A six-digit multiplexed display is illustrated in Fig. 10.2-6. The microprocessor activates each digit, in turn. First, it loads the segment data for digit 1 into the segment output port. Then it loads the digit select output port with a value that makes the output connected to digit-driver number 1 logic 0, turning on the first digit of the display. Loading the digit select port also fires the single shot, which is set to a time interval equal to the period of time each single digit in the display is turned ON. When the single shot times out, it sets the interrupt request flip-flop, interrupting the microprocessor. The interrupt service subroutine first turns OFF all digit drivers. Then it sets the segment data for the

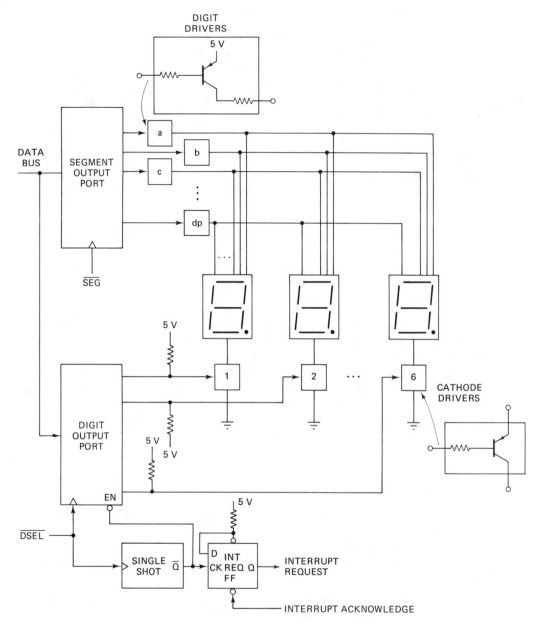

Figure 10.2-6 Six-digit multiplexed LED display.

next digit, outputs it to the segment port, and turns ON the corresponding digit driver by outputting the proper code to the digit select port. After the last digit in the display has been turned ON, the procedure is repeated, starting with the first digit. Each digit is turned ON, or *refreshed*, at a frequency called the *refresh rate*. If a digit is refreshed often enough, it appears to the human eye to be constantly ON. The minimum practical refresh rate is usually 100 Hz. Typically, multiplexed

```
DMAX:   EQU 6
MSDPY:  PUSH B          ;SAVE STATUS
        PUSH D
        PUSH H
        PUSH PSW
        XRA A           ;TURN OFF DISPLAY
        CMA
        OUT DSEL
        LDA DIGIT       ;GET NUMBER OF LAST DIGIT TURNED ON
        CPI DMAX        ;COMPUTE NEXT DIGIT TO BE TURNED ON
        JNZ MDSP1
        XRA A
MDSP1:  INR A
        STA DIGIT       ;SAVE DIGIT NUMBER
        MOV E,A
        MVI D,0
        LXI H,STBLE     ;COMPUTE TABLE ENTRY ADDRESS FOR DIGIT PATTERN
        DAD D
        MOV A,M         ;GET SEGMENT PATTERN
        OUT SEG         ;OUTPUT SEGMENT PATTERN
        MVI A,0FEH      ;COMPUTE DIGIT SELECT PORT BIT PATTERN
MDSP2:  DCR E
        JZ MDSP3
        RLC
        JMP MDSP2
MDSP3:  OUT DSEL        ;TURN ON SELECTED DIGIT
        POP PSW         ;RESTORE STATUS
        POP H
        POP D
        POP B
        EI              ;ENABLE INTERRUPT
        RET             ;RETURN
        .
        .
        .
DIGIT:  DS 1            ;LAST DIGIT TURNED ON
STBLE:  DS 6            ;SEGMENT BUFFER
```

Figure 10.2-7 Multiplexed display driver subroutines.

displays are refreshed at 1 kHz, or higher [1]. For N digits refreshed at f Hz, the maximum ON time, t_p, for each digit is

$$t_p = \frac{1}{fN}$$

The **duty factor** for a single digit—the ratio of the time that the digit is ON with respect to the refresh period—is $1/N$. Therefore, not only is multiplexing efficient in terms of decoding and driving circuitry, it is also the most efficient way of operating an LED. Strobing an LED at a high peak current and low duty factor provides greater light output than DC drive for a given average power dissipation. The service subroutine for the display of Fig. 10.2-6 is shown in Fig. 10.2-7.

The peak segment currents allowable when a display is multiplexed exceed the average allowable currents. Thus, if a digit is left ON for an extended period of time, it is damaged. To avoid damage, in the event that some system failure prevents the timely updating of the display, the output from the single shot also enables the digit select port's output buffers. The outputs are pulled up to logic 1 values by the pull up resistors shown in Fig. 10.2-6. When the single shot times out, all digits turn OFF, providing the desired safeguard.

10.2.2 ICM7218B Multiplexed Eight-Digit Display Driver

Implementation of a multiplexed display is significantly simplified by use of a single-chip display driver. The Intersil ICM7218 series of CMOS eight-digit display drivers includes devices to handle common anode (A, C, and E versions) and common cathode (B and D versions) seven segment LEDs. Each device in the series contains the digit drivers, segment drivers, and all multiplex scan circuitry. The ICM7218 devices also contain an 8×8 SRAM. The microprocessor simply writes the information to be displayed to the ICM7218's SRAM. The ICM7218's internal multiplex scan circuitry multiplexes the information from its SRAM to the LED digits. Information is written to the A and B versions of the ICM7218 in byte serial form. These versions have no address inputs to select specific locations in the 8×8 SRAM. Thus, to change the information displayed by a single digit, the information for all eight digits must be written to the driver. The C, D, and E versions are random access; the information displayed by a single digit is changed simply by writing the location in the SRAM associated with that digit.

The ICM7218B and its interface to a microprocessor system bus is shown in Fig. 10.2-8a. Inputs ID_0–ID_7 are driven from the data bus. The control input, MODE, selects the ICM7218B's control register or a register in its SRAM to be written when a write pulse occurs at $\overline{\text{WRITE}}$. To change the information displayed, a control byte is written followed by 8 data bytes (see Fig. 10.2-8b). The first data byte written corresponds to digit 0 of the display and the last corresponds to digit 7.

The control word (see Fig. 10.2-9) uses bit 7 to indicate that data will be written following the control word. Bits 6 and 5 specify how the ICM7218B will use the data in the SRAM to control the segments in each digit. There are two decode formats, Hexa Code and Code B. These codes use the least significant 4 bits of a data byte to encode the information to be displayed. Hexa Code is the common hexadecimal code. Code B encodes the ten decimal digits plus six special characters. If bit 5 is 0, the decode format will be selected by bit 6. If bit 5 is 1, no decode is selected. With no decode, each bit in a byte directly controls a segment. The association of bits with segments in the display is shown in Fig. 10.2-9. Note that the decimal point is turned ON by a 0, all other segments are turned ON by 1s. Since the no decode option allows segments to be directly controlled, it is possible for the display to contain a mix of seven segment digits and annunciators. The annunciators are simply assigned, as segments of a digit and controlled independently. When bit 4 is 0 the display is shut down to save power. However, the data in the ICM7218's SRAM is maintained.

The outputs of the ICM7218B consist of eight segment strobes and eight digit strobes. These lines are connected directly to the appropriate pins of the seven segment displays.

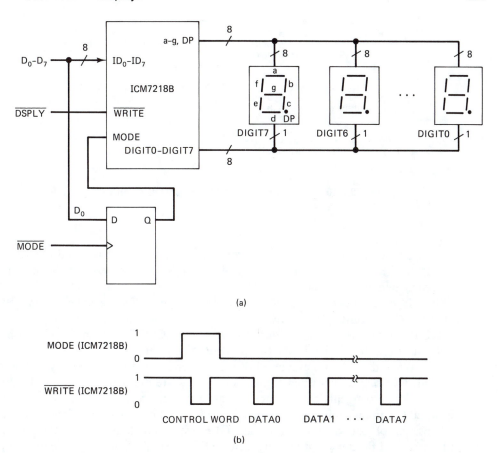

(a)

(b)

Figure 10.2-8 ICM 7218B: (a) interface to microprocessor system bus; (b) control and data byte sequencing.

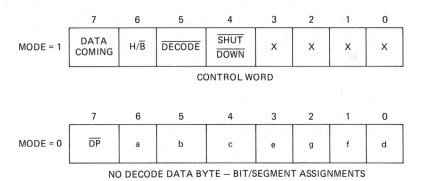

Figure 10.2-9 Control word and no decode data byte bit assignments.

```
UPDATE:  MVI  A,01H     ;SET MODE FF
         OUT  MODE
         MVI  A,0F0H    ;OUTPUT COMMAND TO 7218B
         OUT  DSPLY
         MVI  A,00H     ;CLEAR MODE FF
         OUT  MODE
         MVI  C,8       ;TRANSFER DSPLYI to 7218B
         LXI  H,DSPLYI
UPD1:    MOV  A,M
         OUT  DSPLY
         INX  H
         DCR  C
         JNZ  UPD1
         RET
```

Figure 10.2-10 Subroutine to transfer contents of display image buffer to ICM7218B's SRAM.

One approach to software control of the display is to have an 8-byte display image buffer in the microprocessor system's RWM. The contents of this buffer are manipulated by software to create the bit patterns desired in the ICM7218B's SRAM. After the contents of the display image buffer have been changed, a subroutine is called to update the display. The subroutine, UPDATE, in Fig. 10.2-10, writes the necessary control word to the ICM7218B then transfers 8 bytes of data from the display image buffer, DSPLYI, to the ICM7218B.

When digits in a multiplexed display are controlled by hardware ghosting can occur. *Ghosting* occurs when segments in a digit are dimly lit when they should be OFF. These segments correspond to segments that are to be lit in the next digit turned ON in the multiplexing sequence. This problem is the result of the digit-driver transistor of one digit being turned OFF while simultaneously the digit-driver transistor of the next digit is being turned ON. Since transistors are able to turn ON faster than they can turn OFF, the digit turning OFF starts to display the segment information for the digit turning ON. Ghosting is prevented by having the multiplexing hardware provide a short period of time between digits being turned ON where all digits are OFF. This time is called the *interdigit blanking time*, t_b. The ICM7218B provides an interdigit blanking time of 10 μS. The digit ON time, t_p, is 500 μS. Thus, the refresh period is 8×510 μs = 4.08 mS, and the refresh frequency is 250 Hz.

10.2.3 CRT Displays

A CRT display provides the lowest cost per character when a large number of characters is involved. It uses a cathode ray tube (CRT) to display alphanumeric or graphic information. The CRT generates an electron beam that, when it strikes the phosphor on the face of the CRT, creates a dot of light. Voltages applied to two sets of inputs control the X and Y coordinates of the position at which the beam strikes the CRT face. A third input to the CRT controls the intensity of the light emitted.

The CRT tube, combined with the electronics that control the position of the electron beam and its intensity, comprise a *monitor* (see Fig. 10.2-11). The monitor

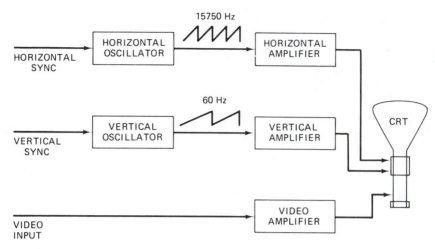

Figure 10.2-11   CRT monitor.

electronics include both horizontal and vertical oscillators that provide ramp outputs. These outputs are amplified by horizontal and vertical amplifiers, respectively. The output voltage from the horizontal amplifier sweeps the beam from left to right across the screen and then back. The sweep from left to right is called the ***horizontal sweep***. The return sweep from right to left is called the ***horizontal retrace***. The vertical amplifier output sweeps the beam from the top to the bottom of the screen and then back. The sweep from top to bottom is the ***vertical sweep***, and the sweep from bottom to top is called the ***vertical retrace***. The electron beam is turned OFF during the horizontal and vertical retraces. The combined action of these two oscillators controlling the CRT beam's position creates a pattern of lines called a ***raster*** (Fig. 10.2-12). Because the horizontal oscillator is run at a higher frequency (typically 15.75 kHz) than the vertical oscillator (typically 60 Hz), the raster consists of a number of horizontal lines if the beam is turned ON for the duration of each horizontal sweep. Each complete sweep of the raster scan from the upper lefthand corner to the lower righthand corner and back is called a ***frame***.

The oscillators that provide the ramp outputs for sweeping the beam's position are usually free running, but they must be synchronized by external signals to provide the raster scan. Low cost CRT monitors have inputs for horizontal and vertical sync pulses. A third input to the monitor, the video input, is amplified by the monitor's video amplifier and controls the intensity of the dot produced by the electron beam. Other monitors accept a composite video signal, which combines the horizontal sync, vertical sync, and video input into a single signal. Circuitry within these monitors separates the composite video signal into its components.

Patterns are made on the CRT screen by turning the beam ON and OFF during the horizontal sweep. Alphanumeric characters are created with dot-matrix patterns. A basic 5×7 dot-matrix character representation on a CRT includes an extra column on the left and right for spacing between characters, as shown in Fig. 10.2-13. An extra row beneath the character can also be reserved for an underline or

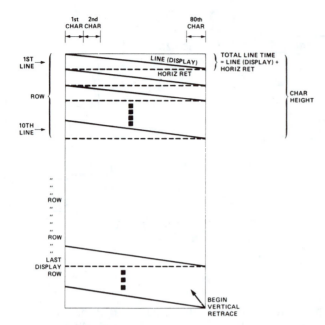

Figure 10.2-12 CRT raster scan. (Courtesy of Intel Corp.)

cursor, and an additional row on the top and bottom for spacing between rows. The final matrix size, then, for this configuration is 7×10.

Each horizontal scan supplies the dots of one line of all the characters on a single character row of the display, as shown in Fig. 10.2-14. In addition to synchronizing the start of the horizontal and vertical traces, circuitry that controls the monitor also supplies the serial video signal which represents the sequence of dots for each horizontal sweep. This signal is the input to the video amplifier of the monitor. The video amplifier output turns the beam ON and OFF to create the required stream of dots for a scan line.

In microprocessor systems, the characters to be displayed on the CRT are stored in 7-bit ASCII code in a reserved block of RWM called, appropriately, the *display memory*. The display memory must contain as many words as character positions in the display format.

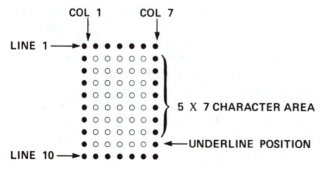

Figure 10.2-13 5×7 dot-matrix character representation.

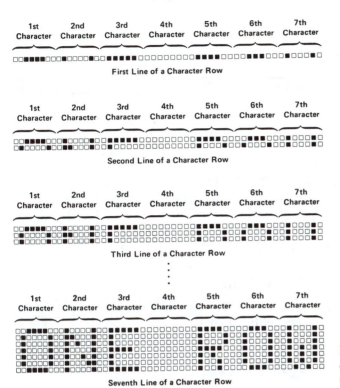

Figure 10.2-14 Single character row of a CRT display. (Courtesy of Intel Corp.)

A block diagram of the hardware interface between a video monitor and a microprocessor system is shown in Fig. 10.2-15. Primarily this interface refreshes the CRT screen by the periodic transfer of information from the display memory to the screen. The displayed information must be written into the screen repetitively, and the process is known as refreshing the screen. The refresh rate is typically 60 Hz, in order to prevent flicker.

There are a number of programmable LSI CRT controllers on the market, including the Intel 8275. See Fig. 10.2-16 [2]. This device sets screen and character formats by the parameters of commands sent to the controller at its initialization. These parameters specify the number of characters per row, the number of rows per frame, the character matrix size, and other attributes of the display.

To write a frame of information to the display, the 8275 requests a DMA operation to transfer one row of ASCII characters from the display memory to one of the 8275's row buffers before the frame begins. When the first horizontal sweep is started, the character codes are output to the character generator in sequence. A character counter, driven by a character clock from the dot generation circuitry, keeps track of the character being displayed. The character code forms the most significant bits of the character generator ROM's address. The least significant bits of the address come from the line counter in the 8275. Each word in the character

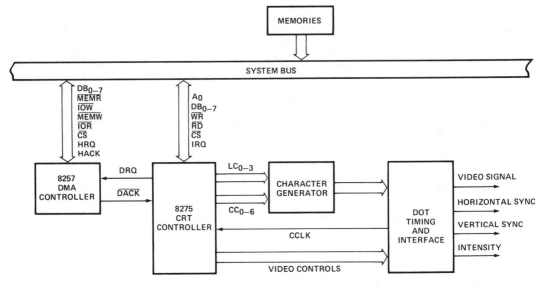

Figure 10.2-15 Block diagram of interface between microprocessor system memory and a CRT monitor. (Courtesy of Intel Corp.)

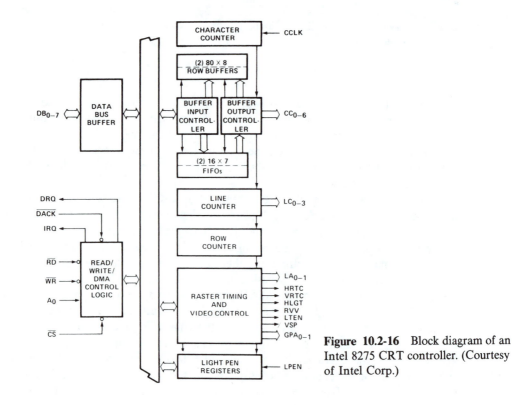

Figure 10.2-16 Block diagram of an Intel 8275 CRT controller. (Courtesy of Intel Corp.)

generator ROM contains the dot pattern for a single line of a single character. The 8275 holds the line count fixed while outputting the character codes during each horizontal sweep. During the horizontal retrace, the line counter is incremented, and the entire row of character codes is output again during the next sweep.

The character generator ROM outputs a 7-bit code corresponding to the line of the particular character being addressed. This code is the dot pattern for that line. The dot timing and interface circuitry converts the parallel dot pattern to a serial signal that controls the video signal. Thus, the video signal for a horizontal sweep corresponds to a serial version of the dot patterns for a single line of an entire character row.

At the initiation of the first horizontal sweep of a character row, a DMA operation is requested by the 8275 to fill the second of its two row buffers with the ASCII codes for the next row of characters to be displayed.

After all the lines of the character row being displayed have been scanned, the roles of the two row buffers are reversed. The most recently filled buffer now drives the display with the next character row. The recently displayed buffer is then filled with the next row of characters from the display memory via a DMA operation. With two buffers DMA operations obtain the data for the next character row from the display memory while concurrently outputting character data to the display for the present character row. Thus, the necessary speed requirements for refreshing the CRT are met.

This role reversal of the row buffers continues until all the character rows have been displayed. At the end of the frame, the 8275 interrupts the microprocessor and requests reinitialization of the DMA controller for the next frame.

For data entry, software maintains pointers to the display memory that define the location of a character on the screen and the cursor position. When a character is input from a device such as a keyboard, these pointers store it in the appropriate display memory location. Operations such as scrolling the display are carried out in software by changing the value of a pointer to the top of the display memory buffer. This value is used when the DMA controller is reinitialized at the completion of a frame.

The 8275 is also equipped with a light pen input and light pen registers. A light pen contains a light sensor that is activated by a microswitch when the pen is pressed against the face of the CRT. As the light beam strikes the sensor, the pen outputs a logic signal that can be input to the 8275. At this signal, the 8275 stores the row and character positions in the light pen register. These registers can be read under software control, thus identifying the position of the character pointed to by the operator.

10.3 PRINTERS

Printers produce hard copy output and vary widely in terms of product type and performance. They are classified either as serial or line. *Serial printers* print a single character at a time, while *line printers* print a group of characters simultaneously. Actually, printing only appears to be simultaneous because the groups of characters

Figure 10.3-1   LRC 7040 printer, shown with optional paper handling mechanism. (Courtesy of LRC, Inc.)

on a single line are printed so quickly. The method of character generation also categorizes printers either as impact or nonimpact. *Impact printers* strike the medium with the printing element to form a character. *Nonimpact printers* generally use thermal or electrostatic techniques that do not require impact. Character formation techniques provide yet another way to classify printers. *Character printers* use fully formed characters, whereas *matrix printers* use combinations of either dots or lines to form complete characters.

Serial dot-matrix impact printers are particularly applicable for low cost microprocessor systems. These printers provide low to medium range printing rates of 30 to 330 characters per second. For example, the LRC 7040 is a dot-matrix impact printer [3] (see Fig. 10.3-1). The print element consists of seven solenoids and print wires. The solenoids are arranged in a circle; however, the print wires driven by the solenoids are arranged in a column at the point where they impact the ribbon and paper. The printing element is driven across the paper via a spirally grooved plastic drum, which is, in turn, driven by a synchronous AC motor. The design is such that the printing element travels across the paper at a constant speed of 10.75 inches per second. The timing diagram for the LRC 7040 is shown in Fig. 10.3-2.

In its simplest configuration, the LRC 7040 has eight inputs. Seven control the seven print solenoids, and the eighth turns the main drive motor ON or OFF. To print a line, the main drive motor is turned ON. To control the solenoids with TTL logic levels, solenoid drivers are required that take TTL logic inputs and drive the

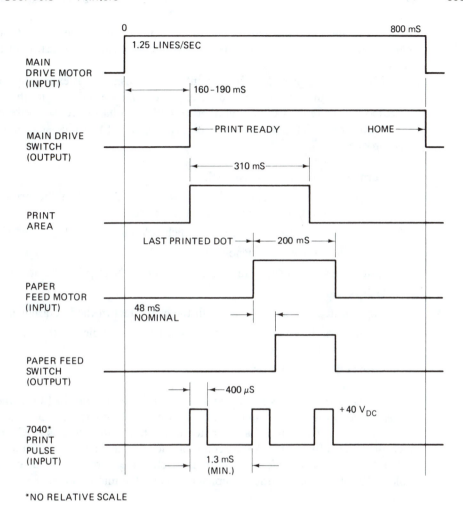

*NO RELATIVE SCALE

Figure 10.3-2   LRC 7040 printer timing diagram. (Courtesy of LRC, Inc.)

inductive load of the solenoid with the proper current levels. A motor driver is also required to allow a TTL level to control the AC line power to the synchronous motor.

A microswitch (main drive switch or home switch) output from the printer indicates when the printhead has reached the lefthand margin of the print area. At that point, printing can begin. Characters are printed when external circuitry pulses the solenoids. The printable area is 3 1/3 inches wide, and thus the print element transverses the print area in 310 mS. The maximum rate at which the solenoids can be pulsed is once every 1.3 mS. If a 5 × 7 dot matrix is used for character formation with a one column space between characters, a maximum of 40 characters can be typed on a line. The main drive motor is kept ON until the main drive switch changes state again, indicating that the printing element has returned to its home position.

Thus, the 7040 provides a basic printer mechanism that is externally controlled by methods ranging from direct control by the microprocessor to the use of a dedicated hardware controller—another example of a hardware/software trade-off.

With direct microprocessor control, printing a line is a nine-step process. The microprocessor

1. Turns the main motor drive ON.
2. Samples the input from the home switch to detect when the printhead has reached the lefthand margin of the print area.
3. Outputs a byte of data specifying which solenoids are to be turned ON.
4. Turns on the selected solenoids for 400 μS.
5. Determines which solenoids are to be turned ON to print the next column.
6. Delays 900 μS.
7. Repeats steps 3 through 6 until all the characters in the line are printed.
8. Samples the input from the home switch until it indicates that the printhead has returned to its home position.
9. Turns OFF the main drive.

To carry out these steps using a minimum amount of hardware, the microprocessor polls the home switch and uses software delays to time out the 400 and 900 μS intervals. To print a character stored in a buffer in RWM as ASCII code, the microprocessor obtains the ASCII code for each character from the buffer, in turn, and obtains bit patterns for the columns of characters from a character generator table in ROM. These activities completely occupy the microprocessor while it prints a line.

If, however, the home switch interrupts the microprocessor and a programmable timer times out the necessary delays and interrupts the microprocessor, a much smaller percentage of the microprocessor's time is required to control the printer, and concurrent processing is possible. The smallest amount of processor time is taken up when a dedicated hardware controller is used. Several LSI single-chip controllers are available for the LRC 7040 printer: the Intel 8295, the Rockwell RC7000, and the Cybernetic Micro Systems CY480.

These controllers are similar in overall function to the Intel 8295. This dot-matrix printer controller, a 40-pin IC, allows serial or parallel transfer of commands and data from the microprocessor to the printer controller. Commands set the format of characters to be printed and control other printer operations such as tab, line feed, and carriage return. The controller also contains a 40-character buffer. When the buffer is full or a carriage return is received, a line is printed. The controller also contains the character generator ROM and provides the solenoid drive outputs along with a properly timed strobe for the solenoids.

REFERENCES

1. Applications Engineering Staff, Hewlett Packard Optoelectronics Division, *Optoelectronics Application Manual* (New York: McGraw-Hill, 1977).

2. *Microsystems Components Handbook* (Santa Clara, Calif.: Intel Corporation, 1986).

3. *LRC Model 7040 Printer Manual* (Riverton, Wyo.: LRC, Inc., n.d.).

PROBLEMS

10-1. Design the hardware interface and write a program for a microprocessor system that measures the contact bounce (in milliseconds) of single-pole/single-throw switches. Both the operate and release contact bounce times should be measured and each displayed on two two-digit seven-segment displays.

10-2. Analyze the cross-coupled RS latch of Fig. 10.1-4 for any input waveform such as that shown in Fig. 10.1-3. Verify that it debounces a single-pole/double-throw mechanical switch.

10-3. A momentary contact switch is used to count events that correspond to the operation of the switch. The switch's output must clock an 8-bit counter each time the switch is released. The counter must be incremented by one for each operation of the switch. The counter is a 74ALSxxx device that counts positive edges. The counter's output is read by the microprocessor through an input port. Draw the block diagram for the interface using isolated I/O. Include any required component values and show their computation. Use 74ALSxxx devices for any required logic. Should the momentary contact switch be SPST or SPDT?

10-4. Two 74LS148 priority encoders and a quad two-input NAND gate can be used to encode the 16 keys of a keypad that has one terminal of each key connected in common. Determine the logic diagram that will accomplish this.

10-5. A four-digit BCD thumbwheel switch is used to enter a control parameter into a microprocessor system while the system is running. Write a subroutine that, when called, checks the BCD switch outputs and updates, if necessary, the value of the control parameter in reserved memory. Assume that the subroutine is called approximately once every 30 seconds. Consider the time required for an operator to alter the value of all four thumbwheel switches before designing a solution.

10-6. Write a subroutine, SCAN, that, when called, scans a 16-key keypad similar to the keypad of Fig. 10.1-10. The subroutine should first detect whether any switch is closed, and, if not, return immediately. If one or more switches are closed, the subroutine should return with the code for the switch or switches in the accumulator.

10-7. Draw the flowchart of a subroutine that scans the keyboard of Fig. 10.1-10 providing two-key rollover. Assume that the subroutine is called less often than the contact bounce period for the key switches used.

10-8. The 74C922 16-key encoder has a DATA AVAILABLE output that makes a 0 to 1 transition when a key is pressed. This signal remains logic 1 until the key is released. An interrupt driven system uses this output to interrupt an 8085A microprocessor via the RST7.5 input. The actual keycode is input through input port KEYSW. Write the sequence of all instructions required in order that the interrupt from the 74C922 can be used. Assume that all other RST interrupts are to be disabled. Write the framework of the service subroutine that services the 74C922. All the necessary instructions are to be shown excluding the actual operations on the data input. However, assume that the operations on the input data modify the contents of the 8085A's general purpose registers. The inputting of the data should be included. Interrupts are not to be nested. Also provide the assembler directive(s) to locate the service subroutine properly in memory.

10-9. A digital potentiometer is to be used with an 8085A in an application where it must interrupt the microprocessor. The RST7.5 interrupt input is to be used. Information indicating the direction of rotation is to be input through the SID input. The service subroutine must increment or decrement the reserved word PARAM. PARAM will be incremented or decremented by one for each interrupt. For clockwise rotation PARAM will be incremented by one; for counterclockwise rotation it will be decremented by one. Output B, of the digital pot, leads output A for clockwise rotation. Draw the logic diagram of the hardware required to interface the digital pot to the 8085A. Write the sequence of instructions in the main program required to enable the interrupt. Write the service subroutine that modifies PARAM as required.

10-10. A control program requires a subroutine LMTSW that scans an 8×8 matrix of limit switches and places an image of the state of each switch in an 8-byte buffer in memory. A parameter is passed to the subroutine in HL, which is a pointer to the beginning of the buffer in memory. The hardware consists of 8-bit output port connected to the rows of the matrix and an 8-bit input port connected to the columns. The top row is connected to bit D_0 of the output port and the right-most column is connected to bit D_0 of the input port. The rows are driven and the columns sensed. The columns have pull-up resistors, and each switch has an isolation diode. Flowchart the subroutine and write the program.

10-11. A common anode seven-segment display is to be directly driven by a 74ALS574 and used to display hexadecimal digits. Diagram the interconnection of the seven-segment display to the 74ALS574. Segments a through g should be driven by bits D_6 to D_0 latched from the data bus. Determine the bit pattern required to display each of the hexadecimal digits.

10-12. An eight-digit multiplexed display is software driven. The display is refreshed at 100 Hz. The display interrupts the microprocessor when it requires service. The interrupt service subroutine requires 60 μS to execute. What is the ON time for each digit? What percentage of time is the microprocessor devoted to servicing the display? At what rate must the display interrupt the microprocessor? What is the duty factor for a digit being ON?

10-13. An eight-digit, multiplexed, seven-segment display is to be refreshed at a refresh rate of 250 Hz. The display is software driven with the segments controlled by an output port, SEG, and the digits controlled by an output port, DIG. Draw the logic diagram and write the initialization routine to use an 8254 to interrupt the microprocessor each time a new digit must be turned on. Assume RST 5.5 is the interrupt input. The 8085 is operated with a 6.144 MHz crystal. How can the 8254 be used to protect the display from damage in a situation where the microprocessor is delayed from responding to the interrupt because of a higher priority task?

10-14. A subroutine BCDSEG is to be written for the ICM7218B multiplexed eight-digit display driver. This subroutine has two parameters passed to it. Register A contains an unpacked BCD digit to be displayed and register C specifies in which digit location it will appear. The digit locations are specified as 0 through 7. The subroutine must convert the BCD digit to the seven-segment pattern required to display the digit, then write this pattern to the appropriate location in DSPLYI.

10-15. A subroutine SEGON is to be written for the ICM7218B multiplexed eight-digit display driver. This subroutine has two parameters passed to it. Register A contains a bit pattern, with a single 1 in it, which corresponds to the segment to be turned ON. Register C specifies which digit this segment is in. The subroutine writes the necessary segment pattern into the specified digit position in DSPLYI. This pattern must not affect any other segments in the digit. Note that the calling sequence can load A symbolically, assuming that constants have been associated with the symbols using equate statements. For example, SEGA EQU 01000000B. Also note that the decimal point segment must be handled differently from the others.

10-16. Repeat problem 10-15 for the subroutine SEGOFF. This subroutine is similar to SEGON but produces the pattern required to turn a segment OFF. Since this subroutine is very similar to SEGON, is it possible to create a single subroutine to handle both cases?

10-17. Draw the block diagram of a hardware interface between the LRC 7040 printer shown in Fig. 10.3-2 and an 8085A system showing the subsystems required. Data transfer is to be accomplished with program controlled I/O. The 8085A outputs ASCII characters using a 6-bit ASCII code. The 8085A uses 1 bit to start the printer's drive motor after which the interface must request data from the 8085A as needed. All timing is to be performed by the interface hardware.

10-18. Draw the block diagram of hardware interface between the LRC 7040 printer (Fig. 10.3-2) and an 8085A system where the hardware interface uses a FIFO buffer to accept ASCII characters from the 8085A. When a carriage return is received, the interface starts the printer and prints one line.

11

Analog Data
Input and Output

A/D converters translate from analog measurements, which are characteristic of most phenomena in the "real world," to digital language, used in information processing, computing, data transmission, and control systems. D/A converters are used in transforming transmitted data or the results of computation back to "real-world" variables for control, information, display, or further analog processing.

D. H. Sheingold*

*Analog-Digital Conversion Notes (Norwood, Mass.: Analog Devices, Inc., 1977).

11.1 ANALOG DATA

The data to be processed by a microprocessor system originates in either of two forms: digital or analog. And the data output from a microprocessor system may be either digital or analog. In electronic systems, digital data is represented by *digital signals*. Each signal is a voltage or current with one of two possible states, logic 1 or logic 0, both corresponding to discrete ranges of voltage or current. For example, for TTL logic, the voltage range for logic 0 is 0 V to 0.8 V, and the voltage range for logic 1 is 2.0 V to 5.0 V. The precise voltage of the digital signal is not important, but it is critical that its value be within one of the two allowable ranges.

Many microprocessor applications involve the determination of the values of physical parameters such as temperature, position, or pressure. For example, whenever a microprocessor is used in a closed loop system to control physical parameters, it must first measure the value of those parameters in order to make the decisions required for control. A transducer appropriate to each of the physical parameters generates an electrical signal that varies in a manner analogous to variations in the physical phenomenon. An electrical signal that is analogous to a physical parameter is an *analog signal*.

Analog data is data that has any one of a continuous set of values within a given range. Analog data is represented in electronic systems by analog signals that have any one of a continuous set of values in a fixed voltage or current range. The precise value of the voltage or current at a given time is important because it carries the information contained in the signal. For example, an analog voltage may have a range of 0 to 10 V and may be interpreted as representing temperatures from 0°C to 100°C. The analog voltage is expected to vary in proportion to the variable it represents; i.e., the variable to which it is electrically analogous.

There are many different types of transducers for various physical parameters [1, 2, 3]. But, in general, a *transducer* simply converts one form of energy to another. Transducers of interest here convert some form of energy to an electrical signal and are classified according to their transduction principle or according to the class of physical parameters that they transduce. *Transduction principles*, the physical principles upon which the operation of the transducer is based, include resistive, capacitive, inductive, piezoelectric, photoconductive, photovoltaic, and electromagnetic, and are used to transduce classes of physical parameters such as acceleration, displacement, flow, force, humidity, light, liquid level, pressure, sound, strain, temperature, and velocity.

Some transducers, those which are *self-generating*, produce an electrical signal directly. A piezoelectric crystal, for example, directly converts a displacement into a voltage. *Non-self-generating* transducers do not directly generate an electrical signal. Instead, they are used as components in an electrical circuit in such a manner that they control an electrical signal. A *thermistor* is a non-self-generating temperature sensitive resistor. When it is used as one of the resistive components in a voltage divider, it controls an electrical signal that varies as the temperature varies.

For the analog signal from a transducer to be processed by a digital system, it must be converted to a digital code. Generally, conversion is handled by several analog electronic subsystems that together comprise a data acquisition system, as

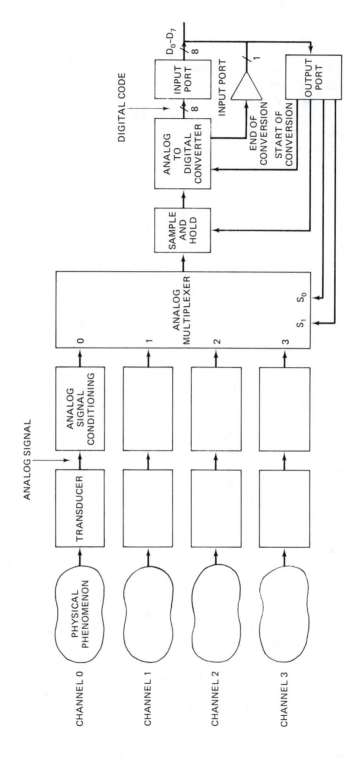

Figure 11.1-1 Multichannel data acquisition system.

shown in Fig. 11.1-1. Each analog input path to the data acquisition system is a *channel*. Data acquisition systems that handle several analog inputs are referred to as *multichannel*.

Many transducers output *low level signals*, those with less than 1 V amplitude. Frequently, such signals are in the millivolt or even microvolt range. Amplification is required to convert these to *high level signals* (1 to 10 V) so they can be further processed and converted. A filter may also be required to eliminate noise or undesired frequency components in a signal. *Analog signal conditioning*, which encompasses such operations as amplification, filtering, and linearization, transforms the transducer's output to a quantity suitable for conversion (see Fig. 11.1-1).

In a multichannel data acquisition system, an *analog multiplexer* selects the analog input for conversion to a digital code. The selected signal is input to a *sample and hold* circuit, which samples the analog input and provides a fixed output at the precise value of the sampled input signal. The sample and hold's output value is held fixed until it can be converted to a digital code. The actual conversion process itself is carried out by an *analog to digital converter*.

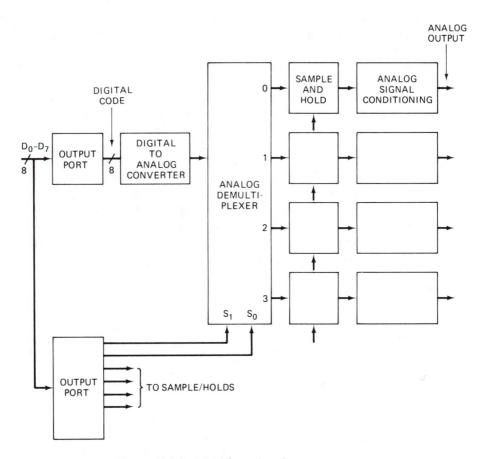

Figure 11.1-2 Multichannel analog output system.

For applications where analog outputs are required, ***digital to analog converters*** generate a piecewise continuous analog output from digital codes. Several analog outputs may be generated using one D/A converter by following it with an analog demultiplexer and a sample and hold circuit for each channel (see Fig. 11.1-2). The analog demultiplexer transmits the output of the digital to analog converter to the selected sample and hold. Signal conditioning is often necessary at the output to amplify, buffer, or scale the analog output signals from the sample and hold circuits.

It is important that the designer of microprocessor systems be familiar with those analog devices that are necessary or useful in microprocessor applications involving analog signals. Such devices include analog to digital converters, digital to analog converters, operational amplifiers, sample and hold circuits, analog multiplexers, and analog demultiplexers.

11.2 OPERATIONAL AMPLIFIERS

Operational amplifiers (op-amps) are analog electronic devices used as components in many of the subsystems in an analog data acquisition system because of their low cost, high reliability, and ease of application. Operational amplifiers are the building blocks for current to voltage converters, voltage amplifiers, buffers, active filters, sample and holds, and a variety of other linear and nonlinear analog signal processing circuits. They are available as separately packaged linear integrated circuits and are used as components in larger integrated circuits.

The characteristics of an operational amplifier are high gain, two analog signal inputs, and one or two analog signal outputs. In addition to the signal inputs and outputs, DC supply voltage(s), usually two of opposite polarity, are required for the op-amp's operation. The basic op-amp circuit symbol is shown in Fig. 11.2-1a. All voltages applied to the op-amp are specified with respect to the circuit's ground terminal. The two signal inputs are the ***inverting input*** $(-)$ and the ***noninverting input*** $(+)$. The voltages at these inputs are labeled v_- and v_+, respectively. Input voltages can be positive or negative for those op-amps operating between two supply voltages of opposite polarity.

11.2.1 The Ideal Op-Amp

For purposes of analysis, the op-amp is assumed to be ideal. The output voltage of an ideal op-amp is a function of the difference between the two input voltages, $v_+ - v_-$, the ***differential*** input voltage. There are three regions of operation of the op-amp. In the linear region, the output voltage, v_0, is the product of the open loop gain, A_{OL}, of the op-amp and the differential input voltage

$$v_0 = A_{OL}(v_+ - v_-)$$

This region is indicated by the diagonal line with slope A_{OL} in Fig. 11.2-1b. The other two regions of operation are the saturation regions. In these, v_0 is fixed at

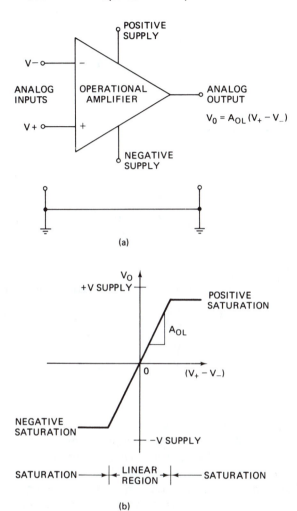

Figure 11.2-1 Operational amplifier: (a) symbol; (b) open loop transfer characteristic.

either the positive or negative saturation voltage and is no longer a linear function of $v_+ - v_-$. The value of the saturation voltage is usually 1 or 2 volts below that of the supply voltage.

The input resistance at the inverting and noninverting terminals is assumed infinite in the ideal op-amp. Therefore, the currents into these terminals are zero: $i_- = i_+ = 0$. The output resistance of the ideal op-amp is assumed zero. A simple equivalent circuit for the ideal op-amp in its linear region of operation is indicated in Fig. 11.2-2. The dependent voltage generator, $A_{OL}(v_+ - v_-)$ models the output as a function of the input.

Open loop gains, A_{OL}, for practical IC op-amps ranges from 10^4 to 10^6. DC supply voltages are usually no greater than ± 15 V. Thus, a limit is placed on the range of the differential input voltage $(v_+ - v_-)$ that can be applied to the op-amp while maintaining linear operation. For a gain of 10^4 and a supply voltage of

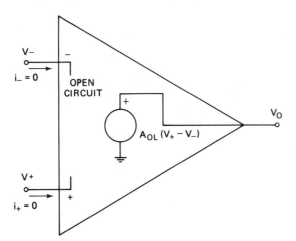

Figure 11.2-2 Equivalent circuit of ideal op-amp.

± 15 V, the maximum differential input voltage is

$$|v_+ - v_-| < \frac{V \text{ supply}}{A_{\text{OL}}}$$

$$< \frac{15 \text{ V}}{10^4}$$

$$< 1.5 \text{ mV}$$

Most applications involve input voltages of a much larger range, and the magnitude of the noise signals present in most environments in applications involving input voltages of very low magnitude cause the output to oscillate or saturate. For these reasons op-amps are not operated open loop in linear applications.

For closed loop operation of an op-amp, a portion of the output signal is fed back to one of the input terminals via an external connection. *Negative feedback*, used in implementing linear circuits, results if the feedback connection is made to the inverting terminal. *Positive feedback* results if the feedback connection is to the noninverting terminal and, under certain conditions, produces nonlinear circuits.

11.2.2 Common Op-Amp Circuits

When an op-amp with a high open loop gain is used with negative feedback to implement a linear circuit, the closed loop gain or transfer characteristic of the circuit and its input and output impedance is, to a first approximation, dictated entirely by the external feedback components. As a result, the analysis and design of linear signal processing circuits with op-amps is relatively straightforward.

There are a number of common op-amp circuits for implementing various functions, and their operations and characteristics, as a function of external components, have been thoroughly analyzed [4, 5, 6, 7]. See Fig. 11.2-3. The analysis of a circuit's transfer characteristics by using *virtual ground analysis* is presented in

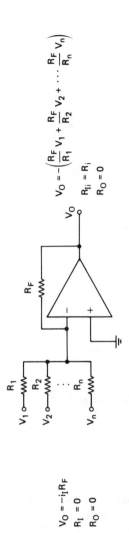

$$V_O = -i_I R_F$$
$$R_I = 0$$
$$R_O = 0$$

(a) CURRENT TO VOLTAGE CONVERTER

$$V_O = V_I$$
$$R_I = \infty$$
$$R_O = 0$$

(b) UNITY GAIN BUFFER

$$V_O = -\frac{R_F}{R_1} V_I$$
$$R_I = R_1$$
$$R_O = 0$$

(c) INVERTING VOLTAGE AMPLIFIER

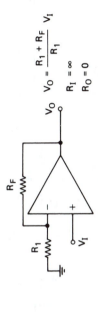

$$V_O = -\left(\frac{R_F}{R_1} V_1 + \frac{R_F}{R_2} V_2 + \cdots \frac{R_F}{R_n} V_n\right)$$
$$R_{Ii} = R_i$$
$$R_O = 0$$

(d) INVERTING SUMMING AMPLIFIER

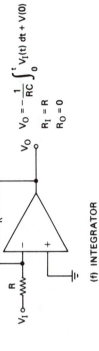

$$V_O = \frac{R_1 + R_F}{R_1} V_I$$
$$R_I = \infty$$
$$R_O = 0$$

(e) NONINVERTING AMPLIFIER

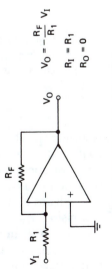

$$V_O = -\frac{1}{RC} \int_0^t V_I(t) \, dt + V(0)$$
$$R_I = R$$
$$R_O = 0$$

(f) INTEGRATOR

Figure 11.2-3 Common operational amplifier circuits.

405

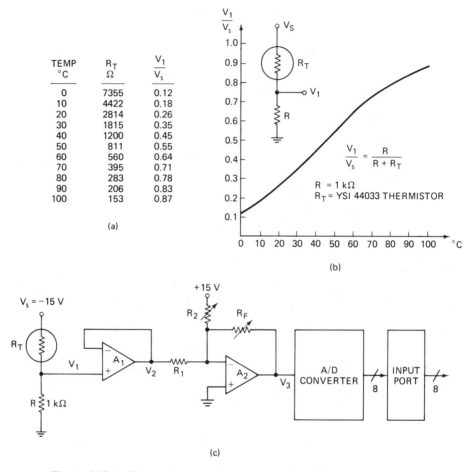

TEMP °C	R_T Ω	$\dfrac{V_1}{V_s}$
0	7355	0.12
10	4422	0.18
20	2814	0.26
30	1815	0.35
40	1200	0.45
50	811	0.55
60	560	0.64
70	395	0.71
80	283	0.78
90	206	0.83
100	153	0.87

(a)

$$\frac{V_1}{V_s} = \frac{R}{R + R_T}$$

$R = 1\ k\Omega$
R_T = YSI 44033 THERMISTOR

(b)

(c)

Figure 11.2-4 Temperature measurement circuit utilizing a thermistor as the temperature transducer: (a) thermistor characteristics; (b) transfer characteristic of voltage divider using thermistor; (c) diagram of complete circuit.

Appendix E. These characteristics are approximations determined from the circuit configuration, with the assumption that the op-amp in the circuit is ideal. However, for most applications, these approximations predict, with sufficient accuracy, the operation of a circuit containing an actual op-amp.

Figure 11.2-4 illustrates the use of op-amps in signal conditioning, where a thermistor, R_T, is used as a temperature sensor. The resistance of the thermistor decreases with an increase in temperature, as shown in Fig. 11.2-4a. The intent is to generate an analog voltage representing temperatures from 0°C to 100°C, convert that voltage to an 8-bit binary code, and input that code to a microprocessor. The A/D converter used is designed to accept input voltages from 0 to 10 V and convert them to a binary code.

Ensuring the proper input to the A/D converter is a two-step process: (1) since the thermistor is not a self-generating transducer, circuitry must be provided to convert the change in thermistor resistance to an analog voltage, and (2) the analog voltage from step 1 must be shifted and scaled so that it corresponds to a 0 to 10 V signal.

The first step is carried out by using the thermistor as part of a voltage divider circuit. The ratio of the output of the voltage divider, V_1, to its excitation voltage, V_S, is plotted in Fig. 11.2-4b. The fact that this transfer characteristic is not linear poses no problem because linearization can be accomplished by a table lookup operation executed by the microprocessor. In the circuit of Fig. 11.2-4c, $V_S = -15$ V. The voltage divider output thus increases negatively for increasing temperature. The output of the voltage divider ranges from -1.8 V at 0°C to -13.05 V at 100°C.

The next step converts the -1.8 V to -13.05 V range to a 0 V to $+10$ V range. Op-amp A_1 s a unity-gain buffer that prevents the following stage of circuitry from loading the voltage divider. Thus, $V_2 = V_1$. The next stage shifts and scales V_2. Voltage V_2 is shifted (biased) by 1.8 V so that a 0 V signal is obtained at 0°C instead of a -1.8 V signal, and its 11.25 V range, $|(-13.05) - (-1.8 \text{ V})|$, is scaled to a 10 V range. Op-amp A_2 and resistors R_1, R_2, and R_F form an inverting summing amplifier, as shown in Fig. 11.2-3d. A value of 10 kΩ is assumed for R_1. At 0°C, $V_2 = -1.8$ V, and the current through R_1 and into the summing junction is $V_2/R_1 = -1.8 \text{ V}/10 \text{ k}\Omega = -0.18$ mA. One side of R_2 is connected to $+15$ V. A value for R_2 is computed that causes a current through R_2, equal to that through R_1. This balances the current through R_1 and causes the current through R_F to be zero and, thus, the output voltage to be 0 V. Therefore

$$\frac{V_2}{R_1} = \frac{15 \text{ V}}{R_2}$$

and

$$R_2 = \frac{15 \text{ V}}{V_2} R_1$$

$$= \frac{15 \text{ V}}{1.8 \text{ V}} 10 \text{ k}\Omega$$

$$= 83.3 \text{ k}\Omega$$

R_2 is an adjustable resistor (potentiometer) with a nominal value of 83.3 kΩ to compensate for slight errors in the actual resistor values and voltages.

The gain of the inverting amplifier circuit to V_2 is $-R_F/R_1$. The desired gain is

$$-\frac{V_3}{V_2} = \frac{10 \text{ V}}{11.25 \text{ V}}$$

$$= -0.888$$

Therefore

$$-\frac{R_F}{R_1} = -0.888$$

$$R_F = 0.888R_1$$

$$= 8.88 \text{ k}\Omega$$

The output V_3 is an analog voltage with a range of 0 to 10 V corresponding to a temperature range of 0°C to 100°C. Note that in Fig. 11.2-4c the reference terminal (ground) with respect to which input and output voltages of the op-amp circuit are measured is omitted from the diagram, as is common practice.

11.2.3 Differential and Instrumentation Amplifiers

Analog signals are divided into two categories: single-ended and differential. A *single-ended signal* appears on a single terminal and is measured with respect to the circuit ground, as shown in Fig. 11.2-5. Single-ended signals are usually high level signals. For short distances, the signal is transmitted over a single wire and referenced to circuit ground. For longer distances, a pair of twisted wires is used to minimize noise pickup. One of the wires in the twisted pair is grounded; the other carries the signal. Alternatively, shielded cable may be used to minimize the effects of noise in the circuit. The circuits shown in Figs. 11.2-3 and 11.2-4 are all designed to accept single-ended inputs and generate single-ended outputs.

    Low level signals are usually handled as *differential signals*, which require two signal wires. The information bearing signal is the difference between the voltages on the two wires, each measured with respect to ground. Most low level transducers generate differential signals. The environment of the transducer may induce electrical noise into the output signal, which may be comparable to or greater in

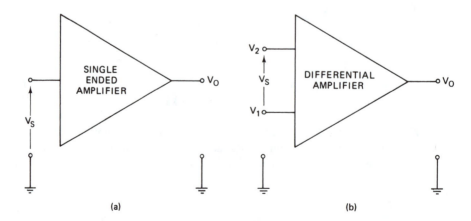

Figure 11.2-5 Generalized amplifier signal connections: (a) single-ended input–single-ended output; (b) differential input–single-ended output.

TRANSDUCER

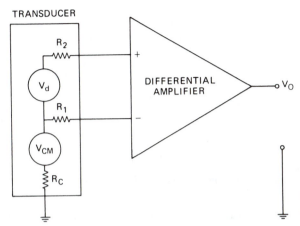

Figure 11.2-6 Simplified transducer model with differential outputs.

magnitude than the signal itself. For our purposes, any signal other than the desired signal is considered noise.

Differential and *instrumentation amplifiers* are designed to handle differential inputs. The output of these amplifiers is usually a high level, single-ended signal that can be processed by single-ended circuits, such as those of Fig. 11.2-3.

Figure 11.2-6 represents the type of application where a differential or instrumentation amplifier is required. The transducer generates a low level output represented by the voltage source, v_d, which is proportional to the physical parameter being measured. In addition, the model of the transducer contains a voltage source v_{CM}, a *common mode voltage*. It is possible for a portion of v_{CM} to result as a function of the design of the transducer, as in the case of a bridge circuit. And, v_{CM} includes noise induced in the conductors between the transducer and amplifier input and/or any difference in potential of the grounds at the transducer and amplifier. If a single-ended connection between the transducer and amplifier is used, V_2 only, the signal amplified is $v_d + v_{CM}$. If v_d is a low level signal, v_{CM} can be of comparable or greater magnitude. This results in a low signal to noise ratio, SNR, at the input of the amplifier, and the noise is amplified along with the signal. However, if a differential signal is obtained from the transducer, an amplifier designed to amplify the differential signal and reject the common mode signal can be used. Then the output is the product of the amplifier gain and the difference of its two input signals:

$$v_0 = G(v_2 - v_1)$$

since $v_2 = v_d + v_{CM}$ and $v_1 = v_{CM}$.

$$v_0 = G(v_d + v_{CM} - v_{CM})$$

$$= Gv_d$$

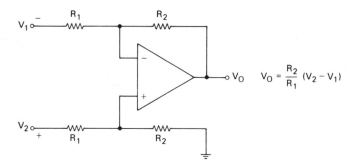

Figure 11.2-7 Differential amplifier constructed from a single op-amp.

Figure 11.2-7 shows the circuit diagram of a differential amplifier constructed from a single op-amp. The output of this circuit is

$$v_0 = (v_2 - v_1)\frac{R_2}{R_1}$$

Thus, the output is the difference of $v_2 - v_1$, multiplied by a gain, $G = R_2/R_1$. A basic drawback of the circuit, however, is that the differential input impedance (i.e., from input to input) is only $2R_1$. This impedance loads the differential signal source and can attenuate it.

The amplifier of Fig. 11.2-7 has other limitations in addition to its low differential input impedance. If high input impedance and high gain are required, the input resistance has to be very large and the feedback resistance even larger, which entails the difficult matching of very high valued resistors. If the matching is not achieved, the common mode signal is also amplified. Also, changing the gain requires changing two matched resistors in the circuit.

An instrumentation amplifier uses three operational amplifiers (see Fig. 11.2-8) to solve these problems. The transfer function of the circuit is:

$$v_0 = \left(1 + \frac{2R_2}{R_1}\right)(v_2 - v_1)$$

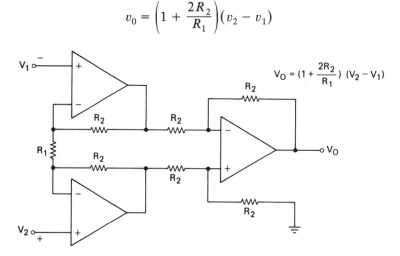

Figure 11.2-8 Instrumentation amplifier constructed from three op-amps.

The two input op-amps provide very high input impedance, since the current into the noninverting terminals is very low, and the gain of the circuit can be adjusted by changing a single resistor, R_1. For high gain, the resistors R_2 that must be matched need not be excessively large. This type of instrumentation amplifier is available as a single IC with R_1 as an external resistor—for example, National Semiconductor's LH0036.

In practical differential and instrumentation amplifiers, the ideal characteristics obtainable, assuming perfectly matched resistors and ideal op-amps, are unachievable. The quality of practical circuits is measured by their common mode rejection ratio, CMRR (or CMR). This is the ratio of the circuit's gain for differential signals, A_d, divided by its gain for common mode signals, A_{CM}.

$$\text{CMRR} = \frac{A_d}{A_{CM}}$$

In the ideal circuit, $A_{CM} = 0$ and the CMRR $= \infty$. In practical IC circuits, CMRRs between 10^3 and 10^6 are typical.

The common mode rejection ratio is often specified in decibels:

$$\text{CMRR (dB)} = 20 \log_{10} \frac{A_d}{A_{CM}}$$

11.2.4 Practical Op-Amp Characteristics

Actual op-amps are not ideal. IC op-amps have such nonideal characteristics as offset voltage, bias and offset currents, drift, finite input and nonzero output impedance, finite response time, and nonzero response to common mode signals. Some op-amps provide terminals to which external components can be added, which partially compensates for some of these nonideal characteristics; others cannot be compensated for completely.

The equivalent circuit of a practical operational amplifier is given in Fig. 11.2-9. The nonzero input currents, the *input bias currents,* I_B, are represented by two current generators. The difference between the values of these two currents is the *input offset current,* I_{IO}. The finite input resistance is represented by the resistor R_I between the two input terminals. The *input offset voltage,* V_{IO}, is represented by the battery in series with the input resistor. This voltage is an internally generated voltage, the value of which is equivalent to the voltage that must be applied to the input terminals to produce an output voltage of 0 V. The nonzero output resistance is represented by the resistor R_0.

Table 11.2-1 lists some typical characteristics for three op-amps. Each of these op-amps represents a different technology. The LM741C is a bipolar device. The AD544K has FET input transistors, which results in a device with very high input impedance and low input currents. The TLC251 is a linear CMOS device that, in addition to having very high input resistance and very low input currents, has very low drift characteristics. *Temperature drift* is the change in a parameter as a function of temperature. The effects of input offset current, input bias current, and

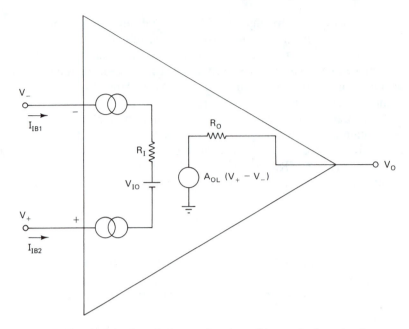

Figure 11.2-9 Practical operational amplifier equivalent circuit.

input offset voltage can be compensated for at a given temperature using external components. However, if the circuit must operate over a wide temperature range external compensation loses its effectiveness. Hence the need, in such applications, for devices that have inherently low drift characteristics. Most op-amps have provisions for connecting an external potentiometer in order to adjust the input offset to zero. Figure 11.2-10 shows a null circuit for the AD544.

Other nonideal characteristics relate to an op-amp's response to time varying inputs. Of particular interest here are settling time, delay time, and slew rate.

Settling time is a parameter that indicates the time response of analog circuits. It is defined as the time elapsing between the application of a full scale step input to the circuit and the output entering and remaining in a specified band of values near

TABLE 11.2-1   PRACTICAL OP-AMP CHARACTERISTICS

| | | Op-Amps | |
Characteristic	LM741	AD544K	TLC251
A_{OL} (open loop gain)	1.5×10^6 i	0.5×10^6	0.28×10^6
I_B (input bias current)	80	.01	.001 nA
I_{IO} (input offset current)	20	.002	.001 nA
V_{IO} (input offset voltage)	2.0	1.0	10 mV
SR (slew rate)	0.5	13	0.6 V/μs
B (bandwidth)	1.5	2	0.7 MHz

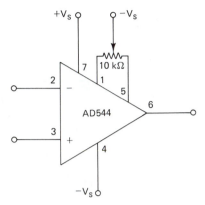

Figure 11.2-10   Offset null configuration for AD544 op-amp.

the final output value. For differential and instrumentation amplifier circuits, a step input is a full scale voltage or current input transition. For other devices, such as D/A converters, analog multiplexers, and sample and holds, the full scale transition involves a switching operation, and thus the settling time includes that switching time.

Settling time for an op-amp is illustrated in Fig. 11.2-11. After the application of a full scale step input, a period of time elapses before the op-amp output starts to change. This time period is known as the *delay time*. The op-amp output then changes at its maximum rate: the *slew rate*, SR. The output eventually reaches the defined error band around the full scale value, and, if the circuit is underdamped, may overshoot and oscillate around the final value. Once the oscillations remain within the error band, the settling time is complete.

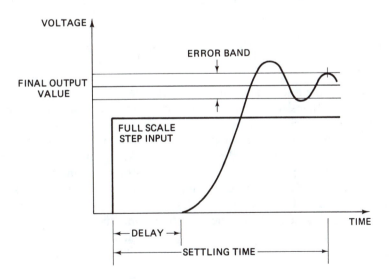

Figure 11.2-11   Settling time of an op-amp.

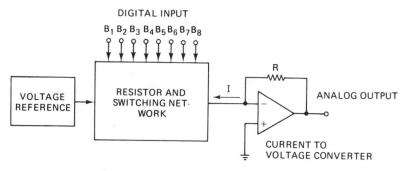

Figure 11.3-1   Digital to analog conversion system.

11.3 DIGITAL TO ANALOG CONVERTERS, DACS

A digital to analog converter (D/A converter or DAC) accepts an n-bit parallel digital code as input and provides an analog current or voltage as output. The DAC's output current or voltage is a function of the code at its input and changes in response to a change in the digital input. Among their many applications, digital to analog converters are used in digitally controlled CRT displays, in digitally controlled power supplies for automatic test equipment, for digital generation of analog waveforms, and for digital control of automatic process control systems. They are, as well, the basis for many analog to digital converter (A/D converter, ADC) designs.

A DAC system typically consists of three basic subsystems: an accurate and stable voltage reference, the basic DAC itself, and an operational amplifier (see Fig. 11.3-1). For an n-bit straight binary[1] input code, the output of an ideal D/A is

$$V_0 = V_{REF}\left(B_1 2^{-1} + B_2 2^{-2} + \cdots + B_n 2^{-n}\right)$$

where B_1 is the msb and B_n the lsb of the binary input.

A DAC consists of electronic analog switches controlled by the input code and a network of precision weighted resistors. The switches control currents or voltages derived from the reference voltage and provide an output current or voltage that is an analog representation of the applied code. An operational amplifier can be used at the output to provide current to voltage conversion and/or buffering. In some high speed applications where a limited output voltage range is acceptable, a resistor, instead of an op-amp, provides current to voltage conversion, thus eliminating the delay associated with the operational amplifier.

The output from an ideal 3-bit DAC that accepts a straight binary code as input is shown in Fig. 11.3-2. As this figure illustrates, the analog output is not

[1] The term "straight binary" is frequently used to refer to the usual (natural) binary code.

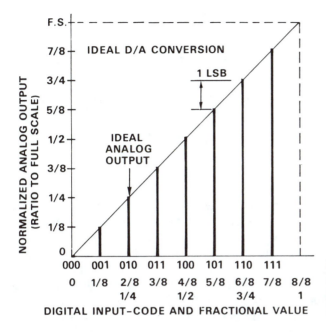

Figure 11.3-2   Conversion relationship for an ideal 3-bit straight binary D/A converter. (Courtesy of Analog Devices.)

continuous but has one of eight possible values. Each value corresponds to one of the eight possible 3-bit codes at the input. These binary inputs are written as numbers ranging from 000 to 111. In actual fact, however, these numbers represent a discrete set of fractions that lie in the range of 0.000 to 0.111, that is, from 0 to the maximum, $1 - 2^{-n}$. The binary point is usually not written. For $n = 3$, as in the present case, the actual maximum output is seven-eighths of the nominal full scale (FS) output. If the 3-bit DAC has a nominal output range of 0 to 10 V, the actual maximum output voltage is 8.75 V. The size of the step at the output, corresponding to a change in the input code of one least significant bit, is $FS/2^n$. For a 3-bit 0 to 10 V converter, the step size is $10/2^3$, or 1.25 V.

The requirements of a particular application dictate the number of bits required in a DAC. In DACs with a larger number of input bits, the number of steps is increased, and step size is reduced. A DAC with an 8-bit straight binary input code, for example, has 256 distinct output values corresponding to the number of distinct input codes possible. For a 10 V FS converter, the step size is 39.06 mV. Table 11.3-1 indicates the resolution of a DAC with straight binary input as a function of the number of input bits. *Resolution* is a measure of the size of the output step associated with a change of 1 lsb at the input. Thus, resolution is a measure of the precision of a DAC and is either expressed in bits or as a percentage. An 8-bit binary converter has a resolution of 1 part in 256 or 0.3906 percent or 3906 ppm (parts per million).

11.3.1 Input Codes

Although straight binary is the most popular, a number of other input codes are used with DACs, including BCD and complementary binary. With binary coded

TABLE 11.3-1 RESOLUTION AS A FUNCTION OF THE NUMBER
OF BITS FOR A BINARY CONVERTER

Number of Bits	Number of Quanta	Percentage	PPM
1	2	50	500,000
6	64	1.6	15,625
8	256	0.4	3,906
10	1,024	0.1	977
12	4,096	0.024	244
16	65,536	0.0015	15

decimal, since 4 bits are required to represent each decimal digit, resolution is lower for a BCD converter than for a binary converter using the same number of bits. This resolution is 1 part in 10^D, where D is the number of BCD digits, and the maximum output voltage is $FS(1 - 10^{-D})$. A 12-bit BCD converter has 1000 output values in a range from 0 to 0.999 FS, with a step size of 0.001 FS and a resolution of 0.1 percent. A 12-bit straight binary converter has 4096 output values in a range from 0 to 0.99976 FS, with a step size of 0.00024 FS and a resolution of 0.024 percent. Thus, the resolution of a 12-bit binary converter is better by a factor of 4 than the resolution of a 12-bit BCD converter.

Because of their method of construction, monolithic (integrated circuit) DACs sometimes use complementary binary or complementary BCD codes (Table 11.3-2). In these codes, all bits are represented by their complements. Thus, in the previous case of a 3-bit binary DAC, 0 output is represented by 111, half scale by 011, and full scale (less 1 lsb) by 000.

The D/A converters previously mentioned are unipolar; i.e., they provide a single polarity output. However, bipolar D/A converters that provide positive and negative output voltages are also available. The input codes of such converters correspond to those that represent positive and negative numbers in digital systems. These include sign-plus-magnitude, two's complement, and one's complement. Also used is a code called *offset binary*, which is identical to two's complement except that the msb is complemented. Table 11.3-3 illustrates the outputs for a bipolar converter with a nominal ±5 V range as a function of the offset binary and two's complement codes.

TABLE 11.3-2 BINARY CODING FOR 8-BIT UNIPOLAR CONVERTERS

Scale	+10 V FS	Straight Binary	Complementary
+FS − 1 lsb	+9.96	11111111	00000000
+3/4 FS	+7.50	11000000	00111111
+1/2 FS	+5.00	10000000	01111111
+1/4 FS	+2.50	01000000	10111111
+1/8 FS	+1.25	00100000	11011111
+1 lsb	+0.04	00000001	11111110
0	0.00	00000000	11111111

TABLE 11.3-3 BINARY CODING FOR 8-BIT BIPOLAR CONVERTERS

Scale	± 5 V FS	Offset Binary	2's Complement
+ FS − 1 lsb	+ 4.96	11111111	01111111
+ 3/4 FS	+ 3.75	11100000	01100000
+ 1/2 FS	+ 2.50	11000000	01000000
0	0.00	10000000	00000000
− 1/2 FS	− 2.50	01000000	11000000
− 3/4 FS	− 3.75	00100000	10100000
− FS + 1 lsb	− 4.96	00000001	10000001
− FS	− 5.00	00000000	10000000

11.3.2 Weighted Resistor D/A Converters

The *weighted resistor method* is a straightforward one for D/A converter implementation. This method creates an output current, I_T, which is the summation of several weighted currents. The selection of those currents to be summed is controlled by the bits of the digital code. An example of a weighted resistor circuit for straight binary codes is shown in Fig. 11.3-3. Its output is from an op-amp connected as an inverting summing amplifier. Thus

$$V_{\text{OUT}} = -I_T R$$

The input to the circuit is a 3-bit digital word, $B_1 B_2 B_3$, which represents a straight binary fraction. B_1, the most significant bit, has a weight of 2^{-1}; B_2 has a

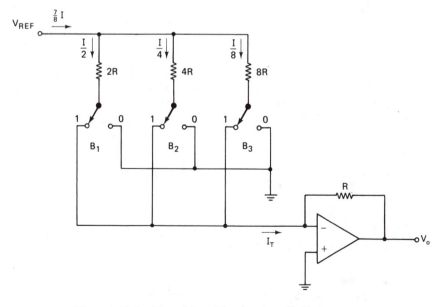

Figure 11.3-3 Three-bit weighted resistor D/A converter.

weight of 2^{-2}; and B_3, the least significant bit, has a weight of 2^{-3}. Each bit controls an analog switch. When bit B_i is 1, its corresponding analog switch passes a current through a resistor of weight $2^i R$ and into the summing junction of the operational amplifier. The summing junction is held at ground by the action of the negative feedback through R. The value of the component of current into the summing junction for bit $B_i = 1$ is

$$I_i = \frac{V_{\text{REF}}}{2^i R}$$

When bit B_i is 0, the analog switch directs the current through the associated resistor to the circuit ground instead of into the op-amp's summing junction.

Proper selection of the resistor ratios allows each bit of the digital word to control a properly weighted current. The resistors are weighted so that their resistances are inversely proportional to the numerical significance of the corresponding bit. In terms of the digital word, the output of the weighted resistor D/A converter of Fig. 11.3-3 is

$$\begin{aligned}
V_{\text{OUT}} &= -I_T R \\
&= -\left(\frac{V_{\text{REF}} B_1}{2R} + \frac{V_{\text{REF}} B_2}{4R} + \frac{V_{\text{REF}} B_3}{8R} \right) R \\
&= -V_{\text{REF}} \left(\frac{B_1}{2} + \frac{B_2}{4} + \frac{B_3}{8} \right) \\
&= -V_{\text{REF}} \left(B_1 2^{-1} + B_2 2^{-2} + B_3 2^{-3} \right)
\end{aligned}$$

The output voltage is, therefore, directly proportional to the digital code. The factor of proportionality is equal to V_{REF}. If V_{REF} is -10 V, the D/A converter's output ranges from 0 V to $+8.75$ V (seven-eighths of full scale), corresponding to input codes from 000 to 111, respectively. This output is identical to that of Fig. 11.3-2, with FS = 10 V.

This circuit can be expanded to handle straight binary codes with a greater number of bits by the simple inclusion of additional analog switches and properly weighted resistors. Weighted codes other than straight binary can be converted by proper choice of the weighting resistor. As the number of bits increases, however, the range of the weighted resistors becomes prohibitively large for accurate implementation as an integrated circuit.

11.3.3 *R-2R* Ladder D/A Converters

A D/A converter that uses resistors of only two values, R and $2R$, is illustrated in Fig. 11.3-4. This type of converter is advantageous in that it does not require a large range of resistor values with precise ratios for a large number of input bits. But it does require twice as many resistors for the same number of bits as the weighted resistor network.

Like the weighted resistor D/A converter, this circuit creates an output current, I_T, proportional to the input code. An operational amplifier converts the

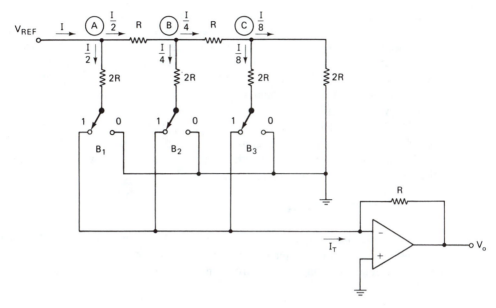

Figure 11.3-4   Three-bit R-$2R$ ladder D/A converter.

current to an output voltage; therefore

$$V_{\text{OUT}} = -I_T R$$

where I_T is the current into the summing junction of the operational amplifier. I_T, in turn, consists of the sum of the weighted currents through the analog switches in the logic 1 position.[2]

Due to the virtual ground effect, which is valid for the operational amplifier in its negative feedback configuration, the noninverting terminal is effectively at ground potential. Thus, each analog switch is connected to ground in either its 0 or 1 position, and the bottom of each $2R$ vertical resistor is grounded. If the Thevenin equivalent of the resistor ladder is computed by looking into the terminal connected to V_{REF}, the equivalent resistance of the ladder is found to be simply R. Thus, the current into the ladder from the reference supply is always

$$I = \frac{V_{\text{REF}}}{R}$$

When the equivalent resistance of the ladder network to the right of node A, i.e., to the right of the first vertical $2R$ resistor, is computed, it is $2R$. Thus, the current I into node A splits in half, resulting in a current $I/2$, through the vertical $2R$ resistor associated with bit B_1. The other half of the current is through R and

---

[2]A method for determining the ratio of the currents through these switches is outlined here; a thorough analysis of the derivation is found in [7].

into node B. The equivalent resistance to the right of node B is also $2R$. Thus, the current $I/2$ into node B splits, causing a current $I/4$ in the vertical resistor associated with bit B_2. A continuation of this analysis shows that the current splits at each node, resulting in currents through the vertical resistors that are weighted by powers of two. For each switch in the 1 position, the current through its associated resistor flows into the operational amplifier's summing junction. Thus, I_T is the sum of these weighted currents.

Both the weighted resistor and the R-$2R$ D/A converters discussed use an op-amp as a current to voltage converter to provide an output voltage. The output line from the D/A converter, which carries the binary weighted currents, is therefore terminated at virtual ground.

11.3.4 2^nR D/A Converters

A very simple and straightforward approach to D/A conversion is the 2^nR method. An n-bit 2^nR D/A converter requires 2^n resistors of equal value, R, and $2^{n+1} - 2$ analog switches. Although this approach necessitates a large number of components,

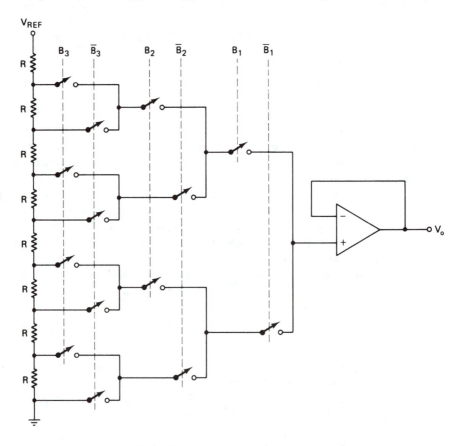

Figure 11.3-5 Three-bit 2^nR D/A converter.

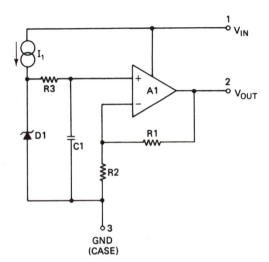

Figure 11.3-6 Equivalent schematic of LH0070 (10 V) and LH0071 (10.24 V) voltage references. These references are available in a 3-lead TO-5 package. (Courtesy of National Semiconductor Corp.)

they are economically manufactured in LSI. As shown in Fig. 11.3-5 the 2^n resistors are connected in series to form a voltage divider that splits the reference voltage into 2^n analog levels. The analog switches are connected to form a tree structure and are controlled by the digital code in such a manner that each code word creates a single path from the voltage divider to the converter output. A unity gain buffer amplifier prevents loading of the voltage divider. The output of this converter is a voltage.

11.3.5 Reference Voltages

In most applications, a stable and accurate voltage reference is essential for the operation of a D/A converter. Some converters have an internal reference voltage derived from the supply voltage by a circuit that uses a temperature compensated zener diode. In addition, these devices allow use of an external voltage reference for greater accuracy. Others have no internal voltage reference and require a separate one for operation.

Voltage references with temperature compensated zener diodes are available in IC form. In these devices, the diode is driven by a current regulator and buffer amplifier. Typically, their output voltages are accurate to ± 0.01 percent. For example, National's LH0070 and LH0071 voltage references (Fig. 11.3-6) provide output voltages of 10.0 and 10.24 V, respectively. With a 10.0 V reference for BCD converters and a 10.24 V reference for binary converters, step size is expressed as multiples or submultiples of 10 mV.

11.3.6 Multiplying D/A Converters

If an external reference voltage input to a D/A converter varies, the output voltage varies accordingly. For a fixed input code some D/A converters are designed so that the change in the output current, I_T, is linear with respect to the variation in the reference voltage. In such cases, the output of the D/A converter is the product of

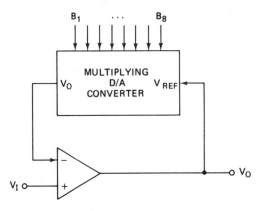

Figure 11.3-7 Multiplying D/A converter used to implement digitally programmed amplifier gain.

the digital input and the reference input. D/A converters designed for this type of operation are called *multiplying D/A converters*.

If a multiplying D/A converter is designed to accept a unipolar digital code and a positive reference voltage, it operates in a single quadrant. If it accepts a bipolar code, it operates in two quadrants. Two-quadrant multiplication also results when the multiplying D/A converter accepts only a unipolar digital code but operates with a reference voltage of either polarity. Four-quadrant multiplication results when a multiplying D/A converter operates with bipolar digital codes and a bipolar reference.

Multiplying D/A converters are used in microprocessor systems for digital gain control. A noninverting digitally controlled op-amp is shown in Fig. 11.3-7. In this system, the multiplying D/A converter controls the fraction of the operational amplifier's output voltage that is fed back to the inverting input. Thus

$$V_I = PV_0$$

where P is the fraction represented by the input code. Then

$$V_0 = \frac{1}{P}V_1$$

If an 8-bit multiplying D/A converter is used, V_0 could range from

$$V_0 = \frac{1}{\frac{255}{256}}V_I$$

$$= 1.004V_I \text{ for a straight binary code, FFH}$$

to

$$V_0 = \frac{1}{\frac{1}{256}}V_I$$

$$= 256V_I \text{ for code 01H}$$

The input code 00H is not acceptable, since the output of the D/A converter would not be a function of the converter's input, thus breaking the feedback connection.

11.4 D/A CONVERTER SPECIFICATIONS[3]

The accuracy of a calibrated DAC is defined in several ways. In each definition, the value referred to as the device's **accuracy** is actually its *inaccuracy*, or error. For example, a device referred to as "having an accuracy of 1 percent" is, in fact, 99 percent accurate. Convention, however, dictates that the device be referred to as "having an accuracy of 1 percent"; "accurate to within 1 percent" would be a better statement.

One definition describes accuracy as the worst case deviation of a DAC output from a straight line drawn between zero and full scale minus 1 lsb. The greatest attainable accuracy of a DAC is no better than $\pm 1/2$ lsb, due to its finite resolution. This definition encompasses all errors in a DAC, including its resolution, and is a measure of how closely its output approaches a desired voltage within the endpoints of its output voltage range.

Accuracy can also be defined as the difference between the actual output of the DAC and the output expected from calculation (see Fig. 11.3-2). This definition does not include resolution error and theoretically, therefore, allows an accuracy of 0 (100 percent).

Most manufacturers' data sheets do not give accuracy specification for DACs. Instead, specifications are given for the component errors that contribute to the accuracy (or inaccuracy) of the device. These include offset, gain, linearity, and differential linearity, and are specified in terms of volts, a fraction of an lsb, or a fraction of full scale.

Two of the errors associated with a DAC, offset error and gain error, can be trimmed to zero at room temperature by using optional external adjustments. **Offset error** is the output of the DAC when the code for zero output is applied. For straight binary this is the code $00\ldots0$. Offset error is specified in millivolts, as a fraction of full scale, or as a fraction of an lsb (see Fig. 11.4-1). **Gain error** or **scale error** is the departure of the actual output from the design output for a given input code, usually full scale code.

A DAC is calibrated to reduce the offset error to zero by applying the zero digital input and adjusting an external offset trim potentiometer to produce zero analog output. To eliminate gain error, the full scale digital input is applied after zeroing the offset error, and an external gain trim potentiometer is adjusted to give full scale output minus 1 lsb. Calibration to eliminate offset and gain errors is only valid for the temperature at which the calibration is made. Changes in this temperature cause a nonzero offset and gain error, referred to as **offset drift** and

---

[3] Resolution (see Section 11.3) differs from D/A converter parameters discussed in this section in that it is a measure of the quality of a D/A converter that is strictly a function of the number of input bits and the code used. It is not a parameter that can be improved by improving the design of a D/A converter. Better resolution for a given type of code requires a converter with a greater number of bits.

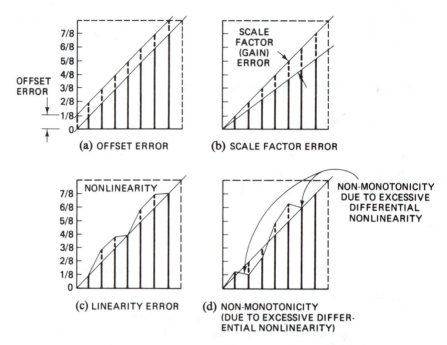

Figure 11.4-1 Typical sources of error for a 3-bit D/A converter. (Courtesy of Analog Devices.)

gain drift, respectively. Offset and gain drift in parts per million per degree centigrade (ppm/°C) specify the sensitivity of a DAC to changes in temperature. Other sources of error in a DAC cannot be trimmed to zero.

Linearity (actually nonlinearity) specifies the deviation of the DAC output from a straight line drawn through the end points of its transfer function and is one of the major measures of a DAC's performance. A curve is monotonic if there is no change in the sign of its slope. For a DAC to be *monotonic*, each step must be greater than zero. The linearity of a DAC must be less than or equal to $\pm 1/2$ lsb for it to be monotonic. Thus a $\pm 1/2$ lsb linearity specification guarantees monotonicity.

Differential nonlinearity indicates the difference between the actual voltage step size and the ideal 1 lsb step size at any code change for the DAC. Differential linearity is a measure of the smoothness of the DAC's output curve.

Other specifications for a DAC relate to its dynamic performance. Settling time is the time required, after a code transition, for the output to settle to within a specified limit of the final value. This limit is frequently $\pm 1/2$ lsb or a percentage of FS (see Fig. 11.2-11). Settling time is primarily a function of the type of switches, resistors, an output amplifier (if any) used in the construction of the DAC. Often, it is defined as the time that elapses from the point at which the output begins to change to the point at which it reaches its final value, within a specified limit. This does not include the delay from the time of the input code changes to the time the output starts to change.

One of the major contributors to the settling time of a DAC, in addition to those normally associated with any electronic device, is the presence of glitches. *Glitches* are spikes in the analog output that may result when, due to the occurrence of an intermediate input state, the output is driven toward a value opposite to its final value. An intermediate state is the result of one or more of the switches in the DAC being faster than the others. Consider the input of an 8-bit DAC being changed from 10000000 to 01111111. If the msb switches faster than the other bits, an intermediate state of 00000000 could occur, which would momentarily drive the output toward 0 V.

11.5 MICROPROCESSOR TO D/A CONVERTER INTERFACE

In principle, any D/A converter can be interfaced to any microprocessor. However, for some D/A converters a substantial amount of additional hardware and software is necessary. For others, the hardware for interfacing to the microprocessor is part of the D/A converter; these are *microprocessor compatible*.

Interfacing an 8-bit microprocessor to a D/A converter that is not directly microprocessor compatible is straightforward if the converter has 8 or fewer bits and accepts TTL inputs. All that is necessary is a latch connected to the data bus to hold the inputs to the D/A converter and the generation of an appropriate device select pulse.

For D/A converters of 9 bits or more, special care is required. Assume that a 12-bit D/A converter is to be interfaced to an 8-bit microprocessor. Since only 8 bits of data can be transferred from the microprocessor at a time, two latches are needed just to hold the 12 bits of data. However, if the two latches that provide the input data to the D/A converter are loaded by two successive instructions or successive write machine cycles of a single instruction, a period of time exists where a portion of the data input to the D/A converter is from the previous word to be converted and a portion is from the new word to be converted. The output of the D/A converter during this period of time is erroneous and produces additional glitch problems.

Double buffering solves the problem, as is shown in Fig. 11.5-1. The 8 low order bits of the 12-bit word are output to latch 1 first. The 4 high order bits are then output to latch 3. The device select pulse, which clocks the 4 bits from the data bus into latch 3, also clocks the output of latch 1 into latch 2. Thus, all 12 bits, $B_0 \ldots B_{11}$, appear at the input of the D/A converter simultaneously.

If memory mapped I/O is used, a single instruction, SHLD, transfers all 12 bits. The first memory write cycle of the SHLD instruction transfers the contents of register L to latch 1. The second cycle transfers the low order 4 bits of register H to latch 3.

Even with double buffering, another source of glitches from data loading can exist. The source of these glitches is the timing relationship between the write strobe

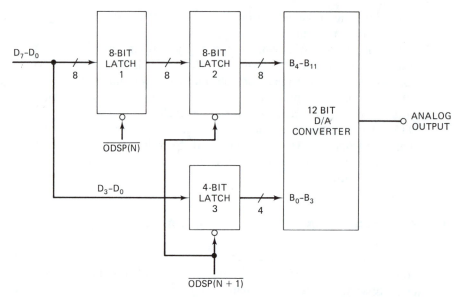

Figure 11.5-1   Double buffering inputs to a D/A converter.

and data during a write or output machine cycle. Many microprocessors bring the write strobe low before driving the bus with valid data. If the D/A's latches are level triggered, they will be transparent as soon as the write strobe goes low and the D/A converter will respond to invalid data until the bus is driven by valid data. For the 8085AH microprocessor this time period is 40 nS maximum. Monolithic A/D converters that contain on-chip registers often use level triggering. Level triggered registers are used so that the D/A converter can also be used in nonmicroprocessor applications simply by hardwiring the latches' clock inputs to the appropriate level leaving the latch transparent.

An example of a monolithic, microprocessor compatible D/A converter is Analog Devices' AD7548. The AD7548 is an 8-bit microprocessor compatible 12-bit multiplying D/A converter in a 20-pin DIP. The input control structure of the AD7548, shown in Fig. 11.5-2, makes it particularly easy to interface. There are two input registers, a least significant byte register and a most significant byte register. Each register has its own chip select input. When $\overline{\text{CSLSB}}$ is low and a $\overline{\text{WR}}$ strobe occurs, the least significant byte register is written. When $\overline{\text{CSMSB}}$ is low and a $\overline{\text{WR}}$ strobe occurs, the most significant byte register is written. The use of two input registers allows the 12-bit data value to be either left-justified or right-justified within the 2 bytes. Data format is selected by the logic value of the CTRL input. Loading the two input registers does not load the D/A. The D/A has its own register, which is loaded from the input registers when $\overline{\text{LDAC}}$ is low and a WR strobe occurs.

This control structure has some important advantages. If the two input registers are loaded separately from the DAC register, the problem of glitches, which results from invalid data on the data bus when $\overline{\text{WR}}$ goes low, is eliminated.

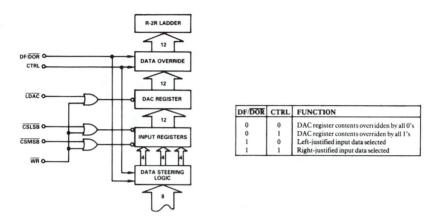

Figure 11.5-2 Simplified AD7548 input control structure. (Courtesy of Analog Devices.)

With this approach, it takes three write or output machine cycles to update the 12-bit output. Another advantage of this approach occurs in applications where several D/As must have their outputs change simultaneously. To accomplish this all the D/As have their $\overline{LDAC}$ inputs connected together. After the input registers of all the D/As have been loaded, a single write to $\overline{LDAC}$ updates all D/As simultaneously.

If the effect of glitches in a particular application is not critical, then the 12-bit output can be updated in two write or output machine cycles In this approach, $\overline{LDAC}$ is connected to either $\overline{CSLSB}$ or $\overline{CSMSB}$. In a memory mapped 8085A application, LDAC can be connected to $\overline{CSMSB}$ and the 12-bit data value can be transferred in one instruction cycle using the SHLD instruction. The addresses associated with CSLSB and CSMSB must be consecutive, with CSLSB having the lower address. Figure 11.5-3 shows the AD7548 configured to produce a 0 to +5 V output from right-justified data. The AD544 operational amplifier is configured as a current to voltage converter. A feedback resistor of approximately 11 K is internal to the AD7548 between the RFB and I_{OUT} pins. The capacitor provides phase compensation and helps prevent overshoot and ringing when high speed op-amps are used. When configured for unipolar operation, as shown, V_{OUT} has a maximum value equal to $-V_{REF}(4095/4096)$. To produce the 0 to +5 V output a -5 V reference is required at the V_{REF} input of the AD7548. The -5 V reference is produced by an AD584 voltage reference. The AD584 has reference voltage outputs of $+2.5$ V, $+5.0$ V, $+7.5$ V, and $+10.0$ V. When connected as shown, with the $+5.0$ V output connected to AGND and the voltage output taken from COM, it produces a -5.0 V output.

An additional feature of the AD7548 is its data override input. The contents of the DAC register can be overridden by bringing the DF/ $\overline{DOR}$ pin low. The state of the CTRL pin then determines whether the DAC register data is overridden by all 0s (CTRL = 0) or all 1s (CTRL = 1). This feature allows the user to perform

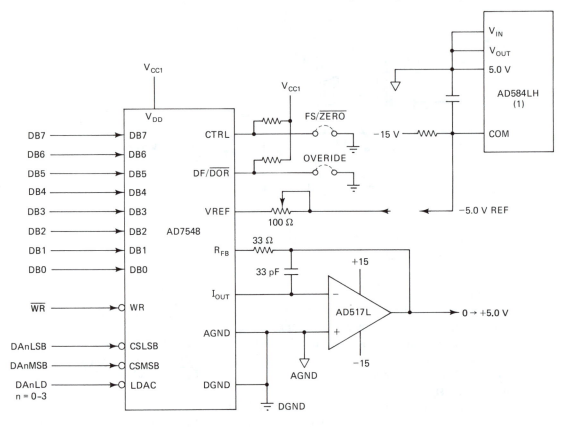

Figure 11.5-3   AD7548 12-bit D/A converter to 8085AH interface.

zero and full scale calibration of the AD7548 without having the microprocessor load the calibration data.

D/A converters with serial data inputs provide another way to transfer data from a microprocessor to the converter. A D/A converter with a serial data input requires fewer pins and can be placed in a smaller DIP, thus requiring less PC board space. The primary disadvantage is that it takes longer to effect the serial transfer of data. This time requirement precludes the use of such D/As in applications where the analog output must be updated at a fast rate.

The Analog Devices' AD7543 is a 12-bit D/A with serial data input. The functional diagram of the AD7543 is given in Fig. 11.5-4. A clear input, $\overline{CLR}$, allows the AD7543's DAC register to be quickly initialized to zero. The serial data is input, most significant bit first, at the SRI input. Four strobe inputs allow the positive edge triggered shift register to be clocked in a choice of ways. Once the shift register is completely loaded, its contents are transferred in parallel to the DAC register using either of the load strobes, $\overline{LD1}$ or $\overline{LD2}$.

Figure 11.5-5 shows a configuration of the AD7543 to interface to an 8085AH. In this interface, the clear and load strobes are device select strobes for the output ports DACLR and DALD, respectively. The data bit is obtained from bit D_7 of the

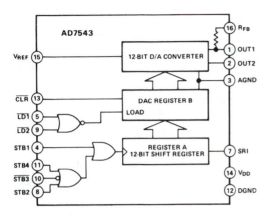

Figure 11.5-4 AD7543 12-bit D/A converter with serial input. (Courtesy of Analog Devices.)

data bus. The clock strobe for the shift register is the device select pulse for output port DATA. The AD7543 has a data setup time requirement of 100 nS and a data hold time requirement of 60 nS for operation over its entire temperature range. These time requirements are met by both the 8085AH and the 8085AH-2 at their maximum speeds. However, the 8085AH-1 does not meet the hold time requirement when operated at a crystal frequency above 10 MHz. An alternative approach would

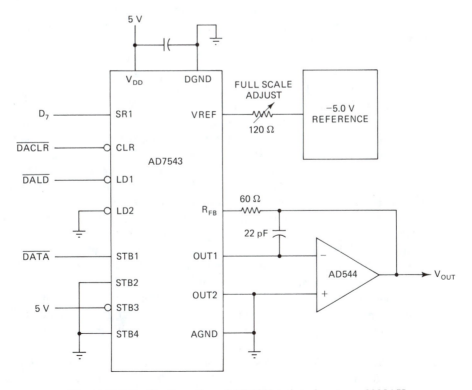

Figure 11.5-5 Configuration of AD7543 to interface to an 8085AH.

be to generate the serial data from the SOD pin of the 8085A and clock the register as before. This approach would alleviate any timing problem when using the 8085AH-1 without the need for additional circuitry.

Fabrication methods other than monolithic are used in D/A converters. Hybrid (multichip) circuit devices and discrete component converters—frequently packaged as potted modules—are common. Discrete component devices are noted for the highest performance, followed by hybrid, then monolithic devices. Binary converters with 6 to 16 bits and BCD converters with 2- to 4-digit resolution are common.

All commercial DACs are characterized by current or voltage output, or both. Voltage references and current to voltage output amplifiers, however, may or may not be included in the package. Frequently, monolithic D/A converters do not include either, as is the case with the AD7548. Those converters that do contain an internal voltage reference, however, often allow it to be bypassed by an external voltage reference when a voltage range other than that provided by the internal reference is desired or when higher accuracy and stability than those of the internal reference are required.

11.6 ANALOG TO DIGITAL CONVERTERS

Analog to digital converters (A/D converters, ADCs) perform two basic operations: quantization and coding. *Quantization* is the mapping of a continuous signal into one of several possible discrete ranges, or quanta. *Coding* is the assignment of a binary code to each discrete range. The same codes used as inputs to D/A converters are used as outputs from A/D converters: binary, BCD, sign-plus magnitude, two's complement, one's complement, and offset binary.

Figure 11.6-1 illustrates the transfer characteristics of a 3-bit straight binary unipolar A/D converter. An n-bit binary A/D converter has 2^n distinct output codes. Thus, the 3-bit converter has eight distinct output codes represented on the vertical axis. The continuous analog input range on the horizontal axis is portioned into quanta by *transition points* or *decision levels*. The size of each quantum is its quantization size: $Q = \text{FS}/2^n$ where FS is the full scale input voltage. The midpoint of each quantum is the analog voltage, which is exactly represented by the output code assigned to that quantum. For example, transition points at $1/16$ FS and $3/16$ FS bracket the $1/8$ FS point. An analog input in the quantum from $1/16$ FS to $3/16$ FS is assigned the output code representing $1/8$ FS (001). Thus, quantization involves an inherent error of $\pm Q/2$. Ideally, the output, M, from an A/D converter indicates that the analog input has a value of $M \pm Q/2$ ($M \pm \text{FS}/2^{n+1}$). The only way that quantization error can be reduced is by using an A/D converter with a larger number of bits. In a practical converter, the placement of the transition points is not precise due to nonlinearity and offset and gain errors, and, therefore, additional error is introduced into the output along with the inherent quantization error.

Errors in A/D converters are defined and measured in terms of the location of the actual transition points in relation to their ideal locations (see Fig. 11.6-2). If the first transition does not occur at exactly $+1/2$ lsb, an offset error results. If the

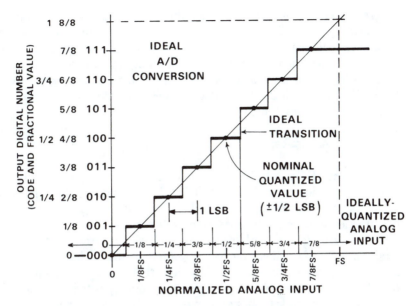

Figure 11.6-1 Conversion relationship for an ideal 3-bit straight binary A/D converter. (Courtesy of Analog Devices.)

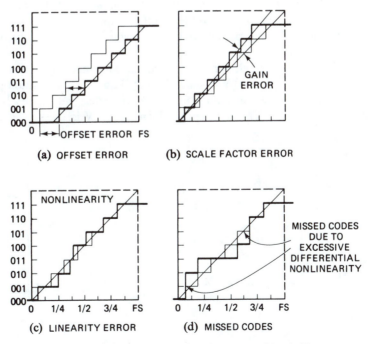

Figure 11.6-2 Typical sources of error for a 3-bit A/D converter. (Courtesy of Analog Devices.)

difference between the points at which the last transition and first transition occur is not equal to FS − 2 lsb, a gain error occurs. A linearity error occurs if the differences between transition points are not all equal, in which case the midpoints of some decision quanta do not lie on a straight line between 0 and FS − 1 lsb. Differential nonlinearity describes the variation in quanta size between adjacent pairs of codes. And if the differential nonlinearity is greater than ±1/2 lsb, then the possibility of missing codes exists.

11.6.1 Comparators

The simplest ADC is a 1-bit converter constructed from a comparator. Even with its large quantization error, it is useful for determining whether an analog signal is above or below some threshold value. It is also used as a component in the construction of direct A/D converters with multibit outputs.

Comparators are available in integrated circuit form and are, essentially, open loop op-amps; i.e., their outputs saturate at the highest positive level if the noninverting input terminal is more positive than the inverting input terminal. If, on the other hand, the inverting terminal is more positive than the noninverting terminal, the output saturates at its most negative value. When providing logic level outputs, the output is clamped at the appropriate levels.

The transfer characteristic of a comparator that has TTL logic level outputs is shown in Fig. 11.6-3. When the comparator is used as a threshold detector, the inverting input is connected to a reference voltage equal to the threshold, and the analog signal is connected to a noninverting input. When the analog signal exceeds the threshold, the comparator outputs a logic 1. When it is below threshold, the output is logic 0.

The conversion relationship of a comparator implementing a 1-bit ADC with a nominal range of 0 to 10 V is shown in Fig. 11.6-4. The transition point is placed at +1/2 lsb, as is the convention for A/D converters with many bits. In the figure, 1 lsb is equal to 5 V. A reference voltage of 2.5 V is the single transition level at

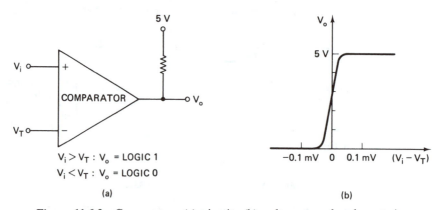

Figure 11.6-3 Comparator: (a) circuit; (b) voltage transfer characteristics.

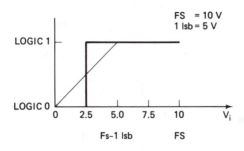

Figure 11.6-4 Conversion relationship of a comparator connected to provide a 1-bit A/D converter with a nominal 0 to 10 V input range.

$+1/2$ lsb, dividing the 0 to 10 V FS range into two quanta. The endpoints of the transfer characteristic are 0 V and 5 V (FS $-$ 1 lsb). The effect of actual full scale being nominal full scale minus 1 lsb is very clear and worthy of note in this example.

To construct A/D converters of n bits, two general techniques are used: direct and indirect conversion. In ***direct conversion***, the analog voltage is repeatedly compared to the output of a reference D/A converter. The D/A converter's output is changed as a function of the comparison, until it eventually corresponds to the unknown analog voltage. The D/A converter's input is then the desired binary code. The various direct conversion techniques differ, however, in the way the inputs to the DAC are changed to obtain the code that represents the analog input value. In all cases the desired binary code has been obtained when

$$|V_I - V_{FS} \sum_{i=1}^{n} b_i 2^{-i}| < \tfrac{1}{2} \text{ lsb}$$

where V_I is the analog voltage to be converted.

With ***indirect conversion***, the analog voltage is transformed to the frequency or time domain, and digital logic converts that time or frequency into a digital output code. Indirect conversion techniques are generally much slower than direct conversion techniques.

11.6.2 Counting A/D Converters

The simplest direct conversion technique is the ***counting converter***. A hardware approach (see Fig. 11.6-5) uses a counter that counts in the desired output code and provides inputs to the D/A converter. To initiate this conversion, the microprocessor generates a start of conversion, $\overline{\text{SOC}}$, device select pulse. This pulse clears the counter and sets the flip-flop, and the Q output of the flip-flop enables the counter. The comparator's output is used as the clock input to the flip-flop. When the D/A converter's output exceeds the analog input, the comparator changes state, clocking a zero into the flip-flop and stopping the counter. The output of the flip-flop sets an end of conversion flag. When this flag is 1, the A/D converter is in operation; when it is 0, the conversion is complete.

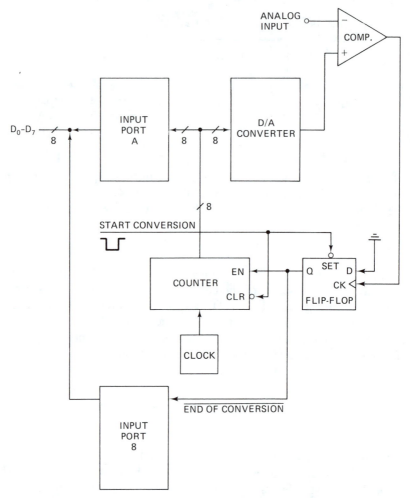

Figure 11.6-5 Hardware approach to a counting-type A/D converter.

The content of the counter is the digital code for the analog input. Conversion time for a counting converter is a function of the analog input value and the clock rate; worst case n-bit conversion time is 2^n clock times.

A software approach to a counting converter replaces the 8-bit input port, counter, flip-flop, and clock with an 8-bit output port (see Fig. 11.6-6). A register in the microprocessor replaces the counter function. The trade-off for hardware savings is that the microprocessor is dedicated to controlling the entire conversion and is, therefore, prevented from doing any other processing during the conversion.

In operation, software first clears the counter, then outputs its contents to the port. The counter is then repeatedly incremented and output, and the comparator is checked for a change of state. When the comparator changes state, the contents of the counter and output port are equivalent to the code representing the analog

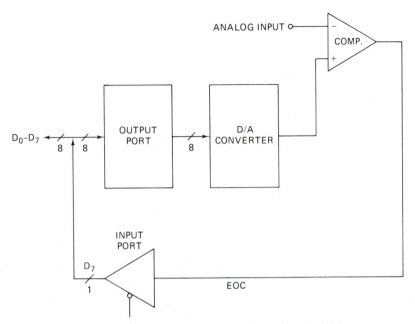

Figure 11.6-6 Basic hardware structure for software A/D conversion routines.

voltage. The settling times of the D/A converter, of its output amplifier, if any, and of the comparator must be accommodated by the software to ensure that the comparator output is stable before it is checked by the microprocessor. The subroutine CNTCV returns the straight binary code for the analog input in register C. The subroutine is written to drive an 8-bit D/A converter.

In order for the counting A/D converter to have the ideal transfer function of Fig. 11.6-1, the D/A converter's output must be offset by $+1/2$ lsb.

```
CNTCV:      MVI C, 0FFH        ;set counter to −1
STEP:       INR C
            MOV A, C
            OUT DAC            ;output code
            NOP                ;delay for settling time
            IN EOC             ;check comparator output
            ORA A
            JP STEP
            RET
```

11.6.3 Successive Approximation A/D Converters

The most popular direct A/D conversion method, known as *successive approximation*, has the advantage of a fixed conversion time proportional to the number of bits, n, in the code. This results in a faster conversion time. The successive

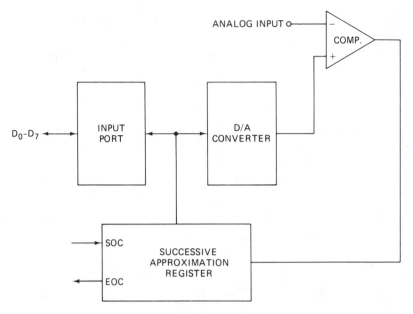

Figure 11.6-7 Hardware approach to successive approximation conversion.

approximation technique generates each bit of the code sequentially, starting with the msb. A hardware approach is similar to that for the counting A/D converter, except that the counter and flip-flop are replaced by a successive approximation register (Fig. 11.6-7). The *successive approximation register*, SAR, is a sequential control that generates inputs to the D/A converter to carry out the following successive approximation conversion algorithm:

1. The msb of the SAR output is set to 1.
2. If the comparator output is 1, this bit is reset; if not, it remains set.
3. If all bits have not been tested, the next most significant bit is set to 1, and then step 2 is repeated; if all bits have been tested, the conversion process is complete.

This algorithm first tests to see whether the analog voltage is greater or less than 1/2 FS. If it is greater, setting the most significant bit does not make the comparator output logic 1. The most significant bit output from the SAR is left logic 1, the next most significant bit is set to 1, and the analog input is tested to see whether it is greater than 3/4 FS. If the previous test of the most significant bit made the comparator output logic 1, then the analog voltage is less than 1/2 FS, and the most significant bit is cleared. The next most significant bit is then set to 1 and tested to determine whether the unknown voltage is less than 1/4 FS. This process is repeated in succession, for each bit until the last bit is tested.

```
SAAD:    LXI B, 8000H      ;SET MSB OF B, CLEAR C
TEST:    MOV A,C           ;CREATE CODE TO BE TESTED
         ORA B
         MOV D,A           ;SAVE NEW TEST CODE-D: test code
         OUT DAC           ;OUTPUT TO D/A CONVERTER
         IN COMP           ;INPUT COMPARATOR OUTPUT
         ORA A             ;SET FLAGS
         JM HIGH
         MOV C,D           ;REPLACE LAST APPROXIMATION WITH NEW
HIGH:    MOV A,B           ;ROTATE TEST BIT AND CHECK FOR END OF
         RRC               ;CONVERSION
         RC                ;RETURN WHEN ALL 8 BITS TESTED
         MOV B,A           ;ESTABLISH NEW TEST BIT POSITION
         JMP TEST
```

Figure 11.6-8 Subroutine for successive approximation A/D conversion using the hardware shown in Fig. 11.6-6.

Integrated circuit successive approximation registers are available and contain all the storage and digital control required for implementing high speed successive approximation A/D converters [8]. Codes other than straight binary are implemented by offsetting the comparator, by changing the weight of the most significant bit, and/or by manipulating the results of the conversion.

Successive approximation A/D conversion can also be implemented in software with the same hardware structure used for the counting A/D converter (see Fig. 11.6-6). The subroutine of Fig. 11.6-8 implements the successive approximation algorithm for an 8-bit conversion, using isolated I/O with an 8-bit output port and a 1-bit input port. For the successive approximation converter to have the transfer function of Fig. 11.6-1, the D/A converter's output must be offset by $-1/2$ lsb.

An interesting variation of this approach uses memory mapped I/O and no input or output ports. The inputs of the D/A converter are connected to the address bus, and the comparator's output is connected through a three-state buffer to the data bus. Thus the converter, comparator, and three-state buffer are treated as a 256×1 ROM. The code to be tested is created in the H and L registers and output to the D/A converter by executing a MOV M, A instruction. During instruction execution, the address bus supplies the input to the D/A converter. One bit of the data obtained in response to the address is the output of the comparator, which is input to the accumulator. The combined settling time of the D/A converter and comparator must be less than 588 nS when used with an 8085AH with $f_c = 6.144$, or a wait state is required. This technique provides a faster conversion time at the expense of a loss in available memory space.

An example of a microprocessor compatible single-chip successive approximation A/D converter is the Analog Devices' AD573, a 10-bit A/D converter. The AD573 includes on one chip, in a 20-pin package, a DAC, voltage reference, clock, comparator, successive approximation register, and three-state output buffers. A 10-bit conversion is accomplished in no more than 30 μS. The functional block diagram of the AD573 is shown in Fig. 11.6-9. The AD573 requires two supply voltages $+5$ V and -12 V to -15 V. The device can be operated as a unipolar converter with an input range of 0 to $+10$ V or as a bipolar converter with an input range of -5 V to $+5$ V. Unipolar operation is obtained by connecting the bipolar

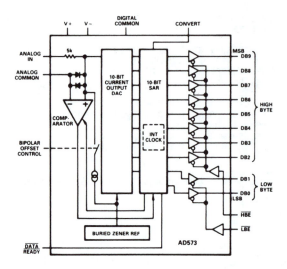

Figure 11.6-9 AD573 10-bit successive approximation A/D converter functional block diagram. (Courtesy of Analog Devices.)

offset input to ground. If this pin is left open, operation will be bipolar. The bipolar data format is offset binary.

Operation of the AD573 is controlled by three inputs: CONVERT, $\overline{\text{LBE}}$, and $\overline{\text{HBE}}$. A conversion is initiated by a positive pulse, of at least 500 nS duration, at the CONVERT input. The rising edge of this pulse resets the internal logic of the AD573 and, within 1.5 μS, sets $\overline{\text{DR}}$ high. The falling edge of the CONVERT pulse starts the conversion cycle. When the conversion is complete, $\overline{\text{DR}}$ goes low, indicating that the data is ready. $\overline{\text{LBE}}$ and $\overline{\text{HBE}}$ are used to enable the output buffers to read the low and high bytes of the result. The output data is left-justified, the high byte contains the most significant 8 bits and bits D_7 and D_6 of the low byte contain the least significant two bits, D_1 and D_0, of the result.

The interface of an AD573 to an 8085AH raises some important timing considerations. If the CONVERT pulse is generated from a device select pulse, it will meet the 500 nS duration requirement of the AD573 only if the crystal frequency of the 8085AH is sufficiently low. The width of $\overline{\text{WR}}$, and thus the device select strobe, is given by the 8085AH parameter t_{CC}:

$$t_{\text{CC}} = (3/2 + N) \times T - 80$$

Since $T = 2/f_c$ and $N = 0$ for no WAIT states, the crystal frequency must be less than 5.2 MHz. WAIT states could be added to increase the $\overline{\text{WR}}$ strobe's duration so that it exceeds 500 nS. Another solution is to use the device select pulse to preset a 74ALS74 flip-flop whose Q output provides the CONVERT pulse (see Fig. 11.6-10). The data input of the flip-flop is grounded and its clock input connected to $\overline{\text{DR}}$ from the AD573. The positive edge of CONVERT causes $\overline{\text{DR}}$ to go high after the AD573 is reset. The positive transition of $\overline{\text{DR}}$ causes the flip-flop to be clocked, bringing CONVERT low and starting the conversion. Of course other solutions are possible, including using a bit from an output port or SOD to generate CONVERT.

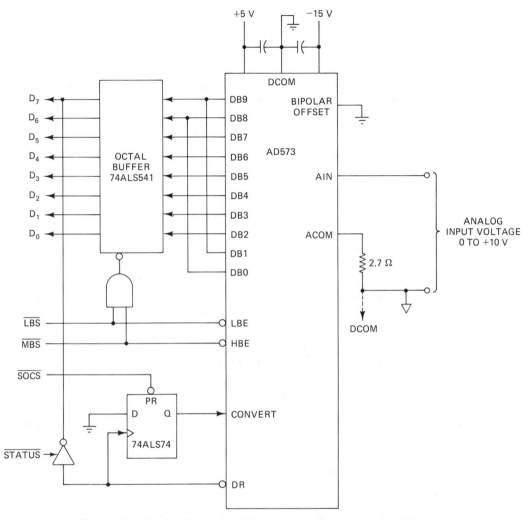

Figure 11.6-10 Interface of AD573 10-bit successive approximation A/D converter to an 8085AH using a 6.144 MHz crystal. Status bit is polled to determine end of conversion.

Another timing consideration involves the data access time of the AD573. The AD573 requires as much as 250 nS to provide stable data after $\overline{\text{LBEN}}$ or $\overline{\text{HBEN}}$ goes low. The corresponding timing parameter for the 8085A is t_{RD}, the time from $\overline{\text{RD}}$ low to valid data. For the 8085AH, this parameter has a value of 300 nS for the highest allowable clock frequency and therefore no timing problem exists. However, for the 8085AH-2 and 8085AH-1, the values at maximum clock rate are 150 nS and 75 nS, respectively. WAIT states must be introduced to increase t_{RD} as necessary.

$$t_{RD} = (3/2 + N) \times T - 150 \quad \text{for 8085AH-2}$$
$$t_{RD} = (3/2 + N) \times T - 175 \quad \text{for 8085AH-1}$$

The final timing consideration concerns the output float delay time of the AD573. The AD573 requires as much as 200 nS before its output buffers are completely in their high impedance state after $\overline{\text{LBE}}$ or $\overline{\text{HBE}}$ goes high. The time elapsed from the rising edge of $\overline{\text{RD}}$ until the 8085AH places the next address on AD_0–AD_7 is given by the parameter t_{RAE}. Any device driving the data bus during a read operation must cease to drive the bus within this time period or a bus conflict will occur between that device and the 8085AH. For the 8085AH at its highest clock frequency, this time is 150 nS, which is insufficient. Examination of the equation for t_{RAE}

$$t_{\text{RAE}} = (1/2) \times T - 10$$

indicates that the introduction of WAIT states will have no effect. The only solution is to place another buffer between the data outputs of the AD573 and the system data bus. This buffer must have a delay time from enabled to disabled less than t_{RAE}. Note that the device select logic that enables the external buffer must do so for both of the addresses assigned to $\overline{\text{LBE}}$ and $\overline{\text{HBE}}$.

The 1/2-bit offset for the AD573 A/D transfer characteristics is accomplished by the 2.7 Ω resistor between the ACOM input and analog signal ground in Fig. 11.6-10.

11.6.4 Voltage to Frequency Converters

One method of indirect conversion transforms the unknown analog voltage to a frequency that is then converted to a digital word. See Fig. 11.6-11. Transformation of the analog voltage is handled by a *voltage controlled oscillator, VCO*. The output

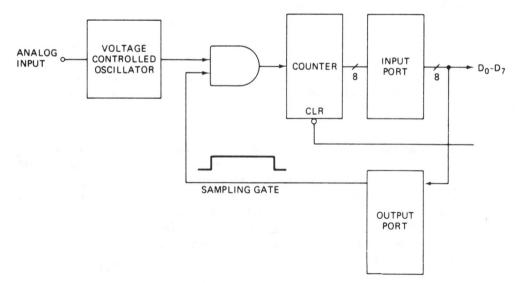

Figure 11.6-11   Voltage to frequency A/D converter.

frequency of a VCO is proportional to its input voltage. Low cost VCOs can be configured from a single IC together with a few discrete components. For example, the interconnection of a National LM131 VCO, seven resistors, and three capacitors constitutes a circuit that accepts an input voltage in the range of 0 to 10 V and outputs a corresponding frequency between 10 Hz and 10 kHz, respectively. This circuit provides a linearity of ± 0.03 percent.

The output from the VCO in Fig. 11.6-11 is gated by a fixed duration sample gate. This sampling gate can be 1 bit of an output port toggled under program control, in which case its duration is controlled by a software delay. The sampling gate could also be the output from a programmable timer. When the sampling gate is logic 1, pulses from the VCO are counted by the counter. At the end of the sample period, the counter contains a value corresponding to the unknown analog voltage.

The resolution of a voltage to frequency converter is partially determined by the number of counter bits. For maximum resolution, the designer must determine the duration of the sample gate corresponding to the largest possible count, without overflow, for the frequency equivalent to full scale VCO output.

11.6.5 Pulse Width Converters

Another approach to indirect conversion transforms the unknown analog signal to the time domain by using the measurand to modulate the duration of a pulse. The width of the pulse changes in proportion to the changes in the measurand. This approach can be implemented with a monostable multivibrator, or single shot, if a transducer is available to transform changes in the measurand to a change in the resistance or capacitance (see Fig. 11.6-12). The duration of the output pulse, T, from the single shot is a function of the external timing components R and C. For example, with a 74121 single shot, $T = RC \ln 2$. Either R is a resistive or C is a capacitive transducer.

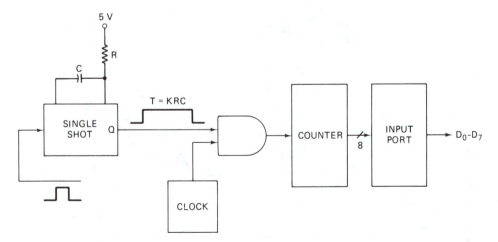

Figure 11.6-12 Pulse width A/D converter.

To carry out a conversion, the counter is cleared, and the single shot is triggered by device select pulses. The output of the single shot gates pulses from a stable, fixed frequency clock to the counter. After the single shot times out, the contents of the counter are used by the microprocessor to determine the desired digital code.

11.6.6 Dual Slope Integrating A/D Converters

Integrating A/D converters use an indirect method of A/D conversion, whereby the analog voltage is converted to a time period that is measured by a counter. There are several variations of the integrating A/D converter: single ramp, dual ramp, and triple ramp. The dual ramp or dual slope-type is employed in many monolithic A/D converters and digital voltmeters.

A dual slope A/D converter circuit is shown in Fig. 11.6-13. An electronic switch selects either an unknown analog voltage or a reference voltage as the circuit's input. At the start of the conversion, the counter is cleared, and the unknown analog voltage is selected as input to the integrator. When the output ramp of the integrator crosses the comparator's threshold, $v_O = 0$ V, the counter is

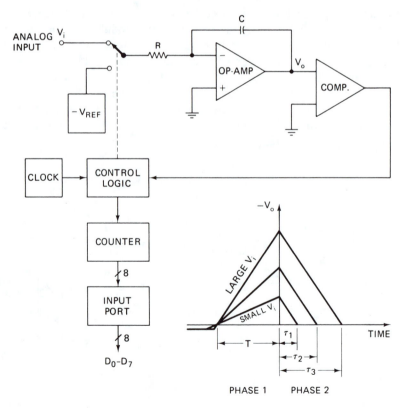

Figure 11.6-13   Dual slope integrating A/D converter.

enabled and counts clock pulses. It counts for a fixed time interval, T, until it overflows. For a constant value analog input, the slope of the integrator's ramp output is proportional to the unknown input, and thus the output voltage of the integrator at the end of the fixed time interval, T, is proportional to the analog input. If the analog input varies during the fixed time interval, the integrator's output at the end of this interval is proportional to the average value (integral) of the input, v_I, over the fixed time interval.

$$v_O(T) = -\frac{1}{RC} \int_0^T v_I \, dt$$

At the end of T, the input of the integrator is switched from the analog input to the reference voltage, making the integrator output a ramp with a fixed positive slope. The counter counts the time required for the integrator's output to reach the comparator's threshold; when it is reached, the counter is stopped. The value left in the counter is the code for the analog voltage. This can be verified by examining the relationship for $v_O(T + \tau)$

$$v_O(T + \tau) = -\frac{1}{RC} \int_T^{T+\tau} (-V_{\text{REF}}) \, dt + v_O(T)$$

$v_O(T)$ is the initial condition at time T; thus

$$v_O(T + \tau) = -\frac{1}{RC} \int_T^{T+\tau} (-V_{\text{REF}}) \, dt - \frac{1}{RC} \int_0^T v_I \, dt$$

Since $v_O(T + \tau) = 0$

$$\frac{1}{RC} \int_T^{T+\tau} V_{\text{REF}} \, dt = \frac{1}{RC} \int_0^T v_I \, dt$$

$$v_{\text{REF}}\tau = \hat{v}_I T$$

$$\hat{v}_I = \frac{\tau}{T} V_{\text{REF}}$$

Thus, the average value of v_I, $\hat{v}_I$, is equal to the ratio of the counts multiplied by V_{REF}, the value remaining in the counter.

Hardware integrating A/D converters are, typically, low-speed devices. However, they are capable of high accuracy at low cost. Commercial integrating A/D converters generally include an additional phase that precedes the first phase of Fig. 11.6-13, during which the device carries out a self-calibrating auto zero operation.

Figure 11.6-14 is the functional block diagram of a 16-bit integrating A/D converter consisting of two Intersil ICs. The analog circuitry is provided by the 14-pin ICL8052 and the digital logic is provided by the 40-pin ICL7104-16. The functions provided by each circuit are shown within the dotted lines in the figure. This converter can convert analog inputs from -10 V to $+10$ V to a 16-bit binary result. The analog input required to produce a full scale output is $V_{\text{IN}} = 2 \times V_{\text{REF}}$.

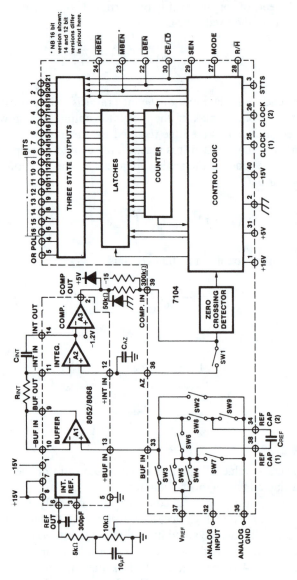

Figure 11.6-14 Functional block diagram of ICL8052/ICL7104-16 16-bit integrating A/C converter. (Courtesy of GE Intersil.)

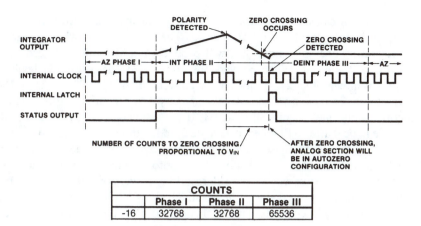

COUNTS			
	Phase I	Phase II	Phase III
-16	32768	32768	65536

Figure 11.6-15 Conversion timing ICL8052/ICL7104-16 16-bit integrating A/D converter. (Courtesy of GE Intersil.)

Either the internal reference, as shown, or an external reference can be used. Two additional output bits indicate the sign of the result, POL, and whether the input exceeded the input range, OR.

This A/D converter will convert its input continuously if the RUN/HOLD input, R/$\overline{\text{H}}$, is held at logic 1 or will convert on demand if the RUN/HOLD input is pulsed. The completion of a conversion is indicated by the status output, $\overline{\text{STTS}}$, being logic 0. Three-state outputs provide the low and high bytes, $\overline{\text{LBEN}}$ and $\overline{\text{MBEN}}$ controls, respectively, of the 16-bit result. The POL and OR bits are accessed as the high byte, $\overline{\text{HBEN}}$.

Conversions are accomplished in three phases (see Fig. 11.6-15). The change in the circuit's configuration for each phase is accomplished by the control section's activation of switches SW1 through SW9. The first phase is the auto zero phase during which the analog input is switched to ground and the auto zero capacitor is charged to a value equal to the offset of the A/D converter's analog input stages, eliminating their error contribution. The reference capacitor is simultaneously charged to the value of the reference voltage. The second phase is the integrate phase during which the analog input is integrated for a fixed number, 32,768, of clock pulses. This corresponds to the first slope of the dual slope conversion previously discussed. If the analog input signal is zero, then the integrator and comparator will see the same voltage that existed at the end of the auto zero phase and the integrator output will not change during this phase. The third phase is the deintegrate phase. During this phase the voltage across the reference capacitor, equal to the reference voltage, is integrated until the integrator's output is zero. Using the reference capacitor and switches, the reference voltage integrated is either positive or negative, depending on the polarity of the integrator's output at the end of the second phase.

An onboard oscillator and an external crystal are used to generate the internal clock. In order to optimize 60 Hz line rejection, the clock frequency is chosen so that 32,768 clock periods, the time during which the unknown is integrated, is an integral multiple of the 60 Hz period. The 60 Hz noise, when integrated over an integral number of its periods, will produce a contribution of zero to the average value of the input. When conversions are carried out continuously, $R/\overline{H} = 1$, the total number of clock periods in a conversion is 131,072. using a 196.608 KHz crystal, a conversion will be completed every 0.67 second. It is possible to reduce the conversion time by controlling $R/\overline{H}$. If the status output is monitored, $R/\overline{H}$ can be made logic 0 after STTS becomes logic 0, indicating the zero crossing in phase three. This will terminate phase three and the auto zero, phase one, will start immediately. If $R/\overline{H}$ is brought to logic 1 a minimum auto zero time is ensured and phase two of the next conversion will begin. The resulting conversion time will then be a function of the analog input value. The relatively long conversion times associated with integrating A/D converters make them good candidates for interrupt driven interfaces.

11.7 SAMPLE AND HOLD CIRCUITS

A *sample and hold* circuit does for analog signals what a D-type flip-flop does for digital signals. At the command of a digital control signal, a sample and hold circuit stores the value of the input analog signal. The stored analog value is available to the circuit's output until the circuit is subsequently commanded to store a new value.

When used at the input to an A/D converter, a sample and hold acquires an analog signal at the precise time dictated by a digital control signal. The A/D converter can then convert the voltage held at the output of the sample and hold. This minimizes inaccuracies in the converted value of an analog signal due to changes in the signal's value during the conversion process. Without a sample and hold, an A/D converter must complete its conversion before the analog input changes $\pm 1/2$ lsb, or the result is inaccurate. Sample and hold circuits are also used at the output of D/A converters to minimize glitches that appear as the output changes from one level to another. Here the circuit samples the output after the settling time of the converter has elapsed.

In its simplest form a sample and hold circuit can be implemented by a switch and capacitor, as shown in Fig. 11.7-1. When the switch is closed, the circuit is in the sample mode and the output signal, v_O, follows the input signal, v_I. Since the circuit in this figure is ideal, the output voltage exactly follows the input voltage. When the switch is open, the circuit is in the hold mode, and the capacitor indefinitely maintains the output voltage at the value that existed at the instant the switch was opened.

Although the switch position in Fig. 11.7-1 is controlled by a logic level signal, a logic gate cannot implement the switch because the precise value of the voltage at the input and output of the switch is important. Instead, an analog switch or analog gate must be used. Analog switches can be constructed from diodes, bipolar transistors, or field effect transistors, and circuits can be constructed by using any

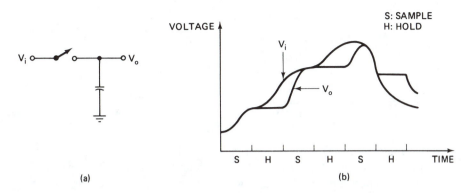

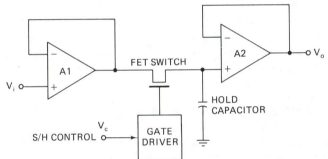

Figure 11.7-1 Idealized representation of a simple sample and hold circuit: (a) circuit; (b) input-output characteristic.

Figure 11.7-2 Implementation of a practical sample and hold circuit.

one of the devices as the switch—as long as the resistance of the switch, when closed, is very small and, when open, is very large.

A practical sample and hold circuit buffers the switch and capacitor from the source and load. See Fig. 11.7-2. In this example, two operational amplifiers configured as unity gain buffers are used. Op-amp A_1 presents a high input impedance to the analog input voltage source and a low output impedance to the switch and capacitor. This allows the capacitor to be charged as rapidly as possible when the switch is closed. The time that elapses from the occurrence of the sample command to the point at which the output has a value within a specified error band around the input value is known as the ***acquisition time*** or ***hold settling time***. After the output achieves this specified error band, it tracks the input. The switch shown in Fig. 11.7-2 is closed when the control voltage, $V_C = 0$ V and is open when $V_C = 2.0$ V. When the control signal switches to 2.0 V, the switch opens, and the sample and hold is in the hold mode. The finite amount of time required between the transition of the control signal to the hold state and the actual opening of the switch is known as the ***aperture time***.

Op-amp A_2 provides a buffer between the storage capacitor and the output. Without A_2, the capacitor could discharge very quickly through the load resistance. With the switch open in the hold mode, the charge on the capacitor, which stores

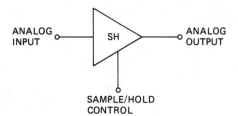

Figure 11.7-3 Symbol for a complete sample and hold circuit.

the analog voltage, decays over a period of time because the resistance of the open analog switch and the resistance of the noninverting input terminal of A_2, although large, are not infinite. Thus, a practical sample and hold circuit cannot indefinitely maintain its output voltage in the hold mode. The rate at which the output voltage decays for a particular sample and hold circuit in the hold mode is its *decay* or *droop rate*. A number of variations exist in the circuit of Fig. 11.7-2 that provide improved operational characteristics.

Numerous integrated circuit sample and hold devices are available that contain buffer amplifiers, an analog switch, and a switch driver in a single package. An external hold capacitor completes the circuit. Such a sample and hold device is represented by the symbol shown in Fig. 11.7-3.

11.8 ANALOG MULTIPLEXERS AND DEMULTIPLEXERS

Although its data inputs and outputs are analog voltages, an analog multiplexer is similar in operation to a digital multiplexer in that a binary code at its address inputs selects one of several possible analog data inputs for transmission to the output. A multiplexer facilitates the handling by an ADC of several analog inputs

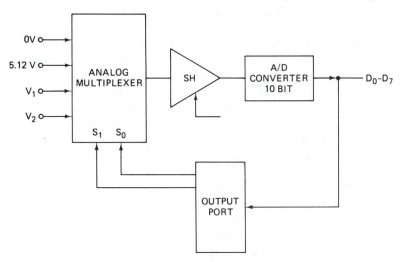

Figure 11.8-1 Data acquisition system with four channel analog multiplexer.

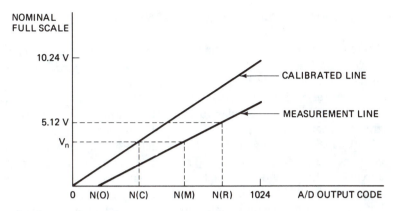

Figure 11.8-2 Graphical representation of calibration relationship for A/D conversion system of Fig. 11.8-1.

on a time multiplexed basis. In Fig. 11.8-1, an analog multiplexer controlled by the microprocessor selects the channel to be input to the A/D converter.

Analog switches similar to the type used in sample and hold circuits (Fig. 11.7-2) can also be used to fabricate analog multiplexers. However, off-the-shelf integrated circuit analog multiplexers are available that include the necessary decoding logic for channel selection, level translators, switch drivers, and the analog switches themselves.

Connecting a voltage reference source, V_R, to one input channel of an analog multiplexer and connecting 0 V to another input of the analog multiplexer provides the capability to correct for offset and gain error in an A/D output, when signals from the multiplexer channels carrying analog information are converted to digital. Ideally, the signal paths from the reference voltage and ground are identical to the signal paths from the analog information sources.

Prior to the conversion of an analog signal, the 0 V and V_R voltages are each converted, and these numbers—$N(0)$ and $N(R)$, respectively—are stored in memory. The analog signal, V_M, is then converted, giving $N(M)$, and this result is used by the microprocessor to compute the corrected measurand voltage.

$$V_M = \frac{N(M) - N(0)}{N(R) - N(0)} V_R$$

Figure 11.8-2 shows this relationship for a system that provides a 10-bit conversion of analog voltages of a nominal 10.24 V FS. The reference input voltage, V_R, is 5.12 V.

Analog demultiplexers are similar in operation to digital demultiplexers, with the exception that the data inputs and outputs are analog voltages. A binary code at the address inputs of the analog demultiplexer selects the channel on which the analog input voltage is output (see Fig. 11.1-2). If the output voltage at a particular channel must be maintained for a period of time, a sample and hold is used at the output.

11.9 MULTICHANNEL DATA ACQUISITION SYSTEMS

There are a multitude of structures for the acquisition and conversion of a number of channels of analog data. These multichannel *data acquisition systems, DAS*, differ in the degree to which their various components are time shared.

Several modular and single board DASs are directly microprocessor compatible. Most of these are similar to the system shown in Fig. 11.1-1 and involve the greatest degree of component sharing. The structure of a typical modular unit, MP20, is shown in Fig. 11.9-1. This structure is implemented as a hybrid circuit contained in a single package. The unit contains an analog multiplexer, which accepts 16 single-ended or eight differential analog signals; an instrumentation amplifier; an 8-bit successive approximation A/D converter; three-state output buffers; and decoding and control logic. Sixteen-channel, single-ended or 8-channel differential operation is determined by external hardwired connections between the multiplexer output and instrumentation amplifier input. The gain of the instrumentation amplifier is programmed by a single external resistor, allowing input signal ranges as low as ± 10 mV.

This module is designed to be interfaced to a microprocessor using memory mapped I/O. Eleven address select lines are externally hardwired to establish the address to which the module will respond. The address decoder uses bits A_4–A_{15} to select the DAS. The remaining four address bits, A_0–A_3, select the channel to be converted. Each analog input channel occupies one memory location. An LDA or MOV instruction inputs the results of a conversion from one channel, or the LHLD instruction can input data from two channels. A READY signal places the microprocessor in the WAIT state until the conversion is complete. Conversion time is 35 μS per channel on the ± 5 V or 0 to 5 V input range to achieve an absolute accuracy of ± 0.4 percent.

Single board DASs provide additional capabilities such as software selectable gains for an instrumentation amplifier, allowing the selection of different gains for different channels or different gains for varying input levels on the same channel. Thus, the dynamic range of a 12-bit converter can be expanded to 15 bits if gains of 1, 2, 4, and 8 are selectable. Real-time clocks called *pacer clocks* are available on some systems to generate precisely timed pulses that trigger the accurately spaced A/D conversions.

Certain single board systems are designed to treat each analog channel as a memory location. Conversion is triggered by a memory read instruction, and the microprocessor is placed in a WAIT state until the conversion is complete. In systems that operate under program control, commands control those registers on the DAS that select the channel and gain and initiate the conversion. An end-of-conversion bit in a status word is checked to determine completion of the conversion. Alternatively, a pacer clock may initiate the conversion and generate an interrupt when the conversion is complete. Other multichannel data acquisition structures are implemented with integrated and modular components.

In contrast to the structure of multichannel DASs that utilize maximum sharing of components, in parallel structures each channel has its own signal conditioning, sample and hold, and A/D converter. Signals are multiplexed into the

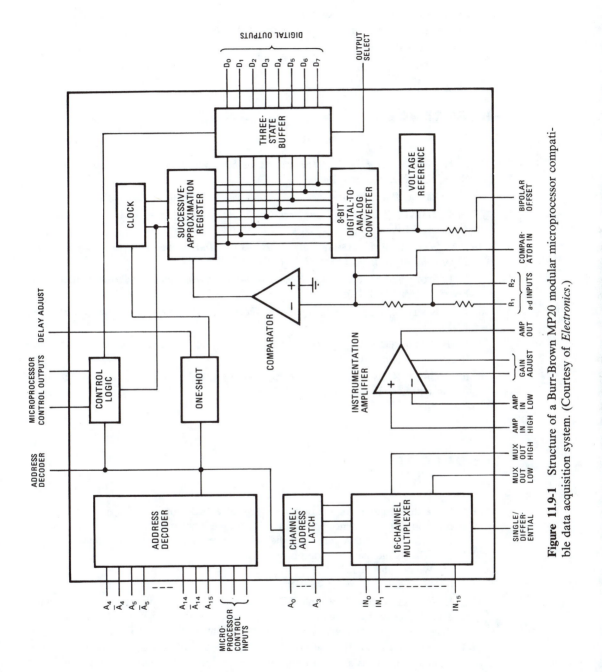

Figure 11.9-1 Structure of a Burr-Brown MP20 modular microprocessor compatible data acquisition system. (Courtesy of *Electronics*.)

451

microprocessor by using a digital multiplexer. With the low cost of IC analog components, such a structure is economically feasible in many applications and provides a very high throughput.

REFERENCES

1. H. N. Norton, *Handbook of Transducers for Electronic Measuring Systems* (Englewood Cliffs, N.J.: Prentice-Hall, 1969).

2. F. J. Oliver, *Practical Instrumentation Transducers* (Rochelle Park, N.J.: Hayden, 1971).

3. G. F. Harvey (Ed.), *ISA Transducer Compendium* (New York: Instrument Society of America, IFI Plenum, pt. 1, 1969; pt. 2, 1970; pt. 3, 1972).

4. J. V. Wait, L. P. Huelsman, and G. A. Korn, *Introduction to Operational Amplifier Theory and Applications* (New York: McGraw-Hill, 1975).

5. D. F. Stout and M. Kaufman, *Handbook of Operational Amplifier Circuit Design* (New York: McGraw-Hill, 1976).

6. J. K. Roberge, *Operational Amplifiers: Theory and Practice* (New York: John Wiley, 1975).

7. D. F. Hoeschele, Jr., *Analog-to-Digital and Digital-to-Analog Conversion Techniques* (New York: John Wiley, 1968).

8. R. C. Ghest, *A Successive Approximation Register* (Application Note). Sunnyvale, Calif.: Advanced Micro Devices, Inc.).

PROBLEMS

11-1. Write the equation for the output voltage of a two-digit BCD D/A converter as a function of the reference voltage, V_{REF}, and the input bits d_1 to d_8, where d_1 is the most significant bit. Assume that the D/A converter uses a 10 V reference:
  (a) What is the maximum output voltage?
  (b) What is the step size?
  (c) What is the percent resolution?

11-2. Using a single chip 8-bit binary D/A converter with a 10 V output and op-amp(s), design an 8-bit two's complement D/A converter with a -5 V to $+5$ V output. Also design an appropriate interface for the D/A converter to an 808A system.

11-3. An 8-bit binary multiplying D/A converter is used in the feedback loop of a buffer amplifier circuit as shown to implement a programmable gain amplifier. The A/D converter has a 0 to 10 V input range.
  (a) What is the equation for V_0 of the programmable gain amplifier as a function of its analog and digital inputs?
  (b) What code should be applied to the programmable gain amplifier, for each channel in the following diagram, in order to provide maximum resolution?

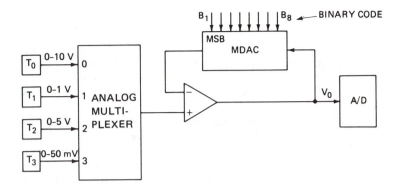

11-4. Draw the circuit diagram of a two-digit weighted resistor D/A converter that uses a single op-amp. Indicate the values of all resistors used in the circuit. Each of the input digits is coded in the 2421 code below. The smallest input resistor to be used is 1 kΩ. The output of the D/A converter is to be 0 to 10 V, nominal. What is the resolution and step size of the converter?

Decimal Digit	Code 2421	Decimal Digit	Code 2421
0	0000	5	1011
1	0001	6	1100
2	0010	7	1101
3	0011	8	1110
4	0100	9	1111

11.5. A 10-bit binary analog to digital (A/D) converter is to be interfaced to an 8085A microprocessor using linear selection. The A/D converter has a control input, SOC, which, when triggered by the leading edge of a positive pulse, begins a conversion of the analog input. The signal, EOC, from the A/D converter goes low when a conversion is in progress, and becomes logic 1 at the end of the conversion. Using isolated I/O, draw a logic diagram of the hardware and write a subroutine that causes a conversion, inputs the converted data, and stores it in 2 bytes of reserved memory labeled DATA.

11-6. An A/D converter similar to the one in Problem 11-5 but with an 8-bit output is to be interfaced to an 8085A. In this case synchronization is to be accomplished using the microprocessor's READY line. Draw the logic required for interfacing, and write the necessary driver subroutine.

11-7. Draw the logic diagram of a hardware structure to support software driven A/D conversion. A 10-bit D/A converter, comparator, three-state buffer, and logic for device selection are all the hardware to be used. The D/A converter is to be treated as if it were a 1024 × 1 block of memory. The data inputs of the D/A converter are to be connected to the address bus. Describe the timing constraints on the circuit for it to operate properly. Write a subroutine that implements a counting type A/D converter with this hardware.

11-8. Draw a flowchart of a successive approximation A/D conversion that uses the hardware of Fig. 11.6-6.

11-9. A voltage to frequency A/D converter is to be designed using a voltage to frequency converter with a 0 to 10 V input range and a corresponding output range of 10 Hz to 10 kHz. The A/D converter is to provide a 10-bit binary output to an 8-bit microprocessor. The gate strobe is to be provided as 1 bit of an output port controlled by the microprocessor.

    (a) Draw a block diagram of the A/D converter and the circuitry required to interface it to an 8-bit microprocessor. It is not necessary to show address decoding.

    (b) What is the duration of the gate strobe for maximum resolution? For this value of gate strobe duration, what is the A/D output count for the following input voltages: 0 V, 2.5 V, and 5 V?

11-10. Using as little additional hardware as possible, design using an op-amp, analog multiplexer, and comparator a 10-bit dual slope integrating A/D converter.

11-11. Write a subroutine that uses the circuit of Fig. 11.8-1 and the relationship of Fig. 11.8-2 to correct the binary result of the conversion of unknown voltages.

11-12. Draw the block diagram of a 10 V FS 4-bit successive approximation A/D converter that is driven by a microprocessor under software control. Draw the graph of the ideal conversion relationship for the converter showing only the first three quanta and first three binary outputs. Show clearly the transition points. Label the quanta and transition points as a fraction of full scale and in volts. To achieve the ideal conversion relationship, what must be the output of the D/A converter when its input is 0000B? For an input voltage of 6.65 V, determine the sequence of binary values output to the D/A converter during the conversion sequence.

11-13. Draw the block diagram of a dual slope integrating A/D converter showing the integrator in detail. The converter produces a 14-bit result and has a 0 to +10.0 V input range. If the converter has a clock frequency f_c, write an expression that gives the maximum conversion time. If the maximum clocking rate of the hardware is 400 KHz, what is the highest value of f_c that can be used to provide optimal rejection of 60 Hz line noise?

12

Programmable Logic Devices

The need to design more compact digital circuits than is possible with SSI/MSI components — but without increasing design time and cost and hampering design flexibility — led to the development of programmable logic.

Programmable Logic: A Basic Guide for the Designer. Data I/O Corporation, © 1983.

The maximum utilization of VLSI, LSI, and MSI devices, in the design of micro-processor systems, results in lower cost and higher reliability. However, as can be seen from previous hardware examples, random logic is usually required in order to tie together various VLSI, LSI, and MSI devices. This logic, implemented with SSI gates, is often referred to as "glue logic." Glue logic can substantially contribute to the number of IC packages in a design.

In addition, some applications require the implementation of special combina-tional or sequential functions that are not available as catalog VLSI, LSI, or MSI devices. These functions may be required to preprocess high speed data before it is input by the microprocessor. Such special functions, when implemented with SSI or MSI devices, may require a substantial number of IC packages.

Programmable logic devices, PLDs, provide arrays of AND gates and OR gates on a single chip. The interconnection of these gates can be programmed to implement combinational functions. Some PLDs, *registered PLDs*, include flip-flops in addition to the AND and OR gates. The inclusion of flip-flops in a PLD allows sequential functions to be implemented. A number of advantages result from the use of PLDs to replace random logic: reduction of the number of ICs in a design, increased reliability, and reduced cost. Also, since PLDs are user programmable, modification of their function in completed designs can usually be accomplished by programming changes without requiring PC board modification.

12.1 BASICS OF PROGRAMMABLE LOGIC DEVICES

Figure 12.1-1a is a block diagram of a general combinational logic network. The outputs of a combinational circuit are a function of its present inputs. Any combinational function can be represented by a *sum-of-products, SOP*, Boolean equation and implemented by a two-level AND-OR circuit. This assumes that both the normal and complement forms of the input variables are available. If not, inverters are necessary. Figure 12.1-1b represents the general form of a clocked sequential circuit. The outputs of the sequential circuit are a function of both the present inputs and the past sequence of inputs. This past sequence of inputs is represented by the bit patterns stored in the memory cells of the sequential circuit. These memory cells can be implemented with D-type flip-flops. Thus, any clocked sequential circuit can be implemented by a two-level AND-OR circuit and D-type flip-flops.

PLDs contain an array of AND gates and an array of OR gates, either or both of which have programmable input connections. In addition, some PLDs have feedback, three-state outputs, and flip-flops. A concise notation is used to represent AND gates and OR gates in PLDs. This notation provides a one-to-one correspon-dence between the chip layout and the logic diagram. Figure 12.1-2 shows the distinctive shape logic symbol representation and the PLD representation of a three-input AND gate and a three-input OR gate. The PLD representation of the gate uses a single line as the gate input. The single line input to an AND gate is the *product line* and the single line input to an OR gate is the *sum line*. Crossing the product line or sum line is a line for each of the input variables. An X at the

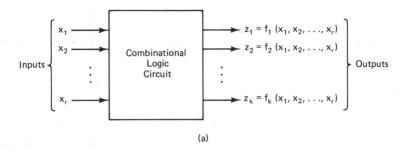

(a)

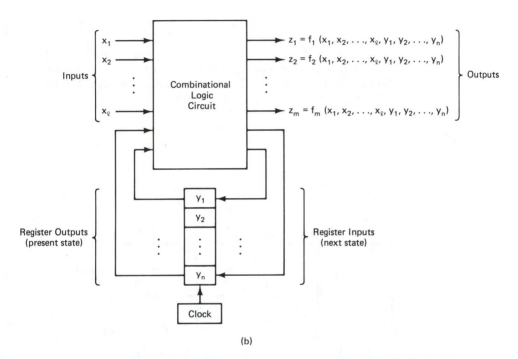

(b)

Figure 12.1-1 (a) General representation of a combinational logic circuit. (b) General representation of a clocked sequential circuit.

intersection of an input variable line and the product line, or a input variable line and the sum line, indicates that the input variable is an input to the gate. Several input variable lines with an X at their intersection with the product line (or sum line), indicates that each variable exists as an input to the gate. This does not imply that the input variable lines are actually connected together!

A PLD consists of an array of AND gates followed by an array of OR gates (see Fig. 12.1-3). The inputs to the AND gates are derived from the external input pins of the PLD. Each external input is buffered and made available to the product line in its normal and complement form. The outputs of the AND gates provide the inputs to the OR gates. The PLD of Fig. 12.1-3 has two inputs, two product terms (AND gates), and two outputs (OR gates). An X appears at the intersection of all

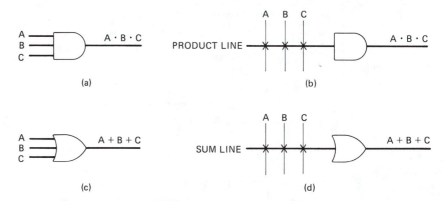

Figure 12.1-2 PLD notation for gates: (a) distinctive symbol representation of a three-input AND gate; (b) PLD representation of a three-input AND gate; (c) distinctive symbol representation of a three-input OR gate; (d) PLD representation of a three-input OR gate.

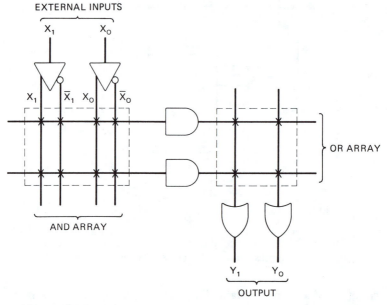

Figure 12.1-3 Two-input, two-output programmable logic device with two product terms.

external input lines and product lines and all AND gate outputs and sum lines. This corresponds to the unprogrammed state of the PLD. Programming the device involves selectively breaking or opening the connections, represented by Xs, in order to realize the desired function.

Since all connections exist in the unprogrammed device of Fig. 12.1-3, it is conceptually possible to program both the AND array and the OR array in this

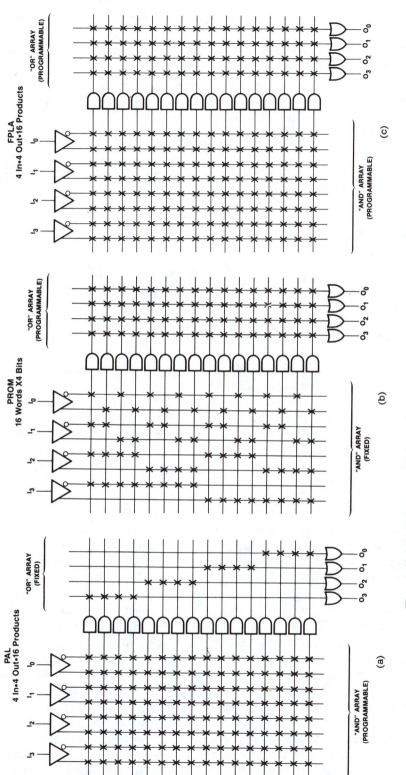

Figure 12.1-4 Programmable logic device structures: (a) programmable AND-fixed OR; (b) fixed AND-programmable OR; (c) programmable AND-programmable OR. (Courtesy of Monolithic Memories.)

459

example. PLDs can be categorized based on which of the arrays can be programmed and which are fixed. The possibilities are

1. Programmable AND-fixed OR; PALs, EPLDs, and GALS
2. Fixed AND-programmable OR; PROMs
3. Programmable AND-programmable OR; FPLAs

These three categories are represented by the structures in Fig. 12.1-4 and are discussed in the following sections.

12.2 PROGRAMMABLE AND-FIXED OR DEVICES

There are several PLD devices that have a programmable AND-fixed OR basic architecture. These include PALs, EPLDs, and GALs, which are discussed in the following sections.

12.2.1 Programmable Array Logic, PALs

Monolithic Memories originated a family of devices called *programmable array logic, PALs*, that have a programmable AND-fixed OR architecture [1]. These devices are available in TTL and CMOS. The least complex group, consisting of a variety of devices, are the 20 pin PALs, some of which are shown in Fig. 12.2-1. Included in this group are devices with active high outputs, active low outputs, complementary outputs, feedback, and registered outputs. The description of each device in Fig. 12.2-1 is given in Table 12.2-1. Each of these PALs can typically replace four or more SSI packages.

A simple device without registers is the 10L8. This PAL has ten inputs and eight active low outputs. The logic symbol of the 10L8 in Fig. 12.2-1 indicates its logic structure. This structure is shown in more detail in the logic diagram of Fig. 12.2-2. Pins 1 through 9 and pin 11 are inputs. Each input is buffered, providing both the normal and complement form of each input variable to the product lines. For example, the input variable associated with pin 1 has its normal form available on vertical line 2 and its complement form on vertical line 3. Each horizontal line is the product line for a 20-input AND gate. The outputs of each group of two AND gates are inputs to an OR gate. The inputs to the OR gates are not programmable and are represented as separate inputs rather than using a sum line. The output of each OR gate is inverted, providing an active low output. The eight outputs of the PAL are pins 12 through 19. Pin 10 is the ground pin and pin 20 is the 5.0 V supply pin.

Logically, the 10L8 is capable of implementing eight SOP equations. Each equation can contain a maximum of two 10 variable product terms. Each product term has 20 variables available. However, since 10 of the variables are complements of the other 10, at most only one form of each variable would appear in any product term. Use of both forms of a variable in a single product term forces that term

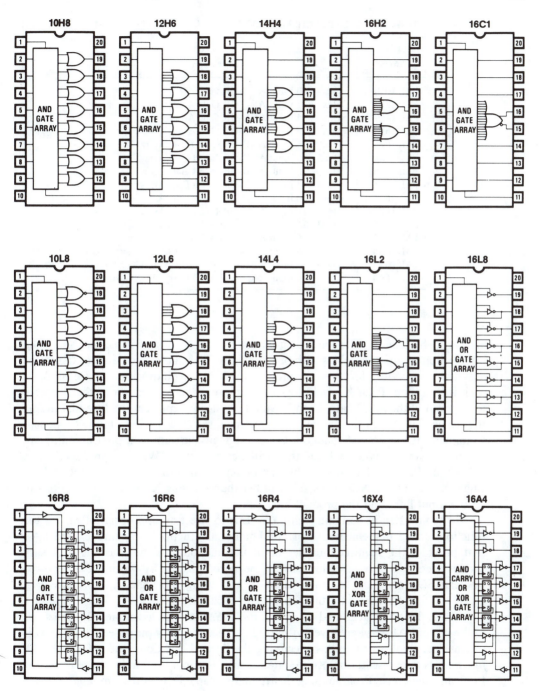

Figure 12.2-1   20-pin PALs. (Courtesy of Monolithic Memories.)

TABLE 12.2-1 DESCRIPTION OF 20-PIN PALS FROM FIG. 12.2-1

Part Number	Description
PAL 10H8	Octal 10 Input AND-OR Gate Array
PAL 12H6	Hex 12 Input AND-OR Gate Array
PAL 14H4	Quad 14 Input AND-OR Gate Array
PAL 16H2	Dual 16 Input AND-OR Gate Array
PAL 16C1	16 Input AND-OR/AND-OR-Invert Gate Array
PAL 10L8	Octal 10 Input AND-OR-Invert Gate Array
PAL 12L6	Hex 12 Input AND-OR-Invert Gate Array
PAL 14L4	Quad 14 Input AND-OR-Invert Gate Array
PAL 16L2	Dual 16 Input AND-OR-Invert Gate Array
PAL 16L8	Octal 16 Input AND-OR-Invert Gate Array
PAL 16R8	Octal 16 Input Registered AND-OR Gate Array
PAL 16R6	Hex 16 Input Registered AND-OR Gate Array
PAL 16R4	Quad 16 Input Registered AND-OR Gate Array
PAL 16X4	Quad 16 Input Registered AND-OR-XOR Gate Array
PAL 16A4	Quad 16 Input Registered AND-Carry-OR-XOR Gate

always to be logic 0. The logic diagram of the 10L8 as shown has no Xs at the intersection of input variables with product lines. This allows the designer to use the diagram as a coding form. An unprogrammed PAL would actually have an X at each intersection. Each X would logically represent the connection of that variable to an input of the AND gate. Each X would physically represent the fuse that makes the connection. When the device is programmed, selected fuses are burned (opened) to implement the desired function. Using the logic diagram as a programming aid, Xs are drawn to indicate fuses that will be left intact. When a product line is unused, all fuses are left intact. This can be represented in shorthand notation by a single X inside the AND gate symbol rather than drawing Xs at the intersections of all the input lines and the product line.

The first step in designing with a PAL is to select an appropriate PAL for the functions to be implemented. For combinational functions, an unregistered PAL that provides the required number of inputs and outputs and has the necessary product terms is chosen. Selection can be accomplished by writing the required Boolean SOP equation for each function and using the logic symbols (see Fig. 12.2-1) to find a device with the appropriate capability.

PAL design is facilitated by use of *PALASM*, a PAL assembler [2]. The steps in the use of PALASM are given in Fig. 12.2-3. The primary purpose of PALASM is to translate Boolean equations specifying the desired functions into a fuse map. A *fuse map* is a representation of the states of the fuses in a PAL to implement specific Boolean functions. Programming instruments, capable of programming a PAL, accept the fuse map as input and program the PAL accordingly. The fuse map is transferred from the computer to the programming instrument using RS232 serial communication. PALASM is available as a program for a number of different computers. The version used here is for the IBM PC. The input to PALASM is a

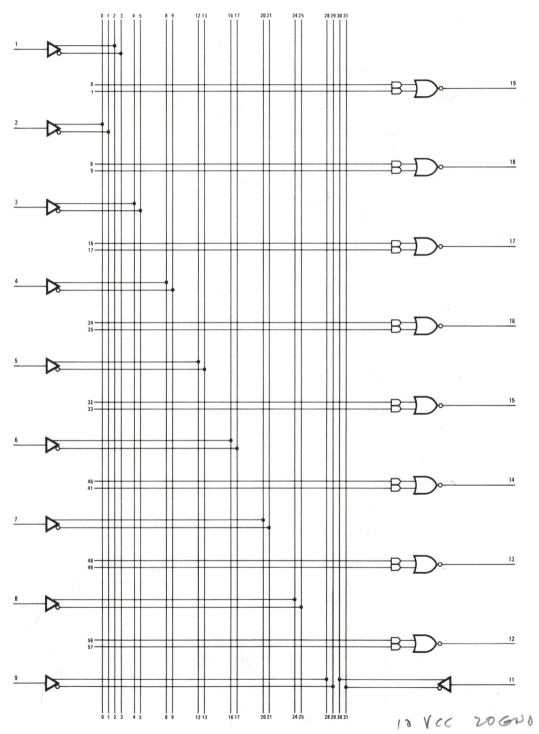

Figure 12.2-2 Logic diagram of 10L8 PAL. (Courtesy of Monolithic Memories.)

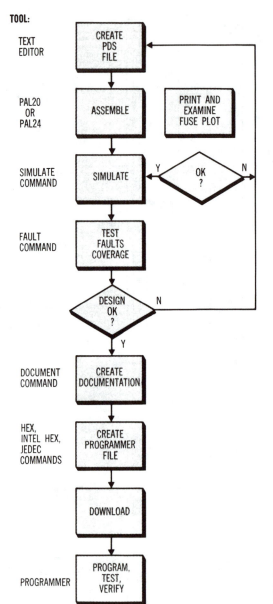

TOOL:

TEXT
EDITOR

PAL20
OR
PAL24

SIMULATE
COMMAND

FAULT
COMMAND

DOCUMENT
COMMAND

HEX,
INTEL HEX,
JEDEC
COMMANDS

PROGRAMMER

Figure 12.2-3 Steps in the use of PALASM, a PAL assembler. (Reprinted with permission from Electronics Products.)

PAL design specification, which is created using a text editor. This input file specifies the PAL to be used, the assignment of input variables to PAL input pins, the assignment of outputs to PAL output pins, and the Boolean equations for each output. Table 12.2-2 details the format of the PALASM design specification. The assembler translates this specification and generates the fuse map.

As an example of the application of a PAL, the address decoding logic of Fig. 2.4-1 is replaced by a PAL. This results in a four-to-one reduction in the number of

TABLE 12.2-2 PALASM DESIGN SPECIFICATION FORMAT (COURTESY OF MONOLITHIC MEMORIES)

The PAL Design Specification is the input file used with PALASM. It is also the recommended data sheet format for describing the function of a PAL once it has acquired the unique personality of a particular fuse pattern. The format for the PAL Design Specification as shown on the opposite page is:

Line 1 PAL part number left justified followed by PAL DESIGN SPECIFICATION

Line 2 User's part number followed by originator's name and the date

Line 3 Device application name

Line 4 User's company name, city, state

Line 5 **Pin List.**
The pin list is a sequence of symbolic names separated by one or more spaces on one or more lines in order of the device pin numbers. Each symbolic name is unique (except for unused pins which may have the same name.) All pins including power and ground must be named. Names may use any printable character except the operator: "=:*+/()". The prefix "/", may be used to logically complement the name.

Line m **Equations.**
The transfer function of the device is expressed in the following three forms:

    1. SYMBOL = EXPRESSION

    2. IF (PRODUCT) SYMBOL = EXPRESSION

    3. SYMBOL: = EXPRESSION

The following terms are used to construct the equations:

SYMBOL	Pin name with optional prefix, "/".
PRODUCT	A sequence of SYMBOLS separated by the AND operator, "*".
IF	Conditional equality, when the PRODUCT is logically true. Otherwise, high impedance (high-Z).
EXPRESSION	A sequence of SYMBOLS separated by operators.

OPERATORS (in hierarchy of evaluation)

;	Comment follows
/	Complement, prefix to a pin name.
*	AND (product)
+	OR (sum)
:+:	XOR (exclusive OR)
:*:	XNOR (exclusive NOR)
( )	Conditional three-state (IF STATEMENT) or fixed symbol
=	Equality
:=	Replaced by after the low to high transition of the clock.

Line n **Function Table.** (optional)
The function table begins with the keyword, "FUNCTION TABLE." It is followed by a pin list which may be in a different order and polarity from the pin list in Line 5. VCC and GND cannot be listed. The pin list is followed by a dashed line; e.g., ---------- (length optional), which in turn is followed by a list of vectors, one vector per line. One state must be specified for each pin name and optionally separated by spaces. A vector is a sequence of states listed in the same order as the pin list and followed by an optional comment. The vector list is followed by another dashed line.

Definition of Function Table States:

H	HIGH LEVEL
L	LOW LEVEL
X	IRRELEVANT
C	TRANSITION FROM LOW TO HIGH LEVEL
Z	OFF (HIGH IMPEDANCE)

Line o **Description.** (Optional if following Function Table).
This section begins with the keyword, "DESCRIPTION." The device operation and application are described here.

ICs required for the decoding. The address decoding logic in Fig. 2.4-1 has six inputs, address bits A_{11} through A_{15} and IO/$\overline{\text{M}}$. Only two outputs are required. The first output, $\overline{\text{EPROMCS}}$, is logic 0 whenever an address in the first 8 K of the memory address space, 0000H through 1FFFH, is generated. This output provides the chip enable to an 8 K $\times$ 8 EPROM. The second output, RWMCS, is logic 0 whenever a memory address from 2000H to 27FFH occurs. This output provides the

```
PAL10L8                                    PAL DESIGN SPECIFICATION
EXAMPLE1                                   KENNETH L. SHORT
ADDRESS DECODE LOGIC
SUNY STONY BROOK
A15 A14 A13 A12 A11 IO NC NC NC GND NC NC NC NC NC NC NC /RWMCS /EPROMCS VCC
EPROMCS = /A15 * /A14 * /A13 * /IO
RWMCS = /A15 * /A14 * A13 * /A12 * /A11 * /IO


FUNCTION TABLE

A15 A14 A13 A12 A11 IO    RWMCS EPROMCS
---------------------------------------
 X   X   X   X   X   H      L     L      ; MEMORY NOT SELECTED
 L   L   L   X   X   L      L     H      ;ALL LOCATIONS IN 8 K EPROM
 L   L   H   L   L   L      H     L      ;ALL LOCATIONS IN 2 K SRAM
 X   X   H   L   H   L      L     L      ;ALL LOCATIONS NOT IMPLEMENTED
---------------------------------------


DESCRIPTION
FULL DECODED ADDRESS DECODER: 8K EPROM, 0000H-1FFFH, 2K SRAM, 2000H-27FFH
```

Figure 12.2-4   PAL address decoder design specification.

chip select to a 2 K × 8 SRAM. The required Boolean equations are

$$EPROMCS = \overline{A_{15}} * \overline{A_{14}} * \overline{A_{13}} * IO \; / \overline{\overline{M}}$$
$$RWMCS = \overline{A_{15}} * \overline{A_{14}} * A_{13} * \overline{A_{12}} * \overline{A_{11}} * IO \; / \overline{\overline{M}}$$

For these equations it can be seen that six inputs and two outputs are required. Since each equation consists of a single product term, only one AND gate is required to provide an input to the OR gate from which each output is obtained. Furthermore, the desired outputs are actually the complements of the functions specified by the SOP equations. These requirements can be met by the 10L8 PAL. The 10L8 has active low outputs, thus providing the required complementation.

A PAL design specification for the address decoder is given in Fig. 12.2-4. This design specification is the input to PALASM. The PAL selected is specified in line 1. Line 5 assigns symbolic names to the PAL's pins. Pin 1 is A_{15}, pin 2 is A_{14}, and so on. The symbol IO has been used in place of $IO/\overline{M}$ since / is reserved as the symbol for the complement operator in PALASM. Input pins that are not used have been labeled NC. The output names are preceded by a / to indicate that they are active low. The SOP equations for the outputs appear in lines 6 and 7. Note that these equations are written for the normal form of the output; the active low output of the 10L8 provides the complement. The function table is optional and will be described later.

Figure 12.2-5 is a brief version of the fuse map generated by PALASM. Only the product lines that have fuses blown are shown. The product line number appears at the left of the row. Only product lines 0 and 8 have fuses blown in this example. The columns are numbered at the top of the fuse map. The columns represent the normal and complement forms of the variables. The correspondence between column numbers and input variables can be obtained from the 10L8 logic diagram in Fig. 12.2-2. Input variable A_{15}, assigned to pin 1, has its normal form on

```
PAL20 V1.7D - PAL10L8   - ADDRESS DECODE LOGIC
                11 1111 1111 2222 2222 2233
   0123 4567 8901 2345 6789 0123 4567 8901
0 -X-X -X   --   --   -X   --   --   ----  /A15 * /A14 * /A13 * /IO
8 -X-X X-   -X   -X   -X   --   --   ----  /A15 * /A14 * A13  * /A12 * /A11 * /IO
```

Figure 12.2-5   Brief version of PALASM fuse map for address decoder.

column 2 and its complement form on column 3. Unblown fuses are represented by an X. Fuses that are blown are represented by a –. Thus, A_{15} is an input to the AND gate associated with product line 0. Blanks are used to represent fuses that do not exist in the PAL. For example, there is no fuse at the intersection of row 0 and column 6; a check of the logic diagram for the 10L8 verifies this. The two product lines associated with the output $\overline{EPROMCS}$, pin 19, are product lines 0 and 1. A detailed examination of the fuses remaining intact in product line 0 shows that it generates the single product term required. This can be verified by labeling Fig. 12.2-2 with the appropriate variables from the pin list on line 5 of Fig. 12.2-4. The product term associated with product line 1 is always logic 0 because both the normal and complement forms of the input variables appear at the input to the AND gate.

Only a portion of the 10L8's capability has been used in this example. The unused outputs of the 10L8 could be used for I/O address decoding. A 10L8 with A_8–A_{15} and IO/$\overline{M}$ as inputs could provide general address decode logic for an 8085A system. The eight outputs can be programmed to decode addresses to select memory devices with a capacity of 256 bytes, or more, and to select isolated IO devices with 1 to 256 registers. This requires that the memory and IO devices have separate chip select, $\overline{RD}$, and $\overline{WR}$ inputs. Alternatively, $\overline{RD}$ and $\overline{WR}$ can be added as inputs to the PAL by removing A_8 as an input. This allows the select outputs to be conditioned by $\overline{RD}$ or $\overline{WR}$. The smallest memory device that can be exhaustively decoded in this case would be 512 × 8, and isolated I/O decoding would not be exhaustive. Another approach is to select a PAL with a larger number of inputs but fewer outputs, such as the 12L6. Thus, in many small systems all address decoding could be implemented by one or a few PALs.

A primary drawback to the use of memory mapped IO is the necessity to decode 16 address bits, when exhaustive decoding is required, for IO devices that have only one register. A 16L2 PAL can provide exhaustive address decoding for two memory mapped IO ports in a single 20-pin package.

An optional part of the PALASM input specification is a function table that is used both to document and verify the design. The function table consists of a pin list of inputs and outputs followed by a list of test vectors. The *test vectors* are sequences of states in the same order as the function table pin list. The states indicate the logic value of the PAL's outputs for specified input states. The states are indicated as high, H, low, L, and don't care. Basically, the function table is the same as a truth table for the functions to be implemented. However, unlike in a truth table, all input combinations do not have to be specified in a function table. The FAULT command in PALASM aids the designer in determining whether the

```
OUTPUT POLARITY WORD XXXXXXXX
LEGEND:  X : FUSE NOT BLOWN (L,N,0)   -: FUSE BLOWN (H,P,1)
NUMBER OF FUSES BLOWN = 54
SECURITY FUSE XX
ADDRESS DECODE LOGIC
    1 XXXXX1XXXXXXXXXXXHH1
    2 000XX0XXXXXXXXXXXHL1
    3 001000XXXXXXXXXXXLH1
    4 XX1010XXXXXXXXXXXHH1
PASS SIMULATION
NUMBER OF STUCK AT ONE (SA1) FAULTS ARE =  2
NUMBER OF STUCK AT ZERO (SA0) FAULTS ARE=  2
PRODUCT   TERM    COVERAGE            =100%
```

Figure 12.2-6   PALASM FAULT command output for address decoder.

function table entries are sufficient to detect all failures in product lines that can fail
by being stuck-at-1 or stuck-at-0. The fault testing procedure determines which
failures the function table entries can and cannot detect. PALASM indicates which
product terms and which types of faults are not detected. Figure 12.2-6 shows the
output of PALASM in response to a FAULT command for the address decoder
example.

PALASM includes a simulator that can check the equations specified against
the function table entries and indicate any discrepancies as errors. All inputs in the
Boolean equations are given the values specified in the function table vectors, and
the equations are evaluated. These results and the outputs specified by the function
table are compared. Don't care, X, entries as test vector input conditions are
replaced with 0s by the simulator. The simulator function translates the function
table vectors into a set of universal test vectors that may be used for functional
testing of a PAL device after it is fabricated.

More complex PAL devices have a variety of possible output structures. The
four structures to be described all provide feedback from output pins. PALs with
programmable I / O allow the same pin to be used as input or output (see Fig.
12.2-7a). The output of the OR gate is buffered by an inverting three-state buffer
before connection to the PAL I/O pin. The three-state buffer is enabled by a
product term. When the buffer is enabled, the I/O pin is an output pin and is
driven by the complement of the OR gate output. If the I/O pin is programmed to
functon only as an output, then PALASM will specify that all fuses in the product
line of the AND gate that controls the three-state buffer be burned. This fixes the
AND gate output at logic 1. The output and its complement are also available as
inputs to the product terms. When the buffer is disabled, the I/O pin is an input
pin, and the AND gates and OR gate associated with the I/O pin are not used.
When an I/O pin is programmed as a fixed input, all the fuses on the product line
of the AND gate are left intact. This fixes the gate output at logic 0. Programmed
I/O allows the designer to change the ratio of inputs and outputs available on a
PAL by allocating some pins for input and others for output. For example, the 16L8
has 10 fixed input pins, 2 fixed output pins, and 6 programable I/O pins. Note that
two of the three-state output buffers don't have feedback connections to the AND

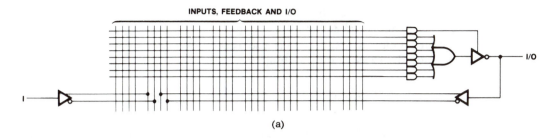

(a)

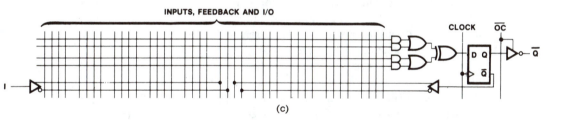

(b)

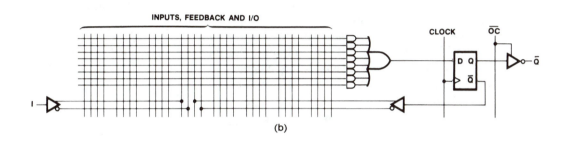

(c)

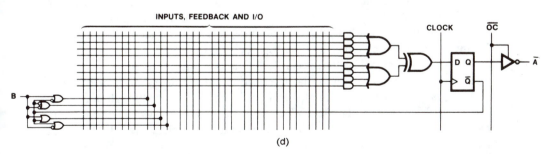

(d)

Figure 12.2-7 PAL output structures: (a) programmable I/O; (b) registered data outputs; (c) EX-OR function; (d) arithmetic gated feedback. (Courtesy of Monolithic Memories.)

array, and therefore can only be used as outputs. Thus, the 16L8 can be configured to have from 10 inputs and 8 outputs to 16 inputs and 2 outputs.

The programmable I/O feature is also used to provide bidirectional I/O. This is accomplished by specifying the output by an equation of the form

IF (PRODUCT) SYMBOL = EXPRESSION

as shown in Table 12.2-2. PRODUCT is the product term that will be implemented by the AND gate controlling the output buffer. When this product term is logic 1, the I/O pin is an output and its value will be logic 0 or logic 1 based on EXPRESSION. Otherwise, the buffer output will be in its high impedance state and the I/O pin can act as an input.

PALs with *registered data outputs* allow the output of the OR gate to be stored in a positive edge triggered D-type flip-flop. See Fig. 12.2-7b. A single input of the PAL provides the clock signal that is common to all the flip-flops on the PAL. Register outputs are specified by an equation of the form

SYMBOL := EXPRESSION

The output of the D-type flip-flop takes the value of EXPRESSION on the rising edge of the clock pulse. Another PAL input controls the three-state outputs of all the flip-flops. The Q output of the flip-flop is fed back through a buffer to provide the normal and complement form of the data stored in the flip-flop to the product terms. This feedback allows the PAL to remember its previous state and makes possible the implementation of state machines.

Another output structure provides the EX-OR function of two SOP expressions in addition to a registered data output (see Fig. 12.2-7c). This type of structure is used in the 16X4. The addition of gated feedback to the EX-OR structure results in the *arithmetic gated feedback* structure (see Fig. 12.2-7d). This structure, which is used in the 16A4, allows arithmetic functions such as addition, subtraction, greater than, and less than to be efficiently implemented.

The features previously described are available on one or more of the 20-pin PALs in Fig. 12.2-1. Other 20-pin PALs have been introduced with additional features. One feature available in some of these devices is registered latched inputs. The input registers are either D-type flip-flops or transparent latches. The input register is programmable so that it can function as a register or simply as an input buffer. Another feature, output polarity selection, allows the polarity of the output to be programmed. This is accomplished by passing the output through one input of a two-input EX-OR gate. The second input of the gate is connected through a fuse link to ground. When the fuse is blown, the input is complemented. PALs are also available with larger numbers of pins, including 24-, 40-, and 84-pin devices.

The *final fuse* feature of a PAL allows a security fuse to be blown after the PAL is programmed and tested. When this fuse is blown, the fuse map of the PAL can no longer be read from the PAL. This prevents unauthorized copying or determination of the function implemented by a programmed PAL.

Second generation PAL architectures use programmable output macrocells, which allow each output macrocell to be individually programmed to implement many of the output structures previously described. For example, Advanced Micro Devices' AmPAL 22V10 is a 24-pin, second generation, fusable link device using a programmable macrocell architecture [3]. Each of its output macrocells can be programmed to any of the following four output configurations: registered/active low, registered/active high, combinatorial/active low, and combinatorial/active high. With this capability the AmPAL can replace many of the 24-pin first generation PALs. Other second generation PALs use macrocell architectures and replace the fusible links with floating gate transistors that allow the devices to be erased and reprogrammed. One of these devices, the EPLD, is discussed in the next section and will be used to describe macrocell structures in more detail.

12.2.2 Erasable Programmable Logic Devices, EPLDs

Erasable programmable logic devices, EPLDs, are programmable AND-fixed OR devices that are user programmable but can be erased, by ultraviolet light, and reprogrammed like EPROMs. EPLDs were introduced by Altera Corporation in 1984. The first EPLD was a 20-pin CMOS device. More complex 24-, 40-, and 68-pin devices are also available.

The first 20-pin EPLD, the EP300, has ten dedicated input pins and eight programmable I/O pins [4]. The EP300 has an effective gate equivalence of 300 gates. Its architecture consists of eight *macrocells*, as shown in Fig. 12.2-8. The detailed structure of a single macrocell is shown in Fig. 12.2-9. Each macrocell consists of a programmable AND array with eight AND gates whose outputs are inputs to a single OR gate. The output of the OR gate is input to an I/O architecture control cell. A ninth AND gate controls the enable input of a three-state buffer that drives the I/O pin of the macrocell.

Inputs to the AND array consist of the normal and complement forms of the signals at the EP300's external inputs and feedback signals from the I/O architecture control cells of each macrocell in the device. One of the EP300's inputs is a clock input that is connected to a positive edge triggered D-type flip-flop, in the I/O architecture control cell, and is available in its normal and complement form to the AND array. Each macrocell contains nine 36-input AND gates. At the intersection of each input line and product line is a floating gate CMOS transistor. The charge on the floating gate of this transistor determines whether there is a connection between the associated input and product line. When erased, all connections are made. Thus, both the normal and complement form of each input are connected to each product line. Selected connections are opened, by charging the associated transistors during the programming process.

The I/O architecture control cell provides the EP300 with substantial I/O versatility (see Fig. 12.2-9). A programmable output multiplexer allows the input to each macrocell's three-state output buffer to be taken from one of four sources: the output of the OR gate, the inverted output of the OR gate, the Q output of the D-type flip-flop, or the $\overline{Q}$ output of the flip-flop. A feedback select multiplexer provides a choice of three sources for the input to the buffer that provides the

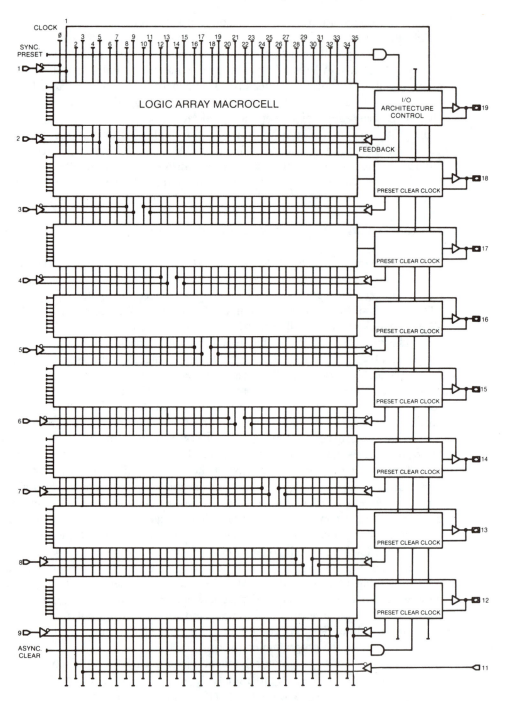

Figure 12.2-8 Architecture of EP300 PLD. (Courtesy of Altera Corp.)

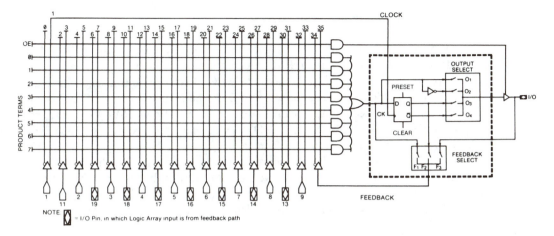

Figure 12.2-9 Detail of one of eight macrocells in EP300. (Courtesy of Altera Corp.)

normal and complement feedback signal to the AND array. The possible sources are the output of the OR gate, the output of the flip-flop, or the I/O pin. Any combination of one switch from the output select multiplexer and one switch from the feedback select multiplexer is valid. The signal at the I/O pin will be the output of the output select multiplexer if the three-state output buffer is enabled or an external input at the I/O pin if the buffer is disabled. Because of the programmability of the I/O architecture control cell, most of the I/O structures available with 20-pin PALs can be achieved with the EP300. Thus, most 20-pin PALs can be replaced by an EP300.

The D-type flip-flops have synchronous preset and asynchronous clear inputs controlled by two additional product terms. All flip-flops share the same synchronous preset and asynchronous clear. When the synchronous preset is asserted, all the flip-flops will be set on the rising edge of the next clock signal. When the asynchronous clear is asserted, all the flip-flops will be cleared independently of the clock. The asynchronous clear overrides the synchronous preset. On power up, the EP300 performs the clear function automatically.

More complex EPLDs provide a larger number of equivalent gates and have a more complex internal architecture. The number of equivalent gates in the EPxxxx family is approximately given by the xxxx designator. Some of the devices in the series are the EP300, EP600, EP1200, and EP1800.

Altera's A + PLUS development software provides design assistance for EPLD users. This software supports multiple design entry methods, including Boolean equations, interactive net list, and schematic diagrams. After the design has been entered, the A + PLUS software performs automatic translation into logic equations, Boolean minimization, and design fitting into the EPLD. The output of the A + PLUS software is a data file in the standard JEDEC format.

12.2.3 Generic Array Logic, GALs

An alternative to using the floating gate transistor structure of the EPROM, to provide reprogrammability in a PAL type structure, is to use the floating gate transistor structure used in EEPROMs. These two floating gate transistor structures are described in detail in Chapters 2 and 13, where their use in EPROMs and EEPROMs is discussed. Lattice Semiconductor Corporation's 16V8 GAL uses this approach [5]. The 16V8 is a 20-pin CMOS device that uses electrically erasable cell technology. Each of its outputs is from a programmable output macrocell. This macrocell is similar, but slightly more complex, than that of the EPLD 300. Electrically erasable cell structures have fast erase times, but the number of write operations that can be performed on a cell is limited. The GAL16V8 is guaranteed for 100 erase/write cycles and to have a data retention exceeding 20 years.

12.3 FIXED AND-PROGRAMMABLE OR, PROMS, PLES

The fixed AND-programmable OR PLD structure is shown in Fig. 12.1-4b. The connections between the normal and complement forms of the inputs and the product lines are fixed. The connections from the AND gate outputs to the sum lines are programmable. This structure is essentially that of a PROM. It is important to note that there is an AND gate for every possible product term. Thus, this structure is appropriate for implementing combinatorial logic where a large number of input combinations is required or a large number of product terms per output is required.

The logic symbol and block diagram of a 2 K × 8 PROM, the PLE11P8, is given in Fig. 12.3-1. The block diagram is similar to that of ROMs presented

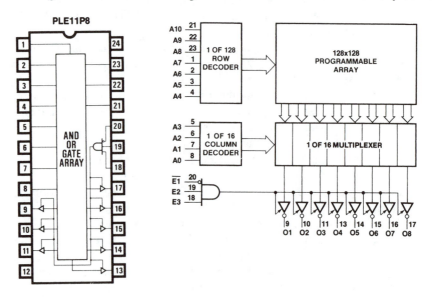

Figure 12.3-1 Logic symbol and block diagram of a 2 K × 8 PROM, the PLE11P8. (Courtesy of Monolithic Memories.)

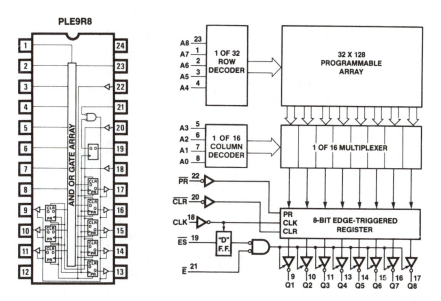

Figure 12.3-2   Logic symbol and block diagram of a 512×8 registered PROM, the PLE9R8. (Courtesy of Monolithic Memories.)

previously, except that there are three enable inputs whose conditions must be satisfied to enable the PROM's three-state output buffers. This device accommodates combinational functions with up to 11 inputs and 8 outputs.

PROMs with registered outputs allow the efficient implementation of sequential circuits. The block diagram of 512×8 registered PROM, PLE9R8, is given in Fig. 12.3-2. The output register has active low preset and clear inputs. Data is transferred to the output registers on the rising edge of the clock (this is not clearly indicated in the block diagram). Data will appear at the outputs provided that both the asynchronous, E, and synchronous, ES, enables are low.

PLEASM is an assembler for PROMs or PLEs and functions similarly to the way PALASM functions for PALs [6]. Logic functions are specified by Boolean equations that PLEASM assembles into a fuse pattern format compatible with commercial PROM programmers. PLEASM also generates a truth table, from the logic equations, that can be used later as test vectors for logic simulation and verification.

12.4 PROGRAMMABLE AND-PROGRAMMABLE OR DEVICES, FPLAS

Programmable AND-programmable OR devices have connections in both the AND array and the OR array programmable, as shown in Fig. 12.1-4c. This allows product terms with from one to all of the input variables represented. However, unlike PROMs, FPLAs usually contain fewer product terms than the maximum possible to conserve chip area. Each OR gate can have from one to all the product

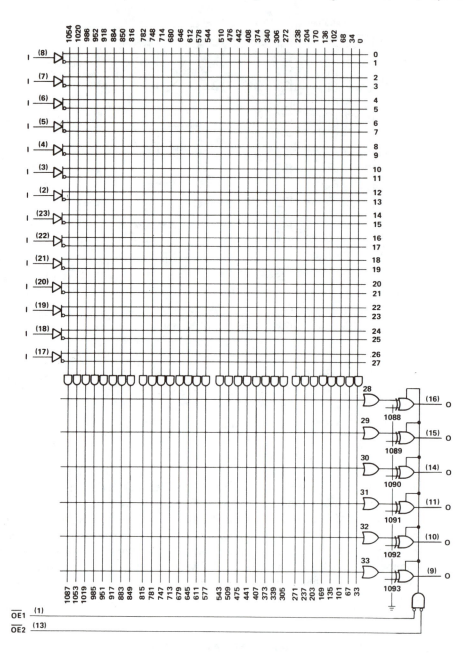

Figure 12.4-1

terms connected to it. This structure is advantageous when implementing logic functions with a large number of product terms of varying sizes or a large number of product terms per output. Although the FPLA architecture is the most flexible for most applications, a large number of the fuses are left intact, in one array or the other, leaving the added flexibility unnecessary.

Figure 12.4-1 is the logic diagram for a $14 \times 32 \times 6$ FPLA, the TIFPLA839. This device has 14 inputs, 32 product terms, and 6 outputs. The maximum possible product terms for 14 inputs is $2^{14} = 16{,}348$, so clearly all possible product terms are not represented.

12.5 HIGH LEVEL PLD DESIGN SOFTWARE

Manufacturers of various PLDs often provide CAD design tools for their specific family or type of PLD. These software packages vary widely in their comprehensiveness and power. For example, Monolithic Memories provides PALASM for its family of PALs and PLEASM for its PROMs. Altera Corporation provides A + Plus for its family of EPLDs. Each of these products is intended to support a single family of devices.

A different level of design support is provided by universal software packages that support a wide variety of PLDs from different manufacturers. Two examples of these are CUPL, from Assisted Technology [7], and ABEL, Advanced Boolean Expression Language, from Data I/O Corporation. Both are high level design languages that allow a design to be specified functionally, without respect to a specific PLD. The functional specification is then compiled to provide a fuse map for a target PLD. The fuse map corresponds to JEDEC standard JC-42.1-81-62 and can be downloaded to programming instruments that accept this standard. Both high level design languages are written in C and are available in versions for the IBM PC and for VAX machines.

REFERENCES

1. J. M. BIRKNER and V. J. COLI, *PAL Programmable Array Logic Handbook*, 3rd ed. (Santa Clara, Calif.: Monolithic Memories, 1983).

2. *The PALASM Manual for Software*, *Release 1.7* (Santa Clara, Calif.: Monolithic Memories, 1984).

3. *Programmable Array Logic Handbook* (Sunnyvale, Calif.: Advanced Micro Devices, Inc., 1984).

4. *EPLD Handbook* (Santa Clara, Calif.: Altera Corporation, 1985).

5. *Lattice Data Catalog* (Beaverton, Oreg.: Lattice Semiconductor Corporation, 1986).

6. *PLE Handbook* (Santa Clara, Calif.: Monolithic Memories, 1984).

7. *CUPL User's Manual* (San Jose, Calif.: Assisted Technology, 1984).

PROBLEMS

12-1. Programmable logic devices consists of an AND array followed by an OR array. Specify which of the arrays is programmable and which is fixed for a PROM, PAL, and FPLA. Using programmable logic conventions, draw the logic representation for an 4×2 PROM whose contents are the following sequence of binary numbers: 11, 01, 00, 10. Using a similar logic structure, show the representation of a "2H2 PAL" with two product terms per output. The PAL should implement the same logic function as the PROM.

12-2. Using the Y_0 output of the programmable logic device in Fig. 12.1-3, show how the AND array and OR array would be programmed (which fuses would be left intact) to implement the following functions of X_0 and X_1: AND, OR, NAND, NOR, and EX-OR. Write the SOP equation for each function.

12-3. Implement the logic required in Problem 3.1 with a 10L8 PAL instead of NAND gates. Write the Boolean equations in the form required by PALASM.

12-4. Using a 10L8 PAL, implement the address decoding logic required in Problem 2-16. Write the Boolean equations required to specify the PAL outputs for PALASM.

12-5. Using a 10L8 PAL, implement the address decoding logic required in Problem 2-17. Write the Boolean equations required to specify the PAL outputs for PALASM.

12-6. Using a 10L8 PAL, implement the address decoding logic required in Problem 2-18. Write the Boolean equations required to specify the PAL outputs for PALASM.

12-7. Using a 10L8 PAL, implement the address decoding logic required in Problem 2-19. Write the Boolean equations required to specify the PAL outputs for PALASM.

12-8. Write the Boolean equations required to implement the logic in Problem 2-20. Can this logic be implemented with one of the PALs in Fig. 12.2-1? If so, indicate which one(s).

12-9. A 10L8 PAL is used to implement various logic functions in a microprocessor system. For each function to be implemented write the appropriate Boolean expression.
   (a) The ROM chip select signals, $\overline{\text{ROM1CS}}$ and $\overline{\text{ROM2CS}}$, are to be generated. The ROMs are each 8 K $\times$ 8 and occupy the first 16 K of address space.
   (b) The signal, $\overline{\text{8254CS}}$, which controls the chip select input, CS, of an 8254 programmable timer, is to be generated. The 8254 is to be located in isolated I/O space with a base address of 6CH. Other inputs to the 8254, which are not generated by the PAL, include $\overline{\text{RD}}$, $\overline{\text{WR}}$, A_0, and A_1.

12-10. Determine the minimum size (number of words and number of bits per word) and the contents of a single ROM programmed to implement all of the following functions:

$$F_1(A, B, C, D) = A'D + BD + B'D$$
$$F_2(A, B, C, D) = (A + B' + C)(A + B')$$
$$(A + C' + D')(A' + B + C + D')$$
$$F_3(A, B, C) = (A' + B)(B' + C)$$
$$F_4(B, C) = A' + B + AB'$$

12-11. Determine the size and contents of a PROM programmed to output the product in binary coded decimal (BCD) of two decimal input digits represented in BCD.

12-12. Determine the size and contents of a PROM that implements a 4-bit comparator (i.e., a comparator that compares two 4-bit words: $A_3A_2A_1A_0$ and $B_3B_2B_1B_0$) that provides three outputs which indicate, by a logic 1 at the appropriate output, one of the following conditions: $A > B$, $A = B$, or $A < B$.

12-13. Design a 4-bit binary up counter using a PROM and D-type flip-flops. Make a provision to clear (set all the outputs to zero) the counter.

12-14. A BCD up-down counter is implemented using programmed logic techniques with a PROM and data latch. The up-down control is represented by the variable U, where $U = 1$ to count up. The output of the counter is $DCBA$, where D is the most significant bit. Draw a block diagram of the system and show the contents of the PROM required to implement the counter.

12-15. Using a PROM and D-type flip-flops, design a 4-bit counter that counts up in binary if its control input equals 0 and counts up in BCD if its control input equals 1. What is the total number of bits required? How many D-type flip-flops are required?

12-16. Modify the design in Problem 1-15 to allow the presetting of the initial value of the count. When this provision is added, what problems may arise and how can they be solved?

12-17. Implement the following state diagram using PROMs and D-type flip-flops. Indicate the state assignment chosen.

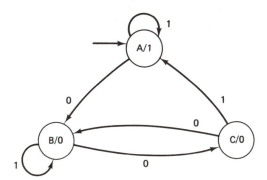

12-18. A PROM implements combinational functions. It has eight inputs and four outputs (256 words, each containing 4 bits). Six of the inputs implement functions $F_1(A, B, C, D, E, G)$ and $F_2(A, B, C, D, E, G)$. Can NAND and EX-OR functions be implemented on inputs X and Y using the same PROM? If so, how?

13

Main and Mass Memory Alternatives

The main memory in a microprocessor system is directly addressable by the microprocessor. This memory is composed of semiconductor devices such as the SRAM and EPROM introduced in Chapter 2. Other types of random access semiconductor memory devices are also used. Each type of device has attributes that make its use preferable in certain applications. Mass memory is used to store large quantities of data. This type of memory is sequentially accessed and not directly addressed by the microprocessor. Data in mass memory is usually transferred, in blocks, to RWM in the microprocessor's main memory, where it is executed as an application program or processed as data.

13.1 DYNAMIC RANDOM ACCESS MEMORIES, DRAMS

Two types of volatile semiconductor read write memory are commonly used in microprocessor systems: static random access memory, SRAMs, and *dynamic random access memory, DRAMs*. The functional operation of SRAMs and their interface to a microprocessor were discussed in Chapter 2. The operation of DRAMs and their interface of a microprocessor differ considerably from those of SRAMs. These differences are a result of the memory cell structures used in the two devices.

13.1.1 Static and Dynamic Memory Cells

The basic six-transistor *MOS static memory cell* is shown in Fig. 13.1-1. This structure, which stores one bit of information, implements a simple RS flip-flop. Transistors Q_3 and Q_4 are biased as resistive loads for transistors Q_1 and Q_2, which

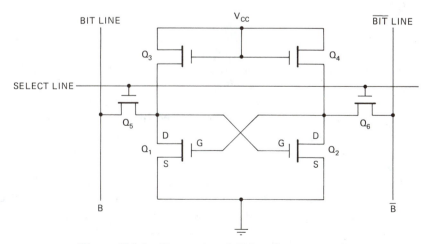

Figure 13.1-1   Six-transistor MOS static memory cell.

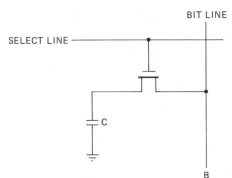

Figure 13.1-2 Single transistor MOS dynamic memory cell.

form a cross-coupled latch. Transistors Q_5 and Q_6 function as transfer gates to connect the drains of Q_1 and Q_2 to the bit lines. If transistor Q_2 is ON, its drain will be at a low voltage. This will cause the gate of Q_1 to be at the same low voltage, turning Q_1 OFF. With Q_1 OFF, its drain will be a high voltage, which will hold Q_2 ON. This state, Q_1 OFF and Q_2 ON, is one of the two possible stable states, and can be defined as the logic 1 state. The logic 0 state would then be the opposite stable state, Q_1 ON and Q_2 OFF. In either state, one of the transistors, Q_1 or Q_2, will be ON and the other will be OFF. With both transistors Q_5 and Q_6 OFF, the memory cell will remain in one of the stable states as long as there is power. If power is removed the stored information is lost. When power is restored the initial state of the memory cell is unknown.

To write data into the memory cell, the cell is selected by placing a high voltage on the select line that turns Q_5 and Q_6 ON. The bit value to be written is placed on bit line B, and its complement on bit line $\overline{B}$. This forces Q_1 and Q_2 into the desired stable state. The cell is then deselected by making the select line voltage low, leaving Q_1 and Q_2 in the state written.

To read the state of the cell, the cell is selected as before. With Q_5 and Q_6 ON, the voltage at the drain of Q_1 can be sensed on B and the voltage at the drain of Q_2 sensed on $\overline{B}$.

The structure of a ***MOS dynamic memory cell*** is shown in Fig. 13.1-2. This cell consists of a single transistor and a capacitor. The state of the memory cell is a function of the charge stored on the capacitor. To write the cell, the bit value is placed on the B line and the cell is selected using the select line. The voltage on the bit line charges the capacitor to write a logic 1 and discharges it to write a logic 0. The state of the memory cell is determined by selecting the cell and sensing the capacitor's voltage on the B line.

The single transistor and capacitor in a dynamic memory cell require much less area on an integrated circuit than the six transistors of a static memory cell. This results in DRAMs with higher bit densities than SRAMs. The dynamic memory cell dissipates almost no power when it is not being written or read. This is in contrast to the static memory cell where one transistor is always ON and therefore dissipating power. Thus, DRAMs require less power than SRAMs.

Unfortunately, this is not the end of the comparison. The charge on the capacitor in the dynamic memory cell will eventually leak off. And after a period of time the data stored in the dynamic cell will be lost. This period of time, the *refresh period*, ranges from 2 mS for early dynamic memory cells to as much as 32 mS for recent CMOS devices.

To prevent the data from being lost, the data must be read from the memory cell and then written back. Peripheral circuitry within a DRAM is designed so that a read operation automatically causes the data read from the cell to be written back. If an application guarantees that each memory cell in a DRAM system is read or written within the refresh period, there will be no loss of data. However, few applications meet this requirement. When this requirement is not met, refresh circuitry external to the DRAM must be used to guarantee that every memory cell is rewritten within the refresh period. This external refresh operation does not require that data actually be output from the memory device.

13.1.2 Dynamic Memory Devices

Dynamic memory devices provide as many as 4 M bits of storage on a single IC. These devices are externally organized as ×1 or ×4. The TMS4416 is a 64 K bit DRAM organized as 16 K × 4 [1]. This device, whose structure and operation is representative of DRAMS in general, will be considered in detail. Figure 13.1-3 shows the pin configuration of the TMS4416. This configuration is substantially different from that of an SRAM. First, a minor but important difference; the TMS4416 requires a single +5 V supply. However, pin 9 is the +5 V supply input and pin 18 is ground. This is the opposite of what is usually the case for a digital circuit in an 18-pin package, but is common with DRAMs.

The TMS4416 is externally organized as 16 K × 4, with common I/O. Pins DQ1–DQ4 are the data pins. With 16 K words, 14 address lines would be expected. However, there are only eight address lines, A0 to A7, on the package. Since DRAMs are used to provide memory systems with high bit density, it is desirable to keep the package size as small as possible. This allows the bit density with respect to printed circuit board area also to be maximized. Therefore, the number of package pins must be minimized. To accomplish this, the 14-bit address is multiplexed into the TMS4416 via the eight address inputs. First, the low order eight address bits, the *row address*, are applied to A0–A7 and strobed into the TMS4416 by the falling edge of the *row address strobe*, $\overline{RAS}$. The high order six address bits, the *column*

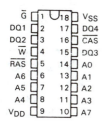

PIN NOMENCLATURE	
A0-A7	Address Inputs
$\overline{CAS}$	Column Address Strobe
DQ1-DQ4	Data In/Data Out
$\overline{G}$	Output Enable
$\overline{RAS}$	Row Address Strobe
V_{DD}	+5-V Supply
V_{SS}	Ground
$\overline{W}$	Write Enable

Figure 13.1-3 TMS4416 16 K × 4 DRAM pin configuration and nomenclature. (Courtesy of Texas Instruments Inc.)

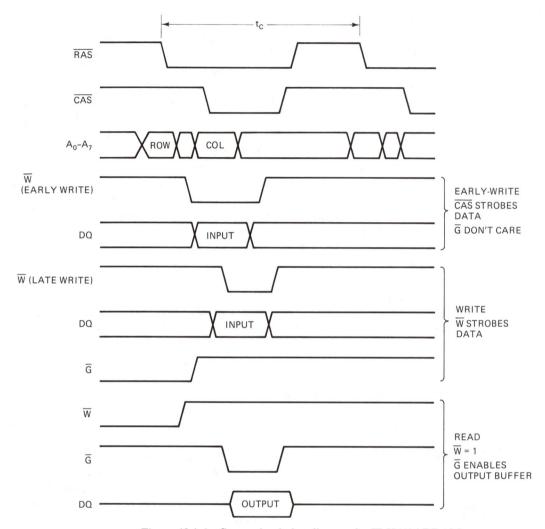

Figure 13.1-4 Composite timing diagram for TMS4416 DRAM.

address, are then applied to A1–A6 and strobed in by the falling edge of the *column address strobe*, $\overline{CAS}$. This relationship is illustrated by the first three waveforms of Fig. 13.1-4. Figure 13.1-5 shows the internal structure of the TMS4416 and the row and column address buffers that latch the address. The two unused column address bits, A0 and A6, are used by a 64 K × 4 DRAM with the same package pinouts.

The TMS4416's square memory array is divided into two halves. Each half consists of 128 rows of 256 bits. The most significant bit of the row address, RA7, selects the upper or lower memory half. The remaining seven row address bits select one of the 128 rows in the selected memory half. The six column address bits control four 1-out-of-64 multiplexers, in the column decode section, which select four of the 256 bits from the selected row to be written or read.

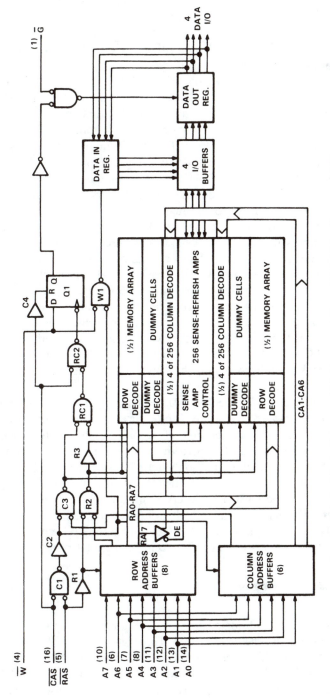

Figure 13.1-5 Block diagram of TMS4416, 16 K × 4 DRAM. (Courtesy of Texas Instruments Inc.)

The timing diagram in Fig. 13.1-4 is a composite diagram showing two types of write cycles and a read cycle. For a write operation the address is strobed into the TMS4416 and the data to be written is placed on the data inputs. Depending on the mode of operation, the falling edge of either $\overline{CAS}$ or $\overline{W}$ strobes the data into the TMS4416. In an *early-write cycle*, $\overline{W}$ is brought low prior to $\overline{CAS}$ and the data is strobed in by $\overline{CAS}$. When $\overline{W}$ goes low prior to $\overline{CAS}$, the data output buffers remain in the high impedance state independently of $\overline{G}$. In the other write cycle, $\overline{CAS}$ goes low before $\overline{W}$ and the data is strobed by $\overline{W}$. In this case $\overline{G}$ must be high before $\overline{CAS}$ goes low to prevent the TMS4416's data bus buffers from being enabled.

A read operation is selected by making the $\overline{W}$ input high. After strobing in the address, data is read from the TMS4416 by bringing $\overline{G}$ low while $\overline{RAS}$ and $\overline{CAS}$ are still low. This will enable the TMS4416's output buffers and provide the addressed data on DQ1–DQ4. Once enabled, the output buffers remain in their low impedance state until $\overline{G}$ or $\overline{CAS}$ is brought high.

On a read access cycle the row address selects a row of 256 bits. This row provides the inputs to one side of 256 *sense-refresh amplifiers*. The inputs to the other side of the sense-refresh amplifiers are the dummy cells from the other side of the memory array. These dummy cells provide a reference voltage for the sense-refresh amplifiers so that the logic level on the 256 storage capacitors of the row can be determined. After this sensing is complete, the output of the sense amplifiers is driven back to the bit lines to refresh the memory cells. This operation is transparent to the user. From the 256 bits that were sensed and restored, four selected by the column address are then output. A write access cycle is similar, except that after sensing, 252 cells are refreshed with the sensed values and four are driven with the four bits to be written.

The refresh period for the TMS4416 is 4 mS. If a read or write operation to one word in each row were guaranteed to occur once every 4 mS, as a result of the application, no further consideration of refresh would be required. If not, an external refresh operation must be performed every 4 mS to retain data. This refresh is accomplished by executing $\overline{RAS}$-only refresh cycles. A *$\overline{RAS}$-only refresh cycle* uses $\overline{RAS}$ to strobe in a row address while CAS is held high for the entire cycle. One $\overline{RAS}$-only refresh cycle must occur every 4 mS for all 256 possible row addresses. Since the output buffers remain in the high impedance state unless $\overline{CAS}$ is applied, the $\overline{RAS}$-only refresh sequence avoids any output during refresh. The time required to refresh the TMS4416 is less than 2 percent of the total refresh period.

13.1.3 DRAM Controllers

DRAMs require external logic to provide address multiplexing, cycle timing, refreshing, and refresh access arbitration. This logic is provided by a dynamic RAM controller. This controller simplifies the interface of DRAMs to microprocessors. The TMS4500A is a single-chip DRAM controller that makes a DRAM system appear as an SRAM to a microprocessor [2]. It can be used, without external latches, to interface directly to microprocessors with multiplexed address data buses, like the 8085A. Figure 13.1-6 shows a TMS4500A used to interface an 8085A to four

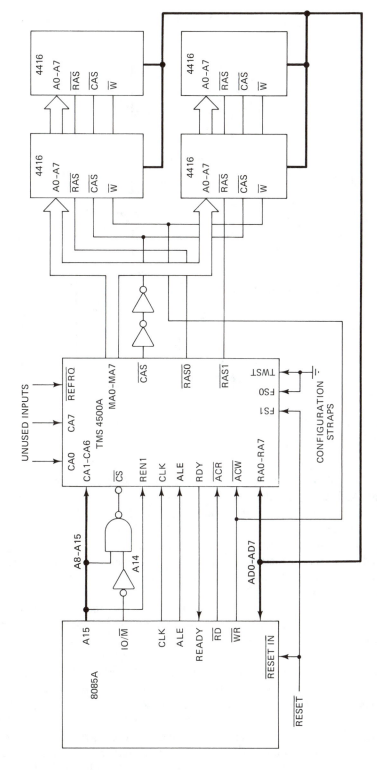

Figure 13.1-6 TMS4500A DMA controller interfacing four TMS4416 16 K × 4 DRAMs to an 8085A.

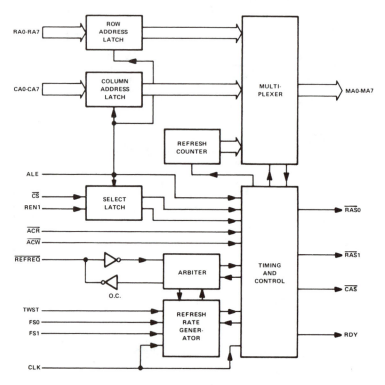

Figure 13.1-7 TMS4500A DMA controller block diagram. (Courtesy of Texas Instruments Inc.)

TMS4416s. This structure provides 32 K × 8 of DRAM starting at address 8000H. The TMS4500A is selected when $A_{15} = 1$ and IO/$\overline{M}$ = 0. The top bank of DRAMs is selected when $A_{14} = 0$, and the bottom bank when $A_{14} = 1$.

The block diagram of the TMS4500A is shown in Fig. 13.1-7. The arbiter selects one of two operational cycles: access or refresh. If a refresh cycle is not due or already in progress, the arbiter instructs the timing and control section to execute an access cycle when the microprocessor addresses a location in the DRAM array and an ALE strobe occurs.

The TMS4500A accepts a 16-bit address at its inputs RA0–RA7 and CA0–CA7. These inputs are latched in the row and column address latches in response to ALE. The occurrence of ALE initiates the access cycle if $\overline{CS}$ is valid. Figure 13.1-8 is a timing diagram that relates the outputs from the TMS4500A to the 8085A signals. The TMS4500A's timing and control block first provides the DRAM array with a row address at MA0–MA7, via its multiplexer, and then generates a $\overline{RAS}$ strobe. The $\overline{RAS}$ strobe will occur at $\overline{RAS0}$ if REN1 = 0, and at $\overline{RAS1}$ if REN1 = 1. Thus, REN1 is controlled by A_{14}. The $\overline{RD}$ and $\overline{WR}$ strobes from the microprocessor provide the access control read, $\overline{ACR}$, and access control write, $\overline{ACW}$, inputs to the TMS4500A. A low at either of these inputs causes the column address to appear on MA0–MA7 and then the column address strobe to be

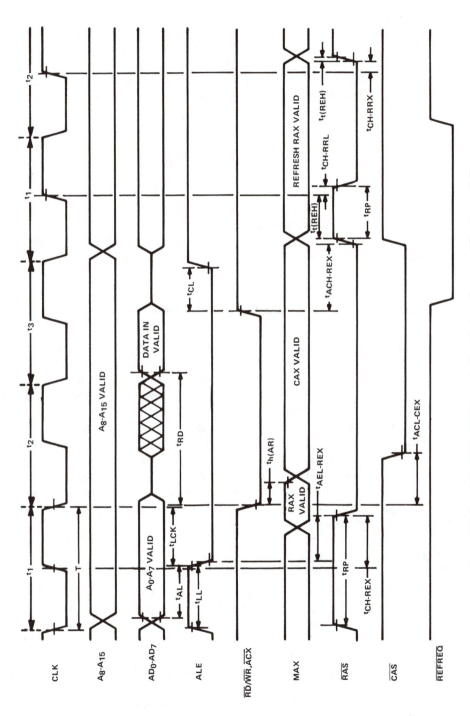

Figure 13.1-8 TMS4500A DMA controller timing diagram. (Courtesy of Texas Instruments Inc.)

489

generated. If the TWST input is logic 1, the RDY output of the TMS4500A will request a WAIT state for every access cycle in order to accommodate slow DRAMs.

The refresh rate generator determines when it is time for a refresh cycle. The refresh generated is a ***distributed refresh***, which spreads the refresh cycles evenly throughout the refresh period. The time between refresh cycles is determined by the clock frequency and the setting of the frequency select straps, FS0, FS1, and TWST. If a refresh cycle is required, any access cycle in progress is completed and then the refresh cycle occurs. The refresh counter maintains the address of the row to be refreshed.

If the microprocessor tries to access the DRAM while a refresh is in progress, the TMS4500A will use its RDY output to force the microprocessor to wait. The REFREQ pin functions as either an input or output. As an output it signals an internal refresh request. As an input it accepts externally generated refresh requests. This allows other refresh modes such as transparent and burst to be implemented using external control. Transparent and burst refresh modes are analogous to transparent and burst DMA discussed in Chapter 9.

13.2 IN-CIRCUIT WRITABLE NONVOLATILE MEMORY

Some applications require nonvolatile memory that can be written without removing it from its circuit. Several types of IC devices are available that meet this need. These devices differ primarily in terms of their write cycle times and the number of write operations allowed. The number of write operations allowed to any single location is specified as the device's ***write endurance***.

All in-circuit writable nonvolatile memory devices must be protected from unstable system control signals that occur when a system is powered up or powered down. Powering down a system may be intentional, system turned OFF, or may be the result of a power failure. When a system is powered up or powered down, the behavior of the system components is unpredictable. It is possible that unstable control signals will accidentally write the memory. ***Write protection circuitry*** must be provided to prevent this.

13.2.1 Battery-Backed CMOS Memory

Because of their low power consumption, CMOS RWM devices can be made nonvolatile by using a battery to back up the AC line power supply. During normal operation from the power supply, the memory can be written and read at its normal speeds. When power is shut OFF or a power failure occurs, the battery provides the backup power necessary to maintain the contents of the memory. In this battery-backed condition, the memory is in its ***data retention mode***, and is not read or written.

Low power versions of most CMOS RWM devices are available. For example, the Toshiba TC5517APL is a low power version of the CMOS SRAM discussed in Section 2.4 [3]. This device will retain data with its V_{CC} as low as 2.0 V. With its

$V_{CC} = 2.0$ V and the device deselected, $\overline{CE} > 1.5$ V, it draws less than 0.2 μA maximum at an ambient temperature of 25°C. At this current level, a 110 mAH battery would retain the data in the memory for 60 years. The current drain increases to 1 μA maximum at 60°C.

Battery backup of a CMOS RWM requires circuitry to handle two major considerations:

1. The memory device's source of power must be switched from the AC line power supply to the battery when the power supply voltage drops below that of the battery.

2. Write protection circuitry must be provided to prevent accidental writes on power up and power down.

These requirements are met by the Dallas Semiconductor's nonvolatile controller, which, when used with a battery, converts CMOS RWM to nonvolatile memory [4]. In Fig. 13.2-1 the DS1210 is used with the TC5517APL to provide 2 K × 8 of nonvolatile RWM. The DS1210 has one input, V_{CC1}, for the AC line power supply and two inputs, V_{BAT1} and V_{BAT2}, for batteries. This allows two batteries to be used for reliability in critical applications. The output, V_{CC0}, which provides power to the memory, is automatically switched to the power supply or the battery, depending on which has the greater output voltage.

The chip select signal from the address decoding logic is input to the DS1210 $\overline{CE}$ input. $\overline{CEO}$ from the DS1210 provides the memory's $\overline{CE}$. The DS1210 constantly monitors the AC line power supply. If the power supply's output drops

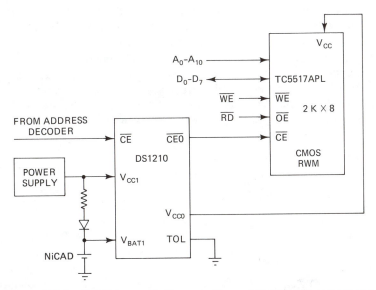

Figure 13.2-1 DS1210 nonvolatile controller and CMOS 2 K × 8 SRAM used together to provide nonvolatile RWM.

below a preselected voltage, $\overline{\text{CEO}}$ is inhibited. This prevents the memory from being inadvertently written during a power failure. When inhibited, $\overline{\text{CEO}}$ will be held to within 0.2 V of the AC line power supply voltage or the battery voltage, whichever is greater. If power supply failure is detected while the DS1210's $\overline{\text{CE}}$ input is low, $\overline{\text{CEO}}$ will remain low until $\overline{\text{CE}}$ returns high. This allows a memory cycle in progress to be completed.

With the tolerance pin, TOL, grounded, power fail detection occurs in the range of 4.75 to 4.5 V. If TOL is connected to V_{CC0}, power fail detection occurs in the range of 4.5 to 4.25 V. The nickel-cadmium battery shown is trickle charged through resistor R. A lithium battery could be used instead, in which case there would be no trickle charge circuit. When operating in standby mode, the DS1210 draws no more than 1 μA from the battery.

The DS1221 nonvolatile controller/decoder is similar to the DS1210 in operation but includes a 1-out-of-4 decoder, allowing it to control the chip enables of four devices. Sixteen devices can be controlled by the DS1212 nonvolatile controller/decoder.

Another approach to battery-backed CMOS SRAM is to include the CMOS SRAM, a lithium battery, write protect circuitry, and power switching circuitry in the same IC package. These devices follow the JEDEC 28-pin universal site standard. External organizations include 2 K $\times$ 8, 8 K $\times$ 8, and 32 K $\times$ 8. Data retention time is typically 10 years for these devices.

13.2.2 Electrically Erasable Programmable Read Only Memory, EEPROM

Electrically erasable programmable read only memories, EEPROMs, employ a special memory cell structure. This structure, shown in Fig. 13.2-2, is somewhat similar to that of an EPROM. However, this cell, called Flotox, uses electron tunneling through a thin oxide to charge and discharge a floating gate [5]. If a positive voltage is applied to the top gate with the drain at 0 V, the floating gate is capacitively coupled to this voltage and electrons are attracted through the tunnel oxide to charge the floating gate. Alternatively, if the gate is grounded and a positive voltage applied to the drain the floating gate will be discharged.

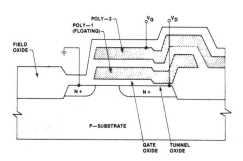

Figure 13.2-2 Flotox cell structure used in EEPROMs. (Courtesy of Intel Corp.)

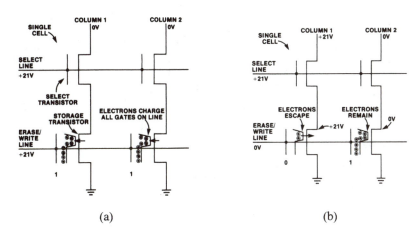

(a)   (b)

Figure 13.2-3 EEPROM memory cell: (a) erase operation; (b) write operation. (Courtesy of Intel Corp.)

The actual memory cell consists of two transistors, as shown in Fig. 13.2-3. One transistor is simply a select transistor that connects the storage transistor, the Flotox cell, to the bit line (column) when the select line is at a positive voltage. To write data into a cell, the cell must first be erased (Fig. 13.2-3a) and then written (Fig. 13.2-3b). Each of these operations takes approximately 10 mS. A 20 V supply voltage is required for these operations. To read the device, only a 5 V supply is required and read cycle times are on the order of 100s of nanoseconds. Thus, the EEPROM has a long write time and short read time. An important characteristic of the Flotox cell is that the threshold voltage difference between the charged and discharged states of the cell decreases the more the cell is written. After approximately 10,000 write operations, this difference is too small for the state of the cell to be distinguished. In effect, the cell wears out. Thus, the write endurance for the cell is 10,000 erase/write operations.

The Intel 2817A is a 2K × 8 EEPROM (see Fig. 13.2-4) [6]. It interfaces easily to a microprocessor because all the support circuitry needed to operate the Flotox cell is on chip. Only a + 5 V supply is required; the higher voltage needed to operate the Flotox cells is generated on chip from the + 5 V. Circuitry is also provided on chip to protect the memory from accidental writes on power up and power down.

A microprocessor writes the 2817A using a normal write cycle. The write time problem is handled by on-chip circuitry that latches the address and data in response to the write strobe. An internal write timer generates the internal write strobes required first to erase the byte to be written and then write it. Once the microprocessor writes a byte of data to the 2817A, it cannot again read or write the device until the 2817A's internal circuitry completes the actual write operation. The 2817A provides a RDY/BUSY output to indicate when this process is complete. This signal is monitored by the microprocessor to determine when the

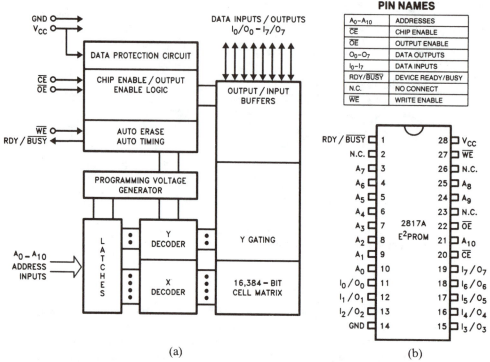

PIN NAMES

A_0-A_{10}	ADDRESSES
$\overline{CE}$	CHIP ENABLE
$\overline{OE}$	OUTPUT ENABLE
O_0-O_7	DATA OUTPUTS
I_0-I_7	DATA INPUTS
RDY/$\overline{BUSY}$	DEVICE READY/BUSY
N.C.	NO CONNECT
$\overline{WE}$	WRITE ENABLE

(a)   (b)

Figure 13.2-4 Intel 2817A 2 K $\times$ 8 EEPROM: (a) functional block diagram; (b) pin configuration. (Courtesy of Intel Corp.)

2718A can again be written. This monitoring can be accomplished by using the RDY/BUSY line to control the microprocessor's READY input, by polling the RDY/BUSY line, or by using it to generate an interrupt.

The 2817A has an endurance of 10,000 erase/write cycles per byte. The data from each write is retained for 10 years. The read access time is 250 nS and the write access time is 120 nS. The write cycle time is 20 mS!

13.2.3 Nonvolatile Random Access Memory, NVRAM

Nonvolatile random access memory, NVRAM, overcomes the long write cycle times associated with EEPROMs. The NVRAM, as shown in Fig. 13.2-5 contains both an SRAM and an EEPROM on a single chip. When system power is up, the SRAM is written and read at typical SRAM speeds. Whenever desired, a *store* operation, which transfers the entire SRAM array contents to the EEPROM array, can be executed. This operation is started by bringing the nonvolatile enable input, $\overline{NE}$, low and generating a write strobe at $\overline{WE}$. $\overline{NE}$ is typically controlled from a bit of an output port. The store cycle takes 10 mS for completion.

The store operation is typically used to save data when a power failure occurs or during power down. This operation is initiated by an interrupt from a power fail

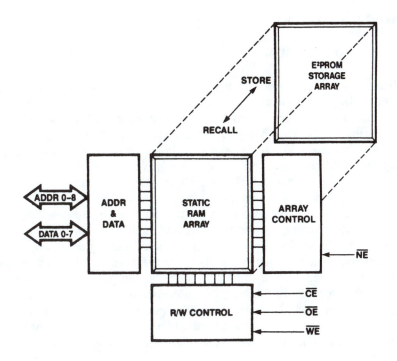

Figure 13.2-5   Intel 2004 NVRAM operational block diagram. (Courtesy Intel Corp.)

detection circuit. The power fail detection circuit detects when the power supply output drops below a specified level. The interrupt service subroutine brings $\overline{\text{NE}}$ low and generates the write strobe to the NVRAM. Since the store cycle takes 10 mS, the design of the V_{CC} supply must be such that it maintains its output for this period of time.

Data is transferred from the NVRAM's EEPROM array to its SRAM array by a *recall* operation. A recall is initiated by bringing $\overline{\text{NE}}$ low and strobing $\overline{\text{OE}}$. A recall operation is automatically performed when the system is powered up.

The 2004 NVRAM is a 512×8 device that requires a single $+5$ V supply for operation [6]. The read and write cycle times are 250 nS. Write protect circuitry is included on chip to preserve data on power up and power down. The EEPROM array uses the same Flotox cell described in the previous section. As a result, the device has an endurance of 10,000 store cycles and a 10-year data retention for each store.

One criterion for choosing an EEPROM and a NVRAM in an application is based on the device's endurance. If the application requires nonvolatile memory that is frequently written, the NVRAM is the choice. If the system is powered up and powered down more often than the nonvolatile memory is written, then an EEPROM is preferable.

3.3 READ ONLY MEMORY

13.3.1 Masked ROM

Read only memories store permanent information; the contents of the memory are fixed during fabrication of the integrated circuit and cannot be altered after manufacture. Both bipolar and MOS technology are used for manufacturing ROMs. The primary difference between bipolar and MOS ROMs is access time: Bipolar access times are as low as 50–90 nS; MOS access times are about ten times higher. Bipolar ROMs are faster and have higher drive capability, while MOS devices are smaller for a given number of bits and consume less power.

Integrated circuits are fabricated on a wafer of silicon. The fabrication involves a number of processing steps, including photo masking, etching, and diffusion, to produce a pattern of junctions and interconnections across the wafer that creates the semiconductor devices. In manufacturing *mask programmed* ROMs, the connection of the coupling cell between the word and the bit lines is determined by a single step in the fabrication. The system designer specifies the desired programming of the ROMs, and this information is used to control a computerized operation that produces the mask used to custom-program the ROM. The nonrecurring cost of developing the customized mask makes mask programmed ROMs economical only in high quantity applications. If an error is made by the system

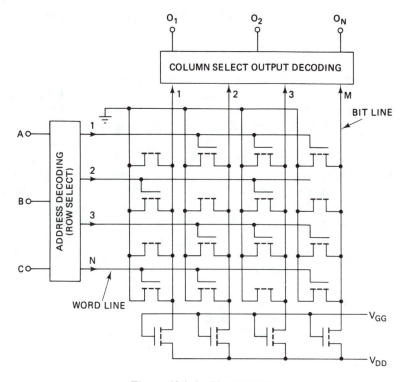

Figure 13.3-1   PMOS ROM.

PROGRAMMABLE EMITTER CONTRACTS

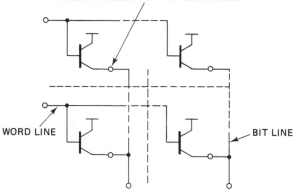

WORD LINE   BIT LINE

Figure 13.3-2   Bipolar ROM array.

designer in determining or specifying the ROM contents, then the manufactured ROMs are useless.

MOS is an ideal technology for the fabrication of ROMs because the very dense geometrical layouts that are possible in MOS permit the design of matrix structures containing many thousands of MOS devices. The basic storage element in a MOS ROM is a MOS transistor. A MOS ROM using P-channel enhancement mode transistors is shown in Fig. 13.3-1. The existence of a MOS transistor coupling the word and bit lines is determined in this particular MOS ROM by the oxide thickness at each transistor location. During fabrication, if the oxide is left thick, no transistor action occurs; where the oxide is thin, a MOS transistor exists between the particular word and bit lines. The existence of a transistor between the word and bit lines corresponds to a logic 1 for that bit position. This insertion or deletion of transistors from the matrix is accomplished by a single photo mask used in the fabrication process.

In bipolar ROMs, the coupling element between word and bit lines is a bipolar transistor. A typical bipolar memory element array is shown in Fig. 13.3-2. A transistor is connected between a word and bit line by making a connection to the emitter of the transistor. Such connections are controlled by a single step in the fabrication process. Sense amplifiers detect the current in a selected column to determine the existence of a logic 1 or logic 0.

13.3.2 Programmable Read Only Memory, PROM

PROMs are *field programmable* read only memories; that is, they are programmed after manufacture.

PROMs can be programmed, written into, only once. PROM programming requires circuits that provide the high currents necessary to burn in the desired bit patterns. These circuits can be constructed by the user, or one of the many commercial PROM programmers can be used. Some PROM vendors provide programming services for their customers. Because of this programming cost, PROMs are generally more expensive than ROMs and are advantageous only in low volume applications.

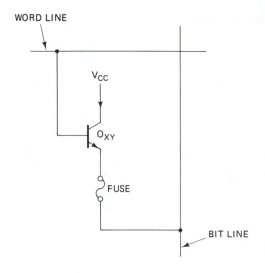

Figure 13.3-3   Typical fuse cell.

A common type of programmable read only memory uses, as a connecting element between the word and bit lines, a transistor in an emitter-follower configuration with a fuse in series with the emitter. A bipolar element with a fusible link is shown in Fig. 13.3-3. The fuse is typically nichrome or polycrystalline silicon. When the word line is selected, the transistor is turned on. If the fuse is intact, the bit line is pulled toward 5 V (V_{CC}); if the fuse is blown or open, the bit line is left floating.

Fusible link PROMs are programmed by selectively blowing the fuses in connecting elements. For example, with the polycrystalline fuse, pulse trains of 20–30 mA amplitude and successively wider duration are applied until the fuse is blown.

13.4 MASS STORAGE SYSTEMS

Mass storage systems store large quantities of information at a lower cost per bit than is possible with semiconductor memory. However, they have significantly longer access times for writing or reading data. The medium on which the data are stored provides nonvolatile storage. In most cases the storage medium can be easily removed from the system and transferred to another compatible storage system, facilitating low cost exchange or portability of large quantities of information. Two common types of mass storage are cassettes and cartridges and floppy disks.

13.4.1 Cassettes and Cartridges

Magnetic tape stores fairly large quantities of digital data. A particularly convenient approach to the use of magnetic tape in microprocessor systems involves either digital cassettes or cartridges that permanently house the tape in a plastic container. These compact containers facilitate the handling and use of a magnetic tape.

Digital cassettes are very similar in appearance to the audio cassettes from which they are descended and come in two sizes: the full size cassette and the

Figure 13.4-1 Full size and minisize data cartridges. (Courtesy of 3M Company.)

TABLE 13.4-1 COMPARISON CHART OF MAGNETIC STORAGE SYSTEMS

	3M Cartridge	3M Mini Cartridge	Philips Cassette	Mini Data Cassette	Floppy (single sided) (single density/ double density)	Single Density Mini Floppy (single sided)
Unformatted capacity (bytes)	2,870 K	772 K	720 K	200 K	400/800 K	110 K
Tracks	4	1	2	2	77	35
Heads	4	1	1	1	1	1
Transfer rate (BPS)	48 K	24 K	24 K	24 K	250/500 K	125 K
Relative head/media velocity (IPS)	30	30	30	30	120 (max)	80
Recording density (BPI)	1600	600	800	800	3200/6400	2600
Average access time (sec)	20	20	20	20	0.286	0.566
Media size (in.)	$4 \times 6 \times 0.67$	$2.4 \times 3.2 \times 0.4$	$4 \times 2.5 \times 0.4$	$2.125 \times 1.375 \times 0.313$	8.00×8.00	5.25×5.25
Error rate	1 bit in 10^8	1 bit in 10^8	1 bit in 10^7	1 bit in 10^8	1 bit in 10^9	1 bit in 10^9

BPS—Bits per Second

IPS—Inches per Second

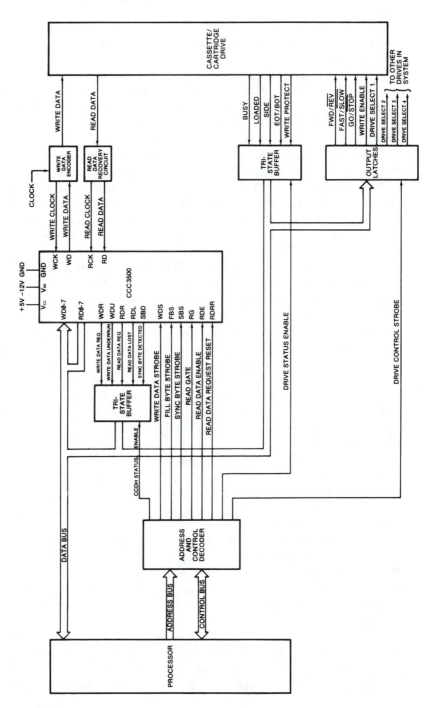

Figure 13.4-2 Cassette/cartridge drive interface to a microprocessor using a CCC3500 LSI cassette/cartridge data handler. (Courtesy of Standard Microsystems Corp.)

minicassette (see Fig. 13.4-1). Full size cassettes contain 282 feet of 0.15 inch tape and store 720 kilobytes of unformatted data. Minicassettes contain 100 feet of 0.15 inch tape and store 200 kilobytes of data.

Data cartridges, which provide higher operating speeds and more storage than cassettes, also come in full size and minisize (see Fig. 13.4-1). A full size cartridge contains 300 feet of 0.25 inch wide tape and stores up to 2870 kilobytes of unformatted data. Minicartridges contain 140 feet of 0.15 inch tape and store 772 kilobytes. Table 13.4-1 summarizes the storage capacities of cassettes and cartridges.

Cassette or cartridge tape drives or transports electromechanically control the direction and speed of the tape and contain the read write heads that record and read data from the tape. Tape drives or transports range from a basic configuration without a read write head or any electronics to systems with all the necessary electronics for interfacing through an RS 232 serial connection. OEM systems that use a parallel interface and contain all the electronics for microprocessor control are also commonly available.

A basic system is shown in Fig. 13.4-2. It includes a cassette or cartridge controller that interfaces to the microprocessor, providing parallel data transfer and a number of control and status signals. The controller encodes and decodes data to and from the read write amplifiers. It also provides motion control commands to the servoelectronics that control servomotors of the tape driver and, thus, its motion.

In digital tape systems data is recorded as changes in tape magnetization. Each change from one magnetic polarity to another is called a *flux change*, which is caused by switching the direction of the write head drive current. When the tape is read, the flux changes on the tape induce a voltage into the read head. The drive's read write electronics amplify and shape the signals so that (1) digital logic levels representing flux transitions are obtained when reading, and (2) logic levels control the write head current when writing.

The coding scheme used by a particular digital tape system determines the way in which flux changes on the magnetic tape represent logic values. Coding schemes also prevent any loss of information due to the nonideal characteristics inherent in all systems. Many coding schemes have been devised with one or two flux changes representing each bit of digital data.

Encoding methods are either clocked or self-clocking. In *clocked encoding*, an extra recording track next to the data track provides synchronizing pulses that define the data cells on the tape. The clock track is either prerecorded or recorded concurrently with the data. With *self-clocking* techniques, on the other hand, a data encoding pattern changes state regularly and thus provides synchronization without the necessity of an extra clock track.

A popular self-clocking encoding technique is *phase encoding*, and the most widely used form of phase encoding is called *bi-phase-level (B-Φ-L)*, split phase, or Manchester II + 180.[1] This technique represents each bit of data by a data cell. Flux changes may occur at the beginning (phase time) of a cell and always occur at the middle (data time) of the cell (Fig. 13.4-3).

---

[1] Bi-phase-level is the encoding technique used in ANSI recording standards for cassettes and cartridges [7, 8]. Many nonstandard cassette and cartridge systems use other recording techniques.

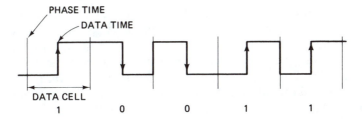

Figure 13.4-3   Phase encoding.

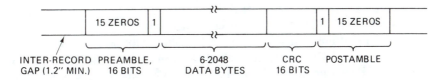

Figure 13.4-4   ANSI standard tape format for cartridges.

The information stored in a data cell on the tape is specified by the direction of the flux change at data time. A south to north flux change represents a logic 1, and a north to south, logic 0. A flux change occurs at phase time to establish the right polarity for the following flux change at data time only if the preceding bit is the same as the next bit to be written.

Encoding electronics generate the proper flux changes for the tape as a function of the serial data received. Decoding circuitry reconstructs the clock from the flux changes on the tape and converts the flux changes occurring at data time into serial digital data.

Independent of the encoding scheme, data is placed on the tape according to some specified format. Usually it is recorded in blocks called **records**. These records are separated from each other by regions of erased tape called **interrecord gaps**. The lengths of the records and gaps depend on the standard or convention followed.

For example, in the proposed ANSI standard X3B144 for cartridges, the record starts with a 16-bit preamble consisting of 15 zeros followed by a single 1 (see Fig. 13.4-4). The preamble is followed by a minimum of 6 to a maximum of 2048 data bytes. These bytes are, in turn, followed by a 16-bit cyclic redundancy character, CRC, used for error detection. Finally, a postamble consisting of a single 1 followed by 15 zeros completes the record. The interrecord gap that precedes the next record has a minimum length of 1.2 inches.

Cyclic redundancy is a common method of error detection for serial data. Cyclic encoding and decoding schemes are based on modulo-2 arithmetic operations on the data stream interpreted as a polynomial. The bits of an n-bit block of data are treated as coefficients of a polynomial of order $n - 1$ in the dummy variable X. During encoding, this data or message polynomial is divided, using modulo-2 arithmetic, by a generating polynomial. The remainder, after this division, is the cyclic redundancy check character. It is appended to the end of the data.

For error checking, the bit stream, containing the data and CRC bits, is divided by the polynomial used to generate the CRC bits. If this division results in a remainder of zero, then no detectable errors exist in the bit stream.

Various standards specify particular generating polynomials. For example, the polynomial $X^{16} + X^{15} + X^2 + 1$, referred to as CRC-16, is used in standards for cassettes and cartridges. It leaves a 16-bit remainder after dividing the data stream. This 16-bit remainder comprises the two 8-bit CRC characters that become part of the data block in the tape format.

In modulo-2 arithmetic, the division of the data stream can be carried out in hardware by using a feedback shift register that incorporates exclusive OR gates in the feedback paths. A circuit that implements CRC-16 is shown in Fig. 13.4-5. As the data stream is transmitted, it is simultaneously shifted into the shift register. When all the data bits have been shifted into the shift register, its contents—the CRC bits—are then shifted out and appended to the data bits.

Several CRC generator/checker integrated circuits carry out the above functions. For example, the Fairchild 9401 CRC Generator/Checker is contained in a 14-pin DIP. The 9401 has three select inputs through which it generates or checks serial data with any one of eight generator polynomials. The circuit in Fig. 13.4-5 is the equivalent circuit for the 9401 when its select inputs $S_2 S_1 S_0 = 000$. Figure 13.4-6 shows the additional logic required with the 9401 to generate and append the CRC bits to a data stream.

When used to check a message being received, the data and check bits are monitored. They are input to the 9401 while simultaneously being stored by the receiver. After the last check bit is entered, the error output, ER, is logic 1 if a detectable error has occurred.

A tape drive controller interfaces the microprocessor and the tape drive. Commands and data to be written on the tape are sent to the controller by the microprocessor, and status and data read from the tape are sent to the microprocessor by the controller. The controller also handles the timing considerations necessary to operate the tape drive properly. It formats for writing, including generating CRC characters the encoding the data. It also decodes data, removing

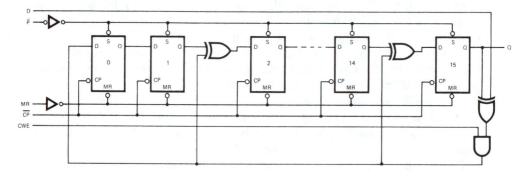

Figure 13.4-5 Circuit for implementing CRC-16. (Courtesy of Fairchild Camera and Instrument Corp.)

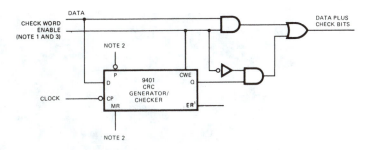

NOTES:
1. Check word Enable is HIGH while data is being clocked, LOW during transmission of check bits.
2. 9401 must be reset or preset before each computation.
3. CRC check bits are generated and appended to data bits.

Figure 13.4-6   Check word generation circuit using the 9401 CRC generator/checker. (Courtesy of Fairchild Camera and Instrument Corp.)

the preamble and postamble, and carries out the cyclic redundancy check on data read from the tape.

The design of cassette and cartridge controllers is simplified by using an LSI cassette/cartridge data handler like Standard Microsystems CCC3500 (see Fig. 13.4-2).

13.4.2 Floppy Disks

A floppy disk is another form of magnetic medium used for mass storage. Unlike paper and magnetic tape, however, it essentially provides random access to the data stored upon it. Floppy disks are made of a flexible, heavy, Mylar-based magnetic material. The disk is permanently housed in a thin, semistiff jacket or cartridge with a low friction liner. Floppy disks (see Fig. 13.4-7) come in two sizes: the full size

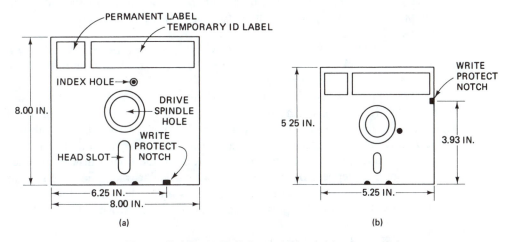

Figure 13.4-7   (a) Full size and (b) minisize floppy disks.

Figure 13.4-8 Full size and minisize floppy disk drives. (Courtesy of Shugart Associates.)

floppy, which is housed in an 8×8 inch cartridge, and the minifloppy,[2] which is housed in a 5.25×5.25 inch cartridge. The floppy disks shown in Fig. 13.4-7 are single-sided, i.e., designed for recording on one side only.

Three holes cut in the cartridge allow access to the floppy disk. One is the spindle hole through which the floppy disk drive spindle protrudes when the disk is loaded into the drive. The spindle turns the floppy disk inside its plastic jacket. Through the head access hole the floppy disk drive read write head comes into contact with the floppy disk.[3] The index hole in the jacket allows the index hole in the floppy disk to be optically sensed for the purpose of generating a synchronization signal.

Information is recorded on the floppy disk in concentric circles called *tracks*. The outermost track is track 00, and the innermost is track 76 for the full size floppy or, in the case of a minifloppy, track 34.

The floppy disk drive has a door that covers a slot into which the floppy disk is placed (see Fig. 13.4-8). When the door is closed, the disk is clamped to the rotating spindle. Usually the read write head is moved radially across the disk above the head access hole by a stepper motor and lead screw mechanism. It is moved in increments equal to the distance between tracks on the floppy disk each time the stepper motor is stepped. In order to access a particular track, the head is brought to track 00 and its position detected by a limit switch. The head is then stepped n tracks to its destination by pulsing the stepper motor. Moving the head to the

---

[2] Minifloppy is a registered trademark of Shugart Associates.

[3] Double-sided floppy disks, those that can be recorded on both sides, have head access holes on both sides of the cartridge. The discussion in this text focuses on single-sided floppy disks.

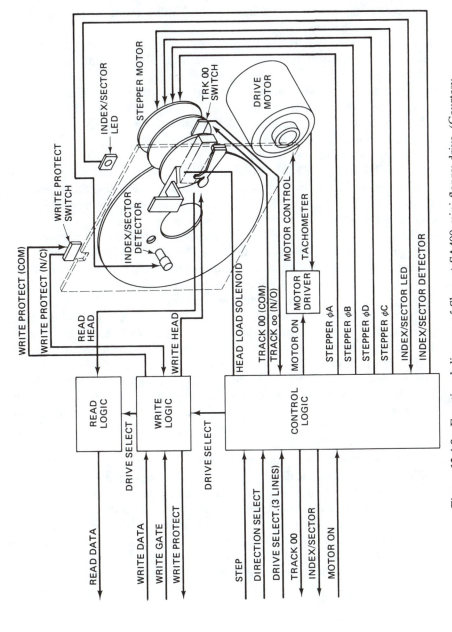

Figure 13.4-9 Functional diagram of Shugart SA400 mini floppy drive. (Courtesy of Shugart Associates.)

507

proper track is called a *seek operation*. When the head is over the desired track, a control mechanism in the drive *loads the head*, causing it to come into contact with the floppy disk. Data can then be written onto or read from the disk. After writing or reading data, the head is unloaded from the disk to minimize wear on both the disk and the read write head.

A set of primary interface signals to a floppy disk drive for the Shugart SA 400 minifloppy is shown in Fig. 13.4-9. The DRIVE SELECT lines allow any one of three drives to respond to the drive control signals. The MOTOR ON input turns the drive motor ON for reading or writing, and the DIRECTION SELECT line controls the direction of the read write head motion when the STEP line is pulsed. When the TRACK 00 signal is logic 0, the read write head of the drive is positioned at track 0. When the WRITE GATE is logic 0, data is written onto the disk; when it is logic 1, data is read from the disk.

The INDEX/SECTOR output from the drive provides a logic 0 pulse each time the sector hole in the floppy disk is sensed by the index/sector photodetector of the drive. The WRITE PROTECT output indicates whether a write protected disk is in the drive—the drive prevents writing into a protected disk. The READ DATA line provides the data and clock together as read by the drive electronics. Data to be written on the disk is input on a WRITE DATA line. A flux reversal is written onto the disk during each transition from logic 1 to logic 0 on this line.

Data is recorded on a floppy disk in either single or double density. Single density, for a full size disk, is 3200 bpi (bits per inch) and double density is 6400 bpi. For a minifloppy, single density is 2581 bpi. In both single and double density encoding, the data is divided into bit cells. The manner in which 0 or 1 is encoded in the bit cell depends on the encoding scheme. For single density recording, a frequency modulated, FM, encoding scheme is used whereby each bit cell begins with a flux transition or pulse. The bit cell representing logic 1 has an additional flux transition at its center; the bit cell representing logic 0, on the other hand, does not (see Fig. 13.4-10). This FM encoding scheme is called *double frequency recording* because a string of logic 1 data bits creates a frequency of pulses twice the frequency of a string of logic 0 data bits.

Double density recording uses MFM (modified FM) or M2FM (modified MFM), which doubles the density of data bits without increasing the number of flux reversals per inch. Both MFM and M2FM have rules for eliminating the need for some clock bits, as a function of the data bit stream, when they are not necessary for synchronization [9]. For example, by MFM rules, a 1-bit cell has a pulse at its center, and a 0-bit cell has one at the beginning of the bit cell except when preceded by a 1, in which case no pulse at all occurs during the bit cell.

Full size disk drives rotate the disk at 360 rpm. In single density recording, data is transferred to or from the disk at a nominal rate of 250 K bits per second; in

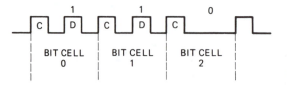

Figure 13.4-10   FM encoding.

double density, 500 K bits per second. Since each revolution of the disk takes 167 mS, the average time to access a particular record is 83 mS, assuming the read write head is already located on the track. In general, the time required to access a randomly located record is dominated by the time it takes to move the read write head to the appropriate track—a function of the track to track access time and the head loading time. Track to track access and head loading times vary with the electromechanical design of the specific disk drive. For the full size drive shown in Fig. 13.4-8, these times are 8 mS and 35 mS, respectively.

Minifloppy drives rotate the disk at 300 rpm and, for single density recording (2581 bpi), data is transferred to or from the disk at 125 K bits per second. For the minifloppy drive shown in Fig. 13.4-8, the track to track access time is 40 mS, and the head loading time is 75 mS.

Data is written on a floppy disk in a particular format. The format divides each track into a number of smaller, fixed-length areas called *sectors*. Division is either soft sectored or hard sectored. Soft sectored disks have a single index hole, and sectors are identified by addresses that are permanently written onto the disk. Hard sectored disks contain a number of sector holes around the disk in addition to the index hole. These sector holes are sensed to identify the beginning of each sector.

The first floppy disk system was developed by IBM. This system, the IBM 3740, has become a de facto standard for single density, full size, soft sectored systems. The IBM 3740 format is shown in Fig. 13.4-11. Each track contains the same sequence of control, address, and data fields. Data is written on the disk with frequency modulation encoding.

The preamble consists of 46 gap bytes. A gap byte is a sequence of 1s and 0s. Address marks indicate that the byte following the preamble is the beginning of an address or data field and are distinguished by missing clock bits. The last 3 bits in an address mark indicate whether the information that follows is deleted data, regular data, or an index, or ID, byte.

The index address mark indicates that 32 bytes follow before the first byte of the first sector. Each track contains 26 sectors of 188 bytes. The last sector is followed by the postamble.

Each of the 26 sectors is, in turn, subdivided into a number of fields—the first byte of the sector is the ID address mark, which indicates that the track/sector ID field follows. This field consists of a 1-byte track number, then a byte of zeros followed by a 1-byte sector number, followed by another byte of zeros. The track/sector ID field is terminated by a 2-byte checksum. A 17-byte ID gap precedes the 1-byte data address mark, which itself indicates that the 130-byte data field follows. The sector is terminated by a 33-byte data gap. Out of a total of 188 bytes in a sector, only 128 bytes are actual data.

The Shugart minifloppy uses a modified IBM type format. The gap structure in this format differs somewhat from the 3740 format, and there are only 18 sectors per track.

A floppy disk controller interfaces the microprocessor and the floppy disk drive. It receives commands and data from and provides status and data to the microprocessor. In response to the commands, the floppy disk controller provides

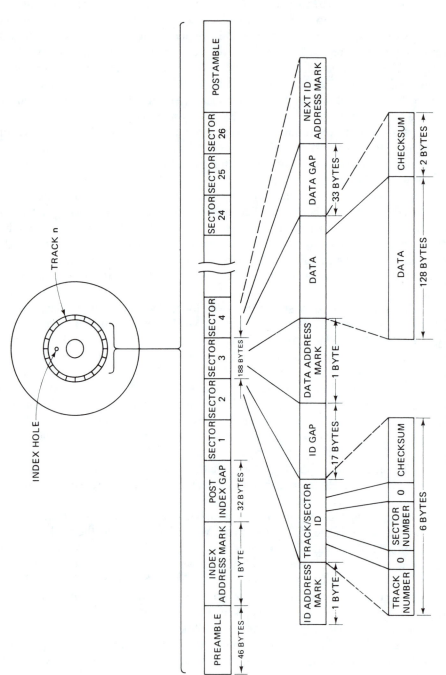

Figure 13.4-11 IBM 3740 floppy disk format.

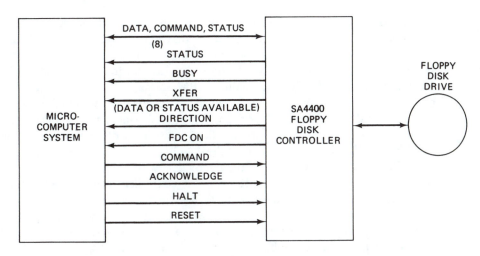

Figure 13.4-12   Shugart SA400 mini floppy controller interface.

TABLE 13.4-2   COMMANDS FOR SHUGART SA4400 CONTROLLER

Function Name	Function	Description
INIT	System reset	Resets controller and all floppy disks in system, and controls disk drive motor on/off.
SEEK	Position head on track	Steps head to specified track.
READ	Read disk sector	Reads a sector of data from specified sector.
READID	Read next ID	Reads the next sector ID information.
WRITE	Write disk sector	Writes a sector of data with normal data AM* to specified sector.
WRDEL	Write sector of deleted data	Writes a sector of data with deleted data AM to specified sector.
FORMAT	Format track	Writes address marks, gaps, and data on entire track per modified IBM-type format.
STATUS	Drive status	Returns status for addressed drive.

*Address mark

signals to the disk drive, which controls the reading and writing of data. The controller also carries out formatting of the disk and a CRC check for data errors.

The Shugart SA4400 is a typical minifloppy disk controller (see Fig. 13.4-12). It transfers data between one, two, or three disk drives and a microprocessor. It also formats disks according to the modified IBM format. An 8-bit bidirectional data bus transmits commands to the controller, transfers data between the microprocessor and controller, and provides floppy disk status to the microprocessor. Additional control status lines initiate floppy disk control operations and provide handshaking signals for transfers over the data bus.

The microprocessor controls the floppy disk with only eight commands. These commands are listed in Table 13.4-2. The controller itself contains a preprogrammed microprocessor that implements the commands.

It also contains a 128-byte sector buffer that allows the host microprocessor to transfer data to the buffer at its own rate and subsequently allows data to be transferred from the sector buffer to the disk, independent of the host. For read operations, the host microprocessor requests that data be transferred from the disk to the sector buffer and, subsequently, can read the buffer at its own rate.

Alternatively, data can be transferred directly between the host microprocessor and disk, byte by byte. Here the XRF and ACK lines are used for handshaking.

To store and read data as files, software interfaces the file commands of the user and the commands recognized by the floppy disk controller. Such software constitutes a floppy disk operating system. One portion of this system, called the *file manager*, keeps a directory of the location of all the files and remaining free space. When files longer than one sector are stored, the file manager breaks the block of data into single sectors. When the file is to be read, the file manager combines the data from various sectors into the original file.

REFERENCES

1. *MOS Memory Data Book* (Dallas, Tex.: Texas Instruments, Inc., 1984).

2. *TMS4500A Dynamic RAM Controller Users Manual* (Dallas, Tex.: Texas Instruments, Inc., 1982).

3. *MOS Memory Products* (Tustin, Calif.: Toshiba America, Inc., 1983).

4. *Product Data Book* 1985–86 (Dallas, Tex.: Dallas Semiconductor, 1985).

5. W. S. JOHNSON, G. L. KUHN, A. L. RENNINGER, and G. PERLEGOS, "16-K EE-PROM Relies on Tunneling for Byte-Erasable Program Storage," Electronics, February 28, 1980.

6. *Memory Components Handbook* (Santa Clara, Calif.: Intel Corporation, 1986).

7. *Magnetic Tape Cassettes for Information Interchange* (New York: American National Standards Institute, Inc., 1977).

8. *Unrecorded Magnetic Tape Cartridge for Information Interchange* (New York: American National Standards Institute, Inc., 1977).

9. D. J. KALSTROM, "Simple Encoding Schemes Double Capacity of a Flexible Disc," *Computer Design*, (September 1976), 98, 100, 102.

14

Microprocessor System Design

...we suggested that implementation, maintenance, and modification would be minimized if the system could be designed in such a way that its pieces were small, easily related to the application, and relatively independent of one another. This means, then, that good design is an exercise in partitioning and organizing the pieces of a system.

By partitioning we mean the division of the problem into smaller subproblems, so that each subproblem will eventually correspond to a piece of the system. The questions are: Where and how should we divide the problem? Which aspects of the problem belong in the same part of the system, and which aspects belong in different parts? Structured design answers these questions with two basic principles:

● Highly interrelated parts of the problem should be in the same piece of the system, i.e., things that belong together should go together.

● Unrelated parts of the problem should reside in unrelated pieces of the system. That is, things that have nothing to do with one another don't belong together.

E. Yourdon and L. L. Constantine*

Structured Design: Fundamentals of a Discipline of Computer Program and Systems Design (Englewood Cliffs, N.J.: Prentice-Hall, 1979).

Previous chapters are primarily concerned with the design of systems that implement functions of limited complexity, systems whose operation can be specified in at most a few pages of natural language description, flowcharts, timing diagrams, or some combination of these. In most cases, however, these systems are actually subsystems of a larger system.

Although a few of these, such as memory subsystems, are strictly hardware, the majority can be implemented through various combinations of hardware and software. Where several designs meet the system's requirements, the rule of thumb is: use the most economical.

The hardware portion of a subsystem consists of an interconnection of small, medium, and large scale ICs and, usually, a few discrete components. Each IC or discrete component can, in itself, be considered a subsystem. Each implements a well-defined function and interacts with other subsystems that connect to it via an interface of electrical signals. When these smaller subsystems are SSI circuits, formal digital system synthesis techniques are used to determine the most economical interconnection to implement the function. When the subsystems are MSI or LSI devices, few formal procedures are available to specify their interconnection, making the synthesis techniques heuristic.

The software portion of a subsystem consists of an interconnection of assembly language instructions, macros, and subroutines. Like the hardware, each of these software structures can be considered a subsystem that implements a well-defined function and interacts in a predetermined manner with the other subsystems to which it is connected. This interaction is carried out through registers, flags, and calling sequences. Software interaction not only takes place with other software but also with the hardware that supports it and with the hardware it controls.

The technique of viewing a system as a subsystem or component in a larger system and the converse—viewing a system as a collection of smaller subsystems—provides a basis for the specification, design, implementation, testing, and documentation of complex systems.

A systematic, five-stage methodology implements system synthesis:

> Stage 1: Requirements definition
> Stage 2: Systematic design
> Stage 3: System implementation
> Stage 4: Testing and debugging
> Stage 5: Documentation and maintenance

14.1 REQUIREMENTS DEFINITION

The requirements definition involves a statement of the problem, the system features required to solve that problem, the boundary conditions or environment in which those features must operate, and a justification for using the proposed system as opposed to any other.

The importance of a complete requirements definition cannot be overemphasized. It is easy at this stage to put off finding answers to difficult questions in the hope that they will somehow answer themselves as later stages progress. However, it is far more likely that serious problems will arise to confront the designer who has postponed thorough analysis.

A requirements definition, the first stage of the five-stage methodology, is itself divided into three functions: context analysis, functional specification, and design constraints.[1]

14.1.1 Context Analysis

The purpose of a context analysis is to develop a clear statement of the problem that the system is intended to solve and to understand thoroughly the technical, operational, and economic environment in which the system will be used.

Although not necessarily involved in the original context analysis, it is important that the designer be completely familiar with both the results of the analysis and the reasoning that lead to those results.

14.1.2 Functional Specification

The system functional specification designates the overall purpose of the system—what it is to accomplish—*not* how it will be accomplished or what will be used to accomplish it.

A functional specification includes the following:

1. A complete description of what the system should do
2. The performance requirements it must meet
3. Specific details of the operator/system interaction
4. A specification of the system's interface with the external environment
5. Procedures for handling errors and diagnosing malfunctions

The operational description is drawn up in terms of required and, often, desirable features. Its purpose is to facilitate implementation decisions in later stages of development. Performance requirements of the system must also be specified completely and in detail.

Operator/system interaction may be as simple as pressing a run button or as complex as having the system monitor the commands provided by the operator and indicate errors in those commands. Or the system may prompt the operator by requesting commands or parameter values. A functional specification of the hardware interface of a system to its operating environment includes designating the characteristics of all input and output signals. Some of these characteristics are listed in Table 14.1-1. The software interface primarily involves parameter passing conventions, data transmission protocols, data formats, and data structures.

---

[1] These specific three terms were used by Ross and Schoman in [1]. The operations thus named, however, are applied universally by system designers.

TABLE 14.1-1 CHARACTERISTICS OF SYSTEM INPUT
AND OUTPUT SIGNALS

1.	Number and function
2.	Number of bits per input/output
3.	Code/format
4.	Data rate
5.	Duration
6.	Data transfer method—program I/O, interrupt, or DMA
7.	Handshaking/control signals
8.	Service priorities
9.	Voltage levels
10.	Buffering
11.	Multiplexed signals

The functional specification must determine the types of errors likely to occur in the operation of the system and designate a method of system recovery, i.e., the system's response to these error conditions. Errors may be caused by the operator, by communication or transmission difficulties, or by mechanical or electrical failures.

The aim of error diagnosis and recovery is a system that is easy both to service and to maintain.

14.1.3 Design Constraints

The specification of design constraints sets forth the way in which the system is to be constructed and implemented. It does not specify the components that will be in the system; rather, it identifies the boundary conditions by which the components will be selected.

The designer must also consider the effect of the operating environment on the system. This manifests itself in terms of physical size constraints, temperature range of operation, and such hostile environmental conditions as electrical noise and corrosive atmosphere.

14.2 SYSTEMATIC DESIGN

The aim of a formulated design approach, in applications of increased system complexity, is a conceptually integrated system consisting of appropriate subsystems. These subsystems or subfunctions should be modular in nature. A system composed of interconnected modular subsystems is easier to design, document, debug, and modify.

One method, which for years has been used by engineers for designing all types of systems, has lately been given the name "top-down design." Essentially, top-down design identifies the total system function, then partitions it into less complex subfunctions, each of which performs a specific task. These subfunctions are, in turn, subdivided or partitioned into subfunctions of even less complexity (see Fig. 14.2-1). The partitioning process continues until relatively low complexity subfunctions amenable to easy implementation are reached.

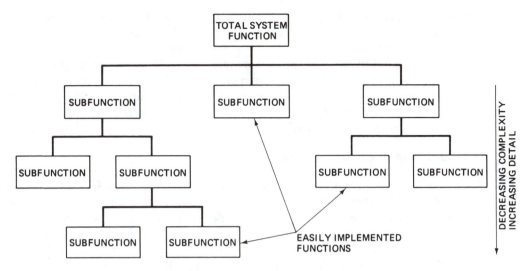

Figure 14.2-1   Partitioning of system function into less complex subfunctions.

14.2.1 Partitioning

Each level of partitioning involves increased detail. Partitioning decisions made at any particular level are constrained by decisions made at higher levels and, in turn, constrain partitioning decisions made at lower levels.

The first level partition determines the basic system structure. At its simplest, this level consists of three basic subfunctions: input, processing, and output. These are specified according to function and according to the method of interfacing with other subfunctions at the same level. Subfunctions of a modular nature, those that require minimal interfacing, are advantageous because they can be individually optimized, in terms of hardware/software trade-offs, without seriously affecting the rest of the design. Also, at lower levels, partitioning is generally influenced by readily available software and hardware subfunctions, e.g., standard LSI.

14.2.2 Selection of an Overall Implementation Method

As partitioning continues, a sufficient amount of information is generated to reach a decision about implementation methods. At a given level, one subfunction might be implemented by one method and another by a different method. Possible choices include nonprogrammed logic approaches, such as random logic design, or implementation with MSI or LSI. These are appropriate in low complexity systems or if standard MSI or LSI circuits easily implement the functions. They are also appropriate when very high speed operation must be achieved, possibly by parallel execution of subfunctions. Programmed logic approaches include programmable logic devices (PLDs) and ROM based sequential machines. In other applications, custom LSI may be appropriate. These two methods are frequently used when the system is not of sufficient complexity to justify use of a microprocessor.

Microprocessor systems are, however, appropriate for an extremely wide range of applications. Devices used in such systems range from single-chip microcomputers to complex, high speed microprogrammable bit slice devices. As system requirements increase, several microprocessors may be utilized within a single system. Implementation of multiple microprocessor systems requires special design considerations (see Section 14.6).[2]

14.2.3 Types of Microprocessors

In theory, any microprocessor can be used in any application as long as it is fast enough to meet the system performance requirements. In fact, however, because the choice of a microprocessor to a great extent determines the final cost of the system, microprocessor selection is of paramount importance. Although the microprocessor itself is usually an insignificant fraction of the final system cost, it does affect the selection of memory, interface circuits, power supply, and other hardware and, therefore, greatly affects the total system cost. In addition, the software development cost, the major portion of the total system cost in some designs, is also affected by the choice of microprocessor.

Microprocessors fall into three major categories:

1. Single-chip microcomputers
2. General purpose microprocessors
3. Bit slice microprocessors

14.2.3.1 Single-Chip Microcomputers

Single-chip microcomputers are available in 4-, 8-, or 16-bit word lengths and typically contain the microprocessor, ROM, RWM, I/O ports, and a clock oscillator and timer. Some devices allow off-chip memory and/or I/O expansion; others don't. Many are organized for a specific class of applications; others are basically general purpose in nature. For applications that fit within the available ROM, RWM, and I/O lines, single-chip microcomputers are very cost-effective.

To facilitate system development, some single-chip microcomputers are available in several versions. These microcomputers have identical architectures but differ in terms of the ROM they provide. One version, used in the final system, contains mask-programmed ROM. Another version, used in prototype development, contains EPROM, and still another version, used in the early stages of development, contains no ROM at all but allows the use of external RWM in place of it.

Single-chip microcomputer I/O lines may be fixed as input or output, or their direction may be programmable, either on a bit or word basis. Single-chip microcomputers with individually programmable I/O lines provide the greatest flexibility.

---

[2] The presentation prior to Section 14.6 concentrates on designs where a single microprocessor is utilized.

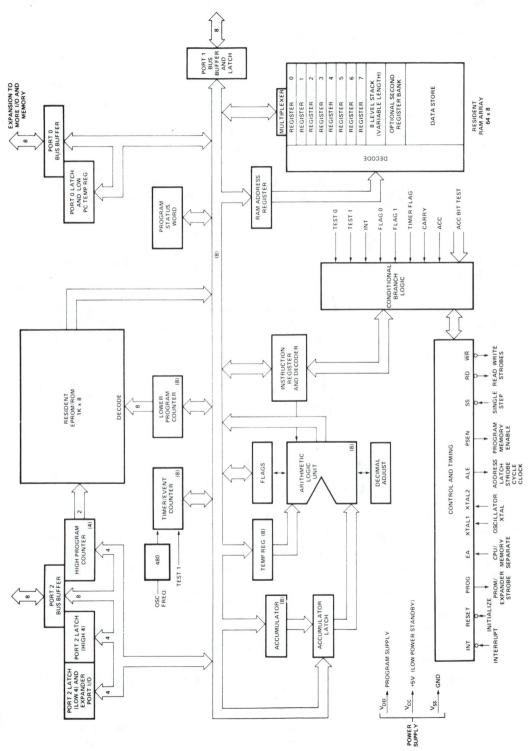

Figure 14.2-2 Architecture of the 8048/8748 single-chip microcomputer. (Courtesy of Intel Corp.)

519

The architecture of Intel's 8048 and 8748 8-bit microcomputer, the first single-chip microcomputer, is shown in Fig. 14.2-2. The architecture of these two microcomputers is identical except the 8748 contains a 1 K × 8 EPROM and the 8048 contains a 1 K × 8 mask-programmable ROM. The 8748 is used for protyping and low volume production; the 8048, for high volume production after the program code has been fully tested.

Also included in this family of devices is the 8035. This device is similar to the 8048/8748 except that it is used with external memory in place of the 1 K × 8 ROM. Thus, the 8035 is not a single-chip microcomputer.

In addition to its 8-bit CPU and 1 K × 8 ROM, the 8048/8748 has a 64 × 8 RWM, three 8-bit I/O ports, an 8-bit timer/event counter, and three test/interrupt inputs.

The 8-bit CPU has 96 basic instructions, including many for bit, nibble, and byte manipulation. These instructions require one or two machine cycles, each consisting of five states. With a 6 MHz clock, instruction execution times are either 2.5 or 5 μs.

Intel also provides an enlarged memory version of the 8048, the 8049. This device provides 2 K × 8 of ROM and 128 × 8 of RWM. In lieu of using the 8049, however, memory expansion is possible with the 8048/8748. By using one of the ports of the 8048/8748 as a multiplexed address/data bus, devices such as the 8755 and 8155 can expand memory and I/O. A latch demultiplexes this address/data bus when standard ROM and RWM are used.

The 8048/8748 is a MOS device requiring a single 5 V supply and typically dissipating 325 mW. For low power applications, CMOS versions of the 8048/8748 are used.

14.2.3.2 General Purpose Microprocessors

The category of general purpose microprocessors encompasses single and multichip devices that use external ROM, RWM, and I/O ports. External ROM and RWM are either standard semiconductor memories or multifunction devices containing a combination of ROM or RWM, I/O ports, and other features. The 8085A, for example, uses either standard memory or special memory and I/O devices such as the 8155 RWM with I/O ports and a timer or the 8355 ROM with I/O ports.

In either case, systems developed around general purpose microprocessors are easily expandable because memory and I/O ports are external. For large systems, separate memory and I/O are usually preferred over devices with a combination of the two, since in most applications the number of I/O ports does not increase in proportion to memory.

General purpose microprocessors are available in word lengths of 1, 4, 8, 12, 16, or 32 bits and typically consist of one to three integrated circuits. Although a wide variety of architectures and instruction sets is available, all general purpose microprocessors contain an ALU with one or more registers that function as accumulators, a control unit, an instruction decoder that handles a fixed instruction set, and general and special purpose registers. The number and universality of general purpose registers varies significantly among devices.

14.2.3.3 Bit Slice Microprocessors

Unlike a typical single-chip microprocessor that contains on a single chip all the elements of a central processing unit—ALU, general purpose and special purpose registers and control—bit slice microprocessors divide these functions among several ICs. For this approach, the registers and ALU are packaged separately from the control; each register and ALU (RALU) package is essentially equivalent to a small—2-, 4-, 8-bit wide—slice of the register and ALU portion of the complete microprocessor. Bit slice microprocessors can be cascaded to produce longer word lengths of 8, 12, 16, 32, or more bits. The control portion of a bit slice microprocessor is constructed from a microprogram sequencer IC and other logic. The *microprogram sequencer* contains an instruction register and additional logic to decode and execute instructions.

When the microprogram sequencer decodes an instruction from the main program memory, it generates a starting address to a special ROM, called a microinstruction ROM or control ROM, CROM. Each instruction in the main program ROM is like a machine language instruction on a single-chip micro-processor. For each such instruction, the microprogram sequencer creates a different starting address in the CROM—beginning at this address is a sequence of memory words, microinstructions, that implements the more complex machine language instruction. Microinstructions directly control the registers and logic of the RALU, causing the execution of the instruction.

Because the control ROM is a separate package or packages, the machine language instruction set can be customized for an application. The designer creates machine language instructions from sequences of primitive operations that are implemented by microinstructions. Creating an instruction set in such a manner or writing an entire application program by using microinstructions is referred to as *microprogramming*. Note that microprogramming is not equivalent to programming a microprocessor. It is a way of implementing the control portion of a CPU and was used on mainframe computers long before microprocessors came into existence.

Designing with a bit slice microprocessor is much more difficult than using a fixed instruction set microprocessor because the designer must configure the CPU and the system hardware as well and microprogram the instruction set. This has already been done by the IC manufacturer in a fixed instruction set microprocessor. In addition, because bit slice microprocessors have both unique architectures and unique instruction sets, few software development aids are available.

However, bit slice microprocessors do have certain advantages in the flexibility they provide for designing a microprocessor. The designer can build a system of any desired word length and create an optimal instruction set for a particular applica-tion. Bit slice devices are also used to emulate other microprocessors or minicom-puters with microprograms that execute the target computer's instruction set.

14.2.4 Microprocessor Selection

A general list of considerations in the selection of a microprocessor or microcomputer is presented in Table 14.2-1. The relative importance of each item in this list varies, depending on the application.

For low complexity systems that can be implemented with a single-chip microcomputer, selection criteria primarily center around the capabilities and limitations of available microcomputers and their software development aids. The largest application of single-chip microcomputers is in small dedicated controllers. The rationale for their use is a system with a minimal package count. To this end, a device is sought that provides the required capability without requiring additional packages.

Before selecting a single-chip microcomputer, a designer's major consideration should be whether the device provides a sufficient number of I/O lines for the application. Although some microcomputers provide I/O expansion capability, the

TABLE 14.2-1 GENERAL CONSIDERATIONS FOR MICROPROCESSOR SELECTION

Software	
word size	:data and instructions
register complement	:number and flexibility
instruction set	:type and number of instructions — suitability for application
instruction cycle time	:instruction execution speed
address capacity	:number of directly addressable memory and I / O ports
addressing modes	:direct, indirect indexed, relative, etc.
stack	:location and length
Hardware	
package size	:number of package pins
minimal system parts count	:number of packages required for minimal system
parts family completeness	:compatible ROM, RWM, and peripheral ICs
power requirement	:number of power supply voltages and power dissipation
logic compatibility	:input and output logic levels
drive capability	:number of unit loads drivable by output pins
interrupt structure	:number and type of interrupt inputs
DMA provisions	:provision for DMA, additional hardware required
second sources	:independent manufacturers of microprocessor and support ICs
availability	:actual availability of microprocessor and required support ICs in small and large quantities
Support	
documentation	:completeness of hardware and software manuals, data sheets
development system	:range, performance, and flexibility of development system
development software	:assemblers, compilers, editors, debuggers, and subroutine library
application notes	:hardware and software device interface and system design examples
prototype hardware	:single and multicard prototype hardware
diagnostic hardware	:device specific system analyzers
application support	:field application engineering support available from vendor

requisite additional devices detract from the minimal package count goal. For those devices with sufficient I/O lines, the flexibility of the I/O lines and the instructions that control them are compared.

Another consideration is program size, since single-chip microcomputers have a fixed amount of ROM within which an application program must fit. Execution speed must also be taken into account in real-time applications.

Systems of medium to high complexity typically use general purpose microprocessors. Here selection criteria encompass total system solutions: the microprocessor, support devices, hardware packaging, and software. The use of powerful programmable I/O interface devices, including interfaces, which are themselves special or general purpose microprocessors, contributes substantially to the complexity of selection. These devices, although generally usable with most microprocessors, are frequently designed for direct compatibility with a particular microprocessor or series of microprocessors.

Response and data rates must also be considered, in terms of interrupt and DMA capability. In some applications, the speed requirements of certain subfunctions may be greater than the capability of any microprocessor. In such instances, external hardware is necessary to preprocess data prior to its input.

Programming ease is another important consideration. The architecture of each microprocessor determines its instruction set. Generally speaking, the more instructions available, the easier the programming and the less memory required for storage. But more important than a large number of instructions is the number that are useful in the particular application under consideration. Programming ease is also facilitated by the number and power of on-chip registers because they allow intermediate data to be stored internally during calculations rather than requiring external references to memory for temporary storage. Internal reference also provides faster execution time.

Most microprocessors are part of a family of LSI components, and completeness of this family is an important hardware consideration. These components, sometimes referred to as *support circuits*—clock drivers, system controllers, peripheral interface adapters, communication interface circuits, DMA controllers—are designed for intrafamily interfacing. And, while it is usually possible to use a device from one family with those of another, the electrical interface between the circuits may require additional logic. Since package count minimization is a design goal, the smallest number of ICs required for a complete system with a specified number of I/O lines is also a selection consideration.

14.2.4.1 Benchmarking

Benchmarking is a technique for evaluating microprocessor performance. As originated in the computer industry, benchmarking involves comparing the performance of several computers in executing a set of programs or benchmarks. The performances are compared in terms of speed and memory requirements. This technique has been adapted for comparing microprocessors for selection.

The designer must first identify tasks critical to the specific application and then write a benchmark program that implements these tasks for each microprocessor under consideration. If the benchmark programs are written in assembly language, their execution speeds are determined by ascertaining the number of states required for the execution of each individual instruction. This number is multiplied by the number of instructions in the benchmark. That product is, in turn, multiplied by the processor state time. This product is the total execution time for the benchmark. Computation of both worst case and typical execution times is helpful for comparison. The amount of memory used by a benchmark program is determined from the number of bytes of memory required for each instruction. Paper and pencil calculations are sufficient for estimating both execution times and memory requirements for some microprocessors.

As adapted for use with microprocessors, benchmarking also evaluates performance in terms of a microprocessor's ability to execute critical subfunctions in the time allotted by the performance requirements and in terms of its ability to meet the performance requirements of a particular subfunction in the overall system. If a microprocessor fails to meet these requirements, either the main program must be optimized or hardware must be added to speed up the processing. If a more efficient routine cannot be written, or if the additional hardware is not economically acceptable, either a faster microprocessor or a change in the functional partitioning of the system is necessary. Benchmarking is also beneficial in that it familiarizes the designer with the ease or difficulty of programing a particular microprocessor.

14.2.4.2 Hardware / Software Trade-Offs

The purpose of a hardware/software trade-off is to optimize performance and minimize cost. It involves determining the amount of hardware versus the amount of software to be used in implementing a particular function. Typically, software is traded off for hardware to increase the speed of execution at a concomitantly higher cost. Hardware is traded off for software to decrease cost, with a concomitantly slower execution time.

There are, basically, two types of speed problems: data transfer rate problems and data manipulation rate problems. And there are several trade-offs possible as solutions to these problems.

For example, the hardware/hardware trade-off involves the selection of hardware having a higher speed than that originally considered. This either means using a different, faster processor than the original selection or a graded, high speed version of the same microprocessor. For example, the nominal clock frequency for an 8085AH in 3 MHz; however, a faster version of this microprocessor, the 8085AH-2, operates at a clock frequency of 6 MHz. If a microprocessor is being used with memory that has a slow access time, such that the microprocessor must wait on the memory, an increase in execution speed is possible by using the same microprocessor with faster memory. Keep in mind, however, that faster hardware costs more.

Data transfer rate problems are the result of a disparity in the rates at which the microprocessor and I/O devices transfer data. In some cases, the transfer rate of the I/O device is much slower than the microprocessor can handle. This is true, for example, where a microprocessor transfers data to or from a terminal or low speed electromechanical device.

In this case, the microprocessor could completely control the transfer, both formatting and timing, with software. However, if many transfers are involved, the system can become I/O bound. When a system is *I/O bound*, or *I/O limited*, it must wait for data transfers from external devices to continue its operation. If the microprocessor still has adequate time to carry out the required data manipulations, then there is really no problem. If, however, additional computation time is needed, the software controlling the serial-to-parallel conversion and formatting can be traded off for a USART. Data can be transferred to the USART under program control, and computation can be carried on concurrently with the USART receiving or transmitting data. Even less processor time can be devoted to the transfer by having the USART interrupt the processor when it has received data or is free to transmit another word of data. This involves trading off that portion of the software that polls the status flags of the USART for any additional hardware required to generate an interrupt to the microprocessor.

Transferring blocks of data at high speed to or from an I/O device is an example of a case where the I/O device data rate is in excess of that of the microprocessor. This necessitates using a DMA transfer, which, of course, requires a DMA controller.

FIFO buffers are another hardware approach to eliminating data transfer rate disparities. FIFOs are useful when the average data rate is low but occasional high speed bursts of data occur. When the I/O data rate is much higher than the microprocessor's, the I/O device transfers data to the FIFO at its transfer rate, and the microprocessor removes it at a lower transfer rate. In the other direction, the microprocessor fills a FIFO at one transfer rate, and the I/O device inputs data from the FIFO at its higher transfer rate.

Data computation rate problems arise when data must be processed within a prescribed time interval. There are two possible solutions: a hardware/software trade-off or a software/software trade-off. The software/software trade-off is essentially the design of a faster algorithm.

The hardware/software trade-off is one of two types. In the first, software is modified to reduce the execution time of the algorithm. This is accomplished by replacing subroutine calls with the instructions that comprise the subroutine's function. This saves the time required to call and return from the subroutine and the time needed for subroutine passing. It also adds more instructions to the program. This hardware/software trade-off requires additional memory only in cases where the additional instructions cross a memory package boundary.

In the second case, software is traded off for hardware that either executes the function faster or preprocesses data. The APU exemplifies the use of hardware to implement functions providing both an increase in execution speed and the possibility of concurrency.

14.3 SYSTEM IMPLEMENTATION

After the system has been functionally partitioned and a microprocessor selected, the actual media with which to implement the hardware and software are selected.

14.3.1 Hardware Implementation

A number of alternatives are available to the designer for developing a hardware prototype and for implementing the final system hardware in production. In any case, the designer can develop the system from the ground up, starting with ICs, or can use either prefabricated printed circuit boards or completely packaged micro-computer systems containing all the hardware (power supplies, front panel, and so on) in a cabinet.

As the complexity and availability of functions implemented in LSI have increased, the difficulty of designing a microprocessor system from ICs has been minimized. This is particularly true when a compatible family of LSI devices is used.

The advantage of designing a system from the chip level is cost-effectiveness. No hardware beyond that absolutely required in the design is utilized. This minimization of package count results in substantial hardware savings where large production numbers are expected. Another advantage in designing a system from the chip level is flexibility in packaging. For small systems, all the hardware can be placed on a single printed circuit board, and an expansion capability can be built in by laying out the PC board to allow for additional RWM, ROM, and I/O. Where the designer foresees a series of models of the same basic system or foresees functionally different systems with essentially the same hardware requirements, a single, sufficiently flexible PC board can be designed to handle the different requirements. Such systems would differ significantly only in their application programs. Note, however, that flexibility via software changes is only possible if provision for the supportive hardware has been made.

In larger systems, hardware is partitioned by function over several PC boards or PC cards. A common bus with address, data, and control signals interconnects the PC cards. The bus can be physically implemented by a ***motherboard***, which is an additional PC card on which the bus connections are laid out and into which other system PC cards plug via card connectors. Or the bus signals can be brought out to edge connectors on each card and connected by flat cable, eliminating the need for a motherboard.

Bus signals can be limited to those necessary to support a particular system, or a complete set of bus signals can be provided for generality. Use of one of the de facto industry standard bus structures popularized by various manufacturers allows use of a number of commercially available prefabricated support cards designed to be compatible with various buses.

Prefabricated boards, which include single board and multicard systems, eliminate the need for much of the hardware design. Single board computers, for instance, contain a complete microcomputer system on a single printed circuit card, including the microprocessor, ROM and RWM, and parallel and serial I/O lines. The most flexible single board computers use programmable peripheral interface and communication devices. Some have connector provision that only bring out the I/O lines; others bring out both the I/O lines and system bus connections.

Multicard prefabricated systems may have one card for the CPU, one for ROM, one for RWM, and another for I/O. In some cases, the CPU card is itself a single board computer with a limited amount of ROM, RWM, and I/O, and with a complete bus structure brought to connectors at the card's edge. Other bus compatible cards include memory cards with extensive amounts of ROM or RWM, and I/O cards with serial and parallel I/O lines having logic level conversion for standard I/O interfaces such as a 20 mA current loop and RS 232. Other special purpose PC cards are available for high speed arithmetic and for controlling floppy disks and CRTs. Various analog data acquisition and control boards are also available, including A/D and D/A converters, optoisolators, and solid state relay boards.

The range of functional cards is so extensive that in many applications the designer can simply select an appropriate set of PC cards, plug them onto a motherboard or into a card cage, and thus have configured the majority of the system hardware. Any special functions not available can be designed and implemented on PC cards compatible with the system's bus structure and mechanical hardware.

Prefabricated boards are economical for low to medium volume production runs, in cases where design time is of primary concern, and where the microcomputer portion of a system represents only a very small fraction of the system cost. Completely packaged microcomputer systems are appropriate for implementing general purpose systems—for instance, low cost data processing or word processing systems. Here the microcomputer is used in the same manner in which minicomputers have traditionally been used. These systems usually have an operating system and use one or more higher level languages.

14.3.2 Software Implementation

Designers can write application programs in assembly language or in a high level language, since translators—which generate object code for specific microprocessors—are available for a number of high level languages. Both approaches have advantages and disadvantages that must be weighed.

High level languages make it possible to program in a natural algorithmic language that is closer to English than assembly language. Many high level languages are structured or block oriented.

PLM, a language similar to PL-1, appeared in 1973 and was the first high level language available for use with microprocessors. It was originally developed by Intel for use with the 8008 and 8080 microprocessors. The high level languages now available for use with microprocessors, include BASIC, FORTH, Pascal, C, and FORTRAN.

An objective of high level languages is machine (microprocessor) independence: their statements should not depend on the architecture of a specific microprocessor. When machine independence is achieved, high level language programs are portable; i.e., they can be run on any microprocessor for which there exists a translator for converting them to the microprocessor's machine language. The question of whether a particular high level language is available for a specific microprocessor is actually a question of whether there is a compiler to translate the particular high level language to machine code for a specific microprocessor. Like assemblers, compilers can be written to run on the microprocessor for which they generate machine code or written to run on a different microprocessor. These are referred to as *self-compilers* and *cross-compilers*, respectively.

The objective of a compiler is to translate a high level source program into *efficient* machine code. Since the statements of the high level language bear no relationship to the microprocessor architecture, the compiler must determine what sequence of machine language instructions best implements those statements. In addition, the compiler must decide how memory is to be allocated, in what memory locations data will be stored, which registers of the microprocessor are to be used for each task, whether the previous contents of these registers must be saved, and what optimizations can be performed.

The output of a compiler can either be machine code or assembly language. If the output is assembly, the statements are then assembled to provide the machine code. Some compilers provide as output a listing of the high level language statements followed by their equivalent assembly language statements and corresponding machine code equivalents.

When a high level language is suitable for a specific application, it has advantages over assembly language. Software development time and cost are significantly reduced because fewer program statements are necessary. Also, programs written in a high level language are generally more reliable than those written in assembly language. This is true for several reasons. Since fewer program statements are required by a high level language, there are fewer chances for error when writing the source program. In fact, errors resulting from the incorrect usage of registers or from the incorrect allocation of registers or memory are entirely eliminated. In addition, if the high level language is of the structured variety, the structure inherently leads to fewer program errors.

However, high level languages do have their drawbacks. For many applications, none of the available high level languages is appropriate. This is particularly true when direct control over the microprocessor's architectural features is required by the designer. One approach to resolving the problem of inapplicability is the use of software development systems that allow software written in high level languages and assembly language to be combined. Another approach is to provide special instructions in the high level language that carry out machine dependent operations. However, use of either of these approaches precludes program portability, as does a third approach: use of a *system implementation language*. This class of machine dependent programming languages contains a mixture of assembly and high level instructions.

Another drawback to using a high level language is that the amount of machine code produced by the compiler is greater than that produced when an equivalent assembly language program is converted to machine code. Thus, high level languages are generally less efficient than assembly language in terms of the memory required for the resultant object code in the microprocessor system.

The trade-off in memory inefficiency versus reduced development costs using a high level language, as opposed to assembly language, is illustrated in Fig. 14.3-1. The figure shows that programming costs are independent of the number of systems produced; however, memory costs are not. Therefore, since an assembly language

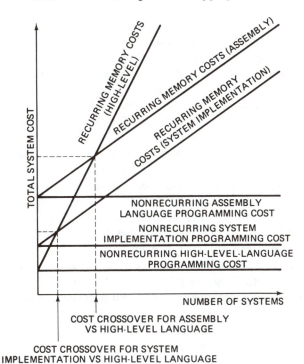

Figure 14.3-1 Effect of programming language choice on system cost.

system typically requires less memory than an equivalent high level language system, the rate of cost increase is less for the assembly language system. This is true, however, only in cases where the additional words of memory required by the high level language program necessitate one or more additional memory packages. If no memory package boundary is crossed, no additional cost is incurred. A crossover point exists such that when the number of systems required is less than n, high level language is the most cost effective, and when the number is greater than n, assembly language is the choice.

Use of a system's implementation language produces an intermediate situation, with a software development cost between that of a high level language and assembly language and memory requirements in some cases no greater than those of assembly language.

14.4 TESTING AND DEBUGGING

Testing a system is the process of determining the existence of errors in the operation of the system;[3] *debugging* is the process of locating the source of those errors and correcting them.

[3] Software testing by using a simulator was introduced in Chapter 5 and expanded on in Chapter 6. This section considers the testing and debugging of an entire system, including hardware and software and their interaction.

For some applications, the only viable strategy is bottom-up testing. A top-down approach requires an inordinate amount of extra programming and equipment. Bottom-up testing is appropriate for finding and correcting hardware, software, and total system errors. With this strategy, the modules comprising the lowest levels of a partitioned system are tested and debugged first. But prior to this, appropriate sets of test data and expected results are determined from the original functional specification for each module. A test is useless if the expected results are not completely known before it is begun.

The testing and debugging of hardware, software, and the total system, in that order, are consistent with the use of low cost tools, which range from simple to sophisticated. The primary focus here is on simple tools because they are readily available, although more costly sophisticated tools allow a great deal of parallelism when checking for and eliminating software and hardware errors.

When a microprocessor system is implemented from the bottom up, each module can be tested and debugged immediately following its completion. Indeed, it is advantageous to determine whether critical modules at the lower levels of a functional partition meet their performance requirements before proceeding with the detailed design and implementation of higher level modules. If they do not, the design can be modified accordingly at an early stage.

14.4.1 Hardware Testing and Debugging

A number of tools are used for testing and debugging a system's hardware: logic probes, multitrace oscilloscopes, logic analyzers, and microprocessor development systems. The simplest of these is, of course, the *logic probe*. A logic probe contains two LEDs that indicate the logic state of any point within a circuit touched by the probe. One LED signals a logic 0 state; the other, a logic 1. Pulse trains, or periodic waveforms, light both LEDs. A pulse stretching feature in the probe allows the observation of nonrepetitive pulses by using a single shot in the probe that, when triggered by the pulse, turns on the LED for sufficient duration to be observed. Probes are commonly available for TTL and MOS logic levels.

An *oscilloscope* displays DC and AC electrical signals in a system. It is the only tool that facilitates observation of the precise characteristics of time varying signals such as rise and fall time and duration of pulses. Multitrace oscilloscopes display the timing relationships among several waveforms, and oscilloscopes with storage features display a single event, such as a pulse, for an extended period of time. Thus, a multitrace storage oscilloscope provides considerably more information than a logic probe—at a considerably increased cost.

The *logic analyzer* is a relatively new instrument, specifically designed for testing digital systems. It does in the digital domain what the multitrace scope does in the analog analog domain; i.e., it provides a display of multiple channels of sequential digital data. Multichannel probes enable the logic analyzer to acquire 4 to 32 channels of digital data simultaneously. The data acquired on a single pass is stored in the memory of the analyzer for indefinite display.

A simplified block diagram of a logic analyzer is shown in Fig. 14.4-1. A multiple channel probe connects to the signals that are to be monitored simulta-

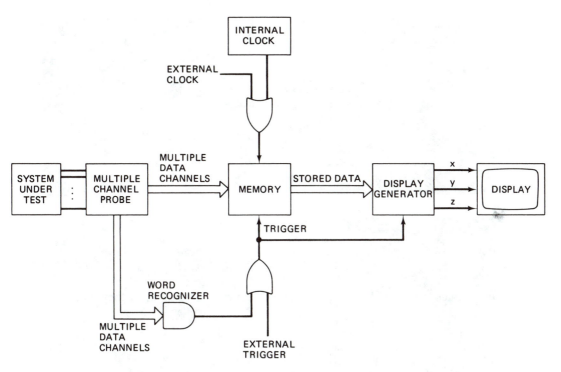

Figure 14.4-1 Simplified block diagram of a logic analyzer.

neously. An external clock or a clock internal to the analyzer continuously inputs the multichannel data into the analyzer's memory until a trigger signal occurs. Word recognition logic can create a trigger signal when a specified bit pattern occurs at the multiple input data channel. Or a delay counter can cause the trigger at some desired time interval following recognition of the trigger word. When the last memory location in the logic analyzer fills with data, writing continues in the first memory location.

The logic analyzer's display generator shows the acquired data on a CRT screen in one of several formats: a binary or hexadecimal state table, a timing diagram, or a map (see Fig. 14.4-2). A map display portrays each stored logic word as a dot. The vertical position of each dot is proportional to the most significant half of the word, and the horizontal position is proportional to the least significant half. The pattern of dots for a given sequence of data words forms a unique signature for that block of data.

The key to successful testing of both hardware and software is to check one thing at a time in a modular fashion. When making corrections, make one at a time, then retest. When a system is being prototyped from LSI devices, it is generally brought up in the following order:

1. Wire the microprocessor, its immediate support circuitry, and a minimal amount of RWM and ROM memory into the system.

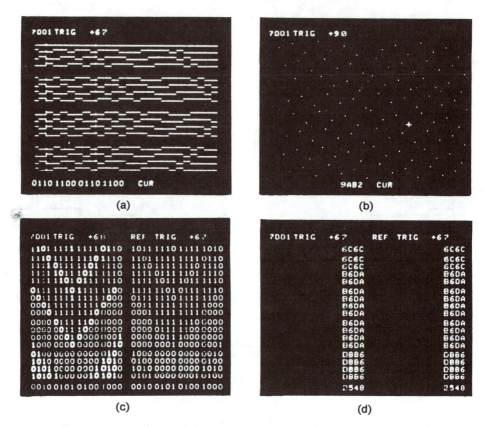

Figure 14.4-2 Logic analyzer display formats: (a) timing; (b) map; (c) binary; (d) hexadecimal. (Courtesy of Tektronix, Inc.)

2. With the integrated circuits removed from their sockets, check for proper power supply voltages at the appropriate socket pins. Also check for a good ground connection at the sockets and an absence of voltage at nonsupply connections.

3. Insert the IC circuits and again check for proper power supply levels and ground.

4. If the microprocessor uses an external clock generator, check the clock waveforms with an oscilloscope to determine that they meet the manufacturer's specifications. If the microprocessor provides an external clock out, check for the existence and validity of that signal.

Additional testing of the basic system hardware requires the execution of short diagnostic routines. For the simplest approach, three routines are written and programmed into EPROMs and executed.

The first routine is an instruction that jumps back to itself. It is placed in memory as the first instruction to be executed. This loop creates periodic waveforms on the address, data, and control lines that can be checked with an oscilloscope to verify proper operation. The second routine verifies the operation of the system RWM. A simple program that writes and then reads back patterns of all 0s, all 1s, and checker board patterns is usually adequate. And third, a routine that checks the proper operation of input and output ports is executed with a set of switches providing inputs in place of the actual input devices and a set of LEDs and their drivers replacing the output devices. At this stage, it is sufficient to determine that the output ports can actually be written and that data can be input through the input ports.

Once the basic system is operational, it can be used to check the operation of I/O devices under software control. Eventually, the entire system hardware is interconnected and its basic functionality tested.

14.4.2 Software Testing and Debugging

Thorough testing of a microprocessor system's software is imperative to ensure that the system operates as required by its functional specification. While it may be impossible to find all the bugs in a complex system during the testing and debugging stages, the motivation to do so is great. If systems are produced in large quantities, using masked ROMs, the detection of a software error after the ROMs have been produced leaves the designer with a large collection of useless ROMs. PROMs that have been programmed with unreliable software are also useless. And although EPROMs, if used, can be reprogrammed to correct the errors, even with EPROMs software changes are costly when carried out after the systems have been constructed. These are merely economic considerations; the consequences of unreliable software may be even more drastic, depending on the system's application. A strategy for software testing and debugging should, therefore, be well established early in the design process.

Software designed in a modular fashion can be tested and debugged from the bottom up. In bottom-up software testing, independent modules (subroutines[4]) are tested first; then groups of related subroutines are tested until the entire system's software is tested as a unit.

Partitioning provides functional specifications for each subroutine. From these a set of test cases or input data is established that is sufficiently exhaustive to test every decision statement in the subroutine and to verify that the subroutine operates reliably. Initial subroutine testing begins as soon as the subroutine is written. Syntax errors can be identified and corrected as the subroutine is translated. Test cases can then be run.

Tested and confirmed subroutines are combined into subsystems that, in turn, are tested. At this second stage, testing detects both logic and interface errors. Finally, all the modules are combined, and the complete software system is tested.

As the complexity of the subsystems increases, exhaustive testing becomes an impossibility. One of the problems all designers face is determining how much testing to do, as well as determining an appropriate set of test cases.

---

[4] See Chapters 5 and 6 for the testing of individual subroutines.

14.4.3 System Testing and Debugging

Software is tested initially with a simulator or by execution on a development system. But final testing requires a prototype of the actual system. For most dedicated systems this means transferring the machine code version of the application program to EPROM or PROM. And, depending on the environment in which the system is ultimately expected to operate, simulation of some of the system's inputs and outputs may be necessary. For example, in most process control applications, final testing cannot be carried out while a system is on line, i.e., actually controlling the process.

The objective of the system test is to determine wheter the system operates as required by the functional specification and to determine whether it meets its specified performance requirements. There are several different types of bugs, including logical errors as well as timing, throughput, and capacity errors.

14.5 DOCUMENTATION AND MAINTENANCE

If the requirements definition for a microprocessor system remains unchanged over the useful life of the system, maintenance becomes a continuation of the testing and debugging stage for both the system hardware and software. Hardware maintenance involves two types of system faults: design errors and component failures. The correction of design errors may require engineering changes in the systems already in the field as well as in those to be produced. Component failures can occur that are the result of neither poor design nor of the component being operated beyond its electrical limits. This type of maintenance properly belongs in the category of system repair.

During the initial stage of hardware maintenance, the source of the fault is determined and analyzed. It is at this point, therefore, that the proper documentation of the hardware and its operation has the greatest impact—this is particularly true when maintenance is provided by someone other than the original system designer.

There are also two types of software maintenance: correction of software design errors and system improvement. If the software is complex, in all probability subtle errors will remain even after testing and debugging. Again, if an error is serious enough, it requires correction in existing units as well as in units to be produced. Since such corrections often require field changes of ROMs, they can be very costly.

Modifications in software to implement minor improvements or performance enhancement are easier if the software has been developed in a modular fashion. It is also easier if the software has been well and thoroughly documented. It is difficult and time consuming for a designer to go back, several months later, and understand poorly documented software, and even more difficult, if not impossible, for someone else to understand it. High level languages are advantageous in this respect because, to a limited extent, they are self-documenting.

14.6 MULTIPLE MICROPROCESSOR SYSTEMS

The low cost of microprocessors makes it possible to use more than one in a system. Then the total system function is partitioned into tasks and each task allocated to a different microprocessor. A multiple microprocessor system has many advantages over single microprocessor systems, including higher throughput, faster real-time response, greater modularity, and improved reliability.

Concomitant with these advantages, however, are a number of design problems, including the most effective partitioning of a process into parallel tasks, allocation of these tasks, sequencing and control of the microprocessor's interprocessor connections, and control of shared resources. As a solution, a number of sophisticated schemes for interconnecting multiple processors (micros, minis, or mainframes) have been proposed, and a few have been implemented. Much of the research in this area has been aimed at achieving super computer performance via a number of low cost processors.

Two practical multiple microprocessor architectures—distributed systems and multiprocessor systems—are achievable with off-the-shelf products. These are both in a class called *multiple instruction multiple data, MIMD*, systems. MIMD architectures achieve parallelism by concurrently performing independent tasks on separate data and combining the results when appropriate.

Distributed systems differ from multiprocessor systems in the way that tasks are handled. The tasks assigned to each microprocessor in a distributed system are permanently fixed when the system is designed. In a *multiprocessing system* a complex operating system runs on one of the microprocessors and allocates tasks to microprocessors in a dynamic fashion in order to implement the overall system function in the most efficient manner. Multiprocessing systems are beyond the scope of this text. However, the more commonly used distributed systems are considered briefly.

14.6.1 Distributed Systems

In a distributed system, each microprocessor performs a dedicated function defined during the system partitioning. Software for each processor is developed in a modular fashion with the goal of minimizing the interaction between programs on separate microprocessors.

Each processor in a distributed system has two sets of interfaces: one to the external system and one to the other microprocessors. The external system activity usually involves either controlling an external process or preprocessing or postprocessing data to or from another microprocessor. Microprocessors usually communicate by passing messages or blocks of data through I/O ports or shared memory.

Distributed systems are divided into master/slave and multiple master systems.

14.6.1.1 Master / Slave Distributed Systems

Master/slave distributed systems are the simplest of the multiple processor systems because of the fixed hierarchy of their system microprocessors. A single master microprocessor controls the system. And although each microprocessor has its own I/O interface to any external activities associated with its individual tasks, an additional I/O interface connects each processor to the common system bus, which is controlled by the master. The slave processors communicate with the master, and via the master with other slave microprocessors, through the common system bus. The requests for transferring data over the common bus are arbitrated by the master. Common bus systems are designed to minimize data transfer, and parallelism is achieved by each slave processor handling its processing tasks asynchronously. A master/slave system utilizing a common bus for intercommunication is shown in Fig. 14.6-1.

Any microprocessor can be used as either a master or slave. A slave processor is chosen for its ability to optimally perform certain tasks, and several different types of microprocessors can be used as slaves in a single system. The hardware interfacing between the master and each slave must be bidirectional and must provide the handshaking logic necessary to allow synchronization of data transfers between the asynchronous master and slaves. Devices such as the 8255 programmable peripheral interface are used for master/slave interfacing. Many of the sophisticated peripheral control chips are, in effect, microprocessors that implement fixed, internally microcoded programs to carry out their functions.

Particularly appropriate as slave processors are microcomputer *universal peripheral interface, UPI*, devices. Because these are specifically designed to be used as slave processors, they contain all the logic necessary for interfacing between master and slave. These devices can be programmed to implement the entire control algorithm for a function or peripheral device. For example, the Intel 8041 and 8741 are versions of a singe-chip microcomputer optimized to function as a universal peripheral interface in a multiprocessor environment [2]. Each contains an 8-bit CPU, 64 bytes of RAM, 1024 bytes of ROM, an 8-bit timer/counter, and 18 I/O lines. Whereas the 8041 contains a mask-programmable ROM, the 8741 contains an EPROM and has a hardware single step capability for system development. The

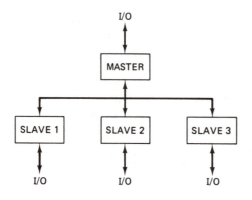

Figure 14.6-1 Generalized master/slave system with a common bus.

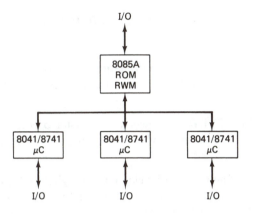

Figure 14.6-2 Master/slave system with 8085A as master and 8041/8741 as slaves.

instruction sets of both contain over 90 instructions and are designed to handle efficiently single bit manipulations in computation and I/O. A master/slave distributed system using an 8085A as the master and UPIs as slaves is shown in Fig. 14.6-2.

Of principal interest here is the interface between the UPI and the master processor (system interface) and between the UPI and its external activity (peripheral interface). The master processor and UPI communicate through an asynchronous *data bus buffer, DBB*, register in the UPI (see Fig. 14.6-3). Data and commands are received by the UPI, and status and data are transferred to the master through the DBB register. The master uses four control lines, $\overline{WR}$, $\overline{RD}$, $\overline{CS}$, and A_0, to read or write the UPI's DBB register. Control signal A_0 specifies whether a command or data word is being sent.

Execution of the program within the UPI is asynchronous to transfers through the DBB register. Thus, the UPI continues to execute its application program while transfers to and from the master are being made through the DBB register.

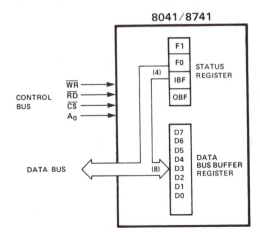

Figure 14.6-3 Communication structure between 8085A and the UPI. (Courtesy of Intel Corp.)

The flags in the 8041/8741 used to synchronize transfers to and from the master are defined as follows:

OBF: The OBF (output buffer full) flag is automatically set when the UPI outputs data to the DBB register and is cleared when the master processor reads the register.

IBF: The IBF (input buffer full) flag is set when the master processor writes data into the DBB register and is cleared when the UPI inputs the data into its accumulator.

F_0: This is a general purpose flag that can be cleared or toggled by UPI software. It can be used as a lockout signal to the master processor to indicate when the UPI is about to load data into the DBB register.

F_1: This flag is automatically set to the condition of the A_0 input line when the master processor writes to the DBB register. The status of the F_1 flag indicates

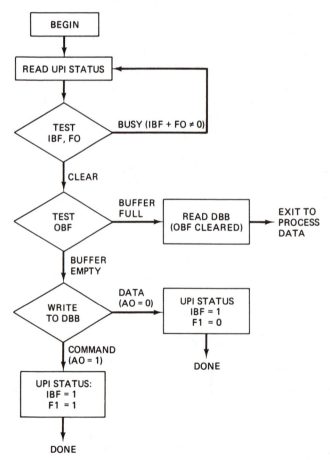

Figure 14.6-4 Master protocol sequence. (Courtesy of Intel Corp.)

whether the transfer is command ($F_1 = 1$) or data ($F_1 = 0$). F_1 can be cleared or toggled by UPI software.

   In applications requiring two-way data transfer between the master and a UPI, simultaneous writing of the DBB must be precluded. And although the UPI does not provide a hardware lockout to prevent such, a software protocol that utilizes the status flags guarantees that each processor can read or write the DBB without interference. The key to this software protocol is the UPI's subservience to the master processor in all DBB operations; i.e., the UPI writes into the DBB register only when commanded to do so by the master. In response to a transfer to the DBB

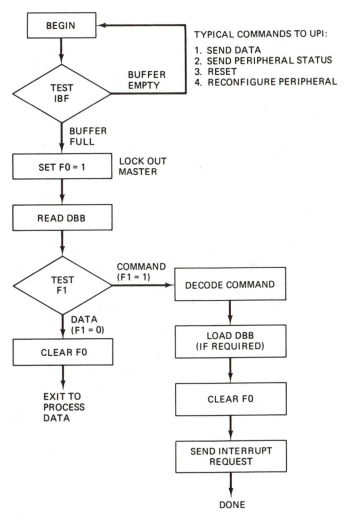

Figure 14.6-5   UPI protocol sequence. (Courtesy of Intel Corp.)

by the master, the UPI sets F_0 to lock out the master until it either loads the DBB with the data or status requested by the master or determines that no response is required.

The master protocol sequence is shown in Fig. 14.6-4. The master reads the UPI status: if the previous character written into the DBB by the master has not been input by the UPI (IBF = 1) or if the UPI has set $F_0 = 1$ to lock out the master, then the master must wait. If both IBF and $F_0 = 0$ and the master is expecting a transfer from the slave, then OBF is 1, and the master reads the DBB, automatically setting OBF to 0. The master then processes this data. Note that the UPI does not set $F_0 = 0$ until after it has loaded requested data or peripheral status into DBB, making OBF equal to 1. If the master is not expecting a transfer from the slave, OBF is 0, and the master can write a command ($A_0 = 1$, causing $F_1 = 1$) or data ($A_0 = 0$, causing $F_1 = 0$) into the DBB. The IBF flag is set when the master writes data into the DBB.

The UPI protocol is shown in Fig. 14.6-5. When the DBB is written by the master, concomitant setting of the IBF flag causes an internal interrupt if the UPI interrupt feature is enabled. Or the UPI can periodically poll its IBF flag. If IBF is set, the UPI sets F_0 to lock out the master. It then transfers the content of the DBB to its accumulator with an IN A, DBB instruction. The UPI checks F_1 for data, $F_1 = 0$, or a command, $F_1 = 1$. If the content is data, the UPI clears F_0 and exits to process it. If the content is a command, the UPI executes it. If the command requires that the UPI return data or peripheral status to the master, it loads the DBB with these before clearing F_0. The UPI can interrupt the master, using a bit from one of its output ports to indicate that the requested data is in DBB. Or the master can poll the UPI by reading the UPI's OBF flag to determine that the requested data is available.

14.6.1.2 Multiple Master Distributed Systems

In a multiple master distributed system, each microprocessor is essentially independent and is able to control the system. In addition, they share the system resources, including common RWM, disk storage, and high speed arithmetic processors. Master processors generally communicate via buffers in common RWM, and access to shared resources is through the common bus. Masters gain control of the common bus on a priority basis; therefore, two primary considerations for the design of a multiple master distributed system are arbitration of bus control requests and mutual exclusion of the simultaneous use of shared resources.

These problems and some approaches to their solution are illustrated by a brief example MULTIBUS structure—a bus structure and bus arbitration logic that allow several microcomputers to share a common bus [3]. The MULTIBUS is implemented on Intel single board computers that can, together with shared resources, be plugged into a common bus structure. Each single board computer has its own microprocessor, memory, and external I/O interconnected by an internal bus on the single board computer (see Fig. 14.6-6). Bus arbitration and control logic facilitate data flow between the single board computer's internal bus and the common bus.

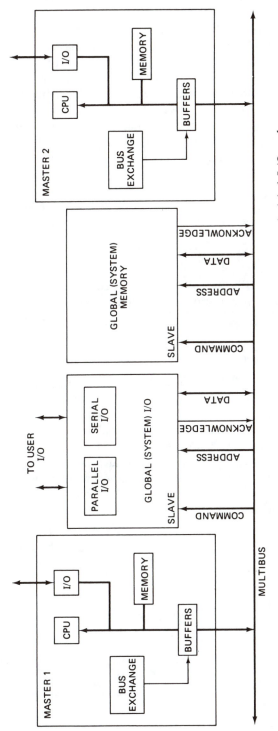

Figure 14.6-6 MULTIBUS structure with two bus masters and global I/O and memory.

Access to MULTIBUS is requested by a master only when a global (resident on the MULTIBUS and accessible by multiple masters) memory location or I/O device is referenced during an instruction execution cycle. Local/global (onboard/offboard) distinction is defined though the value of the physical address referenced. If no other master is currently using the common bus, the new master is granted access immediately; however, if another master is currently using the bus, then the new master must wait. Simultaneous requests by masters for bus control are arbitrated by either of two techniques: serial (daisy chain) or parallel (encoded). Four control lines and a bus clock (all active low) control serial or parallel arbitration:

Bus clock (BCLK/): The negative edge of BCLK/ synchronizes arbitration (minimum bus clock period, 100 nS).

Bus priority in (BPRN/): This indicates to a master that no higher priority master is requesting the use of the bus.

Bus priority out (BPRO/): BPRO/ is passed to the BPRN/ input of the master with next lower bus priority.

Bus busy signal (BUSY/): This signal, driven by the bus master currently in control of multibus, indicates current bus usage. BUSY/ prevents other masters from gaining control of the bus.

Bus request signal (BREQ/): This is used with a parallel bus priority network to indicate that a particular master requires use of the bus for one or more transfers.

The hardware interconnection for serial arbitration is shown in Fig. 14.6-7. When a master requires the common bus, its BPRO/ line inhibits lower priority masters. BUSY/, by the same token, ensures that in-process operations of lower priority masters are not destroyed by asynchronous requests of higher priority masters. In addition, a bus lock function, which asserts the BUSY/, enables a master to retain control of the bus until it issues an unlock command. The bus lock

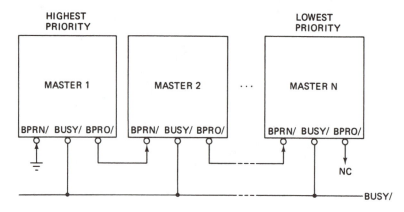

Figure 14.6-7 Serial MULTIBUS arbitration.

function is used in high speed memory or I/O transfers and in critical read modify write operations. Bus transfers normally take place on an interleaved basis (bus arbitration being performed for each cycle). For example, if master$_i$ requires the common bus, it first examines its BPRN/ input; if it is low, it then examines BUSY/. If inactive, master$_i$ asserts it and takes control of the bus. If BUSY/ is active, master$_i$ examines BUSY/ on the falling edge of each BCLK/ until BUSY/ is inactive. Master$_i$ then asserts BUSY/ and takes control of the common bus.

Additional masters can be added as long as the cumulative BPRN/ to BPRO/ propagation delay is such that BPRN/ of the lowest priority master is driven inactive before the next BCLK/ falling edge after the highest priority master requests the bus:

$$\sum_{i=1}^{N-1} \left(t_{\text{BPRN}-\text{BPRO}}\right)_i < t_{\text{BCLK}} - t_{\text{sh}}$$

where $\left(t_{\text{BPRN}-\text{BPRO}}\right)_i$ is the propagation delay for master$_i$, t_{BCLK} is the bus clock period, and t_{sh} is the bus setup and hold time.

Parallel arbitration uses the hardware structure shown in Fig. 14.6-8. In the Intel MULTIBUS structure, each master asserts BREQ/ when it requires access to

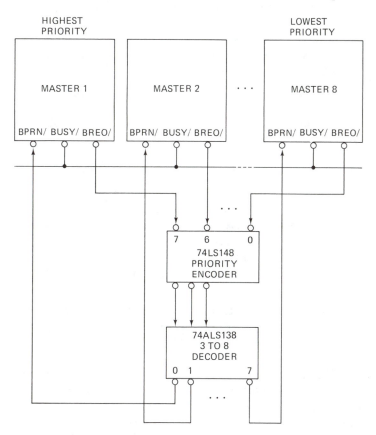

Figure 14.6-8   Parallel MULTIBUS arbitration.

the system bus. The 74LS148 (an 8-line-to-3-line priority encoder) encodes the requests of the highest priority master, and the 74ALS138 (a 3-to-8-decoder) asserts its BPRN/ line. The use of two 74LS148s and two 74ALS138s provides a 16-level priority network.

The second consideration for designing a multiple master distributed system is the mutual exclusion of the simultaneous use of shared resources. Certain segments of a master's program that access shared resources constitute *critical sections*; i.e., to preclude errors in system operation, once entered these sections must be completed before another critical section accessing the same shared resource can begin.

Thus, it is necessary to have a mechanism that allows only one related critical section at a time to be entered and fully executed. Critical sections are related if they utilize the same shared resource.

One method, by which simultaneous access of critical sections to shared resources is prohibited, utilizes a semaphore. A *semaphore*, as used here, is a binary variable. One semaphore is associated with each shared resource and is implemented as a reserved memory location. The use of a semaphore, S, requires two primitive or indivisible operations on the memory location used for that semaphore. An indivisible operation enables the completion of reading, modifying, and writing a memory location prior to access by any other process. The two operations are defined as

1. P(S): If S = 1, S is decremented by 1. Testing and decrementing S is a single indivisible operation. If S = 0, the process that invoked the P operation must wait until it finds S = 1.

2. V(S): S is incremented by 1 as a single indivisible operation.

A semaphore provides mutual exclusion for a shared resource in the following manner:

1. Initially the semaphore is set to 1, S = 1.

2. The related critical sections of each program are preceded by a P operation on S, P(S). If several masters attempt a P operation on S simultaneously, the operations occur sequentially in an arbitrary manner. The first master that finds S = 1 completes the P operation, leaving S = 0, and enters its critical section of code. The remaining master's P operations will be unsuccessful, and they will continually wait in a loop doing P operations on S.

3. The critical section of each program is followed by a V operation on S, V(S). When a master executing in its critical section leaves that section, its V operation sets S = 1. Another master, waiting to use the shared resource, then completes its P operation and enters its critical section.

The remaining problem is how to implement the indivisible P and V operations. The semaphore S is assumed to be a global memory location in common memory. For the V operation, the machine cycles that read S, increment its value, and write it back must be indivisible to prevent other masters gaining control of the common bus. This is accomplished in the MULTIBUS structure by the BUSLOCK operation. For a V operation, once the master controls the MULTIBUS, it locks the bus, increments the semaphore memory location, and then unlocks the bus. For the P operation, when the master gains control of the common bus, it tests the semaphore. If it is 0, the master continues in a wait loop; if 1, the master locks the bus and retests the semaphore. If the semaphore is still equal to 1, it is decremented, the bus is unlocked, and the master enters its critical section of code. If, at the second test, the semaphore is 0, the master unlocks the bus and waits in a loop. The first test for $S = 1$ prevents a master from continually locking and unlocking the bus while $S = 0$.

Semaphores also protect the writing and reading of buffers in common memory that provide communication between masters. In addition, semaphores synchronize masters cooperating in a computation.

REFERENCES

1. D. T. ROSS and K. E. SCHOMAN, JR., "Structured Analysis for Requirements Definition," *IEEE Transactions on Software Engineering*, SE-3 (January 1977), 6–15.
2. *UPI-41 User's Manual* (Santa Clara, Calif.: Intel Corporation, 1979).
3. *Intel Multibus Specification* (Santa Clara, Calif.: Intel Corporation, 1978).

PROBLEMS

14-1. Design a microprocessor system! More specifically, select an application that you are familiar with and that you feel might be appropriately handled by a low to medium complexity microprocessor system. You may wish to select a very simple application for your first microprocessor system design and after its completion repeat this problem attempting a different, more complex, design or a substantial enhancement (second generation) of your first design. Some possible applications are listed below if you need suggestions.

For your design carry out each of the five stages in the five-stage methodology as thoroughly as possible within the limits of time, information, and facilities available to you.

(a) Requirements Definition: Develop a complete written requirements definition. In doing so consider the capabilities and limitations of any existing systems designed for the same applications. Ideally, you should be developing a system that is competitive with existing systems in terms of cost and performance.

(b) Systematic Design: Functionally partition your system. Your partition should take full consideration of existing common LSI subsystems. Select an appropriate microprocessor or microcomputer for your application. Since a low to medium complexity system is being designed, it should be implementable with a single-chip microcomputer or a low end or midrange general purpose microprocessor.

(c) System Implementation: Determine the method of hardware implementation: individual ICs, prefabricated single board computers, or prefabricated card sets. If individual ICs are the chosen approach, select and identify the actual devices and also reconsider the system partition and hardware/software trade-offs in light of the available IC devices. Also consider how your ICs will be physicaly placed among the PC boards. If a prefabricated single board microcomputer or PC card set is the chosen approach, identify the actual parts and determine what special circuitry must be designed and how it will interface with the prefabricated hardware. Draw the logic diagram of any circuitry to be designed.

Determine what language you will program the system in: assembly language or one of the high level languages available for the microprocessor or microcomputer of your choice. For your choice of language, determine what software development aids are available. Flowchart the overall application program logic. Design and code any critical subroutines whose implementation is not readily apparent. If time and facilities permit, write the entire application program.

(d) Flowchart routines for testing and debugging the various hardware subsystems.
(e) Translate and debug the application program to whatever extent is possible with the facilities available to you.
(f) Compile and write the documentation for the system hardware and software.

Possible microprocessor system applications:
1. EPROM programmer
2. Home security system (smoke, fire, and intrusion)
3. Integrated circuit tester
4. Commercial paint mixing system
5. Piece counting by weight system
6. Printed circuit board drilling system
7. Taxi meter
8. Swimming (or running) competition timing and display system
9. Automobile trip computer

A

Open Collector and Three-State Outputs

Regardless of the technology used or the function implemented by an IC logic device, its output can be one of three types: standard totem pole, open collector, or three-state.

The circuit diagram of a simple TTL inverter with a standard totem pole output is shown in Fig. A.1a. The totem pole output stage consists of transistors Q_1 and Q_2. Transistor Q_1 is ON and transistor Q_2 is OFF to provide a logic 1 output. Because of the way it is used, Q_1 is called an active pull-up transistor. When ON, it pulls the output voltage up to its logic 1 level. The output impedance in the logic 1 state is very low. A logic 0 output results when transistor Q_1 is OFF and Q_2 is ON. The output impedance in the logic 0 state is also very low. The design of the circuit is such that one of these transistors is always ON and the other OFF. An advantage of the totem pole output stage is its fast switching speed even when driving highly capacitive loads.

When a logic circuit is constructed from devices with standard totem pole outputs, these outputs are only connected to the inputs of other logic devices. *Outputs of devices with standard totem pole output stages are never connected.* For example, if TTL standard totem pole outputs are connected and one of the outputs is driven low while the other is driven high (as shown in Fig. A.1b, the devices will be damaged. This is due to the fact that one transistor is always ON and the other is always OFF in the standard totem pole output stage. When output A is high, the top transistor is ON, and the bottom transistor is OFF; if output B is low, the top transistor is OFF, and the bottom transistor is ON. With outputs A and B connected, there is only a very small resistance (typically 130 Ω) between V_{cc} and ground, and the resultant current can destroy the devices. Figure A.1c shows, in logic diagram form, the unacceptable connection of the outputs of two TTL inverters with standard totem pole output stages.

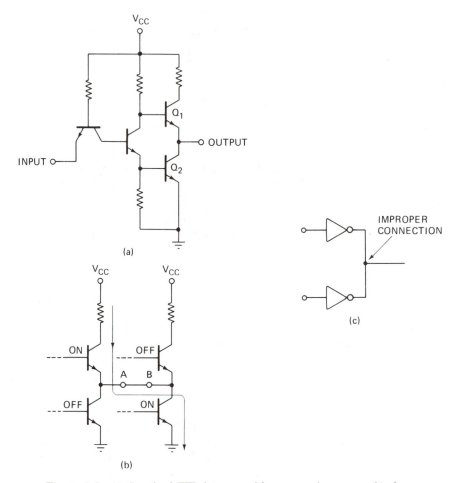

Figure A.1 (a) Standard TTL inverter with totem pole output; (b) short circuit of two inverters with outputs connected; (c) logic diagram of improper connection.

The output stages of open collector devices are not totem pole configurations; nor is a pull-up transistor used. Instead, the output circuit of an open collector device is completed by the addition of an external ***pull-up resistor***. (see Fig. A.2a). The use of a passive pull-up resistor with open collector outputs results in a device that switches more slowly when changing from logic 0 to logic 1 than does a device having an output stage with an active pull up. If the outputs of two or more open collector devices are connected, only a single pull-up resistor is required (see Fig. A2.b). The value of the pull-up resistor is selected so that there is no danger of damage to devices when the outputs are connected (see Fig. A.3). If either device is driven low, its common output, F, is low; if both are high, their common output is high. Thus, $F = A \cdot B$ or $\overline{F} = \overline{A} + \overline{B}$. This connection is frequently referred to as a ***wired AND*** or ***wired OR*** connection. To be more exact, the wired OR reference is actually to a negative logic wired OR. This connection is sometimes represented on

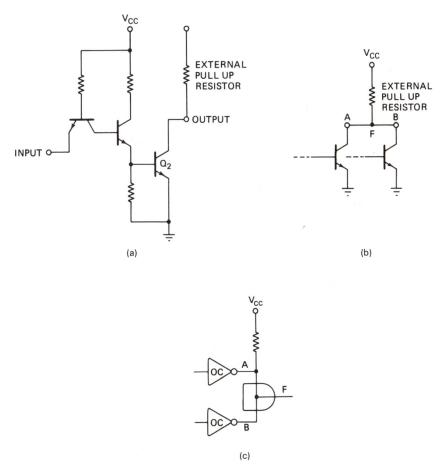

Figure A.2   (a) Open collector TTL output; (b) valid common connection of open collector outputs using a pull up resistor; (c) logic schematic showing dot AND effect of connecting open collector outputs together.

a logic diagram by a gate symbol with a dot in its center. The gate does not exist physically in the system, only the wire connections and the logical effect of the gate exist.

The ability to directly connect the outputs of open collector devices without damage and the logic functions that derive from that interconnection allow the outputs of these devices to be multiplexed without separate multiplexer ICs. This is particularly important when connecting several devices to the same bus. Figure A.4 shows two devices, each with two data outputs. The outputs are provided from output stages consisting of open collector NAND gates. One input to each NAND gate is the complement of the data, and the other is an enable signal. Outputs on a single device have a common enable signal. When the enable signal of one device is logic 0, its outputs are logic 1; if the enable signal of the other device is logic 1, its outputs are the complement of the data inputs to its open collector NAND gates

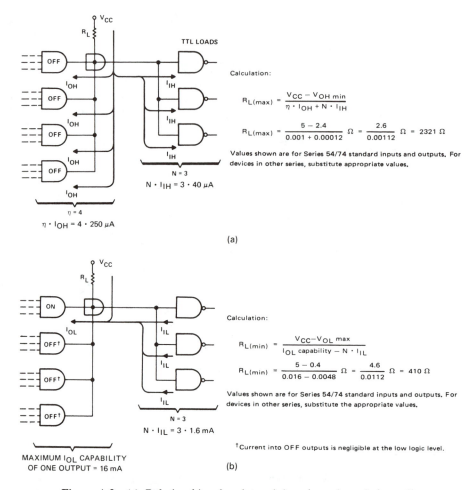

Calculation:

$$R_{L(max)} = \frac{V_{CC} - V_{OH\,min}}{\eta \cdot I_{OH} + N \cdot I_{IH}}$$

$$R_{L(max)} = \frac{5 - 2.4}{0.001 + 0.00012}\,\Omega = \frac{2.6}{0.00112}\,\Omega = 2321\,\Omega$$

Values shown are for Series 54/74 standard inputs and outputs. For devices in other series, substitute appropriate values.

$N = 3$

$N \cdot I_{IH} = 3 \cdot 40\,\mu A$

$\eta = 4$

$\eta \cdot I_{OH} = 4 \cdot 250\,\mu A$

(a)

Calculation:

$$R_{L(min)} = \frac{V_{CC} - V_{OL\,max}}{I_{OL}\text{ capability} - N \cdot I_{IL}}$$

$$R_{L(min)} = \frac{5 - 0.4}{0.016 - 0.0048}\,\Omega = \frac{4.6}{0.0112}\,\Omega = 410\,\Omega$$

Values shown are for Series 54/74 standard inputs and outputs. For devices in other series, substitute the appropriate values.

$N = 3$

$N \cdot I_{IL} = 3 \cdot 1.6\,mA$

†Current into OFF outputs is negligible at the low logic level.

MAXIMUM I_{OL} CAPABILITY
OF ONE OUTPUT = 16 mA

(b)

Figure A.3 (a) Relationships for determining the value of the pull-up resistor in open collector circuits: high level circuit conditions; (b) low level circuit conditions. (Courtesy of Texas Instruments, Inc.)

and drive the common bus. For example, if ENX = 1 and ENY = 0, then $Z_0 = X_0$ and $Z_1 = X_1$.

The output stages of devices with three-state outputs provide three possible output conditions. Two are identical to those of standard TTL, and one of these two conditions exists whenever the device is enabled: a low impedance output with a high voltage level (logic 1) or a low impedance output with a low voltage level (logic 0). The third state, a high impedance output, exists when the device is not enabled. The output stage of a three-state device is similar to that of a standard totem pole TTL output stage except it includes circuitry that allows an enable signal to turn both output transistors OFF simultaneously, providing a high impedance output state (Fig. A.5a and b). The high impedance state makes the output function as if it is not electrically connected to any other device to which it is actually physically

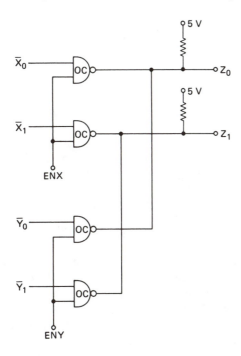

Figure A.4 Multiplexing signals to a common bus using NAND gates with open collector outputs.

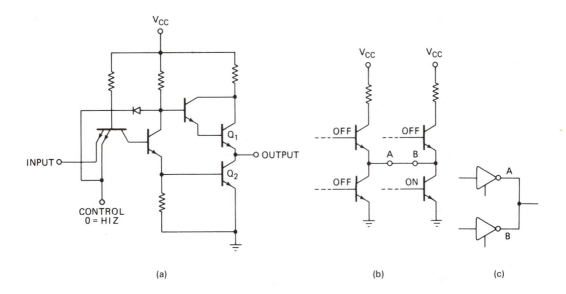

Figure A.5 (a) Three-state TTL circuit; (b) common connection of three-state outputs—only one gate enabled; (c) logic schematic showing connection of three-state outputs.

(a)

(b)

(c)

(d)

Figure A.6   Three-state buffers: (a) noninverting buffer with active high enable; (b) noninverting buffer with active low enable; (c) inverting buffer with active high enable; (d) inverting buffer with active low enable.

connected. If several three-state outputs are connected, all but one must be disabled; only the enabled output determines the logic level of the connection. If the outputs of two three-state devices are enabled simultaneously, a situation similar to that in Fig. A.1b is possible, and the devices are subject to damage. Three-state outputs allow the multiplexing of several outputs without the use of multiplexer ICs or pull-up resistors. The symbol for a three-state output buffer is shown in Fig. A.5c. This device is enabled with a logic 1 at the enable input. The output of this device is the complement of its input. This is one of four possible variations of enable levels and output levels. The logic symbols for all four variations of three-state buffers are shown in Fig. A.6.

Many logic devices are designed with three-state outputs so they can be multiplexed to a bus easily. For devices that do not have three-state outputs, separate three-state buffer ICs between the output of the device and the bus carry out the same function at the cost of an additional package.

B

Octal and Hexadecimal Numbers

The octal (base 8) and hexadecimal (base 16) numbers and their binary (base 2) and decimal (base 10) counterparts from 0 to 15 are as given in the accompanying table.

Decimal (base 10)	Binary (base 2)	Octal (base 8)	Hexadecimal (base 16)
00	0000	00	0
01	0001	01	1
02	0010	02	2
03	0011	03	3
04	0100	04	4
05	0101	05	5
06	0110	06	6
07	0111	07	7
08	1000	10	8
09	1001	11	9
10	1010	12	A
11	1011	13	B
12	1100	14	C
13	1101	15	D
14	1110	16	E
15	1111	17	F

The octal number system has eight digits (0–7), and the hexadecimal system contains 16 digits (0–9 an A–F). Because both 8 and 16 are powers of 2, conversion between binary and octal (2^3) or binary and hexadecimal (2^4) numbers is very simple. To convert a binary number to octal, the bits of the binary number are grouped in threes starting at the binary point and moving left for integers and right for fractions. Each group of three is then converted to the proper octal digit. For example

binary	11	011	101	000 ·	010	11
octal	3	3	5	0 ·	2	6

Note that zeros are assumed to the extreme left and right of the binary number to make the leftmost and rightmost groupings consist of the necessary three digits.

Octal numbers are written with a subscript 8 or a suffix 0 or Q to indicate that they are octal numbers:

$$3350.26_8 = 3350.26Q$$

Binary numbers are converted to hexadecimal numbers by separating the binary number into groups of 4 bits and converting each group to a hexadecimal digit. For example

binary	110	1110	1000 ·	0101	1
hexadecimal	6	E	8 ·	5	8

Hexadecimal numbers are written with a subscript 16 or a suffix H to indicate that they are hexadecimal numbers:

$$6E8.58_{16} = 6E8.58H$$

To convert an octal or hexadecimal number to its binary equivalent, each octal or hexadecimal digit is replaced by its binary equivalent. An example of converting an octal number 743.16Q to binary is

octal	7	4	3 · 1	6
binary	111	100	011 · 001	110

Similarly, for the hexadecimal number A29.C4H

hexadecimal	A	2	9 · C	4
binary	1010	0010	1001 · 1100	0100

Octal and hexadecimal numbers are commonly used to represent bit patterns in a concise manner in microprocessor systems. Hexadecimal is preferred over octal because it is the most concise, and register sizes in microprocessor systems are multiples of 4 bits (4, 8, 12, or 16 bits). For example, if register A contains 10110011, it is simply written as B3H. Furthermore, a 16-bit address 0000 0100 0001 1101 is written 041DH.

C

The Intel 8085A Instruction Set

INSTRUCTION SET ENCYCLOPEDIA

In the ensuing dozen pages, the complete 8085A instruction set is described, grouped in order under five different functional headings, as follows:

1. **Data Transfer Group** — Moves data between registers or between memory locations and registers. Includes moves, loads, stores, and exchanges. (See below.)
2. **Arithmetic Group** — Adds, subtracts, increments, or decrements data in registers or memory. (See page 4-13.)
3. **Logic Group** — ANDs, ORs, XORs, compares, rotates, or complements data in registers or between memory and a register. (See page 4-16.)
4. **Branch Group** — Initiates conditional or unconditional jumps, calls, returns, and restarts. (See page 4-20.)
5. **Stack, I/O, and Machine Control Group** — Includes instructions for maintaining the stack, reading from input ports, writing to output ports, setting and reading interrupt masks, and setting and clearing flags. (See page 4-22.)

The formats described in the encyclopedia reflect the assembly language processed by Intel-supplied assembler, used with the Intellec® development systems.

Data Transfer Group

This group of instructions transfers data to and from registers and memory. **Condition flags are not affected by any instruction in this group.**

MOV r1, r2   (Move Register)
(r1) ← (r2)
The content of register r2 is moved to register r1.

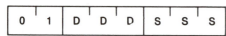

0	1	D	D	D	S	S	S

Cycles: 1
States: 4
Addressing: register
Flags: none

MOV r, M   (Move from memory)
(r) ← ((H) (L))
The content of the memory location, whose address is in registers H and L, is moved to register r.

0	1	D	D	D	1	1	0

Cycles: 2
States: 7
Addressing: reg. indirect
Flags: none

MOV M, r   (Move to memory)
((H)) (L)) ← (r)
The content of register r is moved to the memory location whose address is in registers H and L.

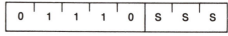

0	1	1	1	0	S	S	S

Cycles: 2
States: 7
Addressing: reg. indirect
Flags: none

MVI r, data   (Move Immediate)
(r) ← (byte 2)
The content of byte 2 of the instruction is moved to register r.

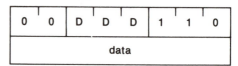

0	0	D	D	D	1	1	0
data							

Cycles: 2
States: 7
Addressing: immediate
Flags: none

MVI M, data   (Move to memory immediate)
((H) (L)) ← (byte 2)
The content of byte 2 of the instruction is moved to the memory location whose address is in registers H and L.

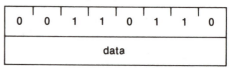

0	0	1	1	0	1	1	0
data							

Cycles: 3
States: 10
Addressing: immed./reg. indirect
Flags: none

(All mnemonics copyright Intel Corporation 1976.)

Figure C.1

Page 115.   LXI HL 464
00100001 — 214
00000110 —
00000100 — 06 H
                  04 H

THE INSTRUCTION SET

LXI rp, data 16 (Load register pair immediate)
(rh) ← (byte 3),
(rl) ← (byte 2)
Byte 3 of the instruction is moved into the high-order register (rh) of the register pair rp. Byte 2 of the instruction is moved into the low-order register (rl) of the register pair rp.

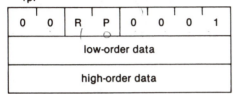

| 0 | 0 | R | P | 0 | 0 | 0 | 1 |

low-order data

high-order data

Cycles: 3
States: 10
Addressing: immediate
Flags: none

LDA addr   (Load Accumulator direct)
(A) ← ((byte 3)(byte 2))
The content of the memory location, whose address is specified in byte 2 and byte 3 of the instruction, is moved to register A.

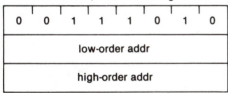

| 0 | 0 | 1 | 1 | 1 | 0 | 1 | 0 |

low-order addr

high-order addr

Cycles: 4
States: 13
Addressing: direct
Flags: none

STA addr   (Store Accumulator direct)
((byte 3)(byte 2)) ← (A)
The content of the accumulator is moved to the memory location whose address is specified in byte 2 and byte 3 of the instruction.

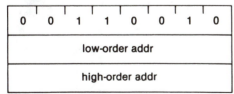

| 0 | 0 | 1 | 1 | 0 | 0 | 1 | 0 |

low-order addr

high-order addr

Cycles: 4
States: 13
Addressing: direct
Flags: none

LHLD addr   (Load H and L direct)
(L) ← ((byte 3)(byte 2))
(H) ← ((byte 3)(byte 2) + 1)
The content of the memory location, whose address is specified in byte 2 and byte 3 of the instruction, is moved to register L. The content of the memory location at the succeeding address is moved to register H.

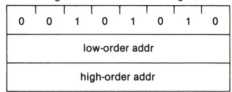

| 0 | 0 | 1 | 0 | 1 | 0 | 1 | 0 |

low-order addr

high-order addr

Cycles: 5
States: 16
Addressing: direct
Flags: none

SHLD addr   (Store H and L direct)
((byte 3)(byte 2)) ← (L)
((byte 3)(byte 2) + 1) ← (H)
The content of register L is moved to the memory location whose address is specified in byte 2 and byte 3. The content of register H is moved to the succeeding memory location.

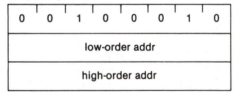

| 0 | 0 | 1 | 0 | 0 | 0 | 1 | 0 |

low-order addr

high-order addr

Cycles: 5
States: 16
Addressing: direct
Flags: none

LDAX rp   (Load accumulator indirect)
(A) ← ((rp))
The content of the memory location, whose address is in the register pair rp, is moved to register A. Note: only register pairs rp = B (registers B and C) or rp = D (registers D and E) may be specified.

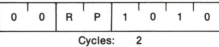

| 0 | 0 | R | P | 1 | 0 | 1 | 0 |

Cycles: 2
States: 7
Addressing: reg. indirect
Flags: none

(All mnemonics copyright Intel Corporation 1976.)

Figure C.2

THE INSTRUCTION SET

STAX rp   (Store accumulator indirect)
((rp)) ← (A)
The content of register A is moved to the memory location whose address is in the register pair rp. Note: only register pairs rp = B (registers B and C) or rp = D (registers D and E) may be specified.

0	0	R	P	0	0	1	0

Cycles: 2
States: 7
Addressing: reg. indirect
Flags: none

XCHG   (Exchange H and L with D and E)
(H) ↔ (D)
(L) ↔ (E)
The contents of registers H and L are exchanged with the contents of registers D and E.

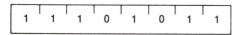

1	1	1	0	1	0	1	1

Cycles: 1
States: 4
Addressing: register
Flags: none

Arithmetic Group

This group of instructions performs arithmetic operations on data in registers and memory.

Unless indicated otherwise, all instructions in this group affect the Zero, Sign, Parity, Carry, and Auxiliary Carry flags according to the standard rules.

All subtraction operations are performed via two's complement arithmetic and set the carry flag to one to indicate a borrow and clear it to indicate no borrow.

ADD r   (Add Register)
(A) ← (A) + (r)
The content of register r is added to the content of the accumulator. The result is placed in the accumulator.

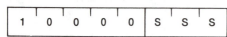

1	0	0	0	0	S	S	S

Cycles: 1
States: 4
Addressing: register
Flags: Z,S,P,CY,AC

ADD M   (Add memory)
(A) ← (A) + ((H) (L))
The content of the memory location whose address is contained in the H and L registers is added to the content of the accumulator. The result is placed in the accumulator.

1	0	0	0	0	1	1	0

Cycles: 2
States: 7
Addressing: reg. indirect
Flags: Z,S,P,CY,AC

ADI data   (Add immediate)
(A) ← (A) + (byte 2)
The content of the second byte of the instruction is added to the content of the accumulator. The result is placed in the accumulator.

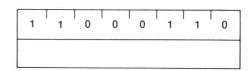

1	1	0	0	0	1	1	0

Cycles: 2
States: 7
Addressing: immediate
Flags: Z,S,P,CY,AC

ADC r   (Add Register with carry)
(A) ← (A) + (r) + (CY)
The content of register r and the content of the carry bit are added to the content of the accumulator. The result is placed in the accumulator.

1	0	0	0	1	S	S	S

Cycles: 1
States: 4
Addressing: register
Flags: Z,S,P,CY,AC

(All mnemonics copyright Intel Corporation 1976.)

Figure C.3

THE INSTRUCTION SET

ADC M   (Add memory with carry)
(A) ← (A) + ((H) (L)) + (CY)
The content of the memory location whose address is contained in the H and L registers and the content of the CY flag are added to the accumulator. The result is placed in the accumulator.

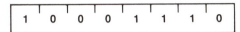

1	0	0	0	1	1	1	0

Cycles:	2
States:	7
Addressing:	reg. indirect
Flags:	Z,S,P,CY,AC

SUB M   (Subtract memory)
(A) ← (A) − ((H) (L))
The content of the memory location whose address is contained in the H and L registers is subtracted from the content of the accumulator. The result is placed in the accumulator.

1	0	0	1	0	1	1	0

Cycles:	2
States:	7
Addressing:	reg. indirect
Flags:	Z,S,P,CY,AC

ACI data   (Add immediate with carry)
(A) ← (A) + (byte 2) + (CY)
The content of the second byte of the instruction and the content of the CY flag are added to the contents of the accumulator. The result is placed in the accumulator.

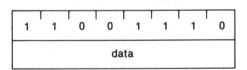

1	1	0	0	1	1	1	0
data							

Cycles:	2
States:	7
Addressing:	immediate
Flags:	Z,S,P,CY,AC

SUI data   (Subtract immediate)
(A) ← (A) − (byte 2)
The content of the second byte of the instruction is subtracted from the content of the accumulator. The result is placed in the accumulator.

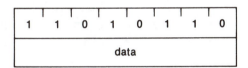

1	1	0	1	0	1	1	0
data							

Cycles:	2
States:	7
Addressing:	immediate
Flags:	Z,S,P,CY,AC

SUB r   (Subtract Register)
(A) ← (A) − (r)
The content of register r is subtracted from the content of the accumulator. The result is placed in the accumulator.

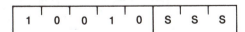

1	0	0	1	0	S	S	S

Cycles:	1
States:	4
Addressing:	register
Flags:	Z,S,P,CY,AC

SBB r   (Subtract Register with borrow)
(A) ← (A) − (r) − (CY)
The content of register r and the content of the CY flag are both subtracted from the accumulator. The result is placed in the accumulator.

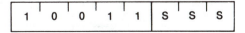

1	0	0	1	1	S	S	S

Cycles:	1
States:	4
Addressing:	register
Flags:	Z,S,P,CY,AC

Figure C.4

THE INSTRUCTION SET

SBB M   (Subtract memory with borrow)
(A) ← (A) − ((H) (L)) − (CY)
The content of the memory location whose address is contained in the H and L registers and the content of the CY flag are both subtracted from the accumulator. The result is placed in the accumulator.

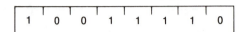

1	0	0	1	1	1	1	0

Cycles:	2
States:	7
Addressing:	reg. indirect
Flags:	Z,S,P,CY,AC

SBI data   (Subtract immediate with borrow)
(A) ← (A) − (byte 2) − (CY)
The contents of the second byte of the instruction and the contents of the CY flag are both subtracted from the accumulator. The result is placed in the accumulator.

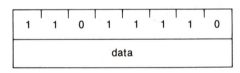

1	1	0	1	1	1	1	0
data							

Cycles:	2
States:	7
Addressing:	immediate
Flags:	Z,S,P,CY,AC

INR r   (Increment Register)
(r) ← (r) + 1
The content of register r is incremented by one. Note: All condition flags **except CY** are affected.

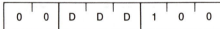

0	0	D	D	D	1	0	0

Cycles:	1
States:	4
Addressing:	register
Flags:	Z,S,P,AC

INR M   (Increment memory)
((H) (L)) ← ((H) (L)) + 1
The content of the memory location whose address is contained in the H and L registers is incremented by one. Note: All condition flags **except CY** are affected.

0	0	1	1	0	1	0	0

Cycles:	3
States:	10
Addressing:	reg. indirect
Flags:	Z,S,P,AC

DCR r   (Decrement Register)
(r) ← (r) − 1
The content of register r is decremented by one. Note: All condition flags **except CY** are affected.

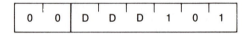

0	0	D	D	D	1	0	1

Cycles:	1
States:	4
Addressing:	register
Flags:	Z,S,P,AC

DCR M   (Decrement memory)
((H) (L)) ← ((H) (L)) − 1
The content of the memory location whose address is contained in the H and L registers is decremented by one. Note: All condition flags **except CY** are affected.

0	0	1	1	0	1	0	1

Cycles:	3
States:	10
Addressing:	reg. indirect
Flags:	Z,S,P,AC

(All mnemonics copyright Intel Corporation 1976.)

Figure C.5

THE INSTRUCTION SET

INX rp   (Increment register pair)
(rh) (rl) ← (rh) (rl) + 1
The content of the register pair rp is incremented by one. Note: **No condition flags are affected.**

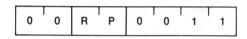

0	0	R	P	0	0	1	1

Cycles: 1
States: 6
Addressing: register
Flags: none

DCX rp   (Decrement register pair)
(rh) (rl) ← (rh) (rl) − 1
The content of the register pair rp is decremented by one. Note: **No condition flags are affected.**

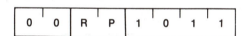

0	0	R	P	1	0	1	1

Cycles: 1
States: 6
Addressing: register
Flags: none

DAD rp   (Add register pair to H and L)
(H) (L) ← (H) (L) + (rh) (rl)
The content of the register pair rp is added to the content of the register pair H and L. The result is placed in the register pair H and L. Note: **Only the CY flag is affected.** It is set if there is a carry out of the double precision add; otherwise it is reset.

0	0	R	P	1	0	0	1

Cycles: 3
States: 10
Addressing: register
Flags: CY

DAA   (Decimal Adjust Accumulator)
The eight-bit number in the accumulator is adjusted to form two four-bit Binary-Coded-Decimal digits by the following process:

1. If the value of the lease significant 4 bits of the accumulator is greater than **9 or** if the AC flag is set, 6 is added to the accumulator.

2. If the value of the most significant 4 bits of the accumulator is now greater than 9, **or** if the CY flag is set, 6 is added to the most significant 4 bits of the accumulator.

NOTE: All flags are affected.

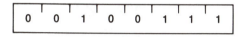

0	0	1	0	0	1	1	1

Cycles: 1
States: 4
Flags: Z,S,P,CY,AC

4.6.3 Logic Group

This group of instructions performs logical (Boolean) operations on data in registers and memory and on condition flags.

Unless indicated otherwise, all instructions in this group affect the Zero, Sign, Parity, Auxiliary Carry, and Carry flags according to the standard rules.

ANA r   (AND Register)
(A) ← (A) ∧ (r)
The content of register r is logically ANDed with the content of the accumulator. The result is placed in the accumulator. **The CY flag is cleared and AC is set.**

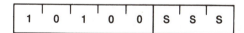

1	0	1	0	0	S	S	S

Cycles: 1
States: 4
Addressing: register
Flags: Z,S,P,CY,AC

(All mnemonics copyright Intel Corporation 1976.)

Figure C.6

THE INSTRUCTION SET

ANA M   (AND memory)
(A) ← (A) ∧ ((H) (L))
The contents of the memory location whose address is contained in the H and L registers is logically ANDed with the content of the accumulator. The result is placed in the accumulator. **The CY flag is cleared and AC is set.**

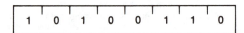

1	0	1	0	0	1	1	0

Cycles: 2
States: 7
Addressing: reg. indirect
Flags: Z,S,P,CY,AC

ANI data   (AND immediate)
(A) ← (A) ∧ (byte 2)
The content of the second byte of the instruction is logically ANDed with the contents of the accumulator. The result is placed in the accumulator. **The CY flag is cleared and AC is set.**

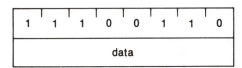

1	1	1	0	0	1	1	0
data							

Cycles: 2
States: 7
Addressing: immediate
Flags: Z,S,P,CY,AC

XRA r   (Exclusive OR Register)
(A) ← (A) ⊻ (r)
The content of register r is exclusive-OR'd with the content of the accumulator. The result is placed in the accumulator. **The CY and AC flags are cleared.**

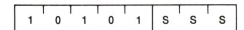

1	0	1	0	1	S	S	S

Cycles: 1
States: 4
Addressing: register
Flags: Z,S,P,CY,AC

XRA M   (Exclusive OR Memory)
(A) ← (A) ⊻ ((H) (L))
The content of the memory location whose address is contained in the H and L registers is exclusive-OR'd with the content of the accumulator. The result is placed in the accumulator. **The CY and AC flags are cleared.**

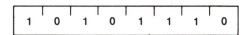

1	0	1	0	1	1	1	0

Cycles: 2
States: 7
Addressing: reg. indirect
Flags: Z,S,P,CY,AC

XRI data   (Exclusive OR immediate)
(A) ← (A) ⊻ (byte 2)
The content of the second byte of the instruction is exclusive-OR'd with the content of the accumulator. The result is placed in the accumulator. **The CY and AC flags are cleared.**

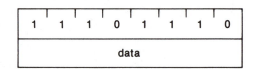

1	1	1	0	1	1	1	0
data							

Cycles: 2
States: 7
Addressing: immediate
Flags: Z,S,P,CY,AC

ORA r   (OR Register)
(A) ← (A) ∨ (r)
The content of register r is inclusive-OR'd with the content of the accumulator. The result is placed in the accumulator. **The CY and AC flags are cleared.**

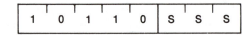

1	0	1	1	0	S	S	S

Cycles: 1
States: 4
Addressing: register
Flags: Z,S,P,CY,AC

(All mnemonics copyright Intel Corporation 1976.)

Figure C.7

THE INSTRUCTION SET

ORA M   (OR memory)
(A) ← (A) V ((H) (L))
The content of the memory location whose address is contained in the H and L registers is inclusive-OR'd with the content of the accumulator. The result is placed in the accumulator. **The CY and AC flags are cleared.**

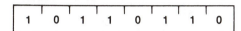

| 1 | 0 | 1 | 1 | 0 | 1 | 1 | 0 |

Cycles: 2
States: 7
Addressing: reg. indirect
Flags: Z,S,P,CY,AC

ORI data   (OR Immediate)
(A) ← (A) V (byte 2)
The content of the second byte of the instruction is inclusive-OR'd with the content of the accumulator. The result is placed in the accumulator. **The CY and AC flags are cleared.**

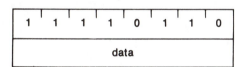

| 1 | 1 | 1 | 1 | 0 | 1 | 1 | 0 |
| data |

Cycles: 2
States: 7
Addressing: immediate
Flags: Z,S,P,CY,AC

CMP r   (Compare Register)
(A) − (r)
The content of register r is subtracted from the accumulator. The accumulator remains unchanged. The condition flags are set as a result of the subtraction. **The Z flag is set to 1 if (A) = (r). The CY flag is set to 1 if (A) < (r).**

| 1 | 0 | 1 | 1 | 1 | S | S | S |

Cycles: 1
States: 4
Addressing: register
Flags: Z,S,P,CY,AC

CMP M   (Compare memory)
(A) − ((H) (L))
The content of the memory location whose address is contained in the H and L registers is subtracted from the accumulator. The accumulator remains unchanged. The condition flags are set as a result of the subtraction. **The Z flag is set to 1 if (A) = ((H) (L)). The CY flag is set to 1 if (A) < ((H) (L)).**

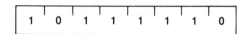

| 1 | 0 | 1 | 1 | 1 | 1 | 1 | 0 |

Cycles: 2
States: 7
Addressing: reg. indirect
Flags: Z,S,P,CY,AC

CPI data   (Compare immediate)
(A) − (byte 2)
The content of the second byte of the instruction is subtracted from the accumulator. The condition flags are set by the result of the subtraction. **The Z flag is set to 1 if (A) = (byte 2). The CY flag is set to 1 if (A) < (byte 2).**

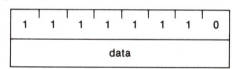

| 1 | 1 | 1 | 1 | 1 | 1 | 1 | 0 |
| data |

Cycles: 2
States: 7
Addressing: immediate
Flags: Z,S,P,CY,AC

RLC   (Rotate left)
$(A_{n+1}) \leftarrow (A_n) ; (A_0) \leftarrow (A_7)$
$(CY) \leftarrow (A_7)$
The content of the accumulator is rotated left one position. The low order bit and the CY flag are both set to the value shifted out of the high order bit position. **Only the CY flag is affected.**

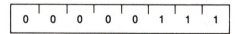

| 0 | 0 | 0 | 0 | 0 | 1 | 1 | 1 |

Cycles: 1
States: 4
Flags: CY

Figure C.8

THE INSTRUCTION SET

RRC　　　　　(Rotate right)
$(A_n) \leftarrow (A_{n+1})$; $(A_7) \leftarrow (A_0)$
$(CY) \leftarrow (A_0)$
The content of the accumulator is rotated right one position. The high order bit and the CY flag are both set to the value shifted out of the low order bit position. **Only the CY flag is affected.**

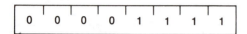

```
Cycles:    1
States:    4
Flags:     CY
```

RAL　　　　　(Rotate left through carry)
$(A_{n+1}) \leftarrow (A_n)$; $(CY) \leftarrow (A_7)$
$(A_0) \leftarrow (CY)$
The content of the accumulator is rotated left one position through the CY flag. The low order bit is set equal to the CY flag and the CY flag is set to the value shifted out of the high order bit. **Only the CY flag is affected.**

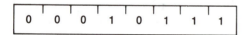

```
Cycles:    1
States:    4
Flags:     CY
```

RAR　　　　　(Rotate right through carry)
$(A_n) \leftarrow (A_{n+1})$; $(CY) \leftarrow (A_0)$
$(A_7) \leftarrow (CY)$
The content of the accumulator is rotated right one position through the CY flag. The high order bit is set to the CY flag and the CY flag is set to the value shifted out of the low order bit. **Only the CY flag is affected.**

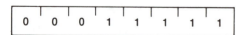

```
Cycles:    1
States:    4
Flags:     CY
```

CMA　　　　　(Complement accumulator)
$(A) \leftarrow (\overline{A})$
The contents of the accumulator are complemented (zero bits become 1, one bits become 0). **No flags are affected.**

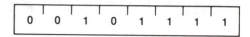

```
Cycles:    1
States:    4
Flags:     none
```

CMC　　　　　(Complement carry)
$(CY) \leftarrow (\overline{CY})$
The CY flag is complemented. **No other flags are affected.**

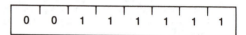

```
Cycles:    1
States:    4
Flags:     CY
```

STC　　　　　(Set carry)
$(CY) \leftarrow 1$
The CY flag is set to 1. **No other flags are affected.**

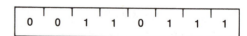

```
Cycles:    1
States:    4
Flags:     CY
```

(All mnemonics copyright Intel Corporation 1976.)

Figure C.9

THE INSTRUCTION SET

Branch Group

This group of instructions alter normal sequential program flow.

Condition flags are not affected by any instruction in this group.

The two types of branch instructions are unconditional and conditional. Unconditional transfers simply perform the specified operation on register PC (the program counter). Conditional transfers examine the status of one of the four processor flags to determine if the specified branch is to be executed. The conditions that may be specified are as follows:

CONDITION		CCC
NZ —	not zero ($Z = 0$)	000
Z —	zero ($Z = 1$)	001
NC —	no carry ($CY = 0$)	010
C —	carry ($CY = 1$)	011
PO —	parity odd ($P = 0$)	100
PE —	parity even ($P = 1$)	101
P —	plus ($S = 0$)	110
M —	minus ($S = 1$)	111

JMP addr   (Jump)
(PC) ← (byte 3) (byte 2)
Control is transferred to the instruction whose address is specified in byte 3 and byte 2 of the current instruction.

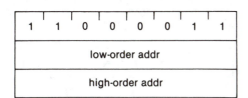

	Cycles:	3
	States:	10
	Addressing:	immediate
	Flags:	none

Jcondition addr (Conditional jump)
If (CCC),
(PC) ← (byte 3) (byte 2)
If the specified condition is true, control is transferred to the instruction whose address is specified in byte 3 and byte 2 of the current instruciton; otherwise, control continues sequentially.

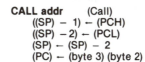

	Cycles:	2/3
	States:	7/10
	Addressing:	immediate
	Flags:	none

CALL addr   (Call)
((SP) − 1) ← (PCH)
((SP) − 2) ← (PCL)
(SP) ← (SP) − 2
(PC) ← (byte 3) (byte 2)
The high-order eight bits of the next instruction address are moved to the memory location whose address is one less than the content of register SP. The low-order eight bits of the next instruction address are moved to the memory location whose address is two less than the content of register SP. The content of register SP is decremented by 2. Control is transferred to the instruction whose address is specified in byte 3 and byte 2 of the current instruction.

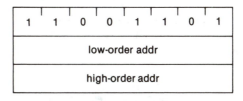

	Cycles:	5
	States:	18
	Addressing:	immediate/ reg. indirect
	Flags:	none

Figure C.10

THE INSTRUCTION SET

Ccondition addr (Condition call)
If (CCC),
    ((SP) − 1) ← (PCH)
    ((SP) − 2) ← (PCL)
    (SP) ← (SP) − 2
    (PC) ← (byte 3) (byte 2)
If the specified condition is true, the actions specified in the CALL instruction (see above) are performed; otherwise, control continues sequentially.

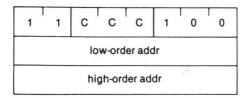

1	1	C	C	C	1	0	0

low-order addr

high-order addr

Cycles: 2/5
States: 9/18
Addressing: immediate/
            reg. indirect
Flags: none

RET   (Return)
    (PCL) ← ((SP));
    (PCH) ← ((SP) + 1);
    (SP) ← (SP) + 2;
The content of the memory location whose address is specified in register SP is moved to the low-order eight bits of register PC. The content of the memory location whose address is one more than the content of register SP is moved to the high-order eight bits of register PC. The content of register SP is incremented by 2.

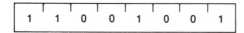

1	1	0	0	1	0	0	1

Cycles: 3
States: 10
Addressing: reg. indirect
Flags: none

Rcondition   (Conditional return)
If (CCC),
    (PCL) ← ((SP))
    (PCH) ← ((SP) + 1)
    (SP) ← (SP) + 2
If the specified condition is true, the actions specified in the RET instruction (see above) are performed; otherwise, control continues sequentially.

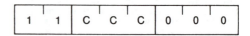

1	1	C	C	C	0	0	0

Cycles: 1/3
States: 6/12
Addressing: reg. indirect
Flags: none

RST n   (Restart)
    ((SP) − 1) ← (PCH)
    ((SP) − 2) ← (PCL)
    (SP) ← (SP) − 2
    (PC) ← 8 * (NNN)
The high-order eight bits of the next instruction address are moved to the memory location whose address is one less than the content of register SP. The low-order eight bits of the next instruction address are moved to the memory location whose address is two less than the content of register SP. The content of register SP is decremented by two. Control is transferred to the instruction whose address is eight times the content of NNN.

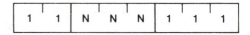

1	1	N	N	N	1	1	1

Cycles: 3
States: 12
Addressing: reg. indirect
Flags: none

15	14	13	12	11	10	9	8	7	6	5	4	3	2	1	0
0	0	0	0	0	0	0	0	0	0	0	N	N	N	0	0	0

Program Counter After Restart

Figure C.11

THE INSTRUCTION SET

PCHL   (Jump H and L indirect —
                    move H and L to PC)

(PCH) ← (H)
(PCL) ← (L)

The content of register H is moved to the high-order eight bits of register PC. The content of register L is moved to the low-order eight bits of register PC.

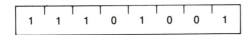

> Cycles: 1
> States: 6
> Addressing: register
> Flags: none

Stack, I/O, and Machine Control Group

This group of instructions performs I/O, manipulates the Stack, and alters internal control flags.

Unless otherwise specified, **condition flags are not affected by any instructions in this group.**

PUSH rp   (Push)

((SP) − 1) ← (rh)
((SP) − 2) ← (rl)
((SP) ← (SP) − 2

The content of the high-order register of register pair rp is moved to the memory location whose address is one less than the content of register SP. The content of the low-order register of register pair rp is moved to the memory location whose address is two less than the content of register SP. The content of register SP is decremented by 2. **Note: Register pair rp = SP may not be specified.**

> Cycles: 3
> States: 12
> Addressing: reg. indirect
> Flags: none

PUSH PSW   (Push processor status word)

((SP) − 1) ← (A)
((SP) − 2)$_0$ ← (CY) , ((SP) − 2)$_1$ ← X
((SP) − 2)$_2$ ← (P) , ((SP) − 2)$_3$ ← X
((SP) − 2)$_4$ ← (AC) , ((SP) − 2)$_5$ ← X
((SP) − 2)$_6$ ← (Z) , ((SP) − 2)$_7$ ← (S)
(SP) ← (SP) − 2   X: Undefined.

The content of register A is moved to the memory location whose address is one less than register SP. The contents of the condition flags are assembled into a processor status word and the word is moved to the memory location whose address is two less than the content of register SP. The content of register SP is decremented by two.

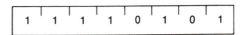

> Cycles: 3
> States: 12
> Addressing: reg. indirect
> Flags: none

FLAG WORD

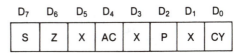

X: undefined

POP rp   (POP)

(rl) ← ((SP))
(rh) ← ((SP) + 1)
(SP) ← (SP) + 2

The content of the memory location, whose address is specified by the content of register SP, is moved to the low-order register of register pair rp. The content of the memory location, whose address is one more than the content of register SP, is moved to the high-order register of register rp. The content of register SP is incremented by 2. **Note: Register pair rp = SP may not be specified.**

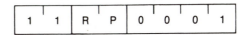

> Cycles: 3
> States: 10
> Addressing: reg.indirect
> Flags: none

Figure C.12

THE INSTRUCTION SET

POP PSW   (Pop processor status word)

$(CY) \leftarrow ((SP))_0$
$(P) \leftarrow ((SP))_2$
$(AC) \leftarrow ((SP))_4$
$(Z) \leftarrow ((SP))_6$
$(S) \leftarrow ((SP))_7$
$(A) \leftarrow ((SP) + 1)$
$(SP) \leftarrow (SP) + 2$

The content of the memory location whose address is specified by the content of register SP is used to restore the condition flags. The content of the memory location whose address is one more than the content of register SP is moved to register A. The content of register SP is incremented by 2.

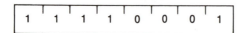

Cycles: 3
States: 10
Addressing: reg. indirect
Flags: Z,S,P,CY,AC

XTHL   (Exchange stack top with H
                 and L)

$(L) \leftrightarrow ((SP))$
$(H) \leftrightarrow ((SP) + 1)$

The content of the L register is exchanged with the content of the memory location whose address is specified by the content of register SP. The content of the H register is exchanged with the content of the memory location whose address is one more than the content of register SP.

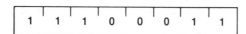

Cycles: 5
States: 16
Addressing: reg. indirect
Flags: none

SPHL   (Move HL to SP)

$(SP) \leftarrow (H) (L)$

The contents of registers H and L (16 bits) are moved to register SP.

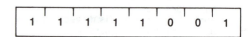

Cycles: 1
States: 6
Addressing: register
Flags: none

IN port   (Input)

$(A) \leftarrow (data)$

The data placed on the eight bit bi-directional data bus by the specified port is moved to register A.

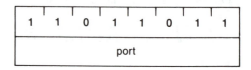

Cycles: 3
States: 10
Addressing: direct
Flags: none

OUT port   (Output)

$(data) \leftarrow (A)$

The content of register A is placed on the eight bit bi-directional data bus for transmission to the specified port.

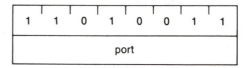

Cycles: 3
States: 10
Addressing: direct
Flags: none

(All mnemonics copyright Intel Corporation 1976.)

Figure C.13

THE INSTRUCTION SET

EI   (Enable interrupts)
The interrupt system is enabled **following the execution of the next instruction.**

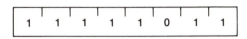

Cycles: 1
States: 4
Flags: none

NOTE: Interrupts are not recognized during the EI instruction. Placing an EI instruction on the bus in response to $\overline{\text{INTA}}$ during an INA cycle is prohibited.

DI   (Disable interrupts)
The interrupt system is disabled **immediately following the execution of the DI instruction.**

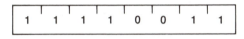

Cycles: 1
States: 4
Flags: none

NOTE: Interrupts are not recognized during the DI instruction. Placing a DI instruction on the bus in response to $\overline{\text{INTA}}$ during an INA cycle is prohibited.

HLT   (Halt)
The processor is stopped. The registers and flags are unaffected. A second ALE is generated during the execution of HLT to strobe out the Halt cycle status information.

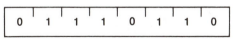

Cycles: 1+
States: 5
Flags: none

NOP   (No op)
No operation is performed. The registers and flags are unaffected.

(All mnemonics copyright Intel Corporation 1976.)

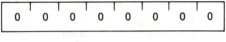

Cycles: 1
States: 4
Flags: none

RIM   (Read Interrupt Masks)
The RIM instruction loads data into the accumulator relating to interrupts and the serial input. This data contains the following information:

- Current interrupt mask status for the RST 5.5, 6.5, and 7.5 hardware interrupts (1 = mask disabled)
- Current interrupt enable flag status (1 = interrupts enabled) except immediately following a TRAP interrupt. (See below.)
- Hardware interrupts pending (i.e., signal received but not yet serviced), on the RST 5.5, 6.5, and 7.5 lines.
- Serial input data.

Immediately following a TRAP interrupt, the RIM instruction must be executed as a part of the service routine if you need to retrieve current interrupt status later. Bit 3 of the accumulator is (in this special case only) loaded with the interrupt enable (IE) flag status that existed prior to the TRAP interrupt. Following an RST 5.5, 6.5, 7.5, or INTR interrupt, the interrupt flag flip-flop reflects the current interrupt enable status. Bit 6 of the accumulator (I7.5) is loaded with the status of the RST 7.5 flip-flop, which is always set (edge-triggered) by an input on the RST 7.5 input line, even when that interrupt has been previously masked. (See SIM Instruction.)

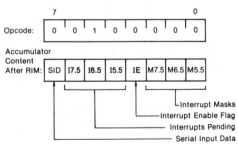

Cycles: 1
States: 4
Flags: none

Figure C.14

THE INSTRUCTION SET

SIM   (Set Interrupt Masks)

The execution of the SIM instruction uses the contents of the accumulator (which must be previously loaded) to perform the following functions:

- Program the interrupt mask for the RST 5.5, 6.5, and 7.5 hardware interrupts.
- Reset the edge-triggered RST 7.5 input latch.
- Load the SOD output latch.

To program the interrupt masks, first set accumulator bit 3 to 1 and set to 1 any bits 0, 1, and 2, which disable interrupts RST 5.5, 6.5, and 7.5, respectively. Then do a SIM instruction. If accumulator bit 3 is 0 when the SIM instruction is executed, the interrupt mask register will not change. If accumulator bit 4 is 1 when the SIM instruction is executed, the RST 7.5 latch is then reset. RST 7.5 is distinguished by the fact that its latch is always set by a rising edge on the RST 7.5 input pin, even if the jump to service routine is inhibited by masking. This latch remains high until cleared by a $\overline{\text{RESET IN}}$, by a SIM Instruction with accumulator bit 4 high, or by an internal processor acknowledge to an RST 7.5 interrupt subsequent to the removal of the mask (by a SIM instruction). The $\overline{\text{RESET IN}}$ signal always sets all three RST mask bits.

If accumulator bit 6 is at the 1 level when the SIM instruction is executed, the state of accumulator bit 7 is loaded into the SOD latch and thus becomes available for interface to an external device. The SOD latch is unaffected by the SIM instruction if bit 6 is 0. SOD is always reset by the $\overline{\text{RESET IN}}$ signal.

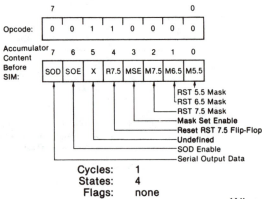

Cycles:	1
States:	4
Flags:	none

(All mnemonics copyright Intel Corporation 1976.)

Figure C.15

D

ASCII Character Set

GRAPHIC OR CONTROL	ASCII (HEXADECIMAL)	GRAPHIC OR CONTROL	ASCII (HEXADECIMAL)	GRAPHIC OR CONTROL	ASCII (HEXADECIMAL)
NUL	00	+	2B	V	56
SOH	01	'	2C	W	57
STX	02	−	2D	X	58
ETX	03	.	2E	Y	59
EOT	04	/	2F	Z	5A
ENQ	05	0	30	[	5B
ACK	06	1	31	\	5C
BEL	07	2	32	]	5D
BS	08	3	33	∧(↑)	5E
HT	09	4	34	−(←)	5F
LF	0A	5	35	ˋ	60
VT	0B	6	36	a	61
FF	0C	7	37	b	62
CR	0D	8	38	c	63
SO	0E	9	39	d	64
SI	0F	:	3A	e	65
DLE	10	;	3B	f	66
DC1 (X-ON)	11	<	3C	g	67
DC2 ~~(TAPE)~~	12	=	3D	h	68
DC3 (X-OFF)	13	>	3E	i	69
DC4 ~~(TAPE)~~	14	?	3F	j	6A
NAK	15	@	40	k	6B
SYN	16	A	41	l	6C
ETB	17	B	42	m	6D
CAN	18	C	43	n	6E
EM	19	D	44	o	6F
SUB	1A	E	45	p	70
ESC	1B	F	46	q	71
FS	1C	G	47	r	72
GS	1D	H	48	s	73
RS	1E	I	49	t	74
US	1F	J	4A	u	75
SP	20	K	4B	v	76
!	21	L	4C	w	77
"	22	M	4D	x	78
#	23	N	4E	y	79
$	24	O	4F	z	7A
%	25	P	50	{	7B
&	26	Q	51	|	7C
'	27	R	52	}(ALT MODE)	7D
(	28	S	53	~	7E
)	29	T	54	DEL (RUB OUT)	7F
*	2A	U	55		

Figure D.1 Seven-bit ASCII code, with the high-order eighth bit (parity bit) always reset.

E

Virtual Ground Analysis

When an op-amp with a high open loop gain is used with negative feedback to implement a linear circuit, the closed loop gain or transfer characteristic of the circuit is to a first approximation dictated entirely by the external feedback connections. As a result, the design of linear signal processing circuits with op-amps is relatively straightforward.

Op-amp circuits with negative feedback can be analyzed and designed through a technique called virtual ground analysis. One of the bases of *virtual ground analysis* lies in the fact that with negative feedback if the output of the operational amplifier is linearly related to its input, and the open loop gain of the op-amp is large, then the voltage $v_+ - v_-$ must be very small (see Fig. E.1). Let $v_+ - v_- = \epsilon$; thus, as a first approximation, $v_+ = v_-$. Then ϵ is approximately zero. This approximation, along with the assumption that the input currents to the op-amp i_- and i_+ are also zero, is the basis of virtual ground analysis. With virtual ground analysis and other elementary circuit laws, such as *Kirchhoff's Current Law, KCL* (the sum of the currents into and out of a node equals zero), and *Kirchhoff's Voltage Law, KVL* (the sum of the voltages around a closed loop is zero), the operation of any operational amplifier circuit using negative feedback can be analyzed. As a case in point, the characteristics of several op-amp circuits commonly used in data acquisition systems are determined below by using virtual ground analysis.

Consider the current to voltage converter circuit in Fig. E.2. Negative feedback is provided between the output and inverting terminals by the feedback resistor, R_F. Because the current into the circuit's input, i_I, cannot flow into the inverting terminal of the operational amplifier, it must flow through the feedback resistor, R_F. The output voltage, v_0, equals the sum of the voltage drop across R_F, v_{R_F}, and the differential input input voltage, ϵ. Thus, since $v_{R_F} = -i_I R_F$

$$v_0 = v_{R_F} + \epsilon$$

$$v_0 = -i_I R_F + \epsilon$$

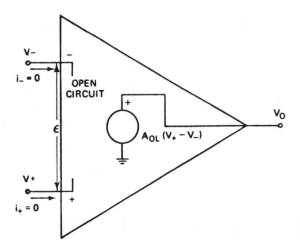

Figure E.1 Equivalent circuit of an ideal op-amp.

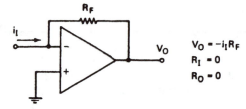

$$v_O = -i_1 R_F$$
$$R_I = 0$$
$$R_O = 0$$

Figure E.2 Op-amp current to voltage converter circuit.

By the virtual ground assumption, $\epsilon = 0$. Thus

$$v_0 = -i_I R_F$$

An important point about one of the virtual ground approximations is illustrated by this example: even though the voltage drop ϵ between the inverting ($-$) and noninverting ($+$) terminals is assumed zero, no current flows between these terminals. The voltage ϵ is approximately zero because of the effects of negative feedback, not because there is a low impedance path between these two terminals. The input impedance for the circuit is also approximately zero. This is because input impedance for the circuit is by definition $R_I = v_I/i_I$, and v_I, in this circuit, is equal to ϵ, which is approximately zero. The output resistance, R_0, of the circuit is essentially equal to or less than the output resistance of the op-amp, and this, in the ideal case, is zero.

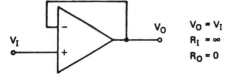

$$v_O = v_I$$
$$R_I = \infty$$
$$R_O = 0$$

Figure E.3 Op-amp unity gain buffer circuit.

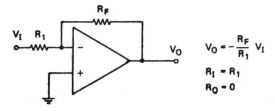

$$v_0 = -\frac{R_F}{R_1} v_I$$

$R_I = R_1$

$R_O = 0$

Figure E.4 Op-amp inverting voltage amplifier circuit.

The unity gain buffer circuit in Fig. E.3 is used as an isolator between other circuits to prevent a circuit with a low input impedance from loading (drawing excessive current from) the output of either a transducer or another circuit. The input impedance of the buffer amplifier is, for all intents and purposes, infinite due to the assumption that the current into the noninverting terminal is zero. $R_I = v_I/i_I \approx \infty$, for i_I approaching zero. The output voltage is

$$v_0 = \epsilon + v_I$$
$$v_0 = v_I$$

Figure E.4 shows an inverting voltage amplifier. The current, i_I, through R_1 is equal to v_I/R_1. This same current flows through R_F, since there is no current into the input terminal of the op-amp. Applying KVL, then $v_0 = -v_{R_F} - \epsilon$. Since $\epsilon = 0$

$$v_0 = -v_{R_F}$$

Substituting $v_{R_F} = i_I R_F$ gives

$$v_0 = i_I R_F$$

and further substituting $i_I = v_I/R_1$ gives

$$v_0 = -\frac{V_I}{R_1} R_F$$

The input impedance of this circuit is $v_I/i_I = R_I$.

A variation of this circuit (see Fig. E.5), uses two or more input resistors and is used to sum several input voltages. The current into the junction at the inverting terminal is the sum of the currents through the input resistances. For this reason, the junction at the inverting input is frequently referred to as the **summing junction** in various op-amp circuits. This current flows through the feedback resistor, R_F.

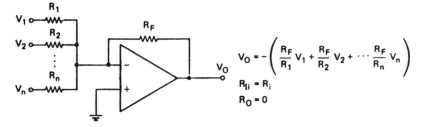

$$v_0 = -\left(\frac{R_F}{R_1} V_1 + \frac{R_F}{R_2} V_2 + \cdots \frac{R_F}{R_n} V_n \right)$$

$R_{Ii} = R_i$

$R_O = 0$

Figure E.5 Op-amp inverting summing amplifier.

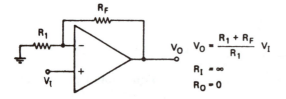

$$v_0 = \frac{R_1 + R_F}{R_1} v_I$$

$R_1 \rightarrow \infty$

$R_0 \rightarrow 0$

Figure E.6 Op-amp noninverting amplifier.

A noninverting voltage amplifier is shown in Fig. E.6. The voltage at the inverting terminal is $v_- = v_0 R_1 / (R_1 + R_F)$ as a result of the fact that R_F and R_1 form a voltage divider that divides the output voltage. The voltage at the inverting terminal, v_-, is the same as that at the noninverting terminal, v_I, since $\epsilon = 0$. Thus

$$v_I = \frac{v_0 R_1}{R_1 + R_F}$$

$$v_0 = \frac{(R_1 + R_F)}{R_1} v_I$$

Since the input current for this circuit configuration is assumed to be zero, the input impedance is infinite.

Operational amplifiers derive their name from their use in constructing circuits used in analog computers for carrying out mathematical operations. One of these circuits, an integrator, is shown in Fig. E.7. The feedback element in this circuit is a capacitor. Using virtual ground analysis, the output voltage is the negative of the voltage drop across the capacitor:

$$v_0 = -v_C$$

And the voltage drop across the capacitor is the integral of the current through it divided by the capacitance:

$$v_0 = -\frac{1}{RC} \int_0^t v_I \, dt + v_i(0)$$

where $v_i(0)$ is the initial voltage across the capacitor at time $t = 0$, and the output of the circuit is the integral of the input voltage.

While virtual ground analysis is an approximation technique, it very accurately predicts the operation of an op-amp circuit with negative feedback under certain

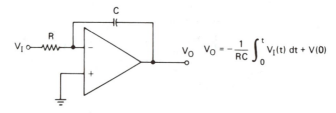

Figure E.7 Op-amp integrator.

conditions. First, the op-amp must have a high open loop gain. Second, the output of the op-amp must be in the linear range. This places a restriction on the allowable closed loop gain and on the input signal range.

The actual effect of negative feedback can be qualitatively illustrated by considering the operation of the inverting amplifier of Fig. E.4. Assume that the circuit is in a stable condition, with input voltage v_I and output voltage v_0, and with $\epsilon \simeq 0$. If the input voltage is increased by a value, Δ, this tends to increase ϵ by Δ from zero. The change in ϵ toward $\epsilon + \Delta$ causes the output to change in the negative direction by a much larger amount—$A_{OL}\,\Delta$. And this causes an increase in the current through R_F and R_1, which in turn increases the voltage drop across R_1, forcing ϵ back toward zero and increasing the voltage drop across R_F. Of course, all these actions occur instantaneously. The net effect is that a change in the input voltage causes the output voltage to change by a factor determined by the external resistances and leaves ϵ near 0 V.

F

Data Sheets

F1 HM6116

F2 2764A

F3 8085AH (Partial)

2048-word×8-bit High Speed Static CMOS RAM

■FEATURES

- Single 5V Supply and High Density 24 Pin Package
- High speed: Fast Access Time   120ns/150ns/200ns (max.)
- Low Power Standby and   Standby: 100µW (typ.)
  Low Power Operation   Operation: 180mW (typ.)
- Completely Static RAM: No clock or Timing Strobe Required
- Directly TTL Compatible: All Input and Output
- Pin Out Compatible with Standard 16K EPROM/MASK ROM
- Equal Access and Cycle Time

■FUNCTIONAL BLOCK DIAGRAM

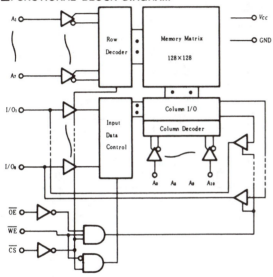

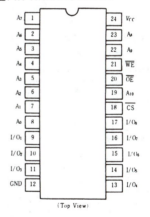

HM6116-2, HM6116-3, HM6116-4

(DG-24)

HM6116P-2, HM6116P-3, HM6116P-4

(DP-24)

■PIN ARRANGEMENT

A_7	1		24	V_{cc}
A_6	2		23	A_8
A_5	3		22	A_9
A_4	4		21	$\overline{WE}$
A_3	5		20	$\overline{OE}$
A_2	6		19	A_{10}
A_1	7		18	$\overline{CS}$
A_0	8		17	I/O_8
I/O_1	9		16	I/O_7
I/O_2	10		15	I/O_6
I/O_3	11		14	I/O_5
GND	12		13	I/O_4

(Top View)

■ABSOLUTE MAXIMUM RATINGS

Item	Symbol	Rating	Unit
Voltage on Any Pin Relative to GND	V_T	−0.5* to +7.0	V
Operating Temperature	T_{opr}	0 to +70	℃
Storage Temperature (Plastic)	T_{stg}	−55 to +125	℃
Storage Temperature (Ceramic)	T_{stg}	−65 to +150	℃
Temperature Under Bias	T_{bias}	−10 to +85	℃
Power Dissipation	P_T	1.0	W

* Pulse Width 50ns : −1.5 V

■TRUTH TABLE

$\overline{CS}$	$\overline{OE}$	$\overline{WE}$	Mode	V_{cc} Current	I/O Pin	Ref. Cycle
H	×	×	Not Selected	I_{SB}, I_{SB1}	High Z	
L	L	H	Read	I_{CC}	Dout	Read Cycle (1)~(3)
L	H	L	Write	I_{CC}	Din	Write Cycle (1)
L	L	L	Write	I_{CC}	Din	Write Cycle (2)

 HITACHI

(F1: Courtesy of Hitachi America, Ltd., Semiconductor and IC Division.)

579

HM6116-2,HM6116-3,HM6116-4,HM6116P-2,HM6116P-3,HM6116P-4 ─────────────

■RECOMMENDED DC OPERATING CONDITIONS ($Ta=0$ to $+70$℃)

Item	Symbol	min	typ	max	Unit
Supply Voltage	V_{CC}	4.5	5.0	5.5	V
	GND	0	0	0	V
Input Voltage	V_{IH}	2.2	3.5	6.0	V
	V_{IL}	-1.0*	—	0.8	V

* Pulse Width : 50ns, DC : V_{IL} min$=-0.3$V

■DC AND OPERATING CHARACTERISTICS ($V_{CC}=5$V$\pm10\%$, GND$=0$V, $Ta=0$ to $+70$℃)

Item	Symbol	Test Conditions	HM6116/P-2 min	HM6116/P-2 typ*	HM6116/P-2 max	HM6116/P-3/-4 min	HM6116/P-3/-4 typ*	HM6116/P-3/-4 max	Unit
Input Leakage Current	$\lvert I_{LI} \rvert$	$V_{CC}=5.5$V, $V_{in}=$GND to V_{CC}	—	—	10	—	—	10	μA
Output Leakage Current	$\lvert I_{LO} \rvert$	$\overline{CS}=V_{IH}$ or $\overline{OE}=V_{IH}$, $V_{I/O}=$GND to V_{CC}	—	—	10	—	—	10	μA
Operating Power Supply Current	I_{CC}	$\overline{CS}=V_{IL}$, $I_{I/O}=0$mA	—	40	80	—	35	70	mA
	I_{CC1}**	$V_{IH}=3.5$V, $V_{IL}=0.6$V, $I_{I/O}=0$mA	—	35	—	—	30	—	mA
Average Operating Current	I_{CC2}	Min. cycle, duty$=100\%$	—	40	80	—	35	70	mA
Standby Power Supply Current	I_{SB}	$\overline{CS}=V_{IH}$	—	5	15	—	5	15	mA
	I_{SB1}	$\overline{CS}\geq V_{CC}-0.2$V, $V_{in}\geq V_{CC}$ -0.2V or $V_{in}\leq0.2$V	—	0.02	2	—	0.02	2	mA
Output Voltage	V_{OL}	$I_{OL}=4$mA	—	—	0.4	—	—	—	V
		$I_{OL}=2.1$mA	—	—	—	—	—	0.4	V
	V_{OH}	$I_{OH}=-1.0$mA	2.4	—	—	2.4	—	—	V

* $V_{CC}=5$V, $Ta=25$℃
** Reference Only

■AC CHARACTERISTICS ($V_{CC}=5$V$\pm10\%$, $Ta=0$ to $+70$℃)

●AC TEST CONDITIONS

Input Pulse Levels: 0.8 to 2.4V
Input Rise and Fall Times: 10 ns
Input and Output Timing Reference Levels: 1.5V
Output Load: 1TTL Gate and C_L = 100pF (including scope and jig)

●READ CYCLE

Item	Symbol	HM6116/P-2 min	HM6116/P-2 max	HM6116/P-3 min	HM6116/P-3 max	HM6116/P-4 min	HM6116/P-4 max	Unit
Read Cycle Time	t_{RC}	120	—	150	—	200	—	ns
Address Access Time	t_{AA}	—	120	—	150	—	200	ns
Chip Select Access Time	t_{ACS}	—	120	—	150	—	200	ns
Chip Selection to Output in Low Z	t_{CLZ}	10	—	15	—	15	—	ns
Output Enable to Output Valid	t_{OE}	—	80	—	100	—	120	ns
Output Enable to Output in Low Z	t_{OLZ}	10	—	15	—	15	—	ns
Chip Deselection to Output in High Z	t_{CHZ}	0	40	0	50	0	60	ns
Chip Disable to Output in High Z	t_{OHZ}	0	40	0	50	0	60	ns
Output Hold from Address Change	t_{OH}	10	—	15	—	15	—	ns

◎ HITACHI

HM6116-2,HM6116-3,HM6116-4,HM6116P-2,HM6116P-3,HM6116P-4

● WRITE CYCLE

Item	Symbol	HM6116/P-2		HM6116/P-3		HM6116/P-4		Unit
		min	max	min	max	min	max	
Write Cycle Time	t_{WC}	120	—	150	—	200	—	ns
Chip Selection to End of Write	t_{CW}	70	—	90	—	120	—	ns
Address Valid to End of Write	t_{AW}	105	—	120	—	140	—	ns
Address Set Up Time	t_{AS}	20	—	20	—	20	—	ns
Write Pulse Width	t_{WP}	70	—	90	—	120	—	ns
Write Recovery Time	t_{WR}	5	—	10	—	10	—	ns
Output Disable to Output in High Z	t_{OHZ}	0	40	0	50	0	60	ns
Write to Output in High Z	t_{WHZ}	0	50	0	60	0	60	ns
Data to Write Time Overlap	t_{DW}	35	—	40	—	60	—	ns
Data Hold from Write Time	t_{DH}	5	—	10	—	10	—	ns
Output Active from End of Write	t_{OW}	5	—	10	—	10	—	ns

■ CAPACITANCE ($f=1$MHz, $Ta=25$°C)

Item	Symbol	Test Conditions	typ	max	Unit
Input Capacitance	C_{in}	$V_{in}=0$V	3	5	pF
Input/Output Capacitance	$C_{I/O}$	$V_{I/O}=0$V	5	7	pF

Note) This parameter is sampled and not 100% tested.

■ TIMING WAVEFORM

● READ CYCLE (1)[1]

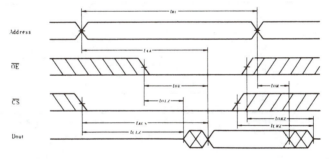

● READ CYCLE (2)[1][2][4]

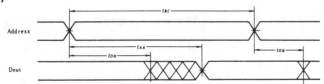

● READ CYCLE (3)[1][3][4]

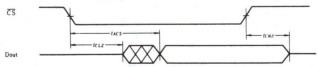

NOTES: 1. $\overline{WE}$ is High for Read Cycle.
2. Device is continuously selected, $\overline{CS} = V_{IL}$.
3. Address Valid prior to or coincident with $\overline{CS}$ transition Low.
4. $\overline{OE} = V_{IL}$.

◉ HITACHI

HM6116-2,HM6116-3,HM6116-4,HM6116P-2,HM6116P-3,HM6116P-4 ——————————

WRITE CYCLE (1)

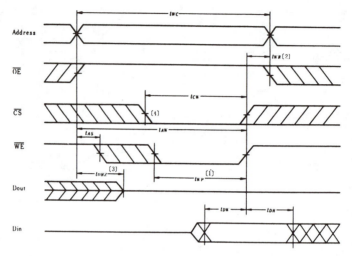

●WRITE CYCLE (2) [5]

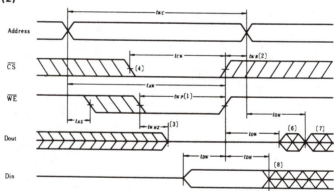

NOTES:
1. A write occurs during the overlap (t_{WP}) of a low $\overline{CS}$ and a low $\overline{WE}$.
2. t_{WR} is measured from the earlier of $\overline{CS}$ or $\overline{WE}$ going high to the end of write cycle.
3. During this period, I/O pins are in the output state so that the input signals of opposite phase to the outputs must not be applied.
4. If the $\overline{CS}$ low transition occurs simultaneously with the $\overline{WE}$ low transitions or after the $\overline{WE}$ transition, output remain in a high impedance state.
5. $\overline{OE}$ is continuously low. ($\overline{OE} = V_{IL}$)
6. D_{out} is the same phase of write data of this write cycle.
7. D_{out} is the read data of next address.
8. If $\overline{CS}$ is Low during this period, I/O pins are in the output state. Then the data input signals of opposite phase to the outputs must not be applied to them.

HITACHI

SUPPLY CURRENT vs. SUPPLY VOLTAGE

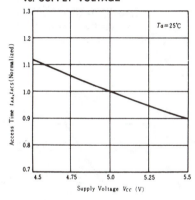

SUPPLY CURRENT vs. AMBIENT TEMPERATURE

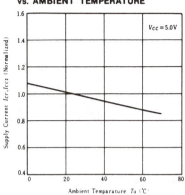

ACCESS TIME vs. SUPPLY VOLTAGE

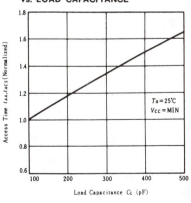

ACCESS TIME vs. AMBIENT TEMPERATURE

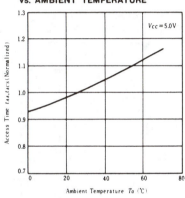

ACCESS TIME vs. LOAD CAPACITANCE

SUPPLY CURRENT vs. FREQUENCY

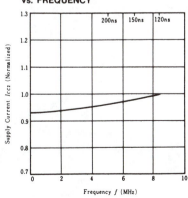

◉ HITACHI

HM6116-2,HM6116-3,HM6116-4,HM6116P-2,HM6116P-3,HM6116P-4 ─────────────

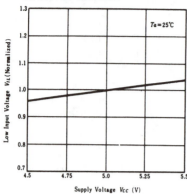

LOW INPUT VOLTAGE vs. SUPPLY VOLTAGE

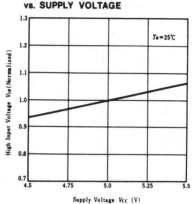

HIGH INPUT VOLTAGE vs. SUPPLY VOLTAGE

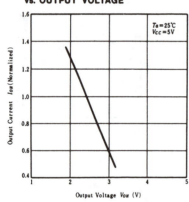

OUTPUT CURRENT vs. OUTPUT VOLTAGE

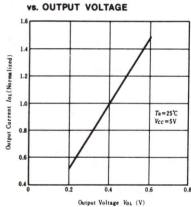

OUTPUT CURRENT vs. OUTPUT VOLTAGE

HITACHI

2764A
ADVANCED 64K (8K x 8)
PRODUCTION AND UV ERASABLE PROMs

- **Plastic P2764A is Compatible with Auto-Insertion Equipment**
- **Fast Access Time—HMOS* II E**
  — 180 ns Cerdip D2764A-1
  — 200 ns Plastic P2764A-2
- **Moisture Resistant**
- **Two-line Control**

- **New Quick-Pulse Programming™ Algorithm For Plastic P2764A**
  — 1 Second Programming
  — int$_e$ligent Programming™ Algorithm Compatible
- **int$_e$ligent Identifier™ Mode**
- **Industry Standard Pinout . . . JEDEC Approved . . . 28 Lead Package**
  (See Packaging Spec, Order #231369)

The Intel 2764A is a 5V only, 65,536-bit plastic production electrically programmable read-only memory (EPROM). The 2764A is fabricated with Intel's HMOSII-E technology which significantly reduces die size and greatly improves the device's performance, power consumption, reliability and producibility.

The P2764A is ideal for high volume production environments where code flexibility is crucial. Plastic packaging is also well-suited to auto-insertion equipment in cost-effective automated assembly lines. Intel's new Quick-Pulse Programming Algorithm enables the P2764A to be programmed within one second. Programming equipment which takes advantage of this innovation will electronically identify the EPROM with the help of the int$_e$ligent Identifier and rapidly program it using a superior programming method. The int$_e$ligent Programming Algorithm may be utilized in the absence of such equipment.

The 2764A provides access times to 180 ns (2764A-1). This is compatible with high-performance microprocessors, such as Intel's 8 MHz iAPX 186 allowing full speed operation without the addition of WAIT states. The 2764A is also directly compatible with the 12 MHz 8051 family.

Two-line control and JEDEC-approved, 28 pin packaging are standard features of all Intel higher density EPROMs. This assures easy microprocessor interfacing and minimum design efforts when upgrading, adding, or choosing between non-volatile memory alternatives.

*HMOS is a patented process of Intel Corporation.

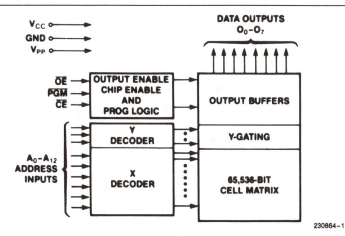

Figure 1. Block Diagram

230864–1

(F2: Courtesy of Intel Corp.)

intel   **2764A**

Pin Names

$A_0 - A_{12}$	Addresses
$\overline{CE}$	Chip Enable
$\overline{OE}$	Output Enable
$O_0 - O_7$	Outputs
$\overline{PGM}$	Program
N.C.	No Connect
D.U.	Don't Use

27916	27513	27512	27256	27128A	2732A	2716
V_{PP}	D.U.	A_{15}	V_{PP}	V_{PP}		
A_{12}	A_{12}	A_{12}	A_{12}	A_{12}		
A_7	A_7	A_7	A_7	A_7	A_7	A_7
A_6	A_6	A_6	A_6	A_6	A_6	A_6
A_5	A_5	A_5	A_5	A_5	A_5	A_5
A_4	A_4	A_4	A_4	A_4	A_4	A_4
A_3	A_3	A_3	A_3	A_3	A_3	A_3
A_2	A_2	A_2	A_2	A_2	A_2	A_2
A_1	A_1	A_1	A_1	A_1	A_1	A_1
A_0	A_0	A_0	A_0	A_0	A_0	A_0
O_0	I/O_0	O_0	O_0	O_0	O_0	O_0
O_1	I/O_1	O_1	O_1	O_1	O_1	O_1
O_2	O_2	O_2	O_2	O_2	O_2	O_2
Gnd	Gnd	Gnd	Gnd	Gnd	Gnd	Gnd

2764A
P2764A

Pin		Pin	
V_{PP}	1	28	V_{CC}
A_{12}	2	27	$\overline{PGM}$
A_7	3	26	N.C.
A_6	4	25	A_8
A_5	5	24	A_9
A_4	6	23	A_{11}
A_3	7	22	$\overline{OE}$
A_2	8	21	A_{10}
A_1	9	20	$\overline{CE}$
A_0	10	19	O_7
O_0	11	18	O_6
O_1	12	17	O_5
O_2	13	16	O_4
GND	14	15	O_3

230864-2

2716	2732A	27128A 27664	27256	27512	27513	27916
		V_{CC}	V_{CC}	V_{CC}	V_{CC}	V_{CC}
		$\overline{PGM}$	A_{14}	A_{14}	$\overline{WE}$	$\overline{PGM/WE}$
V_{CC}	V_{CC}	A_{13}	A_{13}	A_{13}	A_{13}	A_{13}
A_8	A_8	A_8	A_8	A_8	A_8	A_8
A_9	A_9	A_9	A_9	A_9	A_9	A_9
V_{PP}	A_{11}	A_{11}	A_{11}	A_{11}	A_{11}	A_{11}
$\overline{OE}$	$\overline{OE}/V_{PP}$	$\overline{OE}$	$\overline{OE}$	$\overline{OE}/V_{PP}$	$\overline{OE}/V_{PP}$	$\overline{OE}$
A_{10}	A_{10}	A_{10}	A_{10}	A_{10}	A_{10}	A_{10}
$\overline{CE}$	$\overline{CE}$	$\overline{CE}$	$\overline{CE}$	$\overline{CE}$	$\overline{CE}$	$\overline{CE}$
O_7	O_7	O_7	O_7	O_7	O_7	O_7
O_6	O_6	O_6	O_6	O_6	O_6	O_6
O_5	O_5	O_5	O_5	O_5	O_5	O_5
O_4	O_4	O_4	O_4	O_4	O_4	O_4
O_3	O_3	O_3	O_3	O_3	O_3	O_3

NOTE:
Intel "Universal Site"-Compatible EPROM pin configurations are shown in the blocks adjacent to the P2764A pins.

Figure 2. Cerdip/Plastic DIP Pin Configuration

EXTENDED TEMPERATURE (EXPRESS) EPROMs

The Intel EXPRESS EPROM family is a series of electrically programmable read only memories which have received additional processing to enhance product characteristics. EXPRESS processing is available for several densities of EPROM, allowing the choice of appropriate memory size to match system applications. EXPRESS EPROM products are available with 168 ±8 hour, 125°C dynamic burn-in using Intel's standard bias configuration. This process exceeds or meets most industry specifications of burn-in. The standard EXPRESS EPROM operating temperature range is 0°C to 70°C. Extended operating temperature range (−40°C to +85°C) EXPRESS products are available. Like all Intel EPROMs, the EXPRESS EPROM family is inspected to 0.1% electrical AQL. This may allow the user to reduce or eliminate incoming inspection testing.

EXPRESS EPROM PRODUCT FAMILY

PRODUCT DEFINITIONS

Type	Operating Temperature	Burn-in 125°C (hr)
Q	0°C to +70°C	168 ±8
T	−40°C to +85°C	None
L	−40°C to +85°C	168 ±8

EXPRESS OPTIONS

2764A VERSIONS

Packaging Options		
Speed Versions	Cerdip	Plastic
−2	Q	
STD	Q, T, L	T
−3	Q, T, L	T
−25	Q, T, L	T
−30	Q, T, L	

READ OPERATION

D.C. CHARACTERISTICS

Electrical parameters of EXPRESS EPROM products are identical to standard EPROM parameters except for:

Symbol	Parameter	TD2764A LD2764A		Test Conditions
		Min	Max	
I_{SB}	V_{CC} Standby Current (mA)		40	$\overline{CE} = V_{IH}, \overline{OE} = V_{IL}$
I_{CC_1}[1]	V_{CC} Active Current (mA)		100	$\overline{OE} = \overline{CE} = V_{IL}$
	V_{CC} Active Current at High Temperature (mA)		75	$\overline{OE} = \overline{CE} = V_{IL}$ $V_{PP} = V_{CC}$, $T_{Ambient} = 85°C$

NOTE:
1. The maximum current value is with outputs O_0 to O_7 unloaded.

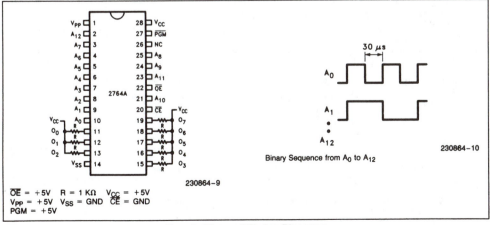

Burn-in Bias and Timing Diagrams

ABSOLUTE MAXIMUM RATINGS*

Operating Temperature
During Read ....0°C to +70°C
Temperature Under Bias ....−10°C to +80°C
Storage Temperature ....−65°C to +125°C
All Inputs or Output Voltages with
Respect to Ground ....−0.6V to +6.25V
Voltage on Pin 24 with
Respect to Ground ....−0.6V to +13.5V
V_{PP} Supply Voltage with
Respect to Ground
During Programming ....−0.6V to +14.0V

V_{CC} Supply Voltage with Respect
to Ground ....−0.6V to +7.0V

*Notice: Stresses above those listed under "Abso-
lute Maximum Ratings" may cause permanent damage to the device. This is a stress rating only and
functional operation of the device at these or any
other conditions above those indicated in the operational sections of this specification is not implied. Exposure to absolute maximum rating conditions for
extended periods may affect device reliability.*

READ OPERATION

D.C. CHARACTERISTICS $0°C \leq T_A \leq +70°C$

Symbol	Parameter	Limits			Conditions
		Min	Max	Unit	
I_{LI}	Input Load Current		10	µA	V_{IN} = 5.5V
I_{LO}	Output Leakage Current		10	µA	V_{OUT} = 5.5V
I_{PP}(2)	V_{PP} Current Read		5	mA	V_{PP} = 5.5V
I_{SB}	V_{CC} Current Standby		35	mA	$\overline{CE}$ = V_{IH}
I_{CC}(2)	V_{CC} Current Active		75	mA	$\overline{CE}$ = $\overline{OE}$ = V_{IL}
V_{IL}	Input Low Voltage	−0.1	+0.8	V	
V_{IH}	Input High Voltage	2.0	V_{CC} + 1	V	
V_{OL}	Output Low Voltage		0.45	V	I_{OL} = 2.1 mA
V_{OH}	Output High Voltage	2.4		V	I_{OH} = −400 µA
V_{PP}(2)	V_{PP} Read Voltage	3.8	V_{CC}	V	V_{CC} = 5.0V ± 0.25V

A.C. CHARACTERISTICS $0°C \leq T_A \leq +70°C$

| Versions(4) | V_{CC} ±5% | 2764A-1 | | 2764A-2 P2764A-2 | | 2764A P2764A | | 2764A-3 P2764A-3 | | 2764A-4 | | Unit | Test Conditions |
	V_{CC} ±10%			2764A-20		2764A-25 P2764A-25		2764A-30 P2764A-30		2764A-45			
Symbol	Parameter	Min	Max	Min	Max	Min	Max	Min	Max	Min	Max		
t_{ACC}	Address to Output Delay		180		200		250		300		450	ns	$\overline{CE}$ = $\overline{OE}$ = V_{IL}
t_{CE}	$\overline{CE}$ to Output Delay		180		200		250		300		450	ns	$\overline{OE}$ = V_{IL}
t_{OE}	$\overline{OE}$ to Output Delay		65		75		100		120		150	ns	$\overline{CE}$ = V_{IL}
t_{DF}(3)	$\overline{OE}$ High to Output Float	0	55	0	55	0	60	0	105	0	130	ns	$\overline{CE}$ = V_{IL}
t_{OH}	Output Hold from Address, $\overline{CE}$ or $\overline{OE}$ Whichever Occurred First	0		0		0		0		0		ns	$\overline{CE}$ = $\overline{OE}$ = V_{IL}

NOTES:
1. V_{CC} must be applied simultaneously or before V_{PP} and removed simultaneously or after V_{PP}.
2. V_{PP} may be connected directly to V_{CC} except during programming. The supply current would then be the sum of I_{CC} and I_{PP}. The maximum current value is with outputs O_0 to O_7 unloaded.
3. This parameter is only sampled and is not 100% tested. Output Data Float is defined as the point where data is no longer driven—see timing diagram on the following page.
4. Model Number Prefixes: No prefix = CERDIP; P = Plastic DIP.

intel   2764A

CAPACITANCE(2) (T_A = 25°C, f = 1 MHz)

Symbol	Parameter	Typ (1)	Max	Unit	Conditions
C_{IN}	Input Capacitance	4	6	pF	V_{IN} = 0V
C_{OUT}	Output Capacitance	8	12	pF	V_{OUT} = 0V

A.C. TESTING INPUT/OUTPUT WAVEFORM

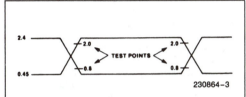

230864-3

A.C. Testing; Inputs are Driven at 2.4V for a Logic "1" and 0.45V for a Logic "0". Timing Measurements are made at 2.0V for a Logic "1" and 0.8V for a Logic "0".

A.C. TESTING LOAD CIRCUIT

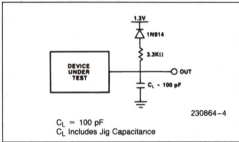

230864-4

C_L = 100 pF
C_L Includes Jig Capacitance

A.C. WAVEFORMS

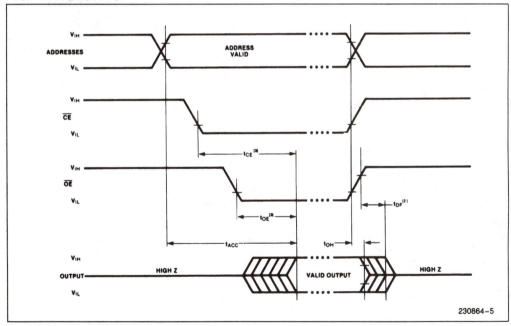

230864-5

NOTES:
1. Typical values are for T_A = 25°C and nominal supply voltages.
2. This parameter is only sampled and is not 100% tested.
3. $\overline{OE}$ may be delayed up to t_{CE}–t_{OE} after the falling edge of $\overline{CE}$ without impact on t_{CE}.

DEVICE OPERATION

The modes of operation of the 2764A are listed in Table 1. A single 5V power supply is required in the read mode. All inputs are TTL levels except for V_{pp} and 12V on A_9 for int$_e$ligent identifier mode.

Table 1. Mode Selection

Mode	$\overline{CE}$	$\overline{OE}$	$\overline{PGM}$	A_9	A_0	V_{PP}	V_{CC}	Outputs
Read	V_{IL}	V_{IL}	V_{IH}	X(1)	X	V_{CC}	5.0V	D_{OUT}
Output Disable	V_{IL}	V_{IH}	V_{IH}	X	X	V_{CC}	5.0V	High Z
Standby	V_{IH}	X	X	X	X	V_{CC}	5.0V	High Z
Programming	V_{IL}	V_{IH}	V_{IL}	X	X	(4)	(4)	D_{IN}
Program Verify	V_{IL}	V_{IL}	V_{IH}	X	X	(4)	(4)	D_{OUT}
Program Inhibit	V_{IH}	X	X	X	X	(4)	(4)	High Z
int$_e$ligent Identifier(3) —manufacturer	V_{IL}	V_{IL}	V_{IH}	V_H(2)	V_{IL}	V_{CC}	5.0V	89H(5) 88H(5)
—device	V_{IL}	V_{IL}	V_{IH}	V_H(2)	V_{IH}	V_{CC}	5.0V	08H

NOTES:
1. X can be V_{IH} or V_{IL}.
2. $V_H = 12.0V \pm 0.5V$.
3. A_1–A_8, A_{10}–A_{12} = V_{IL}.
4. See Table 2 for V_{CC} and V_{PP} voltages.
5. The manufacturers identifier reads 89H for Cerdip EPROMs; 88H for Plastic EPROMs.

Read Mode

The 2764A has two control functions, both of which must be logically active in order to obtain data at the outputs. Chip Enable ($\overline{CE}$) is the power control and should be used for device selection. Output Enable ($\overline{OE}$) is the output control and should be used to gate data from the output pins, independent of device selection. Assuming that addresses are stable, the address access time (t_{ACC}) is equal to the delay from $\overline{CE}$ to output (t_{CE}). Data is available at the outputs after a delay of t_{OE} from the falling edge of $\overline{OE}$, assuming that $\overline{CE}$ has been low and addresses have been stable for at least $t_{ACC} - t_{OE}$.

Standby Mode

EPROMs can be placed in a standby mode which reduces the maximum current of the devices by applying a TTL-high signal to the $\overline{CE}$ input. When in the standby mode, the outputs are in a high impedance state, independent of the $\overline{OE}$ input.

Two Line Output Control

Because EPROMs are usually used in larger memory arrays, Intel has provided 2 control lines which accommodate this multiple memory connection. The two control lines allow for:

a) the lowest possible memory power dissipation, and

b) complete assurance that output bus contention will not occur.

To use these two control lines most efficiently, $\overline{CE}$ should be decoded and used as the primary device selecting function, while $\overline{OE}$ should be made a common connection to all devices in the array and connected to the $\overline{READ}$ line from the system control bus. This assures that all deselected memory devices are in their low power standby mode and that the output pins are active only when data is desired from a particular memory device.

SYSTEM CONSIDERATIONS

The power switching characteristics of EPROMs require careful decoupling of the devices. The supply current, I_{CC}, has three segments that are of interest to the system designer—the standby current level, the active current level, and the transient current peaks that are produced by the falling and rising edges of Chip Enable. The magnitude of these transient current peaks is dependent on the output capacitive and inductive loading of the device. The associated transient voltage peaks can be suppressed by complying with Intel's Two-Line Control and by properly selected decoupling capacitors. It is recommended that a 0.1 μF ceramic capacitor be used on every device between V_{CC} and GND. This should be a high frequency capacitor of low inherent inductance and should be placed as close to the device as possible. In addition, a 4.7 μF bulk electrolytic capacitor should be used between V_{CC} and GND for every eight devices. The bulk capacitor should be located near where the power supply is connected to the array. The purpose of the bulk capacitor is to overcome the voltage droop caused by the inductive effect of PC board-traces.

PROGRAMMING MODES

Caution: Exceeding 14V on V_{PP} will permanently damage the device.

Initially, all bits of the EPROM are in the "1" state. Data is introduced by selectively programming "0s" into the desired bit locations. Although only "0s" will be programmed, both "1s" and "0s" can be present in the data word. The only way to change a "0" to a "1" is by ultraviolet light exposure (Cerdip EPROMs).

The device is in the programming mode when V_{PP} is raised to its programming voltage (see Table 2) and $\overline{CE}$ and $\overline{PGM}$ are both at TTL-low. The data to be programmed is applied 8 bits in parallel to the data output pins. The levels required for the address and data inputs are TTL.

intel

2764A

Program Inhibit

Programming of multiple EPROMs in parallel with different data is easily accomplished by using the Program Inhibit mode. A high-level $\overline{CE}$ or $\overline{PGM}$ input inhibits the other devices from being programmed.

Except for $\overline{CE}$, all like inputs (including $\overline{OE}$) of the parallel EPROMs may be common. A TTL low-level pulse applied to the $\overline{CE}$ input with V_{PP} at its programming voltage (see Table 2) will program the selected device.

Program Verify

A verify should be performed on the programmed bits to determine that they have been correctly programmed. The verify is performed with $\overline{OE}$ at V_{IL}, $\overline{PGM}$ at V_{IH} and V_{PP} and V_{CC} at their programming voltages.

int$_e$ligent Identifier™ Mode

The int$_e$ligent Identifier Mode allows the reading out of a binary code from an EPROM that will identify its manufacturer and type. This mode is intended for use by programming equipment for the purpose of automatically matching the device to be programmed with its corresponding programming algorithm. This mode is functional in the $25°C \pm 5°C$ ambient temperature range that is required when programming the device.

To activiate this mode, the programming equipment must force 11.5V to 12.5V on address line A9 of the EPROM. Two identifier bytes may then be sequenced from the device outputs by toggling address line A0 from V_{IL} to V_{IH}. All other address lines must be held at V_{IL} during int$_e$ligent Identifier Mode.

Byte 0 (A0 = V_{IL}) represents the manufacturer code and byte 1(A0 = V_{IH}) the device identifier code. These two identifier bytes are given in Table 1.

INTEL EPROM PROGRAMMING SUPPORT TOOLS

Intel offers a full line of EPROM Programmers providing state-of-the-art programming for all Intel pro-

grammable devices. The modular architecture of Intel's EPROM programmers allows you to add new support as it becomes available, with very low cost add-ons. For example, even the earliest users of the iUP-FAST 27/K module may take advantage of Intel's new Quick-Pulse Programming Algorithm, the fastest in the industry.

Intel EPROM programmers may be controlled from a host computer using Intel's PROM Programming software (iPPS). iPPS makes programming easy for a growing list of industry standard hosts, including the IBM PC, XT, AT, and PCDOS compatibles, Intellec Development Systems, Intel's iPDS Personal Development System, and the Intel Network Development System (iNDS-II). Stand-alone operation is also available, including device previewing, editing, programming, and download of programming data from any source over an RS232C port.

For further details consult the EPROM Programming section of the Development Systems Handbook.

ERASURE CHARACTERISTICS

The erasure characteristics are such that erasure begins to occur upon exposure to light with wavelengths shorter than approximately 4000 Angstroms (Å). It should be noted that sunlight and certain types of fluorescent lamps have wavelengths in the 3000–4000 Å range. Data shows that constant exposure to room level fluorescent lighting could erase the EPROM in approximately three years, while it would take approximately one week to cause erasure when exposed to direct sunlight. If the EPROM is to be exposed to these types of lighting conditions for extended periods of time, opaque labels should be placed over the window to prevent unintentional erasure.

The recommended erasure procedure is exposure to shortwave ultraviolet light which has a wavelength of 2537 Angstroms (Å). The integrated dose (i.e., UV intensity $\times$ exposure time) for erasure should be a minimum of fifteen (15) Wsec/cm². The erasure time with this dosage is approximately 15 to 20 minutes using an ultraviolet lamp with a 12,000 $\mu W/cm^2$ power rating. The EPROM should be placed within one inch of the lamp tubes during erasure. The maximum integrated dose an EPROM can be exposed to without damage is 7258 Wsec/cm² (1 week @ 12000 $\mu W/cm^2$). Exposure of the EPROM to high intensity UV light for longer periods may cause permanent damage.

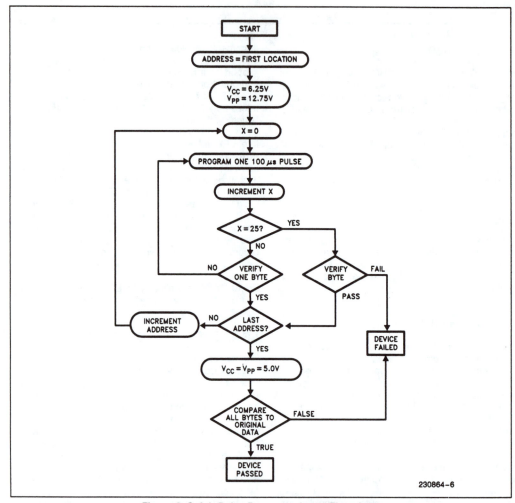

Figure 3. Quick-Pulse Programming™ Flowchart

Quick-Pulse Programming™ Algorithm (Plastic P2764A)

Intel's Plastic and PLCC EPROMs can now be programmed using the Quick-Pulse Programming Algorithm, developed by Intel to substantially reduce the throughput time in the production programming environment. This algorithm allows Plastic P2764A devices to be programmed in under one second, almost a hundred fold improvement over previous algorithms. Actual programming time is a function of the PROM programmer being used.

The Quick-Pulse Programming Algorithm uses initial pulses of 100 microseconds followed by a byte verification to determine when the address byte has been successfully programmed. Up to 25–100 μs pulses per byte are provided before a failure is recognized. A flowchart of the Quick-Pulse Programming Algorithm is shown in Figure 3.

For the Quick-Pulse Programming Algorithm, the entire sequence of programming pulses and byte verifications is performed at $V_{CC} = 6.25V$ and V_{PP} at 12.75V. When programming of the EPROM has been completed, all bytes should be compared to the original data with $V_{CC} = V_{PP} = 5.0V$.

In addition to the Quick-Pulse Programming Algorithm, Plastic and PLCC EPROMs are also compatible with Intel's int$_e$ligent Programming Algorithm.

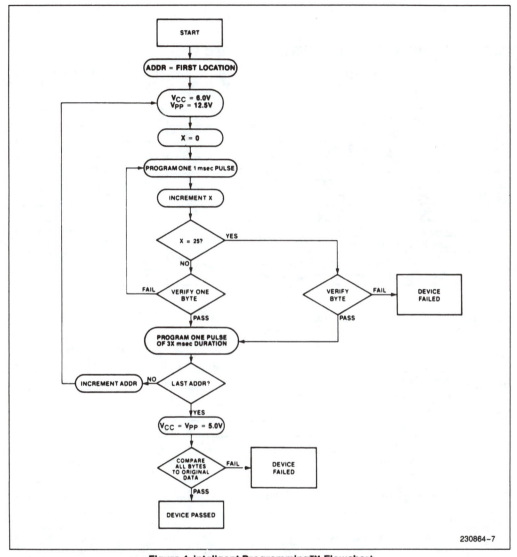

Figure 4. int_eligent Programming™ Flowchart

int_eligent Programming™ Algorithm

The int_eligent Programming Algorithm, a standard in the industry for the past few years, is required for all of Intel's 12.5V CERDEP EPROMs. Plastic and PLCC EPROMs may also be programmed using this method. A flowchart of the int_eligent Programming Algorithm is shown in Figure 4.

The int_eligent Programming Algorithm utilizes two different pulse types: initial and overprogram. The duration of the initial $\overline{PGM}$ pulse(s) is one millisecond, which will then be followed by a longer overpro-

gram pulse of length 3X msec. X is an iteration counter and is equal to the number of the initial one millisecond pulses applied to a particular location, before a correct verify occurs. Up to 25 one-millisecond pulses per byte are provided for before the overprogram pulse is applied.

The entire sequence of program pulses and byte verifications is performed at $V_{CC} = 6.0V$ and $V_{PP} = 12.5V$. When the int_eligent Programming cycle has been completed, all bytes should be compared to the original data with $V_{CC} = V_{PP} = 5.0V$.

Table 2

D.C. PROGRAMMING CHARACTERISTICS $T_A = 25°C \pm 5°C$

Symbol	Parameter	Limits			Test Conditions (see Note 1)
		Min	Max	Unit	
I_{LI}	Input Current (All Inputs)		10	μA	$V_{IN} = V_{IL}$ or V_{IH}
V_{IL}	Input Low Level (All Inputs)	-0.1	0.8	V	
V_{IH}	Input High Level	2.0	V_{CC}	V	
V_{OL}	Output Low Voltage During Verify		0.45	V	$I_{OL} = 2.1$ mA
V_{OH}	Output High Voltage During Verify	2.4		V	$I_{OH} = -400 \mu A$
$I_{CC2}^{(4)}$	V_{CC} Supply Current (Program & Verify)		75	mA	
$I_{PP2}^{(4)}$	V_{PP} Supply Current (Program)		50	mA	$\overline{CE} = V_{IL}$
V_{ID}	A_9 int$_e$ligent Identifier Voltage	11.5	12.5	V	
V_{PP}	int$_e$ligent Programming Algorithm	12.0	13.0	V	$\overline{CE} = \overline{PGM} = V_{IL}$
	Quick-Pulse Programming Algorithm	12.5	13.0	V	$\overline{CE} = \overline{PGM} = V_{IL}$
V_{CC}	int$_e$ligent Programming Algorithm	5.75	6.25	V	
	Quick-Pulse Programming Algorithm	6.0	6.5	V	

A.C. PROGRAMMING CHARACTERISTICS
$T_A = 25°C \pm 5°C$ (see table 2 for V_{CC} and V_{PP} voltages)

Symbol	Parameter	Limits				Test Conditions* (see Note 1)
		Min	Typ	Max	Unit	
t_{AS}	Address Setup Time	2			μs	
t_{OES}	$\overline{OE}$ Setup Time	2			μs	
t_{DS}	Data Setup Time	2			μs	
t_{AH}	Address Hold Time	0			μs	
t_{DH}	Data Hold Time	2			μs	
t_{DFP}	$\overline{OE}$ High to Output Float Delay	0		130	ns	(See Note 3)
t_{VPS}	V_{PP} Setup Time	2			μs	
t_{VCS}	V_{CC} Setup Time	2			μs	
t_{CES}	$\overline{CE}$ Setup Time	2			μs	
t_{PW}	$\overline{PGM}$ Initial Program Pulse Width	0.95	1.0	1.05	ms	int$_e$ligent Programming
		95	100	105	μs	Quick-Pulse Programming
t_{OPW}	$\overline{PGM}$ Overprogram Pulse Width	2.85		78.75	ms	(see Note 2)
t_{OE}	Data Valid from $\overline{OE}$			150	ns	

*A.C. CONDITIONS OF TEST

Input Rise and Fall Times
(10% to 90%) . . . . 20 ns

Input Pulse Levels . . . . 0.45V to 2.4V

Input Timing Reference Level . . . . 0.8V and 2.0V

Output Timing Reference Level . . . . . . 0.8V and 2.0V

NOTES:
1. V_{CC} must be applied simultaneously or before V_{PP} and removed simultaneously or after V_{PP}.
2. The length of the overprogram pulse may vary from 2.85 msec to 78.75 msec as a function of the iteration counter value X (int$_e$ligent Programming Algorithm only).
3. This parameter is only sampled and is not 100% tested. Output Float is defined as the point where data is no longer driven—see timing diagram.
4. The maximum current value is with Outputs O_0 to O_7 unloaded.

PROGRAMMING WAVEFORMS

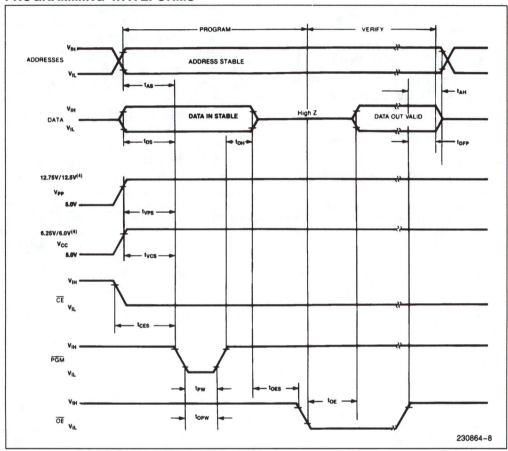

230864-8

NOTES:
1. The input timing reference level is 0.8V for V_{IL} and 2V for a V_{IH}.
2. t_{OE} and t_{DFP} are characteristics of the device but must be accommodated by the programmer.
3. When programming the 2764A, a 0.1 μF capacitor is required across V_{PP} and ground to suppress spurious voltage transients which can damage the device.
4. 12.75V V_{PP} & 6.25V V_{CC} for Quick-Pulse Programming Algorithm; 12.5V V_{PP} & 6.0V V_{CC} for Int$_\text{e}$ligent Programming Algorithm.

8085AH/8085AH-2/8085AH-1
8-BIT HMOS MICROPROCESSORS

- **Single +5V Power Supply with 10% Voltage Margins**
- **3 MHz, 5 MHz and 6 MHz Selections Available**
- **20% Lower Power Consumption than 8085A for 3 MHz and 5 MHz**
- **1.3 μs Instruction Cycle (8085AH); 0.8 μs (8085AH-2); 0.67 μs (8085AH-1)**
- **100% Compatible with 8085A**
- **100% Software Compatible with 8080A**
- **On-Chip Clock Generator (with External Crystal, LC or RC Network)**

- **On-Chip System Controller; Advanced Cycle Status Information Available for Large System Control**
- **Four Vectored Interrupt Inputs (One is Non-Maskable) Plus an 8080A-Compatible Interrupt**
- **Serial In/Serial Out Port**
- **Decimal, Binary and Double Precision Arithmetic**
- **Direct Addressing Capability to 64K Bytes of Memory**
- **Available in EXPRESS**
  - **– Standard Temperature Range**
  - **– Extended Temperature Range**

The Intel® 8085AH is a complete 8 bit parallel Central Processing Unit (CPU) implemented in N-channel, depletion load, silicon gate technology (HMOS). Its instruction set is 100% software compatible with the 8080A microprocessor, and it is designed to improve the present 8080A's performance by higher system speed. Its high level of system integration allows a minimum system of three IC's [8085AH (CPU), 8156H (RAM/IO) and 8355/8755A (ROM/PROM/IO)] while maintaining total system expandability. The 8085AH-2 and 8085AH-1 are faster versions of the 8085AH.

The 8085AH incorporates all of the features that the 8224 (clock generator) and 8228 (system controller) provided for the 8080A, thereby offering a high level of system integration.

The 8085AH uses a multiplexed data bus. The address is split between the 8 bit address bus and the 8 bit data bus. The on-chip address latches of 8155H/8156H/8355/8755A memory products allow a direct interface with the 8085AH.

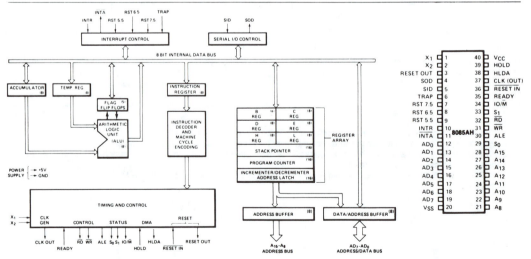

Figure 1. 8085AH CPU Functional Block Diagram

Figure 2. 8085AH Pin Configuration

(F3: Courtesy of Intel Corporation.)

Table 1. Pin Description

Symbol	Type	Name and Function
A$_8$–A$_{15}$	O	**Address Bus:** The most significant 8 bits of the memory address or the 8 bits of the I/O address, 3-stated during Hold and Halt modes and during RESET.
AD$_0$—$_7$	I/O	**Multiplexed Address/Data Bus:** Lower 8 bits of the memory address (or I/O address) appear on the bus during the first clock cycle (T state) of a machine cycle. It then becomes the data bus during the second and third clock cycles.
ALE	O	**Address Latch Enable:** It occurs during the first clock state of a machine cycle and enables the address to get latched into the on-chip latch of peripherals. The falling edge of ALE is set to guarantee setup and hold times for the address information. The falling edge of ALE can also be used to strobe the status information. ALE is never 3-stated.
S$_0$, S$_1$, and IO/$\overline{M}$	O	**Machine Cycle Status:** IO/$\overline{M}$ S$_1$ S$_0$ Status 0 0 1 Memory write 0 1 0 Memory read 1 0 1 I/O write 1 1 0 I/O read 0 1 1 Opcode fetch 1 1 1 Opcode fetch 1 1 1 Interrupt Acknowledge • 0 0 Halt • X X Hold • X X Reset • = 3-state (high impedance) X = unspecified S$_1$ can be used as an advanced R/$\overline{W}$ status. IO/$\overline{M}$, S$_0$ and S$_1$ become valid at the beginning of a machine cycle and remain stable throughout the cycle. The falling edge of ALE may be used to latch the state of these lines.
$\overline{RD}$	O	**Read Control:** A low level on $\overline{RD}$ indicates the selected memory or I/O device is to be read and that the Data Bus is available for the data transfer, 3-stated during Hold and Halt modes and during RESET.
$\overline{WR}$	O	**Write Control:** A low level on $\overline{WR}$ indicates the data on the Data Bus is to be written into the selected memory or I/O location. Data is set up at the trailing edge of $\overline{WR}$. 3-stated during Hold and Halt modes and during RESET.

Symbol	Type	Name and Function
READY	I	**Ready:** If READY is high during a read or write cycle, it indicates that the memory or peripheral is ready to send or receive data. If READY is low, the cpu will wait an integral number of clock cycles for READY to go high before completing the read or write cycle. READY must conform to specified setup and hold times.
HOLD	I	**Hold:** Indicates that another master is requesting the use of the address and data buses. The cpu, upon receiving the hold request, will relinquish the use of the bus as soon as the completion of the current bus transfer. Internal processing can continue. The processor can regain the bus only after the HOLD is removed. When the HOLD is acknowledged, the Address, Data $\overline{RD}$, $\overline{WR}$, and IO/$\overline{M}$ lines are 3-stated.
HLDA	O	**Hold Acknowledge:** Indicates that the cpu has received the HOLD request and that it will relinquish the bus in the next clock cycle. HLDA goes low after the Hold request is removed. The cpu takes the bus one half clock cycle after HLDA goes low.
INTR	I	**Interrupt Request:** Is used as a general purpose interrupt. It is sampled only during the next to the last clock cycle of an instruction and during Hold and Halt states. If it is active, the Program Counter (PC) will be inhibited from incrementing and an $\overline{INTA}$ will be issued. During this cycle a RESTART or CALL instruction can be inserted to jump to the interrupt service routine. The INTR is enabled and disabled by software. It is disabled by Reset and immediately after an interrupt is accepted.
$\overline{INTA}$	O	**Interrupt Acknowledge:** Is used instead of (and has the same timing as) $\overline{RD}$ during the Instruction cycle after an INTR is accepted. It can be used to activate an 8259A Interrupt chip or some other interrupt port.
RST 5.5 RST 6.5 RST 7.5	I	**Restart Interrupts:** These three inputs have the same timing as INTR except they cause an internal RESTART to be automatically inserted. The priority of these interrupts is ordered as shown in Table 2. These interrupts have a higher priority than INTR. In addition, they may be individually masked out using the SIM instruction.

Table 1. Pin Description (Continued)

Symbol	Type	Name and Function
TRAP	I	**Trap:** Trap interrupt is a non-maskable RESTART interrupt. It is recognized at the same time as INTR or RST 5.5-7.5. It is unaffected by any mask or Interrupt Enable. It has the highest priority of any interrupt. (See Table 2.)
RESET IN	I	**Reset In:** Sets the Program Counter to zero and resets the Interrupt Enable and HLDA flip-flops. The data and address buses and the control lines are 3-stated during RESET and because of the asynchronous nature of RESET, the processor's internal registers and flags may be altered by RESET with unpredictable results. RESET IN is a Schmitt-triggered input, allowing connection to an R-C network for power-on RESET delay (see Figure 3). Upon power-up, RESET IN must remain low for at least 10 ms after minimum V_{CC} has been reached. For proper reset operation after the power-up duration, RESET IN should be kept low a minimum of three clock periods. The CPU is held in the reset condition as long as RESET IN is applied.

Symbol	Type	Name and Function
RESET OUT	O	**Reset Out:** Reset Out indicates cpu is being reset. Can be used as a system reset. The signal is synchronized to the processor clock and lasts an integral number of clock periods.
X_1, X_2	I	**X_1 and X_2:** Are connected to a crystal, LC, or RC network to drive the internal clock generator. X_1 can also be an external clock input from a logic gate. The input frequency is divided by 2 to give the processor's internal operating frequency.
CLK	O	**Clock:** Clock output for use as a system clock. The period of CLK is twice the X_1, X_2 input period.
SID	I	**Serial Input Data Line:** The data on this line is loaded into accumulator bit 7 whenever a RIM instruction is executed.
SOD	O	**Serial Output Data Line:** The output SOD is set or reset as specified by the SIM instruction.
V_{CC}		**Power:** +5 volt supply.
V_{SS}		**Ground:** Reference.

Table 2. Interrupt Priority, Restart Address, and Sensitivity

Name	Priority	Address Branched To (1) When Interrupt Occurs	Type Trigger
TRAP	1	24H	Rising edge AND high level until sampled.
RST 7.5	2	3CH	Rising edge (latched).
RST 6.5	3	34H	High level until sampled.
RST 5.5	4	2CH	High level until sampled.
INTR	5	See Note (2).	High level until sampled.

NOTES:
1. The processor pushes the PC on the stack before branching to the indicated address.
2. The address branched to depends on the instruction provided to the cpu when the interrupt is acknowledged.

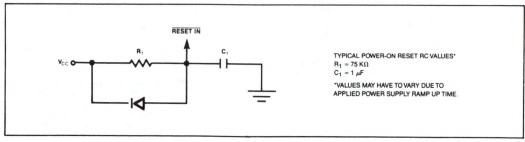

Figure 3. Power-On Reset Circuit

BASIC SYSTEM TIMING

The 8085AH has a multiplexed Data Bus. ALE is used as a strobe to sample the lower 8-bits of address on the Data Bus. Figure 10 shows an instruction fetch, memory read and I/O write cycle (as would occur during processing of the OUT instruction). Note that during the I/O write and read cycle that the I/O port address is copied on both the upper and lower half of the address.

There are seven possible types of machine cycles. Which of these seven takes place is defined by the status of the three status lines (IO/$\overline{M}$, S_1, S_0) and the three control signals ($\overline{RD}$, $\overline{WR}$, and $\overline{INTA}$). (See Table 3.) The status lines can be used as advanced controls (for device selection, for example), since they become active at the T_1 state, at the outset of each machine cycle. Control lines $\overline{RD}$ and $\overline{WR}$ become active later, at the time when the transfer of data is to take place, so are used as command lines.

A machine cycle normally consists of three T states, with the exception of OPCODE FETCH, which normally has either four or six T states (unless WAIT or HOLD states are forced by the receipt of READY or HOLD inputs). Any T state must be one of ten possible states, shown in Table 4.

Table 3. 8085AH Machine Cycle Chart

MACHINE CYCLE		STATUS			CONTROL		
		IO/$\overline{M}$	S1	S0	$\overline{RD}$	$\overline{WR}$	$\overline{INTA}$
OPCODE FETCH	(OF)	0	1	1	0	1	1
MEMORY READ	(MR)	0	1	0	0	1	1
MEMORY WRITE	(MW)	0	0	1	1	0	1
I/O READ	(IOR)	1	1	0	0	1	1
I/O WRITE	(IOW)	1	0	1	1	0	1
ACKNOWLEDGE OF INTR	(INA)	1	1	1	1	1	0
BUS IDLE	(BI): DAD	0	1	0	1	1	1
	ACK. OF RST,TRAP	1	1	1	1	1	1
	HALT	TS	0	0	TS	TS	1

Table 4. 8085AH Machine State Chart

Machine State	Status & Buses				Control		
	S1,S0	IO/$\overline{M}$	A8-A15	AD0-AD7	$\overline{RD}$,$\overline{WR}$	INTA	ALE
T_1	X	X	X	X	1	1	1*
T_2	X	X	X	X	X	X	0
T_{WAIT}	X	X	X	X	X	X	0
T_3	X	X	X	X	X	X	0
T_4	1	0 †	X	TS	1	1	0
T_5	1	0 †	X	TS	1	1	0
T_6	1	0 †	X	TS	1	1	0
T_{RESET}	X	TS	TS	TS	TS	1	0
T_{HALT}	0	TS	TS	TS	TS	1	0
T_{HOLD}	X	TS	TS	TS	TS	1	0

0 = Logic "0"   TS = High Impedance
1 = Logic "1"   X = Unspecified

* ALE not generated during 2nd and 3rd machine cycles of DAD instruction.
† IO/M = 1 during T_4-T_6 of INA machine cycle.

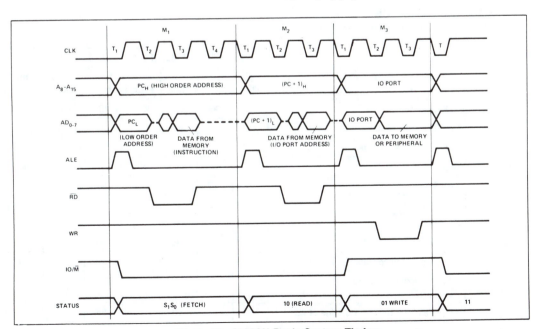

Figure 10. 8085AH Basic System Timing

ABSOLUTE MAXIMUM RATINGS*

Ambient Temperature Under Bias .... 0°C to 70°C
Storage Temperature .... −65°C to +150°C
Voltage on Any Pin
　With Respect to Ground .... −0.5V to +7V
Power Dissipation .... 1.5 Watt

*NOTICE: Stresses above those listed under "Absolute Maximum Ratings" may cause permanent damage to the device. This is a stress rating only and functional operation of the device at these or any other conditions above those indicated in the operational sections of this specification is not implied. Exposure to absolute maximum rating conditions for extended periods may affect device reliability.

D.C. CHARACTERISTICS

8085AH, 8085AH-2: (T_A = 0°C to 70°C, V_{CC} = 5V ±10%, V_{SS} =0V; unless otherwise specified)*
8085AH-1: (T_A = 0°C to 70°C, V_{CC} = 5V ±5%, V_{SS} = 0V; unless otherwise specified)

Symbol	Parameter	Min.	Max.	Units	Test Conditions
V_{IL}	Input Low Voltage	−0.5	+0.8	V	
V_{IH}	Input High Voltage	2.0	V_{CC} +0.5	V	
V_{OL}	Output Low Voltage		0.45	V	I_{OL} = 2mA
V_{OH}	Output High Voltage	2.4		V	I_{OH} = −400μA
I_{CC}	Power Supply Current		135	mA	8085AH, 8085AH-2
			200	mA	8085AH-1 (Preliminary)
I_{IL}	Input Leakage		±10	μA	0 ≤ V_{IN} ≤ V_{CC}
I_{LO}	Output Leakage		±10	μA	0.45V ≤ V_{OUT} ≤ V_{CC}
V_{ILR}	Input Low Level, RESET	−0.5	+0.8	V	
V_{IHR}	Input High Level, RESET	2.4	V_{CC} +0.5	V	
V_{HY}	Hysteresis, RESET	0.25		V	

A.C. CHARACTERISTICS

8085AH, 8085AH-2: (T_A = 0°C to 70°C, V_{CC} = 5V ±10%, V_{SS} = OV)*
8085AH-1: (T_A = 0°C to 70°C, V_{CC} = 5V ±5%, V_{SS} = 0V)

Symbol	Parameter	8085AH[2] (Final)		8085AH-2[2] (Final)		8085AH-1 (Preliminary)		Units
		Min.	Max.	Min.	Max.	Min.	Max.	
t_{CYC}	CLK Cycle Period	320	2000	200	2000	167	2000	ns
t_1	CLK Low Time (Standard CLK Loading)	80		40		20		ns
t_2	CLK High Time (Standard CLK Loading)	120		70		50		ns
t_r, t_f	CLK Rise and Fall Time		30		30		30	ns
t_{XKR}	X_1 Rising to CLK Rising	25	120	25	100	20	100	ns
t_{XKF}	X_1 Rising to CLK Falling	30	150	30	110	25	110	ns
t_{AC}	A_{8-15} Valid to Leading Edge of Control[1]	270		115		70		ns
t_{ACL}	A_{0-7} Valid to Leading Edge of Control	240		115		60		ns
t_{AD}	A_{0-15} Valid to Valid Data In		575		350		225	ns
t_{AFR}	Address Float After Leading Edge of READ (INTA)		0		0		0	ns
t_{AL}	A_{8-15} Valid Before Trailing Edge of ALE [1]	115		50		25		ns

*Note: For Extended Temperature EXPRESS use M8085AH Electricals Parameters.

A.C. CHARACTERISTICS (Continued)

Symbol	Parameter	8085AH[2] (Final)		8085AH-2[2] (Final)		8085AH-1 (Preliminary)		Units
		Min.	Max.	Min.	Max.	Min.	Max.	
t_{ALL}	A$_{0-7}$ Valid Before Trailing Edge of ALE	90		50		25		ns
t_{ARY}	READY Valid from Address Valid		220		100		40	ns
t_{CA}	Address (A$_{8-15}$) Valid After Control	120		60		30		ns
t_{CC}	Width of Control Low ($\overline{RD}$, $\overline{WR}$, $\overline{INTA}$) Edge of ALE	400		230		150		ns
t_{CL}	Trailing Edge of Control to Leading Edge of ALE	50		25		0		ns
t_{DW}	Data Valid to Trailing Edge of $\overline{WRITE}$	420		230		140		ns
t_{HABE}	HLDA to Bus Enable		210		150		150	ns
t_{HABF}	Bus Float After HLDA		210		150		150	ns
t_{HACK}	HLDA Valid to Trailing Edge of CLK	110		40		0		ns
t_{HDH}	HOLD Hold Time	0		0		0		ns
t_{HDS}	HOLD Setup Time to Trailing Edge of CLK	170		120		120		ns
t_{INH}	INTR Hold Time	0		0		0		ns
t_{INS}	INTR, RST, and TRAP Setup Time to Falling Edge of CLK	160		150		150		ns
t_{LA}	Address Hold Time After ALE	100		50		20		ns
t_{LC}	Trailing Edge of ALE to Leading Edge of Control	130		60		25		ns
t_{LCK}	ALE Low During CLK High	100		50		15		ns
t_{LDR}	ALE to Valid Data During Read		460		270		175	ns
t_{LDW}	ALE to Valid Data During Write		200		120		110	ns
t_{LL}	ALE Width	140		80		50		ns
t_{LRY}	ALE to READY Stable		110		30		10	ns
t_{RAE}	Trailing Edge of $\overline{READ}$ to Re-Enabling of Address	150		90		50		ns
t_{RD}	$\overline{READ}$ (or $\overline{INTA}$) to Valid Data		300		150		75	ns
t_{RV}	Control Trailing Edge to Leading Edge of Next Control	400		220		160		ns
t_{RDH}	Data Hold Time After $\overline{READ}$ $\overline{INTA}$	0		0		0		ns
t_{RYH}	READY Hold Time	0		0		5		ns
t_{RYS}	READY Setup Time to Leading Edge of CLK	110		100		100		ns
t_{WD}	Data Valid After Trailing Edge of $\overline{WRITE}$	100		60		30		ns
t_{WDL}	LEADING Edge of $\overline{WRITE}$ to Data Valid		40		20		30	ns

NOTES:

1. A_8–A_{15} address Specs apply $IO/\overline{M}$, S_0, and S_1 except A_8–A_{15} are undefined during T_4–T_6 of OF cycle whereas $IO/\overline{M}$, S_0, and S_1 are stable.
2. *Test Conditions:* t_{CYC} = 320 ns (8085AH)/200 ns (8085AH-2);/ 167 ns (8085AH-1); C_L = 150 pF.

3. For all output timing where $C_L \neq 150$ pF use the following correction factors:
   25 pF $\leq C_L <$ 150 pF: −0.10 ns/pF
   150 pF $< C_L \leq$ 300 pF: +0.30 ns/pF
4. Output timings are measured with purely capacitive load.
5. To calculate timing specifications at other values of t_{CYC} use Table 5.

A.C. TESTING INPUT, OUTPUT WAVEFORM

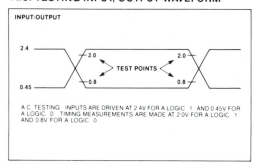

INPUT/OUTPUT

2.4

2.0 — 2.0

TEST POINTS

0.8 — 0.8

0.45

A.C. TESTING. INPUTS ARE DRIVEN AT 2.4V FOR A LOGIC. 1 AND 0.45V FOR A LOGIC 0. TIMING MEASUREMENTS ARE MADE AT 2.0V FOR A LOGIC. 1 AND 0.8V FOR A LOGIC. 0.

A.C. TESTING LOAD CIRCUIT

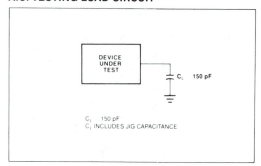

DEVICE UNDER TEST

C_L 150 pF

C_L 150 pF
C_L INCLUDES JIG CAPACITANCE

Table 5. Bus Timing Specification as a T_{CYC} Dependent

Symbol	8085AH	8085AH-2	8085AH-1	
t_{AL}	(1/2) T − 45	(1/2) T − 50	(1/2) T − 58	Minimum
t_{LA}	(1/2) T − 60	(1/2) T − 50	(1/2) T − 63	Minimum
t_{LL}	(1/2) T − 20	(1/2) T − 20	(1/2) T − 33	Minimum
t_{LCK}	(1/2) T − 60	(1/2) T − 50	(1/2) T − 68	Minimum
t_{LC}	(1/2) T − 30	(1/2) T − 40	(1/2) T − 58	Minimum
t_{AD}	(5/2 + N) T − 225	(5/2 + N) T − 150	(5/2 + N) T − 192	Maximum
t_{RD}	(3/2 + N) T − 180	(3/2 + N) T − 150	(3/2 + N) T − 175	Maximum
t_{RAE}	(1/2) T − 10	(1/2) T − 10	(1/2) T − 33	Minimum
t_{CA}	(1/2) T − 40	(1/2) T − 40	(1/2) T − 53	Minimum
t_{DW}	(3/2 + N) T − 60	(3/2 + N) T − 70	(3/2 + N) T − 110	Minimum
t_{WD}	(1/2) T − 60	(1/2) T − 40	(1/2) T − 53	Minimum
t_{CC}	(3/2 + N) T − 80	(3/2 + N) T − 70	(3/2 + N) T − 100	Minimum
t_{CL}	(1/2) T − 110	(1/2) T − 75	(1/2) T − 83	Minimum
t_{ARY}	(3/2) T − 260	(3/2) T − 200	(3/2) T − 210	Maximum
t_{HACK}	(1/2) T − 50	(1/2) T − 60	(1/2) T − 83	Minimum
t_{HABF}	(1/2) T + 50	(1/2) T + 50	(1/2) T + 67	Maximum
t_{HABE}	(1/2) T + 50	(1/2) T + 50	(1/2) T + 67	Maximum
t_{AC}	(2/2) T − 50	(2/2) T − 85	(2/2) T − 97	Minimum
t_1	(1/2) T − 80	(1/2) T − 60	(1/2) T − 63	Minimum
t_2	(1/2) T − 40	(1/2) T − 30	(1/2) T − 33	Minimum
t_{RV}	(3/2) T − 80	(3/2) T − 80	(3/2) T − 90	Minimum
t_{LDR}	(4/2) T − 180	(4/2) T − 130	(4/2) T − 159	Maximum

NOTE: N is equal to the total WAIT states. T = t_{CYC}.

WAVEFORMS

CLOCK

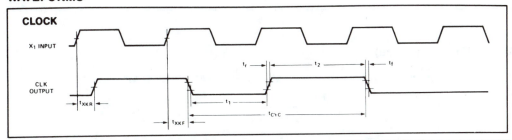

READ

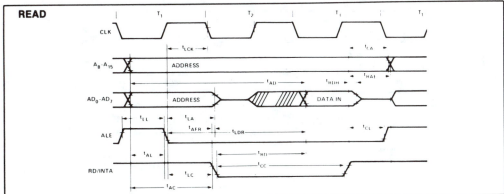

WRITE

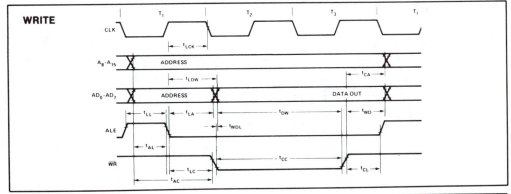

HOLD

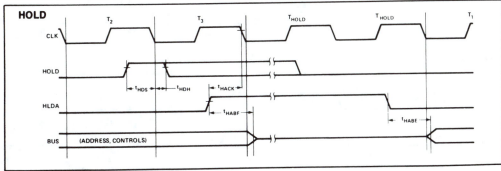

8085AH/8085AH-2/8085AH-1

WAVEFORMS (Continued)

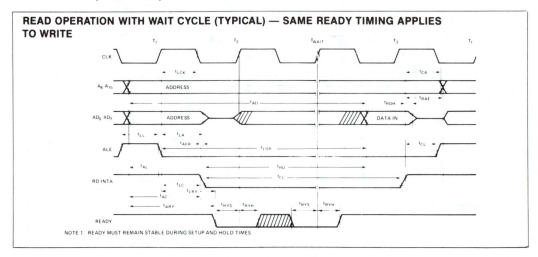

READ OPERATION WITH WAIT CYCLE (TYPICAL) — SAME READY TIMING APPLIES TO WRITE

NOTE 1: READY MUST REMAIN STABLE DURING SETUP AND HOLD TIMES

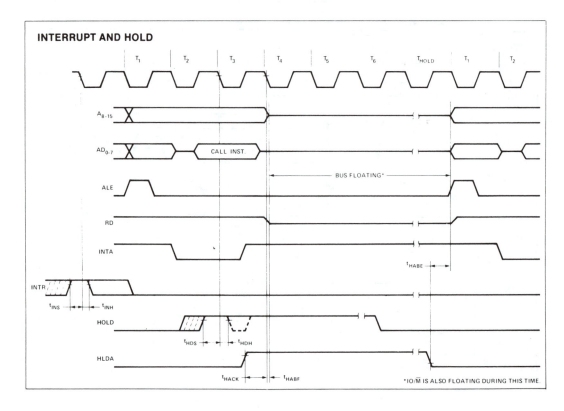

INTERRUPT AND HOLD

*IO/M̄ IS ALSO FLOATING DURING THIS TIME.

G

Unspecified 8085A
Op Codes

Unspecified 8085 op codes enhance programming

by Wolfgang Dehnhardt and Villy M. Sorensen
GSI, Darmstadt, and Sorensen Software, Seeheim, West Germany

Ten operating codes and two flag bits previously unknown to most users of the 8085 microprocessor will enable programmers to write more efficient routines. The new members of the instruction set, which were stumbled upon during the testing of an assembler-disassembler module, include seven op codes that involve the processing of register pairs, two that involve jump operations with one new flag bit, and one that performs a conditional restart on the overflow indication of the other flag bit.

The seven register pair instructions (all with 16-bit operands) consist of a double subtraction, a rotate, a shift, indirect loading and storing of a word, and two offset operations. Either BC, DE, HL, or SP are the designated register pairs used in these op codes.

The mnemonic names of the instructions have been selected to be compatible with the 8085's existing mnemonics. In the double subtraction (DSUB), register pair BC is subtracted from HL. This instruction thus performs the opposite task of DAD B, a well-known instruction. The instruction RDEL rotates register pair DE left 1 bit through the carry. ARHL is an arithmetic shift to the right of HL. It serves to divide HL by 2, except in cases where HL is −1.

All 16 bits of register pair HL can be stored indirectly at the address contained in the DE pair by specifying instruction SHLX. To load HL, LHLX must be employed.

As an example of how this instruction can be used to cut instruction steps, consider the common sequence used for a routine table jump shown in part (a) of the figure. By assigning the register DE for HL and using the LHLX instruction, this sequence can be replaced by the much simpler arrangement shown at the bottom of part (a).

As for adding the contents of register pairs with an additional byte (offset), DE can be loaded with HL plus the byte by selecting the instruction LDHI, which simplifies array addressing. Usually, the architecture of 8080-type systems dictate the addressing of arrays in what are called pages of 256 bytes. This restriction means that the starting address of an array must be placed near the beginning of a page. A typical call is as shown in part (b) of the figure.

The page limitation is bypassed using the LDHI instruction code and constant indexes. The starting address of the array can now be placed anywhere, and addressing occurs as shown at the bottom of part b.

Any additional byte can be combined with register-pair SP in DE if instruction LDSI is specified. This instruction is designed for operating system routes that transfer arguments on the stack. An example sequence, shown in (c), stores HL into the 16-bit word located as the second item below the top of the stack.

The jump and restart instructions work in conjunction with the two discovered flag bits, X5 and V. Op codes JX5 and JNX5 jump depending on the state of the X5 flag. Op code RSTV makes a restart call to hexadecimal address 40 if the V flag is set; otherwise it functions as a no-operation instruction.

Flag bit V indicates a 2's complement overflow condition for 8- and 16-bit arithmetical operations. Flag bit X5 has been named for its position in the condition code byte and not for its function. It does not resemble any normal flag bit. The only use for this bit found thus far are as an unsigned overflow indicator resulting from a data change of FFFF to 0000 on executing the instruction of INX and as an unsigned underflow indicator from a data change of 0000 to FFFF on executing DCX.

The new 8085 instructions are outlined in the table. □

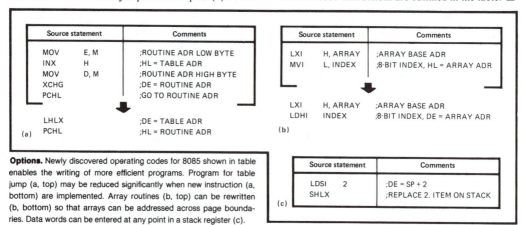

Options. Newly discovered operating codes for 8085 shown in table enables the writing of more efficient programs. Program for table jump (a, top) may be reduced significantly when new instruction (a, bottom) are implemented. Array routines (b, top) can be rewritten (b, bottom) so that arrays can be addressed across page boundaries. Data words can be entered at any point in a stack register (c).

(Reprinted from ELECTRONICS, January 18, 1979. Copyright © 1979, McGraw-Hill Inc. All rights reserved.)

NEW 8085 INSTRUCTIONS

NEW CONDITION CODES: V = bit 1
X5 = bit 5

Condition code format							
S	Z	X5	AC	0	P	V	C

2's complement overflow
Underflow (DCX) or overflow (INX)
$X5 = 01 \cdot 02 + 01 \cdot R + 02 \cdot R$, where
01 = sign of operand 1, 02 = sign of operand 2,
R = sign of result. For subtraction and comparisons,
replace 02 with $\overline{02}$.

DSUB   (double subtraction)

(H) (L) = (H) (L) − (B) (C)
The contents of register pair B and C are subtracted from the
contents of register pair H and L. The result is placed in
register pair H and L. All condition flags are affected.

0 0 0 0 1 0 0 0	(08)

cycles: 3
states: 10
addressing: register
flags: Z, S, P, CY, AC, X5, V

ARHL   (arithmetic shift of H and L to the right)

(H7=H7); (Hn−1) = (Hn)
(L7=Ho); (Ln−1) = (Ln); (CY) = (Lo)
The contents of register pair H and L are shifted right one bit.
The uppermost bit is duplicated and the lowest bit is shifted
into the carry bit. The result is placed in register pair H and L.
Note: only the CY flag is affected.

0 0 0 1 0 0 0 0	(10)

cycles: 2
states: 7
addressing: register
flags: CY

RDEL   (rotate D and E left through carry)

(Dn+1) = (Dn); (Do) = (E7)
(CY) = (D7); (En+1) = (En); (Eo) = (CY)
The contents of register pair D and E are rotated left one
position through the carry flag. The low-order bit is set equal
to the CY flag and the CY flag is set to the value shifted out
of the high-order bit. Only the CY and the V flags are affected.

0 0 0 1 1 0 0 0	(18)

cycles: 3
states: 10
addressing: register
flags: CY, V

LDHI   (load D and E with H and L plus immediate byte)

(D) (E) = (H) (L) + (byte 2)
The contents of register pair H and L are added to the
immediate byte. The result is placed in register pair D and E.
Note: no condition flags are affected.

0 0 1 0 1 0 0 0	(28)
data	

cycles: 3
states: 10
addressing: immediate register
flags: none

LDSI   (load D and E with SP plus immediate byte)

(D) (E) = (SPH)(SPL) + (byte 2)
The contents of register pair SP are added to the immediate
byte. The result is placed in register pair D and E. Note: no
condition flags are affected.

0 0 1 1 1 0 0 0	(38)
data	

cycles: 3
states: 10
addressing: immediate register
flags: none

RSTV   (restart on overflow)

If (V):
((SP)−1) = (PCH)
((SP)−2) = (PCL)
(SP) = (SP)−2
(PC) = 40 hex

If the overflow flag V is set, the actions specified above are
performed; otherwise control continues sequentially.

1 1 0 0 1 0 1 1	(C8)

cycles: 1 or 3
states: 6 or 12
addressing: register indirect
flags: none

SHLX   (store H and L indirect through D and E)

((D)(E)) = (L)
((D)(E)+1) = (H)
The contents of register L are moved to the memory location
whose address is in register pair D and E. The contents of
register H are moved to the succeeding memory location.

1 1 0 1 1 0 0 1	(D9)

cycles: 3
states: 10
addressing: register indirect
flags: none

JNX5   (jump on not X5)

If (not X5):
(PC) = (byte 3) (byte 2)

If the X5 flag is reset, control is transferred to the instruction
whose address is specified in byte 3 and byte 2 of the current
instruction; otherwise control continues sequentially.

1 1 0 1 1 1 0 1	(DD)
low-order address	
high-order address	

cycles: 2 or 3
states: 7 or 10
addressing: immediate
flags: none

LHLX   (load H and L indirect through D and E)

(L) = ((D)(E))
(H) = ((D)(E)+1)
The content of the memory location whose address is in D
and E, are moved to register L. The contents of the succeeding
memory location are moved to register H.

1 1 1 0 1 1 0 1	(ED)

cycles: 3
states: 10
addressing: register indirect
flags: none

JX5   (jump on X5)

If (X5):
(PC) = (byte 3) (byte 2)

If the X5 flag is reset, control is transferred to the instruction
whose address is specified in byte 3 and byte 2 of the current
instruction; otherwise control continues sequentially.

1 1 1 1 1 1 0 1	(FD)
low-order address	
high-order address	

cycles: 2 or 3
states: 7 or 10
addressing: immediate
flags: none

Index